MANAGEMENT SCIENCE

AF647591

Dr. P.G. RAMANUJAM,
B.E., M.B.A., M.Tech., Ph.D., MIE, LMISTE
Principal
Rajamahendri Institute of Engineering and Technology,
Rajahmundry
East Godavari District, Andhra Pradesh.

Dr. B. V. R. NAIDU
M.Com. M.B.A., Ph.D.
Professor and HOD,
School of Management Studies,
Swarnandhra College of Engineering & Technology,
Narsapur, W.G.Dt., Andhra Pradesh.

Prof. P.V. RAMA SASTRY
M.Com. M.B.A., M.Phil.
Professor,
School of Management Studies,
Swarnandhra College of Engineering & Technology,
Narsapur, W.G.Dt., Andhra Pradesh.

HPH

Himalaya Publishing House

MUMBAI • NEW DELHI • NAGPUR • BENGALURU • HYDERABAD • CHENNAI • PUNE • LUCKNOW • AHMEDABAD • ERNAKULAM • BHUBANESWAR • INDORE • KOLKATA • GUWAHATI

© Authors

No part of this publication may be reproduced, stored in a retrieval system, or transmitted in any form or by any means, electronic, mechanical, photocopying, recording and/or otherwise without the prior written permission of the publishers.

First Edition : 2013
Edition : 2014

Published by : Mrs. Meena Pandey for **Himalaya Publishing House Pvt. Ltd.,**
"Ramdoot", Dr. Bhalerao Marg, Girgaon, Mumbai - 400 004.
Phone: 022-23860170/23863863, Fax: 022-23877178
E-mail: himpub@vsnl.com; Website: www.himpub.com

Branch Offices :

New Delhi : "Pooja Apartments", 4-B, Murari Lal Street, Ansari Road, Darya Ganj, New Delhi - 110 002. Phone: 011-23270392, 23278631; Fax: 011-23256286

Nagpur : Kundanlal Chandak Industrial Estate, Ghat Road, Nagpur - 440 018. Phone: 0712-2738731, 3296733; Telefax: 0712-2721216

Bengaluru : No. 16/1 (Old 12/1), 1st Floor, Next to Hotel Highlands, Madhava Nagar, Race Course Road, Bengaluru - 560 001. Phone: 080-22286611, 22385461, 4113 8821, 22281541

Hyderabad : No. 3-4-184, Lingampally, Besides Raghavendra Swamy Matham, Kachiguda, Hyderabad - 500 027. Phone: 040-27560041, 27550139

Chennai : 8/2 Madley 2nd street, T. Nagar, Chennai - 600 017. Mobile: 09320490962

Pune : First Floor, "Laksha" Apartment, No. 527, Mehunpura, Shaniwarpeth (Near Prabhat Theatre), Pune - 411 030. Phone: 020-24496323/24496333; Mobile: 09370579333

Lucknow : House No 731, Shekhupura Colony, Near B.D. Convent School, Aliganj, Lucknow - 226 022. Phone: 0522-4012353; Mobile: 09307501549

Ahmedabad : 114, "SHAIL", 1st Floor, Opp. Madhu Sudan House, C.G. Road, Navrang Pura, Ahmedabad - 380 009. Phone: 079-26560126; Mobile: 09377088847

Ernakulam : 39/176 (New No: 60/251) 1st Floor, Karikkamuri Road, Ernakulam, Kochi – 682011. Phone: 0484-2378012, 2378016; Mobile: 09387122121

Bhubaneswar : 5 Station Square, Bhubaneswar - 751 001 (Odisha). Phone: 0674-2532129, Mobile: 09338746007

Indore : Kesardeep Avenue Extension, 73, Narayan Bagh, Flat No. 302, IIIrd Floor, Near Humpty Dumpty School, Indore - 452 007 (M.P.). Mobile: 09303399304

Kolkata : 108/4, Beliaghata Main Road, Near ID Hospital, Opp. SBI Bank, Kolkata - 700 010, Phone: 033-32449649, Mobile: 7439040301

Guwahati : House No. 15, Behind Pragjyotish College, Near Sharma Printing Press, P.O. Bharalumukh, Guwahati - 781009, (Assam). Mobile: 09883055590, 08486355289, 7439040301

DTP by : Vani Graphics, Hyderabad.

Printed at : M/s Sri Sai Art Printer Hyderabad. On behalf of HPH.

PREFACE

Management constitutes the cutting edge of business strategies of organizations to compete at the global level. In fact, management is universal and all pervasive as it adds quality to every sphere of activity from school management to space project management. Today, it is impossible to find a field of study, wherein the management principles, theories and models are not applied. One cannot imagine an activity of any organization without the management functions of planning, organizing, staffing, directing, controlling, reporting and budgeting etc. Right from a tiny organization to a giant MNC, the grading depends upon the quality of management.

Engineering technology is the engine that drives the economies whereas management is the fuel to run the engine smoothly. Engineering, science and technology invent new ideas, formulas and design through their incessant research. Business organizations by innovation transform the above into products and services to fulfill the needs and comforts of the society. Large scale production and distribution of these goods and services, balancing the demand and supply situation requires expertise knowledge, skills and abilities on the part of the business executives.

Management science performs this function by making the organizations do their business successfully. Management science teaches how to utilize the various resources – men, material, machines, money etc. optimally and productively, how to reduce costs, eliminate wastes and non-valve adding activities to gain competitive advantage and how to maximize the wealth of the organization. Basically management science tells how to do the things in a planned and organized manner to achieve the ultimate objectives. It gives orientation to real life work environment through case studies and explains how quality decisions can be taken for any given situation.

In this context, the authors are delighted to present before the esteemed readers, a comprehensive book on Management Science; embracing all core functional areas of Management viz., Management Theory and Practice, Production and Operations Management, Project Management, Human Resource Management, Marketing Management, Financial Management, Strategic Management, Organizational Behavior, Business Communication, Business Ethics and Contemporary Management Practices etc. Every effort has been made to present the concepts in an easy, clear, lucid and systematic manner. At the end of each chapter, theoretical questions including objective questions covering the entire topics are given.

This book has been specially designed mainly keeping in view the academic requirements of Engineering students, particularly those of JNTU. This book is highly useful for different category of users including the following:

- *All Engineering students studying Management Science as a subject.*
- *For BBM/BBA/MBA students.*
- *For students studying B.Com/M.Com/CA/ICWA/ACS and other business studies.*
- *For teachers of business studies*
- *To all who are interested to know the ABCD..., of Management Science.*

This profusely illustrated and well organized text book with its fine blend of theory and problems would also be useful for the Trainee Managers, Management Practitioners, Practicing Executives and Professionals and Administrative Officers working in public and private sectors with non-management background.

We are confident that with all these features the readers will find it highly useful. We humbly welcome constructive suggestions from the readers for future improvement of the next edition.

Dr. P. G. Ramanujam
Dr. B. V. R. Naidu
Prof. P. V. Rama Sastry

JNTU, KAKINADA SYLLABUS

MANAGEMENT SCIENCE

Unit - I ***Introduction to Management :*** Concept –nature and importance of Management – Functions of Management – Evaluation of Management thought-Theories of Motivation – Decision making process-Designing organization structure-Principles of organization - Types of organization structure

Unit - II ***Operations Management :*** Principles and Types of Plant Layout – Work study-Statistical Quality Control- Control charts (P-chart, R-chart, and C-chart) Simple problems- Material Management: Need for Inventory control- EOQ, ABC analysis (simple problems) and Types of ABC analysis (HML, SDE, VED, and FSN analysis)

Unit - III ***Functional Management :*** Concept of HRM, HRD and PMIR- Functions of HR Manager- Wage payment plans(Simple Problems) – Job Evaluation and Merit Rating - Marketing Management- Functions of Marketing – Marketing strategies based on product Life Cycle, Channels of distributions.

Unit - IV ***Project Management (PERT/CPM) :*** Development of Network – Difference between PERT and CPM - Identifying Critical Path- Probability- Project Crashing (Simple Problems)

Unit - V ***Strategic Management :*** Vision, Mission, Goals, Strategy – Elements of Corporate Planning Process – Environmental Scanning – SWOT analysis- Steps in Strategy Formulation and Implementation, Generic Strategy alternatives

Unit - VI ***Management Ethics :*** Importance of Ethics in Business and Management – Ethics in Marketing - HRM-Financial Management – Business Ethics and Law (Case example)

Unit - VII ***Business Communication :*** Report writing – Cross Cultural Communication, Problems and Challenges- Presentation Skills – Interviews- Video conferences

Unit - VIII ***Contemporary Management Practice :*** Basic concepts of MIS, MRP, Just-in-Time(JIT) system, Total Quality Management(TQM), Six sigma and Capability Maturity Model(CMM) Levies, Supply Chain Management , Enterprise Resource Planning (ERP), Performance Management, Business Process outsourcing (BPO), Business process Re-engineering and Bench Marking, Balanced Score Card.

CONTENTS

UNIT - I

INTRODUCTION TO MANAGEMENT

Introduction :

Every human being has several needs and desires. But no individual can satisfy all his wants. Therefore, people work together to meet their mutual needs which they cannot fulfill individually. Moreover, man is a social being as he likes to live together with other people. It is by working and living together in organized groups and institutions that people satisfy their economic and social needs. As a result there are several types of groups, e.g., family, school, government, army, a business firm, a cricket team and the like. Such formal groups can achieve their goals effectively only when the efforts of the people working in these groups are properly coordinated. The task of getting results through others by coordinating their efforts is known as organizational management.

1.1 CONCEPT OF MANAGEMENT

Management is a key factor for the success of any organized activity and is an essential accompaniment of all social organizations. Management is a discipline and culture. Management is a process, a science, an art and a profession. It is the life-giving, dynamic mechanism of every organization. Management refers to the series of functions, and also to the people who discharge it. As Stafford Beer puts it, the "old world was characterized by the need to manage resources like stone, wood, iron but the new world is characterized by the need to manage complexity as complexity is the very stuff of today's world". Today, management refers to managing changes and challenges crises and complexities; culture and credibility to succeed and to accomplish. Management is the art of getting things done through people for the achievement of organizational goals.

Definition of Management :

It is very difficult to give a precise definition of the term 'management'. Different scholars from different disciplines viewed and interpreted management from their own angles. The economists consider management as a resource like land, labor, capital and organization. The bureaucrats look upon it as a system of authority to achieve business goals. The sociologists consider managers as a part of the class elite in the society.

The definitions by some of the leading management thinkers and practitioners are given below:

(i) Management is the coordination of all resources through the process of planning, organizing, directing and controlling in order to attain stated objectives. **– Henry L. Sisk.**

(ii) Management is the art and science of organizing and directing human efforts applied to control the forces and utilize the materials of nature for the benefit of man. **– American Society of Mechanical Engineers**

(iii) Management is the creation and maintenance of an internal environment in an enterprise where individuals, working in groups, can perform efficiently and effectively towards the attainment of group goals. **– Harold Koontz and Cyril O'Donnel**

(vi) Management is the art of knowing what you want to do and then seeing that it is done in the best and cheapest way. **– F.W. Taylor**

(v) To manage is to forecast and to plan, to organize, to command, to coordinate and to control. **– Henry Fayol**

(vi) Management is the function of executive leadership anywhere. **– Ralph C. Davis**

(vii) Management is a distinct process consisting of planning, organizing, actuating and controlling performance to determine and accomplish the objectives by the use of people and resources. **– George R. Terry**

(viii) Management is guiding human and physical resources into dynamic organizational units which attain their objectives to the satisfaction of those served and with a high degree of morale and sense of attainment on the part of those rendering service. **– American Management Association**

(ix) Management is a multipurpose organ that manages a business and manages managers and manages workers and work. **– Peter F. Drucker**

The Revolution of Management:

For thousands of years, managers have wrestled with the same issues and problems confronting executives today. Around 1100 B.C., the Chinese practiced the four management functions—planning, organizing, leading, and controlling. Between 350 and 400 B.C., the Greeks recognized management as a separate art and advocated a scientific approach to work. The Romans decentralized the management of their vast empire before the birth of Christ. During medieval times, the Venetians standardized production through the use of an assembly line, building warehouses and using an inventory system to monitor the contents.

Till the onset of industrial revolution most managers operated strictly on a trial-and-error basis. But the challenges of the industrial revolution changed that. Management emerged as a formal discipline at the turn of the century. The first university to offer management and business education, the Wharton School at the University of Pennsylvania and the Amos Tuck School at Dartmouth, were founded in the late 19th century. By 1914, 25 business schools existed.

Thus, the management profession today is relatively new when compared to the earlier period. Understanding the origins of management thought will help to grasp the underlying contexts of the ideas and concepts presented.

Out of the great variety of ideas about how to improve management, parts of each approach have survived and been incorporated into modern perspectives on management. Thus, the legacy of past efforts, triumphs, and failures have become a guide for future management practice.

Concepts of Management :

Management is a social process of planning, organizing, co-ordination, commanding and controlling for the purpose of achieving organizational goals by using limited resources efficiently by working with and through people.

The term management has been interpreted in several ways; some of which are given below:

Management as an Activity :

Management is an activity just like playing, studying, teaching etc. As an activity, management has been defined as the art of getting things done through the efforts of other people. But to channelize the group efforts into a unified force, managers have to plan, organize, direct and control the activities of both group and individuals to achieve the objectives of the group and the organization.

The activities of management are:

- Interpersonal activities
- Decisional activities
- Informative activities

Management as a Process

Management is considered a process, because it involves a series of interrelated functions. It consists of getting the objectives of an organization and taking steps to achieve objectives. The management process includes planning, organizing, staffing, directing and controlling functions.

Management as a process has the following implications:

(i) ***Social Process***: Management involves interactions among people. Goals can be achieved only when relations between people are productive. Managing human factor is the most important and complex function of the management.

(ii) ***Integrated Process:*** Management brings human, physical and financial resources together to put into effort. Management also integrates human efforts so as to maintain harmony among them.

(iii) *Continuous Process:* Management involves continuous identification of problems and solving them. It is repeated every now and then till the goal is achieved.

(iv) *Interactive Process:* Managerial functions are contained within each other. For example, when a manager prepares plans, he is also laying down standards for control.

Management as an Economic Resource :

Like land, labour and capital, management is an important factor of production. Management occupies the central place among productive factors as it combines and coordinates all other resources. This is shown in Fig. 1.1.

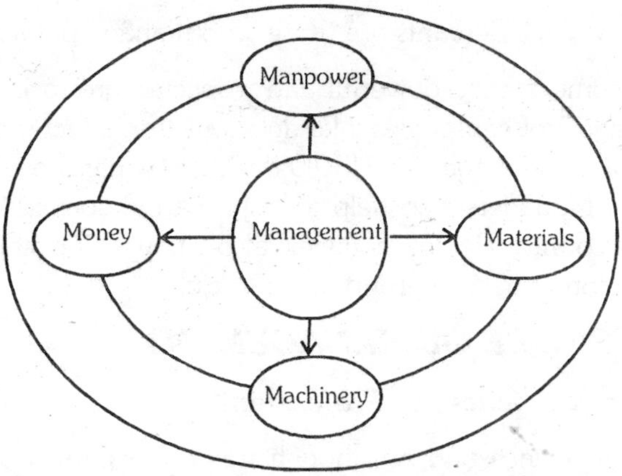

Figure 1.1. : Management as Resource

Management as a Team

As a group of persons, management consists of all those who have the responsibility of guiding and coordinating the efforts of other persons. These persons are called as managers who operate at different levels of authority (top, middle, operating). Some of these managers have ownership stake in their firms while others have become managers by virtue of their training and experience. Civil servants and Defense personnel who manage public sector undertakings are also part of the management team. As a group, managers have become an elite class in society occupying positions with enormous power and prestige.

Management as an Academic Discipline

Management has emerged as a specialized branch of knowledge. It comprises principles and practices for effective management of organizations. Management profession attained glamour and it is evident from the great rush for admission into institutes of management. Management offers a very rewarding and challenging career.

Management as a Group

Management means the group of persons occupying managerial positions. It refers to all those individuals who perform managerial functions. The chief executive, managing director and board of directors, departmental heads, managers, assistant managers, supervisors and so on are collectively known as management.

For example, when one remarks that the management of Infosys is good, it is referring to the persons who are managing the company.

Types of Managers

Managers can be categorized into the following:

(i) ***Family managers***: Family managers are those who have become managers by virtue of their being owners or relatives of the owners of a company.

(ii) ***Professional managers***: Professional managers are those who have been appointed on account of their degree or diploma in management.

(iii) ***Civil Servants***: Civil Servants are those who manage public sector undertakings.

Managers have become a very powerful and respected group in modern society. This is because the senior managers of companies take decisions that affect the lives of a large number of people. For example, if the managers of TISCO decide to expand production it will create jobs for thousands of people. Managers also help to improve the social life of the public and the economic progress of the country. Senior managers also enjoy a high standard of living in society. They have, therefore, become an elite group in the society.

1.2 NATURE AND SCOPE OF MANAGEMENT

Is Management an Art, a Science, or Profession?

Management is both science and art, though it is not a perfect art as music or painting. Similarly, it is not a perfect science as physical or chemical science.

Art: It is bringing about the desired result through application of skills and strategies. The management plans, organizes, directs, coordinates and controls all activities of the organization. Intuition and creativity are often the key ingredients of successful managers.

Science: Science on the other hand, is a systematic body of knowledge acquired by making through observations, experiments and intelligence, which may be verified by researchers. Many theories of management have evolved through experimentation and the results are well structured. Examples are leadership and motivation theories. Many areas of Operations Management such as forecasting, production planning and control, inventory management, etc., are more towards science. Thus, management is both science and arts. Generally, it is the situation which determines the orientation towards science or art.

Profession: Profession is an independent occupation chosen on the basis of one's specialized knowledge and qualifications.For example a lawyer, doctor, tax consultant etc., Every profession has a code of conduct. Now management discipline has transformed into a profession as many consultancies, promotion and ad-agencies are doing good business.

Characteristics of Management

The salient features which highlight the nature of management are as follows:

(i) ***Management is goal-oriented:*** Management is not an end in itself. It is a means to achieve certain goals. Management has no justification to exist without goals.

Management goals are called group goals or organizational goals. The basic goal of management is to ensure efficiency and economy in the utilization of human, physical and financial resources. The success of management is measured by the extent to which the established goals are achieved. Thus, management is purposeful.

(ii) ***Management is universal:*** Management is an essential element of every organized activity irrespective of the size or type of activity. Wherever two or more persons are engaged in working for a common goal, management is necessary. All types of organizations, e.g., family, club, university, government, army, cricket team or business, require management. Thus, management is an all pervasive activity. The fundamental principles of management are applicable in all areas of organized effort. Managers at all levels perform the same basic functions.

(iii) ***Management is an integrative force:*** The essence of management lies in the coordination of individual efforts in to a team. Management reconciles the individual goals with organizational goals. As unifying force, management creates a whole that is more than the sum of individual parts. It integrates human and other resources like money, material and machine.

(iv) ***Management is a social process:*** Management is done by people, through people and for people. It is a social process because it is concerned with interpersonal relations. Human factor is the most important element in management. According to Appley, "Management is the development of people not the direction of things. A good manager is a leader not a boss. It is the pervasiveness of human element which gives management its special character as a social process".

(v) ***Management is multidisciplinary:*** Management has to deal with human behavior under dynamic conditions. Therefore, it depends upon wide knowledge, derived from several disciplines like engineering, sociology, psychology, economics, anthropology, etc., The vast body of knowledge in management science draws concepts and theories from other fields of study.

(vi) ***Management is a continuous Process:*** Management is a dynamic and an on-going process. The cycle of management continues to operate so long as there is organized action for the achievement of group goals.

(vii) ***Management is Intangible:*** Management is an unseen or invisible force. It cannot be seen but its presence can be felt everywhere in the form of results. However, the managers who perform the functions of management are very much tangible and visible.

(viii) ***Management is an art, science, and profession:*** It contains a systematic body of theoretical knowledge and it also involves the practical application of such knowledge. Management is also a discipline involving specialized training and an ethical code is also required arising out of its social obligations.

On the basis of these characteristics, management may be defined as a continuous social process involving the coordination of human and material resources in order to accomplish desired objectives. It involves both the determination and the accomplishment of organizational goals.

FEATURES OF MANAGEMENT

1. Management is a social process:

Management activities are carried out by administrators, politicians, economists, housewives, parents, doctors, lawyers, professors etc., Management is an integral part of social process which facilitates everyone to carry out the activities in a planned way to get success. Management also denotes a body of people involved in decision making.

2. Management is universal and present in all organizations:

Management principles apply to every kind of organization and also to every level in it.

3. Management is inexact science:

In mathematics and pure sciences like physics and chemistry etc., the principles will be static in nature. They will not change and the same result comes in the lab when the particular process is followed. As management theories depend upon social sciences like economics, psychology and philosophy etc., the conditions change very fastly and hence complexity arises

4. It is a complex phenomena

Specialized knowledge and skills are required to find solutions to different problems. Professional approach to managers is essential.

5. Management is situational in nature:

The change in the situation may call for a change in the style of functioning of the manager.

6. Management is an art and also a science

Management can be considered as an art as it satisfies all the criteria of an art as there is scope to apply creativity. Management is a systematic body of knowledge, its principles are universally acceptable, applicable and it stands for logical reasoning, scientific testing and inquiry. Hence management is considered as both science and art.

7. Management is inter-disciplinary:

The subject of management heavily depends upon other disciplines like economics, statistics, operations research, sociology, psychology, mathematics... etc.,

8. Management is a profession:

The managers are professional in their approach and are governed by code of conduct and ethics.

1.3 OBJECTIVES AND IMPORTANCE OF MANAGEMENT:

Objectives of Management:

The objectives of management are narrated as under.

(i) Organizational objectives:

Management is expected to work for the achievement of the objectives of the particular organization in which it exists. Organizational objectives include:

(a) Reasonable profits so as to give a fair return on the capital invested in business

(b) Survival and solvency of the business, i.e., continuity.

(c) Growth and expansion of the enterprise

(d) Improving the goodwill or reputation of the enterprise.

(ii) Personal objectives:

An organization consists of several persons who have their own objectives. These objectives are as follows:

(a) Fair remuneration for work performed

(b) Reasonable working conditions

(c) Opportunities for training and development

(d) Participation in management and prosperity of the enterprise

(e) Reasonable security of service.

(iii) Social objectives:

Management is not only a representative of the owners and workers, but is also responsible to the various groups outside the organization. It is expected to fulfill the objectives of the society which are given below:

(a) Quality goods and services at fair prices to consumers.

(b) Honest and prompt payment of taxes to the Government.

(c) Conservation of environment and natural resources.

(d) Fair dealings with suppliers, dealers and competitors.

(e) Preservation of ethical values of the society.

(f) Protection of environment

Role and Importance of Management

Management is indispensable for the successful functioning of every organization. It is all the more important in business enterprises. No business runs in itself, every business needs repeated stimulus which can only be provided by management.

According to Peter F Drucker, "management is a dynamic life giving element in an organization, and without it the resources of production remain mere resources and never become production".

The importance of management has been highlighted clearly in the following points:

(i) Achievement of group goals:

A human group consists of several persons, each specializing in doing a part of the total task. Each person may be working efficiently, but the group as a whole cannot realize its objectives unless there is mutual cooperation and coordination among the members of the group. Management creates team-work and coordination in the group. It reconciles the objectives of the group with those of its members so that each one of them is motivated to make his best contribution towards the accomplishment of group goals. Managers provide inspiring leadership to keep the members of the group working smart.

(ii) Optimum utilization of resources:

Managers forecast the need for materials, machinery, money and manpower. They ensure that the organization has adequate resources and at the same time does not have idle resources. They create and maintain an environment conducive to highest productivity. Managers make sure that workers know their jobs well and use the most efficient methods of work. They provide training and guidance to employees so that they can make the best use of the available resources.

(iii) Minimization of cost:

In the modern era of cut-throat competition no business can succeed unless it is able to supply the required goods and services at the lowest possible cost per unit. Management directs day-to-day operations in such a manner that all wastage and extravagance are avoided. By reducing costs and improving efficiency, managers enable an enterprise to be competent to face competitors and earn profits.

(iv) Survival and growth:

Modern business operates in a rapidly changing environment. An enterprise has to adapt itself to the changing demands of the market and society. Management keeps in touch with the existing business environment and draws its predictions about the trends in future. It takes steps in advance, to meet the challenges of changing environment. Changes in business environment create risks as well as opportunities. Managers enable the enterprise to minimize the risks and maximize the benefits of opportunities. In this way, managers facilitate the continuity and prosperity of business.

(v) Generation of employment:

By setting up and expanding business enterprises, managers create jobs for the people. People earn their livelihood by working in these organizations. Managers also create such an environment that people working in enterprise can get job satisfaction and happiness. In this way Managers help to satisfy the economic and social needs of the employees.

(vi) Development of the nation:

Efficient management is equally important at the national level. Management is the most crucial factor in economic and social development. The development of a country largely depends on the quality of the management of its resources. Capital investment and import of technical knowhow cannot lead to economic growth unless wealth producing resources are managed efficiently. By producing wealth, management increases the national income and the standards of living of people. That is why management is regarded as a key to the economic growth of a country.

(vii) Ensures economy and efficiency:

Optimum utilization of the resources with possible minimum cost should be the motto of every organization. At the same time quality should not suffer.

1.4 MAJOR FUNCTIONAL AREAS OF MANAGEMENT

Organization means people working in groups together to accomplish the pre-determined goals of an organization. This can be accomplished only when the functions of an organization are scientifically divided and delegated to different groups or departments. The major functional areas of any organization are mainly fourfold in the past. They are production, marketing, finance, and human resource functions. But today we have to necessarily add another function- Information Technology Management, otherwise the organization will be viewed as an outdated one.

i. Production function:

The purpose of creating an organization is to produce goods or services for the benefit of the society. The justification for its existence is producing all such goods and services which satisfy the society needs and maximizes the utility and satisfaction. The success of a manufacturing organization depends upon the quality of the produce and hence meticulous care should be taken in the production process at each and every stage. The main objective of any productive function is to minimize the cost of production and maximize the quality output. Hence in every organization production function is regarded as number one function and production department and manager remain in focus.

ii. Marketing function:

What ever product or service is produced by the production department is for society's consumption. In marketing function, the product or service travels through the marketing channels to ultimately reach the consumer. That means the marketing function delivers standard of living to the people by creating product, price, and place utility. The product or services of the organization are transformed into cash inflows by the sales efficiency of the sales people in the marketing department. Marketing function is also called distribution function. The survival of the organization depends upon the efficiency of marketing function. Creativity and innovativeness are two important qualities a marketing department should possess for the success of the marketing function.

iii. Finance function:

Finance is the life blood of any organization. Finance is required to start and run an organization. The money brought for the purpose of creating an organization is called capital. The capital is used for buying fixed assets like land, plant, building, machinery, etc., and a part of it is required for paying various expenses like raw-material, wages, salaries etc., which is called working capital. Managing successfully the cash outflows and inflows for maximizing profit in the short-run and maximizing the wealth of the shareholders in the long-run is the main objective of the finance function. Finance function is a complex function as it is tied up with various legal obligations. The ultimate objective of finance function is minimizing the cost of funds raised externally and maximizing the benefit to the owners or shareholders of the organization.

iv. Human resource function:

The last but the most important function is human resource function as it is the human resource which has to carry on the production function, marketing function and finance function. In fact organization means people and without people there is no organization or any purpose of the organization. An organization is established by people with people and for the people. The success and survival of any organization depends upon the kind of human resource taken into the organization. The main objective of HR function is to staff the organization with the right kind and quality HR to man all the positions in the organization. The HR function comprises of various sub-functions like recruitment, selection, placement, induction, and training and development etc. The latest development in the global arena is that the human resource is regarded as highly valuable human capital and some of the globally renowned firms are valuing their human resources and showing them in their financial statements like other assets.

v. Information Technology function:

Computerization of almost all organizations has changed the face and pace of all organizational functions right from production to controlling. Now, data is stored in the computer rather than in the files and records. Arranging this information and retrieving the same at the time of need by using different software is the order of the day. Managing information technology is essential for all decision-making which is the essence of management.

1.5 FUNCTIONS OF MANAGEMENT

Functions of management are the activities done by the top level people in the organization. The process of management covers certain functions to be performed in a logical sequence.

Luther Gullick identified "POSDCORB" P-planning, O-organizing, S-staffing, D- directing, Co-coordinating, R-reporting, and B-budgeting as functions of management. Here reporting and budgeting are covered as elements of controlling and planning. So, it is not a standard classification of functions as the most important function, controlling was omitted.

Henry Fayol gave a list of five functions as elements of management process. They are Planning, Organizing, Commanding, Coordinating and Controlling.

According to ***Koontz***, management functions are:

- Planning
- Organizing
- Staffing
- Directing (includes Leadership, Motivation, Communication and Coordination) and
- Controlling

Management is the process of working with people and resources to accomplish organizational goals. Good managers do those things both effectively and efficiently. To be effective is to achieve organizational goals. To be efficient is to achieve goals without waste of resources, that is, effective managers make the best possible use of money, time, materials, and people. Some managers fail on both criteria, or focus on one at the expense of another. The best managers maintain a clear focus on both effectiveness and efficiency.

The context of business and the specifics of doing business are changing, but there are still plenty of timeless principles that make great managers, and great companies. Fresh thinking and new approaches are required now for the 21st-century business environment.

1. Planning: Delivering Strategic Value

Planning refers to the process of preparing for the future by choosing the best course of action to achieve the goals. In detail planning involves essentially four stages:

- Identifying the goals to be achieved.
- Exploring the courses of action or alternatives available to reach each goal .
- Weighing each alternative on the basis of its merits, demerits and costs.
- Selecting the best course of action for implementing.

Elements of Planning:

- ***Forecasts :*** Prediction of what will happen in future on the basis of past and present data.
- ***Objectives :*** Objectives are set for every individual, group and department in the organization.
- ***Policies :*** Policies specify the do's and don'ts of the employees to achieve the given goal.
- ***Strategies :*** Course of action to be followed and how the resources are to be deployed to achieve the given goals.
- ***Programs :*** Specifies what is to be done.
- ***Procedures*** : Outline how a task is to be carried out.
- ***Schedules :*** Indicate what is to be done at a given point of time.
- ***Budgets :*** Estimating the sales budget and other departmental budgets etc.

Features of Planning:

1. Planning is specifying the goals to be achieved
2. Deciding in advance the appropriate actions needed to achieve those goals
3. Planning activities include analyzing current situations
4. Anticipating the future
5. Determining the objectives

6. Deciding in what types of activities the company will engage
7. Choosing corporate and business strategies
8. Determining the resources needed to achieve the organization's goals.
9. Plans set the stage for action and for major achievements
10. Delivering strategic value

Historically, planning describes a top-down approach in which top executives establish business plans and tell others to implement them. Now and in the future, delivering strategic value is a continual process in which people throughout the organization use their brains to identify opportunities to create, seize, strengthen, and sustain competitive advantage. This dynamic process revolves around the objective of creating more and more value for the customer and increasing the wealth of shareholders.

2. *Organizing: Building a Dynamic Organization*

Organizing refers to the process of grouping the related activities and assigning them to a manager with authority to supervise it. Responsibility is fixed to every manager for achieving the given goals. The well defined authority and responsibility are used as tools to evaluate one's performance at work. The functions of organizing provides the manager enough flexibility in the organization to create higher managerial positions that the employees want to reach.

Organizing is assembling and coordinating the human, financial, physical, informational, and other resources needed to achieve goals. Organizing activities include attracting people to the organization, specifying job responsibilities, grouping jobs into work units, marshaling and allocating resources, and creating conditions so that people and things work together to achieve maximum success.

In the past organizing involved creating an organization chart by identifying business functions, establishing and reporting relationships, and having a personnel department that administers plans, programs, and paper and computer work. Now and in the future, effective managers will be using new forms of organizing and viewing their people as perhaps their most valuable resources. They will build organizations that are flexible and adaptive, particularly in response to competitive threats and customer needs. Progressive human resource practices that attract and retain the very best of a highly diverse population will be essential aspects of the successful company.

3. *Staffing:*

Staffing refers to filling the positions in the organization with the right people. Staffing function covers every activity done by a H R Manager in an organization such as recruitment, selection, training, placement, appraisals, training and development promotions and career planning.

4. *Directing or Leading: Mobilizing People*

Directing is a process of issuing orders and instructions to guide and teach the subordinates the proper method of work and ensuring that they perform their jobs as planned.

The manager has to perform the following functions while directing the members of his group.

- ***Leading :*** It is a function of management in which the employees are directed, so that the objectives of the transition will be successfully achieved. It is quite likely that the workers willingly and enthusiastically perform their job, if they like their leader.

- ***Motivating :*** The process of stimulating the employees to perform more effectively using their abilities and full potential is called motivation. It can be broadly categorized into two types 1. Financial and 2. Non financial.

1. Financial factors include competitive salary package, which includes monthly/annual salary, bonus, overtime, allowances, medical & telephone bills, etc.
2. Non financial factors include appreciation from the top, congenial work environment, career growth, flexible working hours, giving work on live projects etc.,
    - ***Communicating :*** It is a process of creating, transmitting and interpreting messages, ideas, facts opinions and feelings.
    - ***Coordinating :*** Coordination refers to the process of arranging group efforts in such a way that the common purpose is achieved efficiently & effectively.

Leading is the ability of a leader to influence people to follow his direction. It includes motivating and communicating with employees, individually and in groups. Leading involves close day-today contact with people and guiding and inspiring them toward achieving team and organizational goals. Leading takes place in teams, departments, and divisions, as well as at the top levels of organizations.

Earlier the leading function was about how managers motivated workers to come to work and execute top management's plans by doing their jobs. Today and in the future, managers must be good at mobilizing people to contribute their ideas and utilize their talents to the maximum. They must rely on a very different kind of leadership that empowers and motivates people. Far more than in the past, great work must be done via great teamwork, both within work groups and across group boundaries. Effective interpersonal and organizational communication will help in achieveing this task.

5. *Controlling: Learning and Changing Controlling:*

It is the process of measuring the current performance of the employee and assess whether the given objectives are achieved or not.

It involves:

- Measuring the actual performance of the employee.
- Comparing it with the target and
- Taking follow up action, that is, corrective or remedial action for improving the performance if necessary

Planning, organizing, staffing and leading are not just sufficient. Controlling function is very important as it monitors performance and implements necessary changes.

Successful organizations, large and small, pay close attention to the controlling function. The key managerial challenges are far more dynamic than in the past as they involve continually learning and changing. Controls must still be in place, but new technologies and other innovations make it possible to achieve controls in more effective ways, and to help all the people throughout the company, and across company boundaries (including customers and suppliers), to use their brains to learn and make a variety of new contributions to build a successful future.

The above management functions apply to an individual also. An individual has to plan for his or her own career, organize all the talents and skills effectively, controlling negative deviations to enhance his or her value in the organization.

Performing all five Management Functions:

For a manager, work will not be neatly divided into the four functions to do them at different times. Situations demand the managers to do many things more or less simultaneously. These activities will include all the management functions. A manager should devote adequate attention and resources to all functions. A manager may be a skilled planner, but if the manager fails to organize the people or fails to motivate them to perform at high levels, the manager will be regarded as an ineffective manager. Likewise, the manager who doesn't really understand where to go or how to do is also an inefficient planner. Good managers don't neglect any management functions as every function is very important.

Foundations of Planning

- Planning is the ongoing process of developing the business' mission and objectives and determining how they will be accomplished. Planning takes in to account both the high level and low level aspects i.e., from vision and mission to strategies and tactics.

Planning is the first function of management. Planning involves defining the organization's goals, establishing an overall strategy for achieving these goals, and developing plans for organizational work activities.

Purposes of Planning

Planning serves a number of significant purposes.

1. Planning establishes goals or standards used in controlling.
2. Planning gives direction to managers for carrying on activities of an organization.
3. Planning reduces uncertainty.
4. Planning minimizes waste.

Planning and Performance linkage:

Most research studies show positive relationships between planning and performance. Effective planning and implementation play a greater part in high performance. Studies have shown that when formal planning has not led to higher performance, the external environment is often the reason.

Goals and Plans in Planning:

Planning is the primary management function. It starts the other functions like organising, leading and controlling. Planning involves two important elements: goals and plans.

Goals are desired outcomes for individuals, groups, or entire organization. They are often termed as objectives.

Types of goals

a. ***Financial goals*** related to the financial performance of the organization.

b. ***Strategic goals*** related to other areas of an organizations performance.

c. ***Stated goals*** are official statements of an organization. The objective of the organization is to create belief in the stakeholders of the organization.

d. ***Real goals:*** Actions pursued by organizational members

Types of Plans

Plans can be described by their breadth, time frame, specificity, and frequency of use

1. ***On the basis of breadth, plans can be strategic or operational plans.***

   a) ***Strategic plans:*** Generally they are long-term plans that apply to the entire organization. They establish the organization's overall goals, and position the organization in terms of its environment.

   b) ***Operational plans:*** These plans are generally called as short-term plans. Operational plans are plans that specify the details of how the overall goals are to be achieved.

2. ***On the basis of time frame plans, can be short-term or long-term plans.***

   a) ***Short-term plans*** are plans that cover one year or less.

   b) ***Long-term plans*** are plans with a time frame beyond three years.

3. ***On the basis of specificity plans, can be specific or directional plans.***

   a) ***Specific plans*** are plans that are clearly defined and leave no room for interpretation.

   b) ***Directional plans*** are flexible plans that set out general guidelines.

4. ***On the basis of frequency of use, plans can be single-use or standing plans.***

   a) ***Single-use plan*** is a one-time plan specifically designed to meet the needs of a unique situation.

   b) ***Standing plans*** are ongoing plans that provide guidance for activities performed repeatedly.

Approaches to Establishing Goals

Goals can be established through the process of traditional goal setting or through MBO (Management by Objectives).

Traditional goal setting is an approach to setting goals in which goals are set at the top level of the organization and then broken into sub goals for each level of the organization.

Traditional goal setting believes that top managers know what is best because of their ability to see the "big picture." Employees are to work to meet the goals for their particular area of responsibility.

This traditional approach requires that goals must be made more specific as they flow down to lower levels in the organization. In striving to achieve specificity, however, objectives sometimes lose clarity and unity with goals set at a higher level. When the hierarchy of organizational goals is clearly defined, it forms an integrated **means-end chain**—an integrated network of goals in which the accomplishment of goals at one level serves as the means for achieving the goals or ends at the next level.

Management by Objectives

Management by Objectives (MBO) is a process of setting mutually agreed-upon goals and using those goals to evaluate employee performance. Studies of actual MBO programs reveal that MBO increases employee performance and organizational productivity. However, Top management's commitment and involvement are important contributions for the success of an MBO program.

The following steps are involved in a typical MBO program:

- Formulation of Objectives and Strategies
- Allocation of objectives to divisions departments and units
- Unit managers collaboratively set specific objectives for their units with their managers
- Specific objectives are collaboratively set with all department members
- Consulting the department members for consensus
- Action plans, defining how objectives are to be achieved, are specified and agreed upon by managers and employees
- Implementation of action plans
- Periodical review of Progress
- Rewarding the Performance

Whether an organization uses a more traditional approach to establish objectives, uses some form of MBO, or has its own approach, managers must define objectives before they can effectively and efficiently complete other planning activities.

Five Characteristics of Well-Designed Goals

1. Measurable and quantifiable
2. Clear as to a time frame
3. Drafted on realistic grounds

4. Challenging, but attainable
5. Communicated to all organizational members

Five Steps in Goals Setting

1. Review the organization's **mission**
2. Evaluate available resources.
3. Determine goals on the basis of inputs from all the relevant people
4. Write down the goals and communicate them to all who need to know.
5. Review results and check whether goals are being met. Make changes as needed.

Developing Plans

The process of developing plans is influenced by three contingency factors and by the particular planning approach used by the organization.

Three Contingency Factors in Planning are:

1. ***Manager's level in the organization:*** Operational planning usually dominates the planning activities of lower-level managers. As managers move up through the levels of the organization, their planning becomes more strategy-oriented.
2. ***Degree of environmental uncertainty***: The greater the environmental uncertainty, the more directional plans should be, with emphasis placed on the short term. When uncertainty is high, plans should be specific but flexible. Managers must be prepared to rework and amend plans or even to abandon their plans if necessary.
3. ***Length of future commitments:*** According to the commitment concept, plans should extend far enough to meet those commitments made today. Planning for too long or for too short a time period is inefficient and ineffective.

Approaches to Planning

In the traditional approach, planning was done entirely by top-level managers who were often assisted by a ***formal planning department***.

Another approach to planning is to involve more members of the organization in the planning process. In this approach, plans are not handed down from one level to the next, but are developed by organizational members at various levels to meet their specific needs.

- ***Organizing:*** Organizing is establishing the internal organizational structure of the organization. The focus is on division, coordination, and control of tasks and the flow of information within the organization. It is in this function that managers distribute authority to job holders.
- ***Staffing:*** Staffing is filling the organization with qualified people in all positions of the organization. Recruiting, hiring, training, evaluating and compensating are the specific activities included in the function. In the family business, staffing includes all paid and unpaid positions held by outsiders and family members.

- ***Directing***: It is influencing people's behavior through motivation, communication, group dynamics, leadership and discipline. The purpose of directing is to channel the behavior of all personnel to accomplish the organization's mission and objectives while simultaneously helping them accomplish their own career objectives.
- ***Controlling***: It is a four-step process of establishing performance standards based on the firm's objectives, measuring and reporting actual performance, comparing the two and taking corrective or preventive action as necessary.

1.6 EVOLUTION OF MANAGEMENT THOUGHT

1.6.1 Introduction

The principles and theories of management have been developed over a period of time as a result of the combination of experiences of management and experiments conducted by management specialists and psychologists. A set of research scholars who have almost supported similar type of perceptions were segregated as a particular school of thought. Those people who believed that scientific management works wonders as per the prophecy of F.W. Taylor come under scientific management school of thought. In the same manner the researchers who supported Henry Fayol's thought as foundation of management science come under administrative school of thought. In the same manner, who followed Elton Mayo advocated that human relations are the most important dynamic factor to decide the productivity and efficiency of the organization come under human relations school. Today, people who believe that systems theory also works out because an organization consists of many subsystems and the success of it depends upon the perfect management of all the systems including information management system come under modern school of management thought.

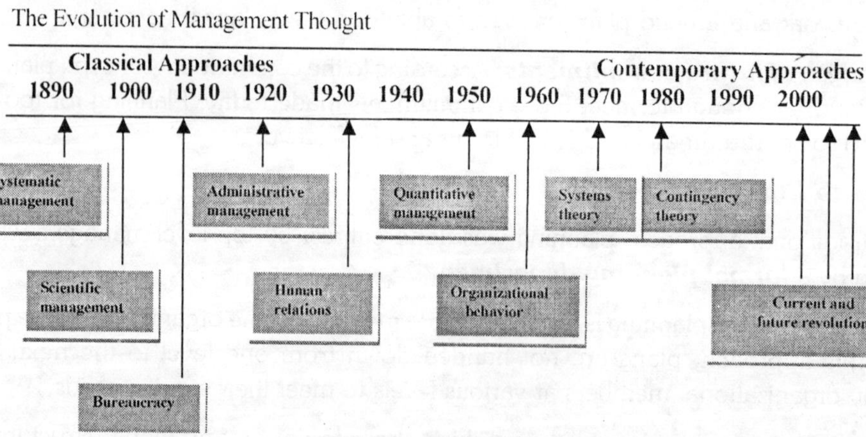

Figure 1.2 : The Evolution of Management Thought

1.6.2 TAYLOR'S SCIENTIFIC MANAGEMENT THEORY

Scientific Management :

Systematic Management failed to lead the production efficiently. This shortcoming became apparent to a young engineer named Frederick Winslow Taylor, who was hired by Midvale Steel Company in 1878. Taylor discovered that production and pay were poor, inefficiency and waste were prevalent, and most companies had tremendous unused potential. He concluded that management decisions were unsystematic and that no research to determine the best means of production existed.

Scientific management was a theory of management that analyzed and synthesized workflows. Its main objective was improving economic efficiency, especially labor productivity. The core ideas of the theory were developed by Frederick Winslow Taylor in the 1880s and 1890s, and were first published in his monographs *Shop Management* (1903) and *The Principles of Scientific Management* (1911).

In response, Taylor introduced a second approach to management, known as ***Scientific management.*** This approach advocated the application of scientific methods to analyze work and to determine how to complete production tasks efficiently.

Taylor identified four principles of Scientific Management:

1. Management should develop a precise, scientific approach for each element of one's work to replace general guidelines.
2. Management should scientifically select, train, teach, and develop each worker so that the right person has the right job.
3. Management should cooperate with workers to ensure that jobs match plans and principles.
4. Management should ensure an appropriate division of work and responsibility between managers and workers.

To implement this approach, Taylor used techniques such as time-and-motion studies. With this technique, a task was divided into its basic movements, and different motions were timed to determine the most efficient way to complete the task.

After the "one best way" to perform the job was identified, Taylor stressed the importance of hiring and training the proper worker to do that job. Taylor advocated the standardization of tools, the use of instruction cards to help workers, and breaks to eliminate fatigue.

Another key element of Taylor's approach was the use of the differential piece rate system. Taylor assumed workers were motivated by receiving money. Therefore, he introduced a system in which workers were paid additional wages when they exceeded a standard level of output for each job. Taylor concluded that both workers and management would benefit from such system.

Frederick Taylor (left) and Dr. Lillian Gilbreth (right) were early experts in management efficiency.

Scientific management principles were widely accepted. Other proponents, including Henry Gantt and Frank and Lillian Gilbreth, introduced many refinements and techniques for applying scientific management on the factory floor. One of the most famous examples of the application of scientific management is the factory Henry Ford built to produce the Model T.

The legacy of Taylor's scientific management approach is broad and pervasive and based on research application of the principles which enhanced productivity and efficiency in manufacturing. The concepts of scientific methods and research were introduced in manufacturing. The piece rate system gained wide acceptance because it more closely aligned effort and reward. Taylor also emphasized the need for cooperation between management and workers. And the concept of a management specialist gained prominence.

Criticism against Scientific Management

1. Critics claimed that Taylor ignored many job-related social and psychological factors by emphasizing only money as a worker incentive.
2. Production tasks were reduced to a set of routine, machinelike procedures that led to boredom, apathy, and quality control problems.
3. Unions strongly opposed scientific management techniques because they believed management might abuse their power to set the standards and the piece rates, thus exploiting workers and diminishing their importance.
4. Scientific management resulted in intense scrutiny of the internal efficiency of organizations, it did not help managers deal with broader external issues such as competitors and government regulations.

Taylor observed that some workers were more talented than others. Even smart workers were often not motivated. He observed that most workers who are forced to perform repetitive tasks tend to work at the slowest rate that goes unpunished. Taylor observed that, when paid the same amount, workers will tend to do the amount of work that the slowest among them does. This reflects the idea that workers have a vested interest in their own well-being, and do not benefit from working above the defined rate of work when it will not increase their remuneration. He therefore proposed that the work practice that had been developed in most work environments was crafted, intentionally or unintentionally, to be very inefficient in its execution. He argued that time and motion studies combined with rational analysis and synthesis could uncover one best method for performing any particular task. Taylor himself prominently acknowledged that if each employee's compensation was linked to their output, their productivity would go up. Thus his compensation plans usually included piece rates.

In the course of his empirical studies, Taylor discovered many concepts that were not widely accepted at the time. For example, by observing workers, he decided that labor should include rest breaks so that the worker has time to recover from fatigue.

Unless people manage themselves, somebody has to take care of administration, and thus there is a division of work between workers and administrators. One of the tasks of administration is to select the right person for the right job.

1.6.3 FAYOL'S PRINCIPLES OF MANAGEMENT

Administrative Management:

The ***administrative management*** approach emphasized the perspective of senior managers within the organization, and argued that management was a profession and could be taught.

An explicit and broad framework for administrative management emerged in 1916, when Henry Fayol, a French mining engineer and executive, published a book summarizing his management experiences. Fayol identified five functions and 14 principles of management. The five functions, are planning, organizing, commanding, coordinating, and controlling.

A host of other executives contributed to the administrative management literature. These writers discussed a broad spectrum of management topics, including the social responsibilities of management, the philosophy of management, clarification of business terms and concepts, and organizational principles. Chester Barnard's and Mary Parker Follett's contributions have become classic works in this area.

The 14 Management Principles from Henry Fayol (1841-1925) are:

1. ***Division of Work***: Specialization allows the individual to build up experience, and to continuously improve his skills. Thereby he can be more productive.
2. ***Authority***: The right to issue commands, along with which must go the balanced responsibility for its function.
3. ***Discipline***: Employees must obey, but this is two-sided: employees will only obey orders if management plays their part by providing good leadership.
4. ***Unity of Command***: Each worker should have only one boss with no other conflicting lines of command.
5. ***Unity of Direction***: People engaged in the same kind of activities must have the same objectives in a single plan. This is essential to ensure unity and coordination in the enterprise. Unity of command does not exist without unity of direction.
6. ***Subordination of individual interest to the organisational interest:*** Management must see that the goals of the organisation are always paramount.
7. ***Remuneration:*** To maintain the loyalty and support of workers, all employees must receive a fair wage for services rendered in the organizations.
8. ***Centralization (or Decentralization):*** Important policy decision relating to whether power and authority be concentrated at the top level or distributed to other levels.
9. ***Scalar chain (Line of Authority):*** A hierarchy is necessary for unity of direction. But lateral communication is also fundamental, as long as superiors know that such communication is taking place. Scalar chain refers to the number of levels in the hierarchy from the ultimate authority to the lowest level in the organization.
10. ***Order***: Both material order and social order are necessary. The former minimizes lost time and useless handling of materials. The latter is achieved through organization and selection.

11. ***Equity***: In running a business a 'combination of kindliness and justice' is needed. Treating employees well is important to achieve equity.

12. ***Stability of Tenure of Personnel:*** Employees work better if job security and career progress are assured to them. An insecure tenure and a high rate of employee turnover will affect the organization adversely.

13. ***Initiative:*** Allowing all personnel to show their initiative in some way is a source of strength for the organization even though it may well involve a sacrifice of 'personal vanity' on the part of many managers.

14. ***Esprit de Corps:*** Management must foster the morale of its employees. He further suggests that: "real talent is needed to coordinate effort, encourage keenness, use each person's abilities, and reward each one's merit without arousing possible jealousies and disturbing harmonious relations." Unity of HR brings strength to the organisation.

Barnard, former president of New Jersey Bell Telephone Company, published his landmark book "The Functions of the Executive" in 1938 and outlined the role of the senior executive in formulating the purpose of the organization, hiring key individuals, and maintaining organizational communications. Mary Parker Follett's 1942 book "Dynamic Organization" extended Barnard's work by emphasizing the continually changing situations that managers face. Two of her key contributions—the notion that managers desire flexibility and the differences between motivating groups and individuals—laid the groundwork for the modern contingency approach.

All the writings in the administrative management area emphasize management as a profession along with fields such as law and medicine. In addition, these authors offered many recommendations based on their personal experiences, which often included managing large corporations. Although these perspectives and recommendations were considered sound, critics noted that they might not work in all settings. Different types of personnel, industry conditions, and technologies may affect the appropriateness of these principles.

1.6.4 MAYO'S HAWTHORNE EXPERIMENTS

HUMAN RELATIONS APPROACH :

Human relations approach was developed during the 1930s. This approach aimed at understanding how psychological and social processes interact with the work situation to influence performance. A human relation was the first major approach to emphasize informal work relationships and worker satisfaction.

This approach owes much to other major schools of thought. For example, many of the ideas of the Gilbreths (scientific management) and Barnard and Follet (administrative management) influenced the development of human relations from 1930 to 1955. In fact, human relations emerged from a research project that began as a scientific management study. Western Electric Company, a manufacturer of communications equipment, hired a team of Harvard researchers led by Elton Mayo and Fritz Roethlisberger, Dickson and Whitehead. They were to investigate the influence of physical working conditions on workers' productivity and efficiency in one of the company's factories outside Chicago. This research project, known as the Hawthorne Studies, provided some of the most interesting and controversial results in the history of management.

The Hawthorne Studies were a series of experiments conducted from 1924 to 1932. During the first stage of the project called (the Illumination Experiments, various working conditions, particularly the lighting in the factory, were altered to determine the effects of those changes on productivity. The researchers found no systematic relationship between the factory lighting and production levels. In some cases, productivity continued to increase even when the illumination was reduced to the level of moonlight. The researchers concluded that the workers performed and reacted differently because the researchers were observing them. This reaction is known as the ***Hawthorne Effect.***

This conclusion led the researchers to believe productivity may be affected more by psychological and social factors than by physical or objective influences. With this thought in mind, they initiated the other four stages of the project. During these stages, the researchers performed various work group experiments and had extensive interviews with employees. Mayo and his team eventually concluded that productivity and employee behavior were influenced by the informal work group.

Human relations proponents argued that managers should primarily concentrate on employee welfare, motivation, and communication. They believed social needs had precedence over economic needs. Therefore, management must gain the cooperation of the group and promote job satisfaction and group norms consistent with the goals of the organization.

Another noted contributor to the field of human relations was Abraham Maslow. In 1943, Maslow suggested that humans have five levels of needs. The most basic needs are the physical needs for food, water, and shelter; the most advanced need is for self-actualization, or personal fulfillment. Maslow argued that people try to satisfy their lower-level needs and then progress upward to the higher-level needs. Managers can facilitate this process and achieve organizational goals by removing obstacles and encouraging behaviors that satisfy people's needs and organizational goals simultaneously.

1.7 MOTIVATION

1.7.1 CONCEPT OF MOTIVATION

Controlling human behavior is the most complex problem a manager or leader encounters during his function. Every individual will have an inner state of a motive that energizes activates, or moves and it also directs the particular individual towards the goal which may be sometimes positive and may also turn into negative depending upon the situations. Rensis Likert calls motivation as the core of management and leadership because different individuals have different needs and perceptions towards work and life. Directing all these different categories of individuals, who form into groups to achieve the ultimate organizational goal is a challenge to every manager. Motivation refers to the way in which urges, drives, desires, aspirations, or needs direct or control the behavior of individuals. A successful manger is one who motivates his employees positively and channelizes all the energy for the betterment of the employees and organization.

Definitions:

As per Encyclopedia of Management, "motivation refers to the degree of the readiness of an organism to pursue some designated goal, and implies the determination of the nature and locus of the forces inducing the degree of readiness"

Edwin B. Flippo defines "motivation as the process of attempting to influence others to do your will through the possibility of gain reward."

Michael J. Jucious defines "motivation as an act of stimulating someone or oneself to get a desired course of action. It is to push the right button to get the desired action."

Koontz and O'Donnell defines "motivation as a general term applying to the entire class of drives, desires, needs, wishes and similar forces that induce an individual or a group of people to work."

Features of motivation:

- Unending process
- A psychological concept
- The whole individual is motivated
- Motivation may be financial or non financial
- Frustrated person cannot be motivated
- Goals are motivators
- Motivation can be positive or negative
- Motivation and job satisfaction are different

1.7.2 NATURE AND IMPORTANCE

Two important factors are necessary to perform any job. They are ability to work and willingness to work. The following are various advantages of motivation.

1. Maximum utilization of factors of production
2. Willingness to work and knowledge and skills enhancement
3. Reduced absenteeism
4. Reduced labour turnover
5. Availability of right personnel
6. Building of good labour relations
7. Increase in the efficiency and output
8. Sense of belongingness
9. Basis for co-operation
10. Helps in realizing organizational goals
11. Improvement in skills and knowledge

Types of Motivation :

1. Negative motivation
2. Positive motivation

3. Extrinsic motivation
4. Intrinsic motivation
5. Financial motivation
6. Non- financial motivation

MOTIVATIONAL THEORIES:

1.7.3 MASLOW'S THEORY OF HUMAN NEEDS / MASLOW'S NEED HIERARCHY THEORY:

The behavior of an individual at a particular moment is usually determined by his strongest need. Psychologists claim that needs have certain priority. As the more basic needs are not met, efforts to satisfy the higher needs should be postponed.

Abraham Maslow a famous social scientist has given a frame work that helps to explain the strength of certain needs. According to him there must be a hierarchy into which human needs are arranged as shown below.

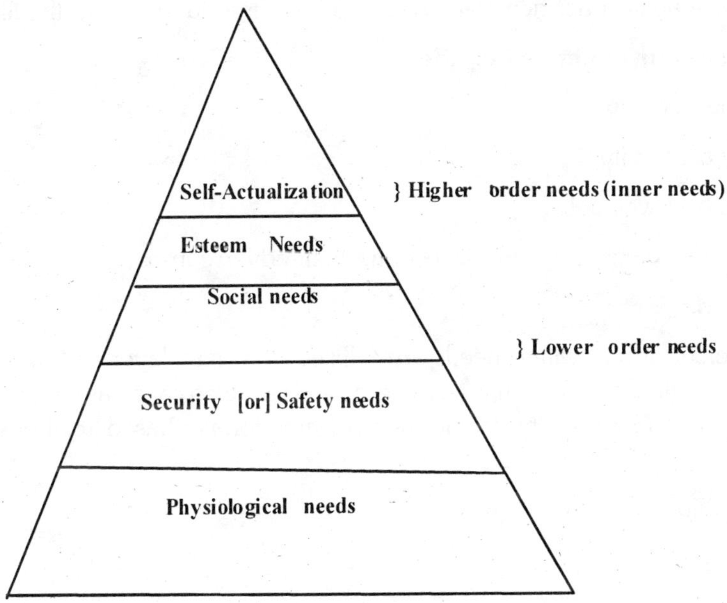

Figure 1.3 : Maslow's Need Hierarchy

1. *Physiological Needs :*

The physiological needs are at the top of the hierarchy because they tend to have the highest strength until they are reasonably satisfied. These needs are also called basic needs. Ex: food, clothes, shelter, water, rest etc.

For the most, physiological needs are obvious and they are the literal requirements for human survival. If these requirements are not met, the human body simply cannot continue to function.

1. *Physiological needs include:*

- Breathing
- Human nutrition
- Water
- Sleep
- Sexual gratification

Air, water, and food are metabolic requirements for survival in all animals, including humans. Clothing and shelter provide necessary protection from the environment.

2. *Safety Needs:*

These needs are also called as 'Security needs'. When the Physiological needs are satisfied to a reasonable level, then the individual's safety needs take precedence and dominate behavior. In the world of work, these safety needs manifest themselves in such things as a preference for job security, grievance procedures for protecting the individual from unilateral authority, savings accounts, insurance against accidents and diseases accommodations, and the like.

Safety and Security needs include:

- Personal security
- Financial security
- Health and well-being
- Safety net against accidents/illness and their adverse impacts

3. *Social Needs:*

After physiological and safety needs are fulfilled, the third layer of human need is social need and involves feeling of belongingness. These needs are also called as love and belongingness needs. This aspect of Maslow's hierarchy involves emotionally based relationships in general, such as:

- Friendship
- Intimacy
- Family

Human need to feel a sense of belongingness and acceptance, whether it comes from a large social group, such as clubs, office culture, religious groups, professional organizations, sports teams, gangs, or small social connections (family members, intimate partners, mentors, close colleagues, confidants). They need to love and be loved by others. In the absence of these elements, many people become susceptible to loneliness, social anxiety and clinical depression. This need for belonging can often overcome the physiological and security needs, depending on the strength of the need.

4. Esteem Needs:

All humans have a need to be respected and to have self-esteem and self-respect. These needs also known as the *belonging need.* Esteem presents the normal human desire to be accepted and valued by others. People need to engage themselves to gain recognition and have an activity or activities that give the person a sense of contribution, to feel accepted and self-valued, be it in a profession or hobby. Imbalances at this level can result in low self-esteem or an inferiority complex.

5. Self Actualization Needs:

Self actualization is the need to maximize one's potential, whenever it may be. This is related with the development of intrinsic capabilities which lead people to seek situation that can utilize their potential. As Maslow has put it "this need height be phrased as the desire to become more and more what one is to become everything that one is capable of becoming". Maslow suggests that the various levels of needs are interdependent and sometimes overlapping each higher-level need emerging before the lower level need has been completely satisfied.

"What a man can be, he must be." This forms the basis of the perceived need for self-actualization. This level of need pertains to what a person's full potential is and realizing that potential.

1.7.4 DOUGLAS McGREGOR'S THEORY X AND THEORY Y

Douglas Mc Gregor Theory X and Theory Y

Prof. Douglas Mc Gregor has introduced two theories in his famous book,' The Human side of Enterprises.' They are called 'X' theory and 'Y' theory. A brief explanation of 'X' theory is given below.

Douglas classified the people within organization into two categories.

(i) People concentrating on basic needs

(ii) People concentrating on higher order needs

He specified the qualities of people in two theories namely Theory X and Theory Y

Theory X:

This theory is based on 'BOSS knows BEST'. In other words, a manager excludes workers from decision-making process. The workers should follow whatever decisions are taken by the manager. Employees are inherently lazy, they require constant guidance and support, sometimes they require even compulsion and control, given an opportunity, they would like to avoid responsibility, they do not show up any ambition but always seek security.

Assumptions of Theory X:

1. Workers have an aversion to work inherently.
2. Workers may do the job half-heartedly.
3. Fear of punishment can motivate the workers into action.

4. No worker is ready to accept any responsibility.
5. A worker prefers to be directed by others.

Features of Theory X:

1. Workers dislike work by themselves.
2. Workers are not ready to accept responsibility.
3. Workers prefer to be directed by others.
4. Workers are un-ambitious.
5. Workers by nature resist changes and want security.
6. Workers lack creativity and fail to solve organizational problems.
7. More focus on the lower level needs of workers i.e., physiological and safety.
8. Strict control is necessary to achieve organizational objectives.
9. Authority is not delegated.
10. Autocrat leadership is followed.

X-Theory is regarded as the means to supervise and control the workers. Workers are forced to follow the decisions.

Theory Y:

Theory Y focus on a totally different set of assumptions about the employees. Theory Y states that employees are capable of directing and controlling performance on their own. They are much committed to the objectives of the organization. Higher rewards make these employees more committed to organization. If given an opportunity, they not only accept responsibility but also look for opportunity to outperform others. Most of them are highly imaginative, creative and display ingenuity in handling organizational issues.

Assumptions of Theory Y:

1. A job is as natural as a play.
2. Once the workers understand the purpose of job, they may extend their co-operation for job completion.
3. Worker has self-direction, self-motivation, self-discipline and self-control.
4. The existing worker has competence to work and can take right decisions.
5. The potentialities of human beings are not fully utilized by any industry.

Features of Theory Y:

1. Workers feel that work is as natural as play.
2. Workers are ready to accept responsibility if proper motivation is available to them.
3. Workers are directed by themselves.

4. Workers are ambitious.
5. Workers are ready to cope with changes
6. Workers have a high degree of creativity and succeed in solving organizational problems.
7. It focuses not only on the lower level needs but also higher level needs i.e., social, esteem and self- actualization of workers.
8. Workers exercise self-control and self-direction to achieve organizational objectives.
9. Authority is delegated.
10. Democratic leadership is followed.

Theory Z:

Prof. William G. Ouchi has developed theory Z. This theory is based on the comparative study of Japanese and American management practices. Theory Z describes how Japanese management practices can be adopted to the environment of other countries especially in United states. Both major and minor decisions are taken through consensus in truly democratic and dynamic management besides, family relationship prevails between the employer and employees. In other words, close co-operative and trustworthy relationship prevails among workers, managers and the other groups.

Features of Theory Z:

1. Trust
2. Life time employment
3. Involvement of employees
4. Integrated organization
5. Restricted promotions
6. Co- ordination
7. No formal structure
8. Motivation
9. Informal control system
10. Good work environment

1.7.5 HERZBERG'S TWO-FACTOR THEORY OF MOTIVATION

Herzberg's Theory of Needs/ Herzberg's Two Factor Theory:

This theory is also known as two factor theory. According to Herzberg, motivational factors are responsible for satisfaction. Hygiene or maintenance factors are responsible for job-dissatisfaction.

Motivational Factors

The presence of some factors creates motivation to the workers and at the same time absence of such factors does not cause dissatisfaction. They are called motivational factors. Herzberg identified some motivational factors as (i) Achievement, (ii) Recognition, (iii) Advancement, (iv) Work itself, (v) Possibility of growth and (vi) Responsibility.

Maintenance Factors

The presence of some set of factors motivate the workers but absence of these factors cause serious dissatisfaction. Herzberg called these factors as Maintenance or Hygiene factors. They are (i) Company Policy And Administration, (ii) Technical Supervision, (iii) Inter Personal relation with sub-ordinates, (iv) Salary, (v) Job Security, (vi)Personal Life, (vii) Working Conditions, (viii) Status, (ix) Inter-personal relations with Supervisors, and (x) Inter-personal relations with peers.

The workers may be motivated:

1. If job is challenging;
2. If there is a possibility of growth;
3. If there is possibility of achievement;
4. If the workers have enough authority and responsibility;
5. If the workers receive recognition; and
6. If the workers are able to advance in the profession

Requirements of a Sound Motivational System:

1. A motivational system should balance the objectives and philosophy of organization workers.
2. Motivation system should be understood by the members of the organization in the right direction.
3. The motivational system should cover all the activities of the workers.
4. The motivational system should have corresponding relationship with efforts and rewards.
5. The motivational system should be flexible. It means that some changes are incorporated in the motivational system from time to time according to the requirements.

1.8 DECISION MAKING PROCESS

Introduction:

All managers continuously make decisions regarding all kinds of problems, issues, opportunities, threats etc. In fact, management is decision-making. In other words, the most important part of management is making decisions. All functions of management, vis., planning, organizing, directing, staffing and controlling involves decision-making. Similarly, all business activities from the beginning to the end, like type of business to start, type of product, sourcing of raw materials, finance, human resources, where to locate the factory, the production process, type of technology, how much to produce, whether to buy or make some of the components, where to market? whom to sell? at what price? How to maintain the relations with the customer? Expansion or diversification of the business in case of getting profits and how to retrench the loss making business operations etc., are important issues for decision- making. There are a number of alternatives for each of these issues. Therefore, managers have to select the best alternative at the right time. This involves decision-making. Decision making depends upon the type of organization structure.

Concept and Definition of Decision-making:

Decision-making is the process of choosing the best alternative among the available alternatives with a purpose under a given set of circumstances.

Harold Koontz and Heinz Weihrich define decision-making as "selection of a course of action from among alternatives and it is the core of planning"

John A Pearce and Richard B. Robinson define decision-making as, "the process of choosing a course of action from two or more alternatives.

Importance of Decision-Making:

Managers perform all their functions and activities through decision-making. Managers have to make not only the right decisions but make them in the right time.

1. Decision-making helps to procure necessary data and information.
2. It helps to initiate and complete the action of all the activities of the management in the right time.
3. Decision-making further helps in the formulation of strategies and implements them.
4. Decision-making helps to avoid the problems
5. Decision-making helps to eliminate crisis situation

Types of Decisions:

Decisions are of different types such as:

1. *Operational Decisions:*

These are based on operational activities of the company which are routine in nature. These are supportive areas of the organization. These decisions require less analysis and concentration. They do not change the organizational direction.

2. *Strategic Decisions:*

These decisions are related to unified, integrated and comprehensive issues of the organization. These decisions are related to contribution to the organizational objectives significantly. These decisions affect the total organization or the major part of it.

3. *Major Decisions:*

These decisions are also called important decisions which affect the policies of the company, the total company or major portion of the company. These decisions influence almost all the functional areas of the company. These decisions do not repeat frequently.

4. *Minor Decisions :*

Minor decisions are also called unimportant decisions. These decisions affect only one functional area to which it belongs. Most of these decisions are made at the lower level.

5. *Programmed Decisions:*

Programmed decisions are those which are made based on the company's policy, budget procedures etc. These decisions are made in response to routine and repetitive situations or problems.

6. *Non-Programmed Decisions:*

Non-repetitive, peculiar, complex and most important, novel and unstructured problems are non-programmed decisions.

7. *Simple Decisions:*

A number of variables affect the decision-making process. If the number of variables affecting the decision are less, such decisions are called simple decisions.

8. *Complex Decisions:*

If the number of variables affecting a decision is more, such decisions are called complex decisions.

9. *Long-Run Decisions:*

Decisions affecting the long-run plans, activities and business are called long-run decisions. These decisions include: plant location, entering new markets etc.

10. *Short-Run Decisions:*

Decisions affecting short-run plans, activities and business are called short-run decisions. These decisions include sources of finances for working capital, over time payment for employees etc.

11. *Individual Decisions:*

Decisions taken by an individual employee or manager are called individual decisions. These decisions are mostly routine, simple, repetitive and programmed decisions.

12. *Group Decisions:*

Decisions made by a group of people are called group decisions. Group decisions include; strategic decisions, non-programmed, complex and strategic decisions. Team decisions and committee decisions are also group decisions.

Process of Decision-making

There are five steps in the process of decision-making. They are:

1. *Problem Awareness (Identifying The Problem):*

Mostly individual employees identify the problems in various areas. Individuals, when they get a feeling that something is wrong, identify the problem. The awareness of problem mostly occurs to employees at the grass root level like sales people, machine operators, finance assistants, human resource assistants etc. Successful business performance depends upon the ability of the management in sensing its environment. Therefore, mangers should respond when the problem is identified by the individual employees at the bottom level.

2. Problem Diagnosis:

After the individual employees are aware of the problem and it is informed to the managers, managers will gather information and define the problem. Information may be gathered in the following ways:

i. Information may be explored to determine the facts of the problem in detail. Such information may be gathered on a verbal and informal basis.

ii. Rationalize the information and stimuli relevant to the problem so as to clarify the situation.

iii. Act diplomatically to establish peer groups or those of political support for individual views of the problem.

Try to define the problem through debates and discussions and also get an organizational view or consensus on the problem to be solved. The problem, then may take clear shape by interviewing experienced managerial of the executives.

3. Development of Alternative Solutions:

After the problems diagnosed clearly, the tendency of managers is that of searching for the readymade solutions. They do this process: i) through memory search in which the managers seek for known, existing or attempted solutions, or (ii) passive search which entails waiting for possible solutions to be offered. If the managers fail in these two searches, they search for the past experience of themselves and other managers. If they fail to find a solution even through this method, they attempt to designing solutions.

They start designing or developing solutions through a vague idea gradually improve it, refine it by recycling it through selection routes back into problem identification or through further searches. This process of developing solutions takes place through discussions, debates, consultations, and brainstorming sessions and by sharing management wisdom and experience. This can take place both in the form of structured and unstructured team works.

4. Evaluation of Alternative Solutions:

After the alternative solutions are developed, the solutions have to be formally evaluated based on their inherent strengths and weaknesses and also based on the environmental threats and opportunities for implementation. The solutions are to be ranked on the basis of their weights' in terms of strengths and opportunities after eliminating the non-viable solutions in view of their weaknesses and environmental threats for implementation.

5. Selection of the Best Solution:

After the formal evaluation and ranking is completed, the managers tend to re-evaluate the solutions based on the managerial judgment followed by political bargaining as the formal evaluation is not the predominant criterion for assessing the feasibility in practice. Therefore, the techniques for evaluation of solutions also include social and political process.

6. Implementation of the Decision:

Implementation of the selected solution is part of the decision-making process as the process may be required to be recycled due to impediments in the process of implementation. The manager should secure the support of the top management for allocation of resources, time etc. regarding the implementation of the decision.

A detailed programme of action should be formulated, specifying the minute details of action, people who will execute it, when it will be implemented, who will provide all necessary resources, how it will be implemented and who will coordinate the work. Employees concerned will be entrusted with the work and relevant information should be fed to them before hand. The managers should also ensure for getting the information back about the progress of implementation. If the decision cannot be implemented due to major hurdles in the implementation process, the process may be recycled for possible modification.

Steps to be an Effective Decision-Maker:

1. Be alert to signals indicating the need for a decision.
2. Make quite uninterrupted time for thinking and reflecting about things to be decided.
3. Set priorities for different decisions.
4. Separate yourself from the problem and solution. How would another person decide the issue?
5. Ask whether the contemplated decision seems honorable and right.
6. Ask whether you will think well of yourself when you review what has resulted from your decision.
7. Have a backing decision, just in case.
8. Take adequate time to reach a decision over the subject. In contrast, don't dig into so many aspects that confusion prevails and no defensive action is taken.

Tools and Techniques of Decision-Making:

The following are the various tools and techniques developed for effective decision-making:

1. Operations Research:

Operations research is the application of specific methods, tools and techniques to operations of systems with optimum solutions to the problems. Operations research presents in the logical approach to a real problem, by quantifying the variables to the problem. It concentrates on goals in a problem area, hurdles to the solution, overcoming the hurdles in reaching the goal. It quantifies all these variables in the process.

2. Decision tress:

Alternative solutions are generated in the decision-making process. Each of these alternative decisions are evaluated before ranking the solutions. The decision tree is a model in the form of a graphic tool that charts the steps to consider in evaluating each alternative solution in the decision-making.

3. Linear Programming:

Linear programming helps in making decisions with regard to optimum allocation of resources, viz., financial, human, material, machines, space, time, etc., among various purposes. It is a mathematical technique which aims at function establishing proportional relationships between/among variables. It establishes the linear relationship of input and output in the same proportion.

4. Game Theory:

Game theory is the logic of rational discussions. It provides solutions for competitive problems taking into consideration the situations, the probable actions by the competitors, expected outcome and choosing a right action.

5. Queuing Theory:

Queuing theory deals with queues or waiting lines of a group of items ready to receive the service or operation in the process. Queuing theory presents a mathematical solution to the problem of long queues vs. a short/queue. This theory considers cost associated, outcome expected, time and alternate use of resources. The characters involved in the decision-making are: i) number of servers waiting at the service stations, ii) capacity and efficiency of the servers, iii) number of service facilities, iv) average arrival rate, v) average service rate, vi) average length of queue, vii) average waiting time and viii) average time spent in the system.

6. Brain Storming :

This technique is used to encourage creative thinking in groups of around eight members. Brainstorming is built on the following lines:

- generate as many ideas as possible
- Be creative, free-wheeling and imaginative
- Build upon, extend or combine earlier ideas and
- Withhold criticism of others ideas.

The success of this technique depends upon the members ability to listen to others, use this interaction as a stimulus to spark new ideas and feel free to express them. Further, even the idiotic and impracticable ideas should also be encouraged. More number of ideas should be encouraged so that eventually higher quality ideas would be generated.

7. Delphi Method:

Members with expertise and relevant information concerning an issue are selected to make the decision regarding that issue. Questionnaires are sent to the group members who record their answers in writing. The group members do not meet face-to-face. Replies of all the members to the questionnaires are summarized and feedback to them is sent for review. They are asked to make the decisions again in view of the additional information. This process is repeated until a satisfactory decision is made.

8. Dialectic Techniques:

This method ensures generation of alternatives seriously, detailed discussion on each of the alternatives and selecting the alternative or developing a new alternative. The incomplete discussions, analysis and making the discussions quickly, discourage some group members from participating in the group decision-making are solved by this.

1.9 DESIGNING ORGANISATIONAL STRUCTURES

An organization in general can be defined as the rational co ordination of the activities of a number of people for the achievement of some common explicit purpose or goal, through division of labor and function, and through a hierarchy and responsibility.

1.9.1 CONCEPT AND CHARACTERISTICS:

It is difficult to give a simple definition of an organization. All of us have spent our lives in various organizations like schools, clubs, community groups, companies and business concerns, government agencies, hospitals, political parties, temples and churches. Yes, it is not easy to state just what constitutes an organization.

According to Theo Haimann " organizing is the process of defining and grouping the activities of the enterprise and establishing the relationships among them. Organization is concerned with order to accomplish the objectives of the enterprise.

Nature of Organization:

To organize man power means to build a structure, not of wood and steel, but of human beings. The people are the material for construction, their loyalty the foundation and their co – operative sprit, the moral that holds the structure together and gives it vitality. The word 'organization' signifies both a process and a result. The process of organization produces an organization and the person who performs the process is termed as 'organizer'. Organization has to deal with the work to be done and persons who are to do it. Combining human beings with segments of work to be done is the major job of the organizer.

For efficient functioning, the activities of a business enterprise may be divided into different departments and sections for the following reasons :

1. The total activities of a business enterprise cannot be performed by one person or group of persons.
2. The benefits of division of labor and specialization can be secured , and
3. Work can be allocated according to importance. But such activities are to be integrated for giving them the commonness of purpose as they are part of an enterprise and they are for achieving a common goal.

Organization is the logical arrangement of work and facilities. To organize the business is to provide it with everything useful for its functioning.

Organization and Designing:

Design of the basic structure involves issues such as division of work in the departments and assigning the same among various positions and the coordination necessary to accomplish total organizational objectives. Organization structure, truly speaking is the totality of both formal and informal relationships. Operating mechanism, or organization process, on the other hand, includes such factors as control procedures, information systems, reward and punishment system, rules and procedures, and so on.

Need for Formal Organization Structure:

1. To facilitate the performance of Management functions such as planning, organizing, staffing, directing, coordinating and controlling,
2. For a planned growth and development an organization structure is needed.
3. For optimum use of technological advancement.
4. For encouraging effective utilization of human assets.
5. For stimulating creativity.

Features of Good Organization Structure:

1. Simplicity
2. Flexibility
3. Clear line of authority
4. Application of ultimate responsibility
5. Proper delegation of authority
6. Minimum possible management levels
7. Principles of unity of direction and command
8. Proper concern and importance to staff

Process of Designing Organization Structure:

1. Identification of activities
2. Grouping of activities
3. Assigning of activities
4. Delegation of authority, responsibility and accountability

Characteristics of Organization:

Organization whether it is a large or small, has the following characteristics:

1. They are large composed of people.
2. They exist to achieve goals.
3. Each has some degree of structure that result in a definition and limitations of the behavior of its members.

Advantages of Organization:

The following are the important advantages of organization. They are:

1. It makes administration easy by dividing duties and responsibilities of individual worker according to his status in the organization.

2. By assigning duties and allotting proper work to individual according to suitability, education and experience. It promotes specialization which results in increased output and efficiency.

3. It keeps co-ordination among the employees of different levels which results in healthy and smooth functioning.

4. It allows sufficient time for top management and administration to work for future expansion, planning and improvement.

5. It increases the margin of profits.

Principles of Organization

The essential guiding principles of organizing are summarized as follows:

1. ***Principle of unity of objective :*** An organization structure is said to be effective if it enables individuals to contribute to enterprise objectives.
2. ***Principle of co-ordination :*** The aim of the objective can be achieved if proper co – ordination exists for different activities among different levels of management.
3. ***Principle of organizational efficiency :*** An organization is efficient, if it is structured to aid the accomplishment of enterprise objective with a minimum of unsought consequences or costs.
4. ***Span of management principle :*** In each managerial position, there is a limit to the number of persons an individual can effectively manage, but the exact number will depend on the efficiency of individual manager.
5. ***Scalar principle :*** The clearer the line of authority from the top management position to every subordinate position, the clearer will be the responsibility for decision making. It results in effective organizational communication.
6. ***Principle of delegation by result expected :*** Authority delegated to all individual managers should be adequate enough to ensure their ability to accomplish the result expected.
7. ***Principle of absoluteness of responsibility :*** The responsibility of subordinates to their superior for performance should be absolute, so that the superior cannot escape responsibility for the organizational activities of his subordinates.
8. ***Principle of parity of authority and responsibility :*** The responsibility for actions cannot be greater than the authority delegated.
9. ***Principles of unity of command :*** The more complete an individual's reporting relationships to a single superior, the smaller the problem of conflicting instructions and the greater the feeling of personal responsibility for results.
10. ***Authority-level principle :*** Maintenance of intended delegation requires that decisions within the authority of individual management should be made by them and not be referred upwards in the organization structure.

11. ***Principle of functional definition:*** Every department should have a clear definition of the results expected and activities to be undertaken for that purpose. It must also have the clear knowledge of the delegation of authority, formal and informal relationships with various other positions to accomplish the organizational objectives.

12. ***Principle of balance:*** The application of principles or techniques must be balanced to ensure the overall effectiveness of the structure in meeting enterprise objectives.

13. ***Principle of flexibility:*** While designing the structure of the organization, proper importance should be given to the factor of flexibility to change as per the needs of the times.

14. ***Principle of leadership facilitation:*** The more an organization structure and its delegation of authority enable managers to design and maintain an environment for performance, the more they will enhance the leadership abilities of managers.

Various Forms of Organization

The main objective of an organization structure is to ensure that efforts of all people working in various sections are to be co-ordinated and integrated for achieving the task in the most efficient and effective way within minimum consumption of resources.

Formal and Informal Organization:

In order to understand the nature of difference between formal and informal organizations, we have to trace out their basic characteristics and how they are created. Comparison between formal and informal organisation is shown in table 1.1.

Characteristics of Formal Organization:

The formal organization is designed to achieve specific objectives. It refers to well-defined jobs, each bearing a definite authority, responsibility and accountability.

According to classical theorists, the formal organization is built on four pillars. They are:

(1) Division of labor

(2) Scalar functional processes

(3) Structure and

(4) Span of control

Characteristics of formal organization are as follows:

1. Organization structure is designed by the top management to fulfill certain requirements for the performance of necessary activities to achieve the organizational goals.

2. Organization structure is based on the principles of division of labour which aims at efficiency in operations.

3. Organization concentrates more on the performance of jobs and not on the individual who is performing the job.

4. The authority and responsibility assigned to each job have to be adhered to by the job-holder. Based on the concept of authority and responsibility, people are placed in hierarchy, and their status is determined accordingly.
5. Co-ordination among members and their control are well specified through processes, procedures, rules, etc.

Characteristics of Informal Organization

Informal organization refers to the natural grouping of people on the basis of some similarities. Whenever people work together, they evolve themselves into groups which are not according to the formal origination. Such relationship may be more complex than the officially prescribed one. This complex system of social relationships is called the informal organization.

Characteristics of Informal organization:

1. Informal organization is a natural outcome at the work place. It is not designed and planned.
2. Informal organization is created on the basis of some similarities and commonness among its members. The basis of similarity may be age, sex, place of origin, caste, religion, personality characteristics, likes and dislikes, etc.
3. Membership in informal organization is voluntary. A person may become member of several informal organizations at the same time.
4. Behavior of members of the informal organization is co-ordinated and controlled by group norms and not by the norms of the formal organization.

Table 1.1 : Comparison between Formal Organization and Informal Organization

Basis of Comparison	*Formal Organization*	*Informal Organization*
Formation	Planned and deliberate	Spontaneous
Purpose	Well–set goals	Social interaction
Structure	Well structured	Unstructured
Nature	Official	Unofficial
Focus on	Positions	Persons
Leadership	Superior	Anyone
Source of power	By delegation	Given by group
Guide lines for behavior	Rules and procedures	Group norms
Sources of control	Reward/punishment	Sanctions

1.9.2 IMPORTANCE OF ORGANIZATION:

Organization is the foundation of management. If the organizational plan is ill-designed, then management becomes difficult and ineffective.

According to Peter F. Drucker, organization is a means of multiplying the strength of an individual. It takes one's knowledge and uses it as the resource for motivating other workers. A good organization facilitates administration, promotes specialization, encourages growth and stimulates creativity.

- ***Facilitates Administration :*** The assumption that manager will manage by instinct or common sense takes too much for granted . The work of management proceeds smoothly only if it is well –defined, systematic, certain and appropriate. Functional groups are provided to help the managers to manage.
- ***Specialization :*** Organization is the medium through which specialization takes place. It allocates different functions among different individuals on the basis of their qualifications and talents. This brings about specialization and diversification. A good organization also makes possible the engagement of specialist.
- ***Growth :*** A Sound organization provides the framework within which a company grows within a time frame.
- ***Creativity :*** A sound organization stimulates creativity, thinking and initiative by providing well – defined areas of work with broad latitude for the development of new and improved ways of doing things.

Significance of Organization

The significance of organization lies in its usefulness and importance which may be stated briefly :

- It provides a means by which human efforts are properly directed more and more to productive, effective and to fruitful results.
- It adds definiteness to the activities to be accomplished by allocating the duties and responsibilities to the individual members of the organization.
- The allocation of duties and responsibilities to the individual members prevents shirking of responsibilities to secure certainty and promptness in the accomplishment of the task.
- It increases managerial efficiency and avoids delay, confusion and misunderstanding in the performance of the work .
- By assembling , integrating and coordinating all activities into a complete whole which ensures necessary communication and instructions to move up, down and sideways without loss of time.
- It secures optimum use of physical, mechanical and human efforts by placing proportionate importance to various activities, men and money .
- It facilitates coordination of activities by welding together structural relationships.
- It provides scope for training, testing and developing expert managers and sound personnel through a wide experience in diverse activities of the business.
- The principle of organization developed in this way helps to consolidate the growth and expansion of a business enterprise. Giant business is the outcome of organizational ability.
- A sound organization provides check against the commission of dishonesty, corruption and malpractices of any sort.

1.9.3 FUNCTIONS OF ORGANIZATION

Process of Organization:

The work of organization looks to the structural as well as functional aspects of business and correlates different factors with their functions. It thus embraces among other things the following important aspects or steps of business :

- It keeps in view the aims, objectives and board policies of business.
- It decides the location and layout of the business undertaking.
- It takes steps for raising finance required for the business.
- It procures land and supervises the construction of building or hires suitable accommodation for business purpose.
- It purchases plant and machinery, furniture, equipments, and so on necessary to carry on the business.
- It engages workers to undertake various types of work.
- It divides the whole work into different departments, sections and also into its component parts.
- It allocates the duties and responsibilities among different departments and employees.
- It establishes the line of authority and responsibility and determines the range of power to be delegated at different levels of authority.
- It establishes the machinery for co operation, coordination and control and ensures team sprit among different grades of employees in order to correlate and coordinate different factors and functions for the successful achievement of the business objectives.

Organization is a mechanism or structure that enable human beings to work together. It is 'the arrangement by which tasks are assigned to men and women so that their individual efforts contribute effectively to some more or less clearly defined purpose for which they have been brought together'.

Functions of Organizations:

Once the objectives have been established, it is then necessary to determine the type of functions or work that must be performed within the organization. A function is the work that can be identified and distinguished from other work.

The basic function or work activities can be defined in any business, government or educational organization. For instance, the major functions of a manufacture would be production, marketing and finance.

Approaches of Organization

There are various approaches to the concept of organisation. They are

1. Classical
2. Bureaucratic

3. Human Relations
4. Systems
5. Contingency
6. Motivational
7. Decision making
8. Biological Mathematical Approach

1. *Classical Approach* :

The classical approach also referred to as the "management process" approach, owes its origin and development to Henry Fayol. It views the organizer as a prescribed pattern of relation among tasks and individuals to reach its goals. The classical theory of organization is based on a number of principles such as :

1. Specialization
2. Unity of direction
3. Functional specification
4. Chain of command
5. Unity of command
6. Parity between authority and responsibility
7. Separation of line and staff
8. Span of control

One of the criticism of the classical theory is that it prescribes what an organization ought to be and makes no attempt to describe or explain it . Second, in the classical view an organisation is, in essence, a machine and an administrator is basically an engineer. It also assumes that its principles are applicable to all kinds of organizations, irrespective of their goals and environments . Third, according to R. Likert, it treats people as rational, inert and passive. Fourth, it ignores the existence of informal structure. Fifth, it emphasizes downward communication and hierarchical control which adversely affects individual morale and activity. Simon advances harsh criticism of classical organisation by characterizing its principles as vague, contradictory. The concept of separation of line and staff has been viewed by Fisch as unrealistic and obsolete. Seventh, in recent years it has been encountering another criticism that the principle of span of control is often attacked as demonstrably untrue since a number of surveys have shown that spans on many successful companies are considerably wider than the classical theory would permit.

Classical are said to believe that the organisation will function harmoniously and effectively when each person in it is being motivated by the hope of reward in the form of pay rises or promotions and is restrained by the fear of penalties in the form of denial of advancement or dismissal. This has been severely criticized by the exponents of behavioral science who claim that classical theory is too mechanistic and ignores major facets of human nature.

2. Bureaucratic Approach :

This theory was propounded by Max Weber. It is based on the identification of its following characteristics: -

1. It is based on the principle of division of labour and specialization.
2. Positions are organized on a – hierarchical structure of authority. It places each position under the supervision and control of another. This hierarchical structure establishes of chain of command running through the organization.
3. Official decisions and actions are governed by a formally established system of rules and regulations.
4. Officials are expected to act in an impersonal manner in dealing with the problems and people.
5. Employment and promotions in organization are based on the universal criterion of proven competence and abilities .

Weber's bureaucratic organization has also been regarded as mechanistic and subjected to much of the same criticism as the classical view of the organization. Nevertheless, all modern organizations are based on the bureaucratic model, according to Blaue and Scott.

3. Human Relations Approach :

The Hawthorne Studies led to the emergence of the Human Relations School. It emphasized the importance of human relations in the organizations. Mc Gregor, Likert and Argyris are the chief exponents of this approach. They view organizations in terms of interpersonal relationship, teamwork, voluntary co – operation, self – control, group – oriented management and inter – group behavior . They gave importance to informal norms and standards , broad span of control with fewer in the organization.

It ignores the basic characteristics of formal organization. This is one severe criticism. It prescribes an universal approach which is not applicable to all kinds of organizations because of difference in their goals and environment.

4. System Approach :

A system is composed of related and independent elements which form a subsystem. In the field of management, the system approach has been applied for developing an appraisal or audit of management. The system approach has an edge over the other approach insofar as its closeness to reality is concerned. The main criticism against the system approach is its utter complexity particularly when it comes to study of large and complex organisation or for that matter the whole management concept and function. Moreover, this approach has been regarded as too theoretical to be of much use to practitioners and too exacting and expensive when used for research.

5. Contingency Approach :

According to this approach, an organisation has multiple goals . It attempts to attain its goals by attempting to make a rational choice within the constraints imposed by its internal and external environments. Organisations, the theory postulates, respond to as well as manipulate their environment. The ability of an organisation to respond to its environment depends to the "strategic choices" it makes. These strategic choices or decisions determine organizational goals, its form structure and the manner in which it adapts to and influence its environment. This approach is the latest and the most widely accepted view of organisation. It emphasizes that the goals, design and structure of an organisation are the function of the environment with in which it operates. It attempts to achieve its goals by coping with uncertainty resulting from dynamic nature of its environment.

6. Motivational Approach :

In a sense, all the behaviorist organisation specialists take a motivational approach to the company structure . They are concerned with the ways in which the goals of individuals and those of the organisation can be made to fuse , or at least concede to some extent. There is, however, a special approach which has been christened 'the motivational approach' by its author, Rensis Likert.

Likert approach is based on a number of empirical studies on the differences between good supervisors and bad ones, good supervisors being those groups achieved high productivity, and bad those in charge of low- productivity groups.

Therefore, he believes, management should establish groups that meet these criteria rather than adhere to the traditional man- to – man pattern. These groups in turn should be linked by means of overlapping groups of supervisors.

7. Decision – Making Approach :

Barnard 's theories were further developed by Herbert A. Simon in his book, 'Administrative Behavior'. Likert, Barnard, Simon emphasized that the equilibrium or survival possibilities of an organization depend on its ability to induce co-operation.

Another writer has suggested, what he calls the 'functional teamwork' approach to organisation as a means of ensuring that decisions regarding various areas are made by those experts in the area. He suggests that the distinction between line and staff be done away with and that all functions be given authority and decision – making power in their own functional areas. He writes: There is a logical sequence of decision .... Thus , the first decision relates to the product and service mix; and once that is made, then manpower planning makes decisions about manpower, size of the staff, composition; finance makes decision about financial requirements; manufacturing makes decisions about production schedule; marketing makes decision about its sales effort to achieve the sales result and so on ...There is teamwork, but only to the extent that decision of one function impinge on the operating efficiency of another.

8. Biological Mathematical Approach

An organization has many properties in common with a living organism. To mention just few, it comes in existence, then grows, reaches a peak, then (or even usually) declines, and finally dies. It reacts to its environment and like a biological organism is made up of many parts that interact with each other in varying and complex ways.

This has led some writers to conclude that an organization, like an organism, cannot grow unless the balance between its various parts is maintained in some fairly exact ratio like the ratio in geometry.

Organizational Designing

Modern Trends in Organizational Structure Designs

Organizations in the recent times have been gearing themselves to suit to the growing demands from their stakeholders in terms of responsiveness, flexibility, ability, adaptability etc. In this process, they are following organic structures which are flexible and adaptable to the changing circumstances. Virtual Organizations, cellular organizations, team structure, boundary-less organization and inverted pyramid are different forms of organic structures that are widely seen among most of the sun-rise sectors such as financial services, Information Technology (IT) and IT enabled services. These structures have been contributing to the organic growth of the organization. The main focus of organic structures is to do away with those activities which do not directly contribute to the growth of the organization and focus only on those activities which directly lead the organization for the achievement of the given goals. These are discussed below:

1.9.4 DEPARTMENTATION

The first real task in designing an organization structure is identification of activities and to group them properly. The process of grouping the common activities is known as departmentation. The terms used to denote the departments that result from departmentation vary a great deal. In business organizations, such terms as division, department bureau and section; in military these are referred to as battalion, group, company, etc. The terms used to designate department may vary in different organizations of same nature, however, the process of departmentation will be the same.

"Departmentation is the process of dividing the work of organization into various units of departments."

Bases of Departmentation:

Basic function : In a manufacturing organization production and the values they create are indispensable. Henry Fayol has divided all the operations of business organization into six functions: they are Technical, Commercial, Financial, Security, Accounting and Management function.

Secondary function : When the departments are created on the basis of major functions, and a manager's span of management is too large to manage effectively, for example marketing department may be classified and grouped into advertising, sales, market research, Product, Territory, Customers, Process, Time, etc.

Choosing a basis for Departmentation:

- Specialization
- Coordination
- Control

- Economy
- Recognition of local conditions
- Adequate attention
- Human considerations

Span of Management

Factors determining Span of Management:

- Capacity of superior
- Capacity of subordinates
- Nature of work
- Degree of decentralization
- Planning
- Use of staff assistance
- Communication techniques
- Supervision from others

Delegation of Authority

Authority:

Authority is the right to give orders and the power to extract obedience. It is the right to decide what one should do or what one should get from others. An authority is the power to command or to extract action from others in the process of discharging the delegated responsibility. Authority and responsibility go hand in hand.

Important Principle of Authority:

Authority and responsibility should be in equal proportion. In other words, the required amount of authority should be delegated to discharge responsibility. This principle avoids misuse of authority and at the same time helps in the proper discharge of responsibility.

Principles of Delegation

- Functional definition
- Delegation of result expected
- Parity of authority and responsibility
- Unity of command
- Absoluteness of responsibility

Responsibility:

Edwin B. Flippo defines responsibility as "one's obligation to perform the functions assigned to the best of one's ability in accordance with directions received. Responsibility is derived function which is the origin for relationship. Hence, it is called functional derivative. The important principles which could be observed in delegating responsibility are:

- Absence of overlapping responsibility i.e., one function should not be assigned to more than one individual employee.
- Functional similarity which facilitates specialization should be taken into consideration while delegating responsibility.
- Clear identification of responsibility limits.
- Avoidance of gaps in delegation of responsibility.
- Unnecessary function or responsibility which does not contribute to organizational goals should not be entrusted

Though, a certain part of the responsibility is delegated to the original and entire amount of the responsibility still rests with the superior.

Accountability:

Accountability is the requirement of answerability for one's performance.

Authority and Responsibility

A manger's primary function is to get work done through people. Lack of delegation of authority causes extra amount of work to the manager. By delegating work and the authority necessary to accomplish the work can substantially reduce manager's work load.

Authority: Authority is defined as right to make decision, give orders and be obeyed in relation with the task assigned.

Responsibility: Responsibility is the obligation to do the assigned work in a suitable manner or to ensure that the work assigned is done in a specified manner.

Duty vs. Responsibility: Activities that a person has to do himself are called duties, whereas duties delegated to others comes under responsibility. Responsibilities can be reassigned or delegated but cannot be relinquished.

Delegation of Authority:

Delegation of authority involves breaking down of the executive responsibility and transmission of a part or the whole to other persons.

Features of Delegation of Authority

- Delegation gives the manager the authority to act in a certain manner. It also prescribes the limitations for the manager.
- Authority once delegated can be enhanced, reduced or withdrawn depending upon the situation and requirement.
- The process of organizing creates the delegation of authority.
- A manager delegates the authority out of the authority restored in him.

- Delegation of authority is specific when courses of actions for particular objectives are specified and it is general when these are not specified, though objectives maybe specified.

Process of Delegating:

The entire process of delegation of authority can be completed through the following four steps:

1. ***Establishment of goals:*** The subordinates will feel interested in the acceptance of delegated authority if they are informed of the objectives underlying the assignment of tasks to them. Successful delegation is marked by prefixed objectives.
2. ***Assignment of Duties:*** Duties can be described in two ways. Firstly, these can be described in terms of an activity or set of activities. Secondly, duties can be described in terms of results that are expected from the performance of activities.
3. ***Authorization for Action:*** This aspect involves granting of permission for the use of resources to take all the necessary steps for the successful completion of given assignment.
4. ***Creation of obligation:*** This is the last aspect of delegation. In this step the superior who is delegating must be able to create a feeling of obligation and commitment in the subordinate to complete the work assigned as per the expectations of the superior.

Measures of Effective Delegation:

The distribution of authority at various points of the organization will enable the manager to take necessary actions.

- ***Making the delegate feel secured:*** The superior should inculcate a feeling of security in the delegate as far as the job, position and his actions are concerned. In other words the delegate must get the confidence and courage to do the assigned work in his own way.
- ***Creating Awareness for need of delegation:*** Many managers are not aware of the need of delegation. Thus proper education and training are required for such managers to convince them about the need for better delegation.
- ***Decision about the tasks to be delegated:*** Delegation may adversely affect when there is no clarity about what is to be delegated. Usually those tasks that are relatively less important and more time consuming should be delegated to the subordinates so as to save the managers precious time.
- ***Establishment of an ideal work climate:*** A manager's most important responsibility is to create an ideal climate for effective work. This is possible by eliminating fear and frustration from the workers mind.
- ***Choosing the delegate wisely:*** Even when the delegate fails it is regarded as the failure of the person who has delegated the work. Hence, a superior must be doubly careful and wise in selecting a right delegate to complete the task.

- ***Connecting Delegation with planning:*** Authority should never be delegated to the managers before the objectives are clear. Specific results and objectives for each activity can be defined when there is open planning in the organization.
- ***Delegation for whole job:*** It is better to give the delegate a chance to participate in a complete job or assignment. Such assignment serves as an effective means of testing a man's ability to manage and it enhances his confidence.
- ***Developing proper control techniques:*** Delegators remain responsible even for the tasks he has delegated to his subordinates. Therefore control and monitoring techniques should be developed to ascertain that delegated authority is properly used or not.

Organization Chart:

L.A. Allen defines an organization as "the process of identifying and grouping the work to be performed, defining and delegating responsibility and authority and establishing relationships for the purpose of enabling the people to work most effectively together in accomplishing objectives. The relationships that exist in an organization may be formal and informal.

The manager describes organizational relationships in a written and graphic manner. He tells the participants to do certain things in a specified manner, to obey orders from designed individuals, and to work co-operatively with others. Formal organization is built on the relationships of authority, responsibility, accountability, span of management, delegation, centralization and decentralization.

Since organization structure is represented by organization charts, it should be designed considering various aspects discussed in the chapter. It should also consider internal and external environment of the organization. Internal environment include workers, managers, working conditions, culture etc., while external environment includes the suppliers, customers, competitors, government agencies etc.

Steps for Designing Organization Structure:

1. Understanding and formulating the objectives and goals of the organization.
2. Determining the necessary functions for achieving the objectives and goals.
3. Grouping of functions related to each other.
4. Positioning the personnel for different groups and departments.
5. Preparation of Job description, duties and responsibilities of each position.
6. Preparation of organizational chart showing the work-related relationships.

The structure provides for appropriate authority and responsibility relationships. The organization structure is generally shown as an organizational chart. The organization structure varies with the organization and the functions to be performed, and depends upon the goals and objectives for which the organization is established. A model of an organizational chart is presented below.

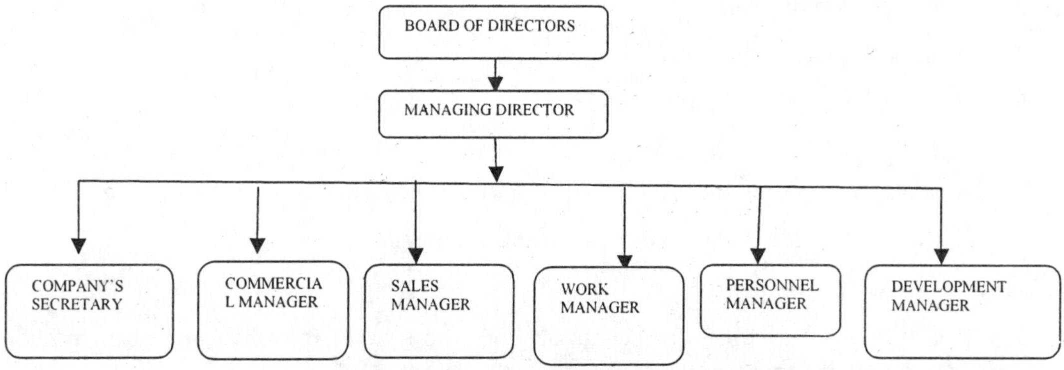

Figure 1.4 : Organisation Chart

1.9.5 CENTRALIZATION AND DECENTRALIZATION

Concepts of Centralization and Decentralization:

Centralization and decentralization are two important aspects of an organization. In management centralization identifies concentration of authority and decentralization identifies dispersion of authority.

Allen has defined both the terms centralization and decentralization.

Centralization is a systematic and consistent reservation of authority at central points within an organization.

Decentralization applies to the systematic delegations of authority in an organization from the higher-levels of management to the lower-levels

The concepts of centralization and decentralization are two extreme points in the matter of distribution of authority in the organization.

Advantages of Centralization

1. Provides opportunity for personal leadership.
2. Facilitates integration of efforts.
3. Quick decisions are possible.
4. Emergencies can be handled very easily.
5. It makes communication and control easier in the organization.
6. Helps in reducing unnecessary efforts by avoiding duplication.
7. It brings about coordination easily.

Advantages of Decentralization

1. It reduces the burden of the top management.
2. Facilitates growth and diversification in the organization.

3. It motivates managers.
4. It encourages development of managers.
5. It emphasizes on horizontal growth of the organization thereby reducing the number of management levels.
6. It clearly describes the objectives to be achieved by each unit of the organization.
7. It grooms leadership qualities among subordinates

Problems of Decentralization

1. The higher the degree of decentralization, the greater the problems of integration, coordination and control.
2. It tends to increase costs by making most units autonomous.
3. Decentralization requires high degree of self-motivation and self-control because of autonomy given to the managers.

Factors Determining Degree of Decentralization:

1. Vision, Mission, Policies and philosophy of the organization.
2. Size of Organization
3. History of the Organization
4. Management Philosophy
5. Availability of Managers
6. Pattern of Planning
7. Control Techniques
8. Decentralized Activities
9. Rate of Change in Organization
10. Environmental Influences

1.9.6 ORGANIZATIONAL OBJECTIVES

The objectives are very important for any organisation. The objectives occupy an important place in the process of management. Generally the objectives give the direction for the future events which occur in the organization. An objective has an inherent power to stimulate action and directs the path towards the end results. It helps to secure a clear vision, a singleness of purpose and spirit in accomplishing the end results of the enterprise. According to Ansoff objectives are decisions and rules, which enable the management to guide and measure the firm's performance towards its objectives. So, the objectives imply, the desired end results. In olden days, the objectives of management are either profit maximization or wealth maximization. The developments in management science have created additional objectives like social responsibility towards society and environment which have broadened the scope of organizational objectives.

Classification of Organizational Objectives:

1. Economic objectives
2. Social objectives
3. Human objectives

1. ***Economic objectives :*** Business enterprises are brought into existence with a view to earn profits, which is the first and foremost objective of economic objectives. Profit is the ultimate goal of business performance. A reasonable profit makes the survival of any enterprise and greater profits indicate the more efficiency of the business. Every organization survives in the market based on its profits only, but profits are not the sole objective of any organization.
2. ***Social objectives:*** As a business organization is a part of the society, it will never permit business enterprise which is harmful to the society. Example: organizations which manufacture banned drugs and Steroids etc., which are harmful to society. The social objectives of business demand, good quality that should be produced at reasonable prices.
3. ***Human objectives:*** Understanding and providing human needs for the satisfaction of Human Resource is another important objective.

So, the objectives are the first prerequisite of planning. The planning process starts with the determination of the objectives.

Management by Objectives (M.B.O.)

M.B.O. is a new concept in the philosophy of management. It was first developed by Peter F. Drucker more than a decade ago in his book 'The Practice of Management '. It is also known as management by results and goals setting approach. Initially the M.B.O was considered as a technique of managerial participation, joint goal setting, collective managerial effort for goal accomplishment, managerial motivation and performance evaluation, but now it has become a total philosophy and approach to management.

Meaning of M.B.O.

It is a process whereby superiors and subordinates jointly identify the common objectives, use the contribution of each individual there by integrating individuals with the organization and make the best use of organizational resources.

Koontz and O' Donnel defined M.B.O. as a comprehensive managerial system that integrates many key managerial activities in a systematic manner, consciously directed towards the effective and efficient achievement of the organizational and individual objectives.

Simply speaking the M.B.O. emphasizes the objectives of superiors and subordinates. It also implies the integration of individual and organizational objectives.

Features of M.B.O

1. M.B.O. is an approach and philosophy to the management and not merely a technique.
2. M.B.O. is related to every aspect of the organization.

3. M.B.O. is objective oriented.
4. M.B.O. emphasizes the objectives and helps to measure the results and resources.
5. It helps in maximizing the results by the best utilization of resources.
6. Periodical review of performance is an important feature of the M.B.O.
7. M.B.O. helps in objective setting and performance reviews.
8. M.B.O. provides guidelines, procedures, resource allocation and delegation of authority.

Process of M.B.O.

M.B.O is a system of achieving organizational objectives. It enhances the employee commitment and participation. The clarity and balance of objective participation of the managers characterize the process of the M.B.O. with accountability for results. The process of the M.B.O. involves the following steps.

1. ***Setting of organizational purpose and objectives:*** The first basic step in the M.B.O is defining the purpose and objectives of the organization. In this exercise the objective should be clearly defined from top-level management to the lowest level of management.
2. ***Identification of key result areas:*** After defining the organizational objectives the result areas should be identified. Key result areas indicate the priorities for emphasis in organizational performance for achieving objectives.
3. ***Setting subordinate's objectives:*** The organizational objectives are achieved through the managers and subordinates. Therefore each individual manager must know in advance what he is expected to achieve. The superiors at the top levels and subordinates at the lowest levels must integrate their objectives at this stage. This helps in the achievement of organizational objectives through superior and subordinate relationship and their mutual cooperation and coordination.
4. ***Matching resources with objectives:*** After setting the objectives the resource requirement must be indicated. The allocation and movement of resources, their availability and application should be carried on in consultation with all the concerned.
5. ***Performance appraisal:*** Whether the subordinate is achieving his objectives or not should be appraised in the process of the M.B.O. It helps to find out the deficiency in working and remove it promptly.
6. ***Recycling:*** After appraisal it is possible to use the results for recycling the objectives and other actions.

There are many benefits through the application of the M.B.O. It helps to achieve better management. It provides clarity in organizational action through the identification of key result areas. The M.B.O. provides greatest opportunity for personal satisfaction through achievement. It also acts as a basis for organizational change and betterment on the basis of rational performance appraisal.

Benefits of M.B.O.:

1. **Better Management :** The M.B.O. helps in better management of organizational resources and activities. These are put in such a way as to improve the performance; there are five assumptions about how it improves the performance.

    1. Clarity of objectives.
    2. Role clarity.
    3. Periodic feedback.
    4. Participation of managers in the management.
    5. Realization that there is scope for improvement.

2. **Clarity in organizational action :** Since organizational objectives are defined very clearly, they help in relating the organization with its environment. A key factor in objective setting is the external environment in which the organization operates. Therefore, any change in environmental factors is taken care of at the level of objective setting itself. Thus, it provides basis for long-range planning in the organization. Besides the external factors, the internal factors can also be taken suitably while formulating plans as all the internal factors are made explicit in terms of what the organization can do and where it cannot and how this gap can be overcome.

3. **Personnel satisfaction :** The M.B.O. provides greatest opportunity for employees satisfaction.. When the individuals are involved in objective setting, they derive satisfaction because of the feeling that they are important to the organization. They enjoy considerable authority, which is a source of inspiration for better performance. Besides, they are very sure that their performance will be measured in terms of their actual performance and will not be affected by managerial bias.

4. **Basis for organizational change :** Taking the above factors into consideration the M.B.O. satisfies each and every point. Under the M.B.O. the objectives are clearly understood by each and every individual working in the organization. Everyone knows why he or she is here and for what purpose. Periodic feedback examines both the management and the subordinates whether their approach is in accordance with the objectives set. Participation in the M.B.O. process increases the motivation of the employees, which leads to an increase in their commitment. They will have a sense of feeling that they are achieving their objectives. The M.B.O. provides a base for the philosophy that there is always a scope for improvement.

Problems or Limitations of M.B.O.

M.B.O. is not without its problems and weaknesses. Many organizations have failed to derive the expected results.

1. **Time and cost :** The M.B.O. is not as simple as it appears to be. It is a process, which requires large amount of the scarce resources which are costly and also the precious time of the senior managers. The M.B.O. generates paper work because there is a problem of communication overload. Once the M.B.O. becomes a part of the organizational life, these problems disappear.

2. ***Failure to teach M.B.O. philosophy :*** The M.B.O. is a philosophy of managing organization in a mew way. However, managers fail to understand and appreciate this new approach. They have a number of doubts about the M.B.O. like what purpose is served by the M.B.O. how the performance is to be appraised, and how will it benefit the organization. If corrective action is not taken early, the objectives become sterile.

3. ***Problem in objective setting :*** The M.B.O. requires verifiable objectives against which performance can be measured. However, setting such objectives is difficult at least in some areas. Objectives are more in the form of statement rather than in quantitative form. Some objectives can be quantified and can be broken in terms of time period but others lack this characteristic for further course of action.

4. ***Emphasis on short-term objectives :*** Sometimes in order to be more precise there is a tendency to emphasize on short-term objectives usually for a year or even less. This may help in performance appraisal but there is always a danger in emphasizing short-term objectives at the cost of long term objectives. Sometimes in an organization short-term objectives and long term objectives may be incompatible because of certain specific problems.

5. ***Inflexibility :*** The M.B.O. represents the danger of inflexibility in the organization particularly when the objectives need to be changed. In a dynamic environment a particular objective may not be valid forever. In the context of revised objectives, changed premises of modified policies, it is useless to follow the old objectives. However, many managers often hesitate to change objectives during a period of time. Thus inflexibility created by applying the M.B.O. may cause harm than what it may contribute.

1.10 TYPES OF ORGANIZATIONAL STRUCTURES

An organization can be classified on the basis of authority relationships or on the basis of its departments. The types of organizations based on authority relationships are: (a) Line organization, (b) Line and staff organization,(c) Functional organization, (d) Committee organization, and (e) Matrix organization.

The organization can also be divided into the following groups based on its activities or departments: (a) Functional organization, (b) Production organization, (c) Regional or geographical organization, (d) Customer organization, (e) Committee organization and (f) Matrix organization.

These classifications are more or less need based. In other words, there is no standard list of the types of organizations. The only thing is that the basis of creating the organization should be justifiable.

1.10.1 LINE ORGANIZATION

The Line Organization Structure:

In a line organization, authority is delegated from top to bottom in an unbroken line. There are no staff organizational units. Both staff and line functions are integrated in the work of line units. Each person exercises line authority over own subordinates. Like the small organization everyone in a manufacturing business would be concerned directly with creating, distributing, or financing customer values. Thus in a pure line organization the executives or subordinates would have to act on his own as secretary, purchasing agent, personnel manger and legal adviser in addition to performing his regular duties.

1. The simple, direct lines of responsibility and authority are easy to understand.
2. Discipline and control are facilitated because of this clarity of command.
3. Decisions are made more quickly as there are no complicated organizational relationships.
4. When properly used, the line organization has an inherent flexibility that enables it to adjust to changing conditions.

Under line organization, each department is generally a complete self-contained unit. Such decision making authority is to flow from the top management level to the bottom. The top management people have greater decision authority than the bottom level executives. It should be noted that in this type of organization, an executive is independent of the other executives of the same level (say departmental heads).

Characteristics of Line Organization :

1. It consists of direct vertical relationships.
2. Authority flows from top level to bottom level.
3. Departmental heads are given full freedom to control their departments.
4. Each member knows from whom he would get orders and to whom he should give his orders.
5. Operation of this system is very easy.
6. A senior member has direct command over his subordinates.
7. Existence of direct relationship between superiors and subordinates.
8. Each member knows to whom he is responsible for the accomplishment of objectives of the organization.
9. The superior takes decisions within the scope of his authority.

Advantages of Line Organization :

1. Simplicity
2. Division of authority and responsibility
3. Unity of control
4. Unity of command
5. Speedy action
6. Discipline
7. Economical
8. Co-ordination

9. Direct communication
10. Flexibility

Disadvantages of Line Organization:

1. Lack of specialization
2. Over loading
3. Lack of initiative
4. Scope for favoritism
5. Dictatorial
6. Limited communication
7. Unitary administration
8. Subjective approach
9. Instability
10. Lack of co-ordination

Suitability :

1. This type of organization is suitable to small size business units.
2. Where the activities are of routine nature or machine based.
3. If the business activities are service minded.
4. Where the number of persons working is small.
5. The business operation is simple in nature.
6. Suitable for a business unit which has straight methods of operation.

Application :

1. Such organization is suitable for small and medium size establishments.
2. Suitable for continuous processing units such as sugar, paper, oil, refining, spinning and weaving industries.
3. Suitable where labor problems are not difficult to solve.

Line Type Organization

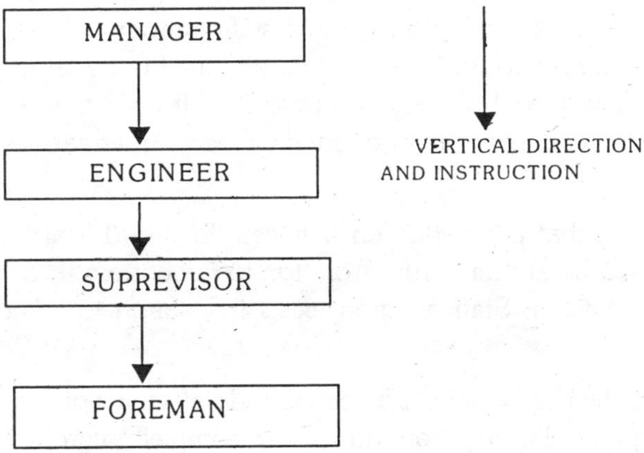

Figure 1.5 : Line Type Organization

Where efforts of large number of people have to be controlled and discipline is of prime importance, line type organization structure will serve the purpose. This is the oldest structure. However, in the present conditions this type of structure has lost the applicability. In this type boss is always right and his orders are to be obeyed at any cost.

1.10.2 STAFF ORGANIZATION

Functions of Staff Officers:

1. The staff officers assist the line officers in the planning of business activity.
2. The board of directors frame the policies of the business on the basis of the recommendations given by the staff officers.
3. The manager can get the advice from the staff officers regarding the selection, 'training', placement and remuneration fixation of the personnel.
4. The staff officers give advice regarding the method of improving the product, the techniques of controlling the cost of production, increasing the profits of the concern etc.
5. The staff officers prescribe the procedures to be followed by the line in the execution of policies and programs.
6. Staff officers of a department help the manager in the preparation of budget of the department.
7. The staff officer may be called to solve the administrative problems encountered by the line officers in general.

1.10.3 LINE VS. STAFF

Line and Staff Type Structure:

The third major type of organization is the line and staff. Line organization represents a direct vertical relationship through which authority flows. In line and staff organization, line authority, moves down in the same manner as in the line organization. In addition, specialists are attached to line managers to advise them on important matters. It is made up of line and staff units exerting what has been described as line and staff authority. The line and staff organization provides for specialized assistance such as that found in the functional organization, yet, it avoids the pitfalls of dual authority and divided accountability. It does this ensuring that there is one source of command for each person, supported by recommendations and advice from staff units.

Some writers argue that the distinction between 'line' and 'staff' should be based on the authority relationships. Line authority runs from top to the bottom through superior-subordinate relations in the organizations. Staff function exists in relation to some line function and not independent of it.

To act is said to be the line manager's functions and staffs function is to think. Taylor advocated separation of thinking and planning from doing. But complete segregation of management into thinking and doing is neither desirable nor feasible. The superior tells his subordinates and is accountable for their work. Therefore, the authority relationship between line and staff is that 'line tells, staff sells'.

Staff units appear when the line manager has no time, the knowledge, or the desire to perform certain functions. By using the staff, the line manager can concentrate on the creation of primary customer values.

As company grows in size, it is not uncommon to find that functional system cannot be applied without taking the help of the line and this type of structure which is combination of line and functional type structure is called line and staff structure.

In medium scale industrial units, large number of specialists like engineers, production experts have raised many problems in the organization. These can be solved by two ways

i. When such specialists are deployed only as advisors without any authority.

ii. When the staff department does not function as a parallel to the line organization.

A line or operating organization unit is one that is actually doing the work that represents the primary mission of the larger organization unit of which it is part. Example - an assembly department in the manufacturing division, a selling branch in the sales division.

A staff or service organization unit is any unit which is helping to do its work, or making it possible for the line to do its work, but is not actually engaged in the work itself. Example: a purchasing unit, a time study unit, a payroll preparation unit, in service training unit etc.

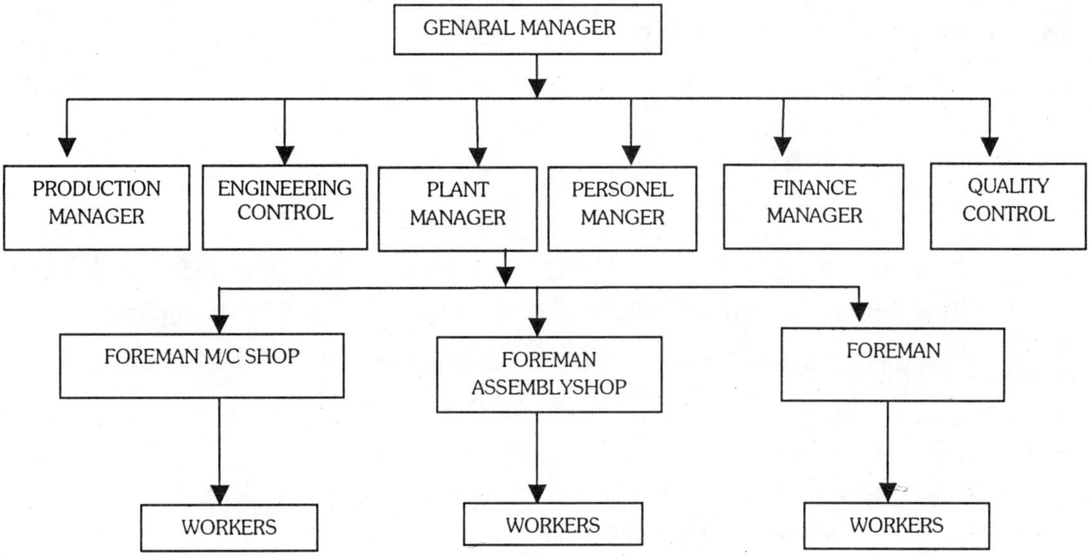

Figure 1.6 : Line and Staff Type Organisation

Advantages

1. It is a planned specialized system.
2. Quality of product will be better.
3. Wastage will be less.
4. Expert knowledge is available.
5. Sufficient time available to general manager for future planning and expansion.
6. Discipline problem is solved because of line relationship.

Disadvantages

1. Sufficient expert knowledge and guidance is not available when it is compared with functional types.
2. Lack of responsibility among higher levels and hence the discipline as a whole will be poor.
3. The over head cost of product may rise, because of high salaried staff.
4. The slackness of any section or department will largely affect the whole organization.

Line and Staff Conflict :

As the staff members are specialists and are highly qualified sometimes the superiority and inferiority complex may creep into the relationship of line and staff. This arises because in the formal organization line people are placed at a higher level with decision making authority. This leads to power conflict. The arguments of both line and staff in this regard are discussed below:

Arguments of Line Officers against Staff Officers :

1. The staff officers have only theoretical knowledge but not practical knowledge.
2. Frequently, the staff officers go beyond their sphere of activity and assume that they have line officers 'authority.
3. Much of the advice given by the staff officers is impractical.
4. Since the staff officers are not responsible for the result, they suggest unfruitful ideas.
5. The staff officers unnecessarily increase the paper work of the line officers.
6. The staff officers give advice without considering the nature of business as a whole.
7. Staff officers are very much interested in becoming line officers of the organization rather than imparting advice to them.
8. Staff officers blame the line officers for the failure of the project but keen on getting credit for the success of the project.

Arguments of Staff Officers against Line Officers :

1. The line officers completely neglect the advice given by the staff officers.
2. The line officers hesitate to accept new ideas.
3. The line officers do not follow the advice of staff officers properly.
4. Some line officers simply reject the advice without considering its validity.
5. Some line officers are not ready to ask for any advice from the staff office.
6. The line officers dissuade the management from giving authority to staff officers to implement new schemes.
7. The line officers do not exploit the full services of the staff officers.
8. Though the staff officers are highly qualified they are placed at a low level in the formal structure with low pay. This makes the line to feel that they are superiors to staff.

Resolving the Conflict between Line and Staff :

The conflict between line officers and the staff officers can be settled by the following suggestions:

1. Both the line and staff officers should be counseled to clearly understand the relationship with a positive attitude.
2. A top level management member should be appointed to bring coordination between the line and staff officers.
3. The line officers should be encouraged to use the advice of staff officers.
4. Only qualified and highly experienced persons should be selected and placed as staff officers.

5. The responsibility for result could be fixed on both line officers and staff officers.

6. Staff officers should convince and encourage the line officers to participate in the proposed scheme of change.

7. Remove the suspicion and fear of both line and staff officers by arranging frequent meetings.

8. If the favorable results are obtained, the line and staff officers may be appreciated by the top management.

1.10.4 FUNCTIONAL ORGANIZATION

The functional organization structure is one in which there are number of functional specialists supervising the activities of a single subordinate. The subordinate is supposed to be accountable to and receive orders from all functional specialists, each of whom handles matters associated with his own specialty.

The initial concept of the functional organization is credited to Frederick W. Taylor. In those days the conventional shop foreman in the industry used to perform a variety of duties. Under functional organization, various specialists are selected for various functions.

The need for functional organization arises out of:

(i) The complexity of modern and large-scale organization;

(ii) A desire to use the specialization in full and;

(iii) To reduce the work-load of line managers with complex problems and decision-making.

Characteristics of Functional organization:

1. The work is divided according to specified functions.

2. Authority is given to a specialist to give orders and instructions in relation to specific function.

3. Functional authority has right and power to give command throughout the line with reference to his specified area.

4. The decision is taken only after making consultation with the functional authority relating to his specialized area.

5. The executives and supervisor discharge the responsibilities of functional authority.

According to Taylor, a foremen should not be burdened with looking after all the activities of his work. Instead, he should be assisted by a number of specialists in solving the problems.

Specialists :

1. Route clerk

2. Instruction card clerk

3. Time and cost clerk
4. Gang boss
5. Speed boss
6. Inspector
7. Repair boss
8. Disciplinarian

Advantages of Functional Organization:

The functional organization has certain advantages:

1. It permits a high degree of specialization.
2. It is easier to fill positions in such an organization since functional specialists are to have only a limited number of talents .
3. It permits each specialist to become an expert in his own field.
4. Application of each expert knowledge
5. Reducing the work load
6. Efficiency
7. Adequate supervision
8. Relief to line executives
9. Co-operation
10. Mass production
11. Economy
12. Flexibility

Disadvantages of Functional Organization:

A functional organization also has the following disadvantages:

1. It suffers from dual authority and violates the principle of single accountability. No organization can run smoothly when a single individual has more than one boss
2. Authority and responsibility often overlap. It is hard to draw a sharp line between functions.
3. It is often difficult to get technical experts to work together smoothly. Each is likely to feel that his area of specialization is the most important .
4. Complex relationships
5. Problem of Discipline
6. Over specialization

7. Ineffective co-ordination
8. Centralization
9. Lack of responsibility
10. Increasing the over head expenses

THE FUNCTIONAL ORGANISATION STRUCTURE

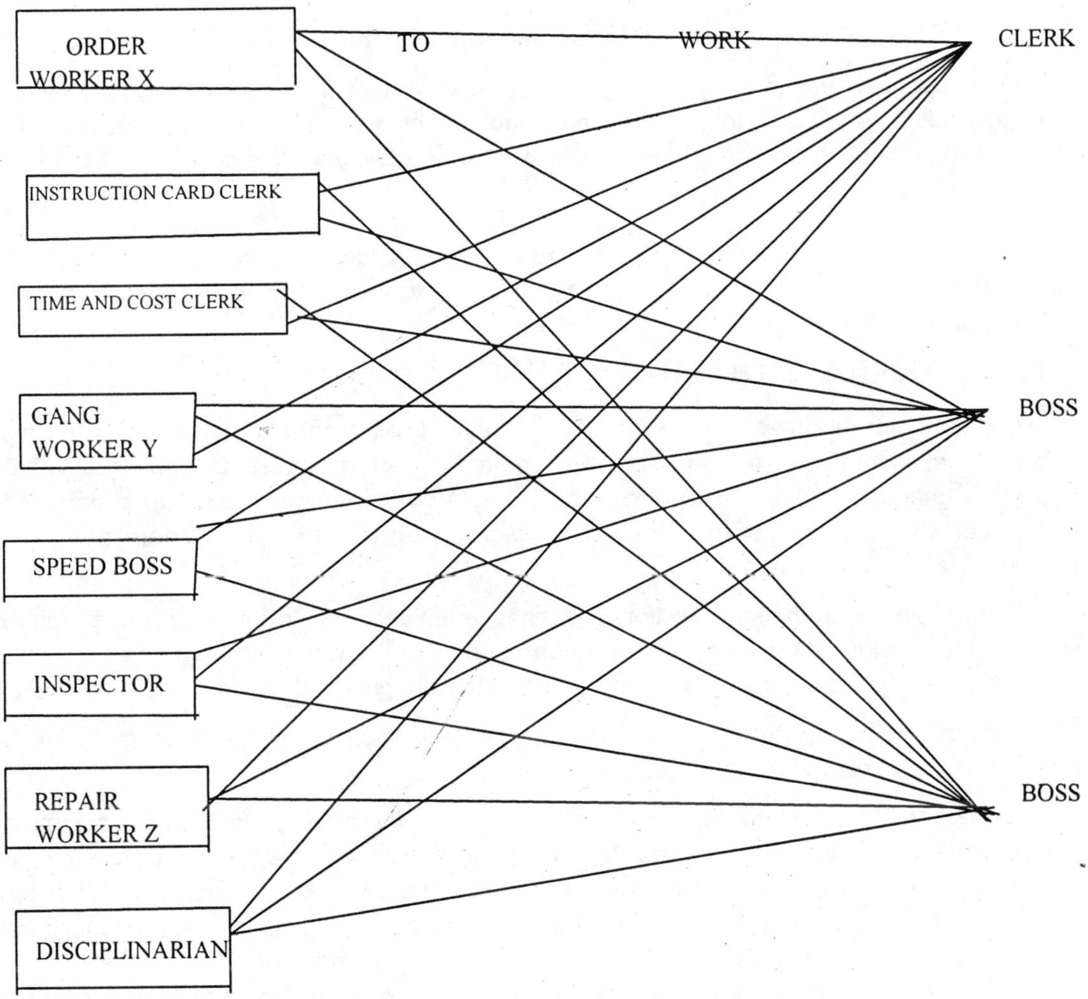

Figure 1.7: The Functional Organisation Structure

Functional Type Structure

This was introduced by F. W. Taylor and is logical extension of the division of labor. In this, authority is delegated to an individual or department to control specified process.

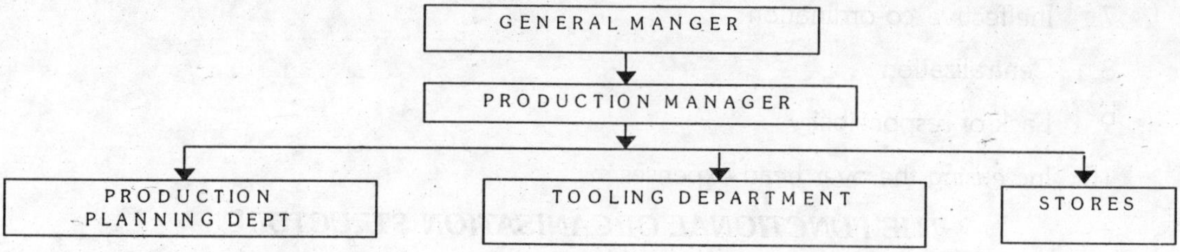

Figure 1.8: The Functional Organisation Structure

In this system planning is separated from performance since the direction of work is divided by various functions in the factory. It has been found that this type of structure become ineffective when the work of department and individuals increase in variety and complexity.

Application

In practice a pure functionalized system is rarely found. In fact a factory where responsibilities are divided on a functional basis, line relationship may also exit. This is suitable for large manufacturing concerns which are capable of expansion in future.

1.10.5 COMMITTEE ORGANIZATION

In the modern business world, some administrative tasks cannot be performed by a single person alone. when two or more persons are required to perform the same administrative task collectively, then committee type of organization is useful. A committee is a group of persons to whom certain managerial functions are assigned and from whom some advice or recommendations are expected.

Webster's New International Dictionary defines committee as a, "Body of persons appointed or elected to consider, investigate or take action upon usually a report concerning some matter or business, as by a court, legislative body or a number of persons".

According to Hicks, "A committee is a group of people who meet by plan to discuss or make a decision for a particular subject".

The duties, authority and responsibility are fixed by the top management and the committee is accountable to the management. The staff system when used with line system corrects to some extent the inefficiencies of the pure line system. It also comments the lack of coordination inherent in the pure functional form of organization. As every piece of work in a department in any enterprise has some connection with a piece of work in other departments, group participation is essential to ensure co-ordination and to promote co-operative relationship, committees are formed for the performance of special duties. Committees are often the most reliable way to make decisions.

Types of Committees:

1. Advisory committee (or) problem solving committee
2. Fact –finding committee
3. Action committee (or) executive committee

Functions of a Committee:

1. Collects the necessary information from different sources and arranges the information in an orderly manner.
2. The collected information is critically analyzed.
3. It drafts a detailed report containing the recommendations for the purpose of implementation.
4. Formulates the standards of performance for future evaluation.
5. Revising the policies of the organization.
6. Directing and controlling the officers at regular intervals to achieve the goals.

Advantages of Committee Organization:

1. The committee can take valuable decisions .The committee members can make use of their experience and knowledge while taking decisions.
2. Hasty decisions are avoided by the committee. Hasty decision are not worthy from a long term point of view.
3. Since "two" heads are better than one, quick and valuable decisions can be taken.
4. By this time schedule and proper following causes speedy action.
5. Decision taken is impersonal which leave the chairman free from personal criticism.
6. There is a stimulus towards co-operative action.
7. Expert knowledge is utilized.

Disadvantages

1. A committee with more members may delay the action and results in waste of time.
2. Committees tend to hang on after its usefulness is over.
3. It functions very slowly.

When the Committee is best used:

1. Where group deliberations and judgment are important.
2. Fear of improper use of authority.
3. Represents interested groups.
4. Motivation though participation.
5. Coordination in planning and implementation.
6. Policy development and interpretation.
7. Administrative communication.
8. Training.

9. Innovation.
10. To avoid or delay decision and action.

When the Committee should not be used:

1. When one manager is better.
2. Fact gathering and research.
3. When fast decision-making is required.
4. Substitute for other weaknesses.
5. Rubber-stamped or predetermined solutions.
6. Present technical reports or printed material which could be circulated .
7. To perform work.

How to have Successful Committee:

1. Define committee objectives, functions and authority.
2. Properly constitute the committee in the Organization.
3. Identify the right persons as Chairman and Members.
4. Appoint a permanent Secretary
5. Schedule regular meetings.
6. Plan agenda and prepare for meetings.
7. Make full use of technical staff.
8. Make use of Sub – committees.
9. Send minutes of the meeting to members.
10. Rely on consensus rather than unanimity.

Applications

This is suitable for the large organizations having too big complicated problems and which are difficult to handle by an individual.

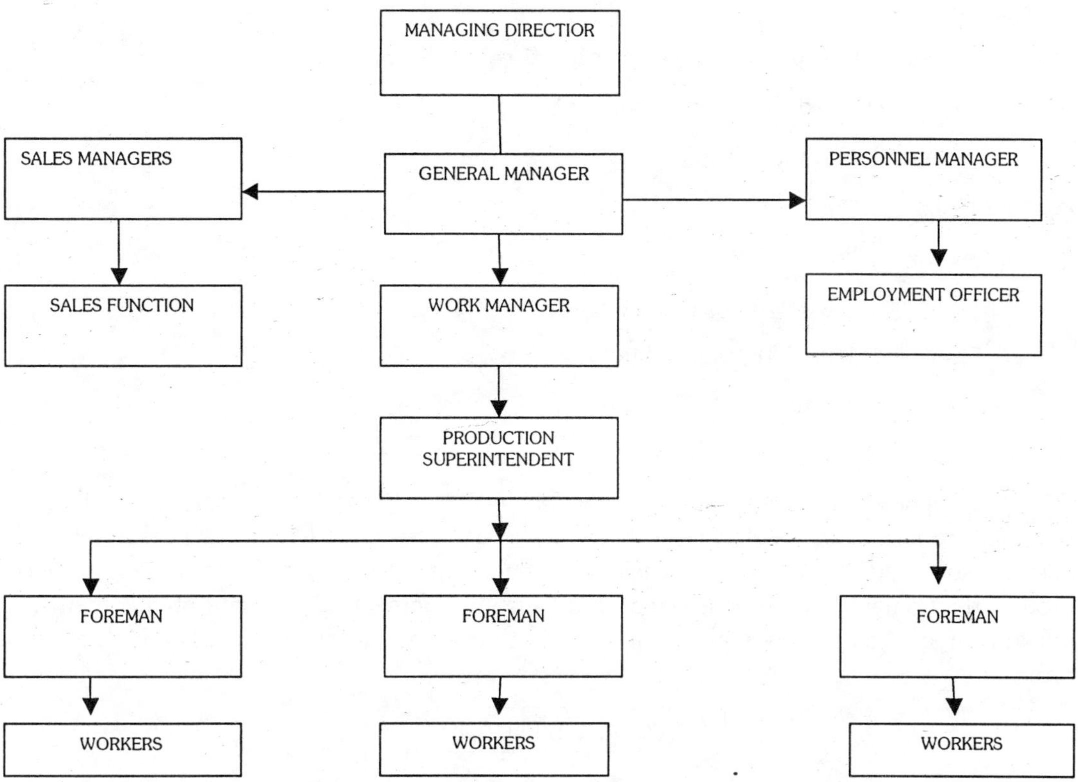

Figure 1.9 : Committee Organization

1.10.6 MATRIX ORGANIZATION

This type of organization assigns each worker two bosses in two different hierarchies. One hierarchy is "functional" and assures that each type of expert in the organization is well-trained, and measured by a boss who is super-expert in the same field. The other is "executive" and tries to get projects completed using the experts.

As an example, a company might have separate individuals with overall responsibility for Product X and Product Y, and different individuals with overall responsibility for Engineering, Quality Control, etc. Individuals responsible for quality control of project X will therefore have two reporting lines. In all the organization structures discussed so far, the communication protocol is vertical in the hierarchy. The information flow is within the hierarchy. The lateral communication between the functions is not permitted. It is a combination of the functional and the product organization.

Advantages:

1. It is a result-oriented structure.
2. Professional identification is maintained.
3. Pin points profit responsibility.

Disadvantages

1. Conflict in organizational authority exists.
2. Possibility of disunity of command.
3. Ineffective human relations.

Applications

1. Construction companies
2. Aerospace (designing) industries
3. Satellites launching organisations
4. Electronic industries

Why Matrix Organization is Used

As companies and customers have become increasingly focusing on end results, that is, in the final product or completed project, there has been pressure to establish responsibility for ensuring such end results. Of course this could be accomplished by organizing along traditional product department lines. This is often done, even in engineering, where a project manager is put in charge of all the engineering and support personnel necessary to accomplish an entire project.

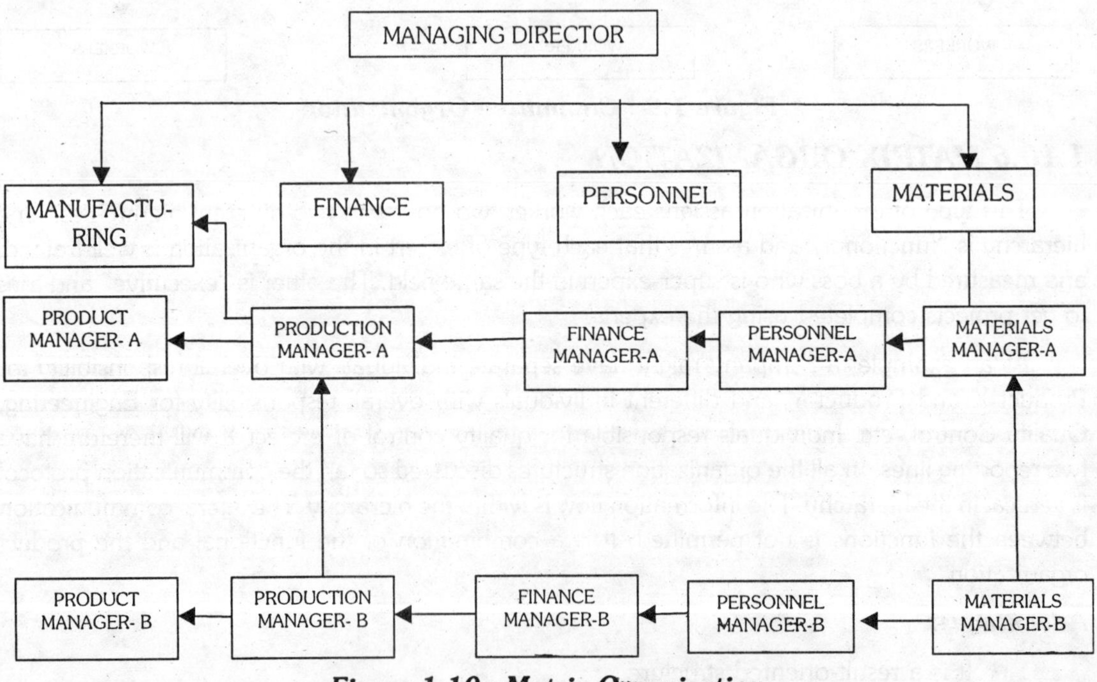

Figure 1.10 : Matrix Organization

1.10.7 VIRTUAL ORGANISATION

Virtual organization is a flexible organization structure which eliminates the traditional boundaries. This form of organization structure helps to increase the competitive capacity of the organizations which join together for a particular business purpose to compete effectively and efficiently at a global level with a particular mission. But the organizations which are coming together must have a common vision, mission, objective and they should share a common culture too. Very often the objective may be to forge a strong global brand which benefits all the participant organizations. Virtual organizations are becoming a reality now because global marketing strategies are formulated to economize the operations. The alliance continues till the operation is completed.

1.10.8 CELLULAR ORGANIZATION

In this form of organization the total production process is divided into different stages and each one is entrusted to a cell. Likewise, all the steps in the production process are undertaken by different units or otherwise called cells. Each cell contains a team of workers which takes the responsibility to maintain and improve the quality and quantity aspects of its products. Each cell will have a self managed team which monitors and corrects the defects in its process of work. These organizations require a small number of staff in its cell and the organization can also reduce the middle management positions.

1.10.9 TEAM STRUCTURE

In this type of organization structure vertical line of authority disappears to give place to team structure. These organizations are identified by horizontal team structures. "We report to each other" is the distinct feature of this type of structure. That means the superior and subordinate concept is eliminated to prevail upon the staff that everyone is equal in the status. Team structures are generally constituted to complete different projects which require specialists from lateral departments also. The team structure may be dissolved when a project is completed and redesigned to take up a new project.

The advantage in this form of organization is that the formal barriers are reduced to the minimum and the members will have more liberty to act as per their need and convenience. But the disadvantage is that when the team was pressurized to finish the task without much preparation, it may fail.

1.10.10 BOUNDARY LESS ORGANIZATION

In this organizational structure all internal and external boundaries in the internal and external environment are eliminated. This form is a combination of teams and network structures with an objective of completing the tasks very efficiently and quickly. The important feature of boundary less organization is spontaneous team work and fast communication. Another feature is that it need not follow the traditional chain of command. The main purpose is finishing the objective even by outsourcing or networking. It is a dynamic organization which requires high level knowledge sharing, absence of bureaucracy and hierarchy. The focus is on acquiring required talent and competencies for task accomplishment without any bureaucratic restrictions. The benefits of this type of organization are creativity, quality, punctuality, enhancement of speed and flexibility. The disadvantages of boundary less organization are lack of communication, cooperation and coordination which makes the organization ineffective.

1.10.11 INVERTED PYRAMID STRUCTURE

Pyramids or Hierarchies

A hierarchy exemplifies an arrangement with a leader who leads other individual members of the organization. This arrangement is often associated with bureaucracy. These structures are formed on the basis that there are enough people under the leader to give him support. Just as one would imagine a real pyramid, if there are not enough stone blocks to hold up the higher ones, gravity would irrevocably bring down the monumental structure. So, one can imagine that if the leader does not have the support of his subordinates, the entire structure will collapse. This is an alternative to the traditional chain of command. This is a structure which is narrow at the top and wide at the base. It includes a few levels of management.

1.10.12 LEAN AND FLAT ORGANIZATION STRUCTURE

Lean Organization Structure :

Lean production is a Japanese system that helps cut down on costs in manufacturing plants and factories. A company that implements lean techniques should also adopt a lean organizational structure. In a lean organizational structure, the organizational arrangement should flow along product and process lines rather than on functional areas. For instance, some lean companies set up integrated product and process teams as self-organized work teams. A dedicated team for each product family could include expertise from different functional areas such as marketing, purchasing, manufacturing, quality assurance and customer relations. Work teams in lean organizational structures should not be set up to report through many layers in a hierarchy. Instead, the reporting structure should focus on a connected set of activities in a horizontal stream. A lean organizational structure helps promote lean objectives such as minimizing waste through continuous improvement. This sort of structure reduces the need for non-essential functions and enhances efficiency and flexibility.

Flat Organization Structure :

A "flat" manufacturing system is one that is bloated with waste. Excesses in inventory and other areas that create unnecessary costs to the organization while providing no value to the customer often go unnoticed within a traditional manufacturing setting. The implementation of a Lean Management System consists of eliminating seven types of waste within your organization. By eliminating waste, your organization can do more with less. To implement a lean management system, there are several steps you must follow to eliminate waste within your manufacturing processes.

1.10.13 PROJECT ORGANIZATION

A project organization is one where common services like finance, purchase etc. are organized at the functional level. But project resources are allocated to the project manager. Since the business responsibility rests with the project manager, necessary authority is given to him with the requisite resources. This type of organization structure helps in making quick decisions for project management and control in terms of cost, resources, quality and time. In a project organization some of the functions are of corporate responsibility and some of them are project manager's responsibility.

Advantages

1. This calls for quick decisions.
2. Placing all the functional resources within the reach of the project manager.
3. Proper co-ordination of the work of different departments for the success of the project.

Disadvantages

1. It tends to increase the problems of control for top management.
2. It is special case of product organization.
3. The organization may get disintegrated with increasing focus on departments and projects.

SHORT QUESTIONS

1. Explain about the classification of organizations.
2. Distinguish between formal organization and informal organization
3. Explain different types of organization structures.
4. Define management?
5. What are the characteristics of management?
6. What are the various functions of management?
7. Explain various principles of scientific management
8. Explain the nature and concept of management.
9. Define role and importance of management?
10. State the characteristics of management.
11. Define functions of management?
12. Explain evolution of management thought.
13. State the various stages of evolution of management.
14. Explain scientific management.
15. Explain principles of management.
16. Explain Hawthorne experiments in human relations approach.
17. What is meant by motivation?
18. Explain theory X.
19. Explain theory Y.

20. Write short note on Maslow's Need Hierarchy theory.
21. Explain the concept of leadership.
22. Define organization.
23. State the essential elements of good organization.
24. Name the various types of organizations.
25. Define organization chart?
26. Explain the terms:
    (a) Formal organization
    (b) Informal organization
27. Explain the classical theory of organization.
28. What is meant by departmentation?
29. Explain the need and importance of departmentation.
30. Define authority and responsibility?
31. What is delegation of authority and give the principles of delegation?
32. What are the features of a good organization structure?
33. Explain line and staff authority.
34. Explain matrix organization structure.

ESSAY QUESTIONS

1. Is management an art or science? Justify your answer by enumerating briefly some of the schools of thought on management.
2. Discuss the important functions of management and which do you consider the most effective in present day context. Name various concepts of management and discuss in detail management by objectives.
3. Explain evolution of management thought.
4. State the contribution of Frank Gilbreth in the evolution of management
5. Define scientific management? What are its objectives and how it is useful to business enterprise?
6. What are the contributions of modern approach to the management?
7. Explain features and importance of Scientific Management.
8. What is meant by management? Explain the principles of management of Henry Fayol.
9. What is the concept of motivation and explain various theories of motivation?
10. What is the significance of Maslow's theory of hierarchy of human needs?

11. Explain Douglas McGregor's theory X and theory Y.
12. Explain briefly Hertzberg's two factor theory of motivation.
13. What is the significance of Hawthorne experiments?
14. Explain the principles and types of organization.
15. "Organization is a tool for achieving enterprise objectives". Discuss.
16. What is an organisation chart? Show the organisation chart of a medium size organisation.
17. Explain organization chart. What are its advantages and limitations?
18. What is an organization? Distinguish between formal and informal organization with suitable examples
19. What are the different types of organization structures and explain each briefly.
20. Name the various types of organisation structures and explain any one of them with its merits and demerits.
21. What is functional organization structure? State the advantages and limitations.
22. What is meant by line and staff organization? Explain in detail.
23. Differentiate between line organisation and functional organisation
24. Why the staff organization is preferred to the line type of organisation in today's industry? Describe the implication of the relation of staff departments with line departments.
25. Why is the line and staff organization preferred to the line type of organization in today's industry?
26. What is committee organisation? State the advantages and disadvantages of committee organization.
27. What do you understand by matrix organization? Under what situations this organisation structure would be appropriate?

FILL IN THE BLANKS

1. The study of application of a combination of management and scientific techniques in an organization is known as................... (Management Science)
2. The art of getting things done through others (people) within an organization is referred to as .... (Management)
3. Father of Management Science is .... (Henry Fayol)
4. Management is both an .... and .... (Art, Science)
5. According to Henry Fayol, the functions of management are ....
(Planning, Organizing, Commanding, Coordination, Controlling)
6. POSDCORB .... (Planning, Organizing, Staffing, Directing, Controlling, Coordinating, Reporting and Budgeting)

7. Determining the future course of action is referred to as.................... (Planning)

8. ....is estimation of expenses in advance to attain the objectives. (Budget and Innovation)

9. The framework of an establishment is called.................... (Organization)

10. The 4M's of management may be identified as...................., ..., ..., ... (Men, Money, Material, Machine)

11. .... consists of verifying whether everything occurs in conformity with the plan, instructions and principles. (Controlling)

12. ....includes selection and training functions of manager. (Staffing)

13. .... is that each group of activities having the same objective must have one head and one plan. (Unity of direction)

14. ....means that an employee should get orders and instructions only from one superior. (Unity of command)

15. The chain of supervisors from the highest level to the lowest level for the purpose of communication is known as..................... (Scalar chain)

16. .... relates to arrangement of things and people in proper places. (Order)

17. ....is a device for achieving the objectives of the enterprise. (Organization)

18. ....is one of the methods to find out the best way of doing the work. (Job analysis)

19. ....is the determination of time a movement takes to complete. (Time study)

20. .... means applying scientific knowledge and scientific methods in systematic, analytical and objective manner. (Scientific Management)

21. ....is the father of Scientific Management. (F.W.Taylor)

22. ....is the father of Modern Management. (Henry Fayol)

23. F.W.Taylor wrote "The Principles of Management" in the year.......................... (1911)

24. Scientific Management's objective is to .... profit with .... inputs. (Maximum, Minimum)

25. Policy making is done by.......................... (Administration)

26. Policy implementation is done by........................... (Management)

27. ....is the executive function. (Management)

28. .... authority remains in charge of administration. (Top level)

29. Low level management is also known as.......................... (Supervisory level)

30. Low level management is concerned with the efficiency in using ....of the organization. (Resources)

31. The level of management which stands between the top management and the supervisory management is called...................... (Middle level management)

32. Basic goals of the organization are established at......................level management. (Top level management)

33. The evidence of the management can be seen from the works of the priests of Mesopotamia in .... era. (Pre-classical)

34. ....era is too mechanistic. (Classical)

35. Empirical school was started by........................ (Earnest Dale)

36. ....school regards organization as a psycho-social system. (Human relations school)

37. ....school emphasized on selecting from possible alternatives, a course of action. (Decisions theory)

38. Operational approach school is known as...................... (Management Process Approach)

39. The grouping of similar activities into small units for the purpose of facilitating administration is called........... (Departmentation)

40. Span of control refers to....................... (Number of Subordinates)

41. The type of span of control which is economical is..................... (Wide span of control)

42. ....helps to secure a unifying spirit in accomplishing the end result of the organization. (Objective)

43. Understanding, providing and satisfaction of human needs is.................... of the business. (Human objective)

44. M.B.O was first developed by .... (Peter F. Drucker)

45. Personnel satisfaction is an advantage of........................ (M.B.O)

46. ....means a process of stimulating people to act to accomplish which will impel employees to strive to attain company goals. (Motivation)

47. Theory of hierarchical needs was explained by.................... (Maslow)

48. The needs realizing one's own potentialities are known as................. (Self-actualization needs)

49. The two separate factors in Herzberg's two factor model of motivation are .... and .... (Maintenance, Motivation)

50. Salary is a...........................factor. (Maintenance)

51. The word POSDCORB is expanded as......................... (Planning, organizing, staffing, directing, coordinating, reporting & budgeting)

52. The functions of management as outlined by Koontz are Planning, Organizing, Staffing, and......................... (Directing and Controlling)

53. .... is the first principle of organizational management (Division of work)

54. An organization principle which enables individuals to contribute to the enterprise's objective is .... (Principles of unity of objective)

55. The organization principle, which talks about the coordination that exists between different activities .... (Principle of coordination)

56. The organization principle, which talks about the clear cut flow of authorities, responsibilities and communication from top to bottom and bottom to top....... (Scalar principle)

57. The organization principle, which talks about the reporting relationship between subordinates and superior (Principle of unity of command)

58. F.W.Taylor introduced a system of working known as .... (Functional organization)

59. The strategies suggested by Tom Peters to deal with chaos are.......... (Participation)

60. Management is an inexact science because .... (The principles are not as exact as science)

61. The school of thought that supports the interchangeability of the term's administration and management is pioneered by.......... (Henry Fayol)

62. The frame work of establishment is called............. (Organization)

63. Organization involves a structure of ....among people working for the desired result (Relationship)

64. It needs organization to provide maximum ....to enable them to be creative (Freedom)

65. The term coined by Luther Gulick to represent management function is....... (POSDCORB)

66. Deciding in advance what is to be done in the future is called......... (Planning)

67. Planning ends with............... (Decision making)

68. The process of determining the course of action to achieve the goals is called..... (Planning)

69. The process of identification and grouping of activates in an organization and assigning them to a manger with authority is called .... (Organizing)

70. The guide like tool to explain how many positions are in the organization and at what level is called.......... (Organization structure)

71. ....function aims at selecting the right person for the right job. (Staffing)

72. The process of estimating the future based on the present and past data is called........ (Forecasting)

73. The process of guiding subordinates to enable them achieve goals is called .... (Directing)

74. To optimize the benefit of effort in direction the leader has to see how well the............... of the group are related to the organization goals (Needs)

75. The process of stimulating the employees to perform more effectively is called .... (Motivating)

76. The orderly arrangement of group effort to provide unity of action in pursuit of a common purpose is called .... (Coordination)

77. In case there is a clash between individual interest and group interest, ...will prevail (Group interest)

78. Unity of command means.......... (One employee- one boss)

79. Esprit de corps refers to............ (Team work)

80. Elton mayo is well known for his ....experiments (Hawthorne)

81. The need to maximize one's potential and accomplish something is covered by ....need in the Maslow's hierarchy of needs (Self actualization)

82. Theory x and theory y was contributed by............... (Douglas Mc Gregor)

83. The framework of relationships; within which the management functions are performed called........... (Organization)

84. The process of grouping the similar activities and assigning responsibility is called............. (Organizing)

86. Different layers in management in the organization is called............ (Hierarchy)

87. The power to use discretion vested in that particular position or job is called ...... (Authority)

88. The process of transferring authority down the levels in the organization is called............ (Delegation)

89. The number of subordinates that can be controlled effectively by a supervisor at a given point of time is called.............. (Span of control)

89. A flat organization is always associated with ....span (Wider)

90. The manager whose role is to support, guide or counsel is called.......... (Staff)

91. The functional organization suggested by Taylor violates one of the basic principles of organization is .... (Line and staff)

92. Dividing the organization on the basis of its department is called........ (Combination of project and functional organization)

93. The process of identifying overall purpose for the organization is called .... (Departmentation)

❖ ❖ ❖

UNIT - II
OPERATIONS MANAGEMENT

2.1 INTRODUCTION TO POM

Introduction

Production management is the branch of management which is concerned with the production function. Production is the center of all activities of an organization. Every organization is engaged in production of either goods or services. All the activities of an organization such as finance, personnel, and marketing etc. exist in an organization because of production activity. Production is the foundation on which every organization is built. Hence, the position of production management in an organization is very important.

Production

Production refers to the sequence of operations that transform materials from a given state to a desired state. ***Production function*** is that part of an organization, which is concerned with the transformation of a range of inputs (men, materials, machines, money, land, information, management, energy, etc) into the desired output (goods / services) having the requisite quality level. The output produced has utility (use) value and economic (money) value.

Production is defined as "the step-by-step conversion of one form of material into another form through chemical or mechanical process to create or enhance the utility of the product to the user." Thus, production is a value addition process. At each stage of processing, there will be value addition.

E. S. Buffa defines production as 'a process by which goods and services are created'. Some examples of production are: manufacturing custom-made products like, boilers with a specific capacity, constructing flats, some structural fabrication works for selected customers, etc., and manufacturing standardized products like, car, bus, motor cycle, radio, television, etc.

Concept of Operations

Operations in an organization can be categorized into manufacturing operations and service operations. Manufacturing operations is a conversion process that includes manufacturing yields, which is a tangible output: a product, whereas, service operation is a conversion process that includes service yields, an intangible output: a deed, a performance, an effort. Operation is that part of an organization, which is concerned with the transformation of a range of inputs into the required output (goods and services) having the requisite quality level.

The operations function consists of all activities directly related to producing goods or providing services. Hence, it exists both in manufacturing and assembly operations, which are goods-oriented, and in areas such as health care, transportation, food handling and retailing, which are primarily service-oriented.

Management

It is the art or science of getting things done by people with satisfaction to employer, employees and public through planning, coordinating, organizing, directing and controlling the activities to meet specified goals. Management is the process, which combines and transforms various resources used in the operations subsystem of the organization into value added services in a controlled manner as per the policies of the organization. Today's manager needs scientific base as well as personal tactics to manage the people under him to achieve the desired goals.

Definition of Production Management

Production management is a function of management, related to planning, coordinating and controlling the resources required for production to produce specified product by specified methods, by optimal utilization of resources.

Production management is defined as management function which plans, organizes, coordinates, directs and controls the material supply and processing activities of an enterprise, so that specified products are produced by specified methods to meet an approved sales programme. These activities are being carried out in such a manner that plant, labour and capital available are used to the best advantage of the organization.

E. S. Buffa defines production management as, "which deals with decision making related to production processes so that the resulting goods or services are produced according to specifications, in the amount and by the schedule demanded and out of minimum cost."

Definition of Production and Operations Management

Production and operations management is the conversion of inputs into outputs using physical resources, so as to provide the desired utility / facilities of form, place, possession or state or a combination thereof to the customer while meeting the other organizational objectives of effectiveness, efficiency and adaptability.

Production/operations management is the process, which combines and transforms various resources used in the production/operations subsystem of the organization into value added product/services in a controlled manner as per the policies of the organization. Therefore, it is that part of an organization, which is concerned with the transformation of a range of inputs into the required output (products/services) having the requisite quality level.

The set of interrelated management activities, which are involved in manufacturing certain products, is called as ***production management***. If the same concept is extended to service operations, then the corresponding set of management activities is called as ***operations management***.

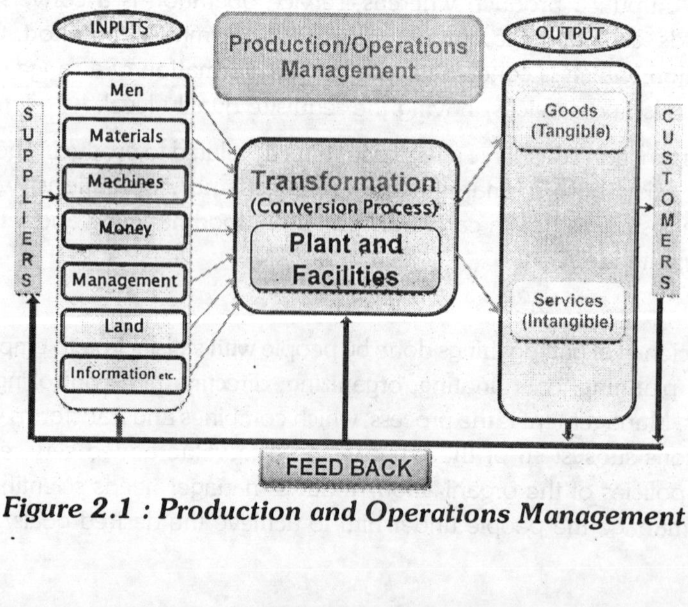

Figure 2.1 : Production and Operations Management

Production management has made a significant contribution to society by playing a role in areas such as providing better quality goods and services, increasing productivity and improving working conditions. Productivity has been increased through such measures as the use of technology and new production methods. Increased productivity permits the more efficient production of goods and services and so helps raise living standards. Better quality goods and services are available through the use of quality initiatives such as total quality management (TQM). The rate of improvement in quality levels is reflected in such programmes as ISO, Zero Defects Programme, Value Analysis, and Six Sigma etc., Improved working conditions are an outcome of the realization that the contribution of people is vital to an organization's success. Job design is used to help enable the full potential of employees.

Production in the organization circuit of activities

- In the first phase, capital or money is used to finance the establishments
- This is followed by the production phase in which the capital is used to procure the physical resources and manufacture goods and services
- The production phase is followed by the marketing phase in which the goods and services produced are marketed or sold
- Here the goods and services are transferred back to money to complete the cycle
- A weakness in any of the activity affects the entire organization

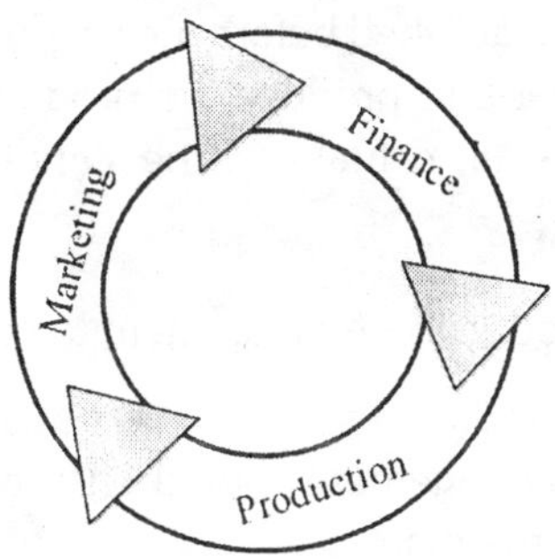

Figure 2.2 : Production in Organization Circuit of Activities

Objectives of Production Management

The objective of production and operations management is to produce the desired product or specified product by specified methods so that the optimal utilization of available resources is met with. Hence, the production and operations management is responsible to produce the desired product, which has marketability at the cheapest price by proper planning, the manpower, material and processes. Production management must see that it will deliver right goods of right quantity at right place and at right price.

Thus, the main objective of production / operations management is to deliver goods of ***right quality*** of ***right quantity*** at ***right place***, ***right time*** and for the ***right price*** which can satisfy the needs of the customer.

1. ***Right Quality***

   The quality of product is established based upon the customers' needs. The right quality is not necessarily best quality. It is determined by the cost of the product and the technical characteristics as suited to the specific requirements.

2. ***Right Quantity***

   The manufacturing organization should produce the products in right number. If they are produced in excess of demand the capital will block up in the form of inventory and if the quantity is produced in short of demand, leads to shortage of products.

3. ***Right Place***

   Products should be made available to the target market through the various channels of distribution, based on the orders made or as and when there is demand from the prospective customers.

4. ***Right Time***

   Timeliness of delivery is one of the important parameter to judge the effectiveness of production department. So, the production department has to make the optimal utilization of input resources to achieve its objective.

5. ***Right Price***

   Manufacturing costs are established before the product is actually manufactured. Hence, all attempts should be made to produce the products at pre-established cost, so as to reduce the variation between actual and the standard (pre-established) cost.

5P's of Production Management

Five important functions of production management to carry out the transformation process effectively, 5P's are

1. ***Product*** – Production management should ensure that the product is manufactured as per specifications and the plan
2. ***Plant*** – Production management has to ensure that the plant meets specifications and is keeping with the requirements
3. ***Process*** – Among the many ways of producing the product, production management has the responsibility of choosing the best way
4. ***Programs*** – The production programme should ensure that the production schedules are met
5. ***People*** – Production management has to ensure that skilled and motivated workers are available for production activity

Functions of Production and Operations Management

The function of production management depends upon the size of the firm. In small firms the production manager may have to look after production planning and control along with personnel, marketing, finance and purchase functions. In medium sized firms, there may be separate managers for personnel, marketing and finance functions. In large sized firms the activities of production management is confined to the management of production activities only.

As such, there is no hard and fast rule to specify the functions of production management, but some of the important functions which are looked after by the production management department can be specified as shown in figure 2.3.

- ***Plant Location***

Plant location can be defined as the determination of that location which when considering all factors of production will provide minimum cost delivered to the customer. Ideal location is the best location which has the lowest cost of production per unit at the time of establishment. A plant is a place where men, material, machine, money are brought together for the transformation process. For a good plant location there should be a balance between various factors affecting plant location.

- ***Plant Layout***

Plant layout is companion problem to plant location. A layout is a physical configuration of departments, workstations and equipment in the conversion process. It is the spatial arrangement of physical resources used to create the product. Plant layout is the physical arrangement of buildings, machines, materials and services facilities required to facilitate efficient operation of the production system. In short, it is the disposition of various facilities and services within the site or location selected previously.

- ***Product Design***

Product design refers to the structure, contents, quality and various other aspects which management consider while designing and developing a product. A product's design has impact on what materials and components would be used, which suppliers will be included, what machines and types of processes will be used to manufacture it, where it will be stored, how it will be transported etc. Marketing is also impacted by product design.

- ***Process Design***

The production process is the key to production. Process design is the complete delineation and description of specific steps in the production process and the linkages among the steps that will enable the production system to produce the products of desired quality, and quantity at the right time for the right price. Product and process design processes are interrelated. There is continuous relation between the two activities.

- ***Productivity***

Productivity is the ratio between the output and the input. It is the ratio of the output of goods and services to input facilities. It represents the overall efficiency of the system. Output means the amount produced and the inputs are the amount of resources used in process of production. The resources may be any combination of materials, machines, labour, capital etc. The input could be the man-hours spent or the amount of material consumed etc. Thus, productivity is a measure of how much input is required to produce a given output.

- ***Materials Management***

Materials Management includes all functions concerned with ordering, storage and movement of materials. It includes several important aspects of management such as material handling, purchasing, storage, inventory control, inspection of material, value analysis etc., In short, it is the term used for controlling the kind, amount, location, movement and timing of various materials used in production process.

- ***Maintenance Management***

In modern industry, equipment and machinery are a very important part of the total productive effort. Therefore, their idleness or downtime becomes very expensive. Hence, it is very important that the plant machinery should be properly maintained.

- ***Inventory Control***

Inventory control aims at keeping track of inventories. It is the technique of maintaining stocks of desired quality and quantity to be made available to different departments as and when they are needed.

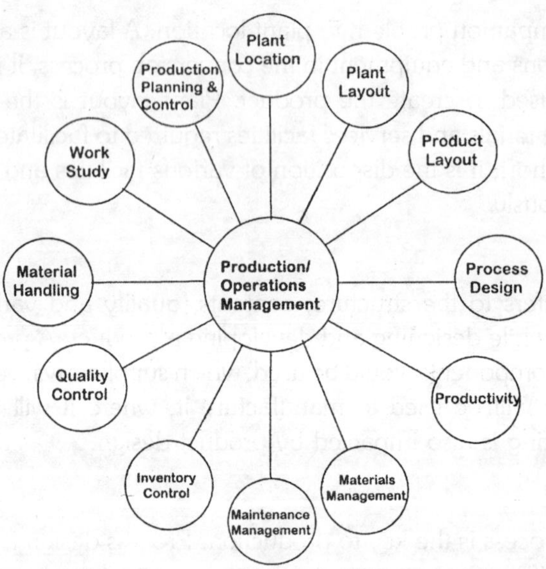

Figure 2.3 : Functions of Production and Operations Management

- ***Quality Control***

Quality control may be defined as 'a system that is used to maintain a desired level of quality in a product or service'. It aims at prevention of defects at the source and corrective action procedure. Quality control is the technique by means of which product of uniform acceptable quality is manufactured. It is the entire collection of activities, which ensures that the operation will produce the optimum quality products at minimum cost.

- ***Material Handling***

Material handling involves the movements of materials, manually or mechanically in batches or one item at a time within the plant with the help of different types of material handling equipment. It is the art and science involving the movements, packaging and storing of substance in any form. Material handling cost can be reduced by proper selection, operation and maintenance of material handling devices.

- ***Work Study***

Work study is the study of work which examines both the method of work and duration. It considers ways to improve methods of doing work so that human efforts may be applied most economically, efficiently, and effectively to achieve higher productivity of an organization. Work study on one hand examines the method of doing the work and on the other hand determines the time required to do the work.

- ***Production Planning and Control***

Production planning and control can be defined as the process of planning the production in advance, setting the exact route of each item, fixing the starting and finishing dates for each item, to give production orders to shops and to follow-up the progress of products according to orders. The principle of production planning and control lies in the statement 'First Plan Your Work and then Work on Your Plan'.

Production and Operations Management underwent three key shifts

1) From cost and efficiency to value creation
2) From mass production to customization
3) From functional specialization to a systems approach to achieving high performance

Upto 1970's the basic focus of Operations Management was on "***Cost reduction***".

However, since the 1990's the focus has been for "***Value creation***"

The value driven approach of operations management focuses on value provided to the customer. The operation function contributes to the 'value' delivery to customers by significant improvements in the cost, quality, timeliness and availability of products and services. Thus, POM constitutes all the activities that an organization conducts in order to deliver value to its customer.

Production and Operations Management's Future Challenges

- Organizations will need an increased ability to customize product for local markets.
- Business will find it increasingly difficult to hire and keep quality workers. The time has come to view employees as a renewable resource and to keep them as long as one can.
- The location of work and workers will be dramatically impacted by communication technologies.
- Investing and mastering the right technologies is a major challenge.
- Technologies to make products more earth friendly should be developed for the protection of the environment.

- ❖ Protection of intellectual property is another challenge. Protection will lie more with the delivery process rather than the product.

Benefits from efficient Production and Operations Management

Efficient production management will give various benefits to the different sections of the society. They are:

1. ***Consumer*** benefits from improved industrial productivity, increased use value in the product - Products are available to consumer at right place, right price, right time in desired quantity and of desired quality.
2. ***Investors*** - They get increased security for their investments, adequate market returns and creditability and good image in the society.
3. ***Employees*** - Get adequate wages, job security, improved working conditions and increased personal and job satisfaction.
4. ***Suppliers*** - Will get confidence in the management and their bills can be released without any delay.
5. ***Community*** - Enjoys benefits from economic and social stability.
6. ***Country*** - Will achieve prospects and security because of increased productivity and healthy industrial atmosphere.

2.2 PLANT LOCATION AND LAYOUT

2.2.1 PLANT LOCATION

Location of facilities is a problem associated with the planning phase of a factory or even a service sector. Small entrepreneur to big industrial houses, hospital to a fashion designer shop and school to a five star hotel start the first planning activity with questions: Where to locate the site so that no change is needed for years to come. It is a very vital decision which has long term implications. This type of decision is called as a strategic decision. The selection of location is a key-decision as large investment is made in building plant and machinery. It is not very easy to answer a location problem. The reasons are: (i) uncertainty in future, (ii) complexity and conflicting factors associated with the site selection problem, (iii) constraints and limitation of resources to produce a site, etc.

Plant location or the facilities location problem is an important strategic level decision making for an organization. One of the key features of a conversion process (manufacturing system) is the efficiency with which the products are transferred to the customers. This fact will include the determination of where to place the plant or facility. The plant location should be based on the company's expansion plan and policy, diversification plan for the products, changing market conditions, the changing sources of raw materials and many other factors that influence the choice of the location decision. The purpose of the location study is to find an optimum location that will result in the greatest advantage to the organization.

Holmes defines plant location problem as one determining "***that location which, in consideration of all factors affecting products delivered-to-customers cost of product (s)***

to be manufactured, will afford the enterprise the greatest advantages obtained by virtue of location". Plant location can be defined as the determination of that location which when considering all factors of production will provide minimum cost delivered to the customer.

Ideal location is the best location which has the lowest cost of production per unit at the time of establishment. It is one which results in lowest production cost and least distribution per unit.The selection of a site is a long term and almost a right line decision for the enterprise. A plant is a place where men, material, machine, money are brought together for the transformation process. For a good plant location there should be a balance between various factors affecting plant location.

Definitions

"Plant location is the function of determining where the plant should be located for maximum operating economy and effectiveness." – ***Prof. R.C. Davis***

"Plant location should be based on nine M's namely money, material, manpower, market, motive power, management, machinery, means of communication and momentum to an early start. In general, "a plant should be located at a place where the innovations are interested in its success, the product can be profitable and the production cost is minimum".

– ***Dr. M. Visweswaryya***

There are three phases in location

1. Selection of the a general territory or region – North / South, States
2. Selection of the community or locality – Urban, Rural, Suburban
3. Selection of the actual or specific site

1. ***Selection of region:*** This refers to the selection of particular geographical zone or state taking into consideration such factors as nearness to market and sources of raw materials, basic infrastructure facilities available, climatic conditions and taxation and laws.

2. ***Selection of a community:*** This refers to the selection of the specific locality within the selected region. The factors that influence the selection of community are availability of labour, community attitude, social structure and service facilities.

   Generally the following alternatives are available:

   (1) Urban area.

   (2) Rural area

   (3) Semi-urban area near the urban area.

3. ***Selection of a particular site:*** This refers to the selection of specific site within the community. The factors that influence the site selection are the cost of the land, availability and suitability of the land. The type of manufacturing process may dictate the site selection.

Considerations in Plant Location

No plant can be located at a place, which fulfills all the criteria of perfect location. Some factors are compromised to take advantage of the other factors. For example, if the raw material is quite bulky and is difficult to transport, then the plant may be located nearer to raw material source. Many iron and steel industries are geographically located near the place where iron-ore is available. Jamshedpur, Bokaro and Rourkela in India are the places where iron-ore is found. To run the power plant, coal is needed. Many NTPC power plants are located near the place where coal is found. Similar observations are valid for oil-fields and location of refineries. However, some others factors may have to be compromised.

Let us consider two sites for location of a new factory. Site A is nearer to market but far from the raw material source; Site B is otherwise. Site A is a rural location with cheap availability of labor; Site B is an urban location with better availability of power. Similarly, we can list many factors: Some are better at site A, while the rest are better at site B. Which site to select? When site selection decision is needed, many options are available with their relative strengths and weaknesses. A careful consideration is needed on an integrated framework before final site is selected.

2.2.2 FACTORS AFFECTING OR INFLUENCING LOCATION:

- Nearness to raw material source (Proximity to suppliers)
- Nearness to potential market (Proximity to markets)
- Transportation facility (Availability of all modes of transport)
- Availability of labour (abundant labour both unskilled and skilled at comparative wages)
- Availability of power and fuel
- Availability of water
- Availability of land for present and future needs (cost, size, leveling etc)
- Supply of capital (Availability of banks and financial institutions)
- Suitable climatic conditions (Agricultural processing units)
- Community and labour attitude
- Environmental considerations and regulations
- Stability of demand
- Integration with other group of companies (Industrial atmosphere)
- Community infrastructure and amenity (Availability of good housing facilities, hospitals, market centers, schools and other recreational facilities)
- Government policy
- Legal requirements and taxation policy
- Initial start and good will

- External economies of scale
- Personal factors
- Natural factors
- Political factors
- Historical factors

Miscellaneous factors

- Drainage and waste disposal
- Construction cost
- Communication facility
- Safety requirements, security
- Strategic factors like dangers of air-attacks.
- Availability of fire-fighting facilities.
- Regional aspirations of people and their political satisfaction.

2.2.3 PLANT LAYOUT

Plant layout is companion problem to plant location. A layout is the physical configuration of departments, workstations and equipment in the conversion process. It is the spatial arrangement of physical resources used to create the product. Plant layout is the physical arrangement of buildings, machines, materials and services required to facilitate efficient operation of the production system. It is the configuration of departments, work centres and equipment in the conversion process. It is a floor plan of the physical facilities, which are used in production. It refers to the physical arrangement of production facilities. In short, it is the disposition of various facilities and services within the site or location selected previously.

Definition: Plant layout refers to the arrangement of physical facilities such as machines, equipment, tools, furniture etc. in such a manner so as to have quickest flow of material at the lowest cost and with the least amount of handling in processing the product from the receipt of raw material to the delivery of the final product.

According to Moore "Plant layout is a plan of an optimum arrangement of facilities including personnel, operating equipment, storage space, material handling equipment and all other supporting services along with the design of best structure to contain all these facilities".

"The overall objective of plant layout is to design a physical arrangement most economically which meets the required quantity and quality". ***– Riggs***

"Plant layout ideally involves the location of space and arrangement of equipment in such a manner that overall operations costs be minimized". ***– J. Zundi***

"Plant layout deals with the arrangement of the physical facilities and the manpower which require manufacturing a product or performing a service". ***– Keith & Gubellini***

Costs associated with plant layout decision are

1. Cost of space
2. Cost of production delays if any, which are indirect costs
3. Cost of spoilage of materials
4. Cost of movement of material from one work area to another
5. Cost of labour dissatisfaction and health risks
6. Cost of changes required, if operational conditions change in the future. This is a long – term cost.
7. Cost of customer dissatisfaction due to poor service (quality, delivery, flexibility, responsiveness cost) which may be due to poor layout.

Importance of Layout Decisions

Production managers are often questioned about the importance of a new or existing facilities layout. In addition to the fact that production managers work for improvement towards design and effective use of operation systems, they should also know the importance of layout decision in terms of money. Some of these are:-

1. Layout decisions require substantial investments of money and effort.
2. Layout decisions involve long-term commitments.
3. Layout decisions have significant impact on cost and efficiency of short-term operations.

The Need for Layout Decisions

Production manager should be aware of the fact that the need for a proper and effective layout facility is always there. The need for layout planning arises both in the process of designing new facilities and in redesigning existing facilities. Some of the common reasons faced by the organization include:

1. In-efficient operations (high cost/bottlenecks that hamper true potential).
2. Accidents or safety hazards.
3. Changes in design of products or services.
4. Introduction of new products or services.
5. Changes in volume of output or mix of output.
6. Changes in methods or equipment.
7. Changes in environmental and legal requirements.

Objectives of Plant Layout

The primary goal of the plant layout is to maximize the profit by arrangement of all the plant facilities to the best advantage of total manufacturing of the product.

A well designed plant layout is one that can be beneficial in achieving the following objectives:

- Minimizing material handling and material handling costs
- Facilitates the manufacturing process
- Minimize overall production time
- Efficient and optimum utilization of men, material and machines
- Proper and efficient utilization of the available floor space.
- Flexibility with regard to changing production conditions. (Future changes in volume of production, range of products, changes in processes etc.)
- Reduced congestion of men, materials and machines
- Effective supervision and control of operations
- Improved work methods and reduced production cycle times
- Simple plant maintenance
- Increased productivity and reduced costs
- Minimize investment in equipment.
- Transportation of work from one point to another point without any delay
- Proper utilization of production capacity.
- Reduced accidents
- Provide for volume and product flexibility
- Provide for employee convenience, comfort, safety and health
- Allow easy maintenance of machines and plant.
- Maintain high turnover of in-process inventory.
- Minimizing damage and spoilage of materials
- Eliminating bottlenecks and delays in production
- Adequate safety and working conditions for the employees
- Facilitate the organizational structure.

2.2.4 PRINCIPLES OF PLANT LAYOUT

1. ***Principle of integration:*** A good layout is one that integrates men, materials, machines and supporting services and others in order to get the optimum utilization of resources and maximum effectiveness.

2. ***Principle of minimum distance:*** This principle is concerned with the minimum travel (or movement) of men and materials. The facilities should be arranged such that, the total distance travelled by the men and materials should be minimum and as far as possible straight line movement should be preferred.

3. ***Principle of cubic space utilization:*** The good layout is one that utilizes both horizontal and vertical space. It is not only enough if only the floor space is utilized optimally but the third dimension, i.e., the height is also to be utilized effectively.

4. ***Principle of flow:*** A good layout is one that makes the materials to move in forward direction towards the completion stage, i.e., there should not be any backtracking.

5. ***Principle of maximum flexibility:*** The good layout is one that can be altered without much cost and time, i.e., future requirements should be taken into account while designing the present layout.

6. ***Principle of safety, security and satisfaction:*** A good layout is one that gives due consideration to workers safety and satisfaction and safeguards the plant and machinery against fire, theft, etc.

7. ***Principle of minimum handling:*** A good layout is one that reduces the material handling to the minimum.

Factors affecting Plant Layout:

- Nature of plant location – size, shape, available floor space and topography of the site affects plant layout
- Nature of product – size, shape, characteristic features of the product, product variety affects plant layout
- Nature of production system – manufacturing process
- Volume of production – large scale or small scale
- Nature of machines, equipments, materials and material handling systems (size, noise, vibration)
- Climatic conditions
- Managerial policies
- Human factor and working conditions – safety and employee facilities.
- Purchasing and inventory policy – storage
- Future requirements (possibility of future expansion)
- Storage of in – process inventory
- Disposal of wastes
- Design of building

Steps in Plant Layout:

Plant layout begins with the plant location and continues through three further levels

- The layout of departments within a site
- Layout of items within the department
- Layout of individual work places.

2.2.5 TYPES OF LAYOUT

There are mainly five types of plant layout:

(a) Product or Line Layout

(b) Process or Functional Layout

(c) Stationary or Fixed Position or Location layout

(d) Cellular or Group Layout

(e) Combination or Hybrid Layout

(a) Product or Line Layout :

In a product layout, various facilities, such as machine, equipment, work force, etc., are located as per the sequence of operations. It is the arrangement of machines and equipment at some definite stage according to the sequence of operations. The position and order in the sequence for a machine performing particular function is fixed. Once a machine is in line, it can perform only the operation which is present in the sequence. Since the machines and equipments are arranged in one line depending upon the sequence of operations required for the product, it is also called line layout.

The material moves to another machine sequentially without any backtracking or deviation i.e. the output of one machine becomes input of the next machine. Since there is continuous flow of materials during the production process from raw materials to finished products, the product layout is used for continuous type of production systems, (i.e.,) producing items of same type continuously on large scale. It is used for mass production of standardized products. Product layout is preferred when production is continuous, part variety is less, production volume is high and part demand is relatively stable. Ex- Assembly line such as automobile factory. A typical product layout is shown in figure 2.4.

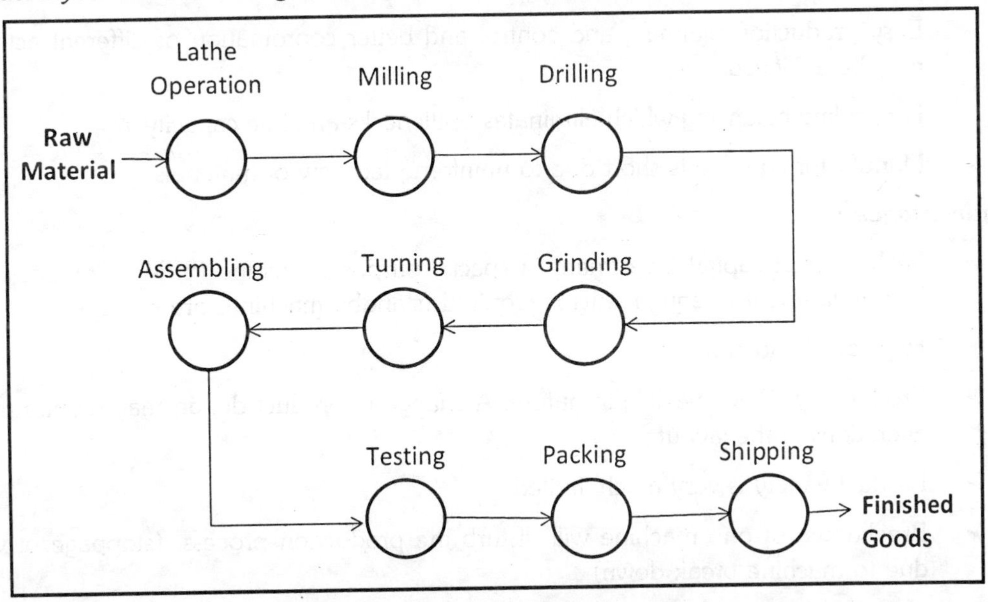

Figure 2.4 : Product Layout

Characteristics

1. High volume of production
2. Low product variety
3. Steady demand in near future
4. Highly standardized products

Advantages:

- Ensures smooth and regular flow of raw materials and finished goods.
- Reduced material handling time and cost due to straight flow and short route and absence of backtracking
- Smooth and continuous operations
- Economy due to short processing time
- Economy in materials and labour by minimizing waste
- Simple and effective inspection of work
- Maximum utilization of available floor space
- Manufacturing costs are low and per unit cost decreases due to large scale and continuous production.
- Compared to process layout, it requires less space for same volume of production.
- The through-put time (or product cycle time) is less as compared to process layout due to fewer chances of congestion and less waiting time on machine.
- Easy production planning and control and better coordination of different activities may be achieved.
- Perfect line balancing which eliminates bottlenecks and idle capacity.
- Manufacturing cycle is short due to uninterrupted flow of materials.

Disadvantages :

- Higher initial capital investment in special purpose machine (SPM). Comparatively high investment in equipments is required (standby machines are required)
- High overhead charges
- Product layout is inflexible in nature. A change in product design may require major alterations in the layout
- Product variety is very much limited
- Breakdown of one machine will disturb the production process. (stoppage of work due to machine break down)
- Requires high capital investment

- Supervision is more difficult
- Since low job variety, lower job satisfaction and more boredom and monotony to the workers

(b) Process or Functional layout:

All machines performing similar type of operations are grouped at one location in the process layout. Process layout is also called as functional layout since machines performing similar type of functions are located in one department. For example, all milling operations are carried out at one place while all lathes are kept at a separate location. Grinding or finishing operation is kept at a separate location. This type of layout is preferred when the product is not standardized and the quantity produced is very small.

The flow paths of material through the facilities from one functional area to another vary from product to product. Usually the paths are long and there will be possibility of backtracking. It is most suitable for intermittent production system i.e., job-shop and batch type of manufacturing systems where small quantities of variety of products are manufactured. This functional grouping of facilities is useful for job production and non-repetitive manufacturing environment. Ex- Drilling machines are grouped together in drilling section, milling machines in milling section, etc.

A typical process layout is shown in figure 2.5.

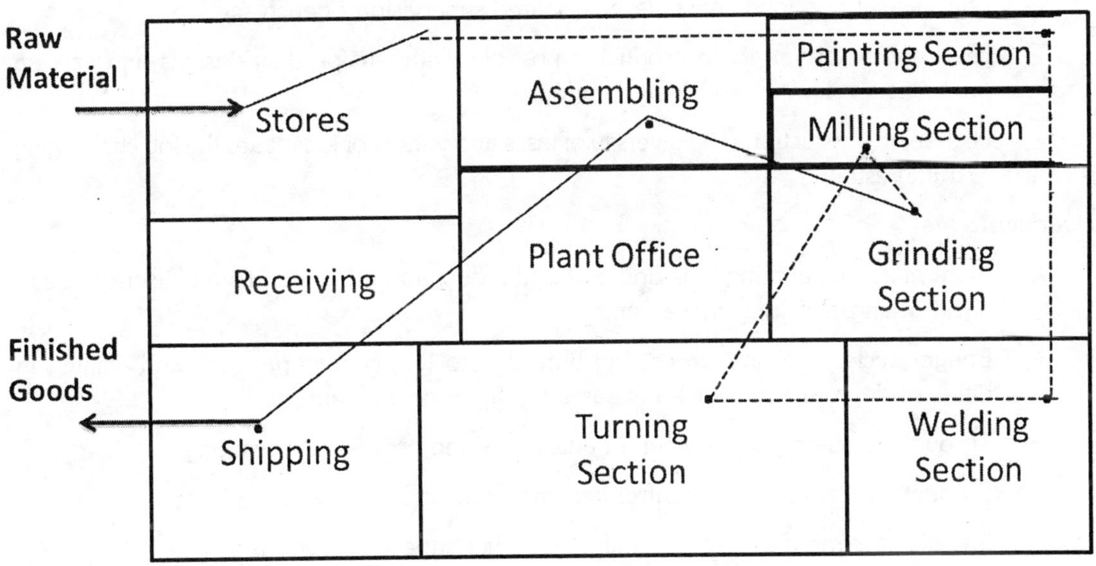

Figure 2.5 : Process Layout

Characteristics

- Low volume
- More product variety
- Demand is small

- Non-standardized product.
- High variety manufacturing environment
- Frequent change in product design

Advantages

- More flexibility in production and scope for expansion (Greater flexibility of resources)
- A high degree of flexibility with regards to work distribution to machines and workers
- Lower initial capital investment is required on account of comparatively less number of machines and lower cost of general purpose machines.
- Lower capital investment in machines.
- The overhead costs are relatively low
- Higher utilisation of production facilities.
- Machine break down does not disturb production schedules and operation (Breakdown of one machine does not disturb the production process).
- In process layout machines are better utilized and fewer machines are required
- Effective supervision is possible. Specialized supervision of each section
- High degree of variety in product is possible. Different product designs and varying production volumes can be easily adopted.
- Higher job satisfaction. The diversity of tasks and variety of job makes the job challenging and interesting

Disadvantages

- More material handling time and cost and reduced material handling efficiency due to backtracking and long movements
- Longer cycle time and processing time due to longer material flow and waiting in different departments which increases the in-process inventory.
- Throughput (time gap between in and out in the process) time is longer.
- Production planning and control becomes difficult
- Inspection is more frequent resulting in higher supervision costs.
- Requires more floor space.
- Require skilled workers to handle product variety and different design resulting in higher labour cost
- Result in large amount of work in process inventory and more storage area. Space and capital are tied up by work-in-process
- Lowered productivity due to number of set-ups

(c) *Stationary or Fixed Position or Location Layout:*

Fixed position layout involves the movement of manpower and machines to the product which remains stationary. Here, men, machines and equipment are moved to the place where the material remains in the fixed position and all the manufacturing activities are carried out. The movement of men and machines is advisable as the cost of moving them would be lesser. This is also called the project type of layout. Example of fixed position layout is shown in figure 2.6.

This type of layout is useful when the product being processed is very big, heavy or difficult to move. When the size of the job is bulky and heavy and where the semi finished goods and finished goods are of such size and weight that their movement from one place to another is not possible then this type of layout is preferred. Example of such type of layout is locomotives, boilers, generators, wagon building, aircraft manufacturing, ship building, bridges, mines etc.

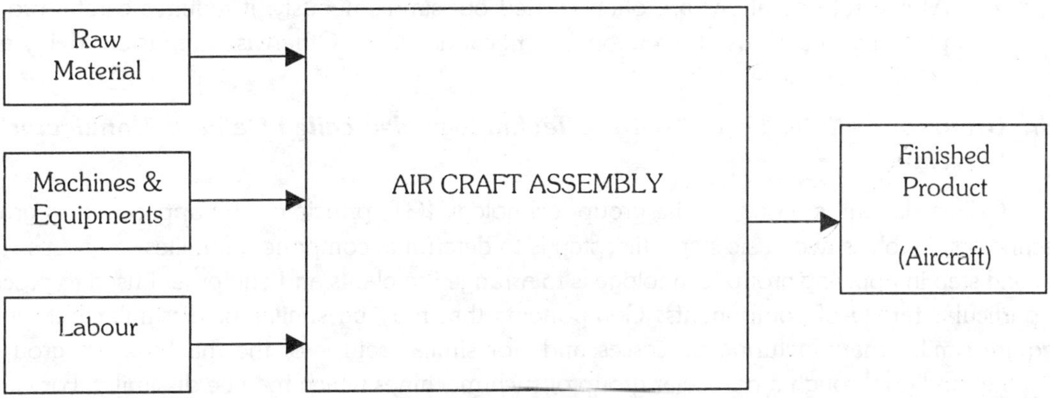

Fixed Position Layout

Figure 2.6 : Stationary or Fixed Position Layout

Advantages

- The investment on layout is very small.
- Lower labour cost and effective labour utilization.
- Lesser floor space and saving in time.
- Movement of material is minimum.
- Layout is simple and flexible
- Flexibility for change in design, operation sequence, labor availability, etc., exists in this layout.
- Large project type of jobs such as construction are suited in this layout
- Adjustments can be made to meet shortage of materials or absence of workers by changing the sequence of operations.
- Easy for products which are difficult to move.

- This layout is very cost effective when many orders of similar type are existing in different stages of progress.
- Helps in job enlargement and upgrades the skills of the operators.

Disadvantages

- Movement of machines and equipment to production centre is costly.
- Highly skilled workers are required.
- High capital investment due to long production period and long duration to complete a product.
- Large space is required for storage of material and equipment near the product.
- As several operations are often carried out simultaneously, it requires careful project planning and focused attention on critical activities. Otherwise confusion, delay and conflict may arise.

(d) Group or Cellular Layout (Group Technology also called Cellular Manufacturing System):

Cellular layout is based on the group technology (GT) principle. The application of group technology involves two basic steps; first step is to determine component families or groups. The second step in applying group technology is to arrange the plants and equipment used to process a particular family of components. Components that may be similar or dissimilar but which require similar manufacturing processes and / or similar setups of the machine are grouped together and go through a particular group of such machines which may be dissimilar. For ex - A turning machine, a drilling machine and a polishing equipment may be put together as a group using which a group of components may be manufactured.

This concept is called Group Technology and each of these groups of machines is called a 'cell'. A cell, thus, consists of a group of machines and a 'family' of related parts being produced on each of this group of machines. Each cell is capable of satisfying all the requirements of the component family assigned to it. Since the manufacturing plant consists of several cells, manufacturing using such Group Technology is also called Cellular Manufacturing System (CMS). Cell is like a mini- factory within the factory, which is managed by a cell team. It is a self- sufficient unit in which all operations required to make the components can be carried out. CMS allows batch production to give economical advantages similar to those of mass production with additional advantages of flexibility, normally associated with job shop production systems.

In group technology layout the objective is to minimize the sum of cost of transportation and cost of equipments. So, this is called as multi-objective layout. Thus, group or cellular layout is a combination of the product layout and process layout since it possesses the features of both. It combines the advantages of both layout systems. Shorter processing times, better team attention to quality problems, reduction of work in process, lower material handling costs and simpler scheduling can be achieved.

A typical group layout is shown in figure 2.7.

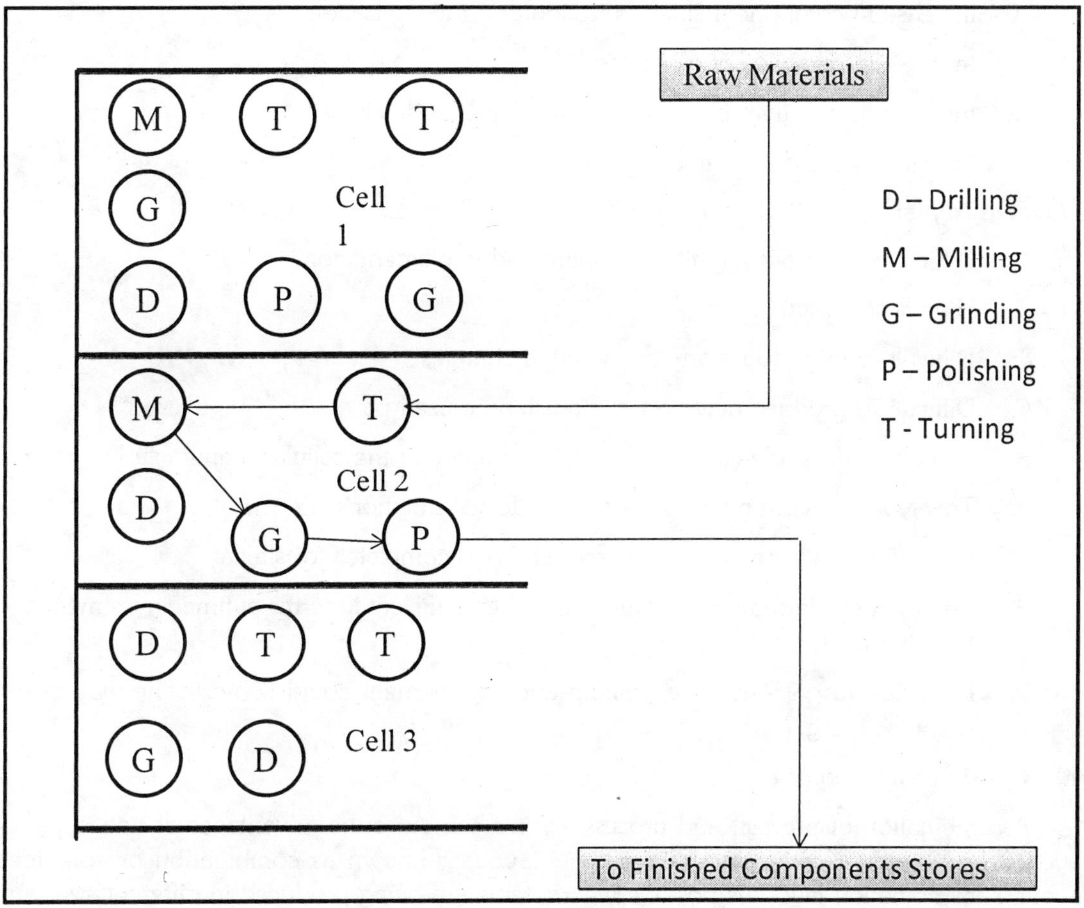

Figure 2.7 : Group Technology or Cellular Layout

Advantages:

1. Processing times are reduced (Shorter processing time)
2. Less work – in – process inventory
3. Product variety is possible
4. Sudden orders can be met without much problem
5. Employees have more job satisfaction and sense of belonging in cell manufacturing.
6. Production control methods could be simpler
7. Quality can also improve because of reduced material handling and effective supervision of cell team
8. Lower material handling time and costs
9. Simpler scheduling.

10. Increase in component standardization and rationalization.
11. Increase in reliability of estimates.
12. Increase in effective machine operation and productivity
13. Increase in customer service

Disadvantages:

1. Difficulty faced during initial planning and implementation.
2. High cost in layout.
3. Difficult to bring too many or too often changes.
4. Difficult to produce new part or non-standardized part.
5. Too much dependence on GT curtails flexibility of the cellular manufacturing system.
6. This type of layout may not be feasible for all situations.
7. It is difficult to form cells if the product mix is completely dissimilar
8. Improper cell formation may turn out to be inefficient in terms of time, investment and humanistic aspect
9. Inadequacies in employee training and involvement could come in the way of cell manufacturing.

(e) Combination Layout

A combination of product and process layouts combines the advantages of both types of layouts. Combination of product and process layout is known as combination or combined layout. A combination layout is possible where items are being produced in different sizes and types. Here machinery is arranged in a process layout but the process grouping is then arranged in a sequence to manufacture various types and sizes of products. It is to be noted that the sequence of operations remains same with the variety of products and sizes. Combined layout is followed in manufacturing concerns where several products are produced in repeated numbers with no likelihood of continuous production. Ex- Files, hack saws etc.

A comparison of product layout and process layout can be illustrated from table 2.1.

Table 2.1 : Comparison of Product and Process Layout

Factor	Product Layout	Process Layout
Investment	Needs high investment in machines and equipments	Comparatively low investment
Manufacturing time	Needs less manufacturing time	Comparatively more manufacturing time
Stoppage of work due to machine breakdown	Break down of any machine stops the whole system	Break down doesn't stop the whole system
Flexibility	Inflexible	Flexible
Floor Space	Requires less space	Requires more floor space
Material handling	Less material handling. Requires less time, money and effort	More material handling, Requires more time, money and effort
Inspection and supervision	More supervision and control	Comparatively less supervision and control
Production planning and control	Easy	Comparatively difficult

2.3 WORK STUDY

Introduction

Work study has contributed immeasurably to the search for better method and the effective utilisation of this management tool has helped in the accomplishment of higher productivity. Work study is a management tool to achieve higher productivity in any organization whether manufacturing tangible products or offering services to its customers. Work study forms the basis for determining job content, changing the job content if necessary, evaluating performance, deriving salary and wage structures, designing incentive schemes and the entire wage and salary administration. Work study concerns itself with better ways of doing things and control over the output by setting standards with respect of time. It is concerned with finding better ways of doing and avoiding waste in all forms.

F. W. Taylor, Frank B Gilberth and Lillian Gilberth and Henry L. Gantt were the pioneers in the field of work study.

- F. W. Taylor (1856-1915) was the first man who evolved the principle of breaking a job into detailed elements to determine the time to be allowed for the job. He initiated the method of measuring work in terms of time units.
- Henry L. Gantt (1861-1919) is famous for his work known as Gantt chart which is widely used in work study and scheduling of works.

Work study on one hand examines the method of doing the work and on the other hand determines the time required to do the work. Both method study and time study resulted from the integration of concepts and practices developed by F W Taylor and by Frank and Lillian Gilbreth.

Work Study Definitions

Work study, as the name suggests, is the study of work. Study of work includes human work as well as dignity of work. In general, it is not restricted to shop-floor; but it may be applicable anywhere: for example, kitchen, writing desk, gardening, etc.

Work study is the study of work which examines both the method of work and duration. It considers ways to improve methods of doing work so that human efforts may be applied most economically, efficiently, and effectively to achieve higher productivity of an organization.

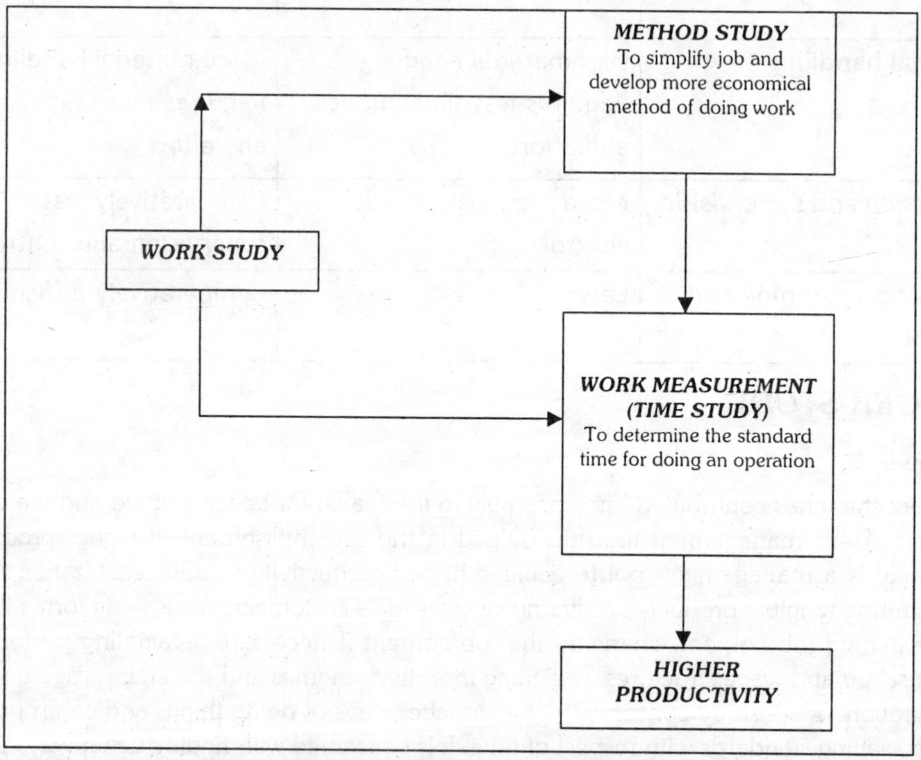

Figure 2.8 : Components of Work Study

Work – Study as a Tool to Improve Productivity

The important functions of production management are setting up the most effective method of performing the operation (standard method) and effective utilisation of resources.

Work study which comprises of method study and work measurement will fulfill these two requirements. Method study aims at determining the most effective method of performing the job, the most logical layout for manufacturing facilities, uninterrupted flow of performing the job, uninterrupted flow of materials throughout the organisation which will help to complete the job in the least possible time and at optimum cost. Work measurement on the other hand determines the time required by an operator to complete the operation or job for the standard method at the defined level of performance.

Work – study is the most effective tool to enhance productivity because of the fact that:

1. It is a straight – forward way of increasing the productive efficiency of the organisation.
2. Considers all the factors influencing productivity.

Work-study is used to associate two sets of techniques:

1. Method Study (Motion Study)
2. Work Measurement (Time Study)

The components of work study can be illustrated in figure 2.8.

These two are distinct approaches, yet they are interdependent. The outcome of both, method-study and work-measurement, thus results in higher productivity. Work study finds applications in industry, marketing, sales and distribution, office stores, material handling, transport, agriculture etc.

Objectives of Work Study:

The purpose of work study is to determine the best or most effective method of accomplishing a necessary operation or function. The prime function of work study is to increase productivity and reduce wastages through the optimum usage of human, machine and material resources available to the organization.

- To analyze the present method of doing a job, systematically in order to develop a new and better method
- To measure the work content of a job by measuring the time required to do the job for a qualified worker and hence to establish standard time.
- To increase the productivity by ensuring the best possible use of human, machine and material resources and to achieve best quality product/ service at minimum possible cost.
- To improve operational efficiency

Benefits of Work Study

- Increased productivity and operational efficiency
- Reduced manufacturing costs
- Improved work place layout
- Better manpower planning and capacity planning

- Fair wages to employees
- Fast and accurate delivery dates
- Better working conditions to employees
- Improved work flow
- Reduced material handling costs
- Provides a standard of performance to measure labour efficiency
- Better industrial relations and employee morale
- Basis for sound incentive scheme
- Provides better job satisfaction to employees

Work Study Procedure:

As can be seen from table 2.2 work study consists of eight basic steps, some of which are common to both method study and work measurement.

Table 2.2 : Steps in Work Study

S. No.	Steps	Method Study	Work Measurement
1	Select	✓	✓
2	Record	✓	✓
3	Examine / Analyse	✓	✓
4	Develop	✓	-
5	Measure	-	✓
6	Define	-	✓
7	Install	✓	-
8	Maintain	✓	-

Basic Work Study Procedure

Work-study consists of an eight-step process. These are:

Step 1: Identify and select the job or process to be studied.

Step 2: Use direct observation for recording everything that happens, using the most effective recording techniques. Ensure that the data is in the most convenient form for further analysis.

Step 3: Data and facts obtained in the previous step are to be examined and analyzed. Critically challenge everything that is done. Consider the purpose of the activity, place and sequence of the job and persons and means to perform the job.

Step 4: Develop the most economical method under prevailing circumstances.

Step 5: Measure the quantity of work involved in the method defined by using appropriate methods of measurement. Calculate standard time for doing it by adding rest allowance. Thus, determine the work content.

Step 6: Define the best method and related time.

Step 7: Install the new method and train personnel so that it conforms to the agreed standard practices.

Step 8: Maintain the standard practice by a proper control mechanism.

Out of above eight steps, steps 1, 2 and 3 are common in every study. However, step 4 is a part of method-study practice and step 5 is a part of work-measurement technique.

2.3.1 METHOD STUDY

The means of improving ways and means of doing things is called method study. Method study is the process of subjecting work to systematic, critical scrutiny to make it more effective and/or more efficient. It helps in analyzing the existing methods and to develop a more efficient method for future. It is one of the keys to achieving productivity improvement. It was originally designed for the analysis and improvement of repetitive manual work but it can be used for all types of activity at all levels of an organization.

Method Study is the systematic recording, analysis and critical examination of existing methods of doing a job in order to develop and install an easy, efficient, effective and less fatigue procedure of doing the same job at lower costs. Thus, the systematic recording and critical examination of ways of doing things in order to make improvements is known as ***method study.***

Motion study is basically concerned with finding the best way of doing work. The study of methods of accomplishing a job by the movement of human limbs and eyes etc is termed as motion study. This is a part of method study.

Objectives of Method Study

- To study the existing proposed method of doing any job, operation or activity
- To develop an improved method to improve productivity and to reduce operating costs
- To reduce excessive material handling or movement and thereby reduce fatigue to workmen
- To improve utilization of resources
- To eliminate wasteful and inefficient motions
- To standardize work methods or processes, working conditions, machinery, equipments and tools.

Purpose of Method Study

It may be noted that method study covers three broad areas:

1. It is a diagnostic tool (location of faults)
2. It is a remedial tool (improvement of situation)
3. It is a constructive tool (sets standard for control)

Benefits of Method Study

1. Better utilization of manpower and other tangible resources
2. Elimination of unnecessary work
3. Reduction in unnecessary fatigue
4. Identification of bottleneck activities and initiative steps to minimize them
5. Improvement of processes and procedures
6. Improvement in layouts and methods of material handling
7. Improvement in working conditions
8. Improvement and simplification in design
9. Improvement and maintenance of quality
10. Improvement in the flow of production and processes
11. Establishing the standardization in methods
12. Improvement in safety standards
13. Establishing a better physical working environment.

Method-study is a well established approach for systematic recording and critical examination of existing and proposed ways of doing work, as a means of developing and applying easier and more effective methods and reducing cost. Still, the greatest thing about this approach is its flexibility with which it may be used in different situations. Following sequence of steps are involved in it:

2.3.2 STEPS IN METHOD STUDY

SREDIM

These six steps are adopted sequentially. The procedure used in method-study involves an approach called SREDIM. The letters in SREDIM stand for a six activities or steps in method study. These steps are:

1. ***S***elect
2. ***R***ecord
3. ***E***xamine
4. ***D***evelop
5. ***I***nstall
6. ***M***aintain

Steps and Procedure to conduct Method Study :

1. ***Select*** the method to be studied.
2. ***Record*** includes direct observation, collection, recording and presentation of necessary information and relevant facts of the present method.
3. ***Examine*** the recorded information and facts of the existing method critically in an orderly sequence, using the techniques best suited to the purpose.

4. ***Develop*** the most practical, economic, effective and improved method of doing things. This is the most important step in method study.

   This can be done in four ways

   ✓ Eliminating all unnecessary movements or activities.

   ✓ Combine operations or elements.

   ✓ Change the sequence of operation so that the work delay is reduced.

   ✓ Simplify the necessary operations/ activity to reduce the work content or time consumption.

5. ***Install*** the new improved method as a standard practice.

6. ***Maintain*** that standard practice by regular routine checks.

The basic procedure of method study is illustrated in figure 2.9.

They are shown diagrammatically on the chart.

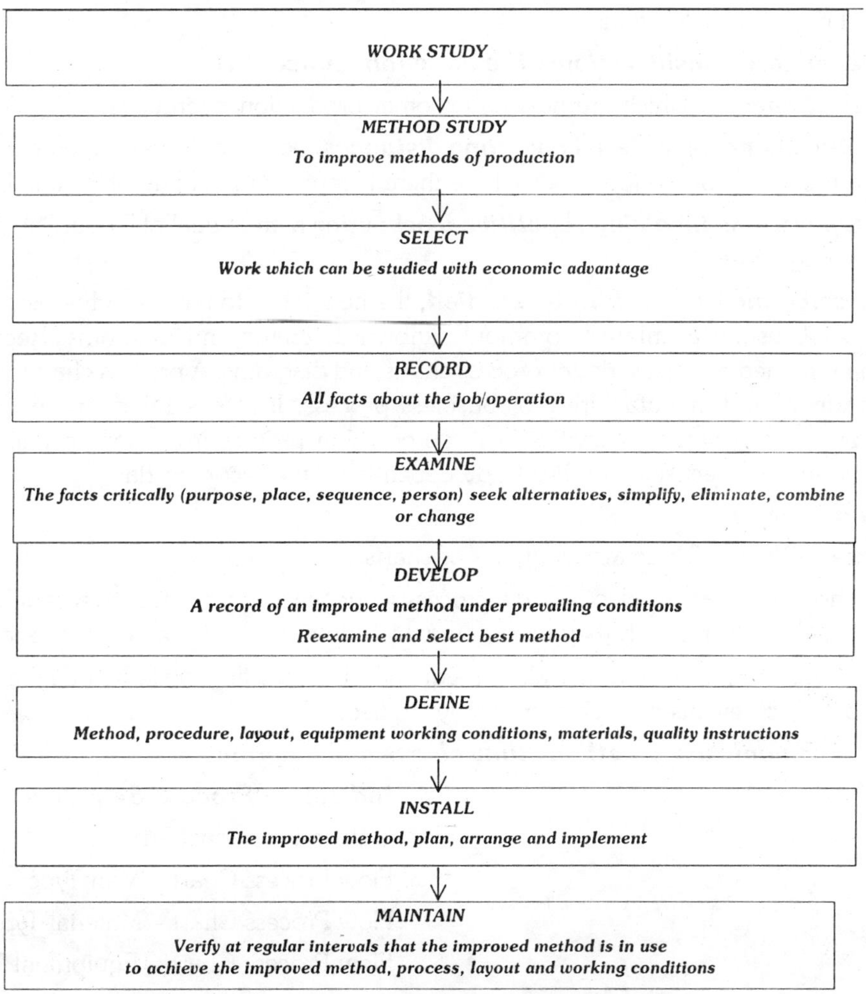

Figure 2.9 : Method Study Procedure

STEPS 1 & 2 of Method Study - Select the method and collect relevant information:

Cost is the main criteria for selection of a job, process, and department for methods analysis. To carry out the method study, a job is selected such that the proposed method achieves one or more of the following results:

- Improvement in quality with lesser scrap.
- Increased production through better utilization of resources.
- Elimination of unnecessary operations and movements.
- Improved layout leading to smooth flow of material and a balanced production line.
- Improved working conditions.

Factors to be considered in selecting a job for method study:

1. Economic Considerations.
2. Technical Considerations.
3. Human Considerations.

Under preliminary considerations, the early job choices are:

- ***Bottlenecks:*** which are holding up other production operations?
- ***Movements of material over long distances:*** between shops or operations involving a great deal of manpower or where there is repeated handling of material.
- ***Operations involving repetitive work:*** using a great deal of labour liable to run for a long time.

After selecting the work to be studied, the next job is to record all the facts relating to the existing job using techniques commonly known as charts and diagrams. Recording the information is carried on by a series of process charts and diagrams. A process chart is a graphical representation of any manufacturing or business process. It represents diagrammatically the sequence or order of various activities in the production process from start to finish. Records must be clear and correct since further study depends on the recorded data.

Charts and Diagrams

Types of Charts: There are two types of charts

1. Those which are used to record a process sequence, i.e., a series of events or happenings in the order in which they occur, but which do not depict the events to scale; and
2. Those which record events, also in sequence, but on a time scale, so that the interaction of related events may be more easily studied.

The most commonly used method study charts and diagrams

A. Charts — ***Indicating Process Sequence***

Outline Process Chart

Flow Process Chart – Man Type

Flow Process Chart – Material Type

Flow Process Chart – Equipment Type

Two – Handed Process Chart

B. Charts

Using a Time Scale

Multiple Activity Chart

Man Machine Chart or Worker-Machine Chart

Simultaneous Motion Cycle (SIMO) Chart

PMTS Chart

C. Diagrams

Indicating Movement

Flow Diagram

String Diagram

Two and Three Dimensional Models

Cyclegraph

Chronocycle Graph

Travel Chart

STEPS 3 & 4 of Method Study - Examine and develop improved method:

The third and fourth steps very often merge to develop the improved methods. Each recorded fact is subjected to a systematic and progressive examination to determine all the aspects regarding that particular operation or activity. The questioning technique is the critical means by which the critical examination is conducted – each activity being subjected in turn to a systematic and progressive series of questions

After critical examination of records is complete, it is necessary to transform the learning's into the development of new methods. Some approaches are:

(a) Eliminate unnecessary activities.

(b) Combine two or more activities. For example, if one uses a combination tool for two operations, say, facing and drilling, the total set-up time will reduce.

(c) Change the sequence of activities so as to reduce time and effort.

(d) Simplify process to reduce number of operations or reduce effort or reduce throughput, etc.

(e) Eliminate or remove the constraints, which are preventing the method to perform better.

There are five sets of primary questions and secondary questions to be determined-

The Primary Questions

- ***Purpose*** – what is being done – is it necessary?
- ***Place*** – where it is being done – why there?
- ***Sequence*** – when it is done – why then?

- ***Person*** – who has done it – why that person?
- ***Means*** – how is it done – why that way?

The Secondary Questions

The secondary questions cover the second stage of the questioning technique, during which the answers to the primary questions are subjected to further query to determine whether possible alternatives to purpose, place, sequence, persons and/or means are practicable or preferable as the means of improvement upon the existing method.

- What else should be done?
- Where else could it be done?
- When else could it be done?
- Who else could do it?
- How else could it be done?

This critical examination seeks to identify possibilities of eliminating, combining, rearranging, or simplifying the recorded activities so that the non-productive time is reduced to the minimum possible. After critically examining and sequential questioning, the improved method is developed and recorded in a flow process chart.

STEPS 5 & 6 of Method Study - Install and maintain:

Installation of new process is a major step towards fulfilling the objective of the entire approach. This involves evolving a time-frame for installing the new (TO-BE) system. Training of the personnel, rearrangement of machine, arrangement of tools and reorientation of workplace are some efforts to install the new system. Making theoretical change is easy. However, making real change requires careful planning and handling of the people involved. Cooperation of every person concerned with the job, educating and training them to accustom to the new method is very essential.

The final step has five stages-

- Acceptability of change at the supervisory level
- Acceptability of change at the manager level.
- Acceptability of change at the workers/union level
- Retention of workers to operate new systems
- Continuous monitoring and maintenance of the new method.

Criteria for Method Improvement :

The improvement in method refers to criteria such as-

- Improved cost performance
- Improved time or delay performance
- Improved worker satisfaction
- Improved standardization of operations and products

Types of Symbols and Charts used in Method Study:

Symbols used in Method Study

The recording of the facts about a job or operation on a process chart is made much easier by the use of a set of standard symbols, which together serve to represent all the different types of activity or event likely to be encountered in any factory or office. The two principal activities in a process are operation and inspection.

Process Chart Symbols

Process charts use five common symbols for recording the nature of events. These symbols were developed by ASME (American Society of Mechanical Engineers) in 1947. The process chart symbols and the description of the events is illustrated in figure 2.10.

Event	*Symbol*	*Description*
Operation	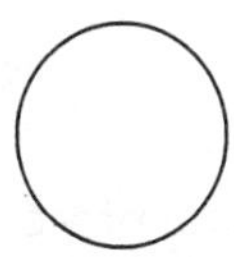	Operation represents an action. Through each operation, the material, component, or service or assembly move towards completion. Ex. pressing, grinding, polishing
Storage	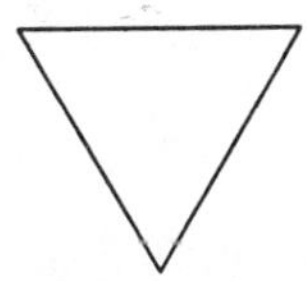	Represents a stage when material awaits an action. This indicates planned and controlled storage of material. Ex. Holding, storing, stocking, or retaining.
Delay or temporary storage	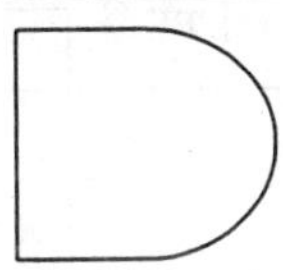	This indicates delay or temporary storage in-between a sequence of operations. Ex.-Waiting for transport or operation etc.,
Transport	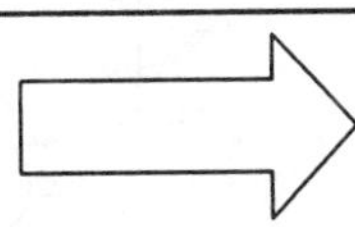	This indicates movement of material, workers, equipment or place of work. Ex: movement, travelling etc.,
Inspection	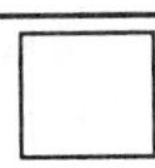	Represents an action of inspection or checking for quality and quantity.
Operation and transportation		This indicates a combined activity. Two events operation and transportation are performed simultaneously.
Inspection and operation	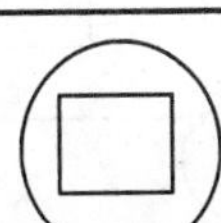	This indicates that two events inspection and operation are performed simultaneously.

Figure 2.10 : Process Chart Symbols

Symbols used in Activity Charts:

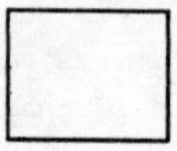
– Blank rectangle is used to show that one of the two, either man or machine is idle.

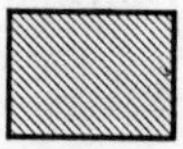
– A striped rectangle shows a combined activity i.e., man and machine are busy

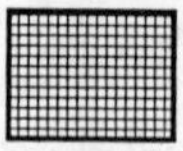
– Rectangle with parallel and vertical lines shows period of independent activity for man / machine is busy.

The charts are generally represented by symbols to produce a better picture and quick understanding of the process.

Types of Charts used in Method Study:

1. Charts indicating Process Sequence:

- ***The Outline Process Chart*** - An outline process chart records an overall picture of the process and records only the main events sequence-wise. It considers only the main operations and inspections. It shows only two principal events:

  (i) Operations, and

  (ii) Inspection

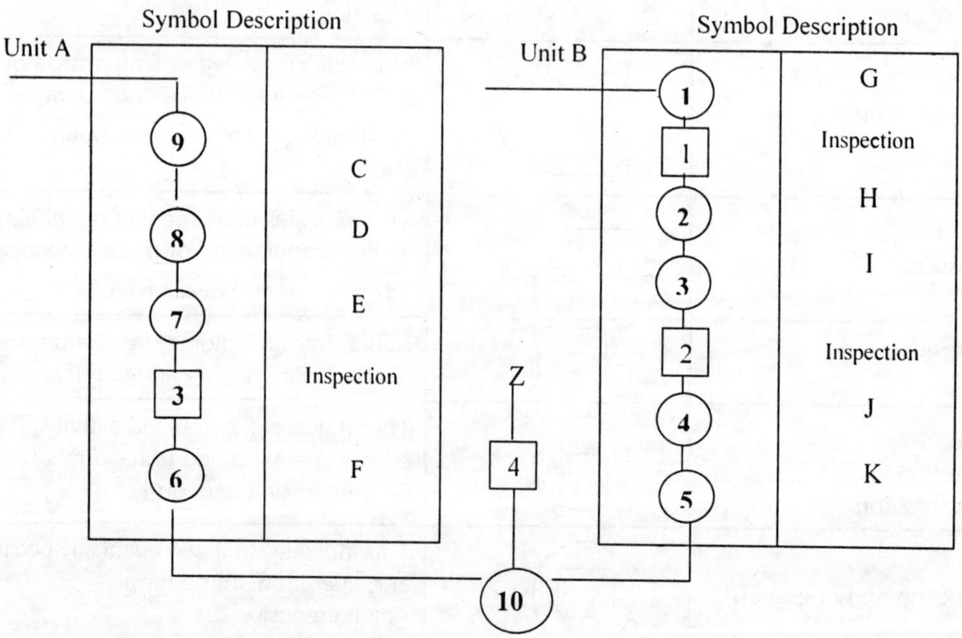

Figure 2.11 : The Outline Process Chart

- ***Operation Process Chart*** - The basic process chart, called an operation process chart, is a graphical representation of the points at which the materials are introduced into the process and of the sequence of inspections and all operations except those involved in materials handling. It includes information considered desirable for analysis such as time required to carry out the operation and the location.
- ***Flow process chart*** - Flow process charts are graphical representation of the sequences of all operations, transportation, inspections, delays and storages occurring during a process or a procedure and include information considered for analysis such as, time required and distance moved. Thus, it is a detailed chart which records all the events. A specimen of the chart is shown in figure 2.12.

There are three types of Flow Process Charts

- ***Man type*** - Flow process chart man type shows the movement of employee. It is a flow chart which records what the worker does.
- ***Material type*** - Flow process chart material or product type shows the sequence of flow of materials. It is a flow chart which records how material is handled or treated.
- ***Equipment type*** - Flow process chart machine or equipment type shows the sequence of usage of machines or equipments. It is a flow chart which records how the equipment is used.

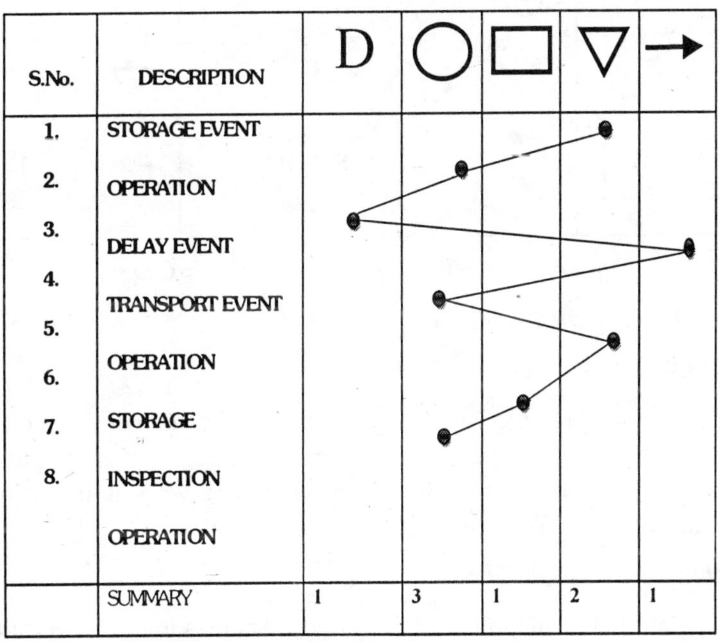

Figure 2.12 : Flow Process Chart

- ***Two handed process chart*** - In this chart, the activities of a worker or operators both hands and limbs are recorded chronographically. It is also called as left and right hand process chart. It records activities of both hands of workers. An illustration of the two handed process chart is shown in figure 2.13.

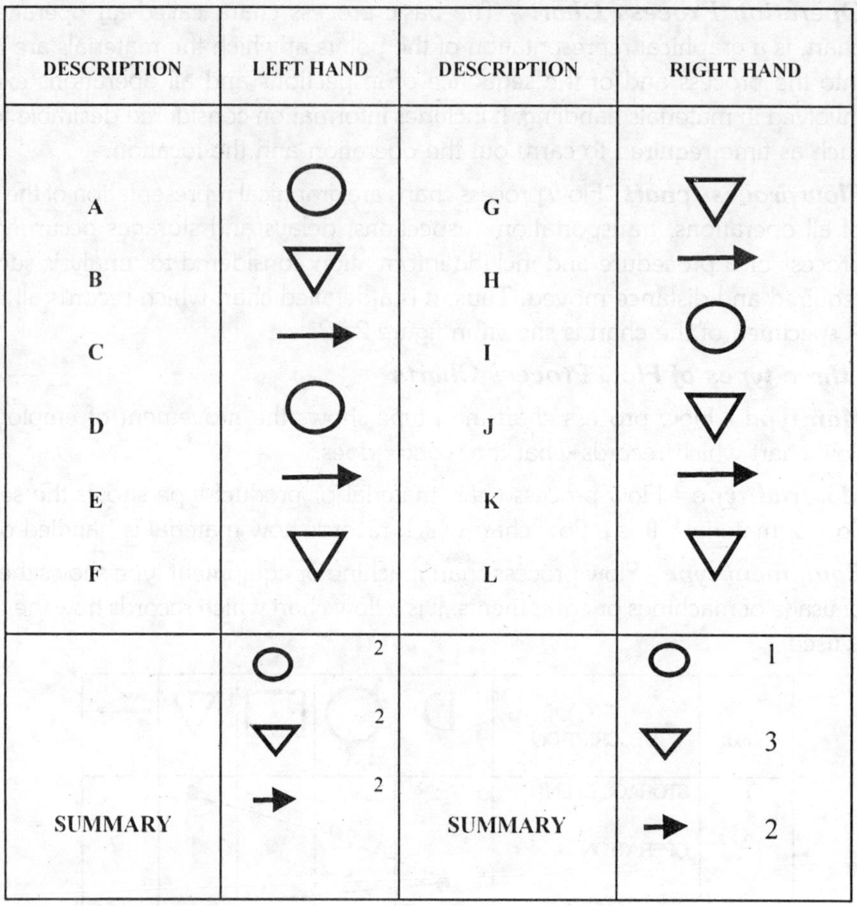

Figure 2.13 : Two Handed Process Chart

2. Charts using Time Scale:

- ***Activity Chart***

This chart shows a breakdown of the process or of a series of operations plotted against time scale. The activity chart is most useful for analysis of maintenance work, job involving people working in gangs and operation where the work is unbalanced and where there is unnecessary idle time.

Objectives of Activity Chart

a. To obtain better utilization of men and machines involved in multiple activity

b. To determine the most effective way of harmonizing the work of the individual with the requirement of the machine or other individuals in the group.

c. To find the most economic pattern or man-machine relationship.

- ***The Multiple Activity Chart***

  Several times a process involves the coordination of various activities and it becomes necessary to study the relationship between these various activities and such inter-relationship is provided by the multiple activity charts. Multiple activity charts is a form of process chart recording the related frequency of work of a number of operators and/or machines on a common time scale.

- ***Man-Machine Chart***

  The man machine chart is a special variant of the multiple activity charts. When the activities of the machine or machines are recorded in relation to that of the operator the chart is known as a man-machine chart. An example of man machine chart may be one worker running two machines simultaneously. This chart shows the movement of men and machines on a common time scale.

- ***Simultaneous Motion Cycle Chart (SIMO chart)*** - It is a type of two handed process chart in which the micro motions (therbligs) of both hands are recorded. It shows the body movements of men on a common time scale. Therbligs indicate the basic motions consisting of three parts, viz.

  (i) When the motion begins.

  (ii) The nature of the motion.

  (iii) When the motion ends.

3. ***Diagrams indicating Movements:***

- ***Flow Diagram*** - The flow diagram is diagram drawn to a scale to show the relative position of a machine or equipment, jigs and fixtures, gangways or aisles and shows the path followed by materials or machines. Flow diagrams show the path of men, materials and equipments.

- ***String Diagram*** - String diagram is a useful tool to record the distance traveled by a worker in the working area. It is scale plan or model on which a string or a thread or colored lines are used to trace and measure the path of workers, materials, machines or equipments during a specified sequence of events

- ***Cyclegraph*** - A cyclegraph is a record of path of movement usually, traced by a continuous source of light on a photograph. A small electric bulb is attached to hand, finger or other part of the body of the operator performing the operation. A photograph is taken by still camera and the light source shows the path of the motive and the path of the photograph is called "cyclegraph".

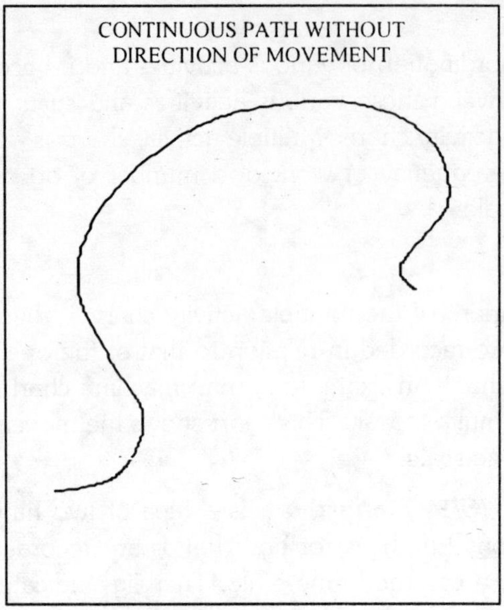

Figure 2.14 : Cyclegraph

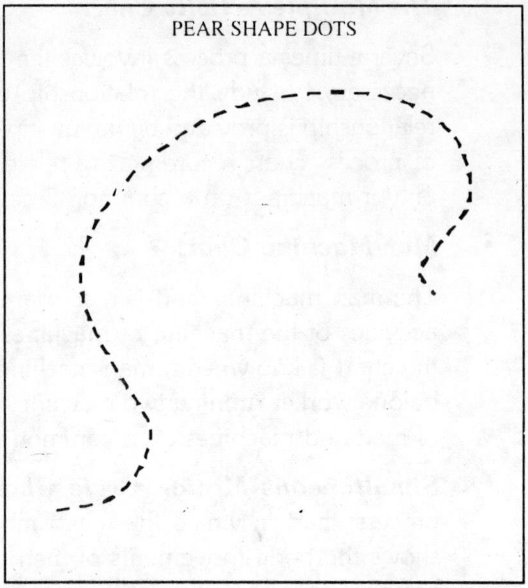

Figure 2.15 : Chronocycle Graph

- ***Chronocycle Graph*** - The chronocycle graph is a special form of cycle graph in which the light source is suitably interrupted so that the path appears as a series of pear-shaped dots, the pointed end indicating the direction of movement and the spacing indicating the speed of movement. The time taken for the movement can be determined by knowing the rate at which the light source is being interrupted and by counting the number of dots.

- ***Travel Chart*** – It is also called as cross chart. It is a tabular record for presenting quantitative data about the movement of workers, materials or equipment between any numbers of places over any given period of time. It shows the movement of material between departments. It is represented as a square matrix: columns indicating origin of movement and rows the destination or vice versa.

Motion Study :

Motion study is the science of eliminating wastefulness, resulting from using unnecessary; ill-directed and inefficient motion. The aim of motion study is to find and perpetuate the scheme of the least waste methods of labor.

Motion-study involves two kinds of analysis for the improvement in method. On the basis of data recorded on motion picture film or video, the approaches are:

1. Micro motion study (or detailed breakdown of motion)
2. Memo motion study (or breakdown of motion at the level of family of micro motions)

2.3.3 WORK MEASUREMENT

Work Measurement (Time Study):

Once the method is established, the next thing to do would be to set the standard times for the work. This aspect of work study is called the time study. In fact, work measurement is a pre-requisite to method study. It is concerned with the determination of the amount of time required to perform a unit of work.

Work measurement is the application of different techniques designed to measure and establish the time required to complete a specific job by a qualified person at the defined level of performance. In brief it is the technique for determining the limited time to perform a specific task.

Objectives / Purposes of Work Measurement:

- It determines the most efficient method which takes the least time besides the man power required for the job
- It results in effective labour control
- Provides a basis for proper balancing of the work distribution
- It helps in calculating delivery dates
- It helps to compare the work efficiency of different operators.
- It provides basis for manpower planning.
- It is used for arriving at job schedules for production planning purposes
- It helps in dividing equipments

Work Measurement Procedure:

1. Select or identify the job to be timed
2. Obtain all the necessary information
3. The whole job is broken down into smallest possible measurable elements
4. Time is determined for each of the elements using appropriate technique and recorded.
5. Provide allowance for relaxation, fatigue, personal and machine delay and other allowances.
6. Calculate the standard or allowed time

2.3.4 TECHNIQUES OF WORK MEASUREMENT:

For the purpose of work measurement, work can be regarded as:

1. ***Repetitive work:*** the type of work in which the main operation or group of operations repeat continuously during the time spent at the job. These apply to work cycles of extremely short duration.
2. ***Non-repetitive work:*** It includes some type of maintenance and construction work, where the work cycle itself is hardly ever repeated identically.

The important techniques of work measurement are

1. Time Study – The important time study equipments are

- A. Stop watch
  - Mechanical Stop watch
    - Decimal minute Stop watch
    - Decimal hour Stop watch
  - Electronic Stop watch

The observation and recording of time using stop watch can be either-

- Continuous or non-fly back
- Fly back or snap back and
- Split hand or split second

B. Motion picture camera

C. 1. Machine using mixing tapes and disks

2. Synthesis from Standard Data
3. Predetermined Motion – Time System (PMTS)
4. Analytical Estimating
5. Estimating
6. Work Sampling
7. Comparative Estimating
8. Rated Activity Sampling

Of all these techniques time study and activity or work sampling are direct observation techniques whereas the other techniques are indirect or pre determined techniques which are data based and analytical in nature

Techniques of Work Measurement:

1. Time Study:

Time study is a work measurement technique for recording the times and rates of working for the elements of a specified job carried out under specified conditions, and for analyzing the data so as to determine the time necessary for carrying out job at a defined level of performance. Time study was developed by F.W. Taylor and is also called stop watch time study as a stop watch is used for making observations. Measuring time by stopwatch is a good old method and is adapted to measure time for elements. Presently instead of mechanical watches, electronic watches are being used. Time study is the original technique of work measurement and it is concerned with the direct observation of work while it is being done.

Applications of Time Study

Stop watch time is employed:

1. For checking time standards obtained by other methods.
2. For timing repetitive operations employed in manufacturing different jobs.
3. Where it becomes necessary to break down an activity (involving motions of head, leg, foot, trunk, etc.) in detail and study.
4. For determining schedules and planning work.
5. For determining standards costs and preparing budgets.
6. For estimating the cost of a product before manufacturing it. Such information is of value in preparing bids and in determining selling price.
7. For determining machine effectiveness, the number of machines which one person can operate, and as an aid in balancing assembly lines.
8. For determining time and standards to be used as a basis for the payment of a wage incentive to direct labour and indirect labour.
9. For determining time standards to be used as a basis for labour cost control

2. Synthesis from Standard Data:

A work measurement technique for building up the time for a job or parts of the job at a defined level of performance by totaling elemental times obtained previously from time studies on other jobs containing the elements concerned from synthetic data. It is estimating the standard time on the basis of previous experience of similar jobs. In this method, work is subdivided into elements for which standard times are available from previously established time studies and these predetermined elements times are totaled with appropriate allowances to compute the standard time for the job as a whole.

The steps involved in synthetic data:

1. Collect all the details about the job (dimensions, tools, methods, conditions.)
2. Analyse jobs into constituent elements (activity grouping to enable synthetic elements to be applied if relevant)
3. Select appropriate basic times from synthetic data covering contingent factors.
4. Select and apply synthetic data covering contingent factors.
5. Verify details of elemental analysis for job method and condition.
6. Total the basic times, rating and allowances to compute standard time for the job.

Advantages of Synthetic Data

Although synthesis was originally developed to establish the work content for short batch production and jobbing work, it can be used to determine times for many other types of work including repetitive work provided necessary data is available.

The main advantage of synthesis is the reduced cost of application. By means of synthesis it is possible to establish times, which are equally satisfactory for planning and production control purpose.

3. *Predetermined Motion Time System (PMTS)*

A work measurement technique whereby times established for basic human motions (classified according to the nature of the motion and condition under which it is made) are used to build up the time for a job at the defined level of performance. It is a technique where times established for basic human motion are used to compute the time for a job at a define level of performance.

A predetermined time system consists of a set of time data and a systematic procedure which analyses and subdivides any manual operation of human task into motions, body motions, or other elements of human performance, and assigns to each the appropriate time value. This system of time data was originally developed from extensive studies of all aspects of human performance through measurement, evaluation and validation procedures. The most commonly used PMTS is known as Methods Time Measurement (MTM).

Advantages of PMTS

1. Short cycle jobs can be timed accurately
2. Rating, the most difficult part of time study is not necessary.
3. The results obtained are consistent
4. A reasonable estimate of work content can be obtained before the task is actually carried out.

4. *Analytical Estimating :*

A work measurement technique, being a development of estimating, whereby the time required to carry out elements of a job at a defined level of performance is estimated partly from knowledge and practical experience of the elements concerned and partly from synthetic data. \

5. *Comparative Estimating:*

It is a technique in which the time for a job is evaluated by comparing the work with the work in a similar series of jobs or bench marks, the work content of which has been measured.

6. *Work Sampling:*

Work sampling was originally developed by L.H.C Tippett in Britain in 1934 for the British Cotton Industry Research Board. Work sampling is a fact finding tool. Work sampling is defined as: "a technique, in which a statistically competent number of instantaneous observations are taken, over a period of time, of a group of machines, processes of workers. Each observation recorded for a particular activity or delay is a measure of the percentage of time observed by the occurrence"

It is a technique in which a large number of observations are made over a period of time of one or group of machines, processes or workers. Each observation records what is happening at that instant and the percentage of observations recorded for a particular activity, or delay, is a measure of the percentage of time during which that activities delay occurs. It is a statistical sampling method which estimates the time devoted to a given type of activity over a certain period of time by means of a large number of random spot observations. It provides an estimate of what proportion of a worker's time is devoted to work activities. It also estimates the time the worker or machine is idle. Thus, the proportion of non – working time is calculated as a percentage of the total time.

Work Sampling Procedure:

1. The first step is to device what activities are defined as 'working'. All other activities comprise of non – working activities
2. Observe the worker at selected intervals and record whether the person is working or not.
3. From this data portion of time working is calculated (i.e.) P

$$P = \frac{\text{No. of observations during which working occurred}}{\text{Total No. of observations}}$$

This calculation of P can be used as a performance standard.

Factors Influencing Choice of Measurement Technique:

- Purpose of the measurement
- Level of detail required
- Time available for predetermined data
- Cost of measurement

Determination of Standard Time

Standard Time may be defined as the amount of time required to complete a unit of work, (a)under existing working conditions, (b) using the specified method and machinery, (c) by an operator, able to do the work in a proper manner, and (d) at a standard pace.

Basic Time is the time required to perform a task by a normal operator working at a standard pace (rate) with no allowance for personal delays, unavoidable delays and fatigue.

Basic Time / Normal Time =

$$\text{Selected observed element time} \times \frac{\text{Observed rating of the operator}}{\text{Standard rating (i.e., 100)}}$$

$$\text{Normal Time} = \frac{\text{Observed time} \times \text{Performance rating (\%)}}{100}$$

Performance Rating

When the time studies observer is making the study, he carefully observes the performance of the operator during the entire course of the study. Performance rating means gauging and comparing the pace rate or the performance of a worker against a standard performance level set by the time study engineer.

The (performance) rating factor is used to convert observed time into basic time. In other words, rating is a leveling factor to convert observed timings into normal timings.

$$\text{Performance Rating} = \frac{\text{Observed time}}{\text{Normal time}} \times 100$$

Basic time

$$\text{Observed time} \times \frac{\text{Performance level of the worker}}{\text{Standard performance level expected}}$$

Allowances: The normal time for an operation does not contain any allowances for the worker. It is impossible to work throughout the day even though the most practicable, effective method has been developed. An amount of time is added to the normal time to provide for personal delays, unavoidable delays and fatigue of the operator. Allowance when added to the normal time, it results in standard time. In other words, standard time is equal to the normal time plus the allowances. The various types of allowances are shown in figure 2.16.

Types of Allowances

The allowances are categorised as:

(1) Relaxation allowance,

(2) Interference allowance, and

(3) Contingency allowance.

Calculate Standard time for the Job

The various allowances are added to the normal time as applicable to get the standard time. Thus, basic constituents of standard time are:

1. Elemental (observed) time.
2. Performance rating to compensate for difference in pace of working.
3. Relaxation allowance.
4. Interference and contingency allowance.
5. Policy allowance.

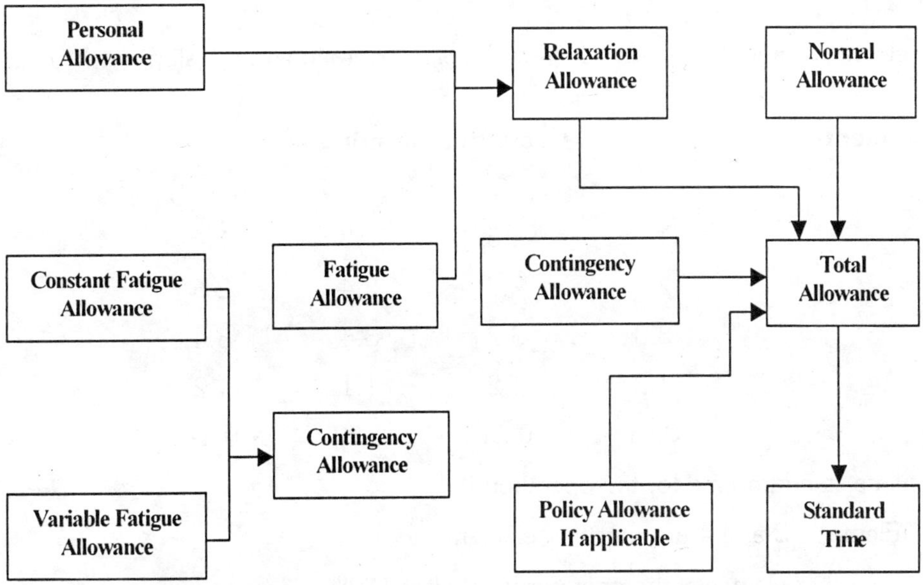

Figure 2.16 : Various Allowances to build Standard Time

Computation of Standard Time

Standard time is the allowed time to an operator to carry out the specified task under specified conditions and defined level of performance. The basic constituents of standard time are illustrated in figure 2.17.

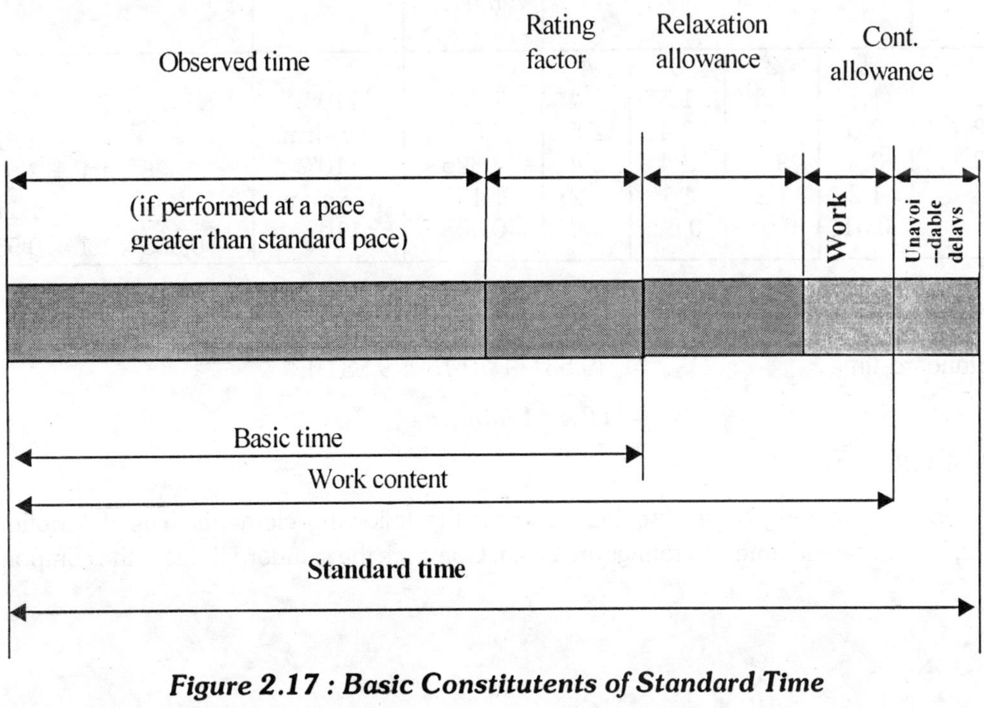

Figure 2.17 : Basic Constitutents of Standard Time

Problem 2.1

The elemental times (in minutes) for 4 cycles of an operation using a stop watch are presented below.

Elements	Cycle time in minutes			
	1	2	3	4
1	1.5	1.5	1.3	1.4
2	2.6	2.7	2.4	2.6
3	3.3	3.2	3.4	3.4
4	1.2	1.2	1.1	1.2
5	0.51	0.51	0.52	0.49

Calculate standard time for the operation if

(i) Elements 2 and 4 are machine elements

(ii) For other elements, the operator is rated at 110%

(iii) Total allowances are 15% of the normal time.

Solution: The normal times are shown in Table 5.3.

Element No.	*Cycle Time (min)*				*Avg. cycle time (3)*	*Rating (4)*	*Normal time = Avg. time x rating*
	1	2	3	4			
1	1.5	1.5	1.3	1.4	1.425	110%	1425 x 1.1 = 1.568
2	2.6	2.7	2.4	2.6	2.575	m/c elem.	= 2.575
3	3.3	3.2	3.4	3.4	3.325	110%	1325 x 1.1 = 3.658
4	1.2	1.2	1.1	1.2	1.175	m/c elem.	= 1.175
5	0.51	0.51	0.52	0.4	0.505	110%	0.505 x 1.1 = 0.555

Normal time for the cycle = 1.568 + 2.575 + 3.658 + 1.175 + 0.555 = 9.531

Standard time = (9.531 + (0.15 x 9.531))

= ***10.484 minutes***

Problem 2.2

A worker operating on a machine performs the following elements. The description of element, their observed time and ratings are given. Compare the standard time for the component.

Element	Description	Observed time	Rating	Relaxation allowance
A	Position the job	0.25	80%	10%
B	Switch 'ON' and lower drill	0.09	100	11%
C	Drill hole	2.8	90	12%
D	Raise drill and switch 'OFF'	0.05	80	10%
E	Remove job from jig	0.15	110	11%

Solution: The relaxation allowance is given separately for each element. So the element wise standard time is to be computed and then added together to get the standard time for the job.

The computation of standard time is shown in the table:

Element	Observed time	Rating	Relaxation allowance	Standard time (min.)
A	0.25	80	.10	0.22
B	0.09	100	0.11	0.099
C	2.80	90	0.9	2.746
D	0.05	80	0.8	0.043
E	0.15	110	1.1	0.183

∴ Standard time for the job = 0.22 + 0.099 + 2.746 + 0.043 + 0.183

= **3.251 minutes**

2.4 QUALITY MANAGEMENT

Introduction

One of the most important issues that businesses have focused on in the last 20-30 years has been quality. As markets have become much more competitive, quality has become widely regarded as a key ingredient for success in business. Quality is important to businesses but can be quite hard to define. Quality is an important dimension of production and operations management. It is not enough to produce goods or service in right quantity and right time. It is important to ensure that the goods and services are produced of right quality. Customers want quality that is appropriate to the price that they are prepared to pay higher price for better quality. Quality is thus, the performance of the product as per the commitment made by the producer to the consumer.

Quality - Quality is first and foremost about meeting the needs and expectations of customers. It is the ability of a product or service to consistently meet or exceed customer expectations. It is defined as customer satisfaction in general and conformance to requirements or fitness to purpose in particular. Quality is some desired or prescribed characteristic present in raw material, semi finished and finished product. It conveys the impression what consumer expects from the product. In short, quality can be defined as fitness for purpose or conformance to the requirement or specifications.

Quality begins with the design of a product in accordance with the customer specifications. Further, it involves the established measurement standards, the use of proper material, selection of suitable manufacturing process and the necessary tooling to manufacture the product, the performance of the necessary manufacturing operations and the inspection of the product to check the manufacturing operations and performance with the specifications.

Defining Quality

Today, there is no single universal definition of quality. Some people view quality as "performance to standards." Others view it as "meeting the customer's needs" or "satisfying the customer." Quality is the totality of features and characteristics of a product or service that bear in its ability to satisfy stated or implied needs. Let's look at some of the more common definitions of quality.

- ***Conformance to specifications*** measures how well the product or service meets the targets and tolerances determined by its designers.
- ***Fitness for use*** focuses on how well the product performs its intended function or use.
- ***Value for price paid*** is a definition of quality that consumers often use for product or service usefulness. This is the only definition that combines economics with consumer criteria; it assumes that the definition of quality is price sensitive.
- ***Support services*** provided are often how the quality of a product or service is judged. Quality does not apply only to the product or service itself; it also applies to the people, processes, and organizational environment associated with it
- ***Psychological criteria*** is a subjective definition that focuses on the judgmental evaluation of what constitutes product or service quality. Different factors contribute to the evaluation, such as the atmosphere of the environment or the perceived prestige of the product.

Quality Characteristics

Quality characteristics can be classified as follows:

(1) Quality of design

(2) Quality of conformance with specifications

(1) Quality of Design - refers to product features such as performance, reliability, durability, maintainability, serviceability and so on. Quality design is a technical term.

Example: All automobiles provide the user with the service of transportation. The various models differ as to size, comfort, appearance, performance, economy, status conferred etc. These differences are in turn the results of intended or designed differences in the size, styling, materials, tolerances, test programs etc.

(2) ***Quality of Conformance*** - means whether the product meets the given quality specifications or not. The design must reflect the needs of fitness for use, and the products must also confirm to the design. The extent to which the product does confirm to the design is called "Quality of conformance"

Example: Two scooters both are produced at the same level of time but one may be 100% according to the drawing and specification of the same design; the second scooter may be 90% according to the drawing and specification and probably a few dimensions may be different from those of drawing. Therefore, quality of conformance of 1st scooter is better than the 2nd scooter even though both are of same design.

Attributes / Dimensions of Quality

The concepts of dimensions of quality represent the fact that customers value a product keeping in mind different dimensions. Operations and Quality Managers come across customer perceptions relating to demand for products which are durable, reliable, performance to a standard and that too in a way that is aesthetically correct.

1. Performance – How well the product functions (main characteristics of the product/ service)
2. Conformance – Product conformance to specifications or standards (how well product/ service conforms to customer's expectations)
3. Features – Other characteristics the product has to enhance its basic function (extra characteristics)
4. Aesthetics – How attractive the product is (appearance, feel, smell, taste)
5. Reliability – How well the product performs for a given time period (consistency of performance)
6. Durability – How long does the product works (useful life of the product/service)
7. Serviceability – How easy is the product to maintain (service after sale)
8. Safety – How little, if any, is the risk to users when the product is in use or after use
9. User – friendliness – How easy is it to use and operate
10. Customizability – How easily the product can be modified to suit the customer's needs
11. Environment – friendliness – How safe is the product for the environment when in use or thrown away after its use.
12. Consistency
13. Value for money
14. Perceived Quality (brand reputation and image)

Importance of Quality

Quality helps to determine a firm's success in a number of ways:

- Customer loyalty – they return, make repeat purchases and recommend the product or service to others.

- Strong brand reputation for quality
- Retailers want to stock the product
- As the product is perceived to be better value for money, it may command a premium price and will become more price inelastic
- Fewer returns and replacements lead to reduced costs
- Attracting and retaining good staff

How to measure Quality

Aside from achievement of standards like BSI, firms can measure quality aspects such as:

- Failure or reject rates
- Level of product returns
- Customer complaints
- Customer satisfaction – usually measured by a survey
- Customer loyalty – evident from repeat purchases, or renewal rates

A detailed analysis of areas such as these would be an important part of quality improvement.

Quality Management - Producing products of the required quality does not happen by accident. There has to be a production process which is properly managed. Ensuring satisfactory quality is a vital part of the production process. Quality management is concerned with controlling activities with the aim of ensuring that products and services are fit for their purpose and meet the specifications.

There are two main parts to quality management

(1) Quality Assurance

(2) Quality Control

Quality Assurance - It refers to the assurance to customers that the products parts, components, tools etc contain specified characteristics and are fit for the intended use. Quality assurance is about how a business can design the way a product of service is produced or delivered to minimize the chances that output will be sub-standard. It refers to the entire system of policies, procedures, and guidelines established by an organization to achieve and maintain quality.

Basic aspects of assuring quality:

- Assurance of incoming raw materials quality
- Assurance that proper processes are operating on the raw materials.
- Assurance of the quality of the outgoing finished goods.

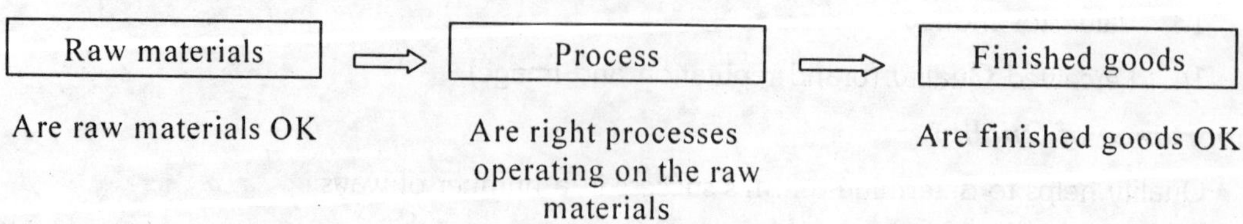

Figure 2.18 : Basic Aspects of Assuring Quality

2.4.1 QUALITY CONTROL

Quality control is the traditional way of managing quality. It is concerned with checking and reviewing work that has been done. Quality control means adherence to a standard or prevention of a change from the standard. It is the process of verification and correction in the quality of the product. Quality control is mainly about "detecting" defective output - rather than preventing it. When the deviations in the quality are found to be more than expected, it is through quality control that measures are taken to see that defective items are not produced at all. Thus, quality control can be defined as that Industrial Management technique by means of which products of uniform acceptable quality are manufactured.

In brief Quality control means

- Adherence to a standard or prevention of a change from the set standard.
- The process of verification and correction in the quality of the product.
- A preventive function to ensure that a product/service is fit for intended use and conform to specifications.

Objectives of Quality Control

(1) To decide about the standard of quality of a product that is easily acceptable to the customer.

(2) To check the variation during manufacturing.

(3) To prevent the poor quality products reaching to customer.

Benefits of Quality Control:

1. Reduction of scrap and wastages.
2. Reduction in inspection.
3. Less customer complaints.
4. Saving excess use of materials.
5. Generates confidence, good will and reputation to the company.
6. Better product design and product quality.
7. Increasing quality consciousness in the organization.
8. Good vendor-vendee relation
9. Customer satisfaction
10. Higher profits

2.4.2 STATISTICAL QUALITY CONTROL

Introduction

With the advent of industrial revolution in the 19th century, mass production replaced manufacturing in small shops by skilled craftsman and artisans. While in the small shops the individual worker was completely responsible for the quality of the work, this was no longer true in mass production where each individual's contribution to the finished product constituted only an insignificant part in the total process. The quality control by the large companies was achieved with the help of quality inspectors responsible for checking a 100 percent inspection of all the important characteristics.

The process of applying statistical principles to solve problem of controlling the quality of a product or service is called SQC. Dr. Walter A. Shewhart, called the father of quality control analysis, developed the concepts of statistical quality control. W.A.Shewart introduced the control charts in 1931 on the basis of statistical principles to determine how far the product confirms to the standard quality and to what extent its quality deviates from the standard.

Defining Statistical Quality Control (SQC)

A quality control system performs inspection, testing and analysis to conclude whether the quality of each product is as per laid quality standard or not. When statistical techniques are employed to control quality or to solve quality control problem, it is called "Statistical Quality Control". SQC makes inspection more reliable and at the same time less costly. SQC is the application of statistical methods to determine how far the product confirms to the standard quality and to what extent its quality deviates from the standard. It is applied by taking samples and drawing conclusions by means of mathematical analysis. Control charts are used to help to achieve the objectives of SQC. Using SQC methods, it can be determined whether variations in output are due to common causes or assignable causes. This technique was recognized in the industry only during the Second World War.

- SQC is often viewed as a productivity improvement tool.
- It is an integral part of management control.
- The techniques of applying statistical methods is based upon the theory of probability to quality control problems with the purpose of establishing quality standard and maintaining adherence to those standards in the most economical manner.

Advantages / Benefits of SQC

- SQC helps to identify the causes for variations in quality and minimize the same
- SQC helps to contorl, maintain and improve quality standards
- It reduces the wastage, scrap, rework, cost per unit and inspection cost
- It gives an early warning of defects
- It gives accurate prediction
- It makes the employees become conscious and efficient
- It facilitates the producer to give guarantee for his products
- It guides the producer when to initiate changes in production settings

Techniques of SQC:

- Process control through control charts
- Acceptance sampling

Process Control

It is a technique of ensuring quality of the products during the manufacturing process itself. If a process produces items consistently with acceptable or tolerable range of specifications, then the process is said to be in control. Process control is carried out through control charts

Control Charts

Control chart (also called process chart or quality control chart) is an important statistical tool used for the study and control of the repetitive processes. Control charts are the tools to determine whether the process is under control or out of control. These charts were developed by W.A Shewart based on the fact that variability does exist in all repetitive processes. Control charts provide a basis for deciding whether the variation in the output is due to common causes (in control) or assignable causes (out of control). The main objective of control chart is to identify process variation and help to reduce the same.

Control chart is a graphical representation of quality characteristics which indicates whether the process is under control or not. It shows whether a sample of data falls within the common or normal range of variation. A control chart has upper and lower control limits that separate common from assignable causes of variation. The common range of variation is defined by the use of control chart limits. Two important lines on a control chart are the upper control limit (UCL) and lower control limit (LCL). If the observed values fall within the limits the process is said to be in control and if they fall outside the limits the process is said to be out of control. Points on the control chart may or may not be connected. Values outside of the control limits provide strong evidence that the process is out of control. Thus, the control chart indicates, whether the process is in control or out of control.

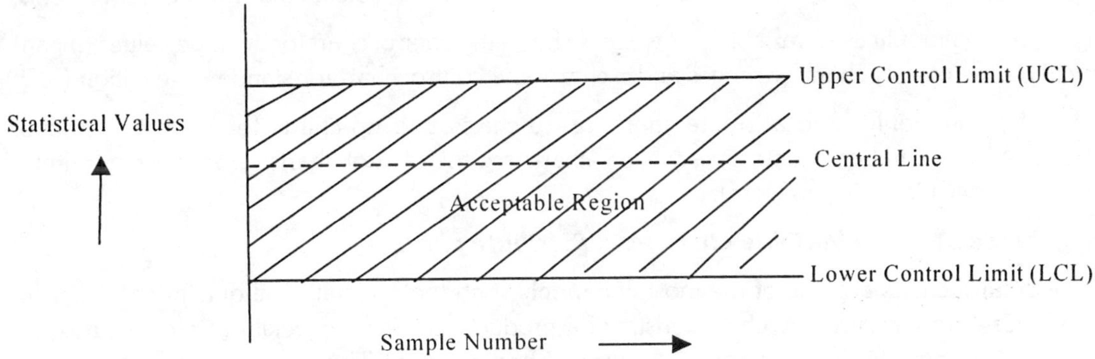

Figure 2.19 : A sample Control Chart

Purpose of Control Charts

Control charts identify when assignable causes of variation or changes have entered the process. For example, the Wheeling Company makes vinyl-coated aluminium replacement windows for older homes. The vinyl coating must have a thickness between certain limits. If the coating becomes too thick, it will cause the windows to jam. On the other hand, if the coating becomes too thin, the window will not seal properly. Thus, a change has occurred in the process. Control charts are useful for detecting the change in process conditions. It is important to know when changes have entered the process, so that the cause may be identified and corrected before a large number of unacceptable items are produced.

2.4.3 TYPES OF CONTROL CHARTS

1. **Control Charts for Variables (Measurement charts)**

   Control charts based upon measurable quality characteristics are called control charts for variables.

   a) $\overline{X}$ chart (Mean chart)

   b) R chart (Range chart)

   c) σ chart (Standard Deviation chart)

2. **Control Charts for Attributes**

   - Control chart for fraction defectives and number of defectives

   a) p – chart (Fraction defectives)

   b) np – chart (Number of defectives)

   - Control chart for no. of defects per unit

   c) c – chart (Number of defects per piece)

   d) u – chart (Number of non conformities per unit)

Like sampling plans, control charts are also based on variables and attributes. In other words, quality can be controlled either through variables or actual measurements (dimensions, weights, etc. or through attributes (Yes/No). When quality characteristics cannot be measured quantitatively, attribute charts are used to classify the items as defective or non defective items.

The commonly used variable charts are X chart - the control chart for average values (mean), R chart - the control chart for ranges and σ chart - the control chart for standard deviation (S.D.)

The commonly used attribute charts are p-charts and np-charts for analyzing fraction defectives and number of defectives while c-charts are the control charts for measuring number of defects per piece (in one item).

Difference between Variable charts and Attribute charts

Control charts are one of the most commonly used tools in statistical quality control. They can be used to measure any characteristic of a product, such as the weight of a cereal box, the number of chocolates in a box, or the volume of bottled water. The different characteristics that can be measured by control charts can be divided into two groups: ***variables*** and ***attributes.***

A control chart for variables is used to monitor characteristics that can be measured and have a continuum of values, such as height, weight, or volume.

A control chart for attributes, on the other hand, is used to monitor characteristics that have discrete values and can be counted. Often they can be evaluated with a simple yes or no decision.

The major differences are

- Variable charts involve measurement of job dimensions. An item is accepted or rejected if the dimensions are within or beyond the fixed tolerance limits.

- Attribute charts only differentiate between a defective item and non defective item
- Variable charts are more detailed and contain more information.
- Attribute charts are less detailed and contain less information
- Variable charts are expensive because of greater cost of collecting measured data.
- Attribute charts are relatively cheaper.

Advantages of Control Charts

The control charts separate out the assignable causes and chance causes for variations and bring substantial improvement in product quality.

1. Control charts indicate whether the process is in control or out of control.
2. It detects unusual variations taking place in the process.
3. It ensures the product quality level.
4. It provides information about selection of process and setting of tolerance limits.
5. Percentage rejections and scrap can be reduced.
6. It builds up the reputation of the organization through customer satisfaction.
7. There is reduction in spoilage of work and rework
8. The inspection work also reduces
9. Control charts can be applied to many businesses including manufacturing

Control Charts for Variables (Measurement charts)

Control charts for variables monitor characteristics that can be measured and have a continuous scale, such as height, weight, volume, or width. When an item is inspected, the variable being monitored is measured and recorded. When observed values go outside the control limits, the process is assumed not to be in control. Production is stopped and employees attempt to identify the cause of the problem and correct it.

$\bar{X}$ chart (Mean chart)

An X chart is used if the quality of the output is measured in terms of a variable such as length, weight, temperature, and so on. X represents the mean value found in a sample of the output. A mean control chart is often referred to as an ***x-bar chart.*** It is used to monitor changes in the mean of a process. To construct a mean chart it is first needed to construct the central line of the chart. To do this take multiple samples and compute their means. Usually these samples are small, with about four or five observations. Each sample has its own mean x. The center line of the chart is then computed as the mean of all X sample means, where X is the number of samples

Range chart

In addition to the central tendency in a sample, it is also required to monitor the amount of variation from sample to sample. A ***range chart*** shows the variation in the sample ranges. It is used to monitor the range of the measurements in the sample. If the points representing the ranges fall between the upper and the lower limits, it is concluded that the operation is in control. According to chance, about 997 times out of 1,000 the range of the samples will fall within the limits. If the range should fall above the limits, it can be concluded that an assignable cause affected the operation and an adjustment to the process is needed.

$\overline{X}$ chart (Control chart for Mean)

To keep a control on the measurable characteristics of an article, $\overline{X}$ chart which involves the mean $\overline{X}$ and the standard deviation σ is used.

The mean of the characteristic, Central Line $\overline{\overline{X}} = \frac{\Sigma\overline{X}}{K}$

Where $\overline{X}$ = Mean of sample means (average value of each sub group'

K = Number of samples (sub groups)

The control charts are set at three standard deviations

1. *Where Standard Deviation is known*

$$UCL_{\bar{x}} = \overline{\overline{X}} + \frac{3\sigma}{\sqrt{N}} = \overline{\overline{X}} + 3\frac{\overline{R}}{d_2}\sqrt{N}$$

$$LCL_{\bar{x}} = \overline{\overline{X}} - \frac{3\sigma}{\sqrt{N}} = \overline{\overline{X}} - 3\frac{\overline{R}^2}{d_2}\sqrt{N}$$

Where $\overline{\overline{X}}$ = Mean of sample means

σ = Standard deviation

N = Number of items or observations in a sample

2. *Where Standard Deviation is not known*

$$\sigma = \frac{\overline{R}}{d_2}$$

Where $\overline{R}$ = Mean of sample range (average range)

d_2 = Quality control factor (constant factor)

3. *Where d_2 is not given*

$$UCL_{\bar{x}} = \overline{\overline{X}} + A_2\overline{R}$$

$$LCL_{\bar{x}} = \overline{\overline{X}} + A_2\overline{R}$$

Where A_2 = Quality control factor (constant factor)

R chart:

The chart for ranges the R chart is obtained from the same sample groups that were used in determining the values of $\overline{X}$. The central line or the mean of the R chart represents the average of the subgroup ranges. Control limits on the range chart can be calculated as

1. *Where σ is known:*

Central line = $\overline{R} = d_2\sigma$

Mean of R = $\overline{R} = \frac{\Sigma\overline{R}}{K}$

$UCL_R = d_2\sigma + 3d_3\sigma$

$LCL_R = d_2\sigma - 3d_3\sigma$

Where ΣR = Sum of sample ranges

K = Total number of samples

N = Number of items in a sample

Where d_2 and d_3 for given n can be determined from statistical tables

2. *Where σ is unknown:*

Central line = $\overline{R} = \frac{\Sigma\overline{R}}{K}$

$UCL_R = D_4\overline{R}$

$LCL_R = D_3\,\overline{R}$

where $D_4 = 1 + 3d_3/d_2$

and $D_3 = 1 - 3d_3/d_2$

D_3 and D_4 can be read for given 'n' from statistical tables

If LCL is negative, it is taken as zero

Table of Constants for $\overline{X}$ and R charts

n	A_2	D_3	D_4
2	1.880	0	3.268
3	1.023	0	2.574
4	0.729	0	2.282
5	0.577	0	2.114
6	0.483	0	2.004
7	0.419	0.076	1.924
8	0.373	0.136	1.864
9	0.337	0.184	1.816
10	0.308	0.223	1.777

Procedure for constructing $\overline{X}$ chart

1. Compute average of averages $\overline{X}$
2. Calculate average range $\overline{R}$
3. Multiply the average range by the conversion factor A_2. This gives $A_2\,\overline{R}$

(i) To obtain the upper control limit, apply the following formula:

Upper control limit (UCL) = $\overline{\overline{X}} + A_2\overline{R}$

(ii) To obtain the lower control limit, apply the following formula:

Lower control limit (LCL) = $\overline{\overline{X}} - A_2\overline{R}$

Procedure for constructing R chart

(a) Compute $\overline{X}$ and $\overline{R}$ for each of the samples obtained

(b) Calculate average range $\overline{R}$

(c) Multiply the average range by the conversion factor (D_4 or D_3).

(i) To obtain the upper control limit, apply the following formula:

Upper control limit (UCL)= $D_4\overline{R}$

(ii) To obtain the lower control limit, apply the following formula:

Lower control limit (LCL) =$D_3\,\overline{R}$

Problem 2.3

Subgroups of five items are taken from a manufacturing process at regular intervals. A certain quality is measured and $\overline{X}$ and R values are computed for each sub group. After 10 sub groups

$\Sigma\overline{X} = 76$

$\Sigma R = 26$

Compute the control chart limits

Solution:

$$UCL\,\overline{X} = \overline{\overline{X}} + A_2\overline{R}$$

$$\overline{\overline{X}} = \frac{\Sigma\overline{X}}{K} = \frac{76}{10} = 7.6$$

$$\overline{R} = \frac{\Sigma R}{K} = \frac{26}{10} = 2.6$$

$$A_2 = 0.577$$

$$UCL_{\overline{X}} = 7.6 + 0.577 \times 2.6 = 9.1002$$

$$LCL_{\bar{X}} = 7.6 - 0.577 \times 2.6 = 6.0998$$

$$UCL_R = D_4\bar{R} = 2.115 \times 2.6 = 5.499$$

$$LCL_R = 0 \times 2.6 = 0$$

Problem 2.4

The following data gives the reading of 10 samples of size 8 each in the production of certain component

Sample	*Mean*	*Range*
1	5.4	0.4
2	5.1	0.7
3	5.4	0.7
4	4.9	0.8
5	5.2	0.9
6	4.7	0.6
7	5.1	0.5
8	5	0.6
9	5	0.7
10	5.2	0.6

Draw the control charts for mean and range and point out which sample if any are out of limits

Solution:

For $\bar{X}$ chart

$\bar{X}$ = 51/10 = 5.1

$\bar{R}$ = 6.5/10 = 0.65

$$UCL_{\bar{X}} = \bar{\bar{X}} + \frac{3\bar{R}}{d_2\sqrt{N}}$$

$$= 5.1 + 3(0.65)/2.847\sqrt{10}$$

$$= 5.1 + 1.95/9.732$$

$$= 5.3434$$

$$LCL_{\bar{X}} = \bar{\bar{X}} - \frac{3\bar{R}}{d_2\sqrt{N}}$$

$$= 5.1 - 3(0.65)/2.847\sqrt{10}$$

$$= 4.8578$$

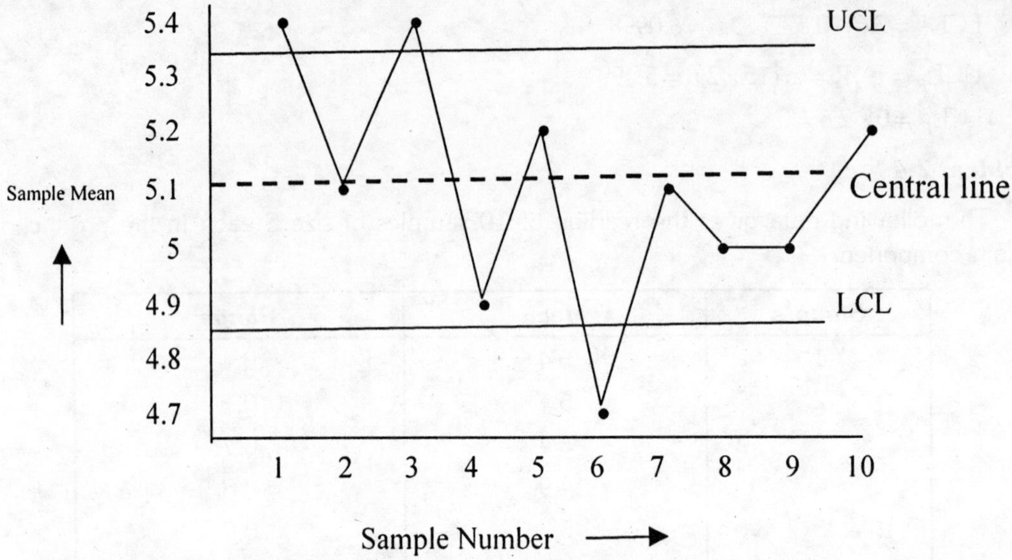

The $\overline{X}$ ***chart*** reveals that the sample numbers 1, 3 and 6 are out of control limits which are indicative of some assignable causes and hence, the process is out of control.

For R chart :

D_4 and D_3 for 8 from stastistical table, D_4 = 1.864, D_3 = 0.136

Central line $\overline{R}$ = 0.65

$UCL_R = D_4\ \overline{R} = 1.864 \times 0.65 = 1.2116$

$LCL_R = D_3\ \overline{R} = 0.136 \times 0.65 = 0.088$

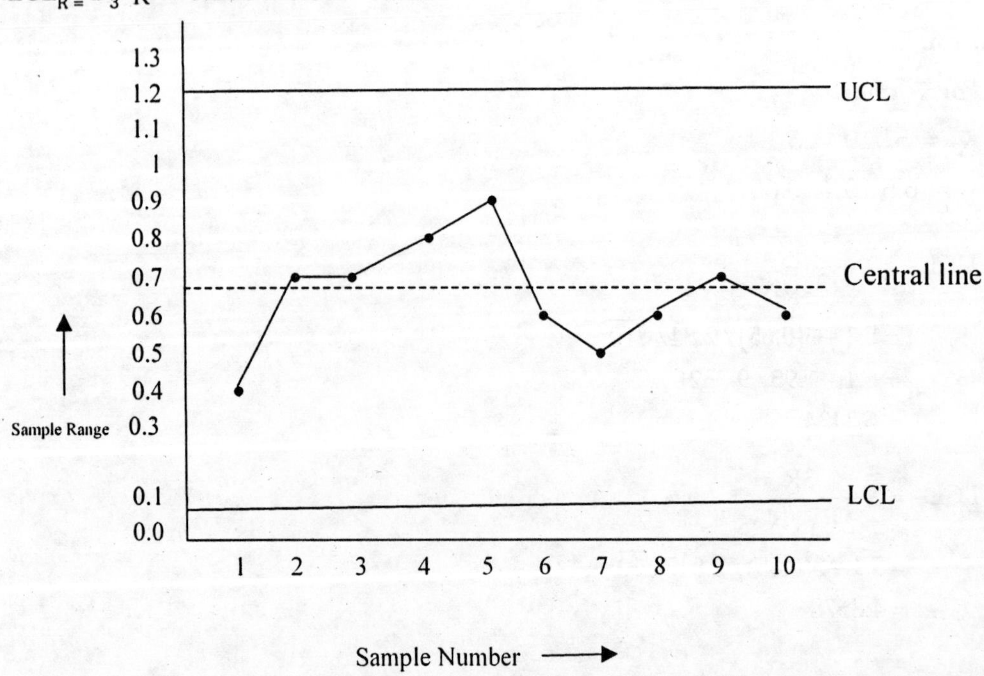

The ***R chart*** reveals that the there is no sample which is out of the control limits i.e., since all samples are within the limits, the process is said to be under control

Problem 2.5

A machine is set to deliver the packets of a given weight 10 samples of size 5 each are examined and the following results were obtained

Sample	*Mean*	*Range*
1	15	7
2	17	7
3	15	4
4	18	9
5	17	8
6	14	7
7	18	12
8	15	4
9	17	11
10	5	5

Calculate the values for the central line and the control limits for the mean chart and range chart. Comment on the state of control.

Solution:

Mean Chart

$$\bar{\bar{X}} = \Sigma\bar{X}/K = 151/10 = 15.1$$

$$\bar{R} = \Sigma R/K = 74/40 = 7.4$$

$$\begin{aligned} UCL_{\bar{X}} &= \bar{\bar{X}} + A_2 R \\ &= 15.1 + 0.577(7.4) \\ &= 4.2698 + 15.1 \\ &= 19.3698 \end{aligned}$$

$$\begin{aligned} LCL_{\bar{X}} &= \bar{\bar{X}} - A_2 R \\ &= 15.1 - 0.577(7.4) \\ &= 10.8302 \end{aligned}$$

R - Chart

$UCL_R = D_4\bar{R}$ = 2.115 x 7.4 = 15.651

$LCL_R = D_3\bar{R}$ = 0 x 7.4 = 0

Inference

The $\overline{X}$ ***chart*** reveals that the sample number 10 is out of control limits which are indicative of some assignable cause and hence, the process is out of control.

The ***R chart*** reveals that the there is no sample which is out of the control limits i.e., since all samples are within the limits, the process is said to be under control

Control chart for attributes

There are two different types of control charts for attributes which are based on the distinction between defectives and defects. There are two control charts for defectives, the p-chart, for the proportion of defectives in the sample and np-chart for the no. of defectives. They are based on binomial distribution. The c-chart is the control chart for no. of defects in a unit and is based on poison distribution. Control charts for attributes are used to measure quality characteristics that are counted rather than measured. That is, we observe the presence or absence of some attribute. Attributes are discrete in nature and entail simple yes-or-no decisions. For example, this could be the number of nonfunctioning light bulbs, the proportion of broken eggs in a carton, the number of rotten apples, the number of scratches on a tile, or the number of complaints issued.

The Attribute Charts are

The p chart – the control chart for fraction rejected as non confirming to specifications (proportion of defectives)

The np chart - the control chart for number of non conforming items (number of defectives)

The c chart - the control chart for number of non conformities (number of defects)

The u chart - the control chart for number of non conformities per unit.

A defective item is defined as one that fails to confirm to specifications in one or more quality characteristics. Defect is a failure of the item to confirm to one specification. A defective item may contain only one defect or many defects.

p-charts

P-charts are used to measure the proportion that is defective in a sample. If the item recorded is the fraction of unacceptable parts made in a larger batch of parts, the appropriate control chart is the percent defective chart. The computation of the central line as well as the upper and lower control limits is similar to the computation for the other kinds of control charts. This chart is based on the binomial distribution and proportions. The central line is at P, the mean proportion defective. The central line is computed as the average proportion defective in the population. This is obtained by taking a number of samples of observations at random and computing the average value of P across all samples.

Use of p-charts

- When observations can be placed into two categories.
  - Good or bad
  - Pass or fail
  - Operate or don't operate
- When the data consists of multiple samples of several observations each

p-chart: This is drawn on the basis of proportion defectives in the lots

Central line $\overline{p}$ = Total number of defective pieces / Total number of pieces inspected

$$UCL_p = \overline{p} + 3\sqrt{\overline{p}(1-\overline{p})/n}$$

$$LCL_p = \overline{p} - 3\sqrt{\overline{p}(1-\overline{p})/n}$$

Where = $\overline{p}$ = Central line

n = Samples size (number of items in a sample)

np- chart

If sub group size is constant the chart for actual number of defectives is called np- chart or pn- char. The construction of np chart is identical with p- chart. After finding the value of $\overline{p}$ this is multiplied with n to get $n\overline{p}$ which indicates the central line

Central line = $n\overline{p}$

$$UCL_{np} = n\overline{p} + 3\sigma np$$

$$LCL_{np} = n\overline{p} - 3\sigma np$$

Where $3\sigma np = 3\sqrt{n\overline{p}(1-\overline{p})}$

Problem 2.6

S. No.	Date	No. of pieces inspected (A)	No. of defectives found (B)	Fraction defective (P=B/A)
1	1st Jan	400	30	0.075
2	2nd Jan	400	25	0.0625
3	3rd Jan	400	30	0.075
4	4th Jan	400	35	0.0875
5	5th Jan	400	40	0.1
6	6th Jan	400	45	0.1125
7	7th Jan	400	35	0.0875
8	8th Jan	400	45	0.1125
9	9th Jan	400	35	0.0875
10	10th Jan	400	40	0.1
Total		***4000***	***360***	***0.9***

Calculate values of central line and control limits

Solution :

Central line $\overline{p}$ = Total no. of defective pieces found/Total no. of pieces inspected

= 360/4000 = 0.09

$$UCL_p = \bar{p} + 3\sqrt{\bar{p}(1-\bar{p})/n}$$
$$= 0.09 + 3\sqrt{\overline{0.09}\,(1-0.09)/400}$$
$$= 0.09 + 3\sqrt{0.0819/400}$$
$$= 0.09 + 3/20 \times 0.2861$$
$$= 0.09 + 0.042927$$
$$= 0.1329$$
$$LCL_p = \bar{p} - 3\sqrt{\bar{p}(1-\bar{p})/n}$$
$$= 0.09 - 0.042927 = 0.0471$$

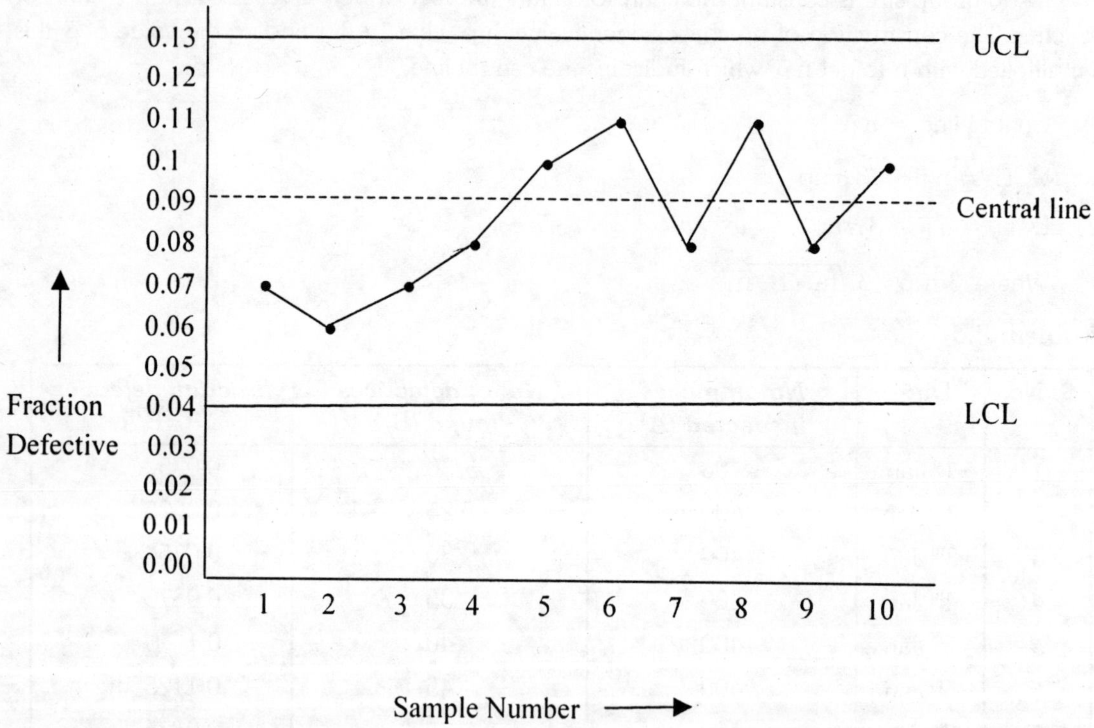

The ***p - chart*** reveals that the there is no sample which is out of the control limits i.e., since all samples are within the limits, the process is said to be under control

Problem 2.7

Date	No. of pieces inspected (A)	No. of defective pieces found(B)	Fraction defective(P=B/A)	% defective (100P)
Nov 4th	300	25	0.0834	8.34
Nov 5th	300	30	0.1000	10
Nov 6th	300	35	0.1167	11.67
Nov 7th	300	40	0.1333	13.33
Nov 8th	300	45	0.1500	15
Nov10	300	35	0.1167	11.67
Nov 11th	300	40	0.1333	13.33
Nov 12th	300	30	0.1000	10
Nov 13th	300	20	0.0666	6.66
Nov 14th	300	50	0.1666	1.66
Total	**3000**	**350**	**0.1166**	

Calculate the value of central line and control limits and draw the control chart. Comment on the state of control

Solution:

Central line $\bar{p}$ = Total no. of defective pieces found/Total no. of pieces inspected

= 350/3000 = 0.1166

$$UCL_P = \bar{p} + 3\sqrt{\bar{p}(1-\bar{p})/n}$$
$$= 0.1166 + 3\sqrt{0.1166(1-0.1166/300)}$$
$$= 0.1166 + 3(0.0185)$$
$$= 0.1166 + 0.0555 = 0.1722$$

$$LCL_P = \bar{p} - 3\sqrt{\bar{p}(1-\bar{p})/n}$$
$$= 0.1166 - 0.0555$$
$$= 0.0610$$

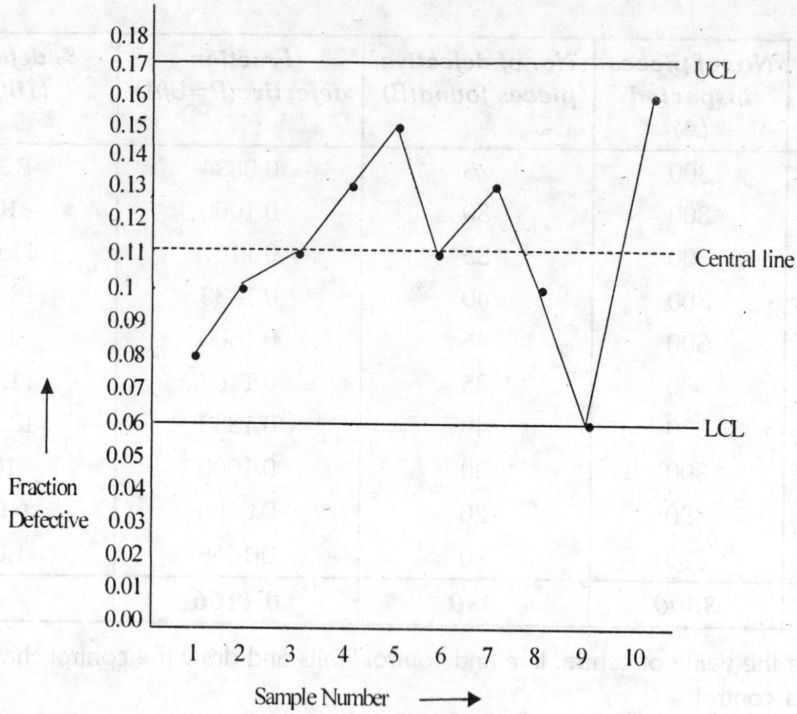

Inference: The ***p - chart*** reveals that the there is no sample which is out of the control limits i.e., since all samples are within the limits, the process is said to be under control

Problem 2.8

An attribute control chart for part 223B shows the average fraction defective as 0.125. Upper control limit is 0.200 and LCL = 0.050. Based on two months of daily data, recently 12 units were sampled each day for 6 days with units defective 2, 1, 2, 0, 3 and 3. Construct a control chart for management and interpret it for management.

Fraction defective = 0.1667, 0.0833, 0.1667, 0, 0.25, 0.25

Central line = $\overline{p}$ = 0.125

$UCL_P = 0.2$

$LCL_P = 0.05$

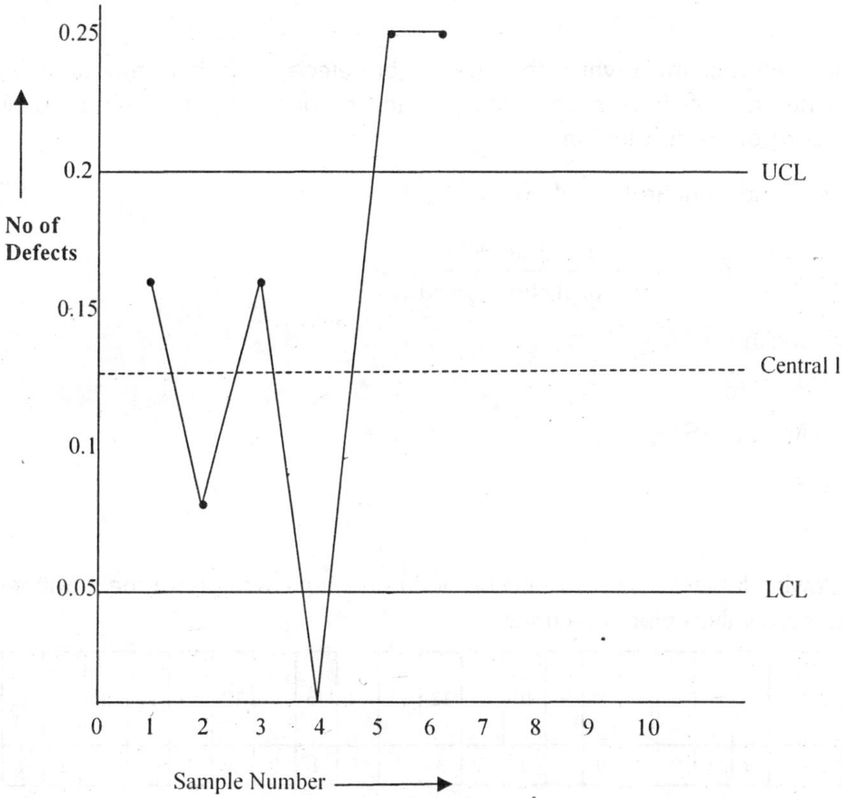

Inference: - The ***p - chart*** reveals that the sample numbers 5 and 6 are out of control limits which are indicative of some assignable causes in the manufacturing process. Hence, the process is out of control.

The control chart for non conformities- c-chart:

c - charts are used to monitor the number of defects per unit. A non confirming article is one that in some way fails to confirm to one or more given specifications (a defective). Each instance of the article's lack of conformity to specifications is the non conformity (a defect). The c-bar chart plots the number of defects or failures per unit. c-chart and u chart are based on poisson distribution.

Use of c - charts

- Used only when the number of occurrences per unit of measure can be counted; non-occurrences cannot be counted.
- Scratches, chips, dents, or errors per item
- Cracks or faults per unit of distance
- Breaks or tears per unit of area
- Bacteria or pollutants per unit of volume
- Calls, complaints, failures per unit of time

c - chart

It is the control chart in which the number of defects in an item are plotted or drawn. It controls the number of defects observed per unit or per sample. c- chart follows poison's distribution. For poison distribution

Mean $= \bar{c}$ and standard deviation $= \sqrt{c}$

$$\text{Central line} = \bar{c} = \frac{\text{Total defects}}{\text{Total no. of items produced}}$$

$$UCL_C = \text{Mean} + 3\,\text{S.D}$$
$$= \bar{c} + 3\sqrt{\bar{c}}$$
$$LCL_C = \text{Mean} - 3\,\text{S.D}$$
$$= \bar{c} - 3\sqrt{\bar{c}}$$

Problem 2.9

The following table gives the inspection of 25 similar glass tubes for the number of defects in them. Using these values plot a C chart.

Glass Table No.	1	2	3	4	5	6	7	8	9	10	11	12	13	14	15	16	17	18	19	20	21	22	23	24	25
Defects	2	1	2	6	8	2	4	9	3	4	5	3	3	7	4	5	2	4	3	7	2	4	5	3	2

Solution:

Central line c = Total defects/ Total number of items produced

= 100/25 = 4

$$UCL_C = \bar{c} + 3\sqrt{\bar{c}}$$
$$= 4 + 3\sqrt{4} = 10$$
$$LCL_C = \bar{c} - 3\sqrt{\bar{c}} = 4 - 6 = -2 = 0$$

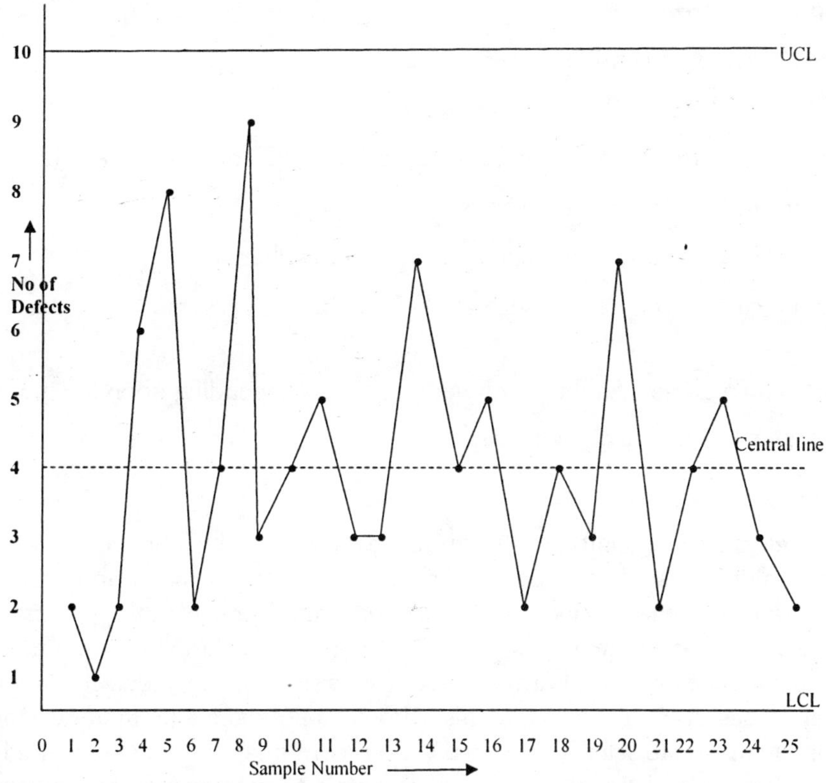

Inference : The c - chart reveals that there is no sample which is out of the control limits (i.e.) All the samples are within the limits. Hence, the process is in control.

Table 2.3 : Comparison of X, R chart and p-chart

X, R chart	***p - chart***
• X, R charts are control charts for variables	• p chart is control chart for attributes
• Data collection costs more	• Data collection costs comparatively less
• Sample size is smaller	• Sample size is comparatively larger
• Variation in sample size influences the control limits more	• Variation in sample size influences the control limits less
• Sensitivity in detecting a shift is poorer comparatively	• Sensitivity in detecting a shift is better
• Separate charts are essential for each measured quality characteristics	• One p chart may be applied to any number of quality characteristics observed in one article at any inspection station
• It is much superior for diagnosing the causes of change in dimension	• It is much inferior for diagnosing of causes of trouble or rejection.

Application of Control Charts

1. Final Assemblies (Attribute charts)
2. Welded and soldered joints (Attribute charts)
3. Defects in parts made of glass, rubber, turbines, IC engines etc (Attribute charts)
4. Bullets and shells (Attribute charts)
5. Punch, press works, spot welding etc. (Attribute charts)
6. Manufactured components such as shafts, spindles, balls, pin holes, slots etc (Variable charts)
7. Incoming material (Attribute and Variable charts depending upon the type of material)

2.5 MATERIALS MANAGEMENT

Introduction

Materials refers to inputs into production process most of which are converted into output. It may be raw material, work in progress, finished goods, spare parts and components and others required for maintenance and repairs. Materials management is the process of planning, organizing and controlling the materials in a given organization. Among government, it is better known as supply management and armed forces as logistics management. It is the total control of goods at all stages in the firms operations. About 20-25 years ago, there was no cut-throat competition in the market to sell the products. Various consumer items manufactured by different industrial undertakings and the availability of materials to manufacture these items were not scarce. Therefore, materials management was not thought to be so important and its separate identity in the organization was not felt. But today it has become an important management activity to streamline production.

Definition

Material management is the function responsible for the coordination of planning, sourcing, purchasing, moving, storing and controlling materials in an optimal manner so as to provide pre decided service to the customer at the minimum cost. Materials management aims for integrated approach towards the management of materials in an industrial undertaking. Its main objective is cost reduction and efficient handling of materials at all stages and in all sections of the undertaking. It is the planning, directing, controlling and coordinating those activities which are concerned with materials and inventory requirements from the point of their inspection to their introduction into the manufacturing process. Materials Management is related to planning, procuring, storing and providing the appropriate material of right quality, right quantity at right place in right time so as to co-ordinate and schedule the production activity in an integrative way for an industrial undertaking.

Materials management embraces all functions concerned with ordering, storage and movement of material. Its function includes several important aspects connected with material, such as, materials requirements planning, purchasing, storage, inventory control, material handling, standardization etc. In short, materials management is the term used for controlling the kinds, amount, location, movement and timing of various materials used in production process. Importance of materials management can be revealed from the fact that every item in stock or in use is nothing but cash in the form of equipment and store. In almost all organizations, material forms the largest part of the expenditure in their budget.

The International Federation of Purchasing and Materials Management defines materials management as a total concept having its definite organization to plan and control all types of materials, its supply, and its flow from raw stage to finished stage so as to deliver the product to customer as per his requirements in time. This involves materials planning, purchasing, receiving, storing, inventory control, scheduling, production, physical distribution and marketing. It also controls the materials handling and its traffic. The materials manager has to manage all these functions with proper authority and responsibility in the material management department.

Average Expenditure on the Materials by various Industries

The various industries, which are spending their money on the materials to produce the products as percentage of average expenditure, are given below.

Table 2.4 : Industry-wise Expenditure on Materials

S. No.	Industries	Average expenditure on materials in percentage
1.	Electrodes, rubber goods, cotton and silk yarns, electric motors, sugar, jute, motor vehicles etc.	65% to 70%
2.	Cotton textiles, cables, wires and utensils	60%to 65%
3.	Engineering goods and non-ferrous metals	55% to 60%
4.	Ship building, cement, chemicals and electricity	50% to 55%
5.	Pharmaceuticals and medicines	45% to 50%
6.	Aircraft, fertilizer and steel	40% to 45%
7.	Other industries	40%

Industries-wise expenditure on materials is given in the above table to show its importance. Average material expenditure is above 60% for cotton textiles, sugar, jute, wool etc. and above 50% for cement, chemicals etc.

Types of Materials

The various types of materials to be managed are:

1. Purchased materials: They are raw materials, components, spare parts, oils, grease, cotton waste, consumables and tools.
2. Work in process (WIP) materials: These are semi-finished and finished parts and components lying on the shop floor.
3. Finished goods: These are the final products either waiting to be assembled in the assembly lines or in stores which are stocked for final delivery waiting to sell.

The various costs involved in these materials are basic price, purchasing costs, inventory carrying cost, transportation cost, materials handling cost, office cost, packing cost, marketing cost, obsolescence and wastages.

Objectives of Materials Management

The objectives of materials management can be categorized in two ways as follows:

1. Primary objectives
2. Secondary objectives

1. ***Primary objectives*** are stated as "making available (supply) of materials in specified quantity and quality at economic cost and maintaining the continuity of supply, minimization of investments in materials and inventory costs and assuring high inventory turnover."

This can be classified as

- Efficient materials planning
- Buying or Purchasing
- Procuring and receiving
- Storing and inventory control
- Supply and distribution of materials
- Quality assurance
- Good supplier and customer relationship
- Improved departmental efficiency

2. ***Secondary objectives*** help to achieve the primary objectives. The secondary objectives can be stated as

1. Purchasing the items from a reliable source at economic price.
2. Reduction of costs by using various cost reduction techniques such as variety reduction, standardization and simplification, value analysis, inventory control, purchase research etc.
3. Co-ordination of the functions such as planning, scheduling, storage and maintenance of materials.

There can be several secondary objectives of materials management. Some of them are given below:

- Efficient production scheduling
- To take make or buy decisions
- Prepare specifications and standardization of materials
- To assist in product design and development
- Forecasting demand and quantity of materials requirement
- Quality control of materials purchased

- Material handling
- Use of value analysis and value engineering
- Developing skills of workers in materials management
- Smooth flow of materials in and out of the organization

To fulfill all these objectives, it is necessary to establish harmony and good co-ordination between all the employees of material management department and this department should have good co-ordination with the other departments of the organization to serve all production centres.

2.5.1 SCOPE OF MATERIALS MANAGEMENT

Materials management encompasses all the aspects of the material. *i.e.*, material costs, material supply and material utilization. Materials management is concerned with material planning and materials control activities. The details of planning and control activities are represented in the below table.

Planning and Control Activities of Materials Management

• Planning	- Right type, quantity of purchasing materials.
• Sourcing	- Selecting a right source of material supply and procurement from the sources.
• Controlling	- Follow up and monitoring, inventory control.
• Storing	- Receiving, inspection, storing and issue of materials.
• Handling	- Flow or movement, packaging, transportation.
• Distribution	- Distribution of finished goods, warehousing and shipping.

Materials management is defined as "the function responsible for the coordination of planning, sourcing, purchasing, moving, storing and controlling materials in an optimum manner so as to provide a pre-decided service to the customer at a minimum cost".

From the definition it is clear that the scope of materials management is vast. As soon as materials are purchased and brought by the organization, its value goes on increasing as the other costs such as carrying the materials in inventory, its maintenance and handling charges must be assigned to the cost of materials before it enters into a product or transformed into some other form. In order to economize all the costs of materials management, the company has to adopt definite method of deciding the quantity of materials to be ordered, quantity to be stored as inventory and work in process inventory. In order to reduce the material cost and all other costs stated above, there has to be some efficient and effective materials management techniques, which must be dynamic to adjust with changing demand and production. The functions of materials management can be categorized in the following way, which is shown in the figure.

1. Material Planning and Control
2. Purchasing or Procurement of materials
3. Stores Management

4. Inventory Control
5. Standardization
6. Simplification
7. Value Analysis
8. Ergonomics
9. Just-in-Time (JIT)

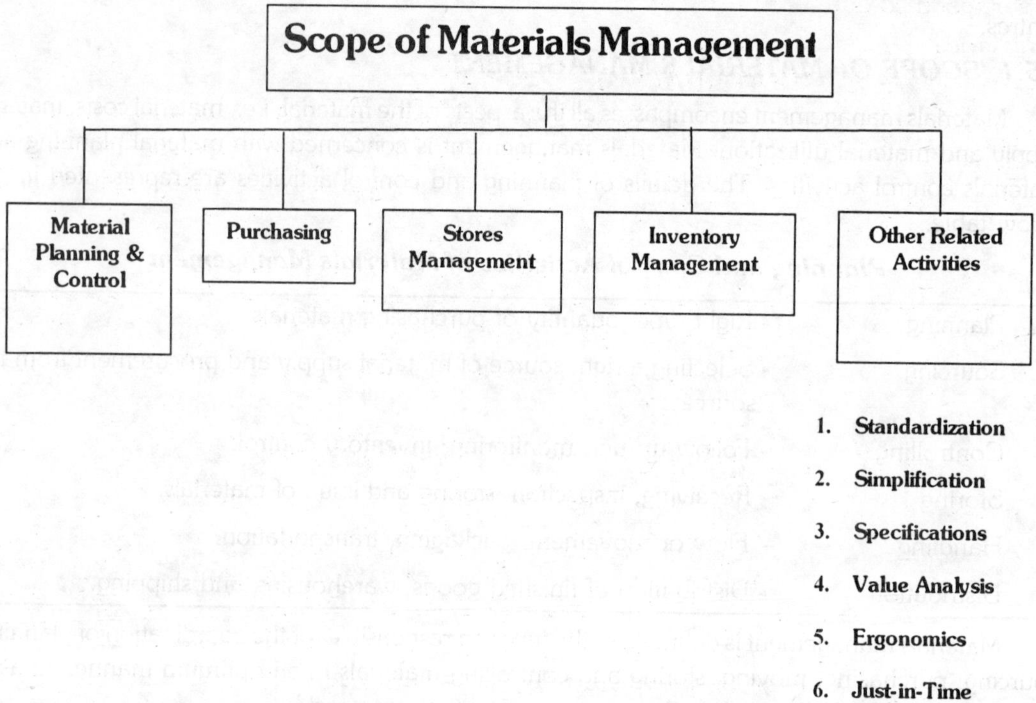

Figure 2.20 : Scope of Materials Management

1. ***Materials planning and control:*** Based on the sales forecast and production plans, the materials planning and control is done. This involves estimating the individual requirements of parts, preparing materials budget, forecasting the levels of inventories, scheduling the orders and monitoring the performance in relation to production and sales.
2. ***Purchasing:*** This includes selection of sources of supply finalization in terms of purchase, placement of purchase orders, follow-up, maintenance of smooth relations with suppliers, approval of payments to suppliers, evaluating and rating suppliers.
3. ***Stores management:*** This involves physical control of materials, preservation of stores, minimization of obsolescence and damage through timely disposal and efficient handling, maintenance of stores records, proper location and stocking. A store is also responsible for the physical verification of stocks and reconciling them with book figures. A store plays a vital role in the operations of a company.

4. ***Inventory control or management:*** Inventory generally refers to the materials in stock. It is also called the idle resource of an enterprise. Inventories represent those items, which are either stocked for sale or they are in the process of manufacturing or they are in the form of materials, which are yet to be utilized. The interval between receiving the purchased parts and transforming them into final products varies from industry to industry depending upon the cycle time of manufacture. It is, therefore, necessary to hold inventories of various kinds to act as a buffer between supply and demand for efficient operation of the system. Thus, an effective control on inventory is a must for smooth and efficient running of the production cycle with least interruptions.

5. ***Other Related Activities***

   (a) ***3S***

   i) ***Standardization**:* Standardization means producing maximum variety of products from the minimum variety of materials, parts, tools and processes. It is the process of establishing standards or units of measure by which extent, quality, quantity, value; performance etc. may be compared and measured.

   ii) ***Simplification**:* The concept of simplification is closely related to standardization. Simplification is the process of reducing the variety of products manufactured. Simplification is concerned with the reduction of product range, assemblies, parts, materials and design.

   iii) ***Specifications**:* It refers to a precise statement that formulizes the requirements of the customer. It may relate to a product, process or a service.

   Example: Specifications of an axle block are, Inside Diameter $= 2 \pm 0.1$ cm, Outside Dia. $= 4 \pm 0.2$ cm and Length $= 10 \pm 0.5$ cm.

   (b) ***Value Analysis:*** Value analysis is one of the major techniques of cost reduction and cost prevention. The idea behind value analysis is to find a substitute giving the same functional value, yet costing the same or less. Value Analysis is an organised approach to identify unnecessary costs associated with any product, material part, component, system or service by analysis of function and efficiently eliminating them without reduction in quality, functional reliability or its capacity to provide service

   (c) ***Ergonomics (Human Engineering):*** The human factors or human engineering is concerned with man-machine system. Ergonomics is concerned with the 'fit' between people and their technological tools and environments. Ergonomics is "the design of human tasks, man-machine system, and effective accomplishment of the job, including displays for presenting information to human sensors, controls for human operations and complex man-machine systems".

   (d) ***Just-in-Time (JIT):*** Just- in- time production is "philosophy that focuses attention on eliminating waste by purchasing or manufacturing just enough of the right items just in time". Proper use of JIT manufacturing has resulted in increased quality, productivity and efficiency, improved communication and decrease in cost and wastes. JIT stands for purchasing / producing necessary quantities at the necessary time.

Stages of Materials Management:

The following are the main stages of materials management activities in an enterprise.

1. **Decision Stage:** Co-ordination of activities, guiding design decisions, introducing new materials and some minor changes in the production process.
2. **Sourcing Stage:** Make or buy decision, procurement facilities etc.
3. **Production planning stage:** Preparation of master schedule and calculation of material requirements etc.
4. **Stage of ordering:** Placing the orders, follow up, packaging and transportation.
5. **Receiving Stage:** Receiving the items, inspection of material, identification of quality etc.
6. **Inventory control:** Determination of economic lot size, safety margins and inventory costs.

Functions of Material Management: It includes all functions concerned with ordering, storage and movement of materials. It includes several important aspects of management of materials such as

- Material planning and control
- Purchasing or procurement of materials
- Stores and inventory control
- Simplification, standardization and value analysis.
- Material handling and transportation
- Disposal of scrap, surplus and obsolete materials.
- Inspection of material
- Value analysis etc.,

Organization structure of Materials Management Department:

To facilitate planning, direction, control and coordination of various activities related to material in an enterprise there should be a separate department of materials management. The organization structure of the department can be

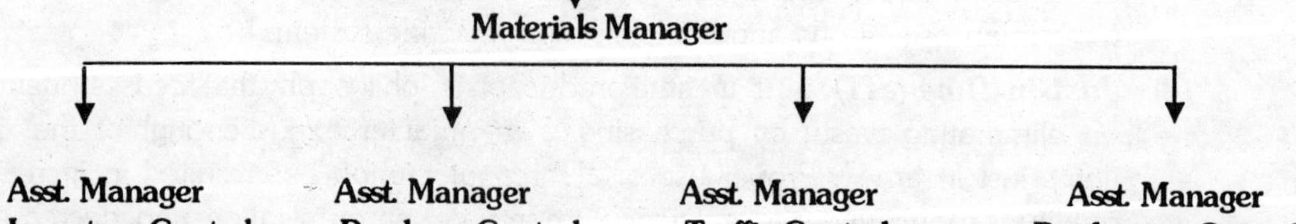

Figure 2.21 : Organisation structure of Materials Management Department

There can be more subsections of the department but in general, materials manager controls the four major sections and is responsible for reporting to the General Manager of the organization.

Duties of Materials Manager:

As materials management embraces all functions concerning with ordering, storage and movement of materials, the responsibilities of materials manager can be described under the following heads.

1. ***Purchasing:*** Its main operations are
   a) Selection of supplies and issue of purchase order.
   b) Acting as a liaison between supplies and other departments of the enterprise.
   c) To look for new products, materials and suppliers that can contribute to companies profits.
2. ***Production Control:*** This is done by
   a) Determining requirements of materials and parts to be purchased and manufactured.
   b) Scheduling production and purchasing processes of material and parts.
   c) Issuing work order to manufacturing departments and purchase order to suppliers.
3. ***Inventory and stores control:***

   It keeps detailed and upto day record of inventory, order status and potential demand for each production part and material. It is also responsible for non productive stores like office suppliers, perishable goods etc.
4. ***Traffic:***

   It controls inbound shipments of purchased materials and outbound shipment of finished goods to consumers. This is done by:
   a) Selection of carriers
   b) Auditing invoices from carriers and filing claims for refund in case of excess charges of damaged shipments.
   c) Developing techniques to reduce the transportation costs.
5. ***Physical distribution:***

   Finished goods are moved from the production line to the warehouse and finally to the customer.

2.5.2 INVENTORY MANAGEMENT

Introduction

Inventory is a quantity or store of goods that is held for some purpose or use (the term may also be used as a verb, meaning to take inventory or to count all goods held in inventory).

Inventory may be kept "in-house", meaning on the premises or nearby for immediate use; or it may be held in a distant warehouse or distribution center for future use. With the exception of firms utilizing just-in-time methods, more often than not, the term "inventory" implies a stored quantity of goods that exceeds what is needed for the firm to function at the current time (e.g., within the next few hours). Inventory is one of the most expensive assets of any company. It represents as much as 40% - 60% of total invested capital.

It is commonly used to indicate materials, work in process, finished goods, spares and others, which are kept in stores, warehouses or plant for some period of time to meet an expected demand or distribution in future.

Inventory is an idle resource which is usable and has value. It may be men, money, materials, plant acquisition, spares and other stocks to meet future demand.

- In any organization inventories add an operating flexibility that would not otherwise exist.
- For many firms, inventory is the largest current asset.
- Inventories should be carefully handled. Excessive inventories can lead to excessive handling or carrying costs.

Inventory is any stored resource that is used to satisfy a current or future need. It is the stock of items held to meet future demand. Raw materials, work-in-process, and finished goods are examples of inventory.

Two basic questions in inventory management are

- ☐ ***How much quantity to order (or produce), and***
- ☐ ***When to place the order (or produce).***

Figure 2.22 : Inventory in an Organisation

From the above the following points stand out with reference to inventory:

- All organizations engaged in production or sale of products hold inventory in one form or other.
- Inventory can be in complete state or incomplete state.

- Inventory is held to facilitate future consumption, sale or further processing/value addition.
- All inventoried resources have economic value and can be considered as assets of the organization.

The nature of inventory depends upon the type of business activity of the firm. For example, a manufacturing firm carries raw material, some purchased or sub-contracted parts, work in progress, and finished goods. It may also carry tools, spare parts, etc., for the next few weeks. For example, a hospital keeps a reasonable stock of medicines, life saving injections, operation and surgical equipments, hospital ward including beds, etc. Even housewives prefer to keep some food-stock in reserve. This is nothing but inventory. A major reason to maintain inventory is that it acts as a buffer so that the intermediate processes do not stop. A major reason to maintain inventory is to keep the operations going without interruptions due to shortages of material. In-process inventory acts as a buffer so that the intermediate processes do not stop due to shortages of material. Finished item inventory is the item ready for consumption by the consumers.

Different Types of Inventory

Inventory of materials occurs at various stages and departments of an organization. A manufacturing organization holds inventory of raw materials and consumables required for production. It also holds inventory of semi-finished goods at various stages in the plant with various departments. Finished goods inventory is held at plant, finished goods, stores, distribution centers etc. Further both raw materials and finished goods those that are in transit at various locations also form a part of inventory depending upon who owns the inventory at that particular juncture. Finished goods inventory is held by the organization at various stocking points or with dealers until it reaches the market and end customers.

Besides raw materials and finished goods, organizations also hold inventories of spare parts to service the products. Defective products, defective parts and scrap also form a part of inventory as long as these items are inventoried in the books of the company and have economic value.

The different types of inventory are

- Raw material
- Semi finished goods
- Bought out components
- Spare parts
- Obsolete
- Waste, scrap and rejects

Need for Inventory:

Inventory control is necessary to ensure.

(a) Uninterrupted supply of materials.

(b) Optimal stock. (Not too much, not too little)

(c) Adequate controls over materials un-used, used.

Functions of Inventory

Despite being blocked capital, certain level of inventory is desirable in most of the situations. This is for the following reasons:

1. ***Inventory is required to meet the anticipated demand*** - Customer generally does purchasing without any pre-information to the seller or producer. Many times, he is undecided about the model, make or quantity of the purchase. He would like to see the performance of all the available models. After judging his need and expenditure, he would select one piece. It is almost impossible to know how many pieces of a product would be needed each day. Therefore, inventory serves as a buffer to the anticipated demand.
2. ***Inventory guards against stock-out situations*** - There could be many exogenous factors due to which the arrival of raw material may be delayed. Inventory works as the safety stock for such situations.
3. ***Inventory ensures smooth flow of production process*** - Satisfaction of customer is dependent on the timely availability of finished goods and spare-parts. Inventory plays an important role in it.
4. ***Inventory management is a high priority area in industry or service sector*** - This is due to conflicting role of inventory. For example, the salesman wants high level of inventory to keep the promises and quick delivery. On the other hand, warehousing people of the same industry will prefer lower finished goods inventory so that less storage space is needed.

Reasons for Keeping Inventories

1. ***To stabilize production:*** The demand for an item fluctuates because of number of factors, e.g., seasonality, production schedule etc. The inventories should be made available to the production as per the demand failing which results in stock out and the production stoppage takes place for want of materials. Hence, the inventory is kept to take care of this fluctuation so that the production is smooth.
2. ***To take advantages of price discounts:*** Usually the manufacturers offer discount for bulk buying and to gain this price advantage that materials are bought in bulk even though it is not required immediately. Thus, inventory is maintained to gain economy in purchasing.
3. ***To meet the demand during the replenishment period:*** The lead time or procurement of materials depends upon many factors like location of the source, demand supply condition, etc. So inventory is maintained to meet the demand during the procurement period.
4. ***To prevent loss of orders (sales):*** In this competitive scenario, one has to meet the delivery schedules at 100 per cent service level, means they cannot afford to miss the delivery schedule which may result in loss of sales. To avoid this, organizations have to maintain inventory.

5. ***To keep pace with changing market conditions:*** The organizations have to anticipate the changing market sentiments and they have to stock materials in anticipation of non-availability of materials or sudden increase in prices.

6. ***Other reasons:*** Sometimes the organization have to stock materials due to other reasons like suppliers minimum quantity condition, seasonal availability of materials or sudden increase in prices.

Inventory Control

Inventory control is defined as the scientific method of providing the right type of material at the right time in the right quantities for the right price to sustain the given production schedule. Inventory control aims at keeping track of inventories. It is the technique of maintaining stocks of desired quality and quantity to be made available to different departments as and when they are needed.

It is important to note that:

(i) Inventory serves as the buffer or safety against ill-planning, sudden demand, continuous production, etc.

(ii) Any form of excess inventory is a sign of inefficiency. The trend today is to go for minimum inventory.

The level of inventory may be reduced by:

(a) Better planning

(b) Continuous monitoring of stock

(c) Reliable vendors

(d) Use of Just-in-Time (JIT) concepts

(iii) Reduced level of inventory is a direct saving in the operational cost of the plant. Fewer inventories also occupy less storage space and less records of stock in the store. Lesser inventory is desirable as this is an opportunity cost, which may be reduced by better planning and control. If inventory is less, there would be fewer chances of theft and loss in store.

Need for Inventory Control:

It is an established fact that through the practice of scientific inventory control, the stocks can be reduced anywhere between 10 percent to 40 percent. The need for inventory control in the organizations is mainly due to the benefits derived such as:

1. Improvement in customer relationship because of the timely delivery of goods and services.

2. Smooth and uninterrupted production and hence no stock out.

3. Efficient utilization of working capital.

4. Helps in minimizing loss due to deterioration, obsolescence and damage.

5. Economy in purchasing.
6. Eliminates the possibility of duplicate ordering.

Inventory Control Tools and Techniques

- EOQ- analysis of cost factors- ordering cost, carrying cost, over stocking cost, under stocking cost etc.
- Re order level
- Lead time analysis
- Forecasting techniques
- Material requirement planning
- Selective inventory controls such as ABC, HML, XYZ, VED, FSN, SDE, GOLF, SOS etc.

Costs associated with Inventory

- Ordering costs/or Set up cost/ Procurement cost
- Holding cost / Inventory carrying cost
- Over stock cost
- Stock out cost/ Shortage cost/ Under stocking cost

Unit Cost of Inventory

Unit cost of inventory is the price, which is paid to the supplier for procuring one unit of the inventory. For parts manufactured inhouse, cost of inventory is the direct manufacturing cost. The unit cost of inventory may be independent of quantity of inventory produced. In this case, unit cost of inventory is irrelevant for the inventory models. This is because the decision regarding how much to order and when to order is independent of the unit cost of inventory.

In some situations, the unit cost of inventory is dependent upon the quantity of inventory. For example, on a bulk purchase, some quantity discount is offered. Quantity discount means that if inventory is purchased in bulk, it is available at a price lower than the normal unit price. In such cases, the cost of inventory affects the decisions regarding when and how much to order. Therefore, in quantity discount model, cost of inventory is considered in the inventory models.

Ordering costs / Set up cost / Procurement cost

- The costs incurred in processing an order includes procurement cost, handling costs, transportation and receiving costs, inspectional testing cost, stationary costs, cost of source development etc. This is the cost associated with the placement of an order for the acquisition of inventories. The expenses, incurred in the purchase department, are its main constituents. Salary of purchase dept, postages bills, telephone, stationary and follow-up measures by the purchase department are clubbed together to determine ordering cost.

If the firm can determine the cost of one set-up or one order, $C_{0.}$ it can determine its annual setup/order cost by multiplying the cost of one set-up by the number of set-ups made or orders placed annually. Suppose a firm has an annual demand (D) of 1,000 units. If the firm orders 100 units (Q) every time it places and order, the firm will obviously place 10 orders per year (D / Q). Hence, annual set-up/order cost can be expressed as C_0 (D / Q).

Cost of procurement and inbound logistics costs form a part of ordering cost. Ordering cost is dependant and varies based on two factors – The cost of ordering excess and the cost of ordering too less. Both these factors move in opposite directions to each other. Ordering excess quantity will result in carrying cost of inventory, whereas ordering less will result in increase of replenishment cost and ordering costs.

Holding costs / Inventory carrying costs

- It includes expenses incurred due to interest on money invested in inventory, storage space cost, depreciation cost, wastages, obsolescence and insurance costs etc. Some examples of holding costs are building rent or depreciation, building operating cost, taxes on building, insurance on building, material handling equipment leasing or depreciation, equipment operating cost, handling manpower cost, taxes on inventory, insurance, etc.

Holding costs are the costs associated with holding or "carrying" inventory over time. Holding costs are incurred due to maintaining an inventory level in the organization. Inventory in excess of current demand frequently means that its holder must provide a place for its storage when not in use. This could range from a small storage area near the production line to a huge warehouse or distribution center. A storage facility requires personnel to move the inventory when needed and to keep track of what is stored and where it is stored. If the inventory is heavy or bulky, forklifts may be necessary to move it around. Storage facilities also require heating, cooling, lighting, and water. The firm must pay taxes on the inventory, and opportunity costs occur from the lost use of the funds that were spent on the inventory. Also, obsolescence, pilferage (theft), and shrinkage are other problems. All of these things add cost to holding or carrying inventory.

If the firm can determine the cost of holding one unit of inventory for one year, $C_{s,}$ it can determine its annual holding cost by multiplying the cost of holding one unit by the average inventory held for a one-year period. Average inventory can be computed by dividing the amount of goods that are ordered every time an order is placed (Q) by two. Thus, average inventory is expressed as Q /2. Annual holding cost, then, can be expressed as C_s (Q /2).

Over stocking cost

- This cost is basically due to investment in inventory for longer period than necessary. The demand for the item has terminated.

Shortage cost or under stocking or Stock out cost

- This cost is due to non availability of the item when there is demand for the item. The cost of not carrying inventory at the time required is called stock out cost.

  When there is a stock-out situation, the customer demand is not satisfied. In case of raw material or work in progress shortages, the production gets disrupted. This causes loss due to emergency purchase. Unsatisfied customer results in loss of goodwill and lost-sale. The lost-sale may be due to two reasons: (1) the customer may postpone or drop the idea to purchase and (2) the customer may go to another producer of similar product/services.

Purchasing Cost

Purchasing cost is simply the cost of the purchased item itself. If the firm purchases a part that goes into its finished product, the firm can determine its annual purchasing cost by multiplying the cost of one purchased unit (*C*) by the number of finished products demanded in a year (*D*). Hence, purchasing cost is expressed as *CD*.

2.5.3 ECONOMIC ORDER QUANTITY

Economic order quantity is the level of inventory that minimizes the total inventory holding costs and ordering costs. It is one of the oldest classical production scheduling models. The framework used to determine this order quantity is also known as Wilson EOQ Model or Wilson Formula. The model was developed by F. W. Harris in 1913. But still R. H. Wilson, a consultant who applied it extensively, is given credit for his early in-depth analysis of the model.

EOQ also known as economic lot size or standard order quantity is the amount of material procured or quantity procured during one production run by an enterprise which can be ordered reasonably and economically at a time. EOQ refers to that quantity for which the sum of both the ordering and inventory carrying cost is minimum. From the figure the ordering cost and the inventory carrying cost are shown with respect to quantity per order. Total cost is calculated by adding carrying cost and ordering cost. Total cost is minimum at the point A and thus A^1 represents the EOQ or Economic lot size.

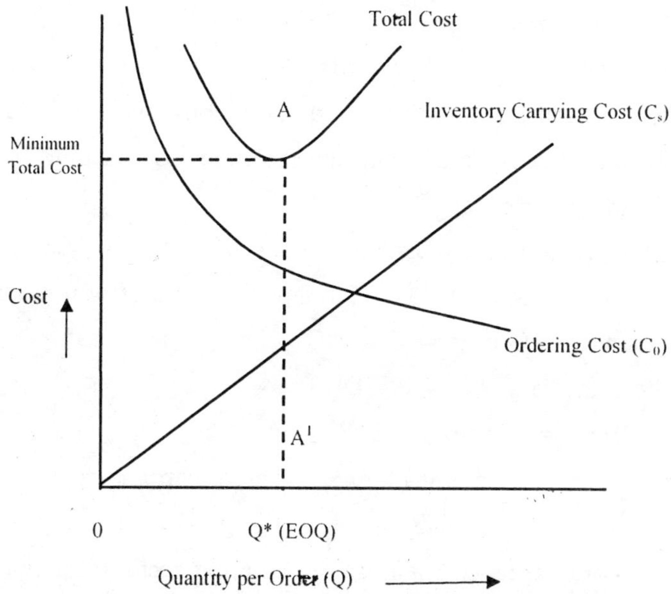

Figure 2.23 : Graph Representation of EOQ

- In this graph, economic order quantity or the optimal order quantity (Q*) occurs at a point where ordering cost (setup cost) is equal to the total (annual) holding cost (carrying cost).
- The total cost is minimum when ordering cost is equal to the total (annual) holding cost (carrying cost)

There are a number of assumptions that must be made with the use of the EOQ. These include:

- Only one product is involved.
- Deterministic demand (Demand 'D' is assumed to be known with certainty).
- Constant demand (demand is stable through-out the year).
- The size of each order is constant
- The ordering cost 'C_0' is assumed to be linearly selected to no. of orders.
- No quantity discounts.
- Constant costs (no price increases or inflation).

While these assumptions would seem to make EOQ irrelevant for use in a realistic situation, it is relevant for items that have independent demand. This means that the demand for the item is not derived from the demand for something else (usually a parent item for which the unit in question is a component). For example, the demand for steering wheels would be derived from the demand for automobiles (dependent demand) but the demand for purses is not derived from anything else; purses have independent demand.

Derivation of EOQ Formula

Let C_o = Ordering cost or cost per order

D = Total quantity ordered in period under consideration (Total demand in time't')

C_s = Inventory carrying cost per unit (Storage cost per unit)

Q = Quantity per order (Order size)

C = Cost per unit of item ordered

Let quantity (or) order size be 'Q'. Then in time't' the no. of order to be placed = D/Q

Total ordering cost for D/Q order= C_o x D/Q

(Cost of D units at the rate of C = C x D)

Mathematically Average inventory = Q/2

Inventory carrying cost =Ave. inventory x Inventory carrying cost/unit

= C_s x Q/2

Min. Total cost T= Ordering cost +Inventory carrying cost+ (Material cost)

Min. Total cost= C_o x D/Q+ C_s x Q/2 [+C x D]

To find the value of Q for which total cost is minimum.

Differentiate total cost 'T' with respect to Q and put it equal to zero.

$$\frac{dT}{dQ} = \frac{d}{dQ}(DC_s / 2)$$

$$O = D \times C_0 / Q^2 \times C_s / 2$$

$$Q^2 = 2DC_0 / C_s$$

$$Q = \sqrt{2DC_0 / C_s}$$

$$\text{Thus, EOQ} = \sqrt{\frac{2 \times \text{Total Quantity order in the period (D)} \times \text{Ordering cost } (C_0)}{\text{Inventory carrying cost per unit } (C_s)}}$$

Finding EOQ under different situations

EOQ when replenishment (Supply of items to inventory is instantaneous)

There is no time lag between placement of an order and supply. This is the most ideal situation.

Problem 2.10

Find EOQ for the following data

Average annual demand =30,000 units

Inventory carrying cost = 12% of the unit value per year

Cost of placing an order = Rs. 70

Cost per unit = Rs. 2

Solution:

D= 30,000, C_o = 70, C_s = 2 x 12/100 = 0.24

$$Q = \sqrt{2DC_0 / C_s}$$

$$= \sqrt{2 \times 30{,}000 \times 10 / 0.24}$$

$$= 4183 \text{ Units}$$

Problem 2.11

A company uses annually 12,000 units of raw material costing Rs. 1.25 per unit. Placing each order costs Rs.15. Carrying costs are 15% per year per unit of average inventory. Find EOQ.

Solution:

D = 12,000

C_o = Rs. 15

C_s = 1.25 x 15/100 = 0.1875

C = 1.25

$$Q = \sqrt{2DC_o/C_s}$$

$$= \sqrt{2 \times 12{,}000 \times 15/0.1815}$$

$$= 1385 \text{ units}$$

Problem 2.12

The annual requirement of a company is estimated at 12,000 units and ordering costs are Rs. 50 per order. In addition to Rs. 1, the carrying costs are 10% per unit of average inventory per year. The purchase price per unit is Rs. 10. Find EOQ and minimum total cost.

Solution :

C_o = 50

C_s = 10/100 x 10+1 =2

D = 12,000

$$EOQ = \sqrt{2DC_0 / C_s}$$

$$= \sqrt{2 \times 12{,}000 \times 0.50 / 2}$$

$$= 775 \text{ units}$$

Minimum Total cost = C_o x D/Q + C x D + C_s x Q/2

= 50 + 12000/775 + 10 x 12000 + 2 x 775/2

= 774 + 12000 + 775

= 1,21,549 Rs.

Problem 2.13

The XYZ Manufacturing Company has determined from an analysis of its accounting and production data for part number 6, 25 that it's cost to purchase is Rs. 36 per order and Rs. 2 per piece. Its inventory carrying cost is 18% of the average inventory. Demand of this part is 10,000 units per annum.

1. What is EOQ
2. What is optimum number of days supplied for order

Solution:

D = 10,000 per annum

C_o = Rs. 36

C_s = 18/100 x 2= 0.36

$$EOQ = \sqrt{2D \times C_0 / C_s} = \sqrt{2 \times 10{,}000 \times 36 / 0.36} = 1414 \text{ units}$$

No. of days for optimum order

No. of orders for 10,000 units per year:

No. of orders per year=D/Q =10,000/1414=7.072

7.072 orders ——365 days

1 order ————?

1/7.072 x 365= 52 days for optimum order

Problem 2.14

The XYZ Company requires 1000 components per month throughout the year for manufacturing automobile generators. Ordering cost is Rs. 25 per day. Unit cost is Rs. 2.50 per component and annual inventory holding cost are charged at 20%. Find EOQ for this component. If the company decides to operate with a back order inventory policy, then taking backorder cost to be Rs. 5 per unit/year, find the new EOQ.

Note: Back Order: An item ordered but unable to be delivered on which the customer will wait for delivery without cancelling the order.

Solution :

Ordering Cost C_o = Rs. 25 per day

Quantity ordered D = 1000 per month = 12000/year

$$EOQ = \sqrt{2DC_0 / C_5} = \sqrt{2 \times 12{,}000 \times 25 / 0.5} = 1095.44 \text{ units}$$

C_1 = Rs. 5

$$\text{New EOQ} = \sqrt{2 \times 12{,}000 \times 25 / 0.5\,(0.5 + 5) / 8}$$

$$= 1149 \text{ units}$$

EOQ when quantity discounts or price breaks are available

$$Q = \sqrt{2DC_0 / C_s}$$

and $T = C_0 \times D / Q + C_s \times Q / 2$

Note : Quantity Discount :

It is the reduction for regular price given by the supplier in return for purchase of large quantities. In this case a balance is to be made between the benefits of discounts and extra stock holding costs. We should compare before and after discount cost of inventory and decide whether the offer should be accepted or not.

Problem 2.15

A manufacturer requirement for raw material is 2000 units per year. The ordering cost is Rs. 10 per order while carrying costs are 19 paisa per unit of average inventory. The purchase price is Re 1/unit. Find EOQ and total inventory cost.

If a discount of 5% is available for orders of 1000 units, should the manufacturer accept this offer? (The carrying cost remains at 16 paisa per unit)

Solution:

$D = 2000$

$C_0 =$ Rs. 10 per order

$C_s = 0.16$ Rs per unit

$EOQ = \sqrt{2DC_0 / C_s} = \sqrt{2 \times 2000 \times 10 / 0.16 \times 1} - 500$

Total Inventory cost $= C_0D/Q + CD + C_s/2 = 10 \times 2000/500 + 1(2000) + 0.16(500/2)$

$= 40 \times 2000 + 40 =$ Rs. 2080

For a discount of 5%

$C_s = 0.16$

$Q = 1000$

$C = 1 - 0.05 = 0.95$

$C_o =$ Rs. 10

Total inventory cost $= C_0 \times D/Q + CD + C_s \times Q/2$

$= 10 + 2000/1000 + 0.95\ (2000) + 0.16\ (1000/2)$

$= 20 + 1900 + 80 = 2000$

Since the total inventory cost is less in second case, we accept the offer.

Reorder Level

The level of inventory at which a reorder should be placed is known as reorder level or reorder point. To place a reorder, the level of inventory should be determined. The best alternative to place an order is before the completion of the stocks.

Reorder level = Maximum Reorder Period × Rate of Consumption

Reorder level = Lead Time × Demand Rate

Max Stock limit : It represents the quantity of material allowed to be kept in store at any time.

Min Stock Limit : It represents the lowest quantity of store below which the stock is not allowed to fall under normal conditions.

Danger level : It is the level below which the stock of material is never allowed to fall

Formula:

1. Max. Stock Level (Maximum Level) = Reorder Level + Reorder Quantity – (Minimum Consumption × Minimum Reorder Period)
2. Minimum Stock Level (Minimum Level) = Reorder Level - (Normal Consumption × Normal Reorder Period)
3. Reorder Level = Maximum Reorder Period x Rate of Consumption

   = Lead Time × Demand Rate
4. Average Stock Level = Minimum Stock Level + 1/2 Reorder Quantity
5. Danger Level = Average Consumption x Maximum Reorder Period for emergency purchases

Lead Time: It is the time gap between placement of an order and time of actual supply

Lead Time = Servicing time + Delivering time + Receiving time

Lead Time Demand: It is the demand during the lead time period

Buffer Stock or Safety Stock - It is the min. level of inventory to cover some unforeseen or uncalled situation. It is the extra inventory held against the possibility of stock out.

Reorder Level = Maximum Reorder Period (Lead Time) × Rate of Consumption (Demand Rate)

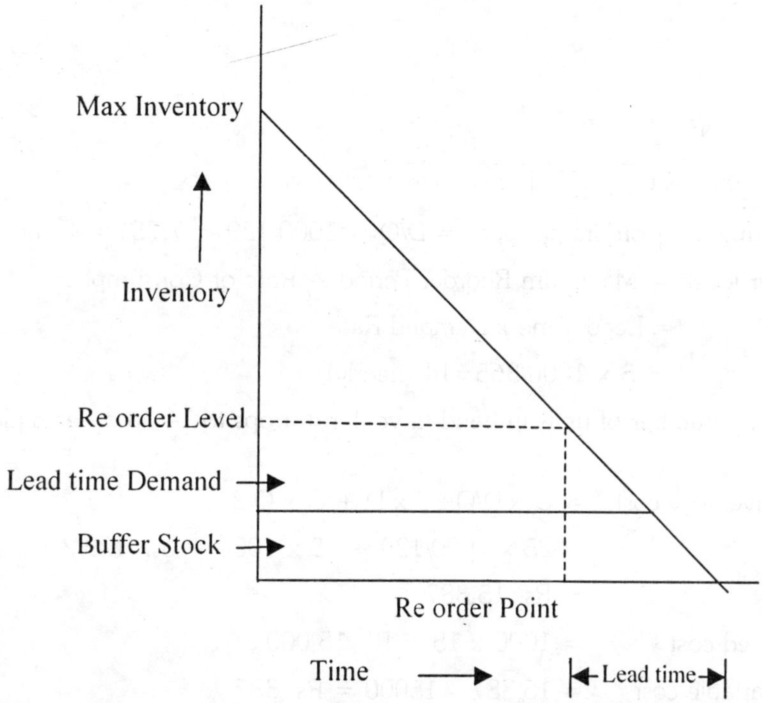

Figure 2.24 : Reorder level, Lead time demand, Buffer stock and Lead time

Determination of Buffer or Safety Stock

1. Situation where demand rate varies

   Buffer stock = Lead Time (Maximum Demand Rate - Average Demand Rate)

2. In case where both lead time and demand rate are fluctuating

   Buffer stock to meet abnormal demand = (Maximum Lead Time x Maximum Demand Rate) - (Average Lead Time x Average Demand Rate)

3. In case lead time varies and demand rate is uniform

   Buffer stock = (Maximum Lead Time – Average Lead Time) x Demand Rate

Problem 2.16

A firm purchases 1000 units of a particular component per year from a vendor at unit cost Rs. 15. The ordering cost is estimated to be Rs. 25 per order and annual carrying cost is taken as Rs. 0.2 per year per rupee of inventory. Lead time of ordering is 5 days. Calculate the following?

1. EOQ
2. Total number of orders per year
3. Reorder level
4. Total variable cost of carrying inventory

Solution:

D = 1000

C_o = Rs. 25

C_s = 0.2 x 15 = Rs. 3

1. $EOQ = \sqrt{2Dc_0 / C_5} = \sqrt{2 \times 1000 \times 25/3} = 129$
2. Total number of orders per year = D/Q = 1000/129 = 7.751 = 8 (nearly)
3. Reorder level = Maximum Reorder Period x Rate of Consumption

   = Lead Time x Demand Rate

   = 5 x 1000/365=14 (nearly)

   When the number of units in hand (inventory) drops to 14 an order is placed for 129 units.
4. Total inventory cost = C_o x D/Q+C x D + C_s x Q/2

   = 25 x 1000/129 + 15 x 1000 + 3 x 129/2

   = Rs. 15,387

   Total fixed cost = 1000 x 15 = Rs. 15,000

   Total variable cost = 15,387 – 15000 = Rs. 387

Problem 2.17

A manufacturing company has determined from analysis of finance and accounting for a certain part that

a. The demand is 9000 units per annum and is uniformly distributed over the year
b. Its cost price is Rs. 2 per unit
c. Its ordering cost Rs. 40 per order
d. The inventory carrying charge is 9% of the inventory value and equal to 8 working days and that the total working days in a year are 300.

Determine

i. EOQ
ii. Optimum number of orders per year
iii. Re –order level
iv. Time of inventory cycle

Solution:

D = 9000

C_o = Rs. 40

C_s = 2 × 9/100 = 0.18

1. $EOQ = \sqrt{2Dc_0 / C_s}$

$$= \sqrt{2 \times 9000 \times 40 / 0.08}$$

$$= \sqrt{2 \times 9000 \times 40 \times 100 / 18}$$

$$= 2000 \text{ units}$$

2. Optimum number of orders per year = D/Q = 9000/2000 = 4.5 orders
3. Reorder Level = Lead Time x Rate of Consumption

   = 8 x 9000/300 = 240

   When the number of units in hand (inventory) drops to 240 an order is placed for 2000 units.
4. Time of inventory cycle = 300/4.5 = 66.7 days

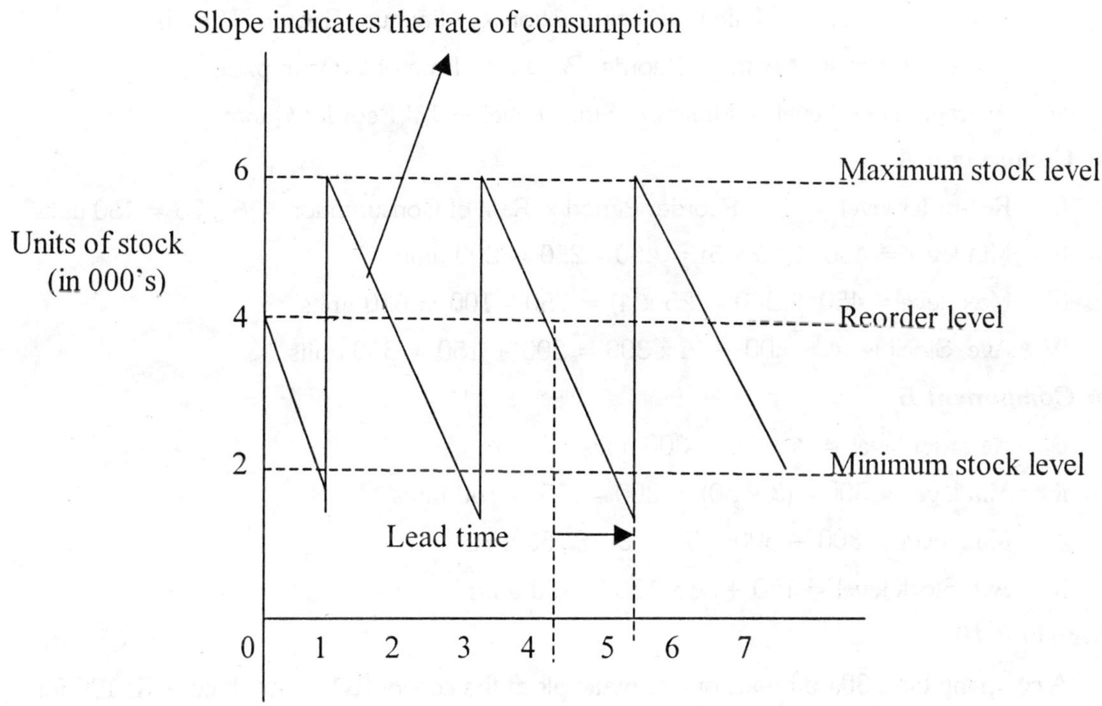

Figure 2.25 : Stock levels, Rate of consumption and Lead time

Problem 2.18

The particulars of two components A and B used in a factory are as follows

Normal Usage = 50 units/ week each

Min Usage = 25 units/week each

Max Usage = 15 units/week each

Re-ordering Quantity = A – 300 units and B- 500 units

Re order period = A - 4-6 weeks and B -2-4 weeks

Calculate for each component

i. Minimum level

ii. Maximum level

iii. Reorder level

iv. Average stock level

Solution:

Formulae:

i. Minimum Level = Reorder Level - (Normal Consumption x Normal Reorder Period)

ii. Maximum Level = Reorder Level + Reorder Quantity – (Minimum Consumption x Minimum Reorder Period)

iii. Reorder Level = Maximum Reorder Period x Rate of Consumption

iv. Average Stock Level = Minimum Stock Level + 1/2 Reorder Quantity

For Component A

I. Re –order level = Max. Reorder Period x Rate of Consumption = 6 x 75 = 450 units

II. Min level = 450 – (50 x 5) = 450 – 250 = 200 units

III. Max. level= 450 + 300 – (25 x 4) = 750 – 100 = 650 units

IV. Ave. Stock level = 200 + ½ x 300 = 200 + 150 = 350 units

For Component B

i. Re order level = 4 x 75 = 300 units

ii. Min level = 300 – (3 x 50) = 300 – 150 = 150 units

iii. Max level = 300 + 500 – (25 x 2) = 750 units

iv. Ave Stock level = 150 + ½ x 150 = 400 units

Problem 2.19

A company buys 30,000 units of raw materials at the cost of Rs10/ unit. It costs Rs 100 for ordering to supply. The holding cost is expected to be Rs. 2 unit. Find EOQ, minimum total cost and maximum inventory.

Solution :

D = 30,000 units

C = 10 Rs.

C_o = 100 Rs.

C_s = 2 Rs.

$$EOQ = \sqrt{2DC_0/C_s} = \sqrt{2 \times 30{,}000 \times 100/2} = 1{,}000 \times 1.732 = 1{,}732 \text{ units}$$

Minimum Total Cost = $C_o \times D/Q + C \times D + C_s \times Q/2$

= 30000/1732 (100) + 10 (30000) + 2 (1732/2)

= 1732 + 3, 00,000 + 1732 = 3, 03464 units

Total Max inventory is nothing but EOQ

Therefore, Max Inventory = 1732 units

Problem 2.20

A diesel engine manufacturing has planned its production schedule for the next year based on forecasting demand, back orders and plant capacities. Instead of manufacturing the piston that goes into the final product, the company has decided to buy the piston from India Pistons Limited. The number of pistons required is at the rate of 60 per day. Ordering costs are estimated to be Rs. 50 per order and carrying cost fraction is 0.15. Also assumptions of basic EOQ model are applicable. The company however can take advantage of one the several quantity discounts. The pricing schedule of India Pistons Ltd is listed as follows.

Quantity order	Unit price (Rs.)
0-1999	65
2000-4999	60
5000- 10,000	55
Over 10,000	50

Assuming 300 working days in a year, determine

i. What is the Optimum order quantity

ii. What is the Min. inventory cost

D = 18,000

C_o= Rs. 50 per order

C_s= 0.15

C = 50

At C =50, EOQ = $\sqrt{2 \times 18{,}000 \times 50/7.5} = 490$

Using the lowest unit price of Rs 50 we get EOQ = 490

But it is not feasible because unit price of Rs. 50 is available only for an order of above 10000 units. Therefore, we try the lowest unit price of Rs. 55

C = 55, EOQ = $\sqrt{2 \times 18{,}000 \times 50/60 \times 0.15} = 467$

With the next lowest unit price of Rs. 55, we get EOQ = 467 units. This again is not feasible.

$C = 60$, EOQ = $\sqrt{2 \times 18{,}000 \times 50/60 \times 0.15} = 447$

With the next lowest unit price of Rs 60, we get EOQ = 447 units. This again is not feasible.

$C = 65$, EOQ = $\sqrt{2 \times 18{,}000 \times 50/65 \times 0.15} = 430$

With unit price of Rs. 65, EOQ =1200. This is a feasible order quantity.

Hence, 430 is a feasible order quantity.

Minimum total cost = $C_o \times D/Q + C \times D + C_s \times Q/2$

= 50 x 18000/430 + 65(18000) + (9.75)430/2

= 2093+11,70,000+2096

= 11,74,189

Now we shall determine the total cost at previous price at Q = 2000, 5000 and 10,000

Minimum total cost = $C_o \times D/Q + C \times D + C_s \times Q/2$

= 50 x 18000/2000 + 60(18000) + 9(2000/2)

=450 + 1080000 + 9000 = 10,89,450

Minimum total cost = 50 x 18000/5000 + 55(18000) + 3.25(5000/2)

= 180 + 990000 + 20625

= 10,10,805.

Minimum total cost = 50 x 18000/10000+50(18000)7.5(10000/2)

= 90 + 90,0000 + 37500

= 9,37,590

i. Optimum order quantity = 10,000 units and above.

ii. Minimum inventory cost= 9,37,590 Rs.

The cost calculations show that the total cost is minimum when an order of 10,000 units is placed. Therefore,

a. Optimal order size = 10,001 units (the order size should be greater than 10,000 to avail the unit price of Rs. 50)

b. The min inventory cost = Rs. 9,37,590

2.5.4 ABC ANALYSIS

ABC Analysis (Always Better Control Analysis)

Firms that carry hundreds or even thousands of different part numbers can be faced with the impossible task of monitoring the inventory levels of each part number. In order to facilitate this, many firm's use an ABC approach. ABC analysis is based on Pareto Analysis, (Italian Economist Wilfred Pareto's Law) also known as the "80/20" rule. The 80/20 comes from Pareto's finding that 20 percent of the populace possessed 80 percent of the wealth. ABC Analysis is similar to the

Pareto principle in that the "A class" group will typically account for a large proportion of the overall value but a small percentage of the overall volume of inventory. This is a type of Pareto analysis and is referred to as Always Better Control approach. The idea is to focus resources on the critical few and not on the trivial many. ABC analysis is the widely used approach for classifying the inventories on the basis of cost and use.

ABC analysis is a business term used to define an inventory categorization technique often used in materials management. It is also known as Selective Inventory Control. ABC analysis provides a mechanism for identifying items which will have a significant impact on overall inventory cost whilst also providing a mechanism for identifying different categories of stock that will require different management and controls

When carrying out an ABC analysis, inventory items are valued (item cost multiplied by quantity issued / consumed in period) with the results and then ranked. The results are then grouped typically into three classes. These classes are called ABC items.

From an inventory perspective: approximately 20 percent of all inventory items represent 80 percent of inventory costs. Therefore, a firm can control 80 percent of its inventory costs by monitoring and controlling 20 percent of its inventory. But, it has to be the correct 20 percent. The top 20 percent of the firm's most costly items are termed "A" items (this should approximately represent 80 percent of total inventory costs). Items that are extremely inexpensive or have low demand are termed "C" items, with "B" items falling in between A and C items. The percentages may vary with each firm, but B items usually represent about 30 percent of the total inventory items and 15 percent of the costs. C items generally constitute 50 percent of all inventory items but only around 5 percent of the costs.

By classifying each inventory item as an A, B or C the firm can determine the resources (time, effort and money) to dedicate to each item. Usually this means that the firm monitors A items very closely but can check on B and C items on a periodic basis (for example, monthly for B items and quarterly for C items).

ABC Classification

An important aspect of inventory management is that items held in inventory are not of equal importance in terms of rupees invested, profit potential, sales or usage volume. ABC classification system controls inventories by dividing items into 3 groups A, B and C respectively. The basic reason underlying ABC analysis is to exercise selective control on inventories. For better economic control of items in the inventory, they are classified according to their value and significance in ABC Analysis. In this analysis, the classification of existing inventory is based on annual consumption and the annual value of the items.

Procedural Steps

1. Identify all the items used in the inventory
2. Compute usage value of each item
3. Rank the items in descending order into high usage value medium usage value and low usage value items and group them into three classes A, B, and C

ABC analysis divides on-hand inventory into three classifications.

1. Class ***A*** - Items having 70% of the value of total inventory but which constitute only 10% of the total inventory items are class A items
2. Class ***B*** - Items having 20% of the value of total inventory and also constitute only 20% of the total inventory items are class B items.
3. Class ***C*** - Items having only 10% of the total inventory value but constitute about 70% of the total inventory items are class C items

Table 2.5 : Selective control procedures to be adopted for A B C items

Category	Value (%)	Volume (%)	Degree of Control
A	70	10	Strict
B	20	20	Moderate
C	10	70	Low

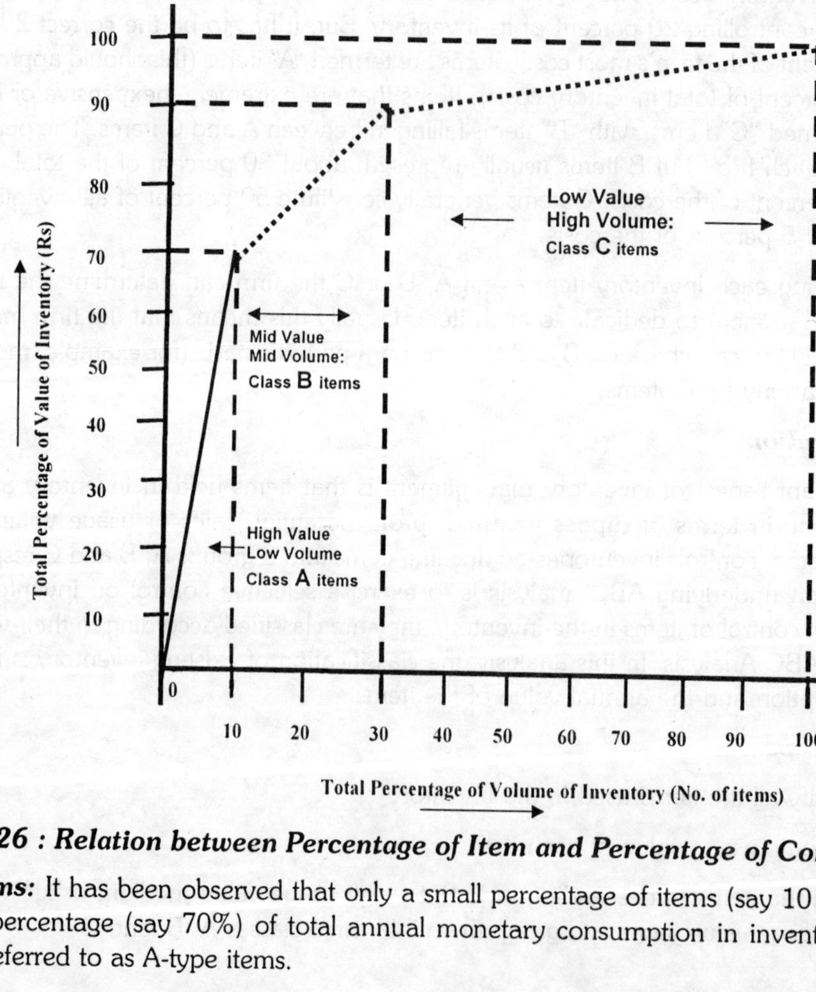

Figure 2.26 : Relation between Percentage of Item and Percentage of Consumption

A items: It has been observed that only a small percentage of items (say 10 %) accounts for major percentage (say 70%) of total annual monetary consumption in inventories. These items are referred to as A-type items.

They are valued but limited in number. This means that their annual consumption is very less but these are very costly items. Despite required less in volume, their annual monetary value is quite high, as these are very costly items. These items need more care and control. Their size of order is based on calculated requirement. A detailed record of their receipt and issue should be kept and proper handling and storage facility should be provided; such items being costly are purchased in small quantity, often and just before their use. Safety stock of less than two weeks may be kept

B items: Items other than A and C type constitute 20-25% in terms of percentage of items and 20 to 25% in terms of their annual consumption value. These are termed as B-type items.

These items cannot be over looked but need lesser degree of control than the A class items. These items being comparatively less costly a safety stock of upto 3 months may be kept. B items also require careful storage and handling.

C items: Majority of the items (say 70%) constitute only a minor fraction of the total annual monetary consumption (say 10%) in inventories. These items are C-type items.

These are low valued items. These items need loose control low records are normally kept and a large safety stock of more than three months may be kept. These items are purchased in large quantities in order to secure purchase discounts and minimize time and money required by clerks, stores, accounts etc. These are the least important items such as pins, clips, washers bolts, nuts etc.,

Different Controls used with different classes

- ***A Items:*** High priority – Tight control including complete accurate records, regular and frequent review by management, frequent review of demand forecast and close follow-up and expediting to reduce lead time.

  "A" items are the most critical ones. These items require tight inventory controls; frequent review of demand forecasts and usage rates; highly accurate part data; and frequent cycle counts to verify perpetual inventory balance accuracy. ABC-analysis recommends careful control of A-type inventory. More periodic review is needed. Involvement of higher level of management is recommended in the review process. A small reduction in the safety stock and EOQ will cause substantial saving for the organizations.

- ***B Items:*** Medium priority – Normal control. Their control and supervision are moderate as compared to A or C type inventories. "B" items are of lesser criticality. These items require nominal inventory controls; occasional reviews of demand forecasts and usage rates; reasonably accurate part data; and less frequent but regular cycle counting.

- ***C Items:*** Lowest priority – Simplest possible control. Perhaps use a two-bin system or periodic review system. Order larger quantities and carry sufficient safety stock. "C" items have the least impact in terms of warehouse activity and financials, and therefore require minimal inventory controls. In fact, depending on the nature of the items, these may be good for free bin stores. Analysis of demand forecasts and usage rates on "C" items is sometimes waived in favor of placing infrequent orders – often in large quantities – to maintain plenty of stock on hand.

The control needed for these items may not be very stringent. Bulk-purchase decisions may be useful as the item cost is less. Therefore, lesser number of orders may be placed. These items may be under the supervision of lower level of management and only exceptional reports or monthly reports are needed by top management.

Applications of ABC Analysis

ABC analysis can be effectively used in material management. It can be applied in various situations and stages such as

- Information of items which require higher degree of control
- Stock records
- Determination of safety stock limits
- Stores layout
- Value Analysis
- To evolve useful re-ordering strategy
- Priority treatment to different items

Steps in Making an ABC Analysis

1. Determine the annual usage for each item
2. Calculate the Annual Usage Value (AUV) of each item
3. List the items according to their AUV (descending order)
4. Calculate the cummulative AUV and the cummulative percentage of items
5. Examine the annual usage distribution and group the items into A, B, C based on percentage of AUV

Table 2.6 : The Control Strategy for ABC items

S. No.	Factors \ Items	A-Type Inventory	B-Type Inventory	C-Type Inventory
1.	Percentage volume	10-20%	20-30%	60-70%
2.	Percentage value	70-85%	10-25%	5-15%
3.	Control	Very close	Moderate	Low
4.	Supervisor	Top management	Middle management	User department
5.	Safety stock	Very-very low	Low	High
6.	Ordering frequency	Frequent	Moderate	Low
7.	Supplier	Staggered but reliable	—	Bulk suppliers
8.	Follow-up report and review	Regular (weekly)	Moderately timed (monthly)	Infrequent (semi-annually)
9.	Forecasting and material planning	Accurate	Moderate	Low quality (rough)
10.	Value engineering effort and waste reduction emphasis	More	Moderate	Less
11.	Type of records	Complete and accurate	Compete and accurate	Simplified

The Advantages of ABC Analysis:

1. ABC analysis helps in reducing clerical costs and result in better planning and improved inventory turnover.
2. A B C analysis helps to rationalise number of orders and reduce average inventory.
3. This kind of categorization of inventory helps to manage the entire volume and assign relative priority to the right category.
4. By controlling 'A' items and doing proper inventory analysis, obsolete stocks are automatically pin pointed.
5. This approach helps the Materials Manager to exercise selective control and focus attention only on a few items.
6. Store personnel are placed better with this analysis i.e. their time can be utilized better.
7. Storing, handling and delivery of materials to production department become better.

Limitations of ABC Analysis

1. ABC analysis, in order to be fully effective, should be carried out with standardization and codification
2. It indicates nothing about their profitability or criticality
3. ABC analysis should be reviewed periodically so that changes in prices product mix and consumption are taken into account.

Problems on ABC Analysis

Problem 2.21

Ten items are kept in the inventory. The details regarding the number of items used per annum and price per unit are given below. Classify the items into A, B and C class

Item No.	*Annual Usage*	*Price*
101	200	40.00
102	100	360.00
103	2000	0.20
104	400	20.00
105	6000	0.04
106	1200	0.80
107	120	100.00
108	2000	0.70
109	1000	1.00
110	80	400.00

***Solution** :*

Compute the Annual Usage Value

Item No.	*Annual Usage Value*	*Rank*
101	200 x 40.00 = 8000	4
102	100 x 360.00= 36000	1
103	2000 x 0.20 = 400	9
104	400 x 20.00 = 8000	5
105	6000 x 0.04 = 8000	10
106	1200 x 0.80 = 960	8
107	120 x 100.00 = 12000	3
108	2000 x 0.70 = 1400	6
109	1000 x 1.00 = 1000	7
110	80 x 400.00 = 32000	2

Item No. Class	Annual Usage	Cum Annual Usage	Cum Usage Value %	% of Item in Class
102	36000	36000	36%	2/10x100=20%
110	32000	68000	68%	A
107	12000	80000	80%	
101	8000	88000	88%	3/10X100= 30%
104	8000	96000	96%	B
108	1400	97400	97.4%	
109	1000	98400	98.4%	
106	960	99360	99.36%	5/10X100 = 50%
103	400	99760	99.76%	C
105	240	100000	100%	

The classification is

Classification	Item Nos.	% of Annual value	% of Item in class
A Class	102, 110	68	20
B Class	107, 101, 104	28	30
C Class	108, 109, 106, 103, 105	4	50

Problem 2.22

Management of a company has the following information about its inventory stock. Find the percentage of items management should place in each class according to the ABC classification method.

Item Number	Annual Usage (Number of Pieces)	Unit Price in Rupees
1	600	20
2	5,600	30
3	60	20
4	2,200	10
5	80	10
6	4,400	20
7	300	10
8	1,600	10
9	1,200	30
10	160	20

Solution:

First step is to calculate annual consumption value and rank them. Afterwards they are arranged in descending order and cumulative percentages are worked out. This is shown in the following two tables. It can be seen that only two items are A class items and 6 are B class items and rest will be C class items.

Item Number	*Cumulative Percentage (Number of Pieces) (2)*	*Unit Price in Rs. (3)*	*Usage Value in Rs. 2 x 3 = (4)*	*Ranking (5)*
1	600	20	12,000	6
2	5,600	30	1,68,000	1
3	60	20	1,200	9
4	2,200	10	22,000	4
5	80	10	800	10
6	4,400	20	8,800	2
7	300	10	3,000	8
8	1,600	10	16,000	5
9	1,200	30	36,000	3
10	160	20	3,200	7

Item Number	*Cumulative Percentage of items*	*Cumulative Usage Value in Rs.*	*Cumulative Percentage of Usage Values*	*Category*
2	10	1,68,000	47.97	**A**
6	20	2,56,000	73.10	
9	30	2,92,000	83.38	
4	40	3,14,000	89.66	
8	50	3,30,000	94.23	**B**
1	60	3,42,000	97.66	
10	70	3,45,200	98.57	
7	80	3,48,200	99.43	
3	90	3,49,400	99.77	**C**
5	100	3,50,200	100.00	

Problem 2.23

The store of an oil engine repair shop has 10 items whose details are shown in the following table. Apply ABC analysis to the store.

Details of Store

Component Code	Description	Price/Unit (Rs.)	Unit/Year (Rs.)
C01	Packing thread	100	100
C02	Tower bolt	200	300
C03	Hexagonal nut	50	700
C04	Bush	300	400
C05	Coupling	500	1000
C06	Bearings (big)	3000	30
C07	Bearing (small)	1000	100
C08	Fuel pump	7000	500
C09	Fixture	5000	105
C10	Drill bit	60	1000

Solution:

The preliminary workings for ABC analysis with the annual consumption for various items are summarized in the below table.

Preliminary Workings

Component Code	Description Component Code	Price/Unit (Rs.)	Unit/Year (Rs.)	Annual Consumption Rs./Year
C01	Packing thread	100	100	10,000
C02	Tower bolt	200	300	60,000
C03	Hexagonal nut	50	700	35,000
C04	Bush	300	400	120,000
C05	Coupling	500	1000	500,000
C06	Bearings (big)	3000	30	90,000
C07	Bearing (small)	1000	100	100,000
C08	Fuel pump	7000	500	3,500,000
C09	Fixture	5000	105	525,000
C10	Drill bit	60	1000	60,000

Rearrange the rows of the table as per the decreasing order of annual consumption (Rs./Yr) and compute the cumulative annual values as shown in the next table.

Final Workings of ABC Analysis

Component Code	Price/Unit (Rs.)	Unit/Year (Rs.)	Annual Consumption Rs./Year	Cumulative Value of Annual Consumption (Rs.)	Class
C08	7000	500	3,500,000	3,500,000	A
C09	5000	105	525,000	4,025,000	
C05	500	100	500,000	4,525,000	B
C04	300	400	120,000	4,645,000	
C07	1000	100	100,000	4,745,000	
C06	3000	30	90,000	4,835,000	
C02	200	300	60,000	4,895,000	C
C10	60	1000	60,000	4,955,000	
C03	50	700	35,000	4,990,000	
C01	100	100	10,000	5,000,000	

The summary of ABC classification from the above table, as per 70% : 20% : 10% of the total consumption value is presented in the below table.

Summary of A, B and C Items

Class	Item Code	Description
A	C08	Fuel pump
B	C09	Fixture
	C05	Coupling
C	C04	Bush
	C07	Bearing (small)
	C06	Bearings (big)
	C02	Tower bolt
	C10	Drill bit
	C03	Hexagonal nut
	C01	Packing thread

2.5.5 SELECTIVE INVENTORY CONTROL TECHNIQUES

The fundamental idea behind selective inventory control technique is to put the efforts where results are worth it. The importance of materials can be due to its costs, its criticality, its availability and its consumption. There are number of methods available for selective control of inventory. Each method emphasizes on a particular aspect. ABC analysis or classification emphasizes on value of consumption. V E D analysis emphasizes criticality of the part. S D E analysis emphasizes on availability etc.

Table 2.7 : Selective Inventory Control Techniques

S. No.	TYPE OF CONTROL	BASIS	MAIN USE
1	**A B C** also known as (Always Better Control or Pareto's Law)	Value of consumption of items concerned (it has nothing to do with unit value of the item)	To control raw materials components and work in progress in normal course of business.
2	**H M L** (High, Medium, Low)	Unit price of the materials (This is opposite to ABC analysis, does not take into account the consumption)	Mainly to control purchases.
3	**X Y Z**	Value of items in storage	To review the inventories, their uses etc. at scheduled intervals
4	**V E D** (Vital, Essential, Desirable)	Criticality of the item	To determine the stocking levels of spare parts.
5	**F S N** (Fast Moving, Slow Moving, Non-Moving)	Consumption of the item	To determine the stocking levels of spare parts.
6	**S D E** (Scarce, Difficult and Easy to obtain)	Problems faced in procurement	Lead time analysis and purchasing strategies.
7	**G O L F** (Government, Ordinary, Local and Foreign Sources)	Source of supply of materials	Procurement strategies
8	**S O S** (Seasonal and Off-Seasonal)	Nature of supplies	Procurement and holding strategies for seasonal items like agricultural products.

HML Analysis

This analysis is similar to ABC analysis but here the criterion is 'price' instead of usage value. The items in this analysis are classified into three groups, i.e., high, low and medium. The management decides the cut off lines or prices for the three categories. This analysis helps to keep control over consumption as per the price and helps to assess storage and security requirements, i.e., the high priced items are to be stored in the cupboards. It helps to outline the buying policies and to delegate authorities to buyers.

This analysis is based on the cost of the item.

H = High Cost Items

M = Medium Cost Items

L = Low Cost Items

SDE Analysis

S.D.E. analysis classifies the items into three groups namely - Scarce, Difficult and Easy. These are based on the problems of procurement.

- Scarce, classification includes items which are in short supply, imported items. Such items are procured once in a year because of effort and expenditure involved in its import.
- Difficult items are those items which are available indigenously but are difficult to procure.
- Easy classification covers those items which are readily available and easy to procure. These are mostly commercially available standard items.

This SDE analysis is applied by purchased department. This classification runs like this:

S = Scarce Items

D = Difficult (to procure) Items

E = Easy (not difficult to get) Items

VED Analysis

This analysis represents classification of items based on criticality. The analysis classifies the items into three groups called vital, essential and desirable.

- Vital items are those items the unavailability of which will stop the production.
- Essential items are those items whose stock out costs is very high.
- Desirable items will not cause any immediate production stoppages and their stock out costs is nominal.

This analysis is mainly carried out to identify critical items. An item which may belong to C-category may be critical from production point of view. The service level for each item may be determined and the inventory can be planned accordingly.

The possible consequences of material stock outs when demand arises form the basis of VED analysis. The cost of shortage depends upon the seriousness of the situation. Items are grouped as V (Vital), E (Essential) and D (Desirable)

Table 2.8 : VED Analysis

Items	*Remarks*	*Strategy*
V	Most critical. High opportunity cost of shortage. Must be available in stock whenever demanded.	Percentage of risk should be quite small. High level of service is called for.
E	Quite critical. Substantial opportunity cost of shortage. Should be available in stock by and large.	Can take a relatively higher risk of shortage.
D	No serious consequences of non-availability. Can be stocked.	Risk that can be taken is even higher.

May be, C class items are vital, and A class items are desirable. Cross-classification is therefore needed giving us distinct groups: first A – V, A – E, A – D, then B – V, B – E, B – D, and last C – V, C – E and C – D. For these groups, the service level can be determined and inventories planned accordingly.

In addition to the intrinsic or market value of materials, which is invested in the materials, there is sometimes a nuisance value to the materials. In ABC analysis, we have seen that annual consumption value: quantity of material consumed and the unit cost plays a vital role. This is to say that ABC analysis deals with the annual consumption value of the item due to their presence and not any other aspect such as the criticality of the material or the nuisance value. The nuisance value is the cost associated with materials due to their absence. Some of the materials are important by their absence and not merely by their presence. In case they are not available, the whole production system may come to a standstill and involve high cost of loss of production.

Here the cost of the item is not the question, but the availability is the matter. The investment in these materials may be small but for non-availability of the item the costs or losses that the company is going to involve will be very high. These are critical items, which are required in adequate quantity.

With the above discussion, we can understand that materials may be classified depending upon their criticality, i.e. on functional bases. The degree of criticality can be stated as whether the material is vital to the process of production or essential to the process of production or desirable for the process of production and this classification is known as VED analysis. V stands for vital, E stands for essential and D stands for desirable items. In addition to the conventional ABC analysis, VED analysis also plays an important role in inventory control.

FSN Analysis

FSN Analysis places the items in three categories: Fast Moving (F), Slow Moving (S) and Non-Moving (N). All the items in the inventory are not required at the same frequency. Some are required regularly, some occasionally and some very rarely. Hence, based on the frequency of requirement, the items are classified in FSN analysis as fast moving, slow moving and non-moving. Inventory policies and models for these three groups are different. Theoretical models have validity for F items with regular consumption. Spares are slow moving (S), and require special management. Disposal policies are designed to control dead-stock.

SHORT QUESTIONS

1. Define production and operations management?
2. State the objectives of production and operations management
3. What are the various merits and demerits of product layout?
4. What are the main objectives of plant layout?
5. What are the different types of plant layouts?
6. Write short notes on product layout and combination layout
7. What do you understand from the terms 'product layout' and 'process layout'

8. What are the objectives of work study?
9. What is meant by method study?
10. State the objectives of method study.
11. What are the various process charts used in method study?
12. Write a short note on flow process chart.
13. What are multiple activity charts? What are the objectives?
14. Define"micro motion study" and state its objectives?
15. Write a short note on flow diagram?
16. What is motion economy?
17. What are advantages of work measurement?
18. What are the objectives of work measurement?
19. What is a "man and machine chart"?
20. Define micro motion study?
21. What is cycle graph and chronocycle graph?
22. What is SIMO chart?
23. What is therbligs?
24. What are the features of quality?
25. What are the uses of inspection?
26. Write briefly about inspection methods.
27. Explain, what is meant by quality control.
28. Define quality control and SQC?
29. List the primary objectives of SQC.
30. How SQC is used to control the 'quality'.
31. What are the advantages and disadvantages of control charts?
32. Name the various types of control charts.
33. Explain briefly X chart and its advantages.
34. Explain briefly R chart and its advantages.
35. What are the advantages of np-chart?
36. What is materials management?
37. Enumerate objectives of materials management.
38. Define functions of material management?

39. What is importance of materials management
40. What is an inventory? What are the types of inventory?
41. What are the reasons for keeping inventories?
42. What are the benefits of inventory control?
43. Explain inventory control system.
44. Write short note on EOQ.
45. Explain ABC Analysis.
46. Define VED analysis.

ESSAY QUESTIONS

1. What is production management and describe its functions?
2. Discuss the role and decisions of production manager
3. Distinguish production function with other functional areas of management
4. What is plant layout? Explain the various principles of plant layout.
5. What general considerations are made in preparing the layout of an industrial concern?
6. How do you classify the different types of layouts? Explain in brief.
7. Give a brief account of fixed position layout, stating its merits and demerits to other types of layouts.
8. Describe a product layout and explain its principle with the help of a neat diagram. What are its advantages and disadvantages?
9. What is plant layout? Write appropriate examples; distinguish between process layout and product layout.
10. Name and describe the various tools and techniques used in layout planning
11. What is fixed position layout and under what conditions do you adopt it? Explain.
12. Define work study. State its objectives and basic procedure
13. What do you mean by work study? Explain the basic procedure involved in method study and work measurement.
14. Differentiate between method study and work measurement.
15. State and explain in brief the steps involved in method study procedure..
16. Briefly describe the various symbols and charts used in method study
17. What is a flow chart? Discuss its utility for method study engineer.
18. Describe briefly "SIMO charts" and state its applications.
19. Distinguish method study and work measurements.

20. a) How can work study and method study enable an organization to improve productivity?
    b) What is SIMO chart?
21. Define work measurement. What are its objectives?
22. Explain the various techniques used in work measurement
23. (a) How is 'standard time' computed

    (b) Write a brief note on "predetermined motion and time systems"
24. What are the steps required in making 'time study'?
25. What is work sampling? Explain the procedure of work sampling
26. Define quality? Discuss the various attributes of quality
27. What is importance of quality control in an industry?
28. What is statistical quality control? Explain with the help of an example. Also point out the circumstances when SQC is a desirable alternative?
29. What is meant by SQC? What are its advantages and benefits?
30. Explain control chart with the help of a figure. Discuss the various types of control charts.
31. What are the advantages of control charts? Differentiate between variable and attribute charts
32. Explain the concepts of SQC and how you can construct control chart for variables.
33. What are the objectives and functions of material management?
34. What are the duties and responsibilities of the materials manager?
35. How will you integrate the various activities of materials management?
36. Give a typical organization structure of materials management department.
37. Discuss the scope and objectives of materials management.
38. (a) Explain the functions of material manager.

    (b) What are the activities that need coordination with other functional areas?
39. Define inventory control. Write the objectives and functions of inventory control.
40. What are the assumptions and basic components of the inventory system? Discuss the significance of each component with the help of a diagram.
41. What is meant by inventory? What is the need for inventory control at different stages of production? What are the different costs involved in maintaining inventory?
42. Explain the important methods of inventory control
43. Briefly discuss the various selective inventory control techniques
44. Discuss briefly the various costs associated with inventory.

45. What is EOQ and describe an example on EOQ? Derive an expression for EOQ.

46. A chemical firm buys 2500 units annually of a particular item from a vendor at a cost of Rs. 3per unit. It has received a price schedule from the vendor which is as follows:

Order Quantity	*Price/Unit*
Less than 500 units	Rs. 3
500 and above	Rs. 2.90
The cost of placing order	Rs. 25 per order
Inventory carrying cost	Rs. 20

What should be the order quantity?

47. Explain ABC analysis and discuss its advantages and limitations

48. Discuss the concept of ABC analysis with the help of a figure and state its applications.

FILL IN THE BLANKS

1. Production can be defined as the process of............. (Conversion of inputs to outputs through the process of transformation)
2. ....refers to a sequence of operations that transform materials from a given state to a desired state. (Production)
3. Plant layout reduces idle......................and idle........................... (Machine time, Man time)
4. Process layout is also known as................................ (Functional Layout)
5. In functional layout, the type of production changes in accordance with........................ (Product)
6. In......................., all the machines are arranged sequentially as required by the particular product. (Product Layout)
7. Process layout is more suitable for.................flow production. (Intermittent)
8. Product layout is employed for .... (Continuous production)
9. The process layout is best suited for .... (Production of small number of non-standardized items)
10. Assembly line balancing is most common type of............... (Line Layout)
11. The type of layout suitable for a hospital is .... (Process Layout)
12. Work study consists of............. and .... (Method study, Work Measurement)
13. ....is mainly concerned with the examination of human work. (Work study)
14. Work study involves the study of both........................and........................ (Method study, Work measurement)
15. Application of techniques to establish time for a qualified worker to carry out a specified job at a defined level of performance is referred to as.......................... (Work measurement)

16. The systematic recording and critical examination of existing and proposed ways of doing work is...... (Method study)
17. Method study is mainly based on..........................whereas the work measurement is based on............................ (Job, time taken to carry out a job)
18. In non fly back stopwatch..........................is present. (Winding knob)
19. Fly back stopwatch is also known as........................ (Decimal minute stop watch)
20. ....is concerned with "The way in which the work is performed". (Method study)
21. The symbol for the event "Transport" is............................ (⇨)
22. Henry Gantt made his best known contribution known as............. (Gantt chart)
23. In milestone chart, every bar shown in .... chart is divided into certain number of milestones. (Gantt)
24. Gilberth is called the Father of Motion study. He devised a system of codifying motions called....................... (Therbligs)
25. The term 'therblig' was proposed by.................. (Gilberth)
26. ....is inspection symbol in process presentation. (Square)
27. SIMO charts are used in micro motion studies which are.......... (Detailed studies of repetitive work)
28. Work study consists of .... (Method and time study)
29. ....is symbol of operation in process presentation. (Circle)
30. The chart which defines the main events sequence wise considering only operation and inspections is called......................... (Outline process chart)
31. The chart which records the activities of the hands of an operator is .... (Two hand process chart)
32. The chart which record one subject in relation to others is known as.......................... (Multiple activity chart)
33. The chart which indicates the routes followed by workers, material or equipment in their execution on a layout diagram is known as .... (Flow diagram)
34. The time taken by a normal worker for a specific task working under moderate condition including allowances is .... (Standard time)
35. The allowance allowed in terms of the time actually taken by the machine operator to perform the operation is............................... (Process allowance)
36. The time that is allowed for the personal needs is (Personnel allowance)
37. The time that is allowed to recover from physical or mental tiresomeness is........................ (Fatigue allowance)
38. When one or more machine are idle in a case where a worker is attending more than one machine, the idle time allowed in this case is.......................... (Interface allowance)

39. SQC stands for................. (Statistical quality control)

40. SPC stands for............... and does control of process through control charts. (Statistical process control)

41. Various types of control charts used are............ and ....charts, and............. (X and R charts, P, C charts)

42. The SQC technique used for incoming inspection of material is called .... (Sampling plans)

43. ....is the application of statistical methods of sampling and tests of significance to ensure that production is under control. (Statistical quality control)

44. Statistical quality control was developed by .... (Walter A. Shewart)

45. Control chart was first developed by........................ (Walter A. Shewart)

46. The characteristics which can be measured are called.............................and which are not measurable are called......................... (Variables, Attributes)

47. Control charts prepared to control variation and standard deviations are.......................... (Control charts for variables)

48. Control charts prepared to control proportion of defective units are........................ (Control charts for attributes)

49. The 'P' chart is used for ....type of data. (Attribute)

50. 'P' chart measures .... (Percentage defective)

51. 'C' chart measures .... (No. of defects)

52. The process of checking the quality of the product whether it meets the standard specified mentioned by the designer or not is .... (Inspection)

53. Inputs that go into the production process are called.............................. (Materials)

54. Materials may consist of raw materials,..................and finished goods. (Work in progress)

55. .... is main objective of material management. (Minimizing the material cost)

56. Materials management helps in reducing.............................. (Materials cost)

57. "To trace the new sources of supply" is the objective of....................... (Materials Management)

58. ....could be raw materials, work-in-progress finished products or spare parts and other indirect materials. (Inventory)

59. "To keep the process continuously running" is the function of............................ (Inventory)

60. The time taken to replenish the stocks is called.................. (Lead time)

61. ....include lubricants and spare parts needed for proper operation, repair and maintenance during manufacturing cycle. (Indirect inventory)

62. The system of providing the right material in the right quantity at the right time is called................ (Inventory control)

63. ....refers to the process whereby the investment in materials and parts carried in stock is regulated within the predetermined limits set in accordance with the inventory policy established by the management. (Inventory control)

64. ....reduces chances of going out of stock. (Inventory control)

65. Inventory control helps in uniform and proper utilization of......................... (Resources)

66. The process of recording stores balances after every receipt and issue is called.................. (Perpetual inventory control)

67. The system of delivery of materials/components immediately before they are due to be processed is called......................... (Just in time)

68. That quantity of order at which the total cost is minimum is called............... (Economic order quantity)

69. ....prescribes the size of the order at right time. (Economic order quantity)

70. ....consists of costs of storage space, insurance and taxes. (Inventory carrying costs)

71. Formula for EOQ: ....
(EOQ= "$2DC_o/C_s$ where D: Annual demand, C_o: Ordering costs, Cs: Carrying costs)

72. EOQ means .... (Economic order quantity)

73. EOQ is criticized because of its...........assumption. (Realistic)

74. Pareto analysis concentrates on........................causes than............................ (Vital few, many trivial)

75. .... items constitutes more costly and valuable items that need close control in ABC analysis. (A)

76. In ABC analysis average usage items are classified into.................category. (B)

77. Reduction in clerical cost and improved inventory turnover are achieved by .... (ABC analysis)

78. ....technique analyzes the distribution of a characteristic by its usage and cost. (ABC analysis)

79. More costly and valuable items are classified as......................... ('A' category)

80. In selective inventory management one of the methodologies used is known as VED analysis. VED stands for................ (Vital, Essential, Desirable)

❖ ❖ ❖

UNIT - III

FUNCTIONAL MANAGEMENT

3.1 ***Human Resource Management***

- 3.1.1 Concept of HRM
- 3.1.2 HRD
- 3.1.3 Personnel Management and Industrial Relations (PMIR)
- 3.1.4 HRM vs. PMIR
- 3.1.5 Nature and scope of HRM
- 3.1.6 Role of HR Manager
- 3.1.7 Basic Functions of HRM
  - 3.1.7.1 Manpower planning
  - 3.1.7.2 Recruitment
  - 3.1.7.3 Selection
  - 3.1.7.4 Placement
  - 3.1.7.5 Induction
  - 3.1.7.6 Training and Development
  - 3.1.7.7 Promotion, Transfer and Separation
  - 3.1.7.8 Wage and Salary Administration
- 3.1.8 Wage Payment Plans
- 3.1.9 Performance Evaluation
- 3.1.10 Job Evaluation
- 3.1.11 Merit Rating

3.2 ***Marketing Management***

- 3.2.1 Nature and Scope of Marketing
- 3.2.2 Benefits of Marketing
- 3.2.3 Marketing Concept / Philosophy
- 3.2.4 Core Marketing Concepts
- 3.2.5 Functions of Marketing

3.1 HUMAN RESOURCE MANAGEMENT

Introduction

Organization means people working together to achieve a specific common purpose/ objective. In fact, group is one of the earliest and most enduring features of human existence on this planet. People love to live and work in groups. That's why the grouping like family, community came into existence. Organization affects the quality of human life. Hence, managing organization means managing HR.

Definition of Leon C Megginson

From the national point of view, human resources are knowledge, skills, creative abilities, talents and attitudes obtained in the population; whereas from the view point of the individual enterprise they represent the total of the inherent abilities, acquired knowledge and skills as exemplified in the talents and aptitude of its employees.

Michael J. Jucius called these resources as human factors which refer to a whole consisting of interrelated, interdependent and interacting physiological, psychological, sociological and ethical components.

Sumantra Ghoshal who is considered as a Management guru says Human Resources is human capital consisting of three types of capital — intellectual capital, social capital and emotional capital.

- Intellectual Capital consists of specialized knowledge, tacit knowledge and cognitive skills, complexity and learning capacity.
- Social capital consists of network of relationships, sociability and trust-worthiness
- Emotional capital consists of self confidence, ambition and courage, risk taking ability and resilience.

Since an organization performs a number of functions to achieve its objectives, it requires human resources of different types which may be categorized on the basis of functional areas like production, marketing, finance. Thus HR across the functional areas may be arranged into top management, middle management, supervisory management and operatives.

HUMAN RESOURCES OF AN ORGANIZATION

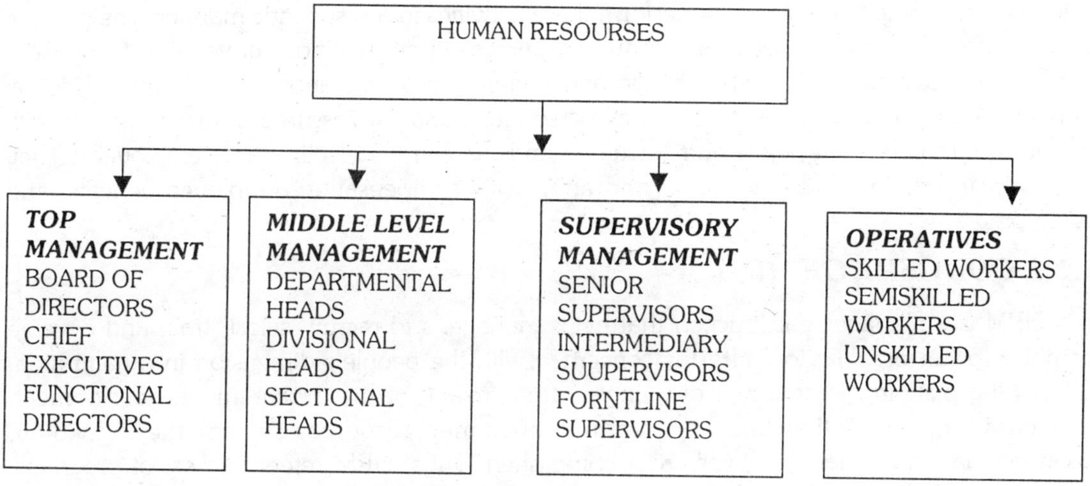

Figure 3.1 : Human Resources of an Organisation

Human Resources Management (HRM) refers to the management of people in the organizations. It comprises of the activities, policies, and practices involved in obtaining, developing, utilizing, evaluating, maintaining, and retaining the appropriate number and skill mix of employees to accomplish the organization's objectives.

The goal of HRM is to maximize employees' contributions in order to achieve optimal productivity and effectiveness, while simultaneously attaining individual objectives such as having a challenging job and obtaining recognition, and societal objectives such as legal compliance and demonstrating social responsibility.

What is Human Resource Management?

Human Resource Management focuses on all issues related to 'people' in the organization. The people in an organization are undoubtedly the most important assets. Therefore special care must be exercised in managing them. Human resource management is concerned with practices involved in the acquisition, development, motivation and maintenance of people. These are essential to achieve the organizational goals.

The people in the organization are instrumental to its success. If human resource management practices are good, then the organization will be effective and efficient. 'Effectiveness' is reflected by the success in goal achievement. 'Efficiency' on the other hand, is reflected by its ability to achieve the output with very little inputs or resources. An organization that is unable to achieve effectiveness or efficiency will eventually die. Survival is dependent on the human resource manager's competence to coordinate the activities of all people in the organization.

Human Resource Management can be termed as the process of acquiring, training, developing, motivating, and appraising a sufficient quantity of qualified employees to perform the activities necessary to accomplish organizational objectives; and developing specific activities and an overall organizational climate to generate maximum worker satisfaction and employee efficiency. While the owner-manager of a small organization is likely to assume complete responsibility for human resource management, larger organizations use company specialists called human resource managers to perform these activities in a systematic manner. The position is becoming increasingly important because of increased competition, government intrusion, emphasis on cost control, complex wage and benefit programs, and a changing work force. Human resource managers, also known as personnel managers, assume primary responsibility for forecasting personnel needs and recruiting and helping in selecting new employees. They also assist in training and evaluation, and administer compensation, employee benefits, and safety programs.

3.1.1 CONCEPT OF HRM

HRM is a management function that helps manager's to recruit, select, train and develop members for an organization. HRM is concerned with the people's dimension in organization. HRM is the planning, organizing, directing and controlling of the procurement, development, compensation, integration and maintenance of human resources so that the individual, organizational and social objectives are accomplished. Thus, HRM refers to a set of programs, functions and activities designed and carried out in order to maximize both employee as well as organizational effectiveness.

HRM is a broad concept whereas Personnel Management (PM) and Human Resource Development (HRD) are part of HRM.

Objectives of HRM:

The basic objective of HRM is to ensure the availability of a competent and willing workforce to an organization. HRM objectives are four fold

1. ***Societal:*** To be ethically and socially responsible to the needs and challenges of the society.
2. ***Organizational:*** To recognize the role of HRM in bringing about organizational effectiveness.
3. ***Functional:*** To maintain department's contribution at a level appropriate to the organization's needs.
4. ***Personal:*** To assist employees in achieving their personal goals.

Table 3.1 : HRM Objectives and its related Supporting Functions

HRM Objectives	Supporting Functions
1. ***Societal objectives***	Legal Compliance Benefits Safety Reservations Union-Management Relations
2. ***Organizational objectives***	HR Planning Recruitment Selection Training And Development Performance Appraisal Placement
3. ***Functional objectives***	Appraisal Placement Assessment
4. ***Personal objectives***	Training And Development Performance Appraisal Placement Compensation Assessment

Other Objectives of HRM:

i. To create and utilize an able work force to accomplish the basic organizational goals.

ii. To establish and maintain sound Structure and desirable working relationships among all the members of the organization.

iii. To secure the integration of individual and groups with the organization to achieve goals.

iv. To create facilities and opportunities for individual and group development.

v. To utilize HR efficiency

vi. To establish a fair compensation policy.

vii. To maintain morale and motivate HR.

viii. To strengthen the organization by innovative HRD programs.

ix. Assisting the organization in obtaining the right number and type of employees to fulfill its strategic and operational goals.

x. Helping to create a climate in which employees are encouraged to develop and utilize their skills to the fullest.

xi. Helping to maintain performance standards and increase productivity through effective job design; providing adequate orientation, training and development; providing performance-related feedback; and ensuring effective two-way communication.

xii. Helping to establish and maintain a harmonious employer–employee relationship.

xiii. Helping to create and maintain a safe and healthy work environment

xiv. Developing programs to meet the economic, psychological, and social needs of the employees

xv. Ensuring that the organization is in compliance with provincial/territorial and federal laws affecting the workplace.

Classification of HRM Functions:

The functions can be broadly classified into two categories

1. ***Managerial functions:***
   a. Planning
   b. Organizing
   c. Leading
   d. Controlling
2. ***Operative functions:***
   a. Procurement
   b. Development
   c. Maintenance
   d. Separation

Two Perspectives on Human Resource Management:

1. Narrow sense : In a narrow sense, it refers to the functions and operations of a single department in a firm: the human resource or personnel department. Most firms with 200 or more employees establish a separate department with the responsibility and authority for selecting and training personnel.

2. Broader sense : In a broader sense, human resource management involves the entire organization. Even though a special staff department exists, general management is also involved in training and developing workers, evaluating their performance, and motivating them to perform as efficiently as possible. The core responsibilities of human resource management are the following:

- Human resource planning
- Recruitment and selection
- Training and management development
- Performance appraisal
- Compensation and employee benefits.

Why is Human Resources Management important to all Engineers and Managers?

Managers and Engineers at all levels are concern themselves with HRM, since they all meet their goals through the efforts of others, which requires the effective management of people. Every supervisor and manager has responsibilities related to a wide range of HRM activities. These include analyzing jobs, planning labour needs, selecting employees, orienting and training employees, managing compensation, communicating and maintaining employee commitment.

They also include ensuring fair treatment, appraising performance, ensuring employee health and safety, building and maintaining good employee/labour relations, handling complaints and grievances, and ensuring compliance with human rights, occupational health and safety, labour relations, and other legislations affecting the workplace. Regardless of field of expertise, learning about employee rights, employer responsibilities, and effective HRM practices is essential for every engineer and manager to perform more effectively.

The Role of the Human Resources Department:

The primary role of the HR department is to ensure that the organization's human resources are utilized effectively and managed in compliance with company policies and procedures, government legislation and collective agreements signed with the unions. To effectively utilize the HR department's assistance and services, all managers should be familiar with its role.

HR department staff members are involved in five distinct types of activities: formulating policies and procedures, offering advice, providing services, monitoring to ensure compliance, and serving as consultant and change agent.

i. ***Formulating Policies and Procedures***

The head of the HR department usually plays a leadership role in initiating and formulating HR policies and procedures that are consistent with overall organizational objectives. These must also be compatible with current economic conditions, collective bargaining trends, and applicable employment legislation.

To maximize effectiveness, HR policies and procedures should be put into writing; they are often compiled in a policy manual or made available online so that they are readily accessible. This helps to ensure that the same information is communicated to all employees, and that there is consistency in employee treatment.

ii. ***Offering Advice:***

In order to cope with increasingly complex HR issues and the ever-changing work environment, managers at all levels frequently turn to the HR department staff for expert advice and counsel. Members of the HR department are expected to be completely familiar with employment legislation, HR policies and procedures, collective agreements, past practices, and the outcome of recent arbitration hearings and court decisions, so that they can provide sound guidance and suggest solutions.

When assisting managers throughout the firm, the HR department staff members must keep their employee advocacy role in mind. This means balancing the department's primary obligation to senior management with the need to ensure that:

(1) Managers understand how they are expected to treat employees,

(2) Employees have mechanisms to contest practices that they perceive to be unfair and

(3) Employees interests are fairly represented when providing guidance and advice.

iii. Providing Services:

The HR department generally provides services in the following areas on an ongoing basis: maintenance of HR records; recruitment, selection, orientation, training and development; compensation and benefits administration; employee counseling and labor relations.

iv. Monitoring to Ensure Compliance

The HR department staff members are generally responsible for monitoring to ensure compliance with established HR policies and procedures. They may analyze data pertaining to absenteeism and turnover or accident rates, for example, to identify problems with policy implementation or failures to comply with specified procedures.

In addition, the HR department staff members play a major role in ensuring compliance with employment legislation. For example, they are generally responsible for collecting and analyzing recruitment, selection, and promotion data to monitor compliance with human rights and employment equity legislation. They also assess salary and benefits data to monitor compliance with employment standards and pay equity requirements, and examine accident investigation and grievance reports to monitor compliance with health and safety and labor relations legislation.

v. Serving as Consultant and Change Agent:

In most firms, HR department staff members serve as in-house consultants to the managers of other departments. Sometimes, HR department staff will recommend using outside consultants for assistance in solving HR issues or handling specialized assignments, such as executive recruitment and job evaluation, or suggest that certain functions or activities be outsourced.

Outsourcing, the practice of contracting with outside vendors to handle specified functions on a permanent basis, has emerged as a worldwide business megatrend.

For better understanding of HR Department, a typical structure of HR Department in a medium and large-sized manufacturing organisation were presented here under :

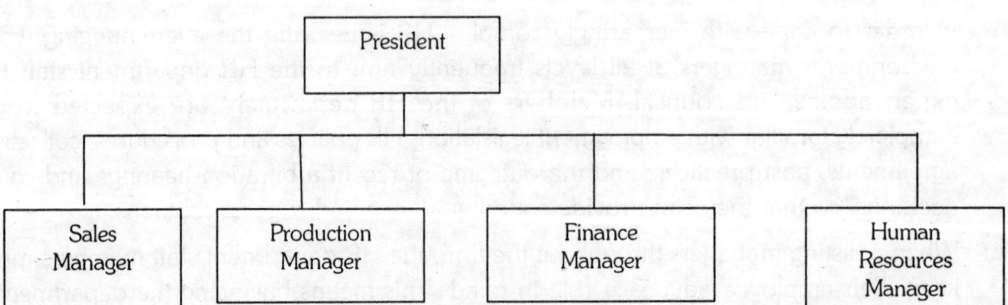

Figure 3.2 : Typical Structure of the Human Resources Function in a Medium - Sized Organization

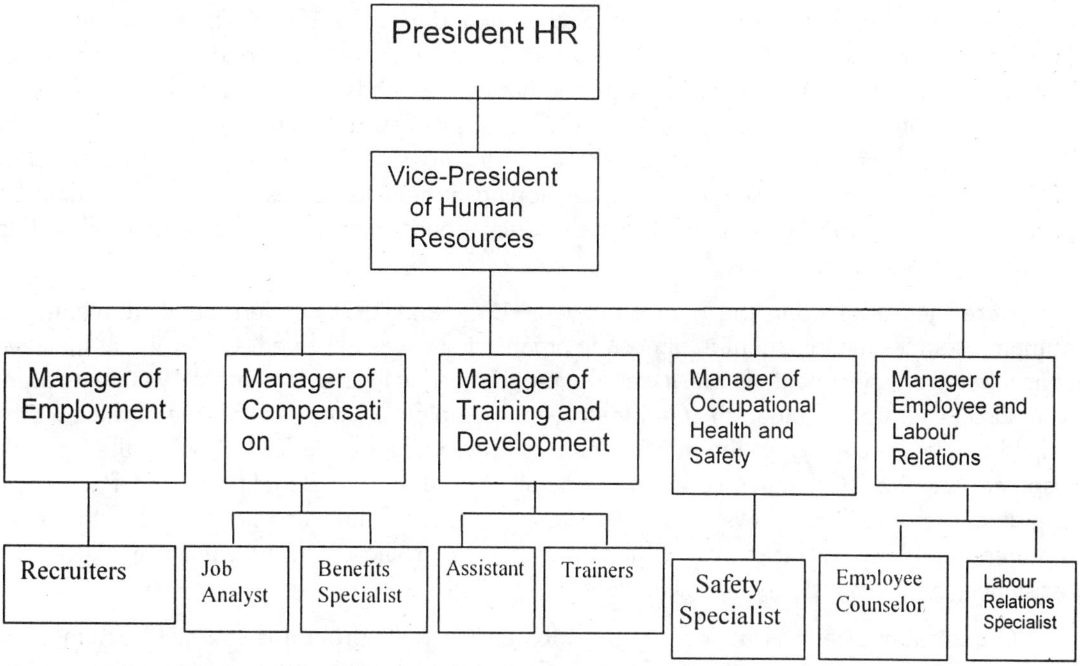

Figure 3.3 : Typical Structure of the Human Resources Department in a Large-sized Manufacturing Firm

History of Human Resources Management

Human Resources Management in its present form has evolved through the years. There are several significant milestones in this transition. Essentially they have been observed in the last two decades. Let us now see these significant milestones. What are their contributions to the development of Human Resources Management as a subject of study?

Early years: Before the twentieth century, there were vague efforts at organizing labor. For the first time, organizations realized the need to organize people. Such organization was considered essential in order to perform jobs. The efforts to organize people gained momentum in the beginning of the industrial revolution.

Mid Years: Between 1900 and 1946 the importance of Personnel Management was recognized. With this came the realization that there is a need to manage employees in order to maintain them on the jobs. This, in turn, was considered crucial to the success of the organisation. Between 1910 and 1920 the focus was on keeping the right person on the right job. Based on Taylor's Scientific Management, work processes were defined more clearly and an attempt to define jobs in terms of sequential activities was begun. The importance of selection was recognized. Organizations attempted to use appropriate selection devices to get the right persons to fit well defined jobs. Simultaneously, Industrial Psychology developed as a subject of interest to psychologists. Scientific experiments were conducted to understand the influence of work conditions and work groups on productivity. One of the most famous studies is the Hawthorne study. The results of these studies have wide ranging implications for practicing managers. They are instrumental in understanding work behaviour even today.

With the onset of the Great Depression of 1930, organizations could not maintain the labor employed. As such, there was large-scale retrenchment during the 1940s. The ill effects of World War II were reflected in the human resources management practices world over. It was widely observed that most organizations were insensitive to the needs of their employees. Of course, some organizations had no choice either. They did not plan for such eventualities. Therefore, they could not keep employees on the rolls even if they desired to. It was at this time, that some of the techniques that are still in use in developing human resources came into existence. In particular, mention must be made of the use of discussions, role-plays, and case method both for developing the skills of employees.

Later years: During the period between 1946 and 1970, government intervention in human resources management in almost all organizations was observed. Government initiatives concentrated on enactment of laws. It was also preoccupied with its enforcement. Welfare measures were also taken up. Together, they did improve the employees' work life. Some of the laws that helped to give a new face to the management of employees are the Factories Act, the Industrial disputes Act, the Workman's compensation Act, the Maternity Benefit Act, the Payment of Gratuities Act etc. These laws have been amended several times to keep pace with current requirements. Welfare measures include the need to provide housing facilities, educational assistance, crèche, subsistence allowance etc.

Organizational efforts at redesigning jobs and benefit programs are still evolving. The motivation techniques and reward systems have started reflecting the changing attitude of the employers. With the result that employers are getting to be more employee oriented.

The early 1970s was witness to an increased intervention by the government in employee's welfare. It was then that Personnel Management was redefined in broader terms as Human Resources Management. It was at this time that trade unions were perhaps most active. Employees were more organized and could demand better treatment. The human resource managers realized that they could not remain silent spectators. They needed to take more active part in making the workplace peaceful. Therefore, the personnel management departments' were transformed into human resource departments. Apart from involving in selection of employees and pay role processing it has evolved into a proactive department encouraging the welfare and development of employees. The most important shift observed since the 1990s, is the belief that the management of human resources is not the exclusive responsibility of the human resource management department alone, but the responsibility of all managers. Now 'Human Resource is considered 'Human Capital'.

Human Resource Information System (HRIS)

Use of computers for collecting, storing, maintaining, retrieving and validating HR data is popularly called ***Human Resource Information System***.

A HRIS is a systematic procedure for collecting, storing, maintaining, retrieving and validating data needed by an organization about its human resources.

The HRIS is usually a part of the organization's larger management information system (MIS). Computerization has its own advantage of providing more accurate and timely data for decision making.

Areas of application of HRIS are training management, risk management, turnover analysis, succession planning, compliance with government and legal requirements, attendance reporting and analysis, Human Resource Planning (HRP), accident reporting and prevention, strategy planning, financial planning etc. HRIS is not just useful in HRP, but its uses extend to whole of HRM.

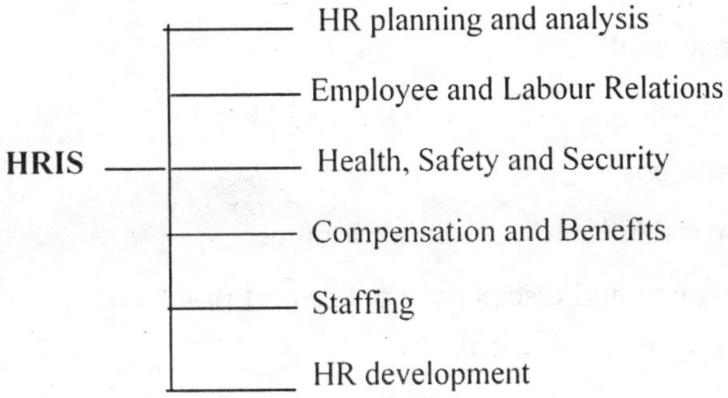

Figure 3.4 : Human Resource Information System

3.1.2 HRD

The term human resource refers to the knowledge, skills, creative abilities, talents, aptitude, values and beliefs of an organization's work force. Enhancement of utilization of human resources depends upon the development of the above ingredients. All the attempts an organization makes through training and developmental programs is called Human Resource Development (HRD). Because of the intense global competition to get success, every organization has to improve its strengths, i.e. the potentialities of its employees for qualitative production of goods and services, minimizing the cost and maximizing the profit to the organization. Especially in the knowledge based industry, the variation in between two organizations can be distinguished on the basis of the HRD. Today HRD has grown into a distinct subject and almost becoming a compulsory educational program for all levels of managers and engineers.

3.1.3 PERSONNEL MANAGEMENT AND INDUSTRIAL RELATIONS (PMIR)

Personnel Management:

Personnel means persons employed in the organisation and the management related to those persons who are employed.

Personnel Management and Industrial Relations:

Personnel management use the employee as an economic entity whose services can be exchanged for wage or salary. Management feels that the employee is a cost factor and wants to control the cost of labor. In this approach employees are mostly used for organizational benefit and personnel function is taken as an auxiliary function.

Industrial Relations (IR):

According to International Labor Organization (ILO), Industrial Relations deal with either the relationship between the state and employers and workers organizations or the relation between the occupational organizations themselves.

Industrial relations are concerned with the relationship between management and workers and the role of regulatory mechanism in resolving any industrial dispute.

IR covers the following areas :

1. Collective bargaining
2. Role of management
3. Role of unions
4. Role of government
5. Machinery for resolution of industrial disputes
6. Industrial grievance and disciplinary policy and practice

Approaches to IR:

The three popular approaches are

1. Unitary approach
2. Pluralistic approach and
3. Marxist approach

Parties to IR:

1. Employee
2. Employee representatives
3. Employees unions
4. Associations of employers
5. Government
6. Courts and tribunals

3.1.4 HRM vs. PMIR

Keeping in view the scope and functions covered a distinction can be drawn in between the personnel management and human resource management which are listed below:

Table 3.2 : Difference between Personnel Management and HRM

PERSONNEL MANAGEMENT	HUMAN RESOURSES MANAGEMENT
1. Personnel Management is a routine maintenance-oriented administrative function.	HRM places emphasis on a continuous development of people at work.
2. PM is mainly reactive and responds to the demands of an organization whenever they arise (It is a firefighting operation)	HRM is a proactive function. It is concerned with present and future needs of organization
3. It is looked as independent function of the organization	HRM is looked as a subsystem linked with all other systems of the supra system of the organization.
4. PM stresses only on improving the efficiency of the personnel.	HRM concentrates on both the efficiency of the worker and creativity for a better work culture.
5. PM emphasizes on economic rewards	HRM emphasizes on creating challenging jobs.
6. PM believes that a happy worker is a Productive worker	HRM is based on the premise that better performance is a source of job satisfaction and high morale.

3.1.5 NATURE AND SCOPE OF HRM

Nature of HRM:

Every organization requires various resources to function and accomplish the goals for which it was established. Out of all the resources required, human resource is the most important one to activate all other resources like machine, material and finance etc. Human resource brings with it not only the knowledge, skills and abilities but also their perceptions, desires, motives, attitudes and values with them. Therefore human resource management is not just the management of technical skills of HR but also the in borne ingredients which affect their performance in the organisation. The success of any organisation depends upon managing the people tactfully and satisfying their inner urges and aspirations. Human resource management policies should lay the guidelines for showing a successful path in this regard.

Scope of HRM:

The scope of HRM is very vast. All major activities from the time the worker enters into the organization until he or she leaves' it, come under the purview of HRM. These activities include – Human Resource Planning, job analysis and design, recruitment and selection, orientation and placement, training and development, performance appraisal and job evaluation, remuneration, motivation and communication, welfare, safety and health, industrial relations (IR) etc...

3.1.6 ROLE OF HR MANAGER

Role of Human Resources Manager:

Human Resources Manager is involved in the process of organizing, developing, motivating and maintaining the human resources in the organization. Acquisition implies a need to put the right people on the right job. It therefore emphasizes the need to select the right person as well as to define jobs clearly and completely. Developing indicates the need to hone the skills of employees in order to enable them to perform well on their job. Motivation is concerned with sustaining the level of performance of each and every employee in the organization. In today's context of high attrition, there is a need to redesign the job which motivates for higher performance. Organizations are realizing that this task is perhaps of prime concern. The maintenance function is concerned with such issues that have a direct impact on building employee relationships.

Main functions of HR Managers

Role of Human Resource Managers

Figure 3.5 : Main functions of HR Managers

Acquisition

Acquisition function begins with manpower planning. It tries to understand the current human resources available with the organization. A forecast of future manpower requirement and supply are made. Any shortages are made up, through recruitment and selection at appropriate time. Acquisition also includes other activities such as induction and socialization of employees.

Development

The development function has four distinct activities. They are employee development, management development, organizational development and career development. Employee development is concerned with developing skills of the employee. It also includes changing the attitudes of the employees into positive. Management development is concerned with enhancement of conceptual abilities and improving knowledge acquisition of employees. Organizational development is concerned with planning and managing change. Career development is concerned with matching the long-term goals of the individual employee and with the organizational requirements.

Motivation

Individual employees are different from each other. Motivation techniques must consider these differences. Therefore this function is concerned with performance appraisal, methods to stimulate performance, linking rewards to performance, compensation administration, and linking rewards to satisfaction. It also takes into consideration issues such as monotony and boredom which have negative impact on performance. It is concerned with disciplining of employees too. The need is to provide challenging, satisfying and personally rewarding jobs.

Maintenance

This function is concerned with ensuring the continuance of employees in the organization. Therefore, it focuses attention on issues such as working conditions, benefits and services to be provided to keep employees happy, so as to ensure their commitment to the organization. For example, the employees stock option plan (ESOP) is a non-cash compensation issued by Infosys that will boost its stock price. A rising stock price gives the employees the drive to work harder and stay longer with Infosys.

3.1.7 BASIC FUNCTIONS OF HRM

3.1.7.1 MANPOWER PLANNING / HR PLANNING

HRP is the process of forecasting a firm's future demand for and supply of the right type of people in the right number. HRP is the process by which an organization ensures that it has the right number and kind of people, at the right place, at the right time capable of achieving the organizations overall objectives. HRP is called as man power planning, personal planning or employment planning.

Definition of HR planning by E.W. Vetter

HRP is "a process by which an organization should move from its current manpower position to its desired manpower position. Through planning, management strives to have the right number and right kind of people at the right places, at the right time, doing things which result in both the organization and the individual receiving maximum long-run benefit."

Objectives of HRP:

i) To recruit required quantity and quality of HR

ii) To foresee and properly manage employee turnover

iii) To meet the needs of expansion and diversification programs

iv) To improve the standard, knowledge, skills and abilities of HR

v) To successfully face the challenges of change in technology and competition

vi) To manage the imbalances of over or under HR utilization.

vii) To rightly estimate the cost and value of HR.

Factors affecting HRP

The important factors influencing HRP are

1) Type and strategy of organization
2) Organization growth cycle and planning
3) Environmental uncertainties
4) Time horizons

5) Type and quality of forecasting information
6) Nature of jobs having filled
7) Outsourcing

Need for HRP:

i) Shortage of certain categories of employees
ii) Need for new skills due to technology change
iii) Change in organizational plans and designs
iv) Demographic changes like changing profile of workforce like age, sex, education etc
v) Government policies like reservation policy, child labour working conditions etc
vi) The labour laws affecting the demand for and supply of labour
vii) Pressure from TUs', politicians, sons of the soil etc.,
viii) Introduction of computers, robots etc.

Benefits of HRP

i) A reservoir of talent which can be tapped at the time of need
ii) Prepares people for future
iii) Easy expansion or contraction of operations
iv) Cuts costs and gets maximum benefits
v) Useful for successive planning
vi) Offsets uncertainty and risks due to changes
vii) Foresees the need for redundancy and plans to check
viii) Enables planning for physical facilities in advance for the HR

3.1.7.2 RECRUITMENT

The human resource manager plays an important role in selecting employees. The recruitment and selection process results from human resource planning and is based on the philosophy, "Don't try to fit a square peg into a round hole!" Adding new employees is expensive, and recruitment costs alone are very high. Interviews and tests are often conducted before selecting new employees. Medical examinations are often required for applicants. Training new people is also costly, and an inefficient worker wastes money.

Recruitment:

Recruitment is the process of locating and encouraging potential applicants to apply for existing or anticipated job openings. Recruitment aims at attracting a large number of qualified applicants who are ready to take up the job when it is offered. According to Edwin B. Flippo recruitment is the process of searching for prospective employees and stimulating them to apply for jobs in the organization.

Dale Yoder considers recruitment as a process to discover the sources of manpower to meet the requirements of the staffing schedule and to employ effective measures for attracting that manpower in adequate numbers to facilitate effective selection of an efficient workforce.

Recruitment is the process of finding and attracting capable applicants for employment. The process begins when new recruits are sought and ends when their applications are submitted. The result is a pool of applications from which new employees are selected. Recruitment is the process of searching for and obtaining applications for jobs, from among whom the right people can be selected. It is a positive linking function.

Factors governing Recruitment:

Recruitment is subject to influence of several factors which include both internal as well as external.

External and Internal factors of recruitment are given hereunder :

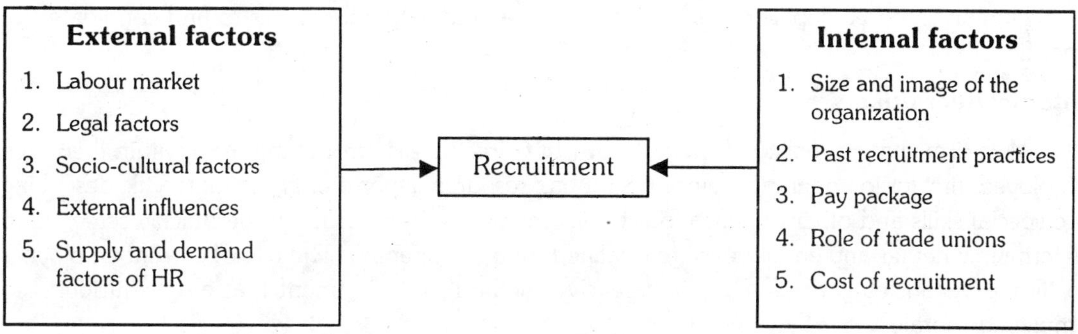

Figure 3.6 : Factors governing Recruitment

Process of Recruitment:

Recruitment is a five step process.

1. Planning
2. Strategy development
3. Searching
4. Screening and
5. Evaluation and control

Objectives and Importance:

1. To determine the present and future manpower requirements of the organization.
2. To increase the pool of job candidates at minimum cost.
3. To increase the success rate of the selection process.
4. To help in retention once applicants are recruited and selected.
5. To meet the organization's legal and social obligations regarding composition of workforce.

6. Identifying potential job applicants.
7. Increase organizational and individual effectiveness in the long run.
8. Evaluate the effectiveness of various recruiting techniques and sources for all types of job applicants.

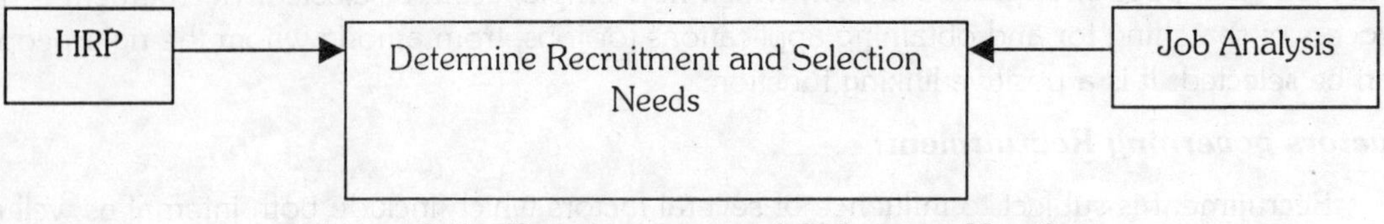

Figure 3.7 : Recruitment and Selection Needs

Sources of Recruitment:

Human resource departments use both internal and external sources to find candidates for specific jobs.

Internal Recruiting

Most firms have a policy of ***hiring from within***—that is, promoting from within their own employees first for job openings. Since the human resource department maintains a file describing the special skills and other qualifications of all employees, its records can be quickly screened to determine whether any employees are qualified for a job opening. The use of current employees to fill job vacancies is a relatively inexpensive method of recruitment that also contributes to employee morale.

External Recruiting

All firms must utilize external sources to some extent in filling vacancies or in adding new employees for newly created jobs. A company may not have qualified employees to fill a certain position, or better qualified people may be available from outside the firm. Sources for potential job applicants outside the company include colleges, advertisements in newspapers and professional journals, public employment agencies, private employment agencies, vocational schools, labor unions, unsolicited applications, and recommendations by current employees. To locate candidates to fill top management positions, a firm may use specialized executive recruiting agencies or advertise in the media. Unskilled workers may be recruited from such sources as public employment agencies, friends of present employees, and walk-ins.

Unions, vocational/technical institutes, recommendations from present employees, and newspaper advertisements may be used in recruiting craft workers and employees with technical skills. Clerical and other white-collar employees are recruited from such sources as private employment agencies and temporary help agencies, present employees, friends of present employees, newspaper advertisements, walk-ins, and educational institutes such as vocational/ technical institutes. Community agencies are effective sources for locating and recruiting handicapped workers.

Sources of Recruitment: Internal and external Recruitment

Internal Sources

i. Present employees promotions

ii. Transfers among the Present employees

iii. Employee referrals

iv. Former employees

v. Previous applicants

External Sources

i. Professionals or trade associations

ii. Advertisements - TV ads, radio, news paper.

iii. Employment exchanges (State or Public)

iv. Campus recruitment

v. Consultants

vi, Contractors (for causal workers)

vii. Displaced persons (rehabilitating the displaced)

viii. Competitors (poaching or raiding)

E –recruitment (internet recruitment)

3.1.7.3 SELECTION

Selection of qualified and competent people is the logical step in the HR process. It is the process of picking the right individuals from the pool of screened job applicants with the help of selection techniques like written tests and interview etc., who can most successfully perform the job from the pools of qualified candidates. It is the process of differentiating between applicants in order to identify those with a greater likelihood of success.

Selection means to choose. Selection is the process of picking individuals who have relevant qualifications to fill jobs in an organization. The purpose of selection is to choose the individual who can most successfully perform the job. It is the look and check whether the needs of the job are matched with the profile of the candidate. It is evaluating the person's fitness to the job.

Dale Yoder defines selection as one or many 'go' or 'no-go' gauges. Candidates are screened by the application of these gauges. Qualified applicants go on to the next hurdle while unqualified are eliminated.

Thomas H.Stone defines selection as the process of differentiating between the applicants in order to identity and hire those with a greater likelihood of success in a job.

Edwin B.Flippo says that selection function tends to be negative because it rejects a good number of those who apply, leaving only the best to be hired.

Process of Selection:

Selection is the long process starting from the preliminary interview of the applicants and ending with the contract of employment.

1. **Rejection of Unqualified Applicants**

A comparison of a completed application form with the job description is enough to determine whether the applicant possess the qualifications needed for the position. A letter or e-mail or telephone call from the company's human resource department informs the applicant of the decision of selection or rejection. In most instances, the letter writer thanks the applicant for contacting the company and seeks to maintain a positive image of the firm for the rejected job-seekers.

2. **Employee Testing**

Employee testing makes the selection process more efficient. Various tests can be used in measuring the aptitude, skills, abilities or knowledge relevant to the jobs that are to be performed. Some companies with testing programs also administer general intelligence or personality tests. Testing serves two main purposes. It helps to eliminate those applicants who are not suited for a particular job, and it helps predict which candidates are likely to be productive employees.

Tools of selection process

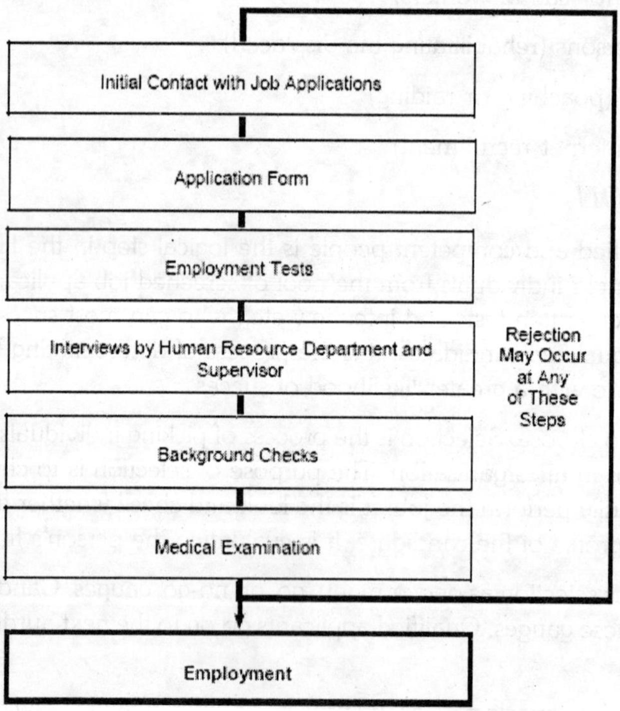

Figure 3.8 : Process of employee testing

3. **Interviewing**

The job applicant's first formal contact with a company is usually an interview with a company representative. This face-to-face contact is another step in the screening of candidates for a job. Trained interviewers are able to obtain considerable insight into the prospective employee's goals, attitudes, and motivations. Job applicants increase their chances of receiving an employment offer through careful preparation before the interview. Answers to anticipated questions should be prepared in advance, and applicants should learn about the company and the position.

4. *Final Selection*

After completion of all the above steps successfully a candidate is considered fit for company employment. A contract of employment will be entered into with that candidate.

Selection Tests

- Ability tests (achievement tests)
- The Thematic Appreciation Test (TAT)
- Aptitude tests
- Psychological test
- Personality tests
- Interest tests
- Graphology test (analyze the handwriting of the individual)
- Medical tests
- Polygraph test (lie detector to ensure accuracy of information)
- Drug tests
- Genetic Screening

Tests must be chosen based on criteria of reliability, validity objectivity and standardization.

Factors affecting Selection:

External factors

Supply and demand of specific skills in the job market, unemployment rate, labor - market conditions legal and political considerations and company image comes under the category of external factors affecting selection.

Internal factors

The internal factor which affects the selection process consists of company's policy, human resource planning and cost of hiring etc.

3.1.7.4 PLACEMENT

Placement is actual posting of an employee to a specific job. In other words it is the effort of right matching of HR with the job. Normally line management of the concerned dept will take this decision. Many organizations place the employee on probation after selection. During this time he will be monitored to find the right job for him. Readjustments are made in the final placement function.

The Human Resource department administers promotions, demotions or transfers to adjust the right person to the right job. Promotion is a reward for efficiency and demotion denotes the weakness of the employee whereas transfer may be for the better utilization of the skills in another position.

Advantages of Proper Placement:

1. Shows good results on the job.
2. Gets along with people easily.
3. Keeps the spirits high and reports regularly for duty.
4. Reduces mistakes and accidents.

Affects of Improper Placement:

1. Leads to poor performance
2. Leads to absenteeism
3. Leads to employee turnover
4. Leads to accidents etc.

3.1.7.5 INDUCTION

Employee Induction / Orientation

Once hired, the employee completes an orientation program, which is the joint responsibility of the human resource department and the department in which the employee will work. The human resource department provides the new worker with a copy of the employee manual, which discusses employee benefits and explains company policy on holidays, leaves, welfare measures, awards, rewards, disciplinary procedures, rest periods, lunch breaks, and so on. The supervisor is responsible for introducing the new employee to fellow workers, explaining the operations of the department, and detailing how the job fits into these operations.

A new employee in a large firm should be put at ease by the supervisor by cordially welcoming. Feelings of loneliness and isolation that often accompany the first days on a new job may lead to frustration, and negative attitude.

The orientation program is designed to convey a sense of belongingness and a feeling of personal integrity. Although the human resource department provides information about company history, products, and benefits, the responsibility for developing a new employee's sense of importance and involvement is primarily that of the immediate supervisor and the other employees in the department.

Induction is

- Systematic and planned introduction of employees to their jobs, their co-workers and the organization.
- Designed to provide a new employee with the information he or she needs to function comfortably and efficiently in the organization.
- Planned introduction of new hires to their jobs, their peers and the company.

Induction conveys three types of information.

- General information about the daily work routine.
- Review of the firms history, objectives etc.
- Detailed presentation of organizations policies ,work rules and employees benefits.

Features of Induction

1. The new employee is provided with information about company and its history
2. About the benefits like leaves, rest periods etc.
3. About the break rooms, restrooms , cafeterias' etc
4. Induction can be done by senior officers of the respective department and the HR Dept.
5. Lectures, handbooks , films , seminars etc are provided
6. The objective is to make the new employee settle down quickly

Objectives of Induction

1. Removes fears in the new employee
2. Creates a good impression
3. Acts as valuable information source

Steps in Induction program

1. Welcome the new employee to the organization
2. Explain about the company
3. Show the work place
4. Introduce him to important persons in positions
5. Give the details of various work groups
6. Give details of various unions
7. Give details about total compensation package
8. Explain about training and development opportunities
9. Explain about career prospects
10. Clarify doubts by encouraging the new employee to ask questions

3.1.7.6 TRAINING AND DEVELOPMENT

Training:

Training is learning that is directed at bringing about a permanent change that improves the person's ability to perform the job assigned. Training involves changing knowledge, skills and attitudes. It also involves changing social skills to suit organizational needs. Training is confined to operatives. Operatives are persons employed in production, maintenance and other clerical jobs. They do not supervise the work of others. Therefore, they need to learn skills required to perform their jobs.

Training and development refers to the imparting of specific skills, ability and knowledge to an employee. It is an attempt to improve current or future employee performance by increasing an employee's ability to perform through learning or increasing skills and knowledge.

Dale S.Beach defines "training as the organized procedure by which people learn knowledge and skills for definite purpose."

Edwin B. Flippo defines "training as the act of increasing skills of an employee for doing a particular job".

Now a definition can be given stating that the main objective of training is learning knowledge, skills and abilities to do a job in a better manner.

Training and development need = Standard performance – Actual performance.

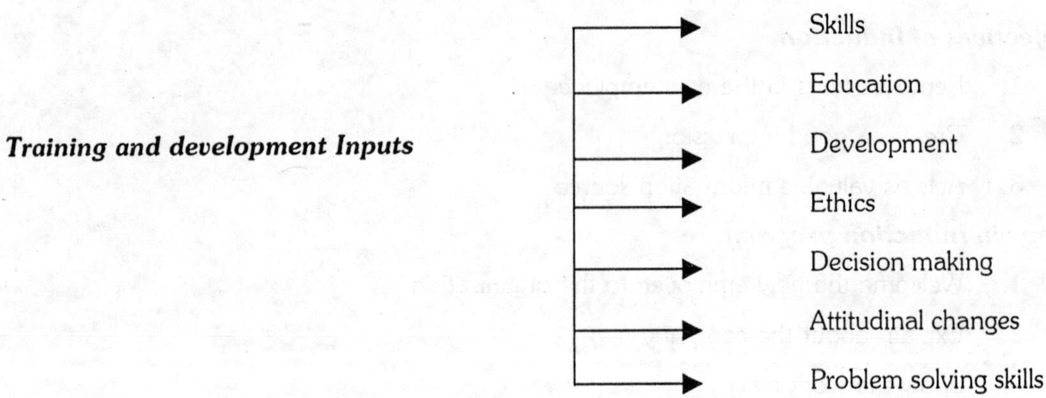

Figure 3.9 : Inputs in Training and Development

The Training Process:

1. Defining organizational objectives and strategies
2. Assessment of training needs
3. Establishing the training goals
4. Designing the training programme
5. Implementation of the programme
6. Evaluation of the results.

Training needs:

1. Newly recruited employees require training to perform their jobs perfectly.
2. To prepare existing human resources for higher level jobs.

3. Existing employees require retraining to replenish their knowledge, skills and abilities.
4. Training is needed for all organizations to cope up with change in technology etc.,
5. Training is necessary to make employees mobile and versatile.
6. Training fills up the gap in between the job need and human attributes.

Methods used in Training Needs Assessment:

1. Groups or organizational analysis
2. Organization goals and objectives
3. Personal skills
4. Efficiency interviews
5. Exit Interviews
6. MBO
7. Quality circles
8. Customer summary
9. Current and projected changes

Importance of Training and Development

Recruiters continuously search for the employee with the right ability for job fitness. However, they are often confronted with the problem of selecting people with skills that fall far below the requirements of the job. The skill gap is reduced through training and development. With experience on the job, the incumbent would be able to meet organizational expectations.

Jobs and job contexts are increasingly complex. Moreover, several changes occur from time to time. Employees therefore need to adapt quickly. Employee training is now more important than ever before. Just look back at the technological changes in the past decade. Let us recall the initial resistance to accept computers as tools for improving efficiency in nationalized banks. So much of resistance to learn computer operations by employees and unions was observed. Of course, there were other fears too besides the doubt whether the older staff would cope with the demands of computerization. Training has erased fears besides improving employee efficiency.

Training is essential for people at all levels. It is important for people planning to change their career. Most people change their careers at least twice during their work life. Some do so voluntarily, others have no choice, and their jobs may simply disappear. There is a need to train to keep them update as per the context. This way, they are able to pick up another job immediately in case of a need.

Considering the importance of learning to the individual and the organization, it is pertinent to understand the concepts of training and development.

Training Methods

Organizations adopt on-the-job and off-the-job methods to train their employees. Let us now see some of the widely used methods.

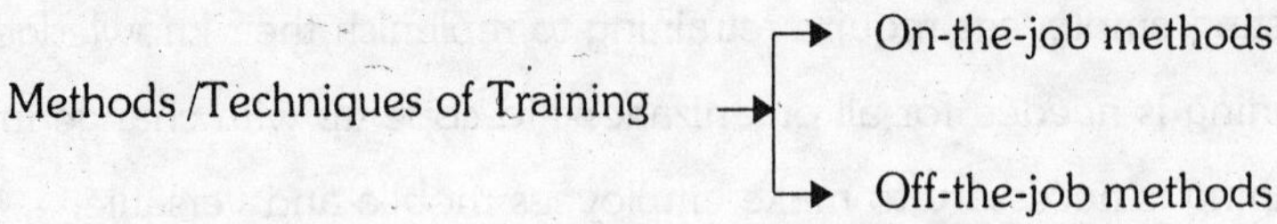

Figure 3.10 : Methods of Training

On-the-Job Training

Two popular on-the job training techniques are:

1. Apprenticeship programs
2. Job Instruction training

Off-the-Job Training

In this method, the training is given at separate place which is away from the workplace. Doing and learning processes are separated. There are a number of techniques used in this method of training. While some are very easy and use simple equipment some others are complex and require sophisticated equipments.

The following are the popular Off-the-job training techniques:

- Lectures
- Films
- Simulation
- Programmed Instruction

Executive Development Methods

On the Job Executive Development Techniques

The popular on-the-job executive development techniques are:

- Coaching
- Understudy Assignment
- Job Rotation
- Committee Assignment

Off the Job Executive Development

- Lectures
- Simulation
- Sensitivity Training
- Role-Plays

3.1.7.7 PROMOTION, TRANSFER AND SEPARATION

Promotion:

Promotion refers to placing of an employee in a higher level job as a reward for exhibiting efficiency in the existing job. Naturally the position carries higher authority, responsibility and higher pay package. The basis of promotion may be merit or seniority or both. Promotion policy defines the criteria to be fulfilled by the employees to get the promotion. As every employee aspires promotion, organizations must try to satisfy this urge of the employee by designing a careful career path for growth.

Transfer:

An employee may be shifted from one position to another position in the same department or in other department almost with similar duties and responsibilities, and then it is called transfer. The pay benefits may also be the same. The objective of transfer may be readjusting the HR in proper positions for better utilization of their potentialities. Sometimes the transfer may be affected at the request of the employee.

Separation:

In this function an employee is separated from his job. This may arise because of the natural retirement, (superannuation) voluntary retirement, death, or incapacitated position of the employee due to illness or accidents etc. Separation may also occur because of disciplinary action taken against the employee by the management for non-observance or violation of rules and regulations of the organization. This separation becomes inevitable when the employee involves in social crimes which are illegal or involves in malpractices or scams etc. Separation also includes dismissals and lay-offs.

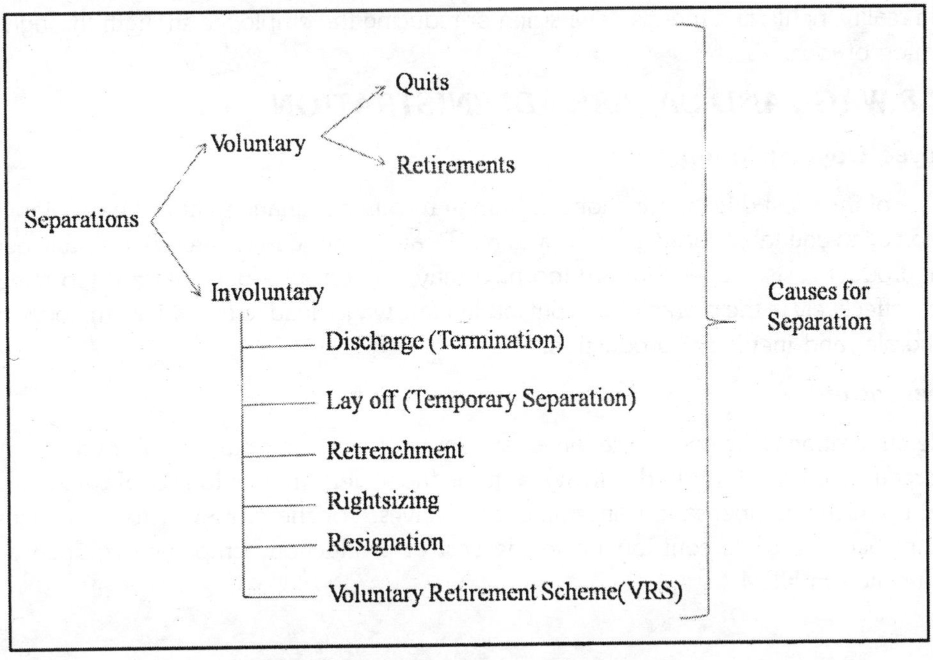

Figure 3.11 : Causes of Separation

Quit – An employee decides to quit where his or her level of dissatisfaction with the present job is high or a more attractive alternative job is awaiting the individual.

Retirements – Occur when employees reach the end of their careers as per the maximum age limit.

Discharge or dismissal – Discharge also called termination takes place when the employer discovers that it is no more desirable to keep an employee any longer. Termination of employment is initiated by the employer which may be due to excessive absenteeism, serious misconduct, false statement of qualifications, theft of company's property etc.

Layoffs – Temporary separation of the employee at the instance of the employer. It may be for a definite period due to shortage of raw materials or power, accumulation of stocks, break down of machinery etc. employer pays a compensation for all the days of the layoff.

Resignation – Termination of employment at the instance of the employee or when employee secures better job elsewhere, or female employees for personal reasons or when an employee suffers ill health.

Retrenchment – Termination of the services of employees because of the replacement of labor by automatic machines or closure of a department or reduction in production operations.

Voluntary Retirement Scheme (VRS) – VRS is used where organizations have surplus labor. VRS sometimes called golden hand shake plan where handsome compensations are paid to employees who opt to leave. This is mainly to reduce strength and easing out unproductive or older workers.

Rightsizing – Reducing the size or increasing it to maintain work force strength at a desired level. In reality, rightsizing means downsizing or reducing the employee strength through planned elimination of jobs.

3.1.7.8 WAGE AND SALARY ADMINISTRATION

Employee Compensation

One of the most difficult functions of human resource management is the development and operation of an equitable compensation system. Because labor costs represent a sizable percentage of total product costs, wages that are too high may result in products that are too expensive to compete effectively in the marketplace. But inadequate wages lead to excessive employee turnover, poor morale, and inefficient production.

Compensation:

Remuneration is the compensation an employee receives in return for his or her contribution to the organization. The standard of living, status in the society, motivation, loyalty and productivity depend upon the compensation an employee receives. For the employer too, compensation is significant because of its contribution to the cost of production. Employee compensation is a major function in HRM.

Components of Compensation:

Remuneration of an employee comprises of the following components:

i. ***Wages and Salary*** : Hourly, daily, weekly, fortnightly and monthly rate of pay

ii. ***Incentives :*** Paid in addition to wages and salaries, also payment by results.

iii. ***Fringe Benefits :*** PF, gratuity, medical care, health and group insurance, canteen, uniform, recreation etc.

iv. ***Perquisites*** : Company car, club membership, paid holidays, furniture, stock option schemes, home etc.

v. ***Non-monetary benefits :*** Recognition of merit, growth prospects, comfortable working conditions, flexi time etc.

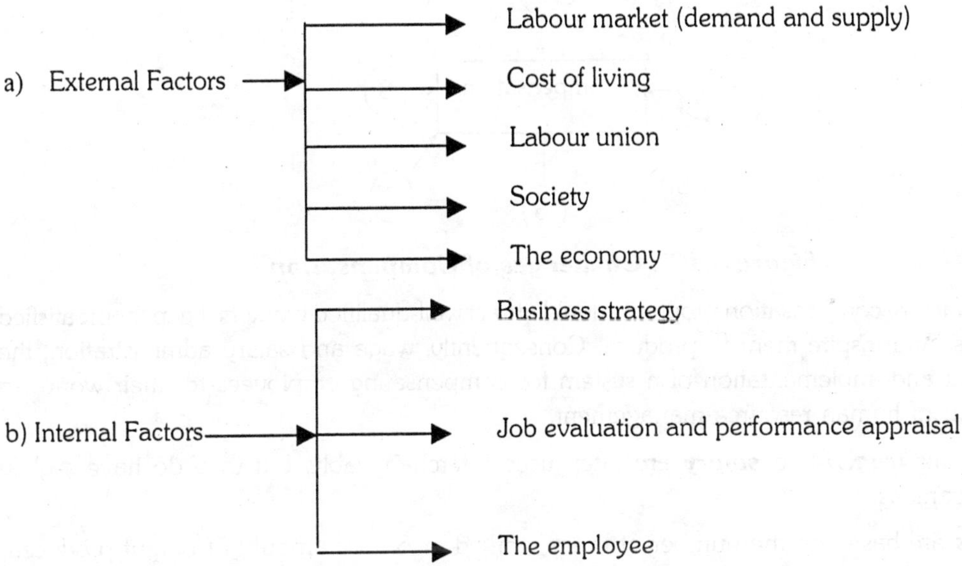

Figure 3.12 : Factors influencing Compensation

Developing a Compensation plan:

Developing a good compensation plan involves the following steps:

1. Job description
2. Job evaluation
3. Job hiring
4. Pay survey
5. Pricing jobs

Challenges of Compensation:

While evolving a just compensation plan, the following challenges should be tackled carefully:

1. Skill- based pay
2. Salary revisions
3. Pay secrecy
4. Comparable worth
5. Employee participation
6. Eclecticism or egalitarianism
7. Below market or above market rates
8. Monetary versus non monetary rewards

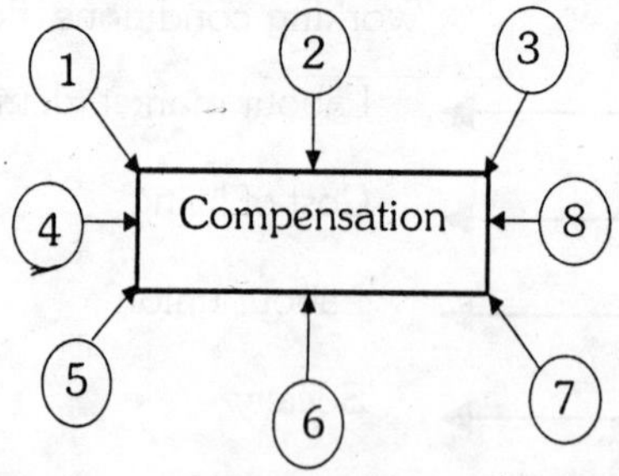

Figure 3.13 : Challenges of Compensation

A satisfactory compensation program should attract well-qualified workers, keep them satisfied in their jobs, and inspire them to produce. Consequently, wage and salary administration, the development and implementation of a system for compensating employees for their work is a vital function of human resource management.

The terms ***wages*** and ***salary*** are often used interchangeably, but they do have slightly different meanings.

Wages are based on the number of hours worked or on the amount of output produced. They, are paid to production employees, retail salespeople and maintenance workers.

Salary is employee compensation calculated on a weekly, monthly, or annual basis. It is usually paid to white-collar workers such as office personnel, executives and professional employees.

The compensation policy of most companies is based on five factors:

(1) Salaries and wages paid by competitive companies

(2) Government legislation

(3) The cost of living

(4) The ability of the company to pay

(5) The workers' productivity.

Concept of Wages:

i. ***Minimum wages***: It is the one providing for sustenance of life plus for preservation of the efficiency of the worker.

ii. ***Fair wages:*** It is sufficient for meeting the necessaries and also comforts. It is one which is paid by the best organization in that field.

iii. ***Living wage:*** It is higher than the fair wages. it is one which should enable the wage earner to provide for him and his family not only the basic need but a measure of frugal comfort and luxuries including education for children, protection against ill health, social needs etc.

There are several practices and applications for motivating employees.

Pay for Performance (Performance Based Incentives)

For most companies, the traditional approach to employee compensation was predictable: wage earners were paid by the hour. Salary earners got paid by the month or the year. And executives—only executives—got bonuses. Every company wants to invent an innovative pay package to attract and motivate its employees.

Incentive compensation: It is designed to reward salaried employees and wage earners for superior performance.

Profit sharing—a type of incentive compensation program in which a percentage of company profits is distributed to employees involved in producing those profits is the most widely used form of incentive pay plans. More than 20 percent of U.S. companies currently use profit sharing to increase company loyalty by creating a feeling of belongingness for employees.

Gain sharing: This approach is aimed at linking employee pay to productivity. Employees are rewarded for results they can directly influence. For instance, producing more garments per hour, attracting more depositors, or collecting more accounts.

Bonus: The bonus is a one-time performance-based payment that does not get built into salaries or wages. Intended as an incentive for increased productivity, bonuses reward employees for exceptional performance.

Besides Financial incentives like Bonus and Profit-sharing, non-Financial incentives mentioned hereunder also count for motivation and effective performance of workforce. They are –

Non-Financial Incentives:

Non-Financial incentives include:

1. Job satisfaction
2. Better and healthy conditions and surroundings
3. Chances of promotion
4. Job security
5. Helpful to cooperative management

6. Respect and recognition in the organization,
7. Training and other employee improvement programmes and
8. Housing, medical, recreational and educational facilities to workers and their families.

Semi financial incentives:

Semi financial incentives include:

1. Provision of subsidized lunch, recreational and medical facilities to the workers and subsidized educational facilities for their children.
2. Pension and other benefits.

Wage Incentive Plans:

Wage incentive plan is a reward to an employee for his good job-performance. The various aspects of job-performance are:

i. Quantity;
ii. Product quality;
iii. Utilization of materials, plant, tools & services, and
iv. Efficiency

Almost all commonly employed Wage Incentive Schemes guarantee a minimum (base) wage plus incentive based upon operator's performance, if it exceeds a plant-wide standard. Normally the wage incentive plans should depend on the standards set by Work Measurement. The Wage Rate may be the result of mutual agreement between employer and employee or formal/informal evaluation of the employee. Operator's Performance depends upon estimates of standard output.

The Requirements of a Sound Wage Incentive Plans are:

1. It should be simple, easy to understand and to operate. It should involve least clerical work.
2. It should be simple well planned and guarantee a minimum wage.
3. A worker should be rewarded in proportion to his efforts and achievements. Rewards should be promptly paid.
4. A worker should get enough and adequate incentive for his contributions.
5. The scheme should preferably be based on Time-study data.
6. It should give incentive both for quantity & quality of production.
7. Standards should be fairly set.
8. The scheme should be just for workers as well as the management.
9. Standards and the allowed time should be altered only when there is a change in the work method.

10. Standardization should preferably be the basis for all incentive schemes. Work methods, material, work place; working conditions, etc., all should be standardized.
11. Worker should not suffer in his incentive for reasons beyond his control.
12. No limit should be put on a worker's incentive earnings.
13. The plan should be installed with the consent of the employees.
14. Once installed, the incentive scheme should be rigidly maintained.

Objectives of Incentives:

1. The incentive scheme should be profitable to both workers and management.
2. It should help increasing production and there by lower the related costs.
3. It should reward workers in proportion to their output for boosting up their morale.
4. The characteristics of an incentive scheme should be such that an able worker is in a position to earn sufficient amount of money to raise his standard of living.
5. An incentive scheme should provide recognition to a worker for his good contribution.
6. An incentive scheme should aid improvements in the utilization of equipment, materials & services.
7. An incentive scheme should furnish a basis for cost control and labor control.
8. An Incentive scheme should help in reducing labor turnover and absentee rate.
9. An incentive scheme should aim at improving relations between workers and management.

Drawbacks:

I. An incentive scheme involves extra cost of :

   1. Standardizing – methods, allowed time, materials, product design, etc.,
   2. Installing and maintaining.
   3. Keeping the records of worker's performance

II. An improperly structured and planned incentive scheme can be a root of all troubles and disputes between the labor and management.

III. Observations showed that groups of workers may have different opinions of an incentive plan and this may give rise to conflict among workmen, between workers and inspectors.

Workers may be classified as:

i. ***Direct workers:*** Direct workers are those who operate the machines and turn out production. A drilling or milling machine operator is a direct worker. It is easy to measure the output of a direct worker and a previous section describes the various incentive schemes applicable to direct workers.

ii. ***Indirect workers:*** Indirect workers are those who assist, guide and supervise the direct workers during production runs. Indirect workers may be categorized as

a) Material handlers, crane operators, set up men, maintenance men etc.

b) Shop inspectors, Foremen and supervisors, and

c) Managers

The main difficulty associated with the incentive payments to indirect workers is that their contribution towards production cannot be accurately measured and hence it is extremely difficult to reward them effectively and suitably. The wage incentive plans applicable to direct workers cannot be usefully employed for indirect workers. However, many organizations have designed incentive schemes to motivate the indirect workers.

Incentives for Direct Workers:

The following are different Wage Incentive Plans for Direct Workers:

- Straight Piece Rate,
- Straight Piece Rate with a Guaranteed Minimum Wage,
- Different Piece Rate System,
- Halsey Plan,
- Rowan Plan,
- Gantt Plan,
- Bedaux Plan,
- Emerson's Efficiency Plan, and
- Group Plan

Incentives for Indirect workers:

The following are the suggested Incentive Schemes for indirect workers :

1. ***Labourers, Crane operators, Set-up men, Maintenance men etc.***

   a) They can be given the same or half the incentive what the direct workers get.

   b) They can be given a bonus at a flat rate, (say 7-10%)

2. ***Supervisory staff***: Supervisory staff can be paid an incentive on the output for which it is responsible. There are a number of factors on which, incentives can be calculated. A supervisor can be given a bonus depending upon the following:

   a) The number of satisfactory units produced by his section/department in one day or one week.

   b) The number of work hours saved in achieving the same output,

   c) Reduction in scrap and wastage,

d) Net cost saved for the organization,

e) Optimum utilization of workers, and

f) The number of orders in whose case delivery dates were met.

3. ***Managerial staff:*** For running a concern effectively, it is highly necessary to maintain the interest and participation of the managerial staff. Incentives to managerial staff may be in the form of:

   a) ***Bonus:*** Bonus may be given to the managerial staff in proportion to their merits, job requirements or salary drawn by them.

   b) ***Issue of Shares:*** Company shares may be issued to managerial staff. The number of shares, naturally, builds up year after year and this induces a sense of discipline, loyalty and cooperation in the managers who start realizing that they are partners in the company and they have to work sincerely and whole heartedly for the same. In this way labor turnover automatically gets minimized.

   c) ***Profit Sharing:*** As per the mutual agreement between the employer and the indirect workers, a proportion of the company's profit may be shared by the indirect workers, in addition to their normal wages. The share of profit which goes to a particular person may depend upon the salary, length of service, merits etc.

   d) ***Fringe Benefits:***

   - Free accommodation
   - Provision of conveyance and phone facilities.
   - Financial assistance at the times of difficulty.
   - Subsidized children education etc.

3.1.8 WAGE PAYMENT PLANS WITH SIMPLE PROBLEMS

Systems of Wage Payment:

There are two principal wage systems:

I. Payment on the basis of time spent in the factory irrespective of the amount of work done. This method is known as ***Time Wage*** system.

II. Payment on the basis of the work done irrespective of the time taken by the worker. This method is called ***Piece Rate*** system.

Time Wage System:

Under this method of wage payment, the worker is paid at an hourly, daily, weekly or monthly rate. Suppose, a worker is paid at the rate of Rs. 10 per hour and he spent 220 hours during a particular month, his wages will be Rs. 2200. This payment is made according to the time worked irrespective of the quantity of work done.

There are five types of this system, each differing only in so far as the fixation of the rate of concerned. They are as follows:

1. ***Flat Time Rate or Time Rate at Ordinary Level:***

   It is the oldest method of wage payment. Under this method, workers are paid at a flat rate on the basis of time they are employed. The flat rate may be per hour, day, week or month. The flat rate is usually fixed keeping in view the rate prevailing in similar trades in the same locality for the same grade and skill.

2. ***High Day Rate or Time Rate at High Wage Level:***

   One of the draw backs of flat rate method that it does not provide any incentive for increased efficiency. This drawback is overcome by adopting high day rate which is usually higher than the average wage rate of the industry. The rate of wages is fixed by hour or day but the rate fixed is relatively higher. Higher rate is given to attract the efficient workers who can easily be motivated to achieve pre-determined standards of efficiency.

3. ***Measured Day Rate:***

   Workers under this method are given a specified work to be performed and the rate is fixed in accordance with the level of performance specified by the employer. Higher rate is fixed for higher level of performance, so it gives incentive to efficient workers.

4. ***Graduated Time Rate:***

   Under this method the rates of wages are linked up with the cost of living index. Thus, the rate per hour or day fixed initially goes on changing with the changes in the cost of living index. This method is liked by workers in a period of rising prices because they are compensated for the increase in the cost of living index.

5. ***Differential Time Rate:***

   Under this method, different rates of wages are fixed for different workers in the same group according to the differences in their personal abilities and skill. Higher rates are given to efficient workers in recognition of their efficient performance. Thus, workers are paid according to their performance and there is a positive incentive for improvement of performance by the workers.

Piece Rate System / Payment by Result

Under this system of wage payment, a fixed rate is paid for each unit produced, job completed or an operation performed. This payment is made according to the quantity of work done and no consideration is given to the time taken by the workers to perform the work. For example, a worker is paid at the rate of Rs.5 per unit and produces 50 units during the day, he will get Rs. 250.

There are four variants of this system, each differing only in so far as the fixation of the piece wage is concerned. They are:

1. ***Straight Piece Rate System:***

   It is the simplest method of payment by result in which payment is made according to the number of units produced at fixed rate per unit. Another type of the straight piece rate method is piece rate with guaranteed time rate in which the worker is guaranteed the time rate with an opportunity of getting piece wages if his earnings if his earnings according to piece rate system are more than his time wage earnings.

2. ***Taylor's Differential Piece Rate System:***

   This system was introduced by F.W. Tylor, the father of scientific management. The underlying principle of this system is to penalize a slow worker by paying him a low piece rate for his production. Taylor was of the view that an inefficient worker had no place in the organization and he should be compelled to leave the organization by paying him a low piece rate for low production. Taylor proceeded on the assumption that through time and motion study, it is possible to fix a standard time for doing a particular task. Hence, Taylor decided to give a large reward to those who would complete the work within or less than the standard time and much less wage to those who would not complete the job within the standard time.

Illustration-1:

Calculate the earnings of workers A and B under Straight Piece Rate system and Taylors Differential Piece Rate System from the following particulars:

Normal rate per hour : Rs. 18

Standard time per unit : 20 seconds

Differentials to be applied:

80% of piece rate below standard

120% of piece rate at or above standard.

Worker A produces 1,300 units per day and worker B produces 1,500 units per day.

Solution:

Standard production per 20 seconds = 1 unit

Standard production per minute = 60/20 = 3 units

Standard production per hour = 3 × 60 = 180 units.

Standard production per day of 8 hours = 180 × 8 = 1,440 units

Normal rate per hour = Rs. 18

Therefore, Normal piece rate = Rs. 18/180 units = 0.10 Re.

Low piece rate below standard production (0.10 x 80)/100 = 0.08 Re.

High piece rate at or above standard (0.10 x 120)/100 = 0.12 Re.

Earnings of worker A:

Under Straight Piece-rate System

1,300units @ 0.10 = Rs.130

Under Taylor's differential Piece rate system

1,300 units @ 0.08 Re. = Rs.104

(Per unit piece rate = 10 x 80% = Re.0.08)

Low piece-rate has been applied because worker A's daily production of 1300 units is less than the standard daily production of 1,440 units.

Earnings of worker B:

Under Straight Piece-rate System

1,500units @ 0.10 = Rs.150

Under Taylor's differential Piece rate system

1,500 units @ 0. 12 = Rs.180

(Per unit piece rate = 10 x 120% = Re.0.12)

High piece-rate has been applied because worker B's daily production of 1500 units is higher than the standard daily production of 1,440 units.

3. *Merrick's Multiple Piece Rate System:*

This method seeks to make an improvement in the Taylor's differential piece rate system. Under this method, three piece rates are applied for workers with different levels of performance. Wages are paid at ordinary piece rate to those workers whose performance is less than 83% of the standard output, 110% of the ordinary piece rate is given to workers whose level of performance is between 83% and 100% of the standard and 120% of the ordinary piece rate is given to workers who produce more than 100% of the standard output.

This method does not guarantee time wages as wages are paid according to pieces produced. Efficient and experienced workers whose performance is more than 100% earn more wages because they got wages at 120% of the ordinary piece rate. The method is not as harsh as the Taylor's piece rate because penalty for slow workers is relatively lower.

Illustration 2 :

Calculate the earnings of workers A, B and C under Straight Piece Rate system and Merrick's Multiple Piece Rate system from the following particulars:

Normal rate per hour	Rs. 18
Standard time per unit	1 minute

Output per day is as follows:

Worker A—384 units; Worker B—450 units; and C—552 units

Working hour per day are 8.

Solution:

Standard output per minute = 1 unit

Standard production per hour = 60 units

Standard production per day of 8 hours = 480 (i., 60 x 8) units

Normal output per hour = 60 units

Normal piece rate = Rs.18/60 = 30 paise

Calculation of level of performance:

Standard output per day	=	480 units (calculated above)
Worker A's output per day	=	384 units
Worker A's level of performance	=	384 × 100/480 = 80%
Worker B's output per day	=	450 units
Worker B's level of performance	=	450 × 100/480 = 93.75%
Worker C's output per day	=	552 units
Worker C's level of performance	=	552 × 100/480 = 115%

Earnings of worker A:

Under Straight Piece Rate System:

For 384 units @ 30 paise per unit = 384 × 0.30 = Rs. 115.2

Under Merrick's Multiple Piece Rate System:

For 384 units @ 30 paise per unit = 384 × 0.30 = Rs. 115.2

Normal piece rate has been applied because worker A's level of performance is 80% which is below 83 %.

Earnings of worker B:

Under Straight Piece Rate System:

For 450 units @ 3 paise per unit = 450 × 0.30 = Rs. 135

Under Merrick's Multiple Piece Rate System:

For 450 units @ 33 paise per unit = 450 × 0.33 = Rs. 148.5

Worker B's level of performance is 93.75% which is between 83% and 100%; so he is entitled to get 110% of normal piece rate (110% of 30 paise is 33 paise per unit)

Earnings of worker C:

Under Straight Piece Rate System:

For 552 units @ 3 paise per unit = 552 × 0.30 = Rs. 165.6

Under Merrick's Multiple Piece Rate System:

For 552 units @ 36 paise per unit = 552 × 0.36 = Rs. 198.7

Worker C's level of performance is 115% which is more than 100% of standard output; so he is entitled to get 120% of normal piece rate (120% of 30 paise is 36 paise per unit)

4. *Gant's Task and Bonus Plan:*

This method is based on careful time and motion study. A standard time is fixed for doing a particular task, worker's actual performance is compared with the standard time and his efficiency is determined. If a worker takes more time than the standard time to complete the task (i.e., his efficiency is below 100%), he is given wages for the time taken by him and if a worker takes the standard time to perform the task (i.e., efficiency is 100%), he is given wages for the standard time and a bonus of 20% on the wages earned. If the worker completes the task in less than the standard time he is given wages for the standard time plus a bonus of 20% of the wages for the standard time. In other words, if a worker's performance is more than 100% he is given piece wages plus bonus at 20% of piece wages. Thus, with every reduction in time, the plan ensures progressive increase in total wages. For this reason, the plan is also known as "Progressive Rate System".

Illustration 3:

From the following data, calculate total monthly remuneration of three workers A, B and C under the "Gant's task and Bonus Scheme".

i) Standard production per month per worker is 1,000 units.

ii) Actual production during the month :

A—850 units, B—1,000 units and C—1,100 units.

iii) Piece work rate –75 paise per unit.

Solution:

Standard production per month is 1,000 units and piece work rate is 75 paise per unit; so guaranteed monthly payment is Rs. 750 (i.e., 1,000 units @ 75 paise).

Level of performance:

Standard output per month	=	1,000 units
Worker A's output	=	850 units
Worker A's level of performance	=	850 × 100/1000 = 85%
Worker B's output	=	1,000 units
Worker B's level of performance	=	1,000 × 100/1,000 = 100%
Worker C's output per day	=	1,100 units
Worker C's level of performance	=	1,100 × 100/1,100 = 110%

Earnings of worker A:

Worker A's level of performance is 85% which is below the standard performance; so he is will get Rs. 750, the guaranteed monthly payment.

Earnings of worker B:

Worker B's level of performance is 100%; so he is will get wages for the standard time and a 20% bonus. Thus, his earnings will be as follows:

Wages for 1,000 units @ 75 paise per unit	— Rs. 750
Add: 20% bonus	— Rs. 150
	Rs. 900

Earnings of worker C:

Worker C's level of performance is 110%, which is more than the standard performance; so he is will get piece wages plus 20% bonus. Thus, his earnings will be as follows:

Piece wage for 1,100 units @ 75 paise per unit	— Rs. 825
Add: 20% bonus (i.e., 825 x 20/100)	— Rs. 165
Total earnings	Rs. 980

Premium and Bonus Plan:

Under this plan, a standard time is fixed for the completion of a specific job or operation and the worker is paid for the time taken by him to complete the job or operation at an hourly rate plus wages for a certain fraction of the time saved on the standard by way of a bonus. The plan is also known as *Incentive Plan* because a worker has the incentive to earn more wages by completing the work in less time. This system of wage payment is in between the time wage system and piece work system.

Some of the important premium plans are discussed below:

i) ***Halsey Premium Plan :***

Under this method, standard time for doing each job or operation is fixed and the worker is given wages for the actual time he takes to complete the job or operation at the agreed rate per hour plus a bonus equal to one-half of the wages of the time saved. In practice, the bonus may vary from 33 1/3% to 66 1/3% of the wages of the time saved. Thus, if S is standard time, T the time taken, R the labour rate per hour, and % the percentage of the wages of time saved to be given as bonus, total earnings of the worker will be:

$$T \times R + \% (S - T) R$$

Under Halsey—Wage plan, the premium is set at 30 % of the time saved.

Illustration 4:

Rate per hour = Rs. 15 per hour

Time allowed for job = 20 hours

Time taken = 15 hours

Calculate the total earnings of the worker under the Halsey Plan. Also find out effective rate of earnings.

Solution:

S (standard time) = 20 hours

T (time taken) = 15 hours

R (rate) = Rs. 15 per hour

Total earnings $= T \times R + 50\% (S - T) R$

$= 15 \times 15 + (50/100)(20 - 15) \times 15$

$= 225 + 37.5$

$= 262.5$

Total wages for 15 hours = Rs. 262.5

Therefore, effective rate of earning per hour = Total wages / Actual time taken

= Rs. 262.5 / 15

= Rs. 17.5

Note: percentage of bonus is to be taken 50% when it is not given.

ii) Rowan Plan :

Under this method, the worker is again guaranteed wages at the ordinary rate for the time taken by him to complete the job or operation. The difference between the Halsey Premium Plan and the Rowan Premium Plan is only in the calculation of the bonus. Under the Halsey Plan, bonus is a fixed percentage of the wages of the time saved whereas under the rowan Plan bonus is that proportion of the wages of the time taken which the time saved bears to the standard time allowed. Thus, bonus under this system will be calculated as:

$$\{(S - T) / S\} T \times R$$

And the total earnings will be calculated as :

$$\{T \times R + (S - T) / S\} T \times R$$

Where S = Standard time,

T = time taken (actual time)

R = rate per hour

Illustration 5:

A Worker completes a job in a certain number of hours. The standard time allowed for the job is 10 hours, and the hourly rate of wage is Re.1. The worker earns at the 50% rate a bonus of Rs.2 under Halsey Plan. Ascertain his total wages under the Rowan Premium Plan.

Solution:

The worker earns Rs. 2 as bonus at 50%; so total bonus at 100% should be Rs. 4. The hourly rate of wages being re.1, the time saved should be 4 hours.

Standard time allowed = 10 hours

Less: time saved = 4 hours

Time taken = 6 hours

Earnings under the Rowan Premium Plan:

Earnings = {T × R+ (S – T) / S} T × R

S = Standard time i.e., 10 hours,

T = Time taken (actual time) i.e., 6 hours,

R = Rate per hour i.e., Re.1

= {(6 × 10) + (10 – 6)/10} 6 × 1

= Rs. 6 + 2.40

= Rs. 8.40

3.1.9 PERFORMANCE APPRAISAL

Employee assessment is one of the fundamental jobs of HRM. Performance appraisal is also known as performance rating, employee assessment, employee performance review, personal appraisal, performance evaluation, employee evaluation and merit rating. Performance appraisal is an objective assessment of an individual's performance against well defined benchmarks.

Performance appraisal may be understood as the assessment of an individual's performance in a systematic way, the performance being measured against such factors as job knowledge, quality and quantity of output, initiative, leadership abilities, and supervisor's co-operation, judgment, health and the like.

Job analysis sets out requirements, which are translated into performance standards, which in turn form the basis for performance appraisal.

Performance management refers to the entire process of appraising Performances, giving feedback to the employee and offering rewards or punishing them.

Objectives of Performance Appraisal:

1. To effect promotions based on competence and performance
2. To confirm the probationary employees

3. To assess the training and development needs of employees
4. To decide upon the pay raise
5. To let the employee know where they stand in so far as the performance is concerned
6. To improve communication
7. To determine whether HR programs such as selection, training and transfers have been effective or not.

Purposes of Performance Appraisal

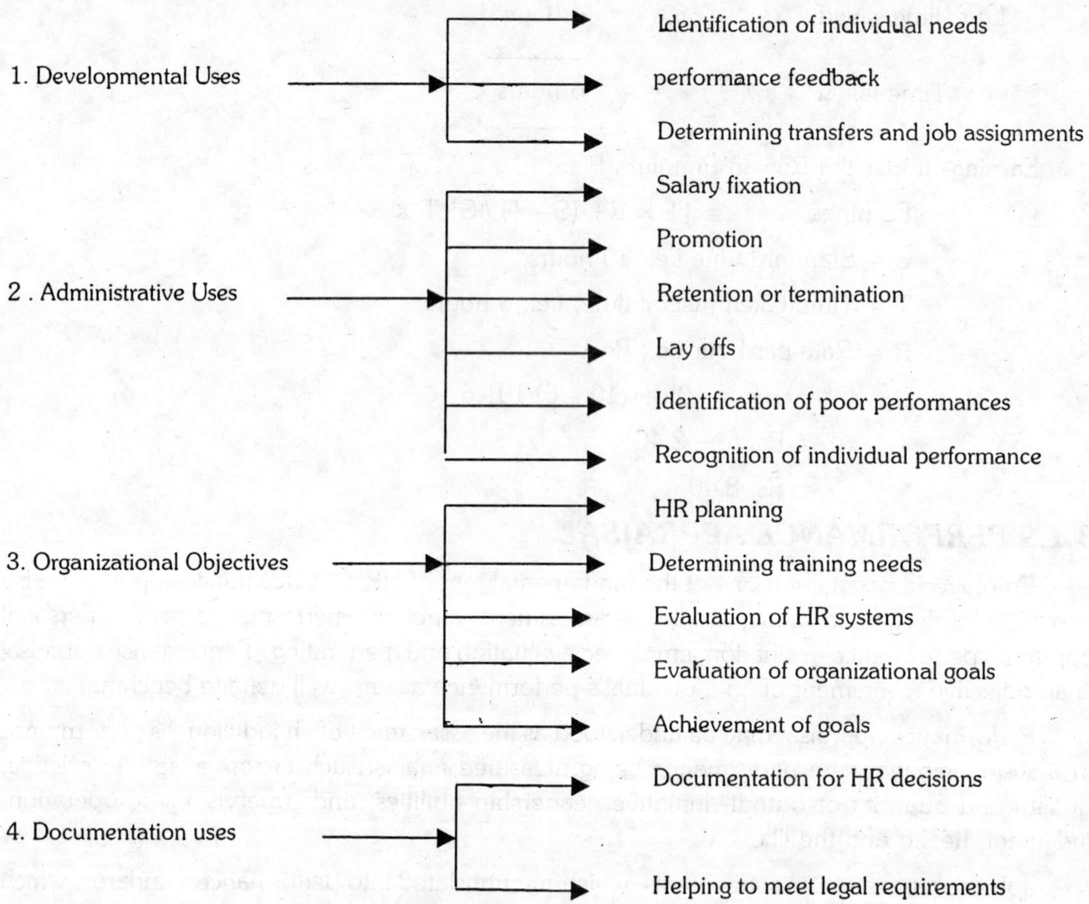

Figure 3.14 : Purposes of Performance Appraisal

Performance appraisal offers competitive advantages to an organisation by improving performance, helps to make correct decisions, ensuring legal compliance, minimizing job dissatisfaction, reduces employee turnover and ensures consistency between organizational strategy and behavior.

Appraisal process:

Formal appraisals occur at specified time periods, once or twice a year. Informal appraisal occurs whenever the supervisor feels the need for communication. Many organizations encourage a mixture of both formal and informal appraisals.

Problems of Rating:

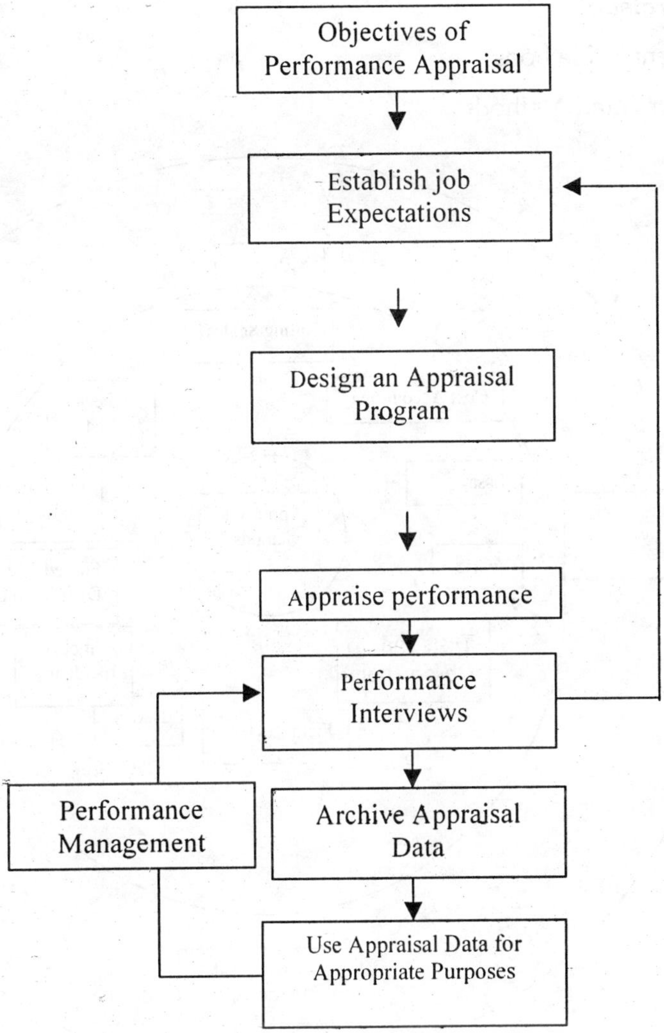

Figure 3.15 : Appraisal Process

Criteria for Assessing Performance:

- Quality
- Interpersonal impact
- Quantity

- Community service
- Timelines
- Cost effectiveness
- Need for supervision

Methods of Appraisal:

1. Past-Oriented Methods
2. Future-Oriented Methods

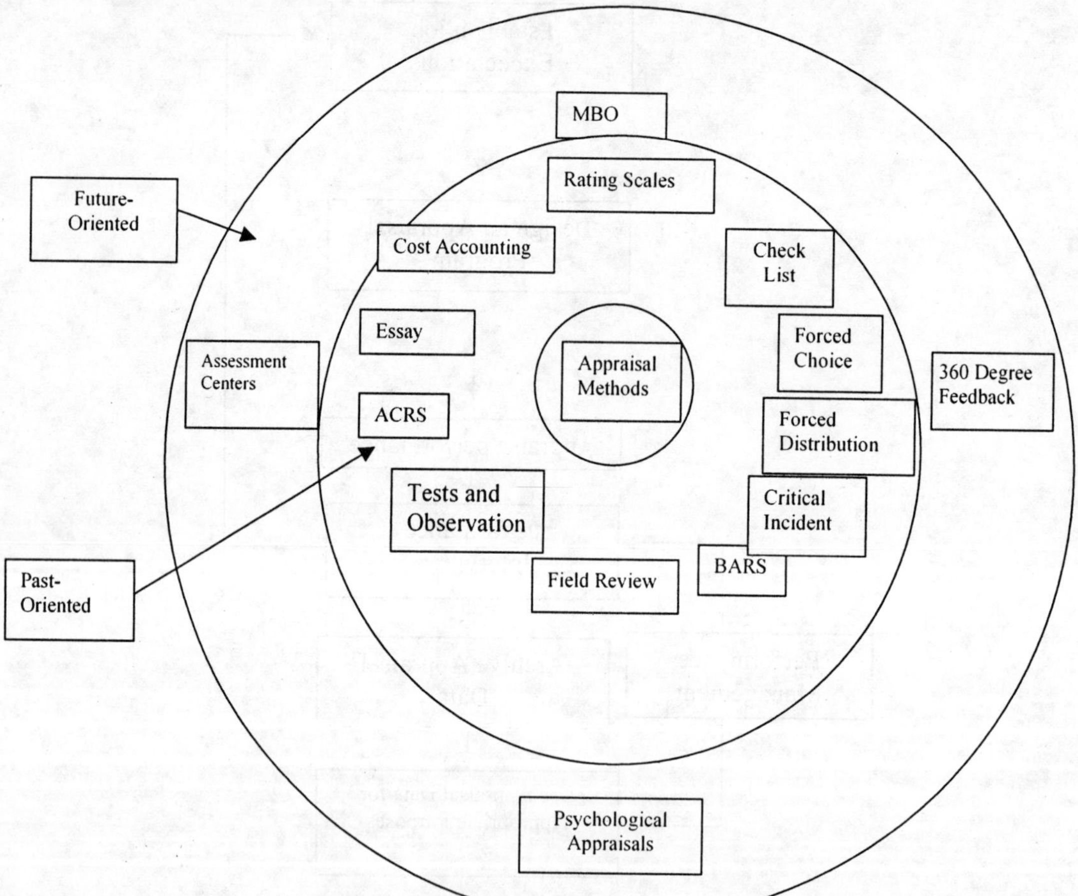

Figure 3.16 : Methods of Appraisal

Past – Oriented Methods:

1. Rating scales
2. Check list
3. Forced Choice Method

4. Forced Distribution Method
5. Critical incident Method
6. Behaviorally Anchored Rating Scales (BARS)
7. Field Review Method
8. Performance Tests and Observations
9. Confidential Records
10. Essay Method
11. Cost Accounting Method
12. Comparative Evaluation Approaches
13. Ranking Method
14. Paired – Comparison Method

Future – Oriented Appraisals:

1. Management by Objectives
2. Psychological Appraisals
3. Assessment Centers
4. 360-Degree Feedback

Performance or Appraisal Interview

Feedback is necessary to effect the improvement of Performance. Appraisal interview is another improvement step in the appraisal process.

Appraisal interview has three goals

1. To change behavior of employees whose performance does not meet organizational requirements.
2. To maintain the behavior of employees who perform in acceptable manner.
3. To maintain superior performance behaviors.

Methods of Feedback:

1. Tell and sell or directive interview
2. Tell and distant interview
3. Problem Solving or participative interview
4. Mixed interview – combination of tell and sell and problem solving interview

Use of Appraisal Data:

The data and information will be useful in following HRM areas

1. Remuneration administration
2. Validation of selection programs

3. Employee training and development programs
4. Promotion, transfer and lay-off decisions
5. Grievance and discipline programs
6. HR planning.

3.1.10 JOB EVALUATION

Introduction

Industrial organizations face the challenging problem of adequately compensating their workers according to the nature of the job they perform. Talented persons will join in an organization only when they get enough wages and incentives. The financial compensations to a worker are dependent on many factors. These factors are: complexity of job, risk and hazard involved in the job, working condition, skill or expertise needed to perform the job, number of subordinates or helpers available to handle the job, etc. Job evaluation is a systematic technique for determining the wage-rate or relative importance of the job by considering various aspects of jobs. It is helpful in determining the wage-rates and incentives.

Job evaluation is a technique to rate a job but not a worker. Therefore, after the job is evaluated, it becomes the starting point to fix the base-wage for a worker so that the wage is fair and equitable. Job evaluation is the criterion for relative differentiation of base-wage rates by establishing the relative worth of various jobs in an organization. The job evaluation of semi-skilled or unskilled workers will be based on the factors, such as: skill, effort, responsibility, job risk, hazard, job conditions, etc. For skilled jobs, factors related to qualification, experience, dynamics of responsibility and complexity in decision-making, leadership quality accountability, etc., are major factors in job evaluation.

Job evaluation is used to analyze and assess the job for ascertaining its relative worth by objective assessment and comparison for determining the basis for a rational wage structure.

It is essential that there should not be any inequity in the salaries of the persons working on the same job in same or in different organizations. Differences in pay lead to resentment amongst the workers which in turn increases labour turnover. Therefore a planned comparison of jobs is necessary to restrict the occurrence of such situations. At this stage job evaluation technique comes to help the management.

Definition and Concept:

Job evaluation is a systematic process of evaluating different jobs of an organization. Depending upon the characteristics and requirements of a job, job evaluation determines its relative worth and attaches a value to it. These relative values of jobs assist in deciding wage rates and salaries for different jobs.

Job evaluation is an attempt to determine and compare the demands which the normal performance of a particular job makes on average workers, without taking into account the individual abilities or performance of the workers concerned.

– International Labor Organization

Job evolution deals with jobs only and is in no way concerned with the persons doing these jobs. For evaluating the merit of the person (say a worker), there is another method known as Merit Rating or performance appraisal.

Objectives of Job Evaluation:

1. To study the relative worth of different jobs in an organization
2. To describe and evaluate new jobs
3. To formulate an appropriate and uniform wage structure.

Uses of Job Evaluation :

(1) Job evaluation is used to determine the relative worth of every job. Relative wages may be fixed on the basis of an objective evaluation and comparison.

(2) It establishes the general wage level, which could be comparable with organisations nearby.

(3) It provides a basis for ranking different jobs.

(4) The relative worth and wage-structure of a new job may be easily established in comparison with the established jobs.

(5) It helps in establishing line of authority, responsibility and accountability.

(6) It provides a sound basis for wage negotiation. It reduces grievances of workers due to improper wages. It eliminates wage inequality within the organization.

(7) Job evaluation is useful in the selection and recruitment process, as skill match with job profile may be achieved.

(8) It is helpful in achieving cordial relations between management and union.

(9) It provides a base for on-the-job training and orientation programs.

Pre-requisites of Job Evaluation

(1) A scientific job analysis should be undertaken furnishing the details of job description, and job-specification.

(2) Top management support and commitment.

(3) Cooperation of union and individual workers.

(4) Comparison of jobs.

(5) Involvement of experts in job-evaluation techniques.

Job Evaluation Procedure:

The job evaluation procedure consists of the following steps:

1. Identifying the jobs to be evaluated.
2. Analyzing the requirements of the job.

3. Writing the skills statement and the responsibilities of the job.
4. Comparing the job with pre-identified key jobs and deciding its level or value.
5. Using the information to evolve suitable wage structure.

For an effective job evaluation, proper description and specification of the job is needed. The main purpose of job evaluation is to decide the base for wage-payment for different categories of jobs:

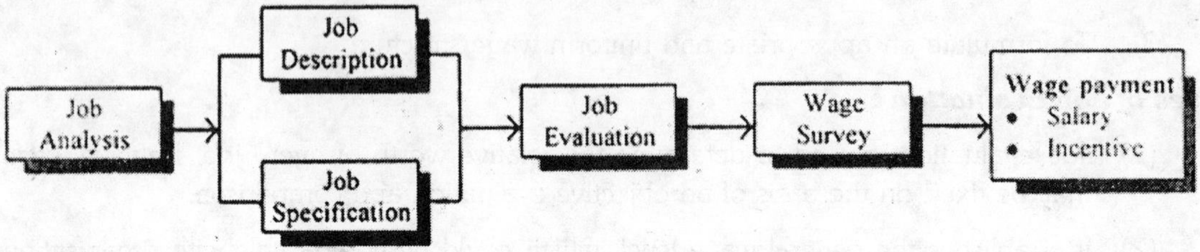

Figure 3.17 : Purpose of Job-Evaluation

Benefits of Job Evaluation:

(1) It helps the management in establishing an objective rationale for acceptable wage-structure.

(2) It takes into account many factors other than the skill difference.

(3) It helps in skill match with job.

(4) It is helpful in the selection, training and promotion of workers.

(5) It establishes cordial labour relationships.

(6) It helps in determining the rate of a new job.

Limitations of Job Evaluation:

(1) Exactness or precision is missing in the job-evaluation. There is no standard table for all the activities. All jobs cannot be measured and compared accurately.

(2) It does not account for many inter-related economic factors.

(3) No special attention is paid for exceptional merit, needed in the performance of the job. Many a times, workers feel frustrated due to this.

(4) The basic assumption in job-evaluation is that a work of equal worth should be equally paid but in reality it's very difficult to implement.

(5) The change in production technology, information system, etc., severely affect the job content. Therefore, a job evaluation conducted few days back may not be valid today.

Methods of Job Evaluation:

The various commonly used methods are:

1. Ranking method,
2. Classification method or grading method,

3. Factor comparison method and
4. Point method.

1. *Ranking Method:*

This is the simplest and most inexpensive way to do job evaluation. This method is suited for small organizations where the evaluators have an intimate knowledge of all the jobs. A committee of experts is constituted for the evaluation of the jobs. Each member should have a complete knowledge of the job-content because job-content forms the basis for the evaluation. The experts evaluate the job-content and job description and then they rank the jobs in hierarchical order on the basis of the relative importance of the job. The decision is on a cumulative perception of the job-content and no specific factor is deeply analyzed. All the rankings of each committee member are averaged to find a final score in terms of relative ranking of each job. The different jobs, depending upon their requirements, responsibilities involved and their importance to the organization are ranked or placed from top to bottom.

Advantages:

1. The method is simple and fast.
2. It can be easily mastered and administered.
3. The method is suitable for small organizations involving lesser number of jobs to be evaluated.
4. Easy to understand and easy to adopt.
5. Inexpensive, as it involves no major cost.
6. It takes less time than any of the other method.

Disadvantages:

1. There is no commonly accepted base for deciding the ranks.
2. The method is not very accurate.
3. It is not useful for large organizations.
4. It is the least used method.

2. *Classification or Grading Method:*

This is a non-quantitative method and suited for organizations that have a large number of activities. This method is an improvement over the ranking method, as a predetermined scale of values is used.

The job evaluation is done by establishing job classes or grade description. An evaluation team is assigned the job of looking into each job description and give weight to it in the light of relevant factors such as, skill, experience, education, etc. Each job is assigned to a particular grade or class. For each grade, different monetary compensation or wage is decided.

Jobs are classified or graded in groups or levels of equal skill, difficulty, responsibility, importance and other requirements. It may be a production job, a sales job or an office job; each job family can be broken into a number of grades. For example, office jobs may be classified in to six grades, namely grade A to grade F. Grade A involves simple tasks like sorting whereas grade F deals with those tasks which require high responsibility and judgment. Each grade carries an appropriate monetary scale.

Advantages:

1. The method resembles ranking method, is simple and can be easily mastered and administrated.
2. It is more accurate as compared to ranking method.
3. A large number of jobs can be handled easily after the grade descriptions are documented.
4. It is relatively simple and inexpensive.
5. It is easy for people to understand in terms of grades or classification.

Disadvantages:

1. Compared to simple ranking system, it takes more time and thus costs more.
2. Compared to point-rating method, it is less accurate.
3. It does not use a detailed job analysis.
4. It is not useful for large organizations.
5. Sometimes it is difficult to correlate and classify grade of the job with the present salary of the worker;

3. *Factor Comparison Method*

This is a quantitative approach for job-evaluation. It resembles the classification method as levels or grades are used in both. Five key-factor scales are used for analysis and evaluating jobs. These factors are: (1) skill, (2) mental effort, (3) physical effort, (4) responsibility, and (5) working conditions.

A composite score is obtained for all factors. Following steps are followed in this method:

Step 1:

Selecting a number of "key" jobs. Recording wages of "key jobs".

Step 2:

Analyzing each "key job" for the five critical-factors, namely: (1) mental requirement, (2) physical requirements, (3) skill requirements, (4) working conditions, and (5) responsibility.

Step 3:

Rank each of the key-jobs within each factor. The rank may vary between factors.

Step 4:

Assign wages according to each factor. It should be in proportion to the requirement of each factor in the job.

Step 5:

Calculate total wage-rate for a job by adding the wage-rate for each factor. This provides a job comparison scale. Insert key-jobs in it.

Step 6:

Evaluate the job under consideration using factor-by-factor in relation to the key jobs on job comparison scale. Then evaluate and compare each job with other jobs in terms of each factor.

Step 7:

Design, adjust and operate the wage-structure.

Advantages of Factor Comparison Method

1. It uses wages of the existing key jobs, which provide standard against which all other jobs are compared.
2. Direct comparison is used for determining wages.
3. A scale for comparing a factor of new jobs is available in this method. This speeds up the evaluation for non-key or new jobs.
4. It is quantitative, yet relatively easy to apply once the factor and levels have been decided.

Disadvantages of Factor Comparison Method

1. It is costly and time-consuming to setup initially.
2. The initial set-up is to be changed every time the wage-structure changes.
3. If unfairly paid jobs are selected as key-jobs, then the entire scaling of factors gives wrong results.
4. Subjectivity in the grading is often challengeable. Different evaluators may give different wages for one factor.

4. Point Method

It is a detailed, quantitative technique, which uses analytical approach to measure the worth of a job. Merrill Lott (1925) developed this method. Each job is broken into different component factors. For each factor, a point or weight is assigned as per its relative importance. The point method bases itself on dividing the jobs into a number of factors which in turn are further sub-divided into grades or degrees. Each degree is awarded certain points and when such points for all the degrees are totaled they indicate the importance of the job in the organization; consequently a suitable wage rate proportional to the total points is determined.

Following steps are adopted:

Step 1: Selecting the jobs to be evaluated.

Step 2: Determining the factors for consideration. These factors may be: (a) skill, (b) effort, (c) initiative, (d) physical requirement, (e) Responsibility, etc. Clearly define each factor.

Step 3: For each factor, determine the number of degrees to be allocated.

Step 4: Assign points for each degree of all factors.

Step 5: Choose few key-jobs and evaluate each by applying Step 1 to Step 4

Advantages

1. Since the method involves points, it is considered to be more accurate and reliable.
2. It is more precise than any other method of job evaluation.
3. Once Grade-Table has been constructed, the chances of subjective discretion decreases.
4. The method can be understood without much difficulty.
5. It is the most widely used method of job evaluation.
6. Most reliable and accurate due to detailed analysis
7. Less chance of subjectivity and judgment is objective based.

Limitations

1. Analysis of factors and grades involve a large amount of work and expertise.
2. Points allocated to each factor base on more or less arbitrary grounds.
3. Time-consuming in establishing initial grade tables.
4. Subjectivity in initial grade table cannot be totally eliminated.

Job Analysis, Job Description and Job Specification:

Human resource planning cannot be accomplished without a clear picture of current and potential employees' skills and qualifications. Three techniques are useful in providing this information: job analysis, job description, and job specification. Job analysis is the process of collecting information about a job. It is the process of collecting job related information.

Job analysis is the systematic, detailed study of a job; it identifies and examines the elements and characteristics of a job and the requirements of the person assigned to the job. From the job analysis, the human resource department develops a job description and job specification.

Job description is a document specifying the objectives of a job, the work to be performed, the responsibilities involved, the skills needed, the relationship of the job to other jobs and the working conditions.

Job specification is a written description of the special qualifications required of a worker who fills a particular job. The specification lists experience, education, special skills, and other requirements. The job specification is typically included as a section of the job description. This type of document is invaluable to human resource departments seeking qualified applicants for job openings. The document also lists qualifications that are desirable but not essential at the time of employment. They may be used by the recruiter or the department manager in evaluating a large number of applicants and selecting a few finalists.

Benefits of Job Analysis are:

1. Foundation for HR planning
2. Foundation for employee hiring
3. Helps in Training and development
4. Useful in Performance appraisal
5. Helpful in Salary and wages fixation
6. Useful in designing Safety and health programs
7. Useful for Job evaluation

Job description implies objectives listing of the job title, tasks, duties and responsibilities involved in a job. Job specification involves listing of employee qualifications, skills and abilities. These specifications are needed to do the job satisfactorily.

The Process of Job Analysis:

Strategic choices → the extent of employee involvement, the level of details, frequency of analysis, sources of job data past oriented vs. future oriented.

Information gathering → methods to be employed for data collection and the officials who should effect

Persons collecting data →
1. Job analysers
2. Supervisors
3. Job holders

Information processing → it is processed to be useful to prepare job description and job specification

Methods of Data Collection (Collecting Job Data):

1. Observation method
2. Interview
3. Questionnaire
4. Check lists
5. Technical conference method
6. Diary method

Job Design:

The logical sequence to job analysis is job design.

Job design involves conscious efforts to organize tasks, duties and responsibilities into a unit of work to achieve certain objectives. Job design follows job analysis.

Job design involves 3 steps:

1. The specification of individual tasks
2. The specification of the method of performing each task
3. The combination of tasks into specific jobs to be assigned to individuals.

While designing a job, requirements of the organization and individual needs of the job holder must be considered.

Factors Affecting Job Design:

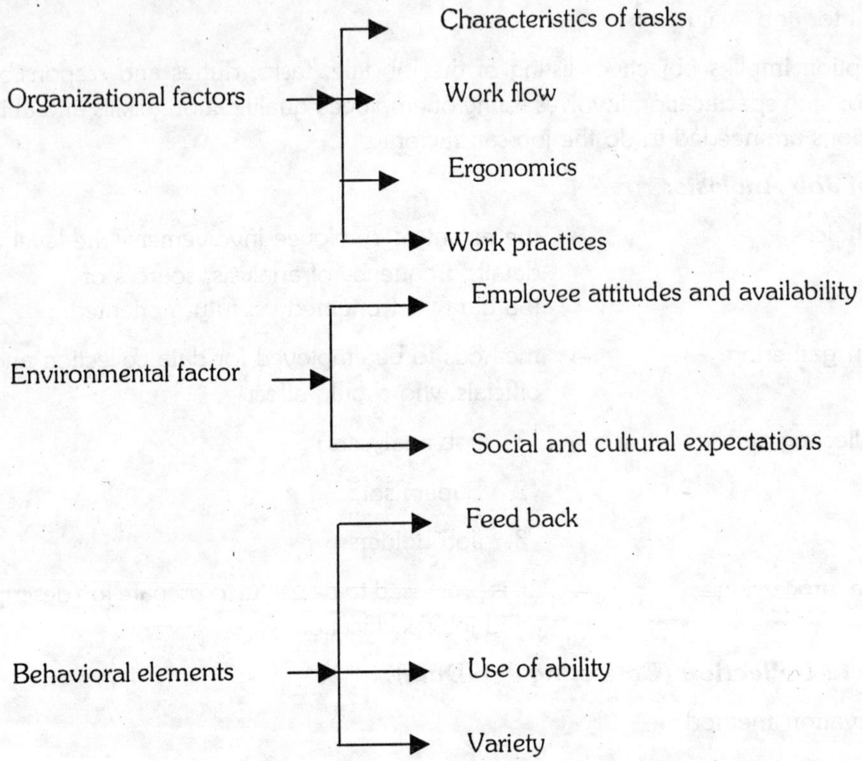

Figure 3.18 : Factors affecting Job Design

Job Design Approaches:

Five popular approaches to job design are

1. Job Rotation
2. Job Engineering
3. Job Enlargement
4. Job Enrichment
5. Socio-Technical Systems

Job Rotation: Refers to moving employees from one job to another job to add variety and reduce boredom by allowing them to perform a variety of tasks. The employee is exposed to different jobs. This helps him to learn the job while he does it. This prepares him to substitute another employee when needed. This takes care of possible short term shortage of skill.

Job Engineering: Focuses on the tasks to be performed, methods to be used, workflows among employees, layout of the workplace, performance standards and interdependencies among people and machines.

Job Enlargement: Refers to the expansion of the number of different tasks performed by an employee in a single job. An enlarged job can motivate individual for five reasons.

1. Task variety
2. Meaningful work modules
3. Ability utilization
4. Worker-paced control
5. Performance feedback.

Job Enrichment: Involves adding more motivators to a job to make it more rewarding. Enrichment makes a job more exciting, challenging and creative. It gives job holder more decision making, planning and controlling powers. It was first coined by Herzberg.

Characteristics of Enriched Job:

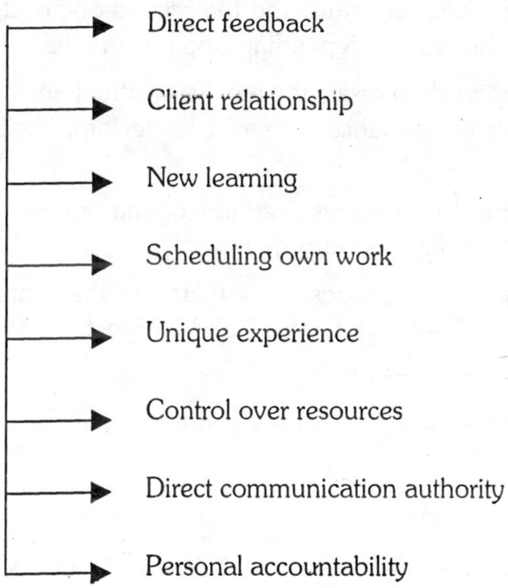

Figure 3.19 : Characteristics of Enriched Job

Outcomes of Job Enrichment:

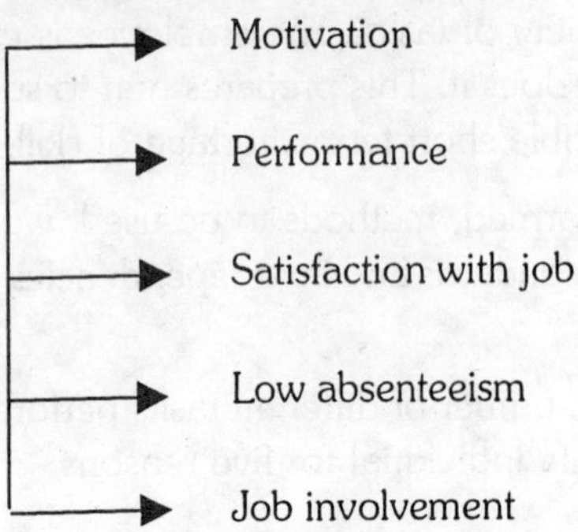

Figure 3.20 : Outcomes of Job Enrichment

3.1.11 MERIT RATING

Introduction

Merit-rating is associated with performance appraisal of an employee. This is a systematic approach for evaluating the performance of an employee on the job. This is also called as performance appraisal, personnel rating and employee evaluation. Merit-rating is a formal, objective procedure for evaluating personality, contributions and potentials of employees in a working organization. Job Evaluation evaluates the job, whereas, Merit Rating assesses the merit of the person doing the job. Merit rating determines the extent to which an employee meets job requirements. Job evaluation and merit rating are two complementary aspects of a sound personnel policy. The first one is a determinant of suitable wage structure and the second one decides the reward an employee should get in addition to his wages, depending upon his merits.

Merit rating is a systematic and orderly approach to assess the relative worth of an employee working in an organization in terms of his job performance, integrity, leadership, intelligence, behavior etc.,

Dale Yoder defines Merit-rating as "all formal procedures used in working organizations to evaluate personalities and contributions and potential of group members".

Performance appraisal (or merit rating) is the process of evaluating the employees' performance on the job in terms of requirements — Scott, Clothier and Spriegel.

Objectives of Merit Rating

1. Helps in executive decisions related to human resource department (HRD).
2. Appraisal of workers.
3. Continuous record for the worth of a worker.
4. Tool for decisions related to training, placement, promotions, confirmation, increment, transfer and counseling of workers.
5. Useful for understanding areas of improvement in a worker
6. Helps in discovering special talent in a worker.
7. Useful in personal research, validation of training objectives and training methodology.

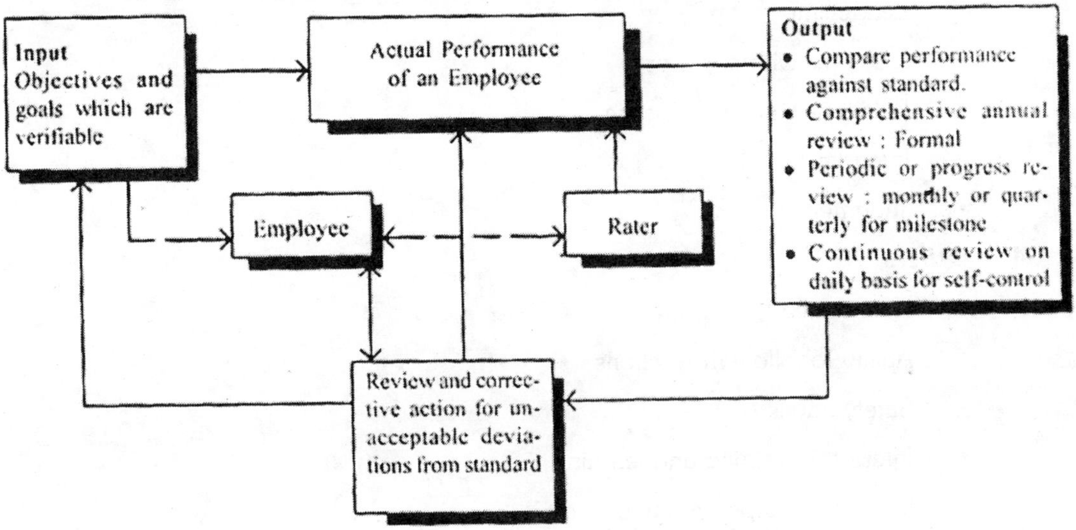

Figure 3.21 : Process of Merit Rating

Criteria for Merit Rating

Employees are rated on the basis of many factors related to personal attributes, leadership quality, on-job performance, interpersonal quality, loyalty, attendance, etc. Some of these factors are:

1. ***Quality of work***
   - Accuracy
   - Rejections and scrap
   - Thoroughness
   - Economy of time
   - House keeping
   - Contribution to quality circle or team
   - Contribution to TQM effort
2. ***Quantity of work***
   - Output
   - Approach in meeting the demand
3. ***Personal Qualities***
   - Team spirit
   - Attitude for work
   - Loyalty

- Leadership
- Relations with superior
- Relations with subordinates
- Integrity
- Judgment

4. ***Others***

- Attendance
- Ability to follow instructions
- Safety habits
- Interest in training and learning
- Interest in corporate culture, etc.

Generally, a rater gives grade on a scale of one to five or remarks such as: exceptional, good, fair, satisfactory and unsatisfactory. All such ratings are added to find the total performance. There are other ways to express in qualitative terms, such as exceptional, good, fair and poor. On the basis of cumulative performance, the overall rating is given which may be above-standard, standard or below standard.

Methods of Merit Rating:

(1) Ranking Method

This is the simplest method in which all the employees are compared with one another. They are ranked in descending order from best to worst. This method has a serious limitation that it is not diagnostic to point the specific areas of weakness and strength of a worker. The method is highly subjective. The difference in rank does not provide the exact nature or the extent of merit-differential. There are chances of personal bias of the rater.

(2) Paired Comparison Method

In this method, each member of the group is compared with remaining other members of the group. Each judgment is recorded in terms of score. These scores are added up to find the final ranking of each person.

This method is an improvement over ranking method. It is a more rational and comprehensive method. The bias of the rater is minimized, yet it may not be over. The method involves large number of comparisons.

(3) Checklist Method

In this method, the evaluator is given a set of statements related to the employee's performance, attitude, behavior and shortcomings. The rater is asked to tick-mark either yes or no. Each yes/no carries certain points, which when added up, give final rating of the employee. Checklist may contain the following statements.

Specimen Checklist

ABC Ltd., BANGALORE		
Employee : Ramakrishna Employee Code : QC-3872 Position :	Department : QCS Date of Rating : 27-06-2010 Rater Code : R-18	
Tick mark (?) the most appropriate box.		
Statements	***True***	***False***
1. Understands work ( )	?	?
2. Assumes responsibility ( )	?	?
3. Makes no mistakes ( )	?	?
4. Innovative in approach ( )	?	?
5. Keeps work area clean ( )	?	?
6. Does not need close supervision ( )	?	?
7. Very regular on work ( )	?	?
Total	4	3
Signature of rater		

Figure 3.22 : Specimen Checklist

(4) Graphic Rating Scale

In this method, the rater marks the rating on a graphic rating scale, the scale containing different degrees of performance in terms of phrases, such as: outstanding, excellent, good, average and poor. For each degree few marks are allotted. Different performance measures are rated on this scale:

(5) Rating by Result

In this method, the rating is done on the basis of achievement of set objectives. Therefore, performance standards are set in advance. It is known to both rater and employee. Under achievement or over achievement is noticed by the rater. Therefore, this method eliminates the personal bias of the rater. Another advantage of this method is transparency in rating. Thirdly, continuous review of rating is possible by both employee and his supervisor. Possibility for improvement may be explored at regular intervals. Since this approach is participative, it instills confidence in employees. The method is more suited for executives and managers as it requires proper education and training.

Advantages of Merit Rating

Merit-rating plays very important role in the human resource administration of a firm. Its advantages are:

(1) Systematic evaluation of employees

(2) Facilitates matching of job with individual.

(3) Facilitates promotion- related decisions.

(4) Facilitates decisions relating to training and development.

(5) Helpful in identifying the weaknesses of the employees which may systematically be removed.

(6) Provides base for guidance and counseling of the employees.

(7) Develops healthy competition among workers to improve performance.

(8) Serves as motivational tool for employees.

(9) Provides objective basis for wage, and salary related decisions including bonus payment and awards and rewards.

(10) Improves employee - employer relationship due to increased trust and confidence.

Limitations of Merit Rating:

(1) Bias of rater may under-rate or over-rate an employee.

(2) Due to bias factor the ratings may not be accurate.

(3) Assessment of irrelevant factors may result in deceptive rating.

(4) Due to improper weightage of factors, the ratings may be improper.

(5) Due to fear, negligence, insufficient time, insufficient information or temperament, the rater may play safe and give average rating to an otherwise good or unsatisfactory employee.

(6) Reward for employee may not follow immediately after a good rating due to organization constraints. This may lead to dissatisfaction.

(7) Many rating factors are very subjective. Due to this, exact rating may not be forthcoming. For example, innovativeness, drive, organizational loyalty, etc., are difficult to be quantified in exact terms.

The Merit Rating/Performance Appraisal Process

Requirements for Success of a Merit Rating System :

A successful merit rating system should be objective. Standard for outputs should be set against which performance should be measured:

For a merit rating system, these requirements are of prime importance:

(1) Commitment and support of top management

(2) Approval of employees and union

(3) Knowledgeable rater

(4) Education and training of employee to understand the rating system

(5) Continuous rating system and periodic review

(6) Grievance redressal system

(7) Administrative support for generating and retrieving necessary information

(8) Sufficient time, fund and formats for the rating

Job Evaluation Vs Merit Rating

Job-evaluation and merit-rating are compared in the following ways:

Table 3.3 : Job Evaluation vs. Merit Rating

Job Evaluation		Merit Rating	
(1)	It evaluates a job or work	(1)	It evaluates a worker
(2)	It is for the purpose of fixing a base-wage for a job.	(2)	It is for the purpose of deciding reward for exceptional merit of worker.
(3)	It is independent of operator or worker. It is impersonal in nature.	(3)	It is independent of job. It is personal in nature.
(4)	Useful for decision regarding wage and salary administration, skill match, etc.	(4)	Useful for decision regarding training, placement, promotion, counseling, etc.

3.2 MARKETING MANAGEMENT

Introduction

Marketing is an essential art and science that is engaged in a vast number of activities by both persons and organizations. Marketing has been gaining a predominant role with the advent of mass production and globalization of economic activity. Marketing is increasingly becoming an important function in all organizations to ensure that demand for a product or service persists along with customer retention. It has become an increasingly vital ingredient in the success of a business. Good marketing is the result of careful planning and execution. The manager today needs a thorough knowledge of marketing to perform their functions in an effective manner. Marketing establishes a vital link between an organization and its consumers.

Meaning of Marketing

Marketing has come to mean many things. It is observed that housewives, who return home after buying vegetables and provisions, state that they have just finished marketing activity. Salesman, who sell the products of their employers by booking orders from the different merchants also refer to their work as marketing. Thus, buying and booking of orders are both referred to as marketing.

To understand the meaning of the term marketing, let us consider a few definitions.

- Marketing is the performance of business activity that direct the flow of goods and services from production centre to consumption centre

  - American Marketing Association.

- Marketing is the process of planning and executing the conception, pricing, promotion and distribution (4 P's) of ideas, goods and services to create exchanges (with customers) that satisfy individual and organizational goals- **American Marketing Association.**

- Marketing is a social and managerial process through which individuals and groups obtain what they need and want through creating, offering and exchanging products and services of value with others **– *Philip Kotler***
- Marketing is the total system of business activities designed to plan, price, promote and distribute want – satisfying products and services to the present and potential customers **– *William J Stanton***
- Marketing is the process of discovering consumer needs and wants and translate them as goods, services and ideas, creating and expanding demand for them **- *Prof. Harry's.***

Other Definitions of Marketing

- Marketing is the creation and delivery of standard of living to the society.
- Marketing is determining the needs and wants of the target customers and delivering the desired satisfactions more efficiently and effectively than the competitors.
- Marketing is the business function that identifies unfulfilled needs and wants, defines and measures their magnitude, determines which target markets the organization can best serve, decides on appropriate products, services and programs to serve these markets and calls upon everyone in the organization to think and serve the customer.
- Marketing is an organizational function and a set of processes for creating, communicating and delivering value to customers and for managing customer relationship in ways that benefit the organization and its stakeholders.
- Marketing starts and ends with the consumer, with information flowing from the consumer to the producer and goods flowing back from the producer to the consumer. Thus, marketing is the whole business seen from the point of view of its final or end result (i.e.) customer satisfaction.

Therefore, marketing involves

- ➢ Creating marketing mix – 4P's (Product, price, place, and promotion)
- ➢ Creating exchange process (Process of obtaining something from someone by offering something in return)

3.2.1 NATURE AND SCOPE OF MARKETING

Marketing is a human activity directed at satisfying needs and wants through exchange processes. Marketing includes such activities as product development, marketing research, communication, pricing, promotion and service apart from selling. Marketing originates with the recognition of a need on the part of a consumer and terminates with the satisfaction of that need by the delivery of a usable product at the right time, at the right place and at an acceptable price.

Marketing is so basic that it cannot be considered a separate function. It is the whole business seen from the point of view of the final result, i.e., from the point of view of the customer. Marketing is a view point which looks at the entire business process as a highly integrated effort to discover, create, arouse and satisfy consumer needs. Marketing is the delivery of standard of living to society. Marketers are involved with marketing several types of entities such as physical goods, services, experiences, events, persons, places, properties, organizations, information and ideas.

Objectives of Marketing: The two main objectives of marketing are

- Ensuring profit to the manufacturers
- Providing satisfaction to the consumers

3.2.2 BENEFITS OF MARKETING

Marketing concept benefits the Organization

The practice of the concept brings substantial benefits to the organization that practices it. For example, the concept enables the organization to keep abreast of changes. An organization practicing the concept keeps feeling the pulse of the market though continuous marketing audit, market research and consumer testing. It is quick to respond to changes in buyer behavior; it rectifies any draw back in its products; it gives great importance to planning, research and innovation and its decisions are no longer based on hunch, but on reliable data relating to the consumers. It does not necessarily stick to one product line; it may diversify and come out with new and improved products or enter totally new areas of business. All these responses, in the long run, prove extremely beneficial to the firm. The base of consumer satisfaction guarantees long term financial success.

Marketing concept benefits the Consumer

The consumer is in fact the major beneficiary of the marketing concept. The attempts of various competing firms to satisfy the consumer put him in an enviable position. The concept prompts the producers to constantly improve their products and to launch totally new products as often as possible; it also prompts them to go in for changes in their business practices. All this results in solid benefits to the consumer such as low price, better quality, improved new products and ready stocks at convenient locations. The consumer can choose, he can bargain, he can complain and his complaint will always be attended to. He can buy on credit, cash or on installments. He can even return the goods if not satisfied with it. When corporations take to the marketing concept, their business practices change in favour of the consumer.

Marketing concept benefits the Society

When more and more corporations resort to the marketing concept, the society is to be benefited. The concept guarantees that only products that are required by the consumers are produced and thereby it ensures that the society's economic resources are channelized in the right direction. It also makes economic planning more meaningful and more relevant to the life of the people.

3.2.3 MARKETING CONCEPT / PHILOSOPHY

It is a basic philosophy/notion/idea/image/view of a company towards marketing efforts. Thus, the marketing concept is the way of life in which all the resources of an organization are mobilized to create, stimulate and satisfy the consumer at a profit. Clearly, marketing activities should be carried out under a well-thought-out philosophy of efficient, effective, and socially responsible marketing. However, there are six competing concepts under which organizations conduct marketing activities: the production concept, product concept, selling concept, marketing concept, customer concept and societal marketing concept.

- The Production Concept
- The Product Concept
- The Sales Concept
- The Marketing Concept
- The Customer Concept
- The Societal Marketing Concept

The Production Concept

The production concept is one of the oldest concepts in business. It holds that consumers will prefer products that are widely available and inexpensive. This concept was built on 'more we make, the more profitable we are'. Managers of production-oriented business concentrate on achieving high production efficiency, low costs and mass distribution. They assume that consumers are primarily interested in product availability and low prices. Some service organizations also operate on the production concept. For example, many medical and dental practices are organized on assembly-line principles as are some government agencies.

However, this does not happen in most cases. As a result, the production concept fails to serve as the right marketing philosophy for an enterprise. This concept is shown in figure 3.23.

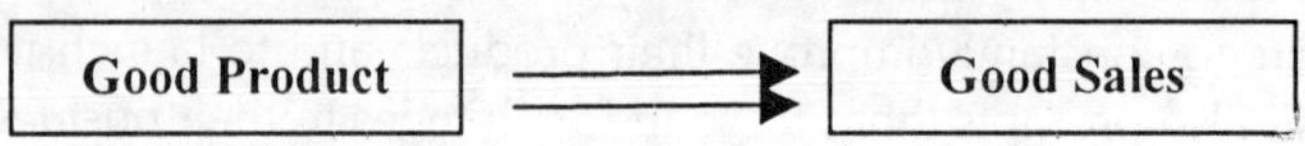

Figure 3.23 : The Product Concept

The Product Concept

The product concept holds that consumers will favour those products that offer the most quality performance or innovative features. If we have good product, consumer response towards our product is definitely favorable. There is no need of any additional promotional efforts.

This concept is based on 'best product could attract buyers automatically'. Product oriented companies assume that consumers would automatically vote for product of high quality. They concentrate on product excellence; they spend their time and money on R&D and bring out many new products. Yet, in many cases they fall in the market place. They do not bother to study the market and the consumer in depth. They fail to find out what the consumers actually need and what they will gladly accept. The product concept can lead to marketing myopia.

Example: A General Motors' executive said years ago

"How can the public know what kind of car they want until they see what is available"? GM's designers and engineers would design the new car. Then manufacturing would make it. The finance department would price it. Finally, marketing and sales would try to sell it. No wonder the car required such a hard sell! GM today asks customers what customers wants what they value in a car and include marketing people in the very beginning stages of design.

The Selling Concept

The selling concept holds that consumers and businesses will ordinarily not buy enough of the organizations products. The organization must therefore, undertake an aggressive selling and promotion effort. We can't sell even the best product without the help of advertising and sales promotion. Its basic consideration is 'a good product does not sell by itself, it has to be pushed. The selling concept is practiced most aggressively with unsought goods, goods that buyers normally don't think of buying, such as insurance, encyclopedia etc. The selling concept is also practiced in the non-profit area by fund-raisers, college admissions etc.

Example: A political party vigorously "sells" its candidate to voters. Large amounts are spent on television advertising, posters etc. The candidate's faults are hidden from the public because the aim is to make the sale.

Most firms practice the selling concept when they have overcapacity. Their aim is to sell what they make rather than make what the market wants. This concept is illustrated in figure 3.24.

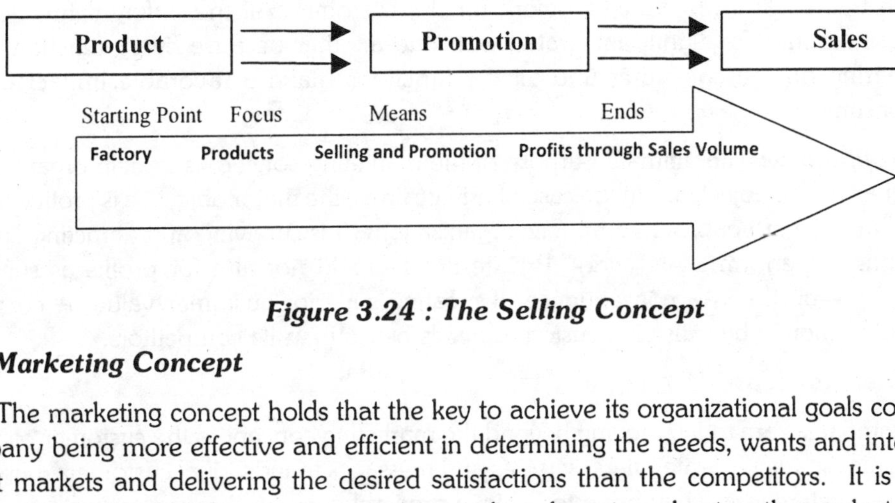

Figure 3.24 : The Selling Concept

The Marketing Concept

The marketing concept holds that the key to achieve its organizational goals consists of the company being more effective and efficient in determining the needs, wants and interests of the target markets and delivering the desired satisfactions than the competitors. It is a customer centric approach which focuses on customer needs and wants and not on the product. "Marketing starts and ends with the customer only". The marketing concept is shown in figure 3.25.

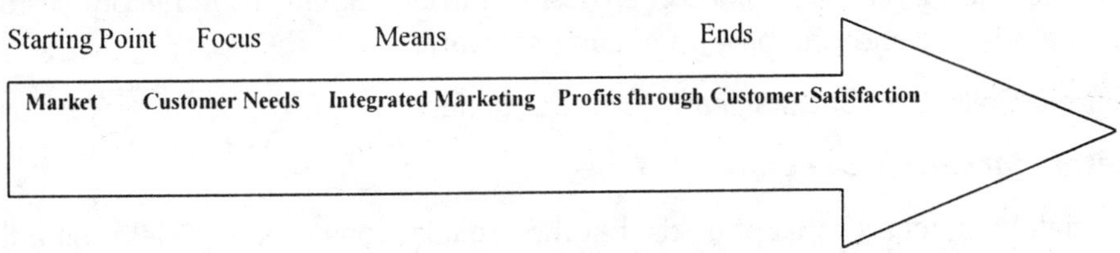

Figure 3.25 : The Marketing Concept

The marketing concept rests on 4 pillars.

1) Target market
2) Needs and wants of the customer
3) Integrated marketing
4) Profitability

1. ***Target Market:*** Companies do best when they choose their target markets carefully and prepare tailored marketing programs.

2. ***Customer Needs:*** Understanding customer needs and wants is not always simple. Some customers have needs of which they are not fully conscious. It is supremely important to satisfy target customer because a company's sales each period come from two groups, new customers and repeat customers. One estimate is that attracting a new customer can cost five times as much as pleasing an existing one. Customer retention is more important than customer attraction.

3. ***Integrated Marketing:*** When all department in the company work together to serve the customers interests, the result is integrated marketing. Unfortunately, not all employees are trained and motivated to work for the customer. All the different functions of business must be tightly integrated with one another because every function has a bearing on the consumer and all the functions make a favorable impact on the consumer.

4. ***Profitability:*** The ultimate purpose of the marketing concept is to help organizations achieve their objectives. In the case of private firms, the major objective is profit whereas in the case of nonprofit and public organizations, it is surviving and attracting enough funds to perform useful work. Private firms should not aim for profits as such but achieve profits as a consequence of creating superior customer value. A company makes money by satisfying customer needs better than its competitors.

The Customer Concept

Many companies are today moving beyond the marketing concept to the customer concept. These companies shape separate offers, services and messages to individual customers, based on their individual preferences. They hope to achieve profitable growth through capturing a larger share of each customer's expenditures by building high customer loyalty and focusing on customer life time. One to one marketing has become possible through advances in factory customization, computers, the internet and database marketing software.

Ex: Barbie Dolls, Levi Strauss Jeans, Dell Computers

The Societal Marketing Concept

The societal marketing concept holds that the organizations task is to determine the needs, wants and interests of the target markets and to deliver the desired satisfactions more effectively and efficiently than the competitors in a way that preserves the consumers and society's well-being.

It is an extended marketing concept. Along with the customer, the company should adopt socially responsible marketing policies and practices. We are still in marketing era, since that is the dominant concept, but increasingly pressure is being put on the companies to adopt the social concept.

Pringle and Thompson define this concept as an "activity by which a company with an image, product or service to market builds a relationship or partnership with a cause or a number of causes for mutual benefit". The comparison of various marketing philosophies is shown in table 3.4.

Table 3.4 : Comparison of Marketing Concepts / Philosophy

Philosophy - Type	View
The Production Concept	Consumers will prefer products that are widely available and highly affordable.
The Product Concept	Consumers will favor those products that offer the most quality, performance and innovative features.
The Sales Concept	Consumers will buy products only if the company promotes/ sells these products
The Marketing Concept	Focuses on needs and wants of target markets and delivering satisfaction better than competitors
The Customer Concept	Focuses on separate offers and services to individual customers based on their individual preferences.
The Societal Marketing Concept	Focuses on needs and wants of target markets and delivering superior value. Holds the view about the consumers and societies well being.

3.2.4 CORE MARKETING CONCEPTS

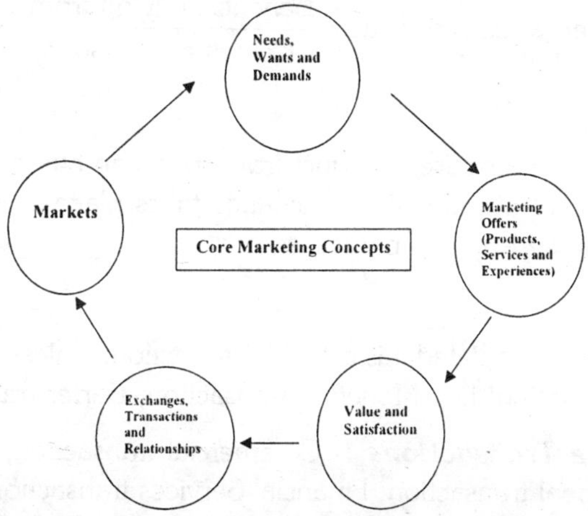

Figure 3.26 : The Core Marketing Concepts

Needs

Customers are motivated by their desire to satisfy complex needs and these needs are the starting point for all marketing activity. Need is basic human requirement. Need refers to something that is deep – rooted in an individual's personality. How individuals go about satisfying that need will be conditioned by the cultural values of the society they belong to.

The human needs can be classified as
- Basic or Primary Needs
- Secondary Needs
- General Needs

Wants

Needs become want when they are directed to specified objects that might satisfy the need. Wants are desires for specified satisfiers of these deeper needs.

Demands

Demands are wants for specific products that are backed by an ability qualification and willingness to buy them. Wants become demand when supported by purchasing power.

Product

Product is anything that can be offered to the market that might satisfy a need or want. Product means anything that can be offered to the market for attention, acquisition, use or consumption which satisfies the need of the customer.

Value

For customers, it is the ratio of perceived benefits to price paid. Customers will evaluate benefits according to the extent to which a product allows their needs to be satisfied.

$$\text{Customer perceived value} = \frac{\text{Benefits deriving from a product}}{\text{Cost of acquiring the product}}$$

Exchange

It is the act of obtaining a desired product from someone by offering something in return. Exchange is a social concept of marketing. Exchange takes place depending on the terms and conditions of exchange agreed by two parties.

Transaction

When the exchange is completed it is called a transaction. Unless there is actual or potential exchange there is no marketing. i.e., Monetary transaction, Barter transaction.

Types of Exchange Transactions : Commercial transaction, Employment transaction, Religious transaction, Global transaction, Financial Services transaction.

Factors affecting Exchange Process

1. Demand and Supply 2. Price 3. Market information with sellers and buyers 4. Legal control and regulations to ensure fair price.

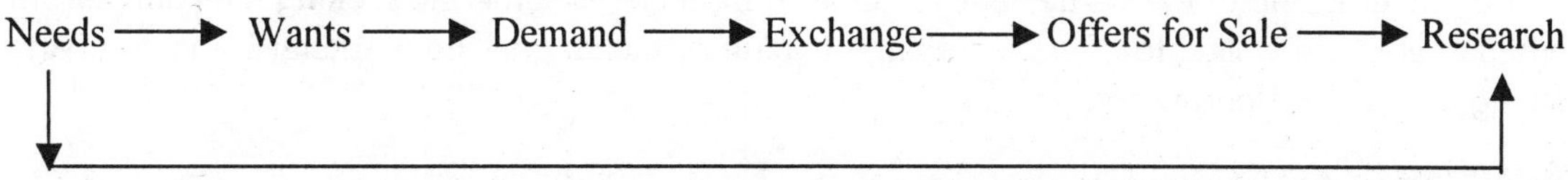

Figure 3.27 : Needs, Wants, Demand and Exchange

The Concept of Exchange

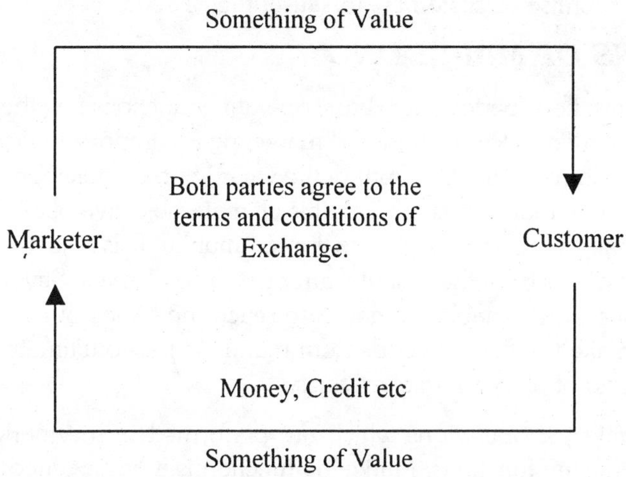

Figure 3.28 : The Concept of Exchange

Market

Market is a place where buyers and sellers gather to exchange goods and services. It can be viewed as any person, group or organization with which an individual, group or organization has an existing or potential exchange relationship.

Markets can be 1. Consumer Market 2. Business Market 3. Global Market and 4. Non – profit and Governmental Marketing.

Types of Consumer Markets

- ***Potential Market*** - Set of customers who possess a sufficient level of interest in a market offer.
- ***Penetrated Market*** - Set of consumers who are buying the company's products.
- ***Target Market*** - A group of individuals whom collectively are intended recipients of an advertised message. A group of customers for whom a seller designs particular goods/services.
- ***Available market*** - Set of customers who have interest, income and access to a particular offer.
- ***Qualified Available Market*** - Set of consumers who have interest, income, access and qualification for the particular market offer.

Marketers

Marketer is one of the parties of exchange. A marketer is someone seeking a resource from someone else and willing to offer something of value in exchange. The marketer is the company serving a market of end users.

Marketing Offers

Marketing offers are combination of products, services, information or experiences offered to a market to satisfy a need or want. It is also called a 'value proposition' which is a set of benefits the marketing people promise to customers to satisfy their needs.

3.2.5 FUNCTIONS OF MARKETING

All business organisations perform two basic operating functions i.e., they produce a product or a service and they market it. Production and marketing are important factors in the economic life of all marketing economies. All efforts put in the varied and complex processes of production are undertaken to satisfy human wants. Unless, this ultimate objective of all economic activities is achieved, production will remain meaningless to the community. This objective is achieved through the process of bringing goods from the manufacturer to the consumers. Several steps are involved in this journey of goods which enable the goods to reach the hands of consumers. All the steps and functions which make the flow of goods from manufacturer to ultimate consumers are very important for the success of all economic activities.

Specialized activities or operations which are performed in the marketing of goods and services are called marketing functions. Marketing function is a homogeneous group of activities which help in the flow of goods from the manufacturer to the consumer. Marketing functions direct and facilitate the flow of goods and services from the producer to the end user. The marketing process starts and ends with these functions.

Marketing functions have been classified by different marketing experts in different ways. However, there is no consensus on the functions of marketing. But, the most acceptable and meaningful classification is given by Clark and Clark which is shown in table 3.5 and figure 3.29.

Table 3.5 : Marketing Functions

Function of Exchange	*Functions of Physical Supply*	*Facilitating Functions*
1. Buying	1. Transportation	1. Financing
2. Selling	2. Storage	2. Risk-Taking
3. Pricing		3. Marketing Information
4. Advertising		4. Marketing Research
5. Sales Promotion		5. Standardization and Grading
		6. Packaging
		7. Branding

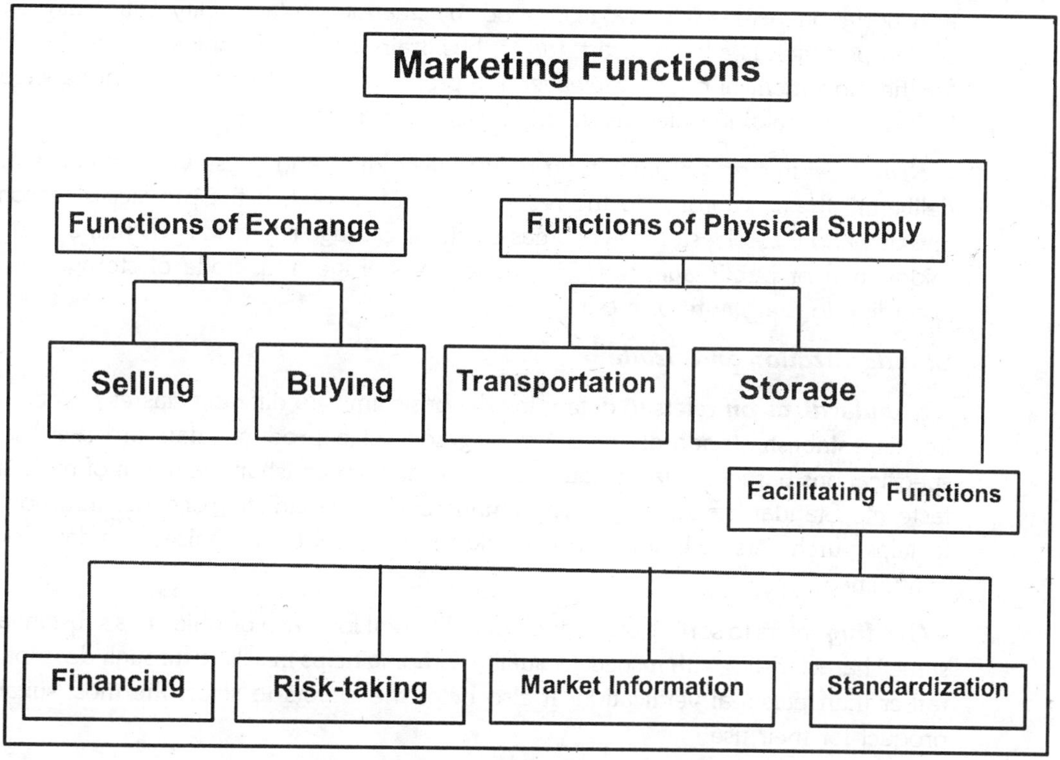

Figure 3.29 : Functions of Marketing

From a theoretical point of view, this classification enjoys maximum acceptance. It is because all the essential functions of marketing are included in this classification and provides an overall idea about the marketing process.

The various functions of marketing are briefly discussed below.

- ***Buying and Selling***

  – ***Buying*** is one of the important functions of 'Exchange'. It requires planning of purchases, search for the sellers, selection of goods to be bought, assembling of goods in right quantity, quality at the right place and time at the right price. In a formal exchange, the buyer has to negotiate terms of purchase and enter into a contract of purchase.

  – ***Selling*** is an important function from the point of view of the seller as well as the consumer. Selling creates demand for a product. Selling function involves product planning and development, finding out or locating the buyers, negotiation of terms of sale such as price, quantity, quality, date of delivery etc. and sale contract leading to transfer of title and possession of goods.

- ***Transportation and Storage***

  – ***Transportation*** is the physical means whereby goods are moved from point of production to the place where they are required for consumption. A good system of transportation increases the value of goods by creation of place utility. Different modes of transportation like bullock cart, trucks, bus, train, aeroplane, ships etc. can be used for the movement of goods. However, the pros and cons of using each mode should be carefully analyzed before selecting the appropriate mode.

– ***Storage*** function provides time utility by holding and preserving products and delivering them according to the requirements of market. If the product is seasonal and demand is stable, storage becomes essential. Storage is provided by manufacturer, middlemen or public agencies. The period of storage and mode of storage varies according to the nature of product.

- ***Standardization and Grading***

  – ***Standardization*** refers to determine the basic limits to different classes of products i.e., to establish standards for different grades of a product. Standard is a list of specifications based on size, colour, appearance, strength, shape, amount of moisture, taste, etc. Standardization plays an important role in the marketing of agricultural goods. It helps purchasers to buy products easily on the basis of recognized standards with confidence.

  – ***Grading*** refers to sorting of products into different lots each of which has substantially same characteristics with respect to quality. Grading helps in selling through description rather than personal verification. It also helps the buyers to select the most suitable product for their use.

- ***Financing*** - Financing is the life blood of commerce. Value of goods is expressed in money and it is denoted by price to be paid by a buyer to a seller. Without finance, the whole marketing activity may come to a standstill. Therefore, for exchange of goods and services and for other marketing activities finance is a vital aspect. The finance for marketing can be obtained from various sources such as banks, financial institutions, individuals, etc. The extent of availability of finance depends on banking policy, credit policy, availability of money from private sources etc.

- ***Risk Management and Insurance*** - One of the important functions of marketing management is risk bearing. In any marketing activity uncertainty is bound to exist. This uncertainty may result in the form of either loss or profit. The unpredictable nature of the consumers, changing fashions, increasing competition and increasing costs of production has led to the concept, "Risk-bearing". All these uncertainties have to be faced in the marketing activity by any producer or entrepreneur. Some of the risks may be avoided by taking insurance coverage.

- ***Marketing Information and Promotion***

  – ***Marketing information*** is a vital resource in business for taking marketing decisions. Information has to be collected, processed and interpreted. Decisions are based on facts and figures. Marketing executives are expected to know the trends in market demand, supply, prices and related market information. If the company is equipped with latest market information, risk of loss can be reduced in marketing, in pricing, in forecasting demand and in facing competition in the market. Securing and using market information is a mark of good marketing management. Modern means of communications such as computer based marketing information system can be adopted for adequate, up-to-date, reliable and timely information.

– ***Sales promotion*** refers to all those marketing activities, other than advertising, personal selling and publicity that stimulate consumer purchasing and dealer effectiveness. Sales promotion techniques are indirect and non personal consumer promotional activities may be in home promotional schemes such as samples, demonstration, coupons, contests, etc., or in store promotional schemes such as temporary price reduction, premium offers, demonstration etc. Dealers' promotional activities include discount on purchases, display and advertisement allowance, prizes, gifts, etc.

3.2.6 PRODUCT LIFE CYCLE CONCEPT

Product Life Cycle

Introduction:

The world of marketing is fast becoming more and more challenging, as marketers try to keep up with the increasing and fast-changing consumer preferences. For a company to be successful, it has to be able to fit its strategies to the changing times, tastes, and technologies. The product life cycle describes the stages that a product goes through. It is often compared to a human being's life cycle. It is considered as a very important tool in marketing, because each stage in the cycle requires different marketing strategies and cause different customer and market reactions. The PLC concept is quite popular in the world of marketing. This concept has been used as a tool for forecasting and also for developing marketing strategy. In other words, this model explains the market response to a new product introduced in the market over a period of time.

The idea of product life cycle is borrowed from biology and an analogy is drawn with the life of an organism, as a living being progresses through the stages of birth, growth, maturity, decline and death. Similarly product also passes through similar stages during its market entry and obvious exist.

Product life cycle has been defined by Phillip Kotler "as an attempt to recognize distinct stages in the sales history of the product". D.T. Kollat, R.D. Balck Well and J.F Robeson have defined it "as a generalized model of sale and profit trends for a product class or category over a period of time. Product life cycle describes the stages in the sales history of a product. The basic features of this theory have propositions that a product has a limited life and a product sales generally follow an 's' curve until sales eventually starts declining. This 's' shaped curve is the most suited for process of life of the product.. The product life cycle (PLC) creates distinct stages in product performance in market place as introduction, growth, maturity, saturation and decline phase.

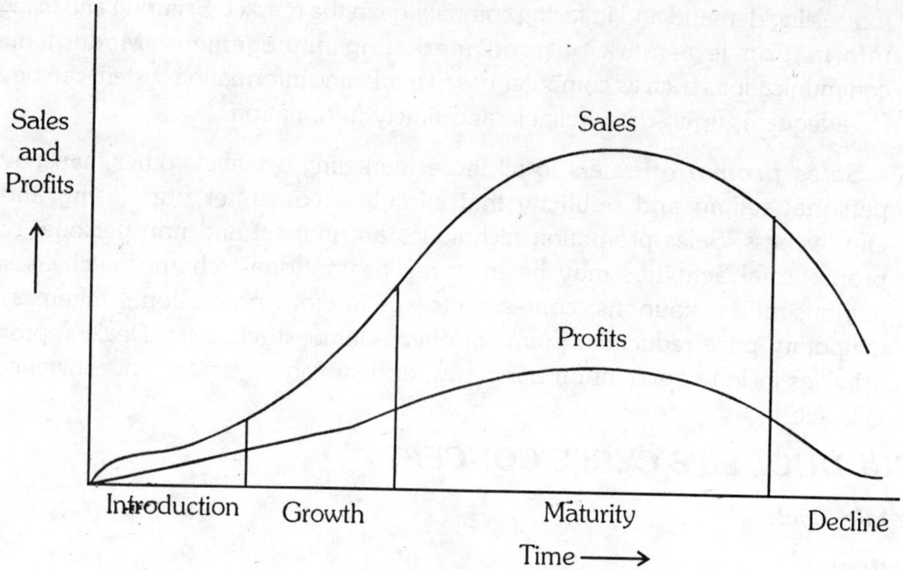

Figure 3.30 : Product Life Cycle

Purpose of PLC

- To take vital product related decisions.
- To estimate the sale/profits of the product at different phases of its life cycle.
- To prolong the profitable phases of PLC

Product Life Cycle Marketing Strategies:

There are distinct opportunities, threats and problems related to each stage of the life cycle of product, influencing the profits of the product and requiring different marketing strategy. A company's differentiating and positioning strategy must change as the product, market and competitors change over time.

To say that a product has a life cycle is to assert four things:

1. Products have a limited life.
2. Product sales pass through distinct stages, each posing different challenges, opportunities, and problems to the seller.
3. Profits rise and fall at different stages of the product life cycle.
4. Products require different marketing, financial, manufacturing, purchasing, and human resource strategies in each stage of their life cycle.

Different stages in Product Life Cycle:

There are four distinct stages in the life cycle of a product. They are

1. Introduction stage.
2. Growth stage.

3. Maturity stage.
4. Decline stage.

1. ***Introduction***: A period of slow sales growth as the product is introduced in the market. Profits are nonexistent in this stage because of the heavy expenses incurred with product introduction.
2. ***Growth***: A period of rapid market acceptance and substantial profit improvement.
3. ***Maturity***: A period of a slowdown in sales growth because the product has achieved acceptance by most potential buyers. Profits stabilize or decline because of increased competition.
4. ***Decline:*** A period where the sales and profits decline to low level or plunge to zero.

3.2.7 MARKET STRATEGIES BASED ON PRODUCT LIFE CYCLE STAGES

1. Introduction Stage:

At the introduction (or development) stage, market size and growth is slight. It is possible that substantial research and development costs have been incurred in getting the product to this stage. In addition, marketing costs may be high in order to test the market, undergo launch promotion and set up distribution channels. It is highly unlikely that companies will make profits on products at the introduction stage. Products at this stage have to be carefully monitored to ensure that they start to grow. Otherwise, the best option may be to withdraw or end the product. This stage is characterized by slow growth, negative or very low profits due to heavy distribution and promotion expenses, few competitors, small number of buyers usually belonging to high income group, high prices due to relatively low production and high production cost and frequent product modification. Hence, a company must choose the strategies carefully and not arbitrarily.

Features:

1. Product is introduced in the market with a full scale of production.
2. Sales are low.
3. High distribution cost.
4. High promotion cost.
5. Profits are low or even negative.
6. Competitors are few.
7. Basic versions of the products are sold.

Strategies:

1. Create product awareness.
2. Build distribution network.
3. Pricing and promotional strategies are crucial.
   a. High priced and low promotion.
   b. Low priced heavy promotion.

Research or engineering skill leads to new product development. The concept of PLC starts from the 'commercialization' stage of new product development. At this stage, product awareness and acceptance among prospective customer are important. Promotional expenditures are at their highest ratio to sales because of the need to

1. Inform potential consumers.
2. Induce product trial.
3. Secure distribution in retail outlets.

Companies that plan to introduce a new product must decide when to enter the market. To create demand for the product is more expensive and risky. Length of the introductory stage will depend on the complexity involved in the product, its degree of newness, its fit into the existing customer need structure, the presence of competitive products either as perfect or imperfect substitutes and the nature, magnitude, superior technology, quality, brand strength and effectiveness of the introductory marketing expenditure.

In this stage, the competition will be in the form of imperfect substitutes available in the market, availability of existing products, two firms working on similar technological plant form may also launch competing products at the same time. When two or more firms launch a product at the same time, then the introductory stage is likely to be shorter.

2. *Growth Stage:*

The growth stage is characterized by rapid growth in sales and profits. In this stage the number of competitors increase and the manufacturers make first major product improvements. The companies use various strategies in the growth stage of their products with a view to sustaining market growth for the longest possible period of time. Profits rise due to an increase in output (economies of scale) and possibly better prices. At this stage, it is cheaper for businesses to invest in increasing their market share as well as enjoying the overall growth of the market. Accordingly, significant promotional resources are traditionally invested in products that are firmly in the growth stage. The product begins to make rapid sales gains because of the cumulative effects of introductory promotion, distribution and word-of-mouth influence. This stage begins when demand grows rapidly. In this the firm uses several strategies to sustain rapid market growth.

Features:

1. Most rewarding stage for the marketers.
2. Sales climb-up rapidly.
3. Marked improvement in profits.
4. Competition intensified.
5. Cost starts declining.
6. Enter into new market and new market segment.

Strategies:

1. It improves product quality and adds new product features and improved styling.
2. It adds new models and flanker products of different sizes, flavors.

3. It enters new market segments.
4. It increases its distribution coverage and enters new distribution channels.
5. It shifts from product-awareness advertising to product preference advertising.
6. It lowers price to attract the next layer of price sensitive buyers.
7. Spend more amount of money on promotional activities.
8. Increased investment lower the current profits.

These strategies strengthen the firm's competitive position. This growth stage also contributes in increasing profit levels.

3. *Maturity Stage:*

The maturity stage is, perhaps, the most common stage for all markets. It is in this stage that competition is most intense as companies fight to maintain their market share. Here, both marketing and finance become key activities. Marketing expenditure has to be monitored carefully, since any significant moves are likely to be copied by competitors. The maturity stage is the time when most profit is earned by the market as a whole.

In this stage, the product covers mass markets. Manufacturers come forward with new product models oriented towards style. There is further decline in prices and dealer margins and profits decrease. Towards the end of this stage, level of sales starts to decline and customers start moving towards other products and substitutes. One of the important marketing strategies pursued by the companies in this stage of their products is market modification. This includes conversion of non users into users, entering new market segments and winning competitors, customers, with a view to expanding the number of brand users, and getting current brand users to increase their usage of the brand by using it more frequently, using more of it per usage occasion and making new and varied uses. Another strategy is product modification under which the marketers take resort to product quality improvement, feature improvement and style improvement. These amounts to product re-launch.

Features:

1. Growth rate of sales slowdown.
2. Competition becomes acute and severe.
3. Market is flooded with many competing products.
4. This stage continues for a reasonable period of time.
5. Cost of inventory leading climb up.
6. Later part of maturity stage will see fall in profits.
7. Consumers start switching to new brands.

Strategies:

1. Market modification.
2. Product modification.
3. Overall change in marketing mix.

At this stage the rate of sales growth will slow because of the declining number of potential customers who remain unaware of the product or who have taken no action.

"Most products are in the maturity stage of the life cycle and most marketing manager's scope is with the problem of marketing the mature product".

The maturity stage divides into three phases.

1. Growth.
2. Stable.
3. Decaying maturity.

In the first phase, the sales growth rate starts to decline. There are no new distribution channels to fill.

In second phase, sales flatten on a per capita basis because of market saturation. Most potential consumers have tried the product and future sales are governed by population growth and replacement demand.

In the third phase, decaying maturity, the absolute level of sales starts to decline and consumers begin switching to other products.

In this maturity stage, the last of the unsuccessful competing brand will tend to withdraw from the market. For this reason, sales are likely to continue to rise while the survivors map up the customers for the withdraw brands. This is the stage in which it becomes difficult to maintain effective distribution and the competition is more on the basis of price than any other component.

4. Decline stage:

In the decline stage, the market is shrinking, reducing the overall amount of profit that can be shared amongst the remaining competitors. At this stage, great care has to be taken to manage the product carefully. It may be possible to take out some production cost, to transfer production to a cheaper facility, sell the product into other cheaper markets. Care should be taken to control the amount of stocks of the product. Ultimately, depending on whether the product remains profitable, a company may decide to end the product.

Features:

1. Sales may come down to zero.
2. Continue at very low levels for some years.
3. Either no profit or low levels of profits.
4. Intensity of competition comes down.
5. The customer switch over to newer better brands increases.

Strategies:

1. Drop the product.
2. Sell the product.

3. Maintain the product.

4. Harvest it.

The sales and profits of all the products ultimately decline, though the decline may be slow in the case of some of them and rapid in the case of others. In this stage, sales are declining for a number of reasons. They are changes in customer preferences, competitive structure in the market, technology, increased domestic and foreign competition and other environmental forces. These factors lead to over capacity, increased price-cutting and profit erosion. Sales begin to diminish absolutely as customers begin to get bored with the product. Profits also decline. A company must continuously watch and review its product and identify the aging ones in the decline stage of their life cycle. Thereafter, it should adopt appropriate marketing strategies to deal with them, depending upon the industry's relative attractiveness and its own competitive strength in the industry to which its product in the decline stage belongs.

According to one study of company strategies in declining industries, five strategies are available to the firm.

1. Increasing the firm's investment.
2. Maintaining the firm's investment level until the uncertainties about the industry are resolved.
3. Decreasing the firm's investment level selectively, by dropping unprofitable customer groups, while simultaneously strengthening the firm's investment in lucrative niches.
4. Harvesting the firm's investment to recover cash quickly.
5. Divesting the business quickly by disposing of its assets as advantageously as possible.

There are another two stages that is saturation and abandonment stages.

The saturation stage is in between maturity and decline stage. The features are

1. Some authors consider saturation in the fourth stage.
2. It comes after maturity.
3. All the features seen under maturity stage are intensified and sales begin to decline.

The abandonment stage is the sixth stage and it is the last stage in the PLC. The features are

1. Marketer has no option, other than drop out the product.
2. Product is totally withdrawn from the market.

The following table 3.6 shows the PLC and its different stages and the various characteristics which they reflect, in the varying stages.

Table 3.6 : Characteristics in different stages of PLC

PLC Elements	Introduction	Growth	Maturity	Decline
Sales	Low	Fast growth	Slow growth	Declining
Profit	Negligible	Peak level	Declining	Low
Cash in flow	Negative	Moderate	High	Low
Competitors	Few	Growing	Many	Declining
Customers	Innovative	Mass market	Mass market	Laggards

Examples

Set out below in table 3.7 are some suggested examples of products that are currently at different stages of the product life-cycle:

Table 3.7 : Examples of Products at different PLC stages

Introduction	Growth	Maturity	Decline
Third generation mobile phones	Portable DVD Players	Personal Computers	Typewriters
E-conferencing	Email	Faxes	Handwritten letters
All-in-one racing skin-suits	Breathable synthetic fabrics	Cotton t-shirts	Shell Suits
Iris-based personal identity cards	Smart cards	Credit cards	Cheque books

Uses of PLC :

1. The product life cycle emphasizes the fact that nothing lasts forever and underlines the fact that companies have to face the fact that products need to be terminated and new products developed to replace them.
2. The PLC helps to identify opportunities for new product development or product improvement and where and when changes to product or process might be needed.
3. The PLC reminds managers that growth will end and suggest when there is need for planning investment in new production facilities.
4. The PLC emphasizes the need to review marketing objectives and strategies as products pass through the various stages.
5. The PLC also stresses the need to analyze the balance of products that a company markets from the point of view of the life cycle stages.
6. The PLC concept highlights the dangers of overpowering.

Limitations of PLC

1. Not all products follow the classic s-shaped curve.
2. The PLC is the result of marketing activities and not the cause.
3. The deviation of the PLC stages is unpredictable.

3.2.8 CHANNELS OF DISTRIBUTION

After products are produced and priced, they must be distributed to the marketplace. All organizations perform the distribution function. The distribution function is vital to the economic well-being of society because it provides the goods and services desired by the consumer. Economists often describe the value of distribution in terms of ownership, place, and time utility. The marketer contributes to the product's value by getting it to the right place at the time the consumer wants to buy it and by providing the mechanism for transferring ownership. Firms that do not perform the distribution function effectively usually fail.

Distribution also provides employment opportunities in the form of salespeople, warehouse managers, truck drivers and operators, all who are involved in distribution. Others service the products provided through a distribution network. Most people involved in distribution are classified as service personnel: Their role is to provide service to some other sector of the economy.

The two major components of an organization's distribution strategy are distribution channels and physical distribution.

Distribution channels are the paths that goods—and title to them—follow from producer to consumer. They are the means by which all organizations distribute the goods and services they are producing and marketing.

The second major component of distribution strategy, ***physical distribution,*** is the actual movement of goods and services from the producer to the user. Physical distribution covers a broad range of activities. These tasks include customer service, transportation, inventory control, materials handling, order processing, and warehousing etc.

Producers normally use a number of marketing intermediaries for taking their products to users. Marketing intermediaries bear a variety of names such as, sole selling agents, marketers, wholesalers, distributors, semi-wholesalers, franchised dealers, retailers, authorized representatives, brokers, commission agents and jobbers. All such intermediaries constitute the distribution channel. The depots, show rooms and other direct outlets of producers also form part of the distribution channel. The process of marketing involves the distribution system which is concerned with the movement of goods from the point of production to the point of consumption.

Meaning and Functions of Channels of Distribution

A channel is live organ of marketing. A channel of distribution is an organized network or a system of agencies and institutions which in combination perform all the activities required to link the producers with users and users with producers to accomplish the marketing task. A channel of distribution is a path way directing the flow of goods and services from producers to consumers composed of intermediaries through their functions and attainment of the mutual objectives.

The word channel has its origin in the French word used for canal. Channels are routes avenues, pathways suggesting movement or flow. Distribution means to distribute, disseminate or spread about. When these words are related to marketing, channels of distribution have been defined in different ways.

According to Richard Bushkirk – "distribution channels are the system of economic institutions through which a producer of goods delivers them into the hands of their users".

The American Marketing Association has defined distribution channel "as the structure of intra company organisation units and extra company agents and dealers, wholesalers and retailers through which a product or service is marketed".

According to William J.Stanton – "a channel of distribution for a product is the route taken by the title of the goods as they move from the producer to the ultimate consumer or industrial users.

According to Philip Kotler – "a channel of distribution is a set of independent organisations involved in the process of marketing a product or service available for use or consumption."

Thus, it is clear from the above definitions that channels of distribution which is also known as trade channels or marketing channels are the means employed by manufacturers and sellers to get their products to the markets in order to reach into the hands of users.

Functions of Channels of Distribution:

Marketing intermediaries enter a channel of distribution that direct products from producers to ultimate consumers. They perform various functions that assist in the operation of the distribution channel. These functions include buying, selling, carrying inventory, storing, financing, transporting, promotion, negotiation and market intelligence etc. Sometimes their efficiency wanes and they must be replaced, but someone in the channel must perform the vital distribution functions. Intermediaries often provide important marketing information with other channel members. By buying a manufacturer's output, intermediaries provide the necessary cash flow for the producer to pay workers and buy new equipment. The importance of distribution channels emanates from the functions performed by them. It is but natural that most business firms consider the channel as a very important component of the marketing mix.

The functions performed by distribution channel are as follows:

1. Distribution channels facilitate the sales process by being physically close to customers.
2. They bridge the makers and users efficiently and economically.
3. Break the bulk and cater to the small size requirements of buyers.
4. Assemble and offer suitable assortments of products as required by buyers.
5. Help sub-distribution.
   a) Selling to sub-distributors
   b) Re-transport
   c) Handling
   d) Accounting

6. Help stock holding
   a) Financing the stocks
   b) Risk bearing
   c) Storage of products
   d) Making available ware house space
   e) Aiding the sales by transforming the static stocks into operational stocks.
7. Provide salesmanship.
8. Provide pre-sale and after-sale service.
9. Assist in sales promotion.
10. Assist in merchandising.
11. Aid the introduction of new products in the market.
12. Aid the price mechanism between the firm and the ultimate customers.
13. Assist in developing sales forecasts for the territory concerned.
14. Provide feedback and market intelligence.
15. Maintain records/registers.
16. Maintain liaison
17. Extend credit to retailers as well as actual users.
18. Transfer technology to the users and act as "change agents".

Steps in Channel Design

- Analysis of customer needs
- Establish channel objectives and constraints
- Identify major channel alternatives
- Evaluate the major alternatives
- Selecting the distribution channel

Selecting a Distribution Channel

The selection of a distribution channel depends on several factors: the market, the product, the producer, the environment and the competition. These factors are often interrelated.

Market Factors - The most important consideration in choosing a distribution channel is that market segment the producer wants to reach. Changes in consumer buying behavior may influence a channel decision. If the product can be marketed to more than one segment, multiple distribution channels may be required. In fact, multiple channels have become increasingly popular in recent years. Market factors such as the existing market structure, the nature of the purchase deliberations, availability of channel and competitor's channel also influence the channel selection decisions.

Product Factors - In general, products that are complex, expensive, custom made, and perishable move through shorter distribution channels whereas the inexpensive and standardized products are typically sold through longer channels. Product variables such as physical and technical nature of the product, the length of product line and the market position must be weighed while selecting a particular channel of production.

Producer Factors - Producers that offer a broad product line and have the financial and marketing resources to distribute and promote their products are more likely to use a shorter channel of distribution. Factors such as the company's financial position, the extent of market control desired, the company reputation and the company marketing policies have bearing on the channel choice.

Environmental Factors - Among the environmental factors, the most significant are three namely economic factors, legal restrictions and fiscal policies. The economic conditions prevailing in the country on one hand, and the world on other, the legislative restrictions imposed by the governments both state and central and the fiscal policies have considerable impact on the channel decisions.

Competitive Factors - In choosing a distribution channel, producers must consider how well an intermediary performs the marketing functions. A producer may become less competitive when an intermediary fails to adequately promote the firm's products.

Marketing Channels

Marketing channel refer to a set of independent organizations which involve in the process of making the product or service available to the consumers for consumption or usage. Marketing channel are a system of economic institutions through which producer deliver their goods to the ultimate consumers. Set of marketing intermediaries include wholesalers, retailers, sole selling agents, commission agents, stockiest, brokers, manufacturer's representatives, jobbers, dealers, transport companies, warehouses, banks and advertising agencies etc.

Marketing channel decisions are critical and influence all other marketing mix decisions. These decisions are often harder to change than price, promotion and product decisions. They are usually long-term and determine product's market presence and ensure customer's accessibility to the product. The same product may require different approaches to set up channel arrangements if different customer segments view it differently. Channels for reaching the consumer may vary over time. Channel selection depends on the circumstances of the market and on consumer needs. Different distribution path alternatives have been developed because a certain channel type may be appropriate for one product but may not be suitable for others.

3.2.9 LEVELS OF CHANNELS

- Direct Marketing Channel
- Indirect Marketing Channel
    - ***One-Level Channel***
    - ***Two-Level Channel***

- ***Three-Level Channel***
- ***Four-Level Channel***

Channels used for Consumer Products

Consumer product channels: Companies producing consumer products may use different types of channels. Producers can choose zero –level channel or direct-marketing channel or the indirect marketing channels such as the one-level channel, two-level channel, three-level channel and four- level channel

Direct Marketing Channel – Direct channel is the simplest and shortest channel through which goods reach the ultimate consumer without the services of middlemen and it is highly applicable in the case of industrial goods. In direct marketing channel the manufacturer sells the goods directly to the consumers without any marketing intermediary.

a) The manufacturer can have own sales depots that directly sell the goods to the consumers. For example: Retail show rooms of the Bata Shoe Company

b) The manufacturer can adopt mail order system of selling in which the producer advertises his products in newspapers and invite direct orders from consumers. Goods can be supplied directly to the consumers by mail, on receipt of orders from the consumers.

c) The manufacturer employs his own sales representatives to visit consumer houses and sell goods directly at their door steps. This is called as door to door selling. For example: The sale of Eureka Forbes Ltd's, Euro clean vacuum cleaner.

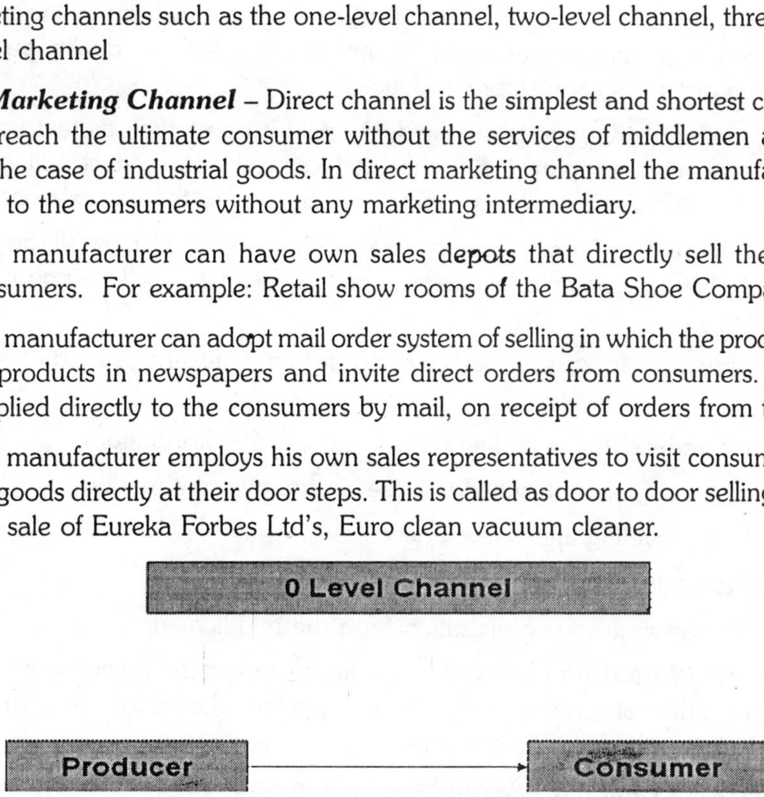

Figure 3.31 : Zero Level Channel

Direct Channel is highly useful in the following circumstances.

i) ***Perishable goods:*** If the manufacturer's goods are perishable in nature, there is every need to dispose of the stock at the earliest. For example: Sale of vegetables, milk, butter, eggs, fish, etc.

ii) ***Less output:*** If the manufacturer's output is less and market is limited then direct channel is desirable. For example: Bakery owners manufacture bread, biscuits, cakes etc., and sell them through their own shops.

iii) ***Special class of people:*** If the goods cater to the needs of a special class of people and are purchased only by them, direct channel is desirable. For example: The X-Ray equipment is purchased only by hospitals and nursing homes and producers intend to sell such equipment directly to them.

iv) ***Technical Nature:*** If the goods produced are technical in nature and require demonstration to the consumers, direct channel is desirable. For example: Sale of heavy machinery goods, computers, and xerox machines etc., i.e. industrial goods.

v) ***New product:*** If a new product is introduced into the market, the manufacturer tries to contact the consumers directly to explain the qualities of the product through his salesmen.

For example: When Henko detergent powder was released in the market, door to door sales was undertaken by the company to explain the quality and superiority of the product over competitor's products.

vi) ***Mail order:*** If the goods can be sent easily by post such as text books or general books exercise equipment etc., the producer can adopt direct selling. For example: Telugu Academy sends the books ordered by post to the desired consumers.

vii) ***Large Network:*** If the manufacturer has a large net work of retail shops, direct selling is desirable. For example: The Bata Shoe Co., DCM etc., sell their goods directly to the consumers.

There has been an increasing use of direct selling in recent years due to the following reasons.

a) Need to reduce the marketing costs by large-scale distribution.

b) Growing competition resulted in close control over the market

c) Need for providing after sales service.

d) Need to undertake special promotional efforts.

e) Exploitation and non co-operation form the middlemen.

- ***Indirect Marketing Channel*** - In indirect channel the manufacturer doesn't sell the goods to the consumer directly. He sells goods to the middlemen. The middlemen in turn sell the goods to the consumers.

- ***One-Level Channel*** - As can be seen from figure 3.32, in this type of channel there is only one intermediary between producer and consumer. This intermediary may be a retailer or a wholesaler/distributor. This type of channel is used for specialty products like washing machines, refrigerators, televisions typewriters, and electric fans etc.

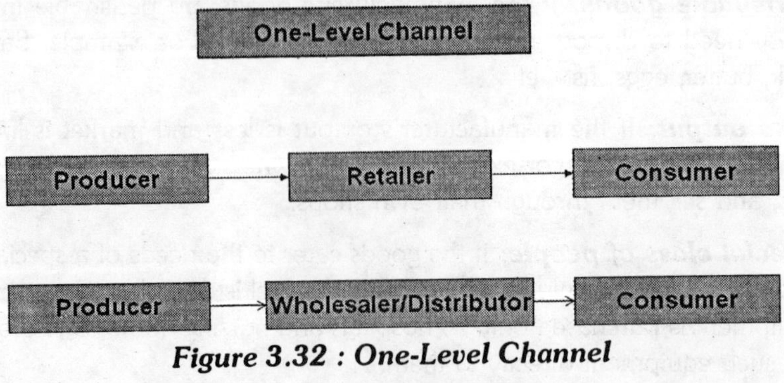

Figure 3.32 : One-Level Channel

- ***Two-Level Channel*** - This type of channel has two intermediaries, namely, wholesaler/ distributor and retailer between producer and consumer. Under this method, the producer sells the goods to the wholesaler, who in turn, sells to the retailers. The retailers in turn sell the goods to the ultimate consumers. This channel is used for consumer durable products. A typical figure of two level channel is shown in figure 3.33.

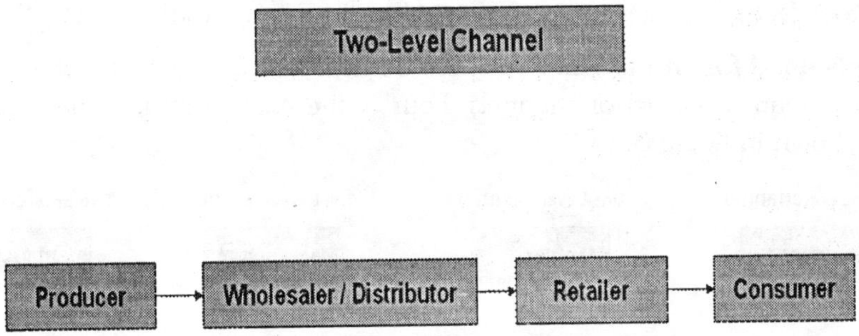

Figure 3.33 : Two-Level Channel

- ***Three-Level Channel*** - As shown in figure 3.34, this type of channel has three intermediaries namely distributor, wholesaler and retailer. In this method, the producer sells his goods to the distributors who sell them to the wholesalers who in turn sells them to the retailers and the retailers sell them to the consumers. This pattern is used for convenience products.

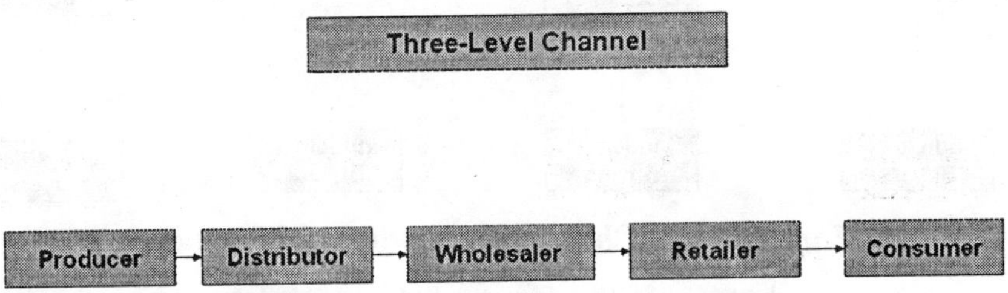

Figure 3.34 : Three-Level Channel

- ***Four-Level Channel*** - This type of channel has four intermediaries, namely agent, distributor, wholesaler and retailer. This type of channel is used for consumer durable products. This type of channel is very popular in agricultural marketing and it is the longest route of distribution. A typical figure of four level channel is shown in figure 3.35.

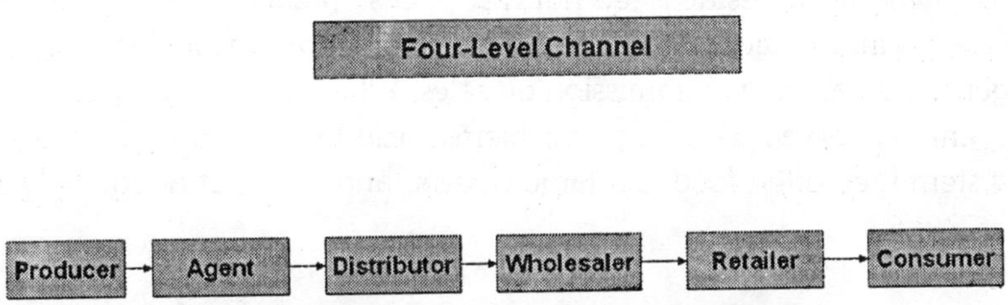

Figure 3.35 : Four-Level Channel

In addition to the above- mentioned channels different types of combinations of channels are also possible. There is no watertight classification of channels. The use or selection of a channel also depends upon the type of product under consideration. For a consumer non-durable and perishable product the channel should be short and for consumer durables it can be longer. While the industrial products are marketed through zero level or direct marketing levels, agricultural products have longer channels due to the distant and distributed location of consumer.

Channels used for Industrial Products Sometimes manufacturers of industrial products work with more than one level of channels. Four of the most common channels for industrial products are shown in figure 3.36.

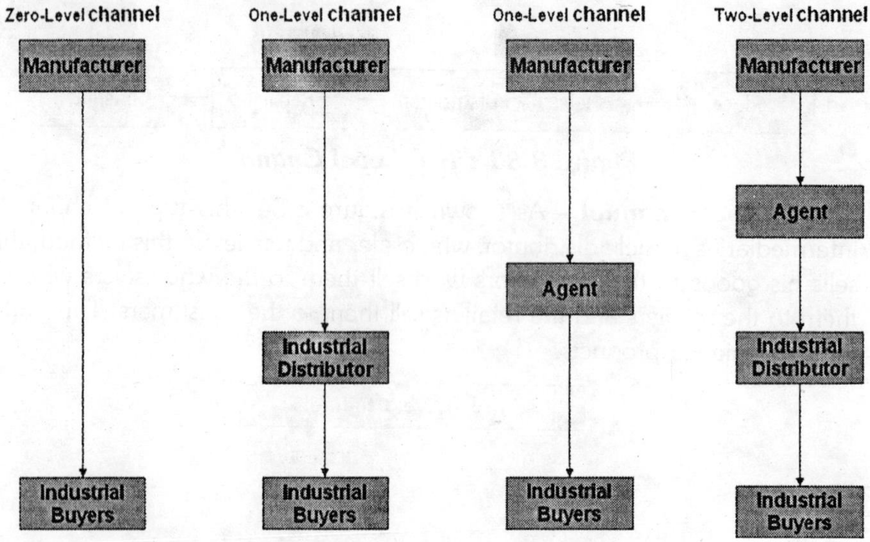

Figure 3.36 : Channels for Industrial Products

A large number of industrial products, particularly producers of expensive and technically complex equipment sell directly to industrial buyer. Industrial distributors may carry a wide variety of products lines and items from different manufacturers, or some may specialize and carry only limited number of lines.

The advantages industrial distributors offer include selling services at low cost, extend credit to customers and develop close relationship with them and provide market intelligence to manufacturers. Agent has an established number of customers and offers the advantage of their considerable market information. They can be very useful for seasonal industrial products, more so because agents are paid only commission on sales. When the company cannot offer a full time sales team, agent can be as asset. The problems include little control on agents, because of commission system they often focus on large buyers, and may not adequately follow up all the customers.

Channel Flows

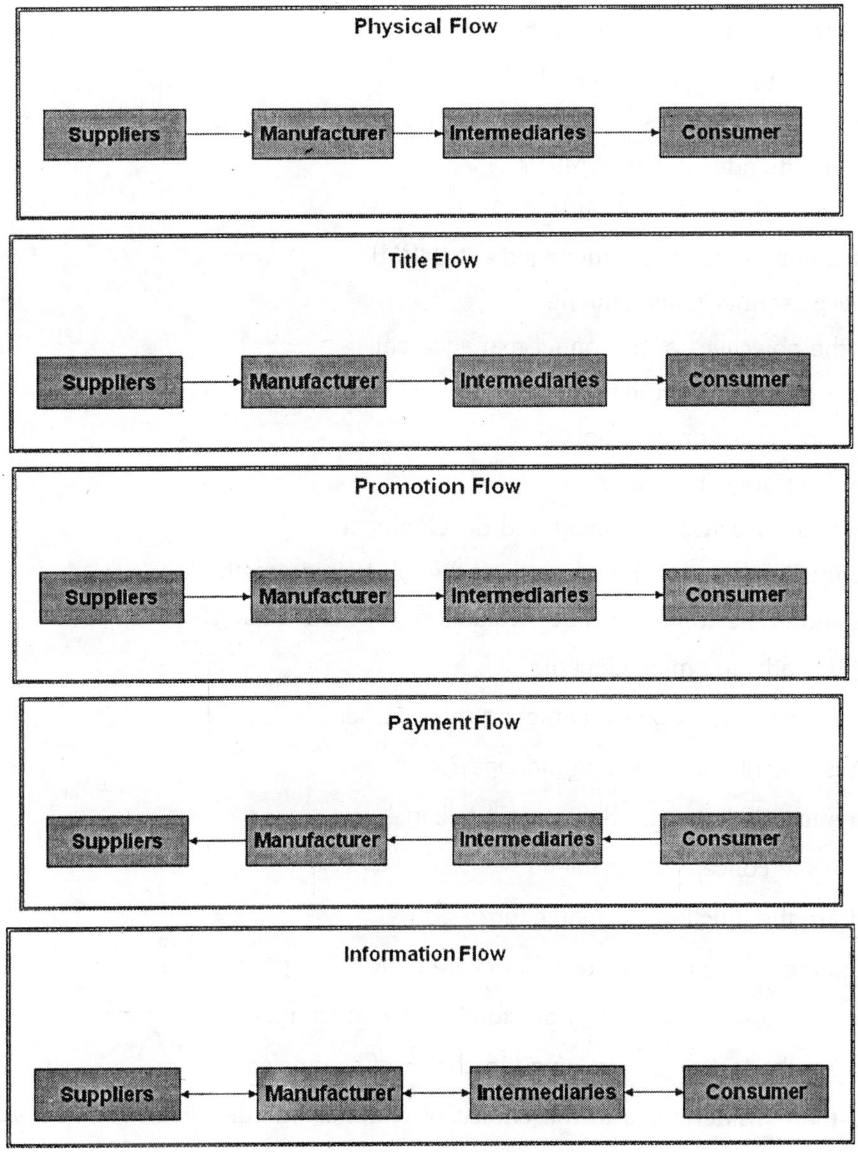

Figure 3.37 : Different types of Channel Flows

SHORT QUESTIONS

1. Write short note on role of HRM in the organization.
2. Explain Role of HR Manager.
3. Differentiate HRM and personnel management.
4. What are the functions of HRM?
5. What are the objectives of HRM?

6. What are the concepts of HRM?
7. What are the features of HRM?
8. What are operative functions of HRM?
9. What is man power planning (MPP)?
10. What are the objectives of MPP?
11. What are the advantages of MPP?
12. What are the problems of MPP?
13. What is human resources management (HRM)?
14. Define personnel management.
15. State the objectives of personnel management.
16. Explain briefly recruitment.
17. Write short notes on selection.
18. Write short notes on interview
19. Distinguish in between training and development.
20. Write briefly about on the job and off the job training methods.
21. Write short notes on : (a) Job Evaluation, (b) Merit Rating.
22. What is marketing management?
23. Write nature and scope of marketing management.
24. What is the role of marketing manager?
25. Differentiate between marketing and selling.
26. Explain the concept of exchange
27. What are the functions of marketing?
28. Discuss the different stages of product life cycle
29. What is meant by channels of distribution in marketing?
30. What are the factors determining the choice of channels?
31. State the considerations in the choice of channels for the distribution for an industrial chemical.

ESSAY QUESTIONS

1. State the principles of personnel management.
2. What is man power planning? Explain the process of manpower planning?
3. What is human resource development? What are the needs and importance of HRD?
4. Explain the sources of recruitment in detail.
5. What recruitment techniques are generally used in India?

6. What is meant by selection? What are the steps in scientific selection process?
7. Training is an ever-continuing process.... Explain briefly and state the objectives of training.
8. What is the significance of salary and wage administration? Explain principles of wage function.
9. Explain the employees' benefits and incentives schemes for increasing productivity of employees.
10. What is job evaluation? Explain the process of job evaluation.
11. What is merit rating? Explain briefly.
12. Distinguish between job evaluation and merit rating.
13. What is merit rating? Explain the uses and significance of merit rating.
14. What are the types of transfer in any organization? What are the reasons and methods of transfer?
15. What are the types of promotion? Write objectives, merits and demerits of promotion.
16. Explain briefly performance appraisal and its objectives.
17. What are the methods of performance appraisal in detail?
18. Explain job evaluation and what are its objectives?
19. What are the procedures and techniques of job evaluation?
20. Welfare administration is necessary in any organization. Explain briefly and what are its objectives and types.
21. Differentiate grievance handling and welfare administration and what are the causes of grievance handling?
22. Define marketing. Explain the importance of marketing in modern world.
23. (a) State the benefits of modern marketing concept.

    (b) Compare selling concept vs. marketing concept.
24. What do you mean by marketing? How is it different from selling?
25. Discuss and compare the various concepts and philosophies of marketing
26. Briefly explain the core concepts of marketing
27. Explain the core marketing concepts and their linkage to one another. Give examples
28. Define marketing and describe the marketing functions of a company.
29. "Marketing should aim at meeting a given consumer need rather than selling a given product." Comment
30. "Consumer is the king." Comment on the statement in the light of marketing concept.
31. Describe different stages of product life cycle and marketing strategies required at each stage.

32. What is product life cycle? Explain briefly various cycles in product development.
33. (a) Describe the various stages of product life cycle.
    (b) Explain how strategies keep changing in time with changes in the stages of product life cycle.
34. What do you mean by channels of distribution? Explain its importance in marketing.
35. Define channel of distribution. State its functions.
36. Discuss critically various channels of distribution used in marketing with appropriate examples. Which channels do you feel most appropriate for selling computers and household refrigerators?
37. Explain the types of alternative distribution channels available to a manufacturing company.
38. How are channels of distribution selected?

FILL IN THE BLANKS

1. ....is the process of achieving the best fit between individuals, jobs, organizations and environment. (Personnel Management)
2. Personnel management is concerned with effective and efficient utilization of........................ (Human Resources)
3. The operating functions of HR Manager are........................, ..., ..., ... (Employment, Development, Compensation, Relations)
4. Motivating, commanding, leading and activating people is the function of .... (Personnel Management)
5. ....deals with the task of blending efforts to ensure a successful attainment of all objectives. (Coordination)
6. ....involves checking, verifying and comparing the actual with plans, identifying deviations and correcting them. (Controlling)
7. The process of study and collection of information relating to operations of a specific job is............... (Job Analysis)
8. The process of searching for prospective employees and stimulating them to apply for jobs in an organization is .... (Recruitment)
9. The relations between the employees, management and trade unions are referred to as........................ (Industrial relations)
10. ....is referred to as foreseeing the human resource requirements of an organization. (Human Resource Planning)
11. ....facilitates inter-changeability of staff among various units or zones. (Centralized Recruitment)
12. ....is well aware of the requirements of the job. (Decentralized Recruitment)
13. Retired employees are included in .... sources of recruitment. (Internal)

14. ....allow flow of skill, latest knowledge, and creative talent into the organization. (External sources)

15. Example of a recruitment technique in external source is......................... (Advertising in Media)

16. ....includes sending the employees from present section/place to a new section/ place. (Transfer)

17. ....sends a representative of the organization to various sources of recruitment and simulate the candidates to apply for job. (Scouting)

18. The objective of..................is to choose right employee for the right job at the right time. (Selection)

19. ....bridges the difference between job requirements and employees present specifications. (Training)

20. Different types of methods of training are....................and.................... (On the job, off the job)

21. ....involves movement of trainee from one job to another job. (Job rotation)

22. Vestibule training comes under......................method of training. (Off the job)

23. The objective of wages and salary administration is...................... (Fair remuneration)

24. Categories of wage payment plans are....................and.................. (Incentive, Non-incentive plans)

25. ....is an arrangement by which employees receive a share, fixed in advance of the profits. (Profit sharing)

26. The mobility of the employee from one job to another in the same level of organizational hierarchy is....................... (Transfer)

27. To make use of employees skill, knowledge where they are required is the objective of.................... (Transfer)

28. An advance of an employee to a better job is known as.................. (Promotion)

29. Types of promotion are......................., ... and .... (Vertical, upgradation, dry)

30. There is no increase in salary in..................promotion. (Dry)

31. Promotion is based on..................... (Employees merit)

32. ....determines the relative worth of jobs. (Job evaluation)

33. To determine the ranks of various jobs is the objective of....................... (Job evaluation)

34. ....method was introduced by Merill R. Lott. (Points rating)

35. In...................... method, the evaluator compares on job with other jobs based on duties, responsibilities, demands and ranks all the jobs. (Ranking)

36. The jobs of similar difficulty are grouped into ....in grading method. (Grades)

37. The objectives of merit rating are..................., ... (Administrative, Self improvement)

38. ....method has only two options (yes/no) for each question. (Checklist method)

39. The process of identifying the customer requirements and satisfying them efficiently and effectively is called......................... (Marketing)

40. Marketing professionals believe that profit is the result of .... (Customer satisfaction)

41. Marketing is the whole business seen from the point of view of its final or end result (i.e.) .... (Customer satisfaction)

42. Marketing starts and ends with the .... (Customer)

43. .... is anything that can be offered to the market that might satisfy a need or want (Product)

44. Value for customers is the ratio of perceived .... to price paid. (Benefits)

45 .... is the act of obtaining a desired product from someone by offering something in return (Exchange)

46. .... is a place where buyers and sellers gather to exchange goods and services. (Market)

47. .... is the physical means whereby goods are moved from point of production to the place where they are required for consumption (Transportation)

48. The .... describes the stages that a product goes through during its life cycle. (Product Life Cycle)

49. Product life cycle is an attempt to recognize distinct stages in the sales history of the .... (Product)

50. The four distinct stages in the life cycle of a product are introduction stage, growth .... and .... (Maturity, Decline stage)

51. .... are the tools used to move goods from production to consumption (Channels of distribution)

52. Zero –level channel is also known as .... (Direct-Marketing Channel)

53. .... consists of one selling intermediary, such as a retailer. (One level channel)

54. .... has two intermediaries, namely, wholesaler/ distributor and retailer between producer and consumer. (Two-Level Channel)

❖ ❖ ❖

UNIT - IV

PROJECT MANAGEMENT

4.1 CONCEPT OF PROJECT MANAGEMENT

Project Management

Project management can be defined as successful completion of project on time within the budgeted cost as per the technical specifications to satisfy the end-users. Project management deals with planning scheduling, controlling and monitoring the complex non-routine activities that must be completed to reach the pre-determined objectives of the project. Project management is the organizing and managing of resources in such a way that these resources deliver all the work required to complete a project within defined scope, time and cost constraints. A project is a temporary and one-time endeavor undertaken to create a unique product or service.

Project management has certain major administrative issues, such as

1. Executive responsibilities
2. Project selection
3. Project manager selection
4. Organizational structure
5. Organizational alternatives
6. Manage within functional unit
7. Assign a coordinator
8. Use a matrix organization with a project leader

Key Success Factors of Project Management

1. Top-down commitment
2. Having a capable project manager
3. Having time to plan
4. Careful tracking and control
5. Good communications

Project management normally involves the knowledge of Project management tools, Work breakdown structure, Network diagram, Gantt charts and Risk management.

Project

A project can be defined as collection of inter-related tasks or activities which must be completed in a specified time according to a specified order on sequence and requires resources such as money, material, man-power, facilities, space etc. Projects are unique, one-time (temporary) operations designed to accomplish a specific set of objectives in a limited time frame. This property of being a temporary and a one-time venture contrast with operations, which are permanent or semi-permanent ongoing functional work to create the same product or service over-and-over again. The management of these two systems is often very different and requires varying technical skills and philosophy, hence requiring the development of project management. Planning, scheduling and controlling the work during the project are the main tasks for any project manager.

Characteristics of a Project

The main characteristics of a project are :

1. Project is a one-time effort non-repetitive in nature
2. It has a definite start and a definite end point

Even if projects are similar in nature, the problems occurring during the life-cycle of the project are different.

Concept of Project

A project is an investment made on a package of inter- related time – bound activities;

Generally, a project becomes a time bound task.

Every project has two phases

1. Preparation and construction
2. Its operation.

Network techniques are primarily used for project planning and controlling.

Planning and controlling involves the following key decisions:

- Deciding which projects to implement
- Selecting a project manager

- ➢ Selecting a project team
- ➢ Planning and designing the project
- ➢ Managing and controlling project resources
- ➢ Deciding if and when a project should be terminated

- Planning is the process of preparing for the commitment of resources in the most economic manner.
- Controlling is the process of making events confirm to schedules by coordinating the action of all the parts of the project to achieve the objective.

Project planning deals with specific tasks, operations or activities, which must be performed to achieve the project goals. Any project that may be considered has an objective, or a set of objectives, to achieve it. It has to be operated within a given set of rules, regulations, constraints and restrictions. Implementation of projects needs resources or inputs. Every project converts the given inputs into outputs through a process of implementation.

Each project has a feedback mechanism. The elements of project management control include programmed objectives, policy restrictions, resource constraints, government regulations, process implementation, review of output, feedback and revision of objectives. e.g. Construction of a dam, overhauling a machine, maintenance of equipment, commission of factory, research on developing a new technology, launching a new weapon system, conducting a war etc. Each of the above cases involves investment of recourses on a package of inter- related, time- bound activities, thereby constituting a project. Thus, project manager involves the coordination of group activity, wherein the manager plans, organizes, staffs, directs and controls to achieve an objective, with considerations on time, cost and performance of the end project.

Project Cycle

Three basic elements must be considered in a cycle.

1. Operations
2. Resources
3. Restraints

1. ***Operations:*** Operations are the objectives or job, which must be performed to meet the project objectives. The activities should be identified and arranged in a logical sequence.

2. ***Resources:*** It can be classified under man power, money, methods, material, machine and time. Time and cost estimates are associated with the methods of performance, where cost estimates resources expenditure to a common measure of costs in money alone and the time estimate defines the expected duration of the resources use.

3. ***Restraints:*** It refers to the externally imposed conditions or restraints, like supply of materials, machines, and designs by outside agencies. The delivery system should be planned carefully in coordination with the activities to be undertaken.

Project Life Cycle

The project life cycle which can be observed in figure 4.1 comprises of a new concept idea for a unique activity which is then evaluated through feasibility reports, planned with certain sequence of activities, execution of activities and terminated after the project has been completed or shelved due to certain unavoidable reasons. What is important is to note that all stages of project life cycle are administered and handled by competent project management team or project managers.

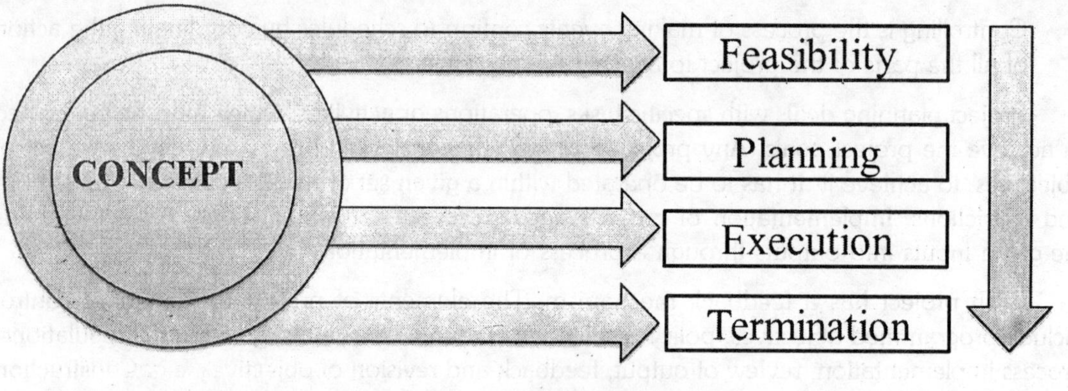

Figure 4.1 : Project Life Cycle

Responsibilities of a Project Manager

Project Manager is normally considered responsible for:

- Project Management
- Technical and Financial Analysis

Project Manager is normally considered to have qualification such as

- PMP Certification
- CFM, CFA and CFP Certification

Project Manager should be skilled enough to carry out or supervise the calculation of

- Financial Evaluation and Investment Analysis
- Cost Benefit Analysis

Project Managers should be able to focus on ethical issues and avoid:

- Temptation to understate costs
- Withhold information
- Misleading status reports
- Falsifying records
- Compromising workers' safety
- Approving substandard work

Work Breakdown Structure

A project is different in its operations due to its unique nature. A good project management practice is to breakdown the project into sublevel or group of similar activities. These sublevel or group of similar activities is called work breakdown structure. The work breakdown structure usually represents a parent child activity with the relationship between a parent and child level being easily identifiable. The work breakdown structure allows a project manager to incorporate more administrative control over the project activities.

4.2 NETWORK ANALYSIS

Network analysis refers to number of techniques for the planning and controlling of complex projects. The basis of network planning is the representation of sequential relationships between activities by means of a network of lines and circles. The idea is to link the various activities in such a way that the overall time spent on the project is kept to a minimum. Network analysis is the generic term for several project planning methods. Network analysis or Network scheduling is a technique used for planning and scheduling large projects in the fields of construction, maintenance, fabrication, purchasing, computer system installation, research and development, designs etc.

In network analysis large and small projects are planned by analysing the project activities. Projects are broken down to individual activities, and are arranged in logical sequence. Time, costs and other resources are allocated to different activities.

Network analysis helps in designing, planning, coordinating, controlling and decision making in order to accomplish the project economically in the minimum available time with the limited available resources.

Network Techniques

A few of the more people popular network techniques are:

P. E. R. T. – Programme Evaluation and Review Technique

C. P. M. – Critical Path Method

R.A.M.P.S. – Resource Allocation and Multi Project Scheduling

P. E. P. – Programme Evaluation Procedure

M. A. P. – Manpower Allocation Procedure

R. P. S. M. – Resource Planning and Scheduling Method

L. C. S. – Least Cost Scheduling

P. C. S. – Project Control System

Of these the most common and the best known and used network techniques are PERT and CPM. These are considered to be most convenient for application to various engineering projects. Most of the other techniques are the variations or developments of these two techniques only.

Objectives of Network Analysis:

The objectives of network analysis are

1. Develops powerful coordinating tool for planning, scheduling and controlling of projects.
2. It helps in bringing out clearly the technological interdependencies of various activities and in integrating the project planning.
3. Effective utilisation of resources.
4. Minimization of total project cost
5. Minimization of total project time
6. Minimization of cost for a given total time
7. Minimization of time for a given cost
8. Minimization of idle resources
9. Minimization of production delays
10. Provides a comprehensive idea of the project
11. Focuses attention on the critical elements of the project

The technique can be applied to many purposeful events involving the use of time, labour and resources. This is mostly used in large industrial and commercial projects of complex nature.

Advantages of Network Analysis

1. Provides a logical picture of the layout and sequence of a complex project.
2. Helps to identity the activities and events, which are critical to the entire project.
3. Provides a basis for working out times, costs and resources involved in the project.
4. Acts as focus point for action and co-ordination.
5. Makes enormous contribution to the planning and especially the control of complex projects.

Applications of Network Analysis

1. The construction of buildings, bridges, factories, highways, stadiums, irrigation projects etc.
2. Budget and auditing procedures
3. Missile development
4. Installation of large computers and machinery
5. Advertisement programmes and for launching a new product.
6. Planning of political campaigns
7. Strategic and tactical military planning

8. Research and development
9. Preparing inventory plans
10. Organization of big conferences, public work etc.

Network Terminology and Network Diagram Representation

1) ***Activity*** - All projects are composed of operations or tasks called activities that require the expenditure of time and resources for their accomplishment. An activity is a task or item of work to be done that requires time, effort and resources for its completion. The head of the arrow shows the sequence or flow of the activities. A new activity cannot begin until the completion of the preceding activity. Activity is denoted by an arrow. $(\rightarrow)$

- ***i) Predecessor activity*** – Activity that is required to be performed before another activity can begin is called predecessor activity to the other activity. Activities that must be completed immediately prior to the start of another activity are called predecessor activities.
- ***ii) Successor activity*** – Activity that is required to be performed after the performance of another activity is called successor activity to that activity. Activities that cannot be started until one or more of other activities are completed.
- ***iii) Concurrent activity*** – Activity that is required to be performed concurrently with the activity is called concurrent activity. Activities that can be accomplished simultaneously are known as concurrent activities. An activity can be a predecessor or a successor to an event or it may be concurrent with one or more of the other activities.
- ***iv) Dummy activity*** - In network analysis when two or more activities in a project have the same head and tail events, dummy activity is introduced. The head events or tail events are joined by dotted line arrow and this is known as dummy activity. Dummy activity may be critical or non critical. It does not consume time.
- ***v) Critical activity*** – A critical activity is an activity that if delayed, affects the completion of entire project. Any activity on critical path will be critical activity.
- ***vi) Non Critical activity*** – A non critical activity is an activity that if delayed to a limited amount of time does not affect completion of the project.

2) ***Event*** - An event is a point in time during a project that signifies the starting or completion of an activity. It is the starting or ending instant of an activity. Activity start and finish points are events. Event consumes neither time nor resources. It is represented by circle in the network.

- ***i) Predecessor event*** - The event that occurs before another event is predecessor event to that event.
- ***ii) Successor event*** - The event that follows another event is called successor event to that event.

3) ***Network*** - It is a graphic representation of projects operations from starting to completion. It is composed of activities.

4) ***Critical Path*** - The longest time path through a network is called the critical path. It is the longest path in the network which consumes maximum resources and maximum time. It is denoted by heavy (double) line.

Rules for Network Constructions

1. The length of the arrow bears no relationship to the time that the activity takes or the resources that the activity consumes.
2. The arrow in a network identifies the logical conditions of dependence. The geometry of arrow diagram is of no significance except that it should be aesthetically pleasing.
3. The direction of the arrow indicates the direction of work flow. The normal convention is to go from left to right.
4. All networks are constructed logically on the principle of dependency.
5. No event can be reached in a project before the activity which immediately precedes is completed. Similarly, no activity can be started until the event which immediately precedes it has been reached.
6. Every activity in the network should be completed to reach the objectives or the end event.
7. No set of activities can form a circular loop.

Numbering the Events and Activity Identification

Rules for numbering events and identification of activities are as follows:

1. All events must be numbered.
2. The one number cannot be used for more than event. This is necessary in order to uniquely identify each activity.
3. Events can be numbered in any order but usually forward numbering system in more familiar. In this method first event in the network is numbered 1(precedes zero) and the second 2 and so on, in such a way that the event number at the tail of each activity arrow is always smaller than the event number at the head of that activity arrow. This implies that the final event of the network will have the latest number and will be equal to the number of the nodes in the network.

Fulkerson's Rule

Fulkerson's rue is used to assign the numbers to the events. The procedure for applying this rule consists of identifying the initial events and then gradually converting the succeeding event by deleting the arrows from the previous preceding events. A number is assigned only when by such deletions; a node is converted into initial event.

This rule devised by D. R. Fulkerson is reduced to following steps:

1. An initial event is that which has arrows coming out of it, but none entering it. There will be one such event in any network, number it '1'
2. Delete all arrows emerging out from event 1. This will create at least one more initial event, number this initial event as number '2'
3. Follow step (ii), and number the new initial event as number 3. Continue until last event is obtained which has no arrow emerging out of it. Forward numbering of events and activities identification in a network.

Use of Dummy Activities

The activities which are used to indicate two activities that starts at the same instant of time. These will become critical if they lie in critical path, otherwise they are non critical. These activities don't consume resources or time. A dummy activity is represented by a dotted arrow.

A dummy is an artificial activity introduced in a network to:

1. Maintain a undue numbering system for different activities.
2. Keep the logical sequence of activities and their inter– relationship correct.

Network Logic

In developing a network diagram, the following questions must be asked for each operation.

1. What activity immediately precedes this operation?
2. What activity should immediately follow this operation?
3. What activities can take place concurrently with this operation?

Based on these questions each activity is connected with one or several of the ways as shown below.

1. ***Sequential*** : Activity B cannot start before activity A is completed or activity B follows activity A or activity A precedes B.

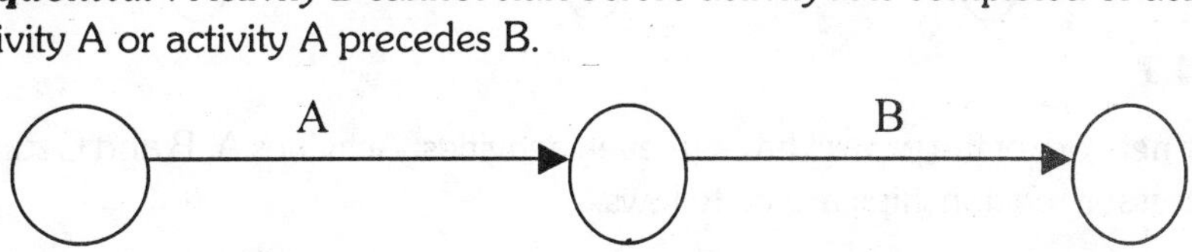

Diverging : Activity Q and R cannot start before the completion of activity P. Activity Q and R could begin at the same time.

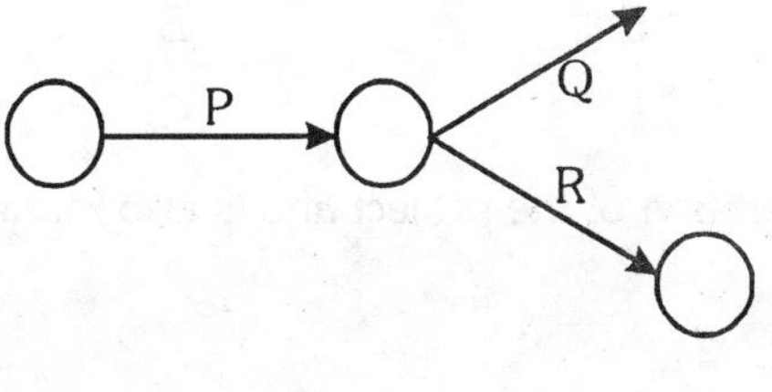

Converging: Activity N cannot start before both the activities L and M are completed.

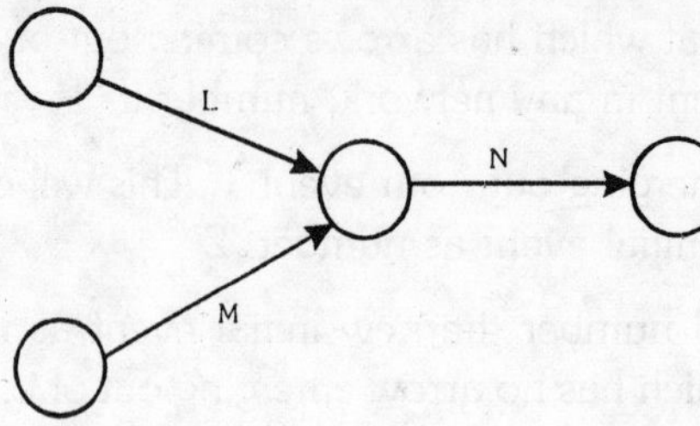

2. ***Mixed:*** Activity A and B should be completed before C and D can both start.

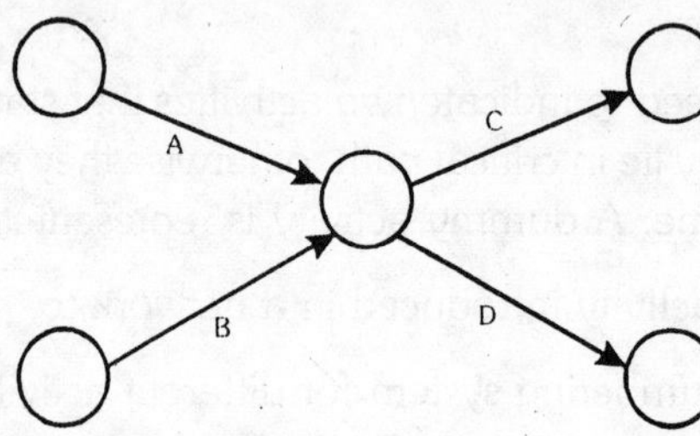

3. ***Parallel:*** In these activity chains B follows A and F follows E but the activity chains are completely independent of each other.

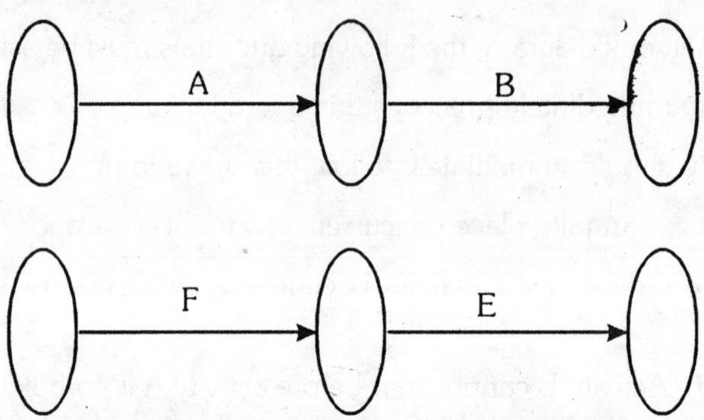

PROBLEM 4.1

Draw the network of the project having seven activities. Activities A, B and C run concurrently. Activity predecessor relationships are as follows.

Activity	*Immediate Predecessor*
D	A
E	B
F	C

Activity G is the last operation of the project and is also immediate successor to D, E and F.

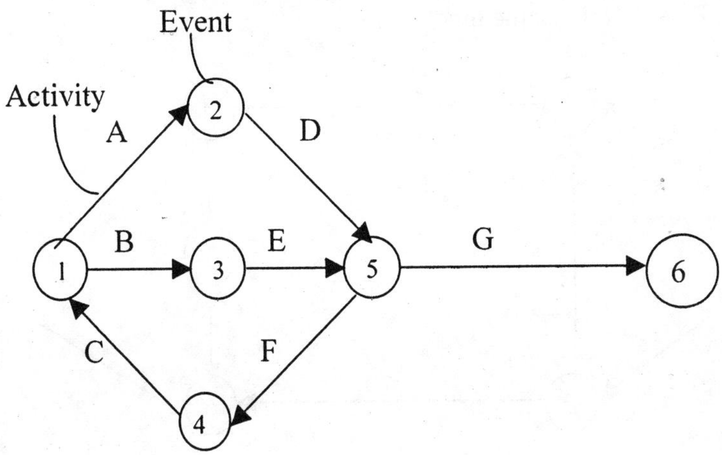

PROBLEM 4.2

Draw the network diagram for the project having 9 activities with the following relationship.

i. C follows D but precedes F

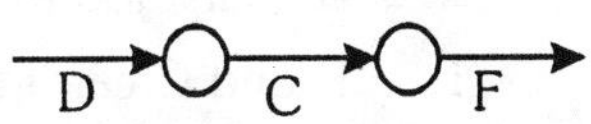

ii. C follows D but prcedes H

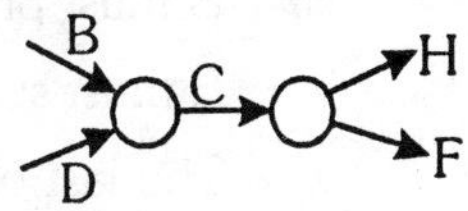

iii. G follows F but precedes I

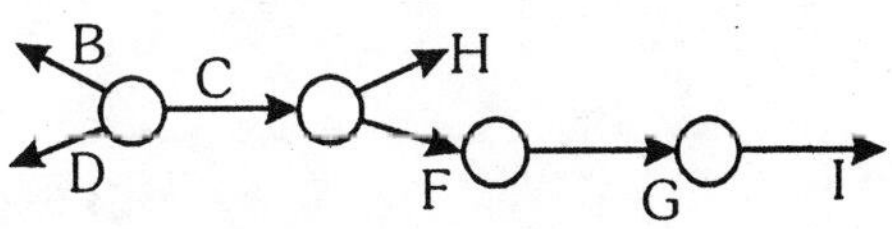

iv. E follows A but precedes I

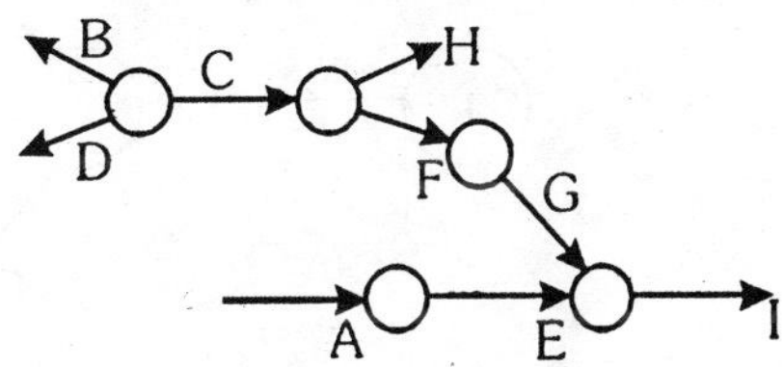

v. D follows A and H and I terminate at the same time

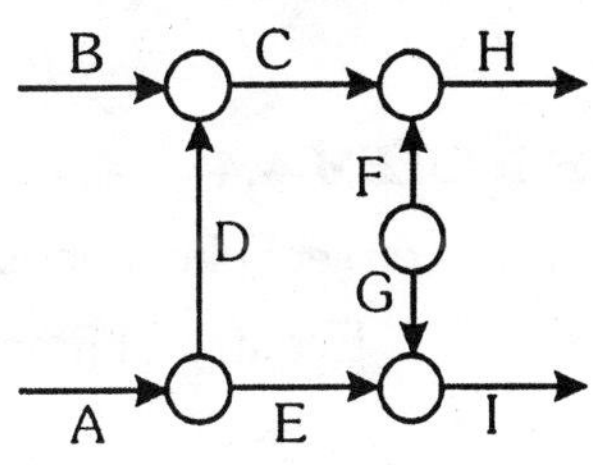

vi. A and B start at the same time

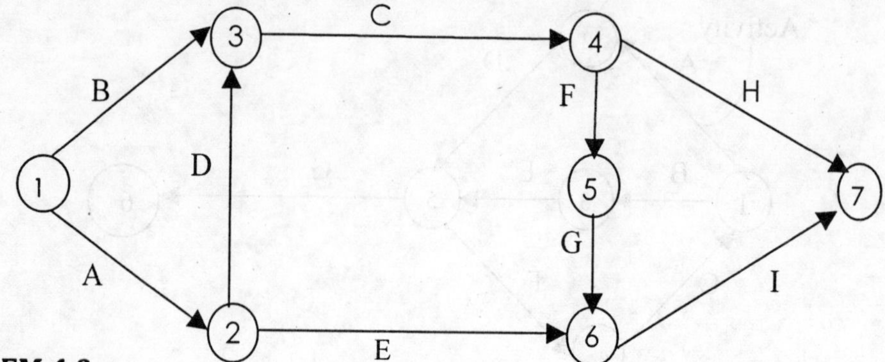

PROBLEM 4.3

A project consists of six activities designed from A to F with the following relationships. Draw the network diagram of the project.

i. A is first job to be performed

ii. B and C can be done concurrently and must follow A.

iii. B must precede D

iv. E must succeed C , but it cannot start until B is complete

v. The last operation F is dependent on completion of both D and E

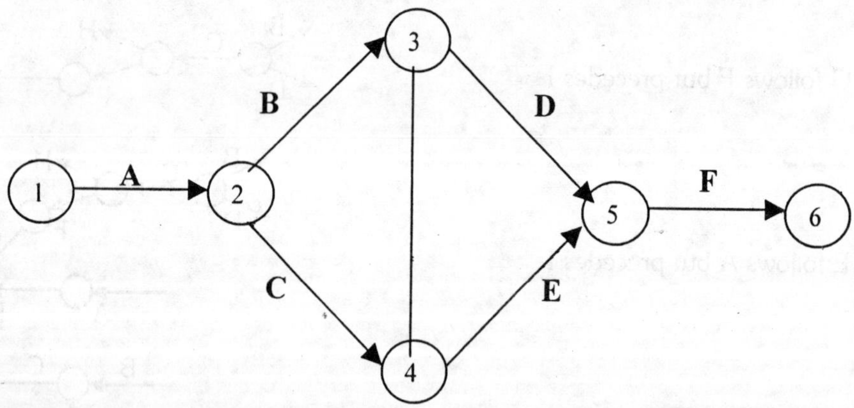

PROBLEM 4.4

A project plan consisting of ten events have predecessor relationships as under

Event	Immediate predecessor	Event	Immediate predecessor
1	—	6	3, 5
2	1	7	3, 4
3	2	8	3, 7
4	2	9	7
5	2	10	3, 6, 8, 9

Draw the network diagram of the project plan

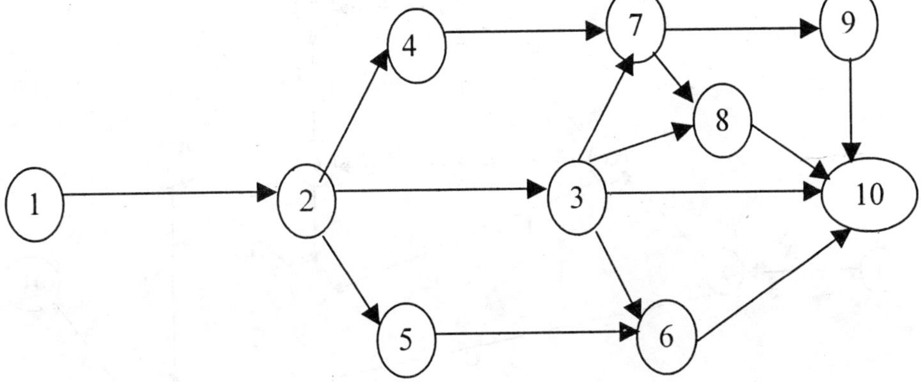

PROBLEM 4.5

A project has 14 activities A through M. The relationships amongst these activities are given below. Construct the network diagram.

i. A is first operation

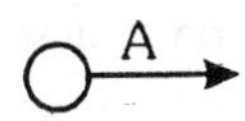

ii. B and C can be performed in parallel and are immediate successors to A

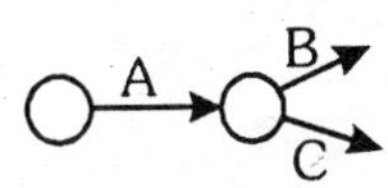

iii. D, E and F follows B

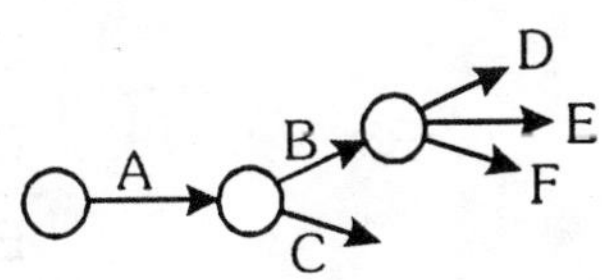

iv. G follows E

v. H follows D, but it cannot start until E is complete

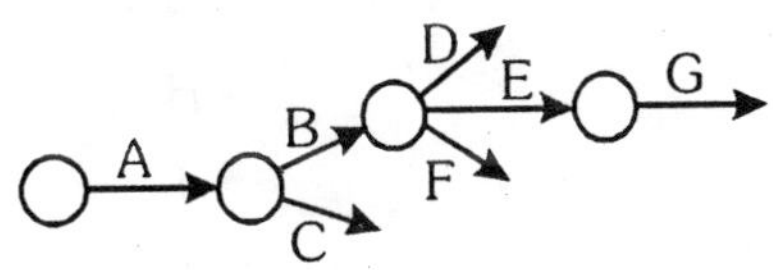

vi. I and J succeed G

vii. F and J precede K

viii. M and I precede L

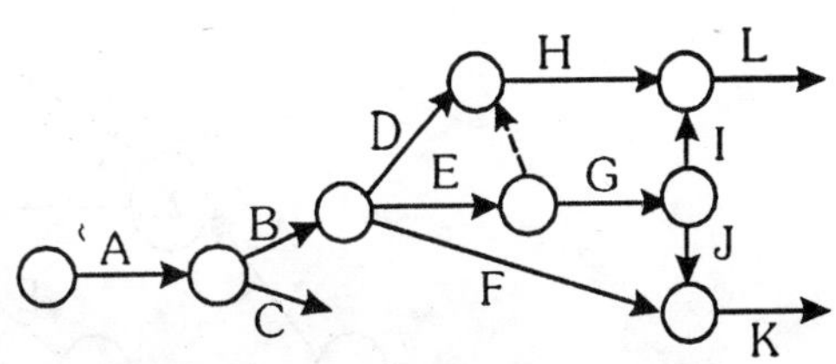

ix. M succeeds L and K

x. The last operation N succeeds M and C

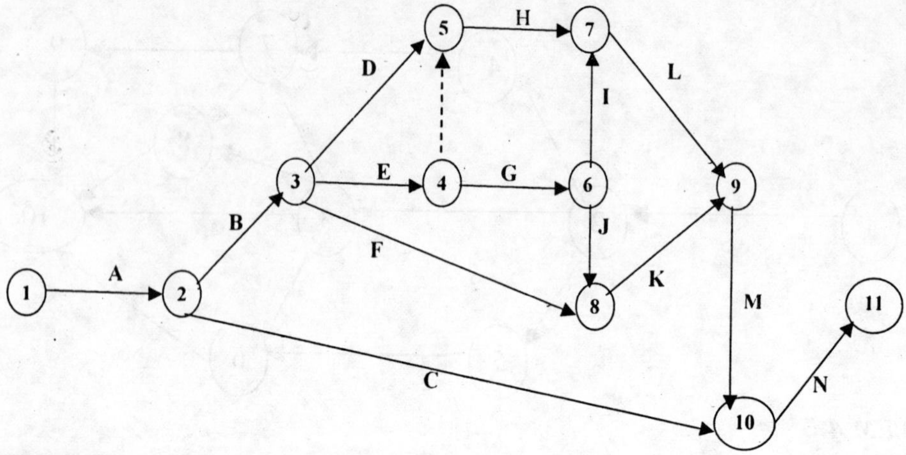

PROBLEM 4.6

Construct an activity – on – arrow (network) diagram for the following dependence table of particular project

Activity	Immediate Predecessor
A	-
B	-
C	A
D	A
E	B
F	B
G	C & E
H	F
I	D, G & H

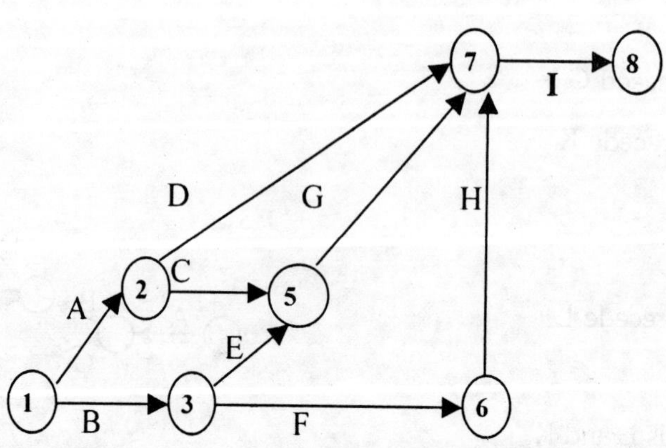

PROBLEM 4.7

A project consists of the activities A, B, C.....M, N. The notation X<Y means that the activity X be completed before Y can start and XY<W means that W will start only after the completion of both the activities X and Y. With this notation construct the network diagram having the following constraints.

A < D, H; B < E ; C < I, F; D <G ; H,L <M; E,I <L; E,F <K ; E,I <J ; G,J, K < N

A, B, C start simultaneously

M, N are end activities

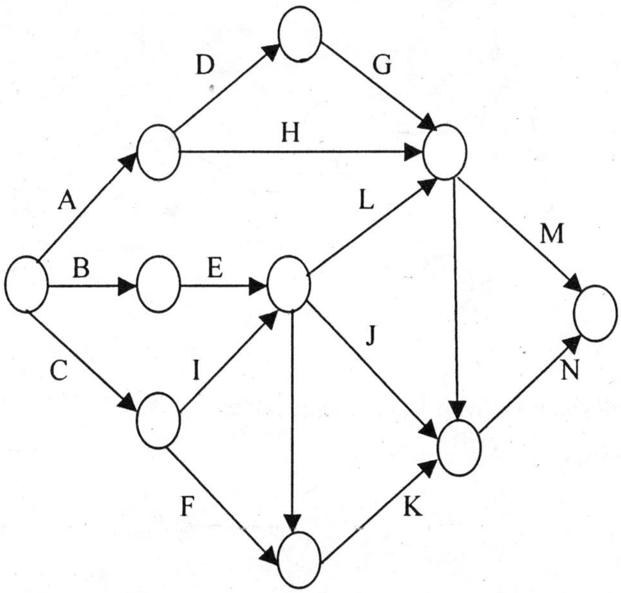

PROBLEM 4.8

Draw an arrow diagram of the following relationship.

Activity	A	B	C	D	E	F	G	H	I	J	K	L	M	N
Immediate Predecessor	–	–	–	A, B	B, C	A, B	C	D,E,F	D	G	G	H, J	K	I, L

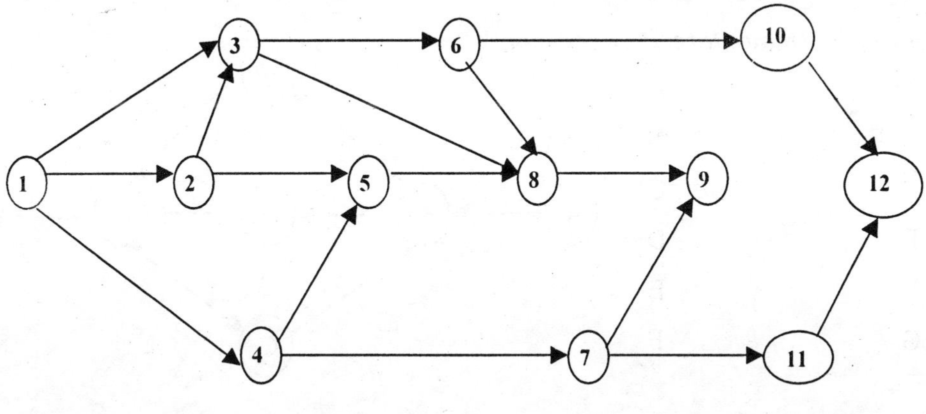

PROBLEM 4.9

Construct a network diagram

Events	*Immediate Predecessor*
2, 3	1
4	2
4, 5	3
6	4
6	5

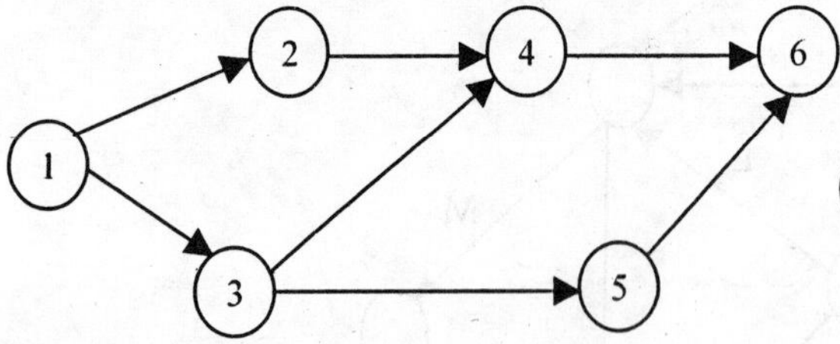
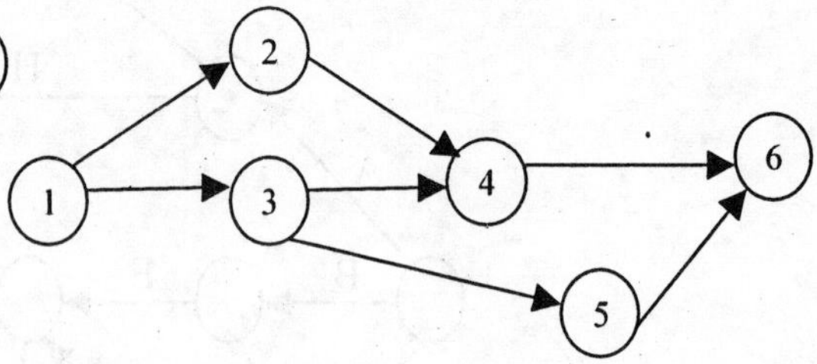

PROBLEM 4.10

Draw the network diagram with the following data

Operation (Event)
A succeeds none
B succeeds A
B precedes C
D succeeds B
C precedes E
E succeeds D

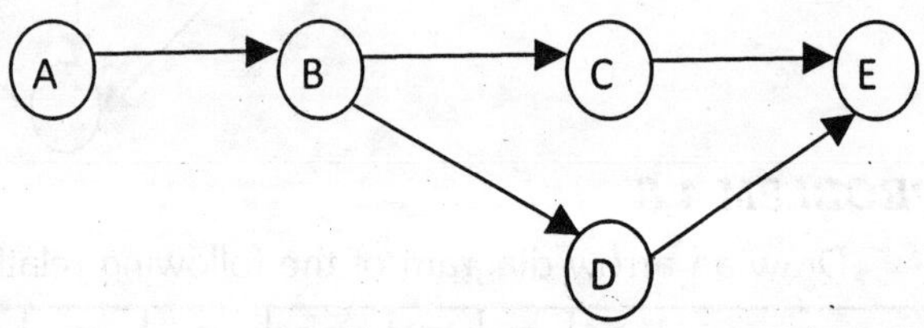

PROBLEM 4.11

Construct the network diagram

Events	*Immediate Predecessor*
B	A
C, D, E	B
F	C
F	D
F	E
G	F

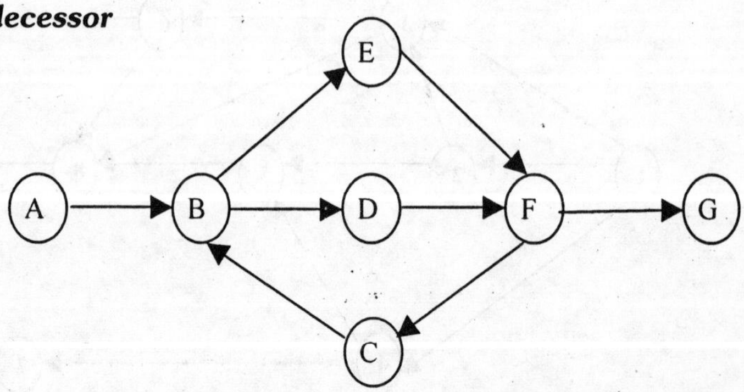

PROBLEM 4.12

Draw a PERT network for the following project.

A is the start event and K is the end event

J is the successor event of F

C and D are successor events to B

B is the successor event of A

D is a predecessor event to G

E and F occur after event C

E precedes F

G starts only after completion of C

H succeeds G

H is predecessor event to J

F restrains the occurrence of H

H starts only after completion of F

K succeeds event J

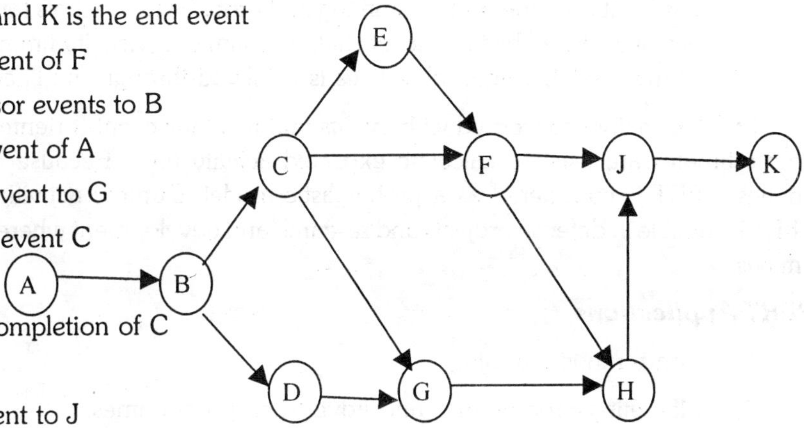

4.3 PROGRAMME EVALUATION AND REVIEW TECHNIQUE (PERT)

Programme Evaluation and Review Technique (P.E.R.T.) is a technique used for scheduling and controlling the projects. PERT is a time – event network analysis technique designed to watch how the parts of a programme fit together during the passage of time and events. PERT was first used in 1957 as a method of planning and controlling the Polaris Missiles Programme by Booz, Allen and Hamilton together with U.S. Naval department. The special project office of the U.S. Navy developed this technique in 1957. It involves the application of network theory to scheduling problems. In PERT it is assumed that the expected time of any operation can never be determined exactly.

PERT finds application in planning and control of complex set of activities functions and relationships. By controlling the critical activities the project can be completed within the scheduled time limit. PERT gives a way of identifying critical activates right at the planning stage so that management is aware of these potentially troublesome areas and exercise proper control over them, so as to complete the project within the scheduled time. PERT, actually cannot be developed as a research and development planning tool where activity timings cannot be estimated with enough certainty. However, it can be employed at those places where a project cannot be easily defined in terms of time or resources required.

As such PERT is more useful and powerful tool in planning the research and development projects and has several distinguished characteristics.

1. It helps the management to handle the uncertainties involved in programmes where standard time, data are available.
2. It gives management the ability to plan the best possible use of resources to achieve a given goal within overall time and cost limitations.

3. It provides the basis for determining manpower, material and capital requirements.
4. Because of the uncertainty of activity timings, PERT acquires the shape of probabilistic model. It uses linear programming and probability concepts for planning and controlling activities. Probability concepts help in estimating activity timings and the maximization of the predetermined objectives is achieved through the linear programming.

PERT is mainly concerned with events and it is thus event- oriented system. In PERT three time estimates are used to calculate expected activity time. Because of uncertainty in activity timings, PERT is considered as a probabilistic model. Dummy activities are required in PERT. PERT is suitable in defense projects and research and development where activities have uncertain timings.

PERT Applications

1. Long- range planning
2. Marketing programmes and advertising programmes.
3. Research and Development
4. Defense projects
5. Installation of machinery
6. Construction programmes
7. Instituting inventory control
8. Designing and manufacturing prototype products

Features of PERT

The following are the main features of PERT:

1. All individual tasks should be shown in a network. Events are shown by circles. Each circle represents an event – a subsidiary plan whose completion can be measured at a given time.
2. Each arrow represents an activity – the time consuming element of a programme, the effort that must be made between events.
3. Activity time is the elapsed time required to accomplish an event.

Advantages of PERT

PERT has the following advantages or merits:

1. PERT forces managers and subordinate managers to make a plan for production because time event analysis is quite impossible without planning and seeing how the pieces fit together.
2. PERT encourages management control by exception. It concentrates attention on critical elements that may need correction.
3. It provides graphic display of activities and identifies critical activities and slack activities

4. It enables forward – working control as a delay will affect the succeeding events and possibly the whole project. The production manager can somehow make up the time by shortening that of some other event.

5. The network system with its sub- systems creates a pressure for action at the right spot and level and at the time.

6. PERT can be effectively used for rescheduling the activities,

Limitations of PERT:

The uses of PERT technique are subject to the following limitations:

1. It is a time – consuming and expensive technique.

2. It is based on beta distribution and the assumption of beta distribution may not always be true.

3. PERT is not suitable when programme is not precise and a reasonable estimate of time schedule is not possible.

4. It is not useful for routine planning of recurring events such as mass production because once a repetitive sequence worked out; elaborate and continuing control is not required.

5. The expected time and the corresponding variance are only estimated values.

6. Important activities may be omitted or the precedence relationships may not be correct

Estimation of Activity Times in PERT

There are three time estimates in PERT. For dealing with uncertainties associated with different activities, PERT approach computes expected activity time from the following three time estimates.

a) Optimistic time (t_o)

b) Most likely time (t_m)

c) Pessimistic time (t_p)

In the original PERT, the three time values are used as follows:

Optimistic time (t_o) – It is the shortest possible time in which an activity can be completed under ideal conditions assuming that everything goes exceptionally well. Hence, it is the minimum possible time. It has low probability of occurrence.

Most likely time (t_m) – The most likely time or most probable time is the time in which the activity is expected to complete under normal conditions. It is the most likely time required to complete the activity taking into consideration all favorable elements. This time estimate lies between the optimistic and pessimistic time estimates.

Pessimistic Time (t_p): It is the time which an activity will take to complete if everything turns out to be against expectation (i.e. under adverse conditions.) Similar to optimistic time it has low probability of occurrence. It is the maximum time that would be required to complete an activity. It is the time which an activity will take to complete in case of difficulty (i.e.) if things go wrong or abnormal conditions prevail. It is the longest of all the three time estimates.

From the practicability point of view, these time estimates of an activity should not vary much from each other. However, greater the uncertainty, the wider would be the range of the estimated completion times. If the probability distribution of these times estimates is drawn, curve would approximately follow beta distribution.

Expected time (T_e) – Expected time or average time (t_e) for an activity is calculated by combining statistically all the three time estimates t_o, t_m and t_p. It is assumed that t_p and t_o is about equally likely to occur whereas the probability of occurrence of t_m is 4 times that of t_o and t_p.

Therefore, $$T_e = \frac{t_o + 4t_m + t_p}{6}$$

In order to maintain the reliability in the time duration (T_e), the variability in the time estimates should be measured and it can be done by standard deviation or variance of their probability distribution. PERT simplifies the calculation of standard deviation of the time.

Variance - It is a measure of the dispersion. Larger the variance, greater will be the uncertainty.

Variance

$$\sigma = \frac{t_p - t_o}{6}$$

and the Variance of (T_e) is given by: $$V(T) = \left\{\frac{t_p - t_o}{6}\right\}^2$$

The greater the uncertainty in time estimates the greater will be the difference in t_o and t_p and high value of 6t represents high degree of uncertainty regarding the activity times. Variance is the square of 6t and if it is small, the indication is that the time estimates are fairly precise with little uncertainly while a large variance indicates a greater uncertainty on the accomplishment of activity.

Steps in PERT

Steps to be followed for accomplishing a project planning in PERT are

1. Dividing systematically the project into different activities.
2. Arranging activities in logical sequence.
3. Drawing network diagram and numbering events and activities
4. Using three time estimates, the expected time for each activity is calculated.
5. Computing standard deviation and variance for each activity
6. Calculating earliest starting times and latest finishing times.
7. Marking expected time, earliest starting times and latest finishing times on network diagram
8. Calculating slack

9. Identifying and marking critical path on network diagram
10. Length of critical path or total project duration is found out.
11. Calculating the probability that the project will finish at due date
12. Analyzing the network from the point of view of resource and if it is deficient, finding alternative ways to use the resources efficiently.
13. Devising project control methods

PROBLEM 4.13

The network of a certain project is shown in the figure. Determine the expected time for each of the path. Find out the critical path.

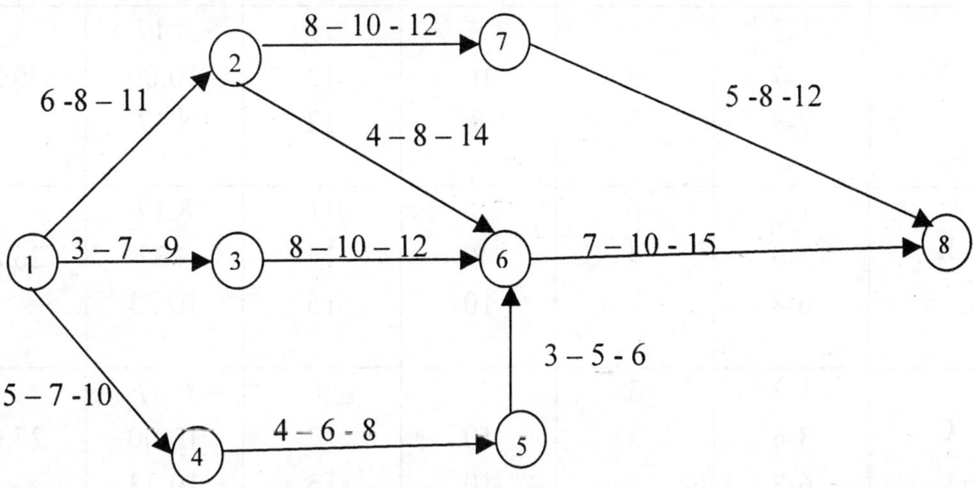

Solution :

In the network event 1 is starting event while event 8 is the end event. There are four paths from the starting event to end event

Path A : 1-2-7-8

Path B : 1-2-6-8

Path C : 1-3-6-8

Path D : 1-4-5-6-8

The optimistic time (t_o) for each path is equal to the sum of all t_o's of the activities of that path. Similarly most likely time and pessimistic time can be found.

	Optimistic time (t_o)	Most likely time (tm)	Pessimistic time (t_p)
Path A : 1-2-7-8	19	26	35
Path B : 1-2-6-8	17	26	40
Path C : 1-3-6-8	18	27	36
Path D : 1-4-5-6-8	19	28	39

From point of view of pessimistic time, path B is critical since it takes longest duration. From optimistic time point of view paths A and D are equally critical. However, from most likely time point of view, path D is the most critical.

In PERT analysis, the expected time Te is taken as the basis for finding critical path.

$$\text{The expected time Te} = \frac{t_o + 4t_m + t_p}{6}$$

The expected time (Te) for any path is equal to ΣT_e of all the activities of that path.

Path	Activity	t_o	t_m	t_p	T_e	ΣT_e
A	1-2	6	8	11	8.17	
	2-7	8	10	12	10.00	26.34
	7-8	5	8	12	8.17	
B	1-2	6	8	11	8.17	
	2-6	4	8	14	8.33	26.83
	6-8	7	10	15	10.33	
C	1-3	3	7	9	6.67	
	3-6	8	10	12	10.00	27.00
	6-8	7	10	15	10.33	
D	1-4	5	7	10	7.17	
	4-5	4	6	8	6.00	
	5-6	3	5	6	4.83	28.33
	6-8	7	10	15	10.33	

From the above table it is found that path D is critical path since ΣT_e for path D is maximum.

PROBLEM 4.14

The owner of a chain of fast food restaurants is considering a new computer system for accounting and inventory control. A computer company sent the following information about the system installation.

Activity Identification	Activity Description	Immediate Predecessor	Optimistic time (t_o)	Most likely time (t_m)	Pessimistic time (t_p)
A	Select the computer model	–	4	6	8
B	Design 4/0,system	A	5	7	15
C	Design monitoring system	A	4	8	12
D	Assemble computer hardware	B	15	20	25
E	Develop the main programs	B	10	18	26
F	Develop 4/op routines	C	8	9	16
G	Create data base	E	4	8	12
H	Install the system	D, F	1	2	3
I	Test and implement	G, H	6	7	8

a) Construct an arrow (network) diagram for this problem

b) Determine the critical path and compute the expected project completion time. Calculate the variances of each activity and variance of the project length

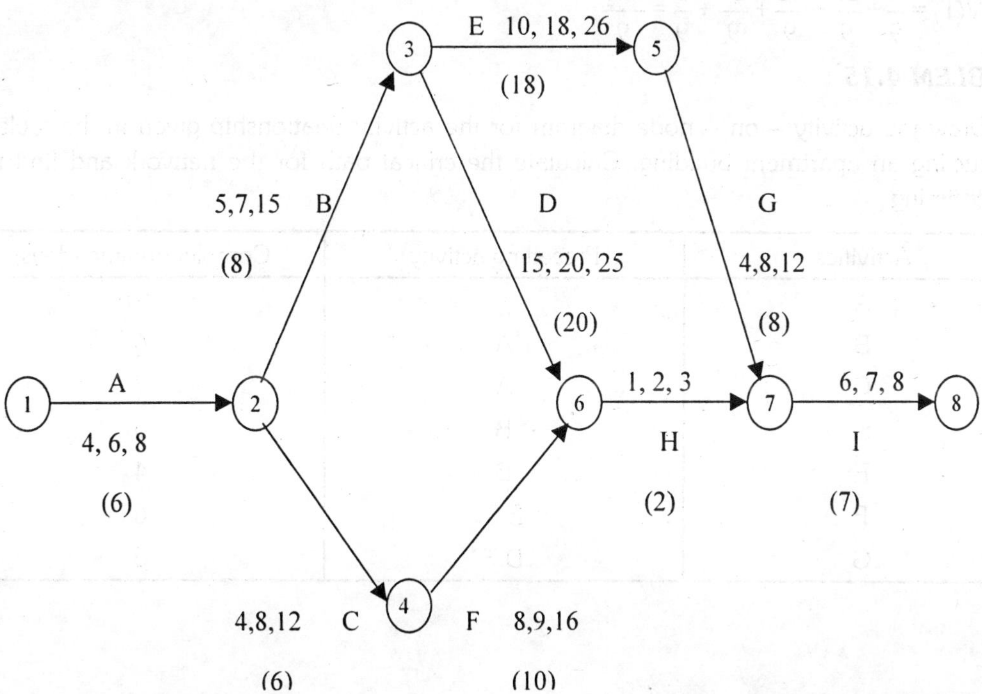

Activity	t_o	t_m	t_p	T_e	σ	σ^2
A	4	6	8	6	4/6	4/9
B	5	7	15	8	10/6	25/9
C	4	8	12	8	8/6	16/9
D	15	20	25	20	10/6	25/9
E	10	18	26	18	16/6	64/9
F	8	9	16	10	8/6	16/9
G	4	8	12	8	8/6	16/9
H	1	2	3	2	2/6	1/9
I	7	7	8	7	2/6	1/9

Using the expected times of activity duration, the critical path is obtained as

A - B –E - G – I (1-2-3-5-7-8)

Thus, the critical path is A – B – E – G – I

The expected project completion time $T_e = T_e A + T_e B + T_e E + T_e G + T_e I$

$T_e = 6 + 8 + 18 + 8 + 7 = 47$ days

Variance of the project length (Critical path)

$V(T) = \sigma 2A + \sigma 2B + \sigma 2E + \sigma 2G + \sigma 2I$

$$V(T) = \frac{4}{9} + \frac{25}{9} + \frac{64}{9} + \frac{16}{9} + \frac{1}{9} = \frac{110}{9}$$

PROBLEM 4.15

Draw the activity – on – node diagram for the activity relationship given in the table for constructing an apartment building. Calculate the critical path for the network and find total project timing

Activities	Preceding activity	Completion time (days)
A	-	10
B	A	6
C	A	7
D	B	6
E	B	4
F	E,C	6
G	D,F	6

For the above conditions, the activity on node diagram is as follows

Activity – Oriented

(CPM NETWORK)

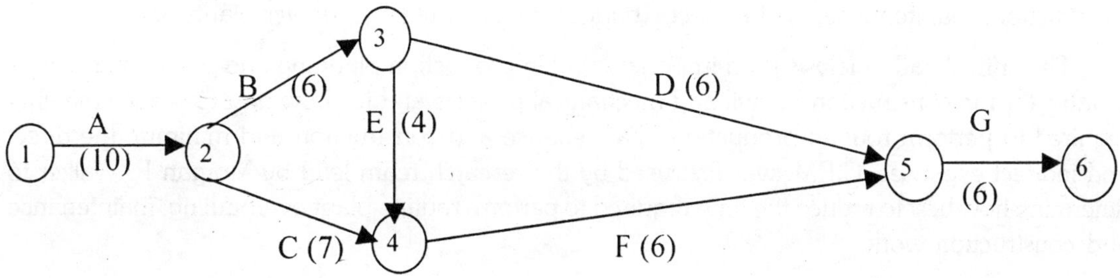

Event Oriented

(PERT NETWORK)

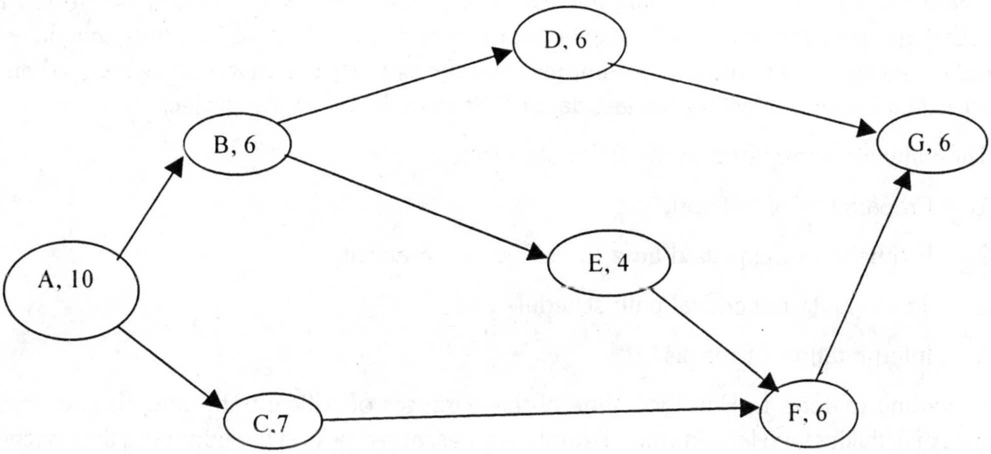

Project timing

Path			***Total time***
A – B – D – G	(10 + 6 + 6 + 6)	=	28 days
A – B – E – F – G	(10 + 6 + 4 + 6 + 6)	=	22 days
A – C – F – G	(10 + 7 + 6 + 6)	=	29 days

So critical path will be A – B – E – F – G

The total project timing T_e = 32 days.

4.4 CRITICAL PATH METHOD (CPM)

The E.I du Pont de Nemours Company (USA) in the year 1958 while working on a chemical plant employed a technique called CPM to schedule and control the project and experienced a good amount of saving.

CPM is an activity oriented approach. In CPM only one time estimate is used. It is a deterministic model with well known activity times based on past experience. It is easy to use and maintain. The use of dummy activities is not necessary in CPM. CPM is employed in projects where minimum overall costs are of primary importance. CPM is suitable for applications like construction, maintenance, civil projects (bridges, dams, buildings, power plants) etc.

The critical path analysis is an important tool in production planning and scheduling. This is suitable for the construction of civil and mechanical projects and for how best to reduce the time required to perform routine production, maintenance and construction and minimize the direct and indirect expenses. C.P.M. was first used by the research team lead by Morgan R. Walker to determine how best to reduce the time required to perform routine plant overhauling, maintenance and construction work.

CPM is used for scheduling special projects where the relationship between the different parts of projects is more complicated than that of a simple chain of task to be completed one after the other. This method (CPM) can be used for both very simple and the most complicated tasks. With the help of C.P.M., manager can know which operation should be started after completing an operation. It also tells at what moment and in what operations time schedules are adhered to strictly so that future programme is not affected and where it may be delayed and up to what extent without affecting the last date of the completion of the project.

The network is prepared in the following phases:

1. Preparation of network
2. Estimation of expected time to perform each activity
3. To compute the critical path schedule and
4. Interpretation of results

According to John L. Burdige, "One of the purposes of critical path analysis is to find the sequence of activities with largest sum of duration times, and thus find the minimum time necessary to complete the project. This critical series of activities is known as the 'critical path'. "It is called critical path because any delay in performing the activities on this path may cause delay in the whole project. So such critical activities should be taken up first. CPM marks critical activities in a project and concentrates on them. It is based on the assumption that expected time is actually the time taken to complete the project.

Main Objectives of CPM

The main objectives are

- To find the difficulties and obstacles in the course of production process.
- To assign time for each operation
- To ascertain the starting and finishing times of the work
- To find the critical path and the minimum duration time for the project as a whole.

Situations where CPM can effectively be used

CPM techniques can be used effectively in the following situations:

- In production planning
- Location of and delivery from a warehouse.
- Road systems and traffic schedules
- Communication network.

Advantages of CPM

The application of CPM leads to the following advantages:

- It provides an analytical approach to the achievement of project objectives, which are defined clearly.
- It identifies most critical elements and pays more attention to these activities.
- It assists in avoiding waste of time, energy and money on unimportant activities.
- It provides a standard method for communicating project plans, schedules and cost

4.5 IDENTIFYING CRITICAL PATH

CPM techniques are a very useful analysis in production planning of a very large project.

Steps in CPM

Steps to be followed for accomplishing a project planning in CPM are

1. Dividing systematically the project into various activities.
2. Naming the activities
3. Arranging all the activities in logical sequence.
4. Construction of arrow diagram
5. The nodes (events) and activities to be numbered
6. Finding time for each activity.
7. Marking activity time in the arrow diagram.
8. Early and late, start an finishing times to be calculated
9. Tabulating various times and mark EST and LFT on the arrow diagram.
10. Calculation of total float for each activity
11. Critical activities are to be identified and critical path marked on arrow diagram
12. Total projects time to be calculated
13. Crashing critical activities of the network, in case the project duration is to be reduced
14. Optimizing the cost
15. Updating Network

CPM Calculations

- ✓ Earliest start time (EST) – It is the earliest possible time at which an activity can begin. It is assumed that all of the predecessors also are started at their E.S.T. It is calculated by moving from first to last event in network diagram.
- ✓ Earliest finish time (EFT) – It is the earliest possible time at which an activity can finish

  EFT = EST + duration of the activity.
- ✓ Latest finish time (LFT) – It is calculated by moving backward (i.e.) from last event to first event of network diagram. It is the last event time of the head event.(It is latest time by which an activity can be finished without delaying the project completion date)
- ✓ Latest start time (LST) – It is the latest possible time at which an activity can start.

  LST = LFT – duration of the activity

Float or slack – Float is used with respect to an activity (i.e.) with CPM and slack with PERT. In general practice both can be used interchangeably. Float is the difference between the time available for completing an activity and the time necessary to complete the same. Float or slack means spare time or a margin of extra time over and above its duration which a non critical activity can consume without delaying the project.

There are three types of floats.

1. ***Total float*** – It is the maximum time by which the completion of an activity can be delayed beyond its EST without delaying the project duration (completion date)

   Total float = (LST – EST) or (LFT – EFT)

   Free Float – It is the amount of time by which the completion of an activity can be delayed beyond the EFT without delaying the EST of subsequent activity. Numerically it is equal to the difference between EFT of an activity and the EST of its immediate successor activity. Free float is always equal to or less than total float of that activity.

   Free float = Total float – float time of the head event.

2. ***Independent Float*** – It is the amount of time by which start of an activity can be delayed without affecting EST of immediately following activities assuming that the preceding activity has finished at its LFT.

   It is equal to EST of succeeding activity minus latest starting time of the activity minus activity duration.

   Independent Float =EST of tail event – LFT of head event – activity duration.

   Independent Float = Free float – Tail event float.

   Independent Float is the excess of minimum available time over the required activity duration

   Critical Path – It is the sequence of activities which add up to the longest overall duration. The longest time path through a network is called critical path.

   Critical Activity – An activity for which total float is zero is a critical activity. The activities on the critical path are called critical activities.

PROBLEM 4.16

A project consists of a series of tasks labeled a, b....h, i with the following relationships. (w< x, y means x and y cannot start until w is completed; x, y< w means w means w cannot start until both x and y are completed). With this notion construct the network diagram having the following constraints. A, B, C start simultaneously.

E, I and H are end activities.

A< D,E; B,D < F; C < G; B,G < H; F,G< I.

Find also the total time of completion of the project when the time (in days) of completion of each task is as follows.

Task(Activity)	A	B	C	D	E	F	G	H	I
Time	23	8	20	16	24	18	19	4	10

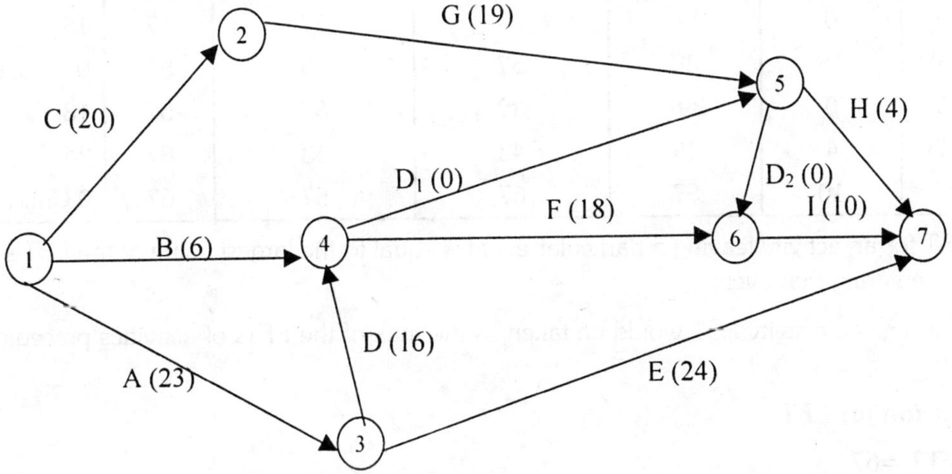

Using the given constraints, the resulting network is drawn. Two dummy activities are introduced to establish the correct precedence relationships. The events of the project are numbered in such a way that their ascending order indicates the direction of progress in the project.

To evaluate the critical activities, all these calculations are put in the following table

Task	*Duration*	*Earliest Start (EST)*	*Earliest Finish (EFT) (EST + Duration))*	*Latest Start (LST) (LFT – Duration)*	*Latest Finish (LFT)*	*Total Float (LST – EST) or (LFT – EFT)*
C(1,2)	20	0	20	18	38	18
A(1,3)	23	0	23	0	23	0 Critical
B(1,4)	8	0	8	31	39	31
G(2,5)	19	20	39	38	57	18
D(3,4)	16	23	39	23	39	0 Critical
E(3,7)	24	23	47	43	67	20
D(4,5)	0	39*	39	57	57	18
F(4,6)	18	39	57	39	57	0 Critical
B(5,6)	0	39*	39	57	57	18
H(5,7)	4	39	43	63	67	24
I(6,7)	10	57	67	57	67	0 Critical

EST for an activity leaving a particular event is equal to the largest value of the EFT's for all activities entering that event

(For a given activity EST would be taken as the max of the EFTs of activities preceding this activity)

Calculation for LFT

LFT7 =67

LFT6 = {LFT7 – T67} = 67 – 10=57

LFT5 = Min {LFT7 – T57, LFT6 – T56} = Min {67 -4, 57 -0} =57

LFT4 = Min {LFT5 – T45, LFT6 – T46} = Min {57 -0, 57 -18} =39

LFT3 = Min {LFT7 – T37, LFT4 – T34} = Min {67 -24, 39 -16} =23

LFT2 = {LFT5 – T25} = 57 – 19 = 38

LFT1 = Min {LFT2– T12, LFT3 – t13, LFT4 – t14} = Min {38 -20, 23 -23, 39 - 8} =0

The activities for which total float is zero are the critical activities. The above table shows that the critical activities for the tasks are (1, 3) (3, 4) (4, 6) and (6, 7)

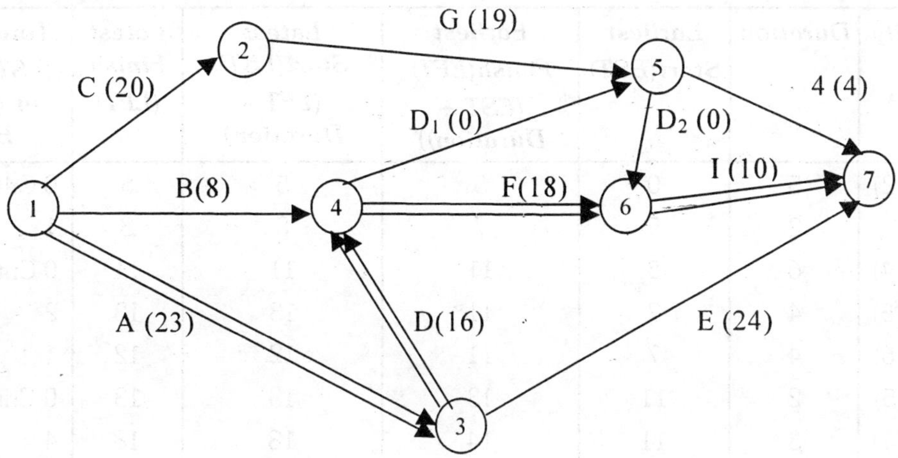

From the figure critical path comprises of the tasks (1, 3), (3, 4), (4, 6) and (6, 7)

Hence, the critical path is A – D – F – I

The total project completion time = 23 + 16 + 18 +10 = 67 days

PROBLEM 4.17

A building project of 10 activities is represented by the network. The normal duration (in days) required to perform various activities of the above project are given below. Compute

a) Activity times

b) Total float.

Also determine the critical path and total project completion time.

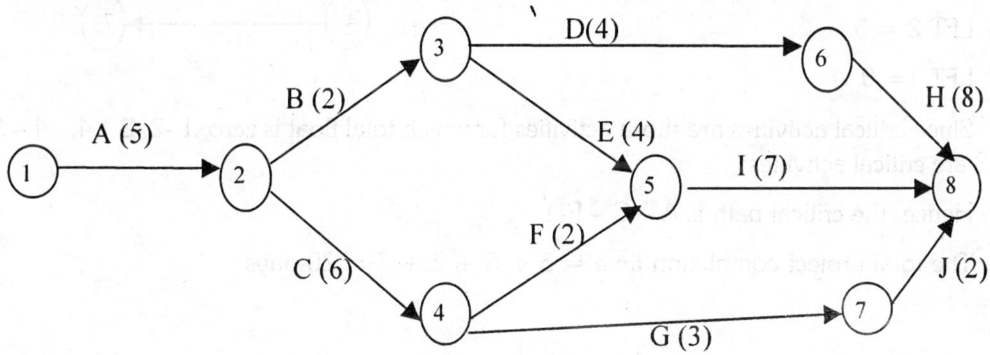

Activity	Duration	Earliest Start(EST)	Earliest Finish(EFT) (EST + Duration))	Latest Start(LST) (LFT – Duration)	Latest Finish (LFT)	Total Float (LST – EST) or (LFT – EFT)
A (1 - 2)	5	0	5	5	5	0 Critical
B (2 -3)	2	5	7	8	8	1
C (2 - 4)	6	5	11	11	11	0 Critical
D (3 - 5)	4	7	11	13	13	2
E (3 - 6)	4	7	11	12	12	1
F (4 - 5)	2	11	13	13	13	0 Critical
G (4 - 7)	3	11	14	18	18	4
H (5 - 8)	7	13	20	20	20	0 Critical
I (6 -8)	8	11	19	20	20	1
J (7 - 8)	2	14	16	20	20	4

LFT 3 = 20

LFT 7 = 18

LFT 6 = 12

LFT 5 = 13

LFT 4 = 11

LFT 3 = 8

LFT 2 = 5

LFT 1= 0

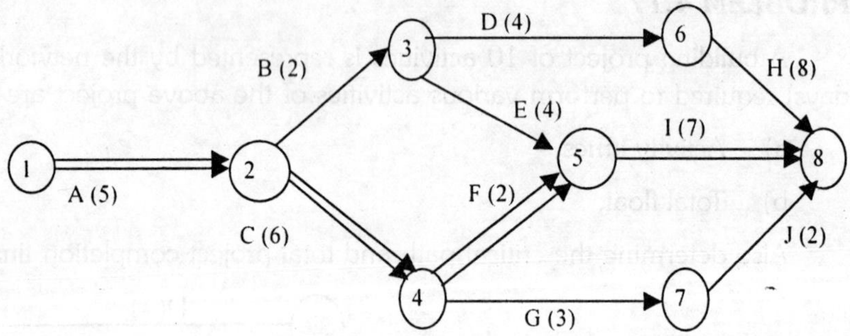

Since critical activities are those activities for which total float is zero, 1 -2, 2 – 4, 4 – 5 and 5 – 8 are critical activities

Hence, the critical path is A – C – F- I

The total project completion time = 5 + 6 + 2 + 7 = 20 days

4.6 Difference between PERT and CPM

PERT	CPM
1. A probabilistic model with uncertainty activity duration	A deterministic model with well- known activity
2. Approach is event – oriented	Approach is activity- oriented
3. Uses words like network diagram, event and slack	Employs words like arrow diagram, nodes and floats
4. Dummy activities are used to represent proper sequencing	Dummy activities are not necessary for usage. The arrow diagram thus becomes slightly simpler
5. Does not demarcate between critical and non- critical activities	Marks critical activities
6. Find application in all those projects where resources are always made available as and when required	Find application in all those projects where overall costs are of primary importance
7. Suitable especially in defense projects and research and development where the activity times cannot be readily predicated.	Suitable for problem in industrial settings plant maintenance, civil constructions projects
8. It has three- times estimates i.e., Optimistic time (t_o), Most likely time (t_m) and Pessimistic time (t_p)	It has one – time estimate
9. It is a control device	It is a planning device

However, over a period of time the difference between the two has narrowed down and there is very little difference between the two as they stand today.

4.7 PROJECT COST ANALYSIS

Introduction

It is the primary objective to complete the project at the earliest to get quicker realization of benefits of the project. As discussed earlier, activities on critical path and sub- critical path need special attention either to complete the project as per schedule or to reduce the completion time. To reduce the scheduled time, non-critical activities can be considered as potential pools of resources for diverting to near critical activities.

In some projects, it is desirable to cut down the total project time, even if it leads to increase in cost. It is generally desired where cost considerations are unimportant or less important than completing the project in absolute minimum time e.g. defense works in emergency. Generally it is possible to reduce the project duration by changing the resources allocated to it. The increase or decrease of the project duration results in decrease or increase of the cost of the project. For this purpose, time and costs are analyzed in a systematic way. This analysis also helps in determining optimum duration of the project.

Project Costs

The total project cost is the sum of direct costs and indirect costs. The direct cost represents the expenditure which can be directly allocated to different activities in a project, like labour material etc. Indirect cost consists of overheads, depreciation, insurance, supervisory cost etc. The longer time the project takes to complete, the higher are the indirect costs.

1. ***Direct costs:*** Costs, like manpower, material, etc. incurred for project execution. This cost is directly proportional to the quality of resources involved during a period. If project normal time is one month and planned to complete within twenty days, more people and machines have to work. It leads to more direct costs. Direct costs are more in crash time.
2. ***Indirect costs:*** Costs like overhead, supervisor's salaries, rent, depreciation, and establishment charges etc. These costs are directly proportionate to the duration of the project.

The total cost of a project is the sum of direct and the indirect costs and is shown in the following figure 4.2.

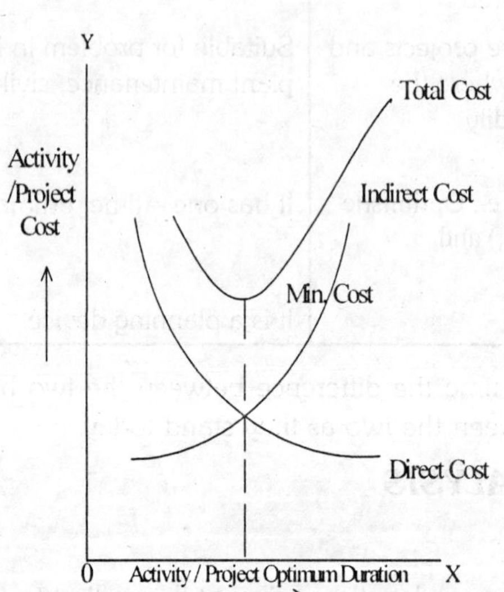

Figure 4.2 : Minimum Cost and Optimum Duration

From the total cost curve shown in the figure 4.2 it is clear that the minimum total cost is obtained at some duration known as the optimum duration. The corresponding cost is known as the minimum cost. If the project duration is increased, total cost will increase, while if the project duration is decreased to the crash value, project cost will be the highest. With the help of above curves, optimum duration is determined, which is also referred as target duration. There is no need to reduce the network i.e.; crashing the duration of any activity. However, if the critical path is longer than the projects optimum duration, then there is need to reduce the duration of some activities so that the critical path is equal to the optimum duration.

These curves help the management to determine following aspects for taking future decisions about the project duration and resource allocation.

a) Determining the project duration, for which the cost is least, i.e.; optimum duration of the project at which the cost is optimum as shown in figure.

b) Determining the least cost of a reduction in project duration to a stipulated date. This is done when the stipulated date is earlier than the optimum time for the project.

c) Determining the time - cost -risk relationship. In this, risk involved in eliminating any activity is calculated. This time – cost risk helps the management to take a decision about most economical solution, based on the circumstances and the objectives of a particular situation.

This shows that the network techniques are an analytical tool for better planning, scheduling, monitoring and decision-making.

4.8 PROJECT CRASHING

In PERT / CPM network techniques, time is related to cost and the objective is to develop optimum time – cost relationship. The ultimate objective of the network techniques is not only to bring improvement in planning scheduling and control of project but also to assess possibility of arriving at a feasible desirable time- cost relationship. The policy of every organization is to reduce the target time so that the time saved can be utilized for additional production or otherwise. Furthermore, every organization wants to accomplish the desired objective at minimum cost also. Sometimes it may be desirable to extend project duration if there is considerable saving in cost. Thus, time – cost relationship is of great significance in project management. The overall project duration can be minimised by reducing the duration of only the critical activities of the project network. To reduce the scheduled time, non – critical activities can be considered as potential point of resources for diverting to critical activities.

The duration of the project can be shortened by systematic analysis of critical path activities, crashing cost and corresponding cost effect of indirect costs. For this time – cost relationship should be critically examined. The project has the highest cost corresponding to the crash duration and has normal cost corresponding to the normal duration. Thus, there are two types of costs and two types of times defined below:

Terms in Crashing

1) ***Normal Costs:*** It is the lowest cost of completing an activity in the minimum time, employing normal means i.e. not using over time or other special resources. The expenditure incurred on normal resources for completing any activity in normal time is known as normal cost.

2) ***Normal Time:*** It is the minimum time required to achieve the normal cost. Normal time is the standard time, associated with normal resources of the organization to perform the activity.

3) ***Crash Costs:*** It is the least cost of completing an activity by employing all possible means like over time, additional machinery, proper materials, etc. The total expenditure incurred on normal and additional resources for crashing the time is known as crash cost.

4) ***Crash Time:*** It is absolute minimum time associated with the crash costs. Crash time is the minimum possible time in which an activity can be completed by employing extra resources. Crash time is that time, beyond which the activity cannot be shortened by any amount of increase in resources.

5) ***Cost Slope:*** In actual practice, we assume the time-cost curve to be linear between crash point A and normal point B. The curve shown in figure shows that there is a change in cost for change in time. The term cost-slope is defined as the "increase in the cost of the activity per unit decrease in the time.

Mathematically, the time – cost relationship can be represented as:

$$\text{Cost Slope} = \frac{\text{Crash Cost} - \text{Normal Cost}}{\text{Normal Time} - \text{Crash Time}}$$

Cost slope represents the extra cost of shortening the duration of the activity by one time unit. For reducing the activity duration, the management may agree for extra expenditure but to keep this expenditure minimum there is a need to concentrate on those activities for which cost slope is minimum. In simple words, cost slope of an activity is the "increase in cost of an activity by reducing the duration by one unit".

It can be observed that shortening the project duration leads to increase in indirect costs but decrease in overhead (indirect) costs and the strategy will be justified only when it results in net saving. The normal time of every manufacturer is to produce at minimum cost and to have most efficient use of human resources. But in emergencies or sudden rush of orders if production is to be increased, then naturally additional resources are to be introduced (e.g. working over time or in two shifts) which will result in additional expenditure. Manufacturer will be tempted to crash the time only when the profit earned from additional production is more than the extra expenditure on crashing.

The following figure 4.3 shows variation in the cost of an activity with time. The figure also indicates that there is critical point in time beyond which it will probably become expensive to try to shorten the time schedule of an activity. It also indicates that lengthening of an activity more than a certain time duration results in negligible cost saving. First such point is crash point while second such point is known as normal point, as shown in figure 4.3.

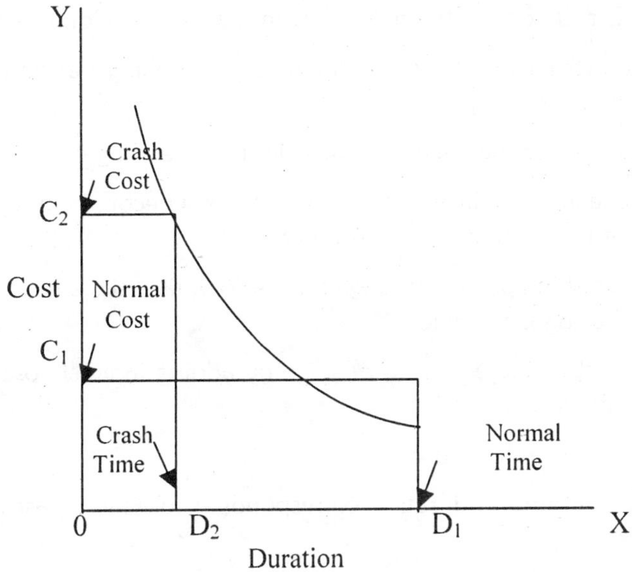

Figure 4.3 : Time - Cost Relationship

Crashing Procedure

The cost slope concept helps in finding lowest cost solution by sequential compressing the activities having lowest cost slope, i.e. having lowest incremental cost on critical path. Some times by crashing one activity, critical path is shifted therefore, at each shift of the critical path, it will be necessary to calculate the cost-slopes of the activities on the new critical path. Then the activity having the lowest cost slope needs to be compressed on this new critical path. This process is repeated until the project crash point is reached.

Procedure for crashing a Project:

a) The ratio of increase in cost to decrease in time for each activity that can be crashed on the critical path is calculated and compared.

b) The activity having the lowest ratio is reduced to the next lower time value.

c) The critical path for the network is again calculated using the new time for crashed activity.

d) Repeat step b and c until the critical path is equal to optimum project duration or equal to prescribed project duration

Steps involved in Time Cost Optimization

The time cost optimization is done in the following steps:

1. ***Establish:*** Direct cost – time relationships for various activities of the project, by analyzing past records.

2. ***Determine:*** Cost slopes for various activities and arrange them in ascending order of cost slope.

3. **Compute:** Direct cost for the network with normal duration of activities.

4. **Crash:** The activities in the critical path as per ranking i.e. starting with the critical activity having lowest slope.

5. **Continue:** Crashing the critical activities in the ascending order of slope.

6. **Crash:** Parallel non – critical activates which have become critical by the critical path reduction due to crashing in steps 4 and 5.

7. **Continue:** Crashing process through steps 4 to 6, till a stage is reached beyond which no further crashing is possible.

8. **Find:** Total cost of project at every stage by adding indirect costs to the direct costs determined above.

9. **Plot:** Total cost duration curve.

10. **Pick up:** The optimum duration corresponding to which least total project cost is obtained.

PROBLEM 4.18

Table gives the information about various activities of network.

Activity	*Normal Duration (Days)*	*Normal Cost (Rs)*	*Crash Duration (Days)*	*Crash Cost (Rs)*
1-2	9	5000	6	6500
2-3	5	2000	3	2500

The project indirect costs are at the rate of 400 per day. Determine

(a) Direct cost-duration relationship

(b) Total cost duration relationship and the corresponding least cost plan(network)

Solution :

Step 1: Cost Slopes : Figure shows the network, with the normal duration of each activity entered below its activity arrow, while the crash duration entered in the bracket.

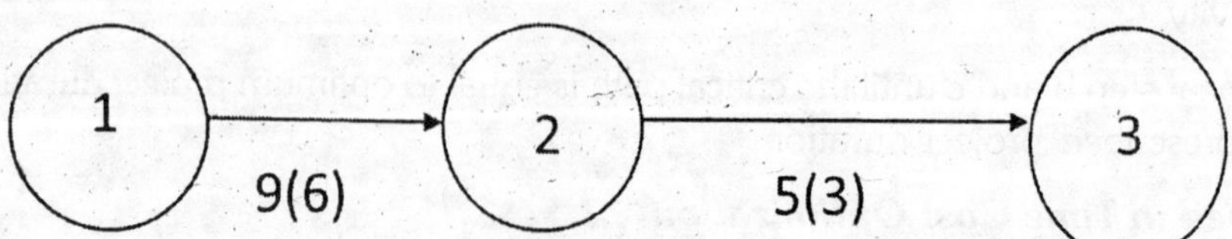

The cost slope for each activity will be calculated as shown in the below table.

Step 2 : Normal duration direct cost.

Activity	*Normal Duration (Days)*	*Normal Cost (Rs)*	*Crash Duration (Days)*	*Crash Cost (Rs)*	Δ C (Rs)	ΔT (Days)	*Cost Slope* $=\Delta C/\Delta T$
1-2	9	5000	6	6500	1500	3	500
2-3	5	2000	3	2500	500	2	250

The normal duration for the project = 9 + 5 = 14 days

Therefore, normal duration cost 5000 + 2000 = 7000

Step 3 :

Activity 2-3 has the least slope. Let us therefore crash it first, though in serial activities network, any activity can be crashed first, or even all the activities can be crashed simultaneously to their corresponding crash durations. Duration by which activity 2-3 can be crashed=2 days

Extra cost of crashing activity = 2 – 3 by 2 days = 250 = 500

Project duration = 9 + 3 = 12 days

Therefore, direct cost for 12 days project duration = 7000 + 500 = 7500

Step 4 :

After having fully crashed activity 2-3, let us crash activity 1-2 from its normal duration of 9 days to its crash duration of 6 days

ΔT = 9 – 6 = 3 days

Extra cost of crashing = 3 × 500 =1500

Project duration= 6 + 3 = 9 days

Therefore, direct cost for 9 days project duration = 7500 +1500 = 9000

The corresponding network with all the activities crashed is shown in the below figure.

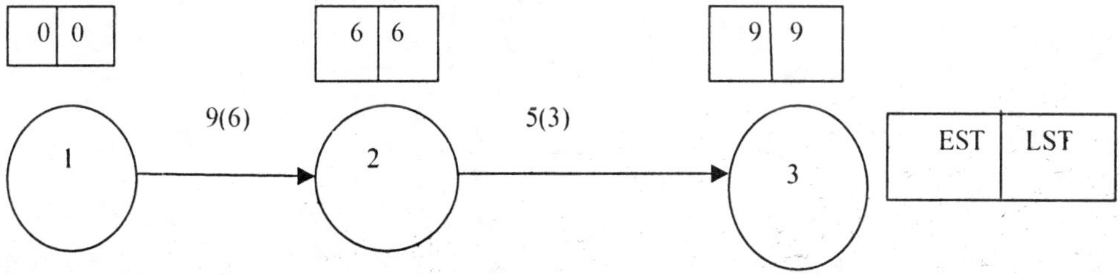

Step 5: Total cost of project: The total cost of the project, for any duration is obtained by adding the indirect costs overheads to the corresponding direct costs. The values are tabulated in the below table.

Duration (days)	14 Normal	12	9
Direct cost	7000	7500	9000
Indirect cost	5600	4800	3600
Total cost	12600	12300	12600

Step 6: Cost duration on curves. From the above table, it is evident that total cost is minimum for project duration of 12 days. Thus, the optimum duration of the project is 12 days and minimum cost corresponding to it is Rs. 12300.

PROBLEM 4.19

For a network shown below, normal time, crash time, normal cost and crash costs are given in the table. Construct the network by crashing it to optimum value and calculate the optimum project cost. Indirect cost is given as Rs. 100 per day.

S. No.	Activity	Normal Time in Days	Normal Cost in Rs	Crash Time in Days	Crash Cost in Rs
1	1-2	3	300	2	400
2	2-3	6	480	4	500
3	2-4	7	2100	5	2500
4	2-5	8	400	6	600
5	3-4	5	320	3	360
6	4-5	6	500	4	520

Solution:

By drawing the network with normal duration, it can be seen that the critical path is 1-2-3-4-5

The project duration is, therefore equal to 18 days. On this path,

Crash time = 13 days (from given data on critical path)

Where normal cost = Rs . 4100 (from above given table)

Crash cost = Rs. 4900 (from above given table).

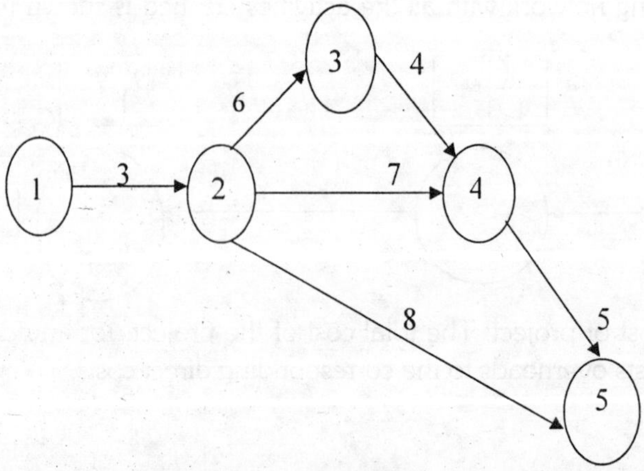

To construct the network, in first stage we should identify those activities on critical path, which have cost – slopes less than the indirect cost. For this purpose cost slopes are calculated as shown in the below table.

S. No.	Activity	Normal		Crash		Cost		Cost Slope
		Time (Days)	Cost (Rs.)	Time (Days)	Cost (Rs.)	ΔC (Rs.)	ΔT (Rs.)	$\Delta C/\Delta T$
1	1-2	3	300	2	400	100	1	100
2	2-3	6	480	4	520	40	2	20
3	2-4	7	2100	5	2500	400	2	200
4	2-5	8	400	6	600	200	2	100
5	3-4	4	320	3	360	40	1	40
6	4-5	5	500	4	520	20	1	20

Critical path activities 2-3 and 4-5 have least slopes. Therefore, these activities are first crashed and network is again drawn.

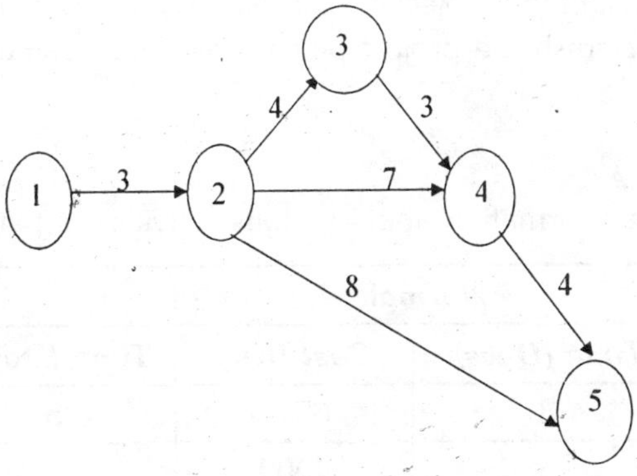

This network shows that, after crashing activities 2-3 by 2 days and 4-5 by 1 day, the critical path is same, i.e.; 1-2-3-4-5 and have 15 days duration.

Now in second stage, the least cost slope in remaining activities is for activity 3-4 on the critical path. By crashing this activity, two paths become critical path, 1-2-3-4-5 and 1-2-4-5 as shown in the following figure

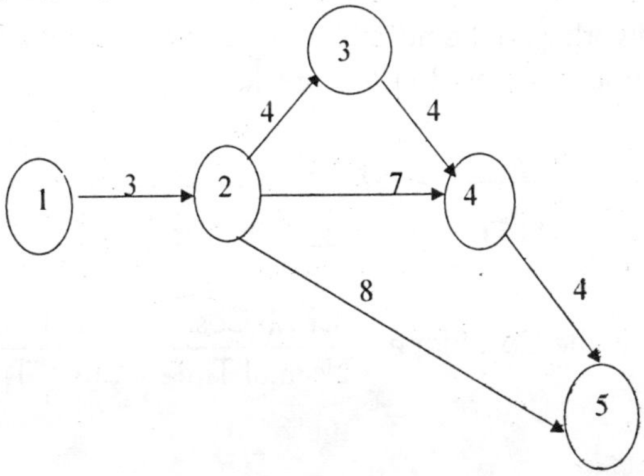

Now, we see that after crashing activities 2-3, 4-5, and 3-4, there is no other activity on both the critical paths, which have cost slopes less than indirect cost. The optimum network and hence optimum project duration is 14 days.

Total direct project cost for this optimum duration

= direct cost for all activities on the network

= cost on activities 1-2; 2-3; 2-4; 2-5; 3-4; 4-5

= 300+520+2100+400+360+520

= Rs. 4200

Indirect cost for 14 days at the rate of Rs. 100 per day = Rs.1400

Total project cost after crashing = 4200 +1400= 5600

Whereas total cost with all normal activities = normal cost + indirect cost for 18 days = 4100+1800 =Rs. 5900

Thus, the optimum cost of the project is Rs. 5600. By crashing to optimum value, we could save Rs 300. If we further crash the project beyond optimum value, the project shall become costlier.

Problem 4.20

Table below gives the ...ormation about various activities of network.

Activity	*Normal*		*Crash*	
	Time (Days)	*Cost (Rs.)*	*Time (Days)*	*Cost (Rs.)*
1 – 2	8	6000	5	7200
2 - 3	6	4000	4	4500

The project overhead costs are at the rate of Rs. 400.00 per day. Determine (a) Direct cost duration relationship (b) Total cost duration relationship and the corresponding least cost plan (network)

Solution:

Figure shows the network with the normal duration of each activity entered below its activity arrow, while the crash duration entered in the bracket.

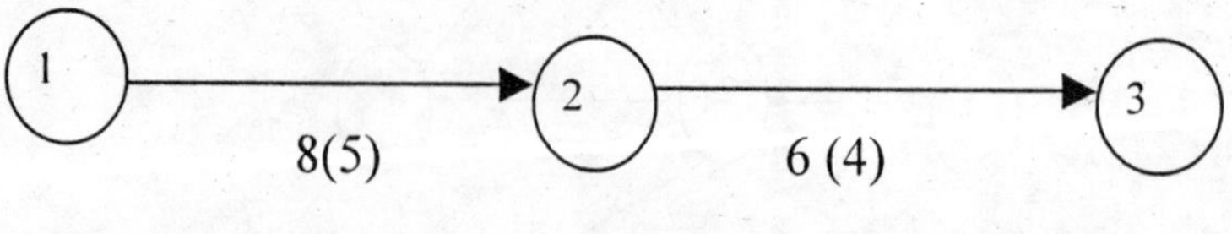

$$\text{Now the Cost Slope} = \frac{\text{Crash Cost} - \text{Normal Cost}}{\text{Normal Time} - \text{Crash Time}}$$

Activity	*Normal Time*	*Normal Cost*	*Crash Cost*	*Crash Time*	*Crash Cost - Normal Cost (ΔC)*	*Normal Time - Crash Time (ΔT)*	*Cost Slope Rs/ Day $\Delta C/\Delta T$*
1 – 2	8	6000	7200	5	1200	3	400
2 – 3	6	4000	4500	4	500	2	250

Now, normal duration direct cost for the project = 8 + 6 = 14 days and

Normal duration cost = 6000 + 4000 = Rs. 10,000/-

The activity 2- 3 has the least slope, let us therefore crash it first

Extra cost of crashing the activity 2 -3 by 2 days = 250 x 2 = Rs. 500

Project duration = 8 + 4 = 12 days

Direct cost for 12 days project duration = 10,000 + 500 = Rs. 10500/-

Total cost = 10,500 + 12 x 400 = 15,300

Let us crash = 3 x 400 = Rs. 1200

Project duration = 5 + 4 = 9 days

Direct cost for 9 days project duration = 10,500 + 1200 = 11700/-

From (1) and (2) it is clear that the total cost is minimum for a project duration of 12 days and the minimum total cost corresponding to it Rs. 10,500/-

PROBLEM 4.21

A project consists of the following six activities:

Activity	*Normal Time (weeks)*	*Crash Time (weeks)*	*Normal Cost (Rs.)*	*Crash Cost (Rs.)*	*Cost Slope Rs. / Week $\Delta C/\Delta T$*
1 - 2	3	2	1600	1800	200
1 - 3	7	5	1400	2000	300
2 - 3	5	3	2500	3000	250
3 - 4	4	3	500	800	300
3 – 5	2	1	4200	4400	200
4 – 5	8	6	1600	2600	500

a. Draw the network for the activities stated above.

b. Identify critical path.

c. What is the total project duration and associated cost?

d. If the duration of the project is to be reduced by one week which activity or activities duration are to be reduced? What will be the total project cost?

e. If the duration is further to be reduced by another week, which activity or activities are to be reduced? What will be the total project cost?

f. If the duration is further to be reduced by one more week, which activity or activities are to be reduced? What will be the total project cost?

g. What is the minimum duration of the project and what will be the associated network? Identify the critical path and the total cost involved.

Solution:

(a) The network for the project is as shown below:

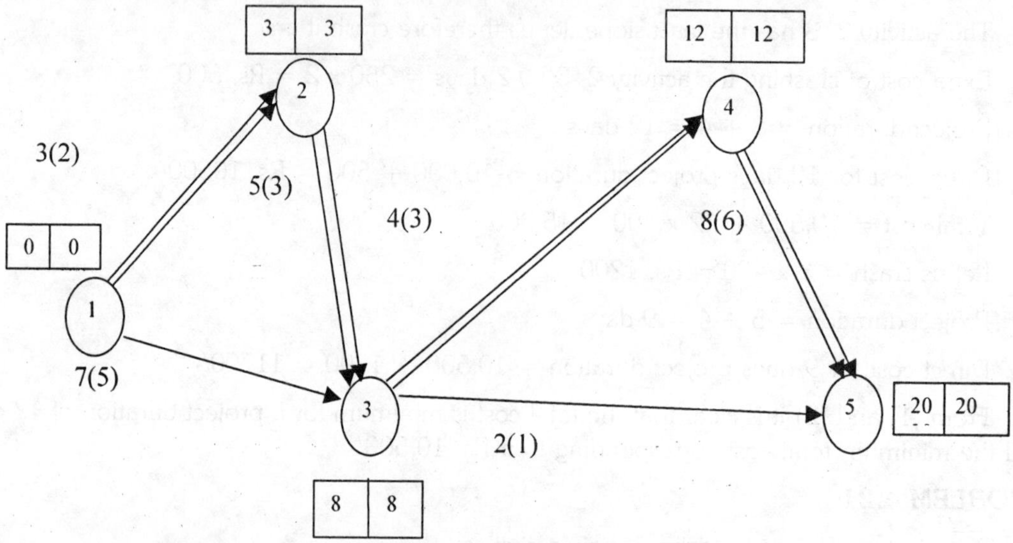

b. The critical path is $1 \rightarrow 2 \rightarrow 3 \rightarrow 4 \rightarrow 5$ (marked by double arrows)

c. The total project duration is 20 weeks.

The project cost if all the activities are carried out as per their normal time

= Normal cost = 1600 + 1400 + 2500 + 500 + 4200 + 1600 = Rs. 11,800

d. Now, the critical path is $1 \rightarrow 2 \rightarrow 3 \rightarrow 4 \rightarrow 5$. To reduce the project duration by one week, select the activity on the critical with lowest cost slope. The activity 1-2 has the lowest cost slope i.e. Rs. 200/- per week. Hence, after crashing this activity by one week the total project duration will be 19 weeks.

The total cost of the project will now be Rs. 11800 + 200 = Rs. 12000/-

e. To reduce the project duration by one more week and bring the project duration to 18 weeks. The next activity on the critical path with lowest cost slope is activity 2 – 3. After crashing activity 2 -3 by one week.

The total cost of the project will now be Rs. 12000 + 250 = Rs. 12250/-

f. To reduce the project duration by still one more week and bring the project to 17days we may again crash activity 2 – 3 by one more day (as the difference between normal time and crash time is 2 weeks)

The total project cost will be, Rs. 12250 + Rs. 250 = Rs. 12, 500/-

The critical path will still remain unchanged.

g. The activities 3 – 4 and can be crashed by 1 week and 2 weeks respectively.

The total project duration will be now 14 days.

The total project cost = Rs. 12500 + 1 × 300 + 2 × 500 = Rs. 13,800/-

SHORT QUESTIONS

1. What is meant by network analysis?
2. What is importance of network analysis in establishing a new project?
3. Explain PERT and its advantages for implementing a new project.
4. Define the term (a) Event (b) Activity (c) Dummy activity
5. Write short notes on :
   a) Network diagram
   b) Critical path.
   c) Float
6. What are the advantages of PERT?
7. What is PERT?
8. Write short note on (a) Total float (b) Free float.
9. Write short note on (a) Pessimistic time (b) Optimistic time.
10. What is meant by CPM?
11. What are advantages of CPM?
12. Explain the uses of float in CPM network.
13. Define the terms CPM and PERT.
14. State the objectives of PERT and CPM.
15. What is meant by project crashing?

ESSAY TYPE QUESTIONS

1. Differentiate between CPM and PERT.
2. What is CPM? What are the essential steps in CPM for project planning?
3. What is PERT? Define optimistic time, pessimistic time and most likely time and explain how you will estimate the expected time to complete the activity in PERT technique.
4. Draw network and calculate project completion time and floats for each activity
5. Explain the use of network analysis in project management.

6. What are the advantages and limitations of network analysis in project management?
7. What is dummy activity? Explain its relevance in network analysis.
8. Explain PERT and its importance in network analysis. What are the requirements for applications of PERT techniques?
9. Draw network and calculate completion time and floats for each activity.

Activity	Activities	Weeks
A	DF	8
B	L	9
C	B,E	10
D	G,H	7
E	G,H	6
F	I,K	9
G	I,K	4
H	L	3
I	L	3
J	G,H	12
K	-	10
L	-	16

10. A project comprises 20 activities whose duration, time estimates (in days) are given below.

S. No.	Activity	Duration
1	1-2	15
2	1-3	13
3	1-4	14
4	2-5	9
5	2-7	8
6	3-5	7
7	3-6	8
8	3-8	34
9	4-6	9
10	4-7	21
11	5-10	22
12	6-9	33
13	6-11	25
14	7-10	10
15	8-9	5
16	8-12	17
17	9-10	17
18	9-11	13
19	10-12	19
20	11-12	18

Draw network for this project and determine the critical path.

11. The following table shows the information about various activities of a project network

Activity	Normal Duration (Days)	Normal Cost (Rs.)	Crash Duration (Weeks)	Crash Cost (Rs.)
1-2	9	8,000	7	150000
1-3	5	5,000	3	8,000
2-3	7	7,000	5	8,600
2-4	8	6,000	6	7,000
3-4	26	9,000	4	11,400

The overhead costs are Rs. 1,300 per day. Determine the optimum cost and duration of the project.

12. The following data pertain to project network:

Activity	Normal Duration (Weeks)	Normal Cost (Rs.)	Crash Duration (Weeks)	Crash Cost (Rs.)
1-2	4	8,000	3	15,500
1-3	8	5,000	5	9,500
2-3	6	7,000	4	9,000
2-4	9	9,000	7	16,000
3-4	5	6,000	3	12,000

The indirect cost of the project is Rs. 3000 per week. Determine the optimum cost and optimum duration of the project. Also draw the least cost network.

FILL IN THE BLANKS

1. A programme is also called a .... (Project)
2. An activity with a specific goal occupying a specific period of time is called.......................... (Project)
3. The technique used for planning, scheduling and controlling large projects is known as .... (Network analysis)
4. PERT stands for................and Review Technique. (Programme evaluation)
5. CPM stands for................ (Critical path method)
6. ....method gives best way of planning and scheduling (CPM)
7. PERT is ....oriented (Event)
8. CPM is...............oriented. (Activity)
9. PERT has .... time estimates. (3)

10. CPM has only..............time estimate. (1)
11. .... is event oriented (PERT)
12. The task or activity which does not consume resources, yet is shown to indicate a logical sequence in a network, is called................. (Dummy activity)
13. All such events carrying a zero slack or minimum slack fall under .... (Critical path)
14. A project must have definite.......... and........points (Start, end)
15. The starting and ending instant of an activity is known as .... (Event)
16. The activity which neither consumes time nor resource is...................... (Dummy activity)
17. The activity when it is delayed leads to delay of the project is .... (Critical activity)
18. The process of reducing the project duration by employing additional resources is known as........................ (Crashing)
19. In beta distribution, standard deviation is equal to .... (Optimistic time estimate)
20. Direct costs are those, which vary with the number of .... in the project. (Activities)
21. Rent and advertisement is an example for .... costs. (Indirect)
22. Total cost is the aggregate of .... and .... costs. (Direct and indirect)
23. Indirect costs are always ....per given unit of time, in the short run. (Fixed)
24. The additional cost per additional unit of time assuming a linear rate of approximation, is called......................... (Cost slope)
25. The time required to complete the project under normal conditions and under normal cost is called............. (Normal time)
26. The three time estimates in PERT are ...., ..., ... (Optimistic(t_o), Most likely(t_m) and Pessimistic(t_p))
27. Crashing of network is.................... (Time-Cost relationship)
28. Normal time is also known as................ (Standard time)
29. Cost slope formula............. (Crash cost-Normal cost/Normal time-Crash time)
30. Shortest possible time in which an activity can be completed is known is ....time (Optimistic)
31. The time in which the activity is normally expected to complete is ...... (Most likely time)
32. Minimum time required to achieve the normal cost is .... (Normal time)
33. Scheduling the activities within the limits of their total floats is .... (Smoothing)

34. The three kinds of floats are........, ..., ...
(Total float, free float and independent float)

35. An activity with a specific goal occupying a specific period time is called.... (Project)

36. ....is event-oriented (PERT)

37. The task or activity which does not consume resource, yet is shown to indicate a logical sequence in a network, is called..................... (Dummy activity)

38. The time estimate, which assumes no hindrances involve its completion, is called.................
(Optimistic time)

39. In beta distribution, standard deviation is equal to............... ((tp-to)/6)

40. All such events carrying a zero slack or minimum slack fall under..............(Critical path)

41. The time required to complete the project under normal conditions and normal cost is called............... (Normal time)

42. ....refers to the duration of such project, which can be reduced to lower period by pumping additional resources (Crash time)

43. The additional cost per additional unit of time assuming linear rate of approximation, is called................... (Cost slope)

44. PERT and CPM are useful for...........and .... (Scheduling, Controlling)

45. In a project network, critical path is the path, connecting the first initial node to last terminal node, of .... (Longest duration)

46. The critical activities have their total float as .... (0)

47. The duration of an activity when everything goes on very well during the project is known as.................................... (Least time estimate)

48. In PERT calculations, the expected duration (t_e) of each activity is assumed to be
($1/6\ (t_o + 4t_m + t_p)$)

49. When the duration of any activity is reduced, the direct costs.................. (Increases)

50. The probability distribution used in PERT which estimates the expected duration and they expect variance of an activity is .... (β -distribution)

51. In PERT analysis, the variance of a job having optimistic time 5, most likely time 8 and pessimistic time 17 is .... (9)

52. If the standard deviations of all the 5 critical activities of a project network are 1, 4, 8, 9, 3 then the standard deviation of the project length is (in times unit)...........................
(13.08)

53. If the critical path of a network is 1 -2 -4 -6 -7 and the variance 1 -2, 2 -3, 2 -4, 4 -5 4 -6, 2 -6, 4 -7, and 6 -7 are 3, 6, 5, 7, 6, 10, 12 what is the variance of the project length? .... (16)

54. The number of time estimates involved in PERT problem is........................ (3)

55. The probability to complete a project in the expected time is........................ (0.5)

56. The cost-time slope of an activity having normal time 4 hours, crash time 2 hours, normal cost Rs.150 and crash cost Rs. 350 is............................ (100)

57. In PERT analysis, the critical path is obtained by joining events having........................ (Positive slack)

❖ ❖ ❖

UNIT - V

STRATEGIC MANAGEMENT

5.1 ***Strategic Management***

- 5.1 Introduction
- 5.1.1 Vision
- 5.1.2 Mission
- 5.1.3 Goals
- 5.1.4 Objectives
- 5.1.5 Policies
- 5.1.6 Strategies
- 5.1.7 Programmes

5.2 ***Elements of Corporate Planning***

- 5.2.1 Process of corporate planning
- 5.2.2 Significance of corporate planning
- 5.2.3 Environmental Scanning
- 5.2.4 SWOT Analysis
- 5.2.5 Steps in Strategy Formulation
- 5.2.6 Strategy Implementation
- 5.2.7 Generic Strategy alternatives

5.1 INTRODUCTION

Running a business was a simple affair during the license raj era. Competition was less severe, where it existed, only domestic firms were competing with each other. There was huge market but scarce supplies. Whatever that was produced, was grabbed by waiting buyers. No wonder, one used to wait for seven years to get a phone connection, and 10 years to get a cooking gas connection.

Not any more, thanks to the economic liberation, set in motion in 1991, things changed significantly. Competition is heating up (from foreign firms include) and margins are falling though volumes are increasing. In this scenario, it has become extremely difficult for any businessman to survive and grow. The businessman needs to be always on the toes. He needs to visualize strategies and execute them according to the need of the hour so that he can enjoy competitive advantage. In other words, today businessman should practice the art and science of strategic Management.

Strategic management provides better guidelines to the entire organization on the crucial point of "what is it we are trying to do and to achieve"?

It makes managers more alert to the winds of change, new opportunities and threatening developments. It also provides managers with a rationale for evaluating competing budget requests for investment capital and new staff. It helps to unify the strategy-related decisions by managers across the organization and creates a more productive management posture and counteracting tendencies for decisions to be creative and defensive.

Thus, among the entire things managers do, few affect a company's performance more fundamentally than how well its management team charts the company's long-term direction. This is where strategic management becomes a disposable factor.

The concept of strategy is central to understanding the process of strategic management. According to Quinn and Rogers, strategy comes from the Greek word, *"strategic"* meaning "generalship" and which described the role of general in the command of the army

From there, the term strategic planning evolved at about the end of World War II as an alternative course of action. Later, this term came to mean the art of the general, i.e. the psychological and behavioral skills with which he performs his role. By the time of Alexandra, it referred to the skill or employment of forces to overcome opposition and to create a unified system of global government. As time went by, it turned out to mean managerial skills in terms of administration, leadership, oration and power.

The end of the cold war brought about the globalization era, gradually turning the world into a global village and a single market where the tenets of strategic planning as in "strategies" or "the commanding army" could not withstand the tidal waves of stiff competition of the managerial skills. This situation paved the way for and/or gave rise to strategic management. Thus, the concept of strategy is central to strategic management.

Strategic management is what managers do to develop the organization's strategies. Strategic management involves all four of the basic management functions—planning, organizing, leading, and controlling.

Strategic management is important for organizations as it has a significant impact on how well an organization performs. In today's business world, organizations of all types and sizes must manage constantly changing situations. Today's companies are composed of diverse divisions, units, functions, and work activities that must be coordinated. Strategic management is involved in many of the decisions that managers make.

"Strategic management is an ongoing process that evaluates and controls the business and the industries in which the company is involved; assesses its competitors and sets goals and strategies to meet all existing and potential competitors; and then reassesses each strategy annually or quarterly [i.e. regularly] to determine how it has been implemented and whether it has succeeded or needs replacement by a new strategy to meet changed circumstances, new technology, new competitors, a new economic environment., or a new social, financial, or political environment."

Managers must carefully consider their organization's internal and external environments as they develop strategic plans. They should have a systematic means of analyzing the environment, assessing their organization's strengths and weaknesses, identifying opportunities that would give the organization a competitive advantage, and incorporating these findings into their planning. The value of thinking strategically has an important impact on organization performance.

According to Arieu (2007), "there is strategic consistency when the actions of an organization are consistent with the expectations of management, and these in turn are with the market and the context." Strategic management includes not only the management team but can also include the Board of Directors and other stakeholders of the organization. It depends on the organizational structure.

Nature of Strategy

The concept of strategy has been borrowed from the military and adapted for use in business. In business , as in the military, strategy bridges the gap between policy and tactics. Together, strategy and tactics bridge gap between ends and means.

Strategy refers to maneuvering troops into position before enemy is actually engaged. Strategy is an art of war during the time of the ancient Greeks through World War II.

Concept of Strategy :

- Strategy is a plan, a " how," a means of getting from here to there.
- Strategy is a pattern in actions overtime; for example, a company that regularly markets very expensive products is using a "high end" strategy.
- Strategy is position ; that is, it reflects decisions to offer particular products or services in particular markets.
- Strategy is perspective, that is, vision and direction.

Strategy means

- a top management decision that directs organization and business towards predetermined goal,

- a carefully crafted plan with a stream of decisions and actions overtime,
- a plan or a course of action that reveals its objectives, purposes, goals, policies and firm is achieved,
- a plan that helps in developing competitive position,
- a term that refers to a complex web of thoughts, ideas, insights, experiences, goals, expertise, memories, perceptions, and expectations that provide general guidance for specific actions in pursuit of particular ends,
- the courses we chart, the journey we imagine and at the same time, it is the course we steer, the troop we actually make.

Definition of Strategy:

Strategy is a "a unified comprehensive and integrated plan designed to ensure that the basic objective of the enterprises are achieved" – ***Glueck.***

Since the word "Strategy" is central to strategic management it is quite in tune and proper to get the meaning of strategy clear before advancing to strategic management. Certainly strategy is not an exact science and organizations can apply their individual rules. The best strategy does not emerge from cook book approach and there are no formulae for calculating the strategy. Strategy is defined in many ways based on the views and experience of the authors. The definitions include:

Anoff (1965) defines strategy as a rule for making decisions under conditions of partial ignorance whereas policy is a contingent decision. Business strategy is the broad collection of decision, rules and guidelines that define business scope and growth direction.

Steiner and Miner (1977), define strategy to mean the formulation of basic organization missions, purposes and objectives, polices and programmer strategies to achieve them, and the methods needed to ensure that strategies are implemented to achieve organization's ends.

Mintzberg (1979) refers to strategy as the interpretation of the environment and the development of consistent patterns in streams of organizational decisions. On the other hand, Porter (1980) sees strategy as a broad-based formula for how business is going to compete, what its goals should be and what policies will be needed to carry out those goals. The essence of formulating competitive strategy is relating a company to its environment.

Quinn's (1980), describes strategic decisions as "those that determine the overall direction of an enterprise and its ultimate viability in light of the predictable and unpredictable and the unknowable changes that may occur in its most important surroundings environment".

However, ***Hax*** (1987) adequately relates strategy to strategic management when he states "the essence of strategy is for a firm to achieve a long term sustainable advantage over its competitors in every business in which it participates".

A firm's strategic management has, as its ultimate objective, the development of its corporate values, managerial capabilities, organizational responsibilities and operational decision making, at all hierarchical levels and across all business and functional lines of authority.

From these definitions one can, like Quinn and Mintzberg state that there is no single universally accepted definition of strategy and there is no one best way to create strategy, nor is there any one best form of organization.

Elements of Strategy

A strategy should have three elements.

1. Objectives and goals to be achieved,
2. Major or key polices that shall guide actions, and
3. Actions, programs that are to be initiated to accomplish the stated goals.

Definitions of Strategic Management:

Strategic management has been defined in many ways by different authors and managers. The following are some of the definitions:

i. Strategic management is that set of managerial decisions and actions that determines the long-run performance of a corporation. It includes environmental scanning, strategy formulation, strategy implementation and evaluation. (Wikipedia, The Free Encyclopedia On-line).

ii. Definition of strategic management is "a stream of decisions and actions, which leads to the strategy management development of an effective strategy to help achieve corporate objectives". – Glueck

iii. Strategic management is a stream of decisions and actions which leads to the development of an effective strategy or strategies to help achieve corporate objectives (Gleck and Juanxh, 1984).

iv. Strategic management is concerned with the over-all long range direction of organizations and consequently provides a framework for operational management (Greenley, 1989).

v. Strategic management is concerned with deciding on strategy and planning how that strategy is to be put into effect via strategic analysis, strategic choice and strategic implementation (Johnson and Scholes, 1993).

vi. Strategic management is the decision process that aligns the organization's internal capability with the opportunities and threats it faces in its environment (Rowe et al, 1994).

From all these, strategic management can be seen as the art or science of formulating, implementing and evaluating cross-functional decisions that enable an organization to achieve its objectives. Other concepts in management that are used sometime or interchangeably with strategic management are strategic planning, business policy and long-range planning.

Strategic Management Techniques:

Strategic management techniques can be viewed in two major ways.

1. Bottom-up Approach:

The first is the bottom-up or collaborative processes. Using this approach, the employees initiate a proposal which they subsequently submit to their managers or their superiors, who put the idea further up in the establishment. These proposals may be assessed based on financial criteria and other concrete economic terms such as cost-benefit evaluation and returns on investment.

2. Top–down Approach:

The second is the top-down approach which is more common than any other method. Here, the chief executive officer and his team decide on the overall direction which the organization should go.

Scope of Strategic Management:

Strategic management covers the major components such as the company mission, vision, policy, profile, objectives and goals. Strategy determination, formulation of alternative strategic choice, implementation and evaluation are part of strategic management.

Some Significant Strategies Formulated by Corporate India in the recent past :

- Tata Steel acquires Corus group (Europe's second largest steel producer) for $4.3 billion, as a "defining moment" for Ratan N. Tata Company and Consistent with its strategy of growth through international expansion. The acquisition is a shared vision of a "global strategy". Tata sail with long proud histories, both companies have compatible culture of commitment to stake holders and complementary strength in technology, efficiency, product mix and geographical spread .Together they will be even better equipped to remain at the leading edge of the fast changing steel industry.
- Vodafone (UK) acquired 67 per cent of Hutchison Essar (Indias fourth largest mobile phone company), with the idea to enable Vodofone's shareholders benefit their increased investment in the Indian mobile phone market.

Key Attributes of Strategic Management

1. Strategic management directs the organization towards overall organizational goals and objectives
2. Strategic management includes multiple stakeholders in decision making
3. Strategic management requires incorporating both long-term and short-term perspective
4. Strategic management involves the recognition of trade-off between effectiveness and efficiency

Characteristics of Effective Strategy

Characteristics of the effective strategy are :

i. Objectives and goals are clearly stated and understood, are decisive and attainable,

ii. There should be scope for initiative and freedom of actions-the chosen strategy should also enhance commitment,

iii. It should be mobilization and use of resources at decisive points in order to ensure success and enhance the superiority of the firm vis-à-vis the competition,

iv. It should have flexibility and maneuverability to facilitate the alteration of a course of action and also to minimize the fixed allocation of resources to defend the firm's position in the market,

v. It must be championed by a committed leadership, in other words, the interests and values of key managers must match the needs of their role,

vi. The strategy must make use of speed, secrecy, and intelligence to initiate a surprise attack on opponent's, with a view to alter the relative competitive position,

vii. The strategy must protect the resource base of the organizations as well as the key operating points from attacks by competitors.

Figure 5.1 : Hierarchical Level of Strategy

The levels of strategy are relevant in a conglomerate - a business having multi- plants and multi-divisions. Where the business has a single unit, only two levels-corporate level and functional level are relevant.

1. *Corporate Level Strategies:*

Corporate level strategy is formulated by Chief Executive Officer (CEO), Board of Directors (BODs), senior executives and other corporate staff.

Tata group is divided into a wide range of business, including Indian Hotels (IHCL), Tata Auto Group systems, Tata chemicals, Tata Coffee, Tata Motors, Tata Tea, Tata Technologies, Tata Consultancy Services, and VSNL. Tata group is headed by Chairman Ratan Tata who decides on overall strategic objectives, allocates resources and decides investment and disinvestment. A part from this he also oversees the performance of business level managers and also acts as a link between manager and its owner (share holders). Therefore corporate level managers are viewed as the guardians of share holders wealth.

2. *Business Level Strategies:*

The second or middle decision making is at the business level. The business is a self – contained division that provides a product or service for a particular market. Business level managers should determine how the firm will compete successfully in the targeted product market, identify new promising market segment, which products and services should be developed in which markets and so on.

3. *Functional (Operational) Level Strategies*:

This level is composed of managers of different functional areas : Human Resources, Finance, Production, Marketing, Customer Service, and Research and Development. Functional level managers are responsible for developing annual objectives and short – term strategies of the concerned areas of operation.

5.1.1 VISION

Vision is the starting point for articulating organization's hierarchy of goals and objectives. A vision statement is a vivid idealized description of a desired outcome that inspires, energizes and helps firm to create a mental picture of its target. It represent a destination that is driven by and evokes passion, but it does not specify the means that will be used to reach the desired destination. The vision provides the point of reference on the horizon – a beacon of light. It seeks to answer the basic question, "what do we want to become?". Developing and implementing a vision is one of the leader's central roles. CEO or top management need to have not only a vision statement but also a plan to implement it.

According to Robinson in 1997, a company vision is sinuous with the company's mission. This means that the alternative name for the company's mission is vision.

Examples of vision:

- Infosys – "To be globally respected Corporation that provides best breed of business solutions, levering technology, vendors and society at large".
- Ford Motor – "To become the world's leading consumer company for automotive products and services".
- Kingfisher – "To deliver a staff, value-based and enjoyable travel experience to all our guests."
- ONGC _ "To be world-class and gas company integrated in energy business with dominate Indian leader ship and global presence".
- Mc Donald's – "To be world's best quick service restaurant".
- P&G – "Be recognized as , the best consumer products and service company in the world".
- Toyota – "To become the most successful and respected car company in each market around the world".
- Disneyland – "To be the happiest place on earth".
- The canon — "Beat Xerox".
- Motorola — "Total customer satisfaction".

The vision statement may also contain slogan, a diagram, or a picture – whatever grabs attention. Take example of Canon's battle with Xerox, How vision created? Creating a vision statement begins with and relies heavily on intuition and dreaming. In the process of creating vision, top management may have brainstorming session with staff or Board. By using this exercise the organization may evolve a vision statement. In the brainstorming session the following questions are debated:

- How do you and your community to be different?
- What role do you and your organization play in your community?
- What will success look like?

The vision may evolve at the end of brainstorming session or it may form in one person's head in the shower one morning . Vision takes form at the end of group discussion or in one person's head, it should consists of two major components. (1) Core ideology, and (2) Envisoned future.

1. *Core Ideology* :

It means the long lasting character of a firm as it passes through the changing circumstances like competition, technology or management style. Generally core ideology rests on the core values and core purposes. By values, we mean the beliefs, business principles , and practices that are incorporate into the way the company operates and the behavior of the organizational personnel. Company value statements generally contain between four and eight values (treatment of employees and customers, integrity, ethics, innovativeness, emphasis on quality service, social responsibility and community citizenship) which ideally, are tightly connected to and reinforce the company's vision, strategy, and operating practices. The typical values statements consists of – Ethics, Trust, Customer Focus, Team work, Example of values, Initiative motherhood.

The following are some examples:

- ***Microsoft:*** As a company and as individuals we value:
  a. Integrity and honesty.
  b. Passion for customers, for our partners, and form technology.
  c. Openness and respect fullness.
  d. Taking on big challenges and seeing them through.
  e. Constructive self- criticism, self – improvement, and personnel excellence.
  f. Accountability to customers, share holders, partners, and employees for committees, result and quality.
- ***Ford Motor Company :***

  The customer is our job one. We do the right thing for customers, our people, our environment and our society. By improving everything we do, we provide superior returns to our share holders.
- ***P&G* :**

  P&G is for its people and values by which we live. We attract and recruit the finest people in the world. We build our organization within promoting and rewarding people without regard to any difference unrelated to performance. We act on the conviction that the men and women of Procter & Gamble will always be our most important asset.

- ***Du Pont Company :***

  Which calls itself " a Science Company," and makes a wide array of products, stresses four values –safety, ethics, respect for people and environmental stewardship. The first three have been in place since the company was founded over 200 years ago by E.I. DuPont.

2. ***Envisioned Future :***

It is consistent long term goal and description of what it would be like to achieve that goal.

Characteristics of an Effective Vision

Strategic Vision must convey something definite about how the organization's leaders intend to position the organization beyond where it is today. Generally, a good vision always needs to be beyond a company's reach, but it should direct towards the vision. The following are the characteristics of effective vision statement :

1. ***Focused :*** Is specific enough to provide managers with guidance in making decisions and allocating resources.
2. ***Graphic*** : Paints a picture of the kind of company that management is trying to create and the market position the company is striving to carve itself.
3. ***Directional*** : Says something about the company's journey or destination and signals the kind of business and strategic changes that will be forthcoming.
4. ***Flexible*** : Is not a once-and – for- all- time pronouncement – vision about a company's future path may need to change as events unfold and circumstances change. Some companies give vision for a specific period of time.
5. ***Feasible :*** Is within the realm of what the company can reasonably expect to achieve in due time .
6. ***Desirable :*** Appeals to the long- term interests of stakeholders particularly shareholders, employees and customers.
7. ***Easy to Communicate*** : Is explainable in less than 10 minutes and ideally can be reduced to a simple memorable slogan. For example, take Henry Ford's famous vision "a car in every garage".

Benefits of having a Strategic Vision

The process and outcome of visioning may seem vague and superfluous. But the long – term benefits are substantial:

1. Breaks you out of boundary thinking.
2. Provides continuity and avoids stumble effect of strategic planning fits and states.

3. Gives direction and sense of purpose.
4. Promotes interest and commitment.
5. Encourages openness to unique and creative solutions.
6. Encourages and Builds confidence.
7. Alerts stakeholders tc needed change.
8. Promotes laser like focus.
9. Builds loyalty through investment (owner ship).
10. Provides competitive advantages through superior efficiency and innovativeness.

Short comings in Vision Statements:

The following are the major shortcomings in company vision statements :

1. ***Incomplete :*** Vision statement is generally short and does not specify where the company is headed or what the organization is trying to create.
2. ***Vague :*** It does not provide much indication of whether or how top management intentions to alter the company's current product/ market/customer/technology focus.
3. ***Bland:*** Lacks in motivation power.
4. ***Not Distinctive:*** Vision statements of companies are stereo typed.
5. ***Too Reliant on Superlatives :*** The vision statements rely on the superlatives such as best, more successful, recognized leader, world best, world's leading, delivering quality products/ services.
6. ***Too Generic :*** The vision statement fails to identity the business and industry to which it belongs is supposed to apply . Anybody whom reads vision statements of a few companies may not be able to identify the business, and the industry the company belongs . The statement could apply to companies in any industry.
7. ***Talk does not result in Walk:*** Vision no doubt arouses great enthusiasm in employees but the euphoria dies down soon as the management says something but does totally different thing. They fail to walk the talk.
8. ***Irrelevance:*** Vision statements of some organizations are prepared without considering the ground realities. "Our vision is to keep all employees happy and contended" may be a statement of a company but the same company is not keeping the employees on regular salaries nor is it able to pay salaries every month.
9. ***Not the Holy Grail :*** Vision can be a cure for all solutions, not a magic word and not an elixir. It is like a rainbow – looking beautiful but not reachable. At the best vision appeals to the emotional instincts of employees. Beyond this, vision has no real significance.

5.1.2 MISSION:

Company Mission

The mission of a company is having fundamental, unique purpose that is setting it apart from other companies of its type and identifies the scope of its operations in product and market terms. The mission also carefully defines what the company does not do. It is a general statement of the company's intent and represents the view that the management has for the future of the company or what they want it to become or achieve. It is the central purpose for the company's existence and implies the image the company seeks to project. It reflects the company's self concept and indicates the principal product or service the company attempts to satisfy. Mission statement defines the aspirations, values, roles, growth, goals, survival and profitability of a company. In short, the mission describes the products, market and technological areas of emphasis for the business in a way that reflects the priorities of the strategic decision maker.

Rader (1994) enumerates seven important features of a powerful mission statement, which are:

- Portraying the imagination with right and powerful images of target outcome
- Employing images that are clear, concise and compelling
- Expressing strong values and beliefs about the future
- Providing guidance for actions that must and must not be done
- Focusing discussion and shaping choices about consequences
- Posing Challenges for present and future performance
- Applying to each and every member of the community.

A company's mission reflects the firm's intention to secure its survival through sustained growth and profitability.

Many organizations have improperly defined mission statements in which some are not complete and in which the essential ingredients of the mission statement are not indicated. Some other companies misuse the mission statement as an external device for public relations rather than an integral part of the strategic management. To be able to achieve its objectives, the mission statement must be understandable, applicable and serves to rule out actions.

Definition:

1. Wheelan and Hunger view that "mission is the purpose or reason for the organization's existence".
2. In Ducker's opinion, "mission focuses the organization on action. It defines the specific strategies needed to attain goal. It creates disciplined organization.... The business purpose and business mission are so rarely given adequate thought, is perhaps the most important single cause of business failure and business frustration".

Mission follows vision creating strategic vision is concerned with "what do we want to become? "On the other hand, a company 's mission statement outlines the core purpose of the organization," why it exists?" That will lay emphasis on business and there by path for development. Generally, mission statement addresses the following questions:

- Why is this firm in business?
- What are our economic goals?
- What is our operating philosophy in terms of quality, company image and self-concept?
- What are core competencies and competitive advantages?
- What customer do and can we serve?
- How do we view our responsibilities to stockholders, employees, communities, environment, social issues and competitors?

Process of Developing Mission Statement :

The top executive takes the initiative and he or she assisted by team of managers. Together, all will brain storm, come out with a draft, after series of revisions, final statement is prepared and that becomes the mission statement of the organization. Unlike vision, mission statement keeps changing.

Mission statements usually give internal direction for the future of the organization. Ambition and visionary zeal are the main constituents of mission. The mission specifies what qualities the organization they will uphold and impart to the society and community. A mission statement is full of enthusiasm.

a. A mission statement is marked by grandeur.

b. It is not time bound because the further envisioned in a mission statement cannot be achieved in a day.

Components of Mission Statement:

Mission statement spells out that an organization's 'purpose of existence'. When strategists raise certain fundamental questions related to business such as:

1. What is our business?
2. Why are we in the business? and
3. What will it be after 5 years?

Then, the need for mission statement arises. The survival of an organization mainly depends on its needs, for satisfying the needs of the society. Mission statement defines the role that an organization plays in a society. For example, BSNL satisfies the communication needs of the society. Mission statement describes what the company stands for its purpose, image and planning and developing mission for its stakeholders. A survey by Bain and Company indicates that planning and developing mission and vision statements are the popular management tools of strategic management.

There are three indispensable components of the corporate mission statement. They are product or service, customer, and the principal technology for production of products or services.

Abell has given almost the same dimensions in his definition for business.

- Who is being satisfied (what customer group)?
- What is being satisfied (what customer needs)?
- How they are being satisfied (by what skills)?

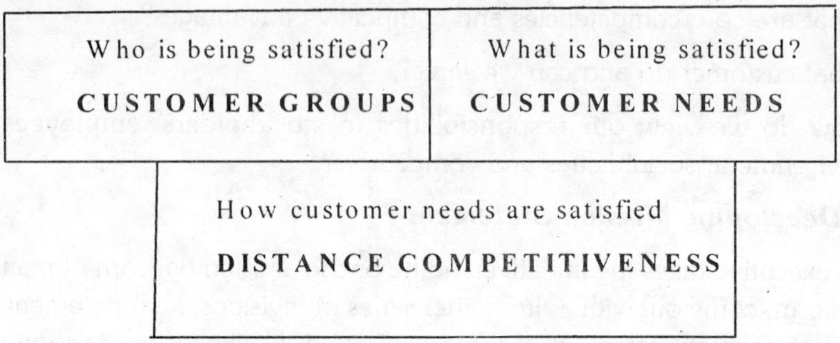

Figure 5.2 : Abell's Framework for Definition of the Business

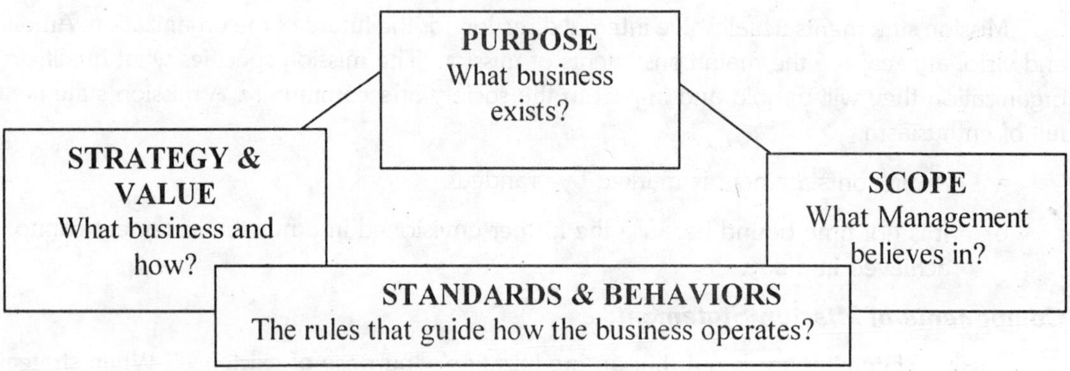

Figure 5.3 : Elements of a Mission Statement

Elements of a Mission Statement:

1. Purpose
2. Strategic scope
3. Standards and behaviors
4. Strategy and values

Characteristics of an Effective Mission Statement:

A mission statement incorporate the basic business purpose and the reason for its existence by rendering some valuable functions for the society.

An effective mission statement should posses the following characteristics.

1. Feasible
2. Precise
3. Motivation

4. Clarity of purpose of the business
5. Distinctive and different from other companies.
6. Define its strategic scope
7. Indicates major components of strategy
8. Measurability of the objectives.
9. Be relevant to the entire firm's stakeholder.
10. Be exciting and inspiring.

Benefits of having Mission Statements:

1. It develops unified purpose of organization.
2. It provides a basis for allocating organizational resources.
3. It helps to establish a general tone or organizational climate
4. It facilitates the translation of objectives into work structure.
5. It specifies organizational purpose, and then to translate these into objectives, in such a way that cost, time, and performance parameters can be assessed and controlled.

Mission Statement in Indian Companies:

Some of the mission statements that carry the required components are given below:

1. ***HPCL :*** 'HPCL will be a fully integrated company in the hydrocarbons sector of exploration and production , refining and marketing".
2. ***Maruti Udyog Ltd :*** "The leader in the Indian Automobile Industry".
3. ***GAIL :*** "Accelerating and optimizing the effective and economic use of NATIONAL GAS and its fractions".
4. ***Kochi Refineries :*** "To enhance shareholder value and maximize returns through the best use of resources".
5. ***Tata Power :*** "To participate in adjacent infrastructure businesses that provide opportunities for growth".
6. ***Gujarat State Fertilizers and Chemicals :*** "To provide quality inputs and services to agriculture and industry at competitive prices".
7. ***TVS MOTORS :*** "TVS MOTORS will have and sustain its cutting edge of technology by constant benchmarking against international leaders'.
8. ***Dr. REDDY's Laboratories :*** "We take utmost care to protect our natural environment and serve the communities in which we live and work ".
9. ***Reliance Industries :*** "Speed and innovation is a way of life".
10. ***L&T :*** "L&T shall be an innovative and attaining global benchmarks".
11. ***Hero Honda Motors :*** "We Hero Honda constantly innovate products and processes".

5.1.3 GOALS

A company's goal describes the desired future position the company wants to reach. The selection of the company's goals is based on the defined mission of the company. In a situation where a strategic planning model separates the goals from the objectives, it means that the goals are broad and timeless statements of the end result that the organization considers that they can use to achieve their mission. A goal should clearly states what is to be achieved and when the results will be accomplished. Company goals do not state how the results will be achieved. Organizations normally have multiple goals and at the same time all existing in a complex hierarchy. An organization may have a series of less permanent goals that define targets for the organization. All strategic goals affect the organization's overall direction and productivity. Profitability is usually the main goal of many business organizations, no matter how it is measured or defined. A goal is a statement of specifics that quantify the objectives.

5.1.4 OBJECTIVES

Vision is a destination whereas mission statements are more specific. Vision and mission statements need to be followed by objectives. Objectives are used to operationalise the mission statement act as yardstick for measuring company's performance.

The organization's objectives establish the intended nature of the enterprise and the direction in which the organization wants to move. Objectives are those ends or results which the organization sets out to achieve through not only its existence but also its operations. A number of different objectives are pursued by business organizations. Some examples include survival, growth, continuity of profit, production at least cost, good quality products or services, quick delivery, meeting target dates, customer and employee satisfaction to mention just a few. Every organization has more than one objective at any given time.

Reasons for establishing objectives:

There are three major reasons why an organization establishes objectives and why these objectives are important in strategic management. The reasons are as follows:

1. Objectives help to define the organization in the environment because they enable the organization to justify its existence and help to attract people who identify with the objectives to work for the organization.
2. Objectives help to co-ordinate decisions and decision makers. This is because objectives help to direct employees to the required standards of behavior and reduce conflicts in decision making since all employees know the objectives of the organization.
3. Objectives also help to provide standards for assessing organizational performance. Without stated objectives it would be difficult for an organization to evaluate itself or for anybody to evaluate the success or failure of the organization. Therefore, an organization's objectives are very crucial to strategic management.

Objectives therefore, indicates management's intentions towards pursing and accomplishing its mission. Usually, objectives and goals address all the areas of the operation of the company including profitability, sales growth, market share, innovation, productivity, physical and financial resources, risk, public responsibility, manager's performance and development.

Objectives / Goals

Objectives are formulated from mission statements. Objectives and goals are used interchangeably in management literature but the recent strategic management literature shows a subtle distinction between these two terms. Objective is the ended statement, which does not quantify what needs to be achieved and the time frame for completion . So 'growth' is a goal whereas an objective is to 'increase growth by 10% in terms of market share and sales over last year'. Usually the long-term goals and short-term objectives are derived from mission.

Significance of Objectives

Objectives form the basis for all other functional decisions such as finance, manufacturing, marketing and human resources. Objectives are split into business wise objectives and functional targets. While setting objectives, the organization encounters the environment and determines the locus it will devise to attain in the environment such as a dominant player, a weak player or one among the heard. Objectives and strategy put together, explain the firm's concept of business. Objectives indicate the organizational performance to be realized and expected over a period of time.

1. ***Canara Bank*** : "The bank's stated objectives are 'growth, innovativeness, high profits as a barometer of efficiency , highly involved employees distinctively charged with pride".
2. ***Maruthi*** : "We don't sell more cars than No. 2. We sell more cars than the entire competition put together".

Areas where Objectives are Set:

Organizations follow multiple objectives such as:

1. Growth
2. Profitability
3. Market Share
4. Productivity
5. Technology
6. R & D and Innovation
7. Corporate Social Responsibility
8. Image
9. Employees Satisfaction

Peter F. Drucker suggested that companies should set goals and objectives in the following areas :

1. Return on Investment
2. Market Share

3. Innovation
4. Productivity
5. Physical and Financial Development
6. Worker Performance and Attitude
7. Social responsibility

In recent times, Management By Objective (MBO) received much attention from the strategists.

Characteristics of Objectives :

Objectives setting is a complex process. Well-formulated objectives possess certain characteristics.

1. ***Specific :*** Instead of stating objective as growth in assets, sales and profits, it is preferable to state 12 per cent increase in sales, 10 per cent increase in profits and 10 per cent increase in assets. Such a specific statement will lead and motivate employees.
2. ***Time bound :*** BPL set the objective of 25 per cent increase of return on net worth by 2002. When an objective is related to a time frame, the managers are forced to act within the duration.
3. ***Measurable :*** Objective should be amenable to measurement. Employee's attraction towards a company is an objective, which can be measured by the following aspects.
   (a) The number of applications received
   (b) The quality of applications received
   (c) The staff turnover
   (d) Average salary offered.

   The objective of employee's attraction for a company can be measured and compared with best companies in the industry .
4. ***Challenging :*** Objectives should be attainable and realistic but challenging for employees. Too high sales target and too low sales are dangerous and misleading the employees and result in frustration and sub optimal performance.
5. ***Objectives form a hierarchy*** : Objectives are usually set at different levels and in different functional areas. All of them are not having the same significance to the firm. Prioritization at different levels is crucial while resources and time are limited. Objectives in functional areas are not equally important so trade-off decisions should be made so that objectives at different levels and different areas support each other and mutually synergetic in nature.
6. ***Constraints :*** Organizations face external constraints like consumer activism, WTO, environmental concern and pollution control and internal constraints like shortage of material resources and human resources. Such internal and external constraints serve as a limitation to objective setting of firms.
7. ***Verifiable*** : Verifiable objectives are measurable irrespective of their qualitative nature.

In order to measure any objective, it should be quantified. Quantifiable objectives alone should be used in strategic management. Canara Bank fulfills its social responsibility objective by setting up training centers for rural youth in several places in India (RUDISET) where industrial training, craft training and skill training are extended to rural youth for setting up their own enterprises .

8. ***Time frame :*** Objectives are generally formulated for different time periods such as long term and short term objectives and such objectives should be integrated with each other. For example long- term objective may be 'growth' whereas it is supported by short-term objectives such as Return on Investment, Return on Asset and specific profit margin on annual basis.

Formulation of Objectives

Formulation of objectives and goals is a complex process. The strategists should consider the four factors while evolving objectives .

1. The forces in the environment
2. Realities of firm's resources and power relationship
3. The values of top management
4. Past strategies

Objectives and Strategic Management

Objectives are important for strategic management for the following reasons:

1. Objectives help to relate the organization in the environmental context. It helps to attract people with identical framework of mind.
2. Objectives help to coordinate decisions. All employees are aware of the objectives and stated objectives proved to be a means of coordination.
3. Objectives serve as standards of appraising organizational performance. They serve as a basis for evaluating or failure of organization.

Kinds of Objectives:

1. Economic and Social Objectives
2. Primary and Secondary Objectives
3. Short- term and Long –term Objectives

Approaches to determine Objectives:

Objectives of an organization may be determined with the adoption of either top-down approach or bottom up approach.

1. ***Top - down approach:*** The top level managers determines the objectives for their subordinates.
   i. Cohesion – It creates cohesion among the strategies and objectives of different division of the organization; and
   ii. Unify Internal Efforts – It helps to unify internal efforts to move the organization alone with the strategic path.

2. ***Bottom - up approach*** : Subordinates determine objectives for their job and the same would be presented to top level managers for consideration.

Areas of Setting Objectives

Drucker says objectives need to be set in the eight prime areas: They are: market standing, innovation, productivity, physical and financial resources, profitability, managers' performance and development, worker performance and attitude, and public responsibility.

Factors affecting Strategic Objective setting:

1. Enhancing Shareholders Value
2. Organizational Availability
3. Value Systems of Top Management
4. Experience of Past Objectives

5.1.5 POLICIES

A policy is a broad guideline for decision making that links the formulation of strategy with its implementation. Companies use policies to make sure that the employees throughout the firm make decisions and take actions that support the corporation's mission, its objectives and its strategies.

Policies are guides to actions. Polices usually indicate how resources are to be allocated. They equally indicate how tasks assigned to the organization can be accomplished. They enable each manager at the functional level such as marketing, accounting or finance, production and personnel to execute the organization's strategy properly. Strategy exists as a collective umbrella for the policy component. Policy should give a broad assessment of the organization's structure, business system and the resources available to the selected strategies. Organization's policies provide a framework for the implementation of any major changes needed to be made in that organization. The policies should provide the key yardsticks or measurements for the expected benefits, the strategy intends to produce or yield, so that the success or the failure of the policies can be readily evaluated. Polices are therefore, rules that express the limits within which action should occur. Policies also exist in hierarchy throughout an organization just the way we have the strategic goals.

5.1.6 STRATEGIES

A strategy is a plan that integrates an organization's major goal, policies and action sequences into a cohesive unit that is achievable. A well formulated strategy helps to enforce and allocate the organization's resources into a unique and viable positive unit based on its relative internal competencies and shortcomings, anticipated changes in the environment and contingent moves by intelligent opponents. Strategy defines the general direction in which the organization chooses to move to meet its goals in order to achieve its mission. Strategies usually include how to move to achieve desired results. Strategies are often constrained by the nature of the organization such as resources available, capabilities, culture, structure and tradition.

Strategy defines how an organization will not achieve its aims. All management decisions can therefore, be trusted against the rejected approach as a measure of acceptability. The strategy should document the strategic opportunities that are deemed most beneficial to pursue. The strategy should be stated in such a way that the organization will make the best use of what is available and also adequately compensate for its limitation. There is no one best way to create strategy, nor is there one best form of organization.

However, Professor R. Andrews in his book, "*The Concept of Corporate Strategy*" describes the central function of the chief executive is leading the continuous process of determining the nature of the enterprise and setting, revising and achieving its goals, it is called "corporate strategy". Professor R. Andrews defines strategy as the pattern of decision in a company that determines and reveals its objectives, purposes or goals, produces the principal policies and plans for achieving those goals, and defines the range of business the company is to pursue, the kind of economic and human organization it is or intends to be, and the nature of the economic and non economic contributions it intends to its shareholders, employees, customers and communities.

So, Corporate Strategy defines the business in which a company will compete, preferably in a way that focuses resources to convert distinctive competence into competitive advantage".

5.1.7 PROGRAMMES

Programmes

- Programmes refer to the logical sequence of operations to be performed in a given job.
- Size of each program is assessed in terms of resources and duration. If a program takes larger resources and time, it is said to be a major program.
- Network techniques like PERT and CPM are used to represent logical sequence of activities with time duration to utilize all the resources effectively.
- In general, goals are derived from mission statement, objectives from goals, strategies from objectives, tactics from strategies and programs from objectives.

5.2 ELEMENTS OF CORPORATE PLANNING

5.2.1 PROCESS OF CORPORATE PLANNING

Corporate Planning:

The success of an organization largely depends on how it defines, understands and faces changes in its environment. In order to do so every organization must have a formal or informal system of planning. A planning system is needed to reappraise the organization and to define the direction it should take.

Some type of planning has been used since long almost in every organization, business or non-business, large or small. Formal and systematic planning is however, relatively a new development. Planning is essentially an analytical process involving an assessment of the future, the determination of desired objectives in the context of the anticipated future, the development of alternative courses of action to achieve the desired objectives and the selection and implementation of a course and action from among these alternatives. Planning results in the commitment of corporate resources. Corporate planning emerged as a distinct, discipline in the U.S.A during 1950's.

Concept and Definitions

Corporate planning is basically the process of determining the objectives to be achieved and selecting the means of achieving the predetermined objectives. Planning is an integral part of a manager's job. Corporate planning is the systematic attempt to increase the rate of growth of an enterprise over the long run. It is a new way to manage, it is a generic process not amenable to precise definition.

According to John Argenti Corporate Planning is "a systematic disciplined study designed to help identity the objectives of any organization or corporate body, determine an appropriate target, decide on suitable constraints and devise a practical plan by which the objective can be achieved.

According to Drucker, Corporate planning is "the continuous process of making present entrepreneurial (risk – taking) decisions systematically and with the best possible knowledge of their futurity, organizing systematically, the efforts need to carry out these decision, and measuring the result, organizing systematically, the efforts need to carry out these decision, and measuring the result of these decision against the expectations through organized, systematic feed – back".

According to Rao and Sarin, Corporate planning is the process of formulating objectives as well as developing and evaluating alternative courses of action to reach these objectives, on the basis of identified external opportunities and treats and internal corporate strengths and weaknesses".

The Nature of Corporate Planning

A careful analysis of the foregoing would reveal the following characteristic feature of corporate planning.

1. Corporate planning is a formal and systematic approach to planning.
2. Corporate planning process is carried out in a sequence of steps.
3. Corporate planning has long –term perspective.
4. Corporate planning is a continuous process.
5. Corporate planning for enterprise as a whole rather than for any component part thereof.
6. Corporate planning is mainly the responsibility of top management.
7. Corporate planning is futuristic involving a forecast of the future.
8. Corporate planning relates the enterprise with its environment.
9. Corporate planning is based on the belief that unless action is taken now desired future state will not occur.
10. Corporate planning is comprehensive consisting of both planning and operational planning.

Elements of Corporate Planning

Mission

- A mission statement defines why the organization exists.
- It may specify the role the company has to play in the society.
- It is an explicit written statement of what an organization wishes to achieve in the years to come.
- Mission statement should be stated in terms of customer –orientation.
- Mission statement should be in specific terms avoiding ambiguity.
- No mission statement can ever be rigid and hard. It should be flexible. If the company finds that the mission is achieved or it is not economical to pursue the mission further, it is free to modify its mission statement.

Goals and Objectives

- Goals are defined as "what to achieve during or by the end of a given period".
- Goals may be classified as long – term or short- term goals.
- Short – term goals are those which are to be achieved in less than a year where as the time frame for long-term goals is more than a year.
- The goals are always set within the scope of the mission statement. Ex: An objective statement like "increase our production rate" is not specific, clear and measurable. It must be stated as 'Increase our production rate from 20% to 25% by next year."
- These objectives acts as basis for control function.
- They motivate the individuals towards the achievement of objectives set for them.

Strategies

Strategy refers to "plan of action" by which organization objectives are realized. Corporate strategy involves the following:

- ***Environmental Appraisal*** : Environmental appraisal includes study and analysis of economic, social, political, legal, and competitive factors to identify opportunities and anticipate possible threats.
- ***Corporate Appraisal :*** It involves the analysis of company's strengths and weaknesses so that strength is well exploited and weaknesses are to be overcome.

Let us suppose the objectives of an organization be "to increase production next year by 10% over the current year".

Then the strategies would be :

- Procure required raw material within given time period.
- Increase number of shifts, if necessary in production department.
- Expand into wide market including market abroad.

Ex: Introduction of 200ml bottles by coke to capture the market of low-income group is a strategy.

Tactics:

- Tactics are means by which a strategy is implemented.

For example there is a strategy to "promote sales effectively in urban areas".

Then tactics would be:

i. Advertise in local magazines and newspapers etc.

ii. Advertise on TV.

Policies

- Policies are guidelines set by top management for the purpose of making decisions at different levels in the organization.
- Organization policy reflects the owner's attitudes to different segments such as creditors, employees, customers, society at large.

Some examples for policies

- Do not accept cash from any source without issuing a receipt (to prevent block money)
- Goods once sold cannot be exchanged or returned.
- Check your cash before you leave the counter.
- Company works only for six days a week. If any of the employees is called for work on holidays, he is entitled for double wages.

Programmes:

- Programmes refer to the logical sequence of operations to be performed in a given job.
- Size of each program is assessed in terms of resources and duration. If a program takes larger resources and time, it said to be a major program.
- Network techniques like PERT and CPM are used to represent logical sequence of activities with time duration to utilize all the resources effectively.
- In general, goals are derived from mission statement, objectives from goals, strategies from objectives, tactics from strategies and programs from objectives.

Constituents of Corporate Planning

The comprehensive nature of the corporate planning process lies in that operational planning, project planning and strategic planning its constituents. Let us examine the nature and scope of each of these constituents.

Operational Planning :

It is necessary so as to ensure that change in the market situation for the existing product line does not adversely affect the earnings of the firm. Thus, operational planning involves study of the market conditions for the existing range of products to maintain and improve the position of the firm in the face of competition. It is essentially a short term exercise and deals with the existing product, market and facilities. The degree of uncertainty in operation planning is of a low order, the time span of discretion is short; choice of alternatives is relatively simple, but the firm can ill-afford to ignore long term changes in the product markets. It has to look for new products, create a market for the same, and utilize the existing facilities and expertise to meet new requirements.

Project Planning :

It is a forward looking exercise concerned with new markets, new products and new facilities. Project planning is, therefore, to deal with greater degree of uncertainty, and demands a higher order of judgment on the part of placement due to risk involved.

Strategic Planning :

It refers to the formulation of a unified comprehensive and integrated plan aimed at relating the strategic advantages of the firm to the challenges of the environment. It is concerned with appraising the environment in relation to the company, identifying the strategies to obtain sanction for one of the alternatives to be interpreted and communicated in all operationally useful manners. Thus, strategic planning provides the frame work within which future activates of the company is expected to be carried out. Compared with project planning, the time span of discretion in strategic planning is much longer, the degree of uncertainty and corresponding risks involved are much greater, and judgment to be exercised is more important.

Strategic planning determines the future direction of company; corporate planning is essentially based on strategic planning, and at the same time takes care of project planning and operational planning.

Nature and Features of Corporate Planning :

1. It is a planning for over all organizations.
2. It is the process of formulating objectives.
3. It consists of strategic planning, programme planning, and operational planning.
4. It is a continuous process.
5. It has long – range planning and short range management.
6. It is mainly related with top management.
7. It helps in decision making.
8. It is against with failures and setbacks.
9. It estimates future trends.

Advantages

1. It helps for finding useful activities.
2. It would spend out a program of execution of plan and achievement.
3. It provides support on rules, procedures and methods of plan implementation.
4. It helps in several entities like finance, marketing, the man power and the research and development.

5. It would declare the strategies in various business functions.
6. It helps to remove elimination of unnecessary activities.
7. It helps in optimum utilization of available resources.
8. It forecasts future challenges.
9. It encourages innovative thought and creativity.
10. It helps to improve the image of the firm in certain period of time.

Limitations

1. Time consuming and cost factor.
2. It is unable to bare rapid changes in company.
3. It is not accurate planning.
4. It is meant for long- range planning, it cannot be started suddenly and to achieve overnight success.
5. It does not give guarantee for success of objectives in adverse situations.
6. Reduces organizational flexibility.

Tactical Planning:

Tactical planning meant for shorter time frames. It involves less uncertainty and hence lower risk compared to strategic planning. It directs how resources of the organization will be utilized to achieve strategic goals. It requires internally generated data. A tactical plan shows how manager will encounter sudden changes in business environment.

Table 5.1 : Strategic Planning vs. Tactical Planning

Strategic Planning	***Tactical Planning***
1. Related to level of management	Developed by lower management
2. Long term planning	Mid or short term planning
3. It depends on forecasting about Technological political and social environment	It depends on pervious performance of the organization.
4. Less detailed	More detailed
5. Planning is done under uncertainty	Planning is done under less uncertainty

Table 5.2 : Strategic Planning vs. Operational Planning

Strategic Planning	***Operational Planning***
1. Long term planning	Short term planning
2. Internal structure is related to external one.	Focus on Internal structure environment
3. Precedes operational planning	Succeeds strategic planning
4. Related to top level management	Developed by low level management
5. Focus is on strategies	Focus is on functional aspects

Strategic Management Process :

Essentially strategic management involves strategy formulation, strategy execution and evaluation of the effectiveness of strategy. Broadly speaking, strategic management comprises the following steps :

1. Developing vision, mission and corporate objectives.
2. Analyze the corporate external competitive environment to identify opportunities and threats.
3. Analyze corporate internal operating environment to identify its strengths and weaknesses.
4. Formulate and select the strategies on the basis of strengths, weaknesses, opportunities and threats (SWOT – Step 2 and 3).
5. Strategy implementation.
6. Strategy evaluation and control.

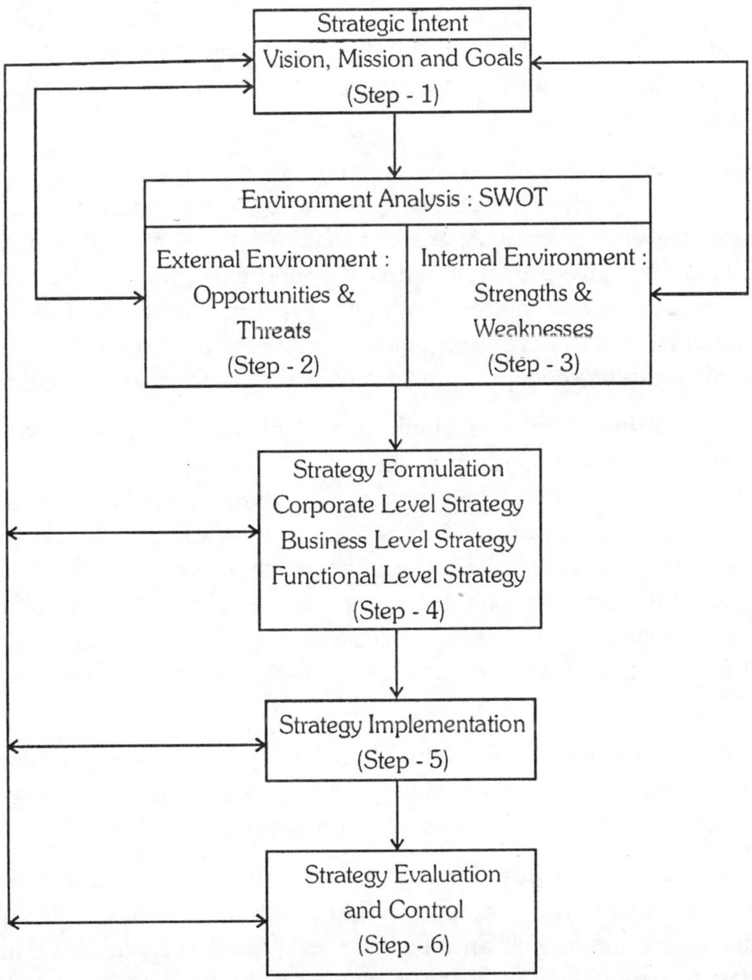

Figure 5.4 : Strategic Management Model

The following steps are identified from the above diagram under strategic management process:

1. Developing Vision, Mission and objectives
2. Analysis of Company's External Environment
3. Analysis of Company's Internal Environment
4. Strategy Formulation
5. Strategy Implementation
6. Strategy Evaluation and Control

The ***strategic management process*** is a six-step process that encompasses strategic planning, implementation, and evaluation.

- ***Identifying the Organization's Current Mission, Objectives, and Strategies:*** Every organization needs a mission, which is a statement of the purpose of an organization. The mission statement addresses the question: What is the organization's reason for being in business? The organization must identify its current objectives and strategies, as well.
- ***External Analysis:*** Managers in every organization need to conduct an external analysis. Influential factors such as competition, pending legislation, and labor supply are included in the external environment. After analyzing the external environment, managers must assess what they have learned in terms of opportunities and threats. Opportunities are positive trends in external environmental factors; threats are negative trends in environmental factors. Because of different resources and capabilities, the same external environment can present opportunities to one organization and pose threats to another.
- ***Internal Analysis:*** Internal analysis should lead to a clear assessment of the organization's resources and capabilities. Any activities the organization does well or any unique resources that it has, are called as strengths. Weaknesses are activities the organization does not do well or resources it needs but does not possess. The organization's major value-creating skills and capabilities that determine its competitive weapons are the organization's core competencies. Organizational culture is important in internal analysis; the company's culture can promote or hinder its strategic actions. *SWOT analysis* is an analysis of the organization's strengths, weaknesses, opportunities, and threats.
- ***Formulating Strategies:*** After the SWOT *analysis*, managers develop and evaluate strategic alternatives and select strategies that are appropriate. Strategies need to be established for corporate, business, and functional levels.
- ***Implementing Strategies:*** Strategy implementation is concerned with translating a decision into action. This presupposes that the strategic choice which ultimately leads to a decision is made with an inbuilt feasibility and acceptability. The allocation of resources to new course of action is needed to be undertaken and there may be a

need for adopting the organization's structure to handle new activities as well as training personnel and devising appropriate systems. Strategic implementation is often called the action stage of strategic management.

- ***Evaluating Results:*** This step is to know how effective the strategies have been and if any adjustments are necessary.

Strategic management process has been presented in various models. However, the most popular model adopted here is that of strategic decision making process preferred by Johnson and Sholes (1993). The model consists of three interacting elements: strategic analysis, strategic choice and strategic implementation.

Johnson and Sholes model presentation is adopted because it is convenient to use, well known and is used by many authors. For instance, it was used by Dress and Miller (1993). It is such a powerful model that can be used to organize our thoughts without losing sight of the interacting nature of the elements. However, it is important to note that the purpose of each model is the same in every case, which is to provide a vehicle through which to explain something complex. The strategic decision making process produces the strategy itself as made up of three interacting elements.

Figure 5.5 is structured around the convenient model for studying and understanding the complexity of the strategic management process as three interacting elements that Johnson and Sholes (1993) present. The figure shows that SMP comprises mainly strategic analysis, choice and implementation.

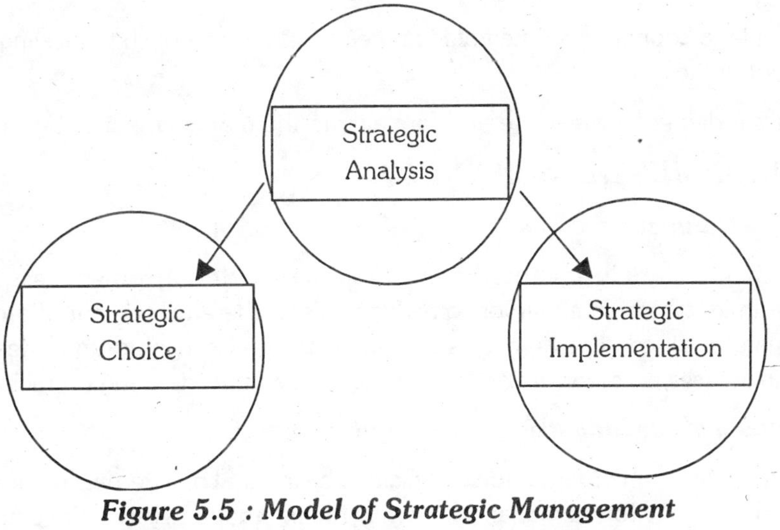

Figure 5.5 : Model of Strategic Management (Adopted from Johnson and Scholes, 1993)

5.2.2 SIGNIFICANCE OF CORPORATE PLANNING

Benefits of Strategic Management:

A survey of nearly 50 corporations in different countries and industries revealed the following three highly rated benefits of strategic management :

1. Clear sense of strategic vision for the firm.
2. Sharper focus on what is strategically important.
3. Improved understanding of a rapidly changing environment.

More specifically, the benefits of strategic management are several.

1. Allow for identification, prioritization and exploitation of opportunities.
2. Provides a frame work to view management problems.
3. Represents a frame work for improved coordination and control of activities.
4. Minimizes the effects of adverse conditions and changes.
5. Allow major decisions to better support established objectives.
6. Allow effective allocation of time and resources among business units.
7. Allows fewer resources and less time to be devoted to correcting erroneous or ad-hoc decisions.
8. Creates a framework for internal communication amòng personnel.
9. Helps to integrate the behavior of individuals into a total effort.
10. Provides basis for classifying individual responsibilities.
11. Encourage forward thinking.
12. Provides a cooperative, integrated and enthusiastic approach to tackling problems and opportunities.
13. Gives a degree of discipline and formality to the management of business.

5.2.3 ENVIRONMENTAL SCANNING

Concept of Environment

'Environment' literally means the surroundings, external objectives, influences or circumstances under which someone or something exists. The environment of any organization is ' the aggregate of all conditions, events and influence that surround and affect it. Since the environment influences an organization in many ways, its understanding is crucial importance.

Meaning of Business or Industry Environment

The environment of an organization could either be internal or external. The external analysis is often referred to as environmental analysis while the internal analysis is the company analysis or strategic advantage analysis. The environment of an organization includes factors outside the firm which can lead to opportunities for or threats to the organization. In business, the environment of an organization is the pattern of all external conditions and influences that effect organization's life and development. The relevant environmental factors include the total business community, the city or town, the entire country and the world at large. They also include technological, economical, physical, social and political factors.

The corporate strategist must be aware of these features in the environment. There should be awareness that change is taking place at varying rates in all the environmental factors. Change usually is fastest in technology, perhaps closely followed by political changes particularly in developing countries which are politically unstable. Change in the environment of business necessitates continuous monitoring of a company's definition of business. Otherwise, it may fail by becoming obsolete at the time it comes on stream. The effect of competition in the company's environment should not be overlooked. The strategist should be able to monitor environmental factors well to determine opportunities for threats to the organization. Environmental diagnosis consists of management decisions made and assessing the significance of the data on the basis of opportunities and threats of the environmental analysis.

Environmental analysis and diagnosis assists a strategist by giving time to anticipate opportunities and plan to take optional responses to the opportunities. It helps the strategist to develop an early warning system to prevent threats or develop strategies, which can turn threat into the organization's advantage. The analysis of the environment is important in that it increases the quality of the strategic decision making.

The strategy of any organization should be directed at exploiting the environmental opportunities and to blocking the environmental threats in a way and manner consistent with the organization's internal capabilities. This is porter's concept of environmental fit which allows the organization to maximize its competitive position.

The success or failure of environmental analysis depends largely on the characteristics of the environment such as the complexity of the environment, the rate of change and the cost of available information about the environment in which an organization floats. The following process may be followed:

(a) Audit the environmental influences.

(b) Assess the nature of the environment to determine the level of complexity of environment.

(c) Identify the key environmental forces.

(d) Identify the competitive position of the organization.

(e) Identify the major opportunities and threats (SWOT analysis).

Nature of the Environment

External Analysis

An organization's environment comprises of all the events, issues and facts which can influence its performance, but over which the organization has little or no influence. The external environment is beyond the control of the organization. The societal environment constitutes conditions that have a broad, rather than direct influence on the organization. These conditions include demographic, natural, political, cultural and economic factors. All these put together constitute the world within the organization functions and operates.

Demographic Factor: This includes aging of population, geographical population shifts, population growth and better educated populous.

Natural Factor: This includes pollution levels, natural resources management, and increased energy cost, raw material availability.

Political Factor: This includes international trade, investment incentives/controls, fiscal/ monetary policies, industrial policies, consumer policies, labor policies and regional policies.

Cultural Factor: This includes status of women and minorities, changes in the family life style, decline in the traditional life style, improved living standard, shifts to less work and more leisure.

Economic Factor: These are gross national product, personal income, employment and unemployment level, inflation rate, government spending and availability of capital.

There is also a task of environment which has a major impact on the organization and its strategic planning. The nature of competition is very important since it impacts on the profitability and scope of strategic manipulations in the market as shown in the following figure.

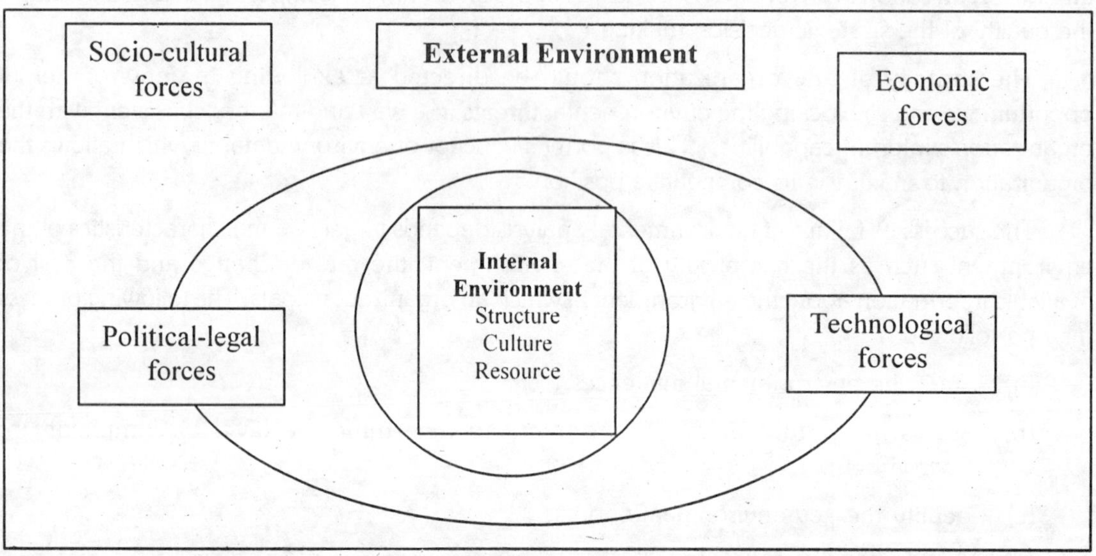

Figure 5.6 : Impact of Environment on the Organization

Among the elements of the external environment as indicated by Wendy Robson are the following:

Socio-Cultural Forces:

These include life-style changes, career expectations, rate of family formation, consumer activities, population growth rate, age distribution, regional shifts, urban-rural migration, birth rates and life expectancies. The strategist must be abreast of the social developments in the environment which may include the increasing rate of crime, demands by women for recognition and opportunity.

Economic Forces:

These include gross national product (GNP) trends, interest rates, money supply, inflation rates, unemployment levels, wage/price control, devaluation/revaluation, availability of energy and cost. The consequences of both national and international economic trends need to be monitored in great detail by any company so that the company will not be taken by surprise by the changing world.

Technological Forces:

Organizational spending on research and development (R&D) focus on technology efforts, patent protection, new products, new development in technology, transfer from laboratory to market place and productivity improvement through automation. Technology developments are the fastest, unfolding the opportunities for any company.

Legal Forces:

These include environmental protection laws, tax laws, special incentives, foreign trade regulations, attitudes towards foreign companies, laws on hiring and promoting etc.,

The importance of political forces to the business must be considered. The relationship between the private companies and government owned establishment is also important.

Also including in the environmental analysis is the task environment which includes the following:

Demand

Among the demand factors are size and growth of the existing market, number/size and distribution of customers, physical distribution channels, nature of market competition (price and non-price competition).

Market structure

Market structure factors include number/size and distribution of competition and suppliers, barriers to entry or exist to market product characteristics and product life cycles. Environmental analysis must include want for the company's products or services. There must be effective market segmentation which will divide the market to pieces that are identifiable, substantial enough to be profitable and defensible against competition.

Technology

This includes the level of technology and likely changes, cost structure including economies of scale, dependence on particular raw material or labor.

Government

Government policies, taxation and legislative apparatus are important in environmental analysis. The impact of particular legislation on the industry relating to product or consumption as well as role of the government as supplier, competitor or customer is a significant environmental factor.

Internal Analysis and Diagnosis

The internal analysis is also called the strategy advantage analysis and diagnosis. It is the process by which the strategist examines the firm's market and distribution, research and development, production and operations, corporate resources and personnel finance and the accounting function to determine where the firm has significant competencies so that it can most effectively exploit the opportunities and also meet the threats to the company's weaknesses which would need to be minimized, if not eliminated, in order to achieve corporate objectives.

Characteristics of Environment

1. Environment is Complex
2. Environment is Dynamic
3. Environment is Multi-faceted
4. Environment has a Far-reaching Impact

Internal and External Environment

The internal environment refers to all factors within an organization that impact strength or cause weak-nesses of a strategic nature. The external environment includes all the factors outside the organization which provide opportunities or pose threats to the organization.

The environment in which an organization exists can, therefore, be described in terms of the strength and weakness existing in the internal environment and the opportunities and threats operating in the external environment. The four environmental influences could be described as below.

Internal environment:

1. ***Strength*** is an inherent capacity which an organization can use to gain strategic advantage. Examples of strength are: good reputation among customers, resources, assets, people, experience, knowledge, data and capabilities.
2. ***Weakness*** is an inherent limitation or constraint which creates strategic disadvantages. Examples of weakness are: gaps in capabilities, financial deadlines, low morale and overdependence on a single product line.

External environment:

3. ***Opportunity*** is a favorable condition in the organization's environment which enables it to consolidate and strengthen its position. Examples of opportunity are: economic boom, favorable demographic shifts, arrival of new technologies, relaxation of regulations, favorable global influences and unfulfilled customer needs.
4. ***Threat*** is an unfavorable condition in the organization's environment which creates a risk for, or causes damage to, the organization. Examples of threat are : economic downturn, demographic shifts, new competitors, unexpected shifts in consumer tastes, demanding new regulations, unfavorable political or legislation, new technology and loss of key staff.

An understanding of the external environment, in terms of the opportunities and threats and the internal environment, in terms of the strengths and weakness, is crucial for the existence, growth and profitability of any organization. A systematic approach for understanding the environment is the SWOT analysis.

Environmental Scanning

Factors to be considered for Environmental Scanning

- Events are important and specific occurrences taking place in different environmental sectors.
- Trends are the general tendencies or the sources of action along which events take place.
- Issues are the current concerns that arise in response to events and trends.
- Expectations are the demands made by interested groups in lights of their concern for issues.

The example is the gas leakage accident that took place way back in December 1984, at the Union Carbide factory at Bhopal. The accident and the resulting disaster was an event. The trend has arisen as a result is a general tendency on the part of the regulatory authorities and organizations.

Approaches to Environmental Scanning:

1. Systematic Approach
2. Ad-hoc Approach
3. Processed-form Approach

Sources of Information for Environmental scanning

1. Documentary or secondary sources of information like different types of publications. These could be newspapers, magazines, journals books, trade and industry association newsletters, government publications, annual reports of competitor companies, commercial data bases, etc.
2. Mass media such as Radio, Television and Internet.
3. Internal sources like company files and documents, internal reports and memoranda, management information system, data bases company employees, sales staff etc.
4. External agencies like customers, marketing intermediaries, suppliers, trade associations, government agencies etc.
5. Formal studies done by employees, market research agencies consultants and educational intuitions.
6. Spying and surveillance through ex-employees of competitors, industrial espionage agencies, or by planting 'moles' in rival companies. The ethicality of these sources is doubt but nevertheless, these are used and so need a mention.

Methods and Techniques used for Environmental Scanning

Krasner outlined nine groups of techniques:

1. Single-extrapolation,
2. Variable extrapolation,

3. Theoretical limit envelopes,
4. Dynamic modes,
5. Mapping,
6. Multivariable interaction analysis ,
7. Unstructured expert opinion,
8. Structured inexpert opinion and
9. Unstructured inexpert speculation.

5.2.4 SWOT ANALYSIS

SWOT analysis was developed by the middle of the 1960s for large organisations to determine the strategic fit between an organization's internal, distinctive capabilities and external possibilities and to prioritize actions. SWOT stands for Strengths, Weaknesses, Opportunities and Threats. In the early 1950s, two Professors of Business Policy at Harvard, George Albert Smith and C. Roland Christensen, began questioning whether a firm's strategy matched its competitive environment.

In 1960, a number of large American enterprises commissioned a long range study at Stanford Research Institute to investigate why their long range planning efforts were unsuccessful. SRI's research team - Marion Dosher, Otis Benepe, Albert Humphrey, Robert Stewart and Birger Lie — interviewed 5,000 managers at 1,000 companies over nine years. They found that the difference between what an organisation planned to do and what they actually accomplished was about 35%. The problem was not the management team's quality of information, but their ability to reach a committed agreement on constructive objectives rather than settling for feeble compromises.

Part of the team's methodology to make strategic decision making more explicit was to determine what the interviewees found positive and negative about the present and the future. The team developed SWOT for this purpose. The SWOT framework was first described in detail in the late 1960's by Edmund P. Learned, C. Roland Christiansen, Kenneth Andrews, and William D. Guth in Business Policy, Text and Cases (Irwin, 1969).

Definition and Meaning of SWOT

This is the analysis and evaluation of strengths, weaknesses, opportunities and threats (SWOT). This concept of SWOT can be used to classify and explain any situation. Strengths and weaknesses fall under the internal environment of an organization and therefore can describe the internal circumstances of such an organization. On the other hand, opportunities and threats adequately express the circumstances of the external environment.

The acronym's definitions are:

1. ***Strengths***

   Those potential factors that make a firm more competitive than its direct competitors;

2. ***Weaknesses***

   Both potential limitations and defects ingrained in an organisation and/or weak factors relative to direct competitors;

3. ***Opportunities***

   Future factors that allow the organisation to improve its relative competitive position

4. ***Threats***

   Those future factors that reduce the firm's relative competitive position.

The steps in the common three phase SWOT analysis process are:

Phase 1: Detect strategic issues

1. Identify external issues relevant to the firm's strategic position in the industry and the general environment at large with the understanding that opportunities and threats are factors that management cannot directly influence.
2. Identify internal issues relevant to the firm's strategic position.
3. Analyze and rank the external issues according to probability and impact.
4. List the key strategic issue factors inside or outside the organization that significantly impact the long-term competitive position in the SWOT matrix.

Phase 2: Determine the strategy

5. Identify firm's strategic fit given its internal capabilities and external environment.
6. Formulate alternative strategies to address key issues.
7. Place the alternative strategies in one of the four quadrants in the SWOT matrix.

   Strategies that combine:

   - Internal strengths with external opportunities are the most ideal mix, but require understanding how the internal strengths can support weaknesses in other areas;
   - Internal weaknesses with opportunities must be judged on investment effectiveness to determine if the gain is worth the effort to buy or develop the internal capability,
   - Internal strengths with external threats demand knowing the worth of adapting the organisation to change the threat into opportunity;
   - Internal weaknesses with threats create an organisation's worst-case scenario. Radical changes such as divestment are required.

8. Develop additional strategies for any remaining "blind spots" in SWOT matrix.
9. Select an appropriate strategy.

Phase 3 : Implement and monitor strategy

10. Develop action plan to implement strategy;
11. Assign responsibilities and budgets;
12. Monitor progress;
13. Start review process from beginning.

SWOT analysis is often presented in matrix form although it is used to explain a complex practical reality. When the two factors internal and external become more vivid, clear strategic analysis as described by Weihrich (1982) is adopted.

Table 5.3 : SWOT Matrix Model

Internal factors	**Strengths** **Opportunities**	**Weaknesses** **Opportunities**
External factors	**Strengths** **Threats**	**Weaknesses** **Threats**

The following process can be followed to be able to fill out matrix:

1. Prepare an enterprise profile showing the kind of business, the geographic domain, the competitive situation and top management orientation.
2. Identify and evaluate the economic, social, political, demographic, products and technology, market and competitive factors.
3. Prepare a forecast; make predictions and assessment of the future.
4. Prepare a strengths and weaknesses audit in the management and organization's operations, finance, marketing and other key areas.
5. Develop alternatives.
6. Make strategic choices by considering strategic tactics and action.
7. Prepare contingency plans.

A careful observation of SWOT analysis indicates that it defines the relationship between the internal and external appraisal in strategic analysis. It concerns the identification and analysis of the environment. When SWOT analysis is properly carried out, and the basic internal strengths and weaknesses of the organization are well analyzed and identified, the organization should be able to know the appropriate strategy or strategies to adopt. Every organization should be able to apply the SWOT analysis to its competitors, suppliers, customers and even to itself. When this is done, the organization will be able to realize its own position within the industry.

Opportunities and Threats in Business Environment

The external forecast can be used to identify opportunities and threats in the business environment. These are illustrated as follows:

Opportunities

These include high growth rate in the served market, government legislation which increases the need for the organization's product, new raw material which can enhance product quality and weak competitor in a served market.

Threats

These include new technologies that obsolete the company's products, industry overcapacity which increases price competition, legislation causing major operating changes and aggressive price competition in a served market.

Strengths and Weaknesses in Business Environment

Just as in opportunities and threats, external forecast can be used to identify strengths and weaknesses in the environment. The analysis of strengths and weaknesses relative to competition require honest assessment. The task involved is analysis of position in the industry, determination of the successes factors in the industry, identification of strengths and weaknesses and assessment of competitive position. At the end of these, such questions like, where are we? where have we been? where are we going? would have been answered.

To be able to adequately identify strengths and weaknesses we need to concentrate on the past and the present. These strengths and weaknesses may include:

Strengths

These include leadership in innovative product design, exceptional employer and employee communication, understanding and relationship. They also cover highest level of automated production in the industry, highly motivated field sales force and superior product quality.

Weaknesses

The weaknesses include antiquated manufacturing and office facilities, out-of-date information systems, cash flow difficulties, limited supply of some raw materials and limited management in-departments.

A major weakness in an environment may be a very strong competitor which will obviously necessitate competitor's analysis. An analysis of key competitors will provide answers to these questions: who are they? what are their resources? who are their customers? why are they so successful?

One should know how competitors will react to our strategies. For instance, how will they react to market changes? where are they most vulnerable? where are they strongest? where is the most appropriate battleground to fight them and how?

One should also know whether the weakness arise from our product lines, selling prices or labor costs.

A company's weaknesses may also be as a result of the weaknesses in its functional areas such as marketing, engineering design and production, manufacturing, financing and human resources. Different strategies will be required for the different observed and identified weaknesses.

As part of the development of strategies and plans to enable the organization to achieve its objectives, then that organization will use a systematic/rigorous process known as corporate planning.

SWOT alongside PEST/PESTLE can be used as a basis for the analysis of business and environmental factors.

- ***Set objectives*** – defining what the organization is going to do
- ***Environmental scanning*** - Internal appraisals of the organization's SWOT, this needs to include an assessment of the present situation as well as a portfolio of products/ services and an analysis of the product/service life cycle
- ***Analysis of existing strategies***, this should determine relevance from the results of an internal/external appraisal. This may include gap analysis which will look at environmental factors
- ***Strategic Issues*** defined – key factors in the development of a corporate plan which needs to be addressed by the organization
- ***Develop new/revised strategies*** – revised analysis of strategic issues may mean the objectives need to change
- ***Establish critical success factors*** – the achievement of objectives and strategy implementation
- ***Preparation*** of operational, resource, project plans for strategy implementation
- ***Monitoring results*** – mapping against plans, taking corrective action which may mean

using SWOT to analyze the market position of a small management consultancy with specialism in HRM.

Table 5.4 : SWOT Analysis

Strengths	***Weaknesses***	***Opportunities***	***Threats***
Reputation in marketplace	Shortage of consultants at operating level rather than partner level	Well established position with a well defined market niche	Large consultancies operating at a minor level
Expertise at partner level in HRM consultancy	Unable to deal with multi-disciplinary assignments because of size or lack of ability	Identified market for consultancy in areas other than HRM	Other small consultancies looking to invade the marketplace

Steps in SWOT Analysis

A simple application of the SWOT analysis technique involves these steps:

1. Setting the objectives of the organization or its unit
2. Identifying its strengths, weaknesses, opportunities and threats
3. Asking four questions
   a. How do maximize our strengths?
   b. How do we minimize our weaknesses?

c. How do we capture the opportunities in our external environment ?

d. How do we protect ourselves from threats in our external environment?

4. Recommending strategies that will optimize the answers from the four questions

The SWOT analysis is usually done with the help of a template in the form of a four – cell matrix, each cell of the matrix representing the strengths, weaknesses, opportunities and threats. The analysis for preparing the SWOT matrix could be done by a group of managers in the work shop session. The session could use the brainstorming technique for generating ideas about the SWOT factors. A typical SWOT analysis matrix for a hypothetical organization is shown in table 5.5.

Table 5.5 : A Typical SWOT Matrix

STREANGTHS	***WEAKNESSES***
Favorable location Excellent distribution network ISO 9000 quality certification Established R & D Centre Good management reputation	Uncertain cash flow Weak management information system Absence of strong USP for major product lines Low worker commitment
OPORTUNITIES	***THREATS***
Favorable industry trends Low technology options available Possibility of niche target market Lack of sustainable financial backing	Unfavorable political environment Obstacles in licensing, new business Uncertain competitors 'intentions Availability of reliable business partners

SWOT analysis has several benefits, among the major being:

- Simple to use
- Low cost
- Flexible and can be adapted easily
- Leads to clarification of issues
- Development of goal oriented alternatives
- Useful as a starting point for strategic analysis

The following could be the pitfalls of using the SWOT analysis indiscriminately:

- Simplicity of use may turn to simplistic by trivializing the reality that may be more complex than represented in SWOT matrices.
- May result in just compiling lists rather than think about what is really important for achieving objectives.
- Usually reflects an evaluator's position and view point that can be misinterpreted to justify a previously decided course of action, rather than be used as a means to open new possibilities.

- Changes exits where strengths may be confused with opportunities or weaknesses with threats.
- May encourage organization to take a lazy course of action of looking for strengths that match opportunities rather than developing new strengths that could match the emerging opportunities.

5.2.5 STEPS IN STRATEGY FORMULATION:

Strategy Formation:

Meaning and Definition:

Strategy formulation is the process through which management develops an organisation's strategic mission, derives specific strategic objectives and chooses a strategy to implement.

Strategic formation is a combination of three main processes which are as follows:

- Performing a situation analysis, self-evaluation and competitor analysis: both internal and external; both micro-environmental and macro-environmental.
- Concurrent with this assessment, objectives are set. These objectives should be parallel to a time-line; some are in the short-term and others on the long-term. This involves crafting vision statements (long term view of a possible future), mission statements (the role that the organization gives itself in society), overall corporate objectives (both financial and strategic), strategic business unit objectives (both financial and strategic), and tactical objectives.
- These objectives should, in the light of the situation analysis, suggest a strategic plan. The plan provides the details of how to achieve these objectives.

Formulation of Strategy and Direction of Organization

Usually, organization's managers have choices about which part to take in achieving strategic objectives. As the age goes, "There are more than one way to skin a cat". So, an organization strategy represents the pattern of choices management has made among the alternative means. A strategy is just the trajectory or the highest path towards the target objective. It is made up of the entrepreneurial competitive and functional area approaches that the management intends to employ in positioning the enterprise and in managing its overall portfolio of activities. Since each organization is unique, strategy formulation is custom-tailored by management to suit or fit all the relevant internal and external circumstances that surround the organization. Also, because the organization's circumstances change, its strategy also changes and is always evolving as the managers either fine-tune or overhaul the ways they try to achieve strategic objectives.

Corporate-Level Strategy

This is senior management's game plan for directing and running the organization as a whole. It cuts across all of the organization's activities such as different businesses, divisions, product line and technologies. The corporate level strategy formulation should involve three tasks, which are:

a. Development of plan for managing the scope and the mix of the organization's various activities in order to achieve or improve corporate performance.

b. Provision of co-ordination among different businesses in the portfolio.

c. Establishment of investment priorities and allocation of corporate resources across the company's different activities.

The portfolio management actions of corporate officers in entering a new or existing business and in pursuing some opportunities more boldly than others are strategically important because they determine the organization's business position.

The strategy to be formulated at this level may be a combination of offensive moves to pursue selected opportunities and build new or stronger business positions, and defensive moves to protect existing positions against emerging threats.

Co-ordination of strategic plans across business units is equally an important task for corporate managers. This is because it is through the co-ordination of the interrelated activities of the corporation's different business units that a corporate-level competitive advantage can be created.

Controlling the level of the pattern of corporate resource allocation is of no less importance. It is very crucial because the number of "worthy projects" and "can't miss opportunities" put forward for funding may entail a lot of capital requirements even beyond the corporate resources. The allocation of the resources must therefore, be genuinely done.

Line of Business Strategy Formulation

This is the managerial action plan for directing and running a particular business unit. The strategy at this level deals explicitly with

a. How the enterprise intends to compete in that specific business.

b. Developing responses to changing industry and competitive conditions.

c. Controlling the pattern of resources allocation within the business unit.

The internal key to good business strategy concerns the development and use of a strategy-supportive distinctive competence. This means the skill or activity that a firm does especially well in comparison to the rival firm. Formulation and selection of a business strategy that is closely matched to the firm's skills resource base is very essential.

For a single business enterprise, corporate strategy and business strategy become one and the same except when the single business is contemplating on diversification.

Functional Area Support Strategy

These are strategic formulation for managing the principal subordinate activities within a business. This should be for each part of the business, production, marketing, finance, research and development and human resources. This task is delegated by the business level manger to the functional area heads. The functional heads then formulate strategies to achieve their set objectives.

Operational–Level Strategy

The operating-level strategies are formulated to enable the departmental and supervisory-level managers carry out fine details of functional area support strategies.

Levels of Strategy Formulation

This is another important aspect of strategic management. This aspect brings into play the critical issue of how the targeted results are to be accomplished. The objectives of the organization are the "ends" while the strategy is the "means" of achieving them. Strategy formulation is a difficult task. It entails taking into account all the relevant aspects of the organization's internal and external situation and coming up with a detailed action plan for achieving the targeted short-run and long-run results consistent with the organization's objectives. Strategy is regarded as a blueprint of all the important entrepreneurial, competitive and functional area actions that are to be taken in pursuing organizational objectives and positioning the organization for sustainable success. Consequently, in formulating strategy, there are issues that must be addressed which include the following:

How to Respond to Changing Strategy Conditions

These conditions include shifts in customer needs, emerging industry trends, how to defend against competitors and other externally imposed threats, etc.

Resources Allocation

In formulating strategy, resources allocation over the organization's various business units, divisions, and functional departments are important. Making decisions that will provoke investment and human resources in the chosen strategic plan are very crucial. To achieve success, a kind of strategy-supportive guidelines for resources allocation must be in place.

Competition within the Industry

This has to do with the decisions on how to develop customer appeal, position the firm against rivals, emphasizes some products and de-emphasizes others to meet some specific competitive threats, which are important for survival and the achievement of a definable competitive advantage.

The actions and approaches to be taken in each of the functional areas of an Operational Department

The different functional and operating level strategies ought to be coordinated rather than be allowed to go off on independent courses. They need to support the creation of a sustainable competitive position and advantage. Strategy formulation should cover the different levels of the organization. There should be strategy for the organization as a whole (which is top management responsibility). There should be strategies for each line of business that the organization is operating and also at functional area level such as manufacturing, marketing, finance and human resources, within each business. There should also be strategy formulation at the operating levels, e.g. for each functional department and unit in order to be able to carry out the details of functional area strategy.

Strategy formulation is mainly an exercise carried out by entrepreneurship. Its contents reflect the entrepreneurial judgments about the long-term direction of the organization: any need for major new initiatives such as increased competitive aggressiveness, diversification moves and divestiture of unattractive activities.

The specific involvement of entrepreneurial aspects of strategy formulation is to:

i. Search actively for innovative ways the organization can improve on what it is already doing

ii. Find out new opportunities for the organization

iii. Develop ways to increase the firm's competitive strength and put it in a stronger position to cope with competitive forces

iv. Devise ways by which to build and maintain a competitive advantage

v. Decide on how to meet threatening external developments

vi. Encourage individuals throughout the organization to put forth innovative proposals and champions those that have promise

vii. Direct resources away from areas of low or diminishing results towards areas of high or increasing results

viii. Decide when and how to diversify

ix. Choose which business or product to abandon, the ones to continue to emphasize and the new ones to add.

So, the entrepreneur needs a critical skill to be able to make strategic choices that will keep the organization in a position of sustainable success.

Other crucial factors in strategy formulation are analysis and judgment. The right strategy formulated and chosen for one organization may not be the right one for another organization, even when they are in the same business and the same environment. This is because situations differ from one organization to another and from time to time. Also, strongly positioned firms can do things which the weak ones dare not do, and weak firms can do things which the strong firms cannot do. A good strategy is one that is right for the organization, considering all the relevant specifics of its situation.

Therefore, in formulating strategies, the entrepreneurial task involves and requires heavy doses of situational analysis and judgment with the aim of achieving "goodness of fit" between the formulated strategy and all the relevant aspects of the organization's internal situation and external environment. In fact, the value of any manager is in his ability to develop customized solutions that fit the unique features of an organization's situation.

In the main, the real purpose, and value, of strategy formulation is to come up with an action plan that will successfully attract buyers, produce a sustainable competitive advantage, boost the firm's market structure, put added competitive pressures on rivals, shape the nature of the competitive battle, influence the direction of industry, change in their favor, and push performance to superior levels. The ideal result and outcome is the one where the firm's formulation strategy propels it to a leadership position above and apart from the rival firms in the industry in a way that earnings prosper and multiply; and its products (services) become the standard or the yardstick for the industry comparison.

Table 5.6 : The Strategy Making Hierarchy of Thompson & Strickland

Strategy Level	Primary Strategy Development Responsibility	Strategy Making Functions and Areas of Focus
Corporate Strategy	CEO, other key Executives (Decisions are typically reviewed and approved by board of directors)	Structuring and managing the portfolio of business units. (Making acquisition, divestitures, strengthening the existing position).
Line-of–Business Strategy	General Manager/head of Business Unit (Decisions are typically Reviewed and approved by senior corporate executives)	Co-ordinating business level strategies. Building business level competitive advantage. Controlling the pattern of resources allocation. Choosing how to compete and what type of competitive advantage to build.
Functional area support strategy	Functional area heads (Decisions are typically reviewed/approved by business units/heads)	Developing response to changing industry and competitive conditions. Co-ordinating the role/thrust of functional area strategies
Operational-level Strategy	Departmental heads/ field unit heads lower level managers within functional areas (decisions are often made after consultation with lateral pears in closely related areas and are reviewed and approved by functional area heads	Controlling the pattern of resource allocation within the business unit. Fleshing out the business strategy as applied to specific functional areas and developing specific functional area action plans to support successful execution of the strategy. Developing action plans to carry out the day-today requirements of functional area support strategies.

Requirements for Developing Effective Strategies:

Alternative strategies are derived from the firm's mission, objectives, external and internal audits. They are consistent with or built upon, past strategies that have worked well. There are many methods of developing effective strategies. The requirements may involve:

1. A Routine Method

This involves looking at what the company has been doing in the past. Caution must however be exercised in adopting this technique since the new challenge or problem may be a break away from the past.

2. Creativity

As a strategist, you may attempt to conceptualize a scenario of the organization and try to develop effective strategy.

3. Brainstorming

Developing effective strategies may also require putting together many experts for a number of days for brainstorming.

4. Consultant Services

Many managers now employ the services of consultants for developing effective company strategies.

5. Holistic Approach

Strategic planning should be initiated by a company's top management because of the broad perspective of these executives. The strategic process works from general to specific. This is called holistic approach to strategic planning.

6. Tactical Approach

Some researchers believe that the holistic approach is inferior to a tactical approach in certain circumstances. With the tactical approach, strategic managers work up through the firm in their study of its potential. Strategic management process must be a people process for it to be successful. Through the involvement in the process, the managers and employees become committed to supporting the organization.

7. Dialogue

Dialogue and participation are also essential ingredients.

8. Informed Employees

Fundamental to effective strategy development are fully informed employees at all levels in the organisation. Every employee must be informed of business objectives, the process of achieving the objectives, customers, competitors and product plans.

9. Global Factors

Global factors must be considered in developing effective strategy. The boundaries of countries can no longer define the limits of people's imaginations. To see the world from the perspective of others has become a matter of survival for business. The price and quality of a firm's product must be competitive on a worldwide basis not just on a local basis.

Based on past experience, judgment and feelings, intuition is essential to making good strategic decisions. Intuition must be integrated with analysis in decision making. This is because analytical thinking and intuitive thinking complement each other. Operating from the "I have already made up my mind, don't bother me with the facts made", is not management by intuition; it is management by ignorance.

Strategy formulation is a process that clearly spells out the organization's mission and defines what the organization actually stands for. It designs specific objectives for the company and states in clear workable terms the strategy to implement in order to achieve the objectives.

5.2.6 STRATEGY IMPLEMENTATION

Introduction

Strategy implementation and execution means that translating a decision into action is essentially an administrative task. It deals with matching organization's strategy implementation with the structure to be able to achieve organization's objectives.

Strategy Implementation

Strategy implementation is concerned with translating a decision into action. This presupposes that the strategic choice which ultimately leads to a decision is made with an inbuilt feasibility and acceptability. The allocation of resources to new course of action is needed to be undertaken and there may be a need for adopting the organization's structure to handle new activities as well as training personnel and devising appropriate systems. Strategic implementation is often called the action stage of strategic management.

Strategy implementation and execution is essentially an administrative task. This is equally true of putting the strategy in place and getting individuals or the whole of the managerial challenge to "make it happen". It involves the following:

a. Building an organization capable of carrying out the strategic plan.

b. Developing strategy–supportive budget and programmes

c. Instilling a strong organization-wide commitment to organizational objectives and the chosen strategy.

d. Linking the motivation and reward structure directly to achieving the targeted results.

e. Installing policies and procedures that facilitate strategy implementation.

f. Developing information and reporting system to track and control the progress of strategy implementation.

g. Exerting the internal leadership needed to drive implementation forward and to keep improving the strategy being executed.

Managers at all levels in the organization are involved in the development of an action agenda for implementation and execution. Each manager starting from the headquarters of the organization down to each operating department is involved in providing answers to such questions as "what is required for us to implement part of our overall strategic plan and how can we best get it done?"

When this is properly done, the tasks will involve scrutinizing every operating activity to see what action can be taken in order to improve strategy practices and behaviors in the organization members.

The task of implementing and executing a strategy is a process of moving deliberately to create a variety of "fits" that provides the organization with strategy. The task of consciously fitting the "way we see things around here" to the requirements of first-rate strategy execution. According to Thompson Strickland, a strategy supports organizational culture and work climate.

In view of the importance of proper implementation and execution of strategy to an organization's success, Thompson and Strickland suggest that a number of fits are required and they include:

1) Strategy and the internal organisational structure
2) Strategy and organisational skills/technical knowhow/ operational capabilities
3) Strategy and the allocation of budgets and staff size
4) Strategy and the organisation's system of reward and incentives
5) Strategy and internal policies, practices and procedures.
6) Strategy and the internal organisation's atmosphere, which are determined by the values and beliefs shared by managers and employees, the philosophies and decision making styles of senior managers, and other factors that make up the organisation's personality and culture.

Broadly speaking, the management task of strategy implementation is done by scrutinizing the whole internal organisation to diagnosis what strategy-supportive approaches would be needed and the actions to take to accomplish such strategies. In this task, the different pieces of the implementation plan need to be arranged into a pattern of action that will produce an orderly change from the old strategy to the new strategy. The management will need to ensure that the necessary changes embarked upon will not create disruption and disaster.

In this regard, both the sequence of actions and the speed of implementation are important aspects of uniting the entire organisation behind strategy accomplishment. The challenge to the leadership of the organisation is how to stimulate the enthusiasm, pride, commitment and dedication of managers and employees such that an organization-wide crusade emerges to carry out the chosen strategy and to achieve the targeted results.

Strategy Implementation and Organizational Structure

The job of a strategy manager is complicated when it comes to implementation due to the number of tasks to be performed and the variety of ways in which each of them can be approached.

For successful implementation of a strategy, it has to be along the organisation's overall condition and setting, the nature of the strategy and the amount of strategy change envisaged. That is to say, shifting to a bold new strategy poses different implementation problems than fine-tuning the strategy already in place. Strategy implementation will also have to be guided along the manager's own skills, style and methods.

Strategy implementation includes developing an affective organisational structure, redirecting marketing efforts, preparing budgets, developing and utilizing information systems and motivating individuals to act. Implementing entails mobilising the employees and managers to put formulated strategies into action. Strategic implementation is the most difficult stage in strategic management. It requires personal and personnel discipline, commitment and sacrifice.

Successful strategy implementation hinges upon the manager's ability to motivate employees, which is more of an art than a science. Strategies formulated but not implemented serves no useful purposes. Strategy implementation activities affect both employees and managers in the organisation. Every department, division or unit must be involved. The challenge of implementation is to stimulate managers and employees throughout an organisation to work with pride towards achieving stated objectives.

For effective and adequate Strategic implementation, some organizations develop corporate culture and whatever strategy is to be implemented must follow that culture. But this may create a problem when the strategist has to make a decision on how to turn around the fortunes of an ailing organization. There must be the right leadership to implement the necessary strategy in order to achieve the corporate objectives. Usually, an organisation's culture is one of the major barriers of strategy as implementation becomes very difficult.

Matching Organisation's Structure with Strategy

A few hard and fast rules must be considered for a strategic implementation to be successful. This is because every strategy is grounded in its own set of key success factors and certain critical tasks. Also, every firm has some historical backgrounds based on the previous organisation's decisions. The easy way out is to design the internal organisational structure around key success factors and critical tasks inherent in the firm's strategy. This implies that the organisation structure must be matched with the formulated strategies for success. To be able to achieve this, Thompson and Strickland highlights five sequence procedures as a useful guide for fitting structure to strategy.

They are:

(i) Pinpoint the key functions and task requirements for successful strategy execution.

(ii) Reflect on how the strategy's critical functions and organizational units relate to those that are routine and to those that provide staff support.

(iii) Make strategic critical business units and functions the main organizational building blocks.

(iv) Determine the degree of authority needed to manage each organizational unit, bearing in mind both benefits and cost of decentralized decision making.

(v) Provide for co-ordination among the various organizations' units. The organizational structure must fit the size of the organization, the strategy, complexity of the environment and personnel characteristics.

Quite often changes in strategy require changes in the way an organization is structured for two major reasons:

i) Structure largely dictates how objectives and policies will be established. Objectives and policies are stated largely in terms of products in an organization.

ii) Structure dictates how resources would be allocated. If an organization's structure is based on customer groups, then resources would be allocated in that manner. A restructuring gives all top managers added responsibilities and encourage the introduction of new products. However, the structure that is good for one organization may not be good for another.

Note that all successful firms in a given industry do not end to organize themselves in a similar way. For example, Small firms tend to be functionally structured i. e., centralized, medium-sized firms tend to be divisionally structured i.e., decentralized and large firms tend to use a matrix structure. As organizations grow, their structure generally change from simple to complex as a result of linking together of several basic strategies.

The transition from strategy formulation to strategy implementation requires a shift in responsibilities from strategist to divisional and functional manager. This shift may create implementation problems in responsibilities especially if strategy formulation decision comes as a surprise to middle and lower level managers.

Managers and employees are motivated more by perceived self interests than by the organization's interests unless the two coincide. So, it is important that divisional and functional managers be involved as much as possible in strategy formulation and implementation. Managers and other employees throughout an organization should participate early and directly in strategy implementation decisions. Top-down flow of communication is essential for developing bottom-up support.

Marketing

In addition to organizing culture and structure, marketing is another crucial matter in strategy implementation. No matter the quality and the price of the organisation's products if there is no adequate market, the company will fail. Marketing must be given serious consideration in strategy implementation.

Personnel

Equally crucial to strategy implementation is the personnel factor. This may require training of staff to get the desired change through their newly acquired skills and knowledge. No matter how good a strategy may be, if there is no right personnel in the leadership position to implement, the strategy will fail.

Symptoms of an ineffective organizational structure include too many levels of management, too many meetings attended by too many people, too much attention directed towards unachieved objectives.

Strategy implementation is seen as translating the decisions made into action. However, for strategy implementation to be successful, it has to be matched with the organization's structure.

Strategy implementation embraces the full range of managerial activities associated with putting the strategy into place, supervising its pursuit and achieving the targeted result. Successful strategy implementation depends on the skills of working through others, organizing, motivating, culture building and creating stronger fits between strategy and how the organization operates.

Strategy Implementation:

Strategy implementation consists of four steps namely

1. Designing appropriate organization structure
2. Designing control systems
3. Matching strategy, structure and controls and
4. Managing conflicts, politics and change

Structure:

Structure involves allocation of duties, responsibilities and decision- making authority and integration among the ranks and files of organization. It is widely believed that structure follows strategy. Some of the options available in this regard are tall structure, flat structure, centralized decision making authority, decentralized decision making authority, autonomous unit and semi autonomous units and different mechanisms for integration of subunits.

Control:

The purpose of strategy control is to determine whether the given strategy is effective in achieving organizational objectives and moving on the right track. The organizational control may be classified as market control, output control, and bureaucratic control. Control system requires the development of perceptible organizational culture .Besides, the type of reward and incentive system also needs to be decided and established towards this end .

Matching Strategy, Structure and Control:

In successful organization a fit among strategy, structure and controls is observed, Different strategies and environment call for different structures and control systems. Cost leadership strategy warrants a simple organization, which lays emphasis on efficiency whereas differentiation strategy revolves around R&D and technical creativity. A fit among strategy, structure and control is essential to ensure success of organizations.

Matching Conflicts, Politics and change:

Conflict is common in organization. The reason for conflicts are resource sharing and different agendas of different subgroups within organizations. Power struggles and coalition building are consequences of such conflicts. The organizational politics plays a key role in strategy implementation. The power and conflict, and inertia should be analyzed and managed effectively so that mission could be fulfilled and change could be introduced smoothly.

Feed back:

Strategic management is an ongoing process. Periodic feedback reveals whether objectives are attainable or implementation is poor or not. The feedback is fed into next round of strategic formulation and implementation. It may reaffirm objectives or suggest changes in goals and objectives.

5.2.7 GENERIC STRATEGY ALTERNATIVES

It is one of the important stages in strategy formulation. In this stage alternatives in broader terms should be developed. The first step is defining the nature of business and developing the generic alternatives is the second step. Here the strategist should address two contradicting issues simultaneously- "should we contract totally or expand the business activity".

There are four types of generic strategy alternatives. They are :

1. Expansion strategy
2. Stability strategy
3. Reduction strategy and
4. A combination of all or some of these strategies.

1. *Expansion strategy :*

Firstly, this may take the shape of expansion of product line, or enhancing the utility of the existing products.

Secondly, searching new territories or markets or adventurously penetrating into the market to grab more share in the market.

Thirdly, by forward and vertical integration of functions to gear-up momentum in the overall functioning or increasing capacities of both men and machine by adding them for increasing the installed capacity.

2. *Stability strategy:*

Re-organize production and marketing processes to enhance the efficiencies, improving total quality management to increase the market value of the share and brand value.

3. *Reduction strategy:*

During recession conditions, reduction strategy may be useful. Instead of high spending cutting down the costs by reducing operations may be the best policy. Withdrawing from uneconomical markets, stopping recruitment and downsizing the HR for rightsizing purpose etc., are some of the important strategies.

4. *Combination of above strategies:*

By sub-contracting or out-sourcing or by entering into joint-ventures organizations can reduce risks.

SHORT QUESTIONS

1. Write short note on 'mission' statement.
2. What do you mean by 'goals'?
3. What do you mean by 'objectives'?
4. Write short note on 'policy'.

5. Explain strategy in detail.
6. Explain procedure in detail.
7. What is meant by 'purpose'?
8. What is meant by 'programme'?
9. Differentiate 'policy' and 'rule'.
10. Explain briefly 'corporate planning'.
11. Define corporate planning?
12. State what are the constituents planning?
13. What is operational planning?
14. What is strategic planning?
15. Explain briefly internal environment.
16. Explain briefly external environment.
17. Environmental scanning is a part of a corporate planning. Explain.
18. What is SWOT analysis?
19. What is the importance of SWOT analysis?
20. Explain briefly strategic formulation.
21. Explain briefly strategic implementation.
22. Explain briefly the process of formulating the strategy.
23. Write short note on evolution of strategy.
24. Write short note on control of strategy.
25. Explain stages in strategic formulation.
26. Explain the implementation process.
27. How strategic formulation used by the corporate in their day-to-day life?

ESSAY QUESTIONS

1. What are the characteristics of mission statement?
2. Explain briefly relationship between mission, goal, objective, strategy and programmes in an industrial environment.
3. Explain the concept of corporate planning. Discuss its importance in industrial environment.
4. Explain the elements of corporate planning process in the industrial environment.
5. How corporate planning is useful in business organizations?
6. 'Policy is a broad guideline set by the top management'. Explain briefly.

7. What are the advantages of strategic management?
8. What do you understand by strategic business unit? Discuss its role and importance in corporate planning?
9. Explain the strategies to improve the sales performance of strategic business unit in pharmaceutical company.
10. What do you understand by SWOT analysis? Discuss how it can be carried for Industrial Business Concerns?
11. Explain briefly environmental scanning. What are its advantages and disadvantages?
12. What are the internal factors that need to be examined for the firm to assess its strength and weaknesses?
13. What are the external factors that need to be examined for the firm to assess its opportunities and threats?
14. Explain types of threats for a PC hardware company vis-a-vis a software company.
15. Explain merits and demerits of organizational capability profile for a business concern.
16. What is the purpose of environmental scanning evaluation? How it is useful to construction industries.
17. Explain advantages and disadvantages of industrial and international environment.
18. Explain briefly SWOT analysis about software industry in India.
19. Define corporate planning give brief idea about corporate planning.
20. State advantages and limitations of corporate planning.
21. Distinguish between strategic planning and operational planning.
22. Distinguish between strategic planning and tactical planning.

FILL IN THE BLANKS

1. The basic reason for the existence of an organization is defined involve it's .... (Mission)
2. Mission statements are communicated down to the lowest level involve the organization to.......... (Develop awareness about vision of the company)
3. What an organization wants to achieve during a given period with a given set of resources called .... (Goal)
4. A unified, comprehensive and integral plan desired to achieve the basic objectives of an enterprise called.......................... (Strategy)
5. ....is an operational tool to achieve the goals set through mission. (Strategy)
6. The logical sequence of the operations it be performance is called .... (Procedure)
7. A single business planned separately from reset of the company is called .... (Strategic business unit)

8. The techniques of reducing the operations if the unprofitable business is called .... (Down sizing)
9. Gaining more market share with current products involve the current market is called......... (Market penetration)
10. The process is identifying technological, socio-economic conditions and others to determine whether they present a threat for the existing strategy or an opportunity for a new strategy is called .... (Environmental scanning)
11. The fluctuating currency exchange rate is an example for.........risk (Financial)
12. The growing income inequalities are an example for.......... risk (Social)
13. The process of examining the firm's internal factors to determine where the firm has significant strength and weakness is called .... (Internal analysis)
14. When there are strengths opportunities the strategy to be followed is.............(Aggressive)
15. When there are strength threats the strategy to be followed is .... (Diversification)
16. When there are strengths weakness-opportunities the strategy to be followed is .... (Turn around)
17. When there are strengths weakness-threats the strategy to be followed............... (winding up or mergers)
18. Involve highly competitive industries particularly the early stage of product life cycle.........strategy followed (Expansion)
19. Strategic management process starts with .... (Mission)
20. Plant location is a ....decision (Strategic)
21. The economies available to all the firms in an industries belt or area are called......economies (External)
22. .... is the determination of basic long term goals objectives (Strategy)
23. .... is continuous (Strategy)
24. SWOT............ (Strength, weakness, opportunity & threat)
25. The final step of strategic management process is .... (Evaluation & control)
26. ....is a line management function (Decision making)
27. The process of identifying the overall purpose for the organization is called................ (Corporate planning)
28. The technique of reducing the operations of the unprofitable business is called............. (Down sizing)
29. A single business planned separately from rest of the company is called............. (Strategic business units)
30. External environment analysis is also called .... Analysis. (Opportunities and threats)

❖ ❖ ❖

UNIT - VI
MANAGEMENT ETHICS

6.1 INTRODUCTION

Managers and executives make number of decisions in an organization everyday in their business dealings and these decisions may be sometimes unethical or illegal. Social thinkers, ethicists and academicians wish the businessman to improve their ethical standards, notwithstanding the pressures and compulsions of competitors.

Definitions:

The word 'Ethics' is derived from the Greek word 'Ethikos' meaning custom or character.

Ethics is defined as the treating of moral questions. **– *Concise Oxford Dictionary***

Ethics is a code of behavior considered correct. **– *Chambers Dictionary***

Ethics is concerned with set of moral principles **– *Oxford Thesaurus Dictionary***

6.2 NATURE OF ETHICS

1. The concept of ethics deals with human beings only. As they only have the freedom of choice.
2. Study of ethics has a set of systematic knowledge about moral behavior and conduct.
3. Science of ethics is a normative science. The value of facts in terms of an idea with judgments of 'what ought to be'.
4. Business is nothing, but the application of ethics in business.
5. Business can be ethical and can still make profits.
6. Now more interest is shown today in the application of ethical practices in business dealings and their implications.
7. Profit maximization and discharging of social responsibilities cannot be done simultaneously as they are at opposite ends.

Goal of Ethics:

The goal of ethics is to determine what is good for individual and for society. Defining what is good, and how to deal with conflicting priorities depends upon the circumstances rather than on some general law.

6.3 OBJECTIVES OF ETHICS

- To study human behavior to make evaluative assessment about what is moral or immoral.
- To establish moral standards and norms of behavior.
- To make judgment upon human behavior based on standards and norms.
- To prescribe moral behavior about how to or how not to behave.
- To express an opinion or attitude about human conduct in general.

Religious Morality:

For the Christian, the ethical rule book is the Bible and for the Muslim it is the Quran, for the Jew it is the Torah and for the Hindu it is the Bhagavadh Gita. God will reward the righteous with the joys of heaven and push the wicked to the torments of hell. Buddhists and Jains have very clearly defined codes of ethics. The purpose of religion is to bind people together.

Indian Ethical Traditions:

India has rich cultural and ethical traditions which were in the scriptures like the Upanishads, Bhagavad-Gita etc. Hindu scriptures speak of the performance of the right duty, at the right time in the right manner. Indian traditions are copied and followed by western countries in their social welfare and organizational conduct.

Gandhian Principles:

The Gandhian principle of trusteeship implies that an industrialist or businessman should consider himself to be a trustee of the wealth he possesses. The trusteeship concept should also be extended to the labor in industry. It does not recognize capital and assets as individual property. This was basically to reduce the conflict between 'have' and 'have not'. The origin of trusteeship can be traced to the concept of non-possession detailed in Bhagawad Gita. Gandhi advocated sarvodaya which means welfare for all. There should be a family atmosphere and harmony in workplace.

Righteousness as the Way in Gita:

The Bhagavad-Gita cites numerous instances of how moral values and ethics can be incorporated in one's work life. The important message of Lord Krishna in Gita is that one has to perform the duty (karma) without expecting any self advantage or immediate result.

In the organizational context too when one is only worried of the result, he or she is likely to fall into improper activities. On the other hand, if one is ready to do the duty to one's ability and is able to set aside the result, he or she will be an ethical person in the organization.

Business and Islam:

All principles covering business are drawn from the Holy Quran. Mohammed, the last prophet and messenger was very much involved in business before he was chosen by God.

Business ethics in Islam focus the following principles :

1. No cheating and fraud
2. No false promises in a sale or sales promotion
3. Need for mutual consent in business agreements
4. Correct weights and measures
5. Very much against monopoly
6. Free enterprise is wished
7. Hoarding is forbidden

8. Against taking interest on capital
9. Muslim investors should invest in clean stocks
10. Should not invest in business dealing with money lending, tobacco, alcohol, pork, etc.,

6.4 BUSINESS ETHICS

Business Ethics is the art and discipline of applying ethical principles to examine and solve complex moral dilemmas.

Ethical solutions to business problems may have more than one right answer. Logical and ethical reasoning is tested in a particular business situation. A company is considered to be ethical only if it tries to reach a balance between its economic objectives and its social obligations. That is obligations to all its stakeholders - the shareholders, employees, customers, government and the environment, where it exists, takes the resources and operates for profit. Business ethics are based on the principles of integrity and fairness.

There is a growing realization that ethics is important for any business and to achieve the progress of any society. It is not the government or law which will protect the society. But ethics alone can protect it. An ethically responsible company is one which has developed a culture of caring for people and environment, a culture which flows downwards from the top managers and leaders. Ethics are the methodical and systematic elaboration of the norms and values we appeal to in our daily activities.

Ethical rules are guides to moral behavior. For example: all societies have ethical rules like forbidding lying, stealing, deceiving and harming others. Ethical code of conduct approves honesty, keeping promises, helping others and respecting the rights of others. These are the basic rules of behavior which are of much use for the preservation and continuation of organized life.

Most of the people find major source of ethical guidance and moral meaning in religious beliefs and organizations. The family institution is equally important as it imparts a sense of right and wrong in children when they grow up in schools and other institutions. Society, culture, traditions, and media (print & electronic) will have lot of influence on the ethical behavior of people.

Ethics is a universal human trait. All the people and the organizations floated by them need rules to govern them on moral and ethical lines.

6.4.1 CHARACTERISTICS OF BUSINESS ETHICS

1. ***Ethics and religion are not one and the same:***

   All religions preach high ethical and moral standards but they do not address all the types of problems people face today.

2. ***Ethics is not exactly equal to law:***

   A good legal system incorporates many moral and ethical standards. However, there are several instances where law deviates from what is ethical. Legal system may vary from society to society depending upon its social, religious and cultural beliefs.

3. ***Ethical standards are different from cultural practices:***

   Ethical standards vary from one culture to the other.

4. ***Ethics is different from feelings:***

   Our ethical choices are based on our feelings. Most people when they do something wrong for the first time, may feel bad. But if they find it to be beneficial or if it brings them pleasure, they make it a habit without feeling bad.

5. ***Ethics is not just a collection of values:***

   Values tend to be under defined and subject to flaw as per human reasoning. Hence, they cannot assure true ethical conduct.

6. ***Ethical issues commonly occur in management:***

   It goes beyond the commonly discussed problems of bribery, collusion and theft, reaching into areas of corporate acquisitions. Ethics want a manager to be honest within one's self and also in the society. The manager has to perform his job well within the frame of professional ethics for the success of a business.

6.4.2 VALUES AND ETHICS IN BUSINESS

Business ethics are related to issues of 'what is right' and 'what is wrong' while doing business. Personal values refer to a conception of what an individual or group regards as desirable. A value is a view of life and judgment of what is desirable that is very much part of a person's personality and a group's morale.

Morality:

Morality is the standard that an individual or group has about what is right and wrong or good and bad. For example, "honesty is the best policy", "Practice non violence and always speak truth".

6.4.3 NEED OF BUSINESS ETHICS

Business operates within the society. It is a part of subsystem of the society. Business's functioning must contribute to the welfare of the society. In order to survive, develop and excel, business must earn social sanction of the society where it exits and functions. Running a business ethically is good for sustaining business. Applying ethics in business also makes good sense. The need of business ethics can be explained with the help of following points

1. ***To bring socialism in business:***

   This means the gains of business must be shared by all concerned and not just by owner of business. Profit is the result of group efforts and hence all concerned must share the same.

2. ***To protect the small firms:***

   Big firms normally try to dominate and eradicate small firms. Business ethics for big firms are required to protect the interest of small business firms.

3. *To catch up with the changes in business market:*

In recent times, structural changes have taken place in the concept of business. In case of many products, sellers market has been converted into buyers market. Under such changed business conditions business ethics is needed to stress the importance of consumer satisfaction and service orientation in place of profit orientation.

4. *To maintain better relations with society:*

Ethics brings to the notice of the business, communicating the importance of honesty, sincerity, fairness which makes them alert and socially conscious.

5. *Necessary to gain trust:*

Ethical behavior is a necessity to gain trust. Lack of ethics would lead to unethical practices in organization as well as in personal life. Ethics is all about developing trust and maintaining it for the health of the organization.

Importance of Business Ethics:

If a society's ethical rule says that dishonesty is unethical and immoral then anyone in business, who is dishonest with employees, customers, creditors, stockholders is acting unethically. Similarly, if protecting people from harm is considered ethical, then business firm that recall a defective and dangerous product is acting in an ethical way.

In most cases, the general public expects business to exhibit high levels of ethical performance and social responsibility. Business that treats their employees with dignity and integrity reap many rewards in the form of high morale and improved productivity.

In spite of the positive benefits of good ethical practices, ethical problems occur for the following reasons:

- Personal gain
- Individual values widely differ with organizational goals
- Managers values and attitudes
- Competitive pressures
- Cross-cultural contradictions

Management of Business Ethics:

Management of any business involves hundreds of decisions. Ethical issues occur in all decision making processes. Conflicts and ethical dilemmas are part and parcel of such processes. The success of any organization depends on revenues, profits, cost-cutting, quality, quantity, efficiency and so on. These objectives of the organization may run concurrently with its social commitment, which is measured in terms of obligations to stake holders, both within and outside the organization. For its survival, it is necessary that the organization should maintain its competitive edge in the market. It should produce useful, safe and quality products and services at affordable prices. While doing so, the organization should ensure that the interests of the stakeholders are not adversely impacted. This requires a fine balancing act on the part of the organization.

Ethical Activities:

Companies are investing millions of dollars on ethics and corporate governance. Fortunes latest survey on various firms regarding ethical activities reveal the following facts:

- Out of 1000 firms surveyed, 78 per cent have a separate code of ethics which is communicated throughout the organization.
- Maximum number of employees received training in ethics and has access to a telephone line for operating problems.
- Value based cultural approach to ethics management works best. This approach requires the sincere commitment of leadership at all levels.
- Reward pro-ethical conduct.
- Penalize the persons and organizations who violate the ethics.

6.4.4 CODES OF CONDUCT

- Company codes
- Company operating policies
- Code of ethics.

Company Codes:

A code of practice may be styled as a code of professional responsibility, which will discuss difficult issues, difficult decisions that will often need to be made, and provide a clear account of what behavior is considered "ethical" or "correct" or "right" in the circumstances. In a membership context, failure to comply with a code of practice can result in expulsion from the professional organization. In 2007 the International Federation of Accountants provided the following working definition: "Principles, values, standards, or rules of behavior that guide the decisions, procedures and systems of an organization in a way that (a) contributes to the welfare of its key stakeholders, and (b) respects the rights of all constituents affected by its operations."

Code of Ethics:

Code of ethics is a statement of values and principles which define the purpose of the company. The first step in designing an ethics program is developing code of ethics. A code of ethics contains norms to be followed. The code and the guidelines are intended to serve as a basis for ethical decision making in the conduct of professional work. Secondly, they may serve as a basis for judging the merit of a formal complaint pertaining to violation of professional ethical standards. Questions related to ethical conflicts can best be answered by thoughtful consideration of fundamental principles, rather than reliance on detailed regulations.

Ethics in Work Place:

An organization has to be ethical in its behavior because it has to exist in the competitive world. There are number of reasons why business should act ethically.

- ➢ To protect its own interest
- ➢ To protect the interests of business community as a whole

- To keep commitment to society to act ethically
- To meet stakeholders expectations
- To prevent harm to general public
- To build trust with key stakeholders groups etc
- To protect themselves from abuse of unethical employees and competitors

Benefits of Ethics in Work Place

Several benefits accrue to an enterprise if it is managed ethically. They are given below:

1. Focus on business ethics has improved our society, social and business organizations.
2. Ethical practice has contributed towards high productivity and strong team work.
3. Ethical training enabled managers to maintain corporations to the changing needs and situations.
4. Ethical practices of organizations created good public image and brand loyalty among employees, consumers and general public.
5. Strong ethical practices act as security for the future function of the business.

6.4.5 ETHICAL MODELS GUIDING DECISION MAKING

Right Theories:

Immanuel Kant underlined the importance of property rights and opined that ethical decisions should protect the legal and moral rights of an individual. An individual is entitled to:

- Free consent
- Freedom of conscience
- Privacy
- Free speech
- Due process

Justice Theories:

It was developed by Greek Philosophers, Plato and Aristotle in the 5th century B.C. These theories advocate that all persons should be guided by fairness, justice, equity and by a sense of impartiality. So people should be treated equitably that is equality based on justice.

Utilitarianism:

This theory holds the view that an action or decision is right if it maximizes utility or produces the greatest good for the largest number of people.

Virtue Approach:

This theory believes that morality in a given context is not only what is normally accepted as moral but also what is acceptable to a mature person endowed with a good moral character.

Virtues are attitudes or character traits that enable us to be and to act in ways that develop our highest potential.

The Common Good Approach:

Life in a community is good in itself and that is every person's moral responsibility to see that effective law and order prevails in the society.

6.4.6 ETHICAL THEORIES IN RELATION TO BUSINESS

Egoism:

The view that associates morality with self interest is referred as egoism. It can be said that egoism is an ethical theory that treats self interest as the foundation of morality. Egoism contends than an act is morally right if it promotes one's long term interests.

Normally the tendency is to equate egoism with individual personal interest but it is equally identified with the interest of the organization or of the society.

Psychological Egoism:

Egoism asserts that the only moral obligation we have is to ourselves though it does not openly suggest that we should not render any help to others. However, we should act in the interest of others if that is the only way to promote our own self – interest.

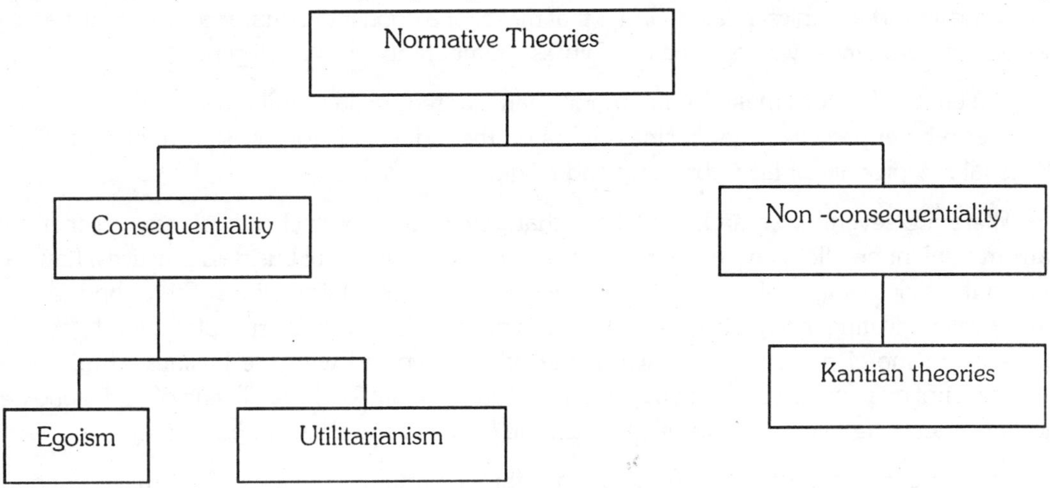

Figure 6.1: Ethical Theories

Utilitarianism:

Two names are associated with utilitarian philosophy. They are Jeremy Bentham who is generally considered the founder of traditional utilitarianism and philosopher cum classical economist John Stuart Mill. According to this philosophy, a decision is ethical if it provides a greater net utility than any other alternative decision. One major problem with the utilitarian theory concerns the measurement of utility. Utility is a psychological concept and is highly subjected. It differs from person to person; place to place and time to time and therefore, it cannot be the basis for a scientific theory.

Kantianism: Ethics of Duty:

Immanuel Kant said that for an action to be morally worth it should reflect goodwill. Kant stressed that the action must be taken only for duties sake and not for some other reason. For Kant ethics is based on reason alone and not on human nature. There are three major influences that have an impact on employee's decision making in business - personal moral standards, their workplace ethics and culture and the nature of issues concerned.

Ethics of Virtues:

Virtue is a quality embedded in the personality of an individual and is expressed in his or her habitual behavior. The ethics of virtues is neither an alternative to the moral principles of utility, rights, justice and care nor an additional factor in judging morality. Ethics of virtue compliment and add to utilitarianism, rights, justice and carry by looking not at the action, people are required to perform, but at the character they are required to have. The role of virtues is to provide a distinctive insight into the ethical perspective of an issue.

Examples of Virtues: Honesty, integrity, trustworthiness, truthfulness, courage etc.,

A moral virtue is an acquired quality that is praised and valued as a part of person's character. It is an indicator of good moral character. According to Aristotle, moral virtue is a habit that enables a human being to act in accordance with the specific purpose of being human.

Some important ethics- related-virtues that make for a good individual or a successful manager are courage, prudence, wisdom, justice, fairness, temperance and intelligence.

The ethics of virtues make for the moral character required by an individual to act ethically. It must also be appreciated that business relies on the individuals for decision making, while an individual is a product of his upbringing and religious beliefs.

There are several laws and regulations that govern the conduct of business, yet there are many fraudulent practices and huge losses to public due to unethical business practices. Laws are important regulators in business, but have their own procedural limitations. Ethics on the other hand, is self regulating mechanism based on one's moral values, moral principles, moral standards and sense of moral responsibility towards the others involved with the business. Ethics is an instrument not only for successful management of a business but for the wellbeing of its stakeholders and the society, the two main pillars on which the business stands and operates.

Ethics can make very good business sense for well rounded success. The ethical standards of an individual are not established by a law-enforcing authority, but are arrived by one's own judgment based on their knowledge, logic, feeling, morality and conscience.

In the context of law and ethics in business, it is necessary to examine :

a) How laws act in business

The law treats modern business organizations as immortal fictitious persons who have the right to sue and be sued, own and sell assets and properties, carry out business on behalf of others and self, enter into a legal ownership and sell assets and properties, carry out business on behalf of others and self, enter into legal contracts in their own name.

The law is enforced in business by holding those individuals accountable who the company has deemed responsible and accountable for its business; unless some other individuals had deliberately and directly acted or colluded to cause the damage. In the eye of law, the person or persons responsible for directing or supervising companies work are made responsible for the consequences of the company's action.

6.5 ETHICS IN MARKETING

Ethics are a collection of principles of right conduct that shape the decisions people or organizations make. Practicing ethics in marketing means deliberately applying standards of fairness, or moral rights and wrongs to marketing decision making, behavior and practice in the organization.

In a market economy, a business may be expected to act in what it believes to be its own best interest. The purpose of marketing is to create a competitive advantage. An organization achieves an advantage when it does a better job than its competitors. Those organizations that develop a competitive advantage are able to satisfy the needs of both customers and the organization.

As our economic system has become more successful at providing for needs and wants, there has been greater focus on organizations' adhering to ethical values rather than simply providing products. This focus has come about for two reasons. First, when an organization behaves ethically, customers develop more positive attitudes about the firm, its products, and its services. When marketing practices depart from standards that society considers acceptable, the market process becomes less efficient, sometimes it is even interrupted. Not employing ethical marketing practices may lead to dissatisfied customers, bad publicity, a lack of trust, loss of business, or, sometimes, legal action. Thus, most organizations are very sensitive to the needs and opinions of their customers and look for ways to protect their long-term interests.

Secondly, ethical abuses frequently lead to pressure by social or government institutions on business and then the business has to assume greater responsibility for their actions. Since abuses do occur in business, consumer interest groups, professional associations, and self-regulatory groups exert considerable influence on marketing. Calls for social responsibility have also subjected marketing practices to a wide range of federal and state regulations designed to protect consumer rights or to regulate trade.

Regulations cannot be developed to cover every possible abuse. Organizations and industry groups often develop codes of ethical conduct or rules for behavior to serve as a guide in decision making. Self-regulation not only helps a firm avoid extensive government intervention; it also permits it to respond in a better manner to changes in market conditions. An organization's long-term success and profitability depends on this ability to respond.

Important issues in Marketing Ethics

- Value-oriented issues: Analyzing ethical problems on the basis of the values which they infringe-for example honesty, autonomy, privacy, transparency.
- Stakeholder-oriented issues: Analysing ethical problems on the basis of whom they affect –for e.g., consumers, competitors, society as a whole.
- Process-oriented issues: Analysing ethical problems in terms of the categories used by marketing specialists-fore.g., research, price, promotion and placement.

6.5.1 ETHICS IN TARGET MARKETING

As very few products can satisfy the needs of all consumers, companies develop different marketing strategies to satisfy different consumer needs. The process is known as target marketing.

It refers to the concentrated marketing of a product to a segment of consumers by creating advertisements which attract different groups.

Ethical issues in Target Marketing:

It involves three step processes - segmenting the market, targeting the market and position the product or service.

1. *Segmentation:*

Segmentation is process of dividing a heterogeneous market, into several sub-markets or segments, each of which tends to be homogeneous in all significant aspects. The division is based on the premise, that different people have different preferences. Market segment is based on the fact that the markets of commodities are not homogeneous but they are heterogeneous. Segmentation identifies groups of customers with common characteristics.

2. *Targeting:*

The market targeting decision identifies the people or organizations in product marketing towards which an organization directs its positioning strategy. Selecting good market targets is a challenge for every organization.

Targeting Strategies:

i. Identifying and analyzing the segments in a product-market.

ii. Decision regarding which segments to target.

iii. Designing and implementing a positioning strategy for each target.

3. *Positioning:*

Brand position is considered as a part of brand identity and value proposition that is to be actively communicated to the targeted audience and that demonstrates an advantage over competing brands.

Positioning is the art of creating a distinct image for a product in the minds of the consumers.

1) Positioning Navaratna hair oil as a stress reliever.

2) Positioning of flavored Parle biscuits as fresh fruit biscuits

3) Positioning Maggi as the fastest food appetizers.

6.5.2 ETHICS IN SALES

Sales ethics:

Ethical issues arise in virtually every aspect of selling. But for many sales people it doesn't matter except selling the product somehow. This may help the company in the short run. But, putting morality aside will prove fatal to the organization. The pragmatic reasons for choosing an ethical approach to any selling situation is possible through trust and credibility. No long-term relationship with a customer is possible without them. Let's look at each and see how they relate to ethical behavior.

Trust:

Trust comes from customer's experience. Trust does not precede your reputation, it follows it. It's built on honesty and on obvious commitment to your customer and the success of business depends on it.

Credibility:

Credibility comes from performance but not just on the basis of your talk. It means possessing and displaying a belief in your company and its products and services creates credibility. It takes long time to build and depends heavily on your professional reputation. If you are not credible, your products aren't saleable.

General guidelines for dealing with customers' successfully:

- Anticipate problems.
- Set high standards from the beginning.
- Avoid legal problems.
- Correct your mistakes.

Ethics in Advertising:

Ethics have always been an important aspect of every business activity. But advertising industry has rarely cared to look beyond immediate marketing objectives of the client company and it is the government's job to judge what is right and what is wrong.

Unethical Advertising:

- When it has degraded or underestimated the substitute or rival's product.
- When it gives false or misleading information on the value of the product.
- When it is immoral and illegal.
- When obscene pictures of women are posted to draw the attention of the other sex.

Remedies to overcome Advertisements:

- Cease-and-desist orders.
- Restitution
- Affirmative disclosures.
- Corrective advertising.

6.5.3 ETHICS OF PRODUCT PLACEMENT

Product placement has always been a bit of a controversial topic in advertising. Some feel that it is unethical pitching of consumer products and brands in mediums meant to entertain and can be seen as disrespectful to the viewer.

Placing real products in television programs and movies makes the films seem more realistic and as long as the brand represented doesn't take artistic control away from the writers, actors, it is a good thing.

Content creators have responsibility to determine whether it adds value or not in the mindset of the customer. Product placement is becoming more and more necessary as the industry changes but ethical considerations must also be taken into consideration.

6.5.4 ETHICS RELATED TO ADVERTISING

The term 'advertising' is derived from the original Latin word 'advert ere' which means ' to turn' the attention. Every piece of advertising turns the attention of the readers or the listeners or the viewers or the onlookers towards a product or a service or an idea.

According to Walter Thomson," Advertising is like electricity, which not only illuminates but electrocutes. Its worth to civilization depends upon how it is used."

There is nothing wrong with advertising but there are advertisers who abuse or misuse advertising. All advertising aims to influence customers. Mostly all people attempt to influence the desires and options of others. When they attempt to influence another by reasons and arguments their persuasion is acceptable. Attempts like exploitation of prospective customers by cheating or by exploitation of their weaknesses or seducing them with false claims are immoral and inappropriate.

6.5.5 MORAL RESPONSIBILITIES IN ADVERTISING

1. Ensure that none is harmed or irritated by the picture or narration in advertisements.
2. Highlight the good points and avoid criticizing other products.
3. Ensure that consumer gets fair treatment and are not misguided.
4. Local laws, socio-cultural values or norms should be respected and there should be no direct or indirect violation.
5. Avoid using similar or same logos, names and punch lines that are already used by competitors.
6. Avoid display of women in a derogatory manner.
7. Only product related aspect to be explained rather than covering other news and views.

Area's concerned in Advertising Regulation:

1. Morality :

Moral principles are the rules or the stands of what is right and wrong. The word morality is quite comprehensive than the word 'ethics' because moral values include ethical values which speak what is good or bad. The concept of morality is not rigid.

2. *Untruthful Advertising :*

It is but natural that the consumers reject those ads which they think that they are untruthful. Such advertisements raise the consumer expectations which are false and misleading. The concept of truth is really very elusive.

In the word of advertising, the word truth has four colors or degrees. These are

- Literal truth.
- Deceptive truth.
- Truth exaggerated.
- The whole truth.

3. *Advertisement as Environment Pollutant:*

Consumer resentment crops up as a result of it's over persuasiveness. This objection stems from the fact that too much of advertising that pollutes the mental environment is just as harmful as effluent and poisonous gases emanating from a factory chimney pollute the physical environment.

6.5.6 UNETHICAL ISSUES OF ADVERTISING

There are various unethical issues in advertising ranging from the question of validity of claims made in the advertisements such as:

1) Highly appealing and enticing harmful products advertisement
2) Over persuasive advertising to children and young
3) Advertising in poor taste.
4) False claims made in the advertisements.
5) Excessive use of exaggeration.
6) Unhealthy brand comparison.
7) Use of testimonials by celebrities from cinema and sport fields.

Advertising's main purpose is to make consumers aware of new products and services.

Beneficial Effects of Advertising:

1. *Educating the Consumer:*

Advertising aims at educating the buyers about new products and their diverse uses. In this process, it introduces new standards of life to the people at large and prompts them to give up their old habits.

2. *Motivation for Better Performance:*

Advertising gives the employees that feeling of pride in their jobs and the products they produce or help to produce, which is basic to high morale. It inspires executives and workers to improve performance.

3. *Creation of Goodwill:*

By constantly associating the name of the company with certain standards of quality, advertising builds a fund of goodwill for the organization.

4. *Improvement in Quality:*

Goods are generally advertised under brand names. When a person is moved by the advertisement to use the product, they proceed on the hope that the articles of the particular brand will be better than the other brands of the same goods.

5. *Sustaining the Press:*

When advertising made its beginning, advertisements generally occupied small place in the corners of the newspapers. The present situation is just the reverse. The newspapers, periodicals, journals and the television channels look to advertisements for support and sustenance.

Adverse Effects of Advertising:

1. *Deceptive Advertising:*

Advertising should win the confidence of the consumers to perform its job effectively.

➢ ***Harmful Effects :*** Advertising has harmful effects on the society. Sex, nudity, violence and bad habits etc., intruding into the minds of the children and the young, is turning as a social menace.

i) *Taste:*

Many people have criticized advertising on the ground that it is in bad taste. It has adverse effects on culture and social traditions.

ii) *Appeal:*

The appeal to sex and drugs has become the most adverse aspect of advertising. Advertising has employed obscenity, nudity to increase emotional appeal.

iii) *Intrusiveness:*

Advertising repeats several messages number of times over the TV channels. It may turn into monotony and the advertisement loses the appeal.

iv) *Impact on Children:*

Advertising makes an adverse impact on children, who are more susceptible to deception because they lack the perceptual defense of adults.

➢ ***Confuses the People:*** Advertising creates confusion in the minds of the people. Multiple and repetitive advertisements irritate people. Customers do not take a rational decision.

ii) *Power of Advertising :*

Advertising has the potential to maintain consumers. It stimulates the customers to make repeated purchases.

iii) ***Creating Differentiation among Brands :***

Advertising encourages unnecessary differences in various brands of products and hence customers are confused.

iv) ***Uniformity and Conformity :***

'Uniformity' refers to the individuals looking to others and the mass media. Customers are guided by neighbors, friends and relatives. Conformity is a sort of others directedness being guided by the purchasing habits of friends, relatives and mass media instead of by one's self.

v) ***Interpersonal and Group Relationship :***

Advertising destroys interpersonal relationship and develops group relationship. The individual has no place in an advertising campaign.

vi) ***Comparison :***

Advertising creates unnecessary comparison between two products.

- ***Forceful Selling :*** Customer may be forced to buy though he or she may not be in need of that product immediately because of the recall of advertisement which he has recorded in his mind sometime back.

i. ***Motivation :***

Motivation research uncovers hidden motives of consumers and has become a powerful tool for the expansion of the marketing function.

ii. ***Emotional Appeals :***

Advertisers understand the emotions and sentiments of the people. They use them to induce prospective buyers to buy their products. Emotional appeals have changed the buying habits of the people.

iii. ***Unwanted Products :***

Advertisers try to sell those goods, which are not required by the consumers. They create wants and convert the needs into wants.

- ***Media Misuses :*** Advertising misuses the media of information, news papers, magazines etc. by overcrowding them with advertisements and the cost of the advertising will be thrown on the heads of the consumers.

6.6 ETHICS IN HUMAN RESOURCE MANAGEMENT

Organization means people working together to achieve a specific common purpose or objective. In fact, group life is one of the earliest and most enduring features of human existence on this planet. People love to live and work in groups and that is why groups like family, community and society came into existence. Humans have created organizations to improve their quality of life.

The concept of Human Resource as per Leon C Megginson:

From the national point of view human resources are knowledge, skills, creative abilities, talents and attitudes obtained in the people: whereas from the view point of the individual enterprise they represent the total inherent abilities, acquired knowledge and skills as exemplified in the talent and aptitude of its employees.

'All HR practices have an ethical foundation. HR deals with the practical consequences of human behavior'. Despite these moral appreciations of human resource management (HRM), there is a strong tradition in business that insists that business should not be concerned with ethics. As Milton Friedman, a vociferous proponent of this position has put it: 'The social responsibility of business is to its shareholders. The business of business is business'. The core concern of business proponents of the market economy argue that the main goal is to secure the best possible return on any investment.

Some entrepreneurs like Infosys Narayana Murthy, Wipros Azim Premji and Tatas Ratan Tata and other management professionals have all expressed the view that standards of behavior within business need to be evaluated and improved.

A case can be made that negative consequences are a result of poor ethical standards:

While short-term goals may be achieved through the cut-throat tactics of free market principles, business will survive better if good standards of conduct are maintained in the long run. Ethical business creates a positive environment to buy and sell, as corruption, poverty and lack of respect for the environment generate problems for the business community in the long term.

The ethics of HRM revolves around those ethical issues arising out of employer- employee relationship, such as the rights and duties owed between them. There is no denying the fact that the executives have to play an active role to provide ethical leadership in the organization. Such leadership arises not only out of their responsibility to keep the organization out of trouble from the government machinery and various regulations and acts but also to gain respect from the employees.

6.6.1 ETHICAL ISSUES CONCERNING HRM POLICIES

Most of the ethical issues concerning HRM policies and activities are universal in nature. Some of them have greater relevance in the Indian context. They are:

- Discrimination issues.
- Suppression of democratization in the work place.
- Privacy issues.
- Safety and health.
- Performance appraisals.

Discrimination Issues:

Most of the discrimination issues centre on age, gender, race, religion, disabilities, weight and attractiveness. These discriminations are clearly exhibited by Indian corporations in the matter of recruitment and promotions by seeking only "experienced" persons. Some companies may not give importance to youth. There are companies that do not recruit lady candidates. There are several companies that choose candidates belonging to a particular community. But they deny this discrimination.

Suppression of Democratization in the Work Place:

Corruption often suppresses the democratic rights and representation of employees in bodies that would promote the latter's collective interest. Tempting and bribing the union leader, breaking the strike by unethical means are normally used by them to defeat the purpose of collective bargaining and other democratic rights of the worker.

Privacy Issues:

Privacy refers to protect a person's private life from intrusive and unwarranted action by others. Privacy issues are being increasingly important in organization where people work long hours together and share official secrets. In HRM, practices such as recruitment, performance appraisal, employee discipline management, adherence to code of conduct, performance monitoring and exit interviews are some of the important areas to be handled with care.

Recruitment and Selection:

Taking advantage of their position in the organization and the vulnerability of job seekers, a lot of questions are asked by HR officers. These questions may sometimes threaten the new incumbent's privacy, forcing them to disclose confidential information about past employer and his secret business strategies.

Performance Tracking:

It is another area where privacy of employees is often intruded. In case of new age industries like BPO's, call monitoring and other electronic monitoring mechanisms are widely used to track on every detail about the employee which can be used for the inconvenience of the job performer.

Privacy Issues of Computerized Employee Records:

It is a worrisome factor that unauthorized persons could access employee information of a confidential nature.

Electronic Surveillance:

Surveillance of employees, using a broad range of electronic tools like CC cameras and tapping phones etc., by an employer is increasingly becoming a menace to privacy of employees even in advanced countries. With no relevant legislation, technologies are exposing the individual worker to scrutiny as opposed to the earlier prevalent group evaluation and in some cases employer may resort to blackmailing on the basis of this information.

Safety and Health:

HRM executives have the responsibility to provide a safe and conducive environment at the work place. However, in actual practice this is hardly done. It is well known that much of the industrial work is hazardous. Accident injuries and illness are very common in the very nature of some jobs. In many cases serious attention is not paid by the HR person which is unethical.

Performance Appraisals:

Another area which generates unethical practices from executives relates to performance appraisal. It is difficult to quantify an employee's performance where a number of value judgments are involved in the evaluations. The overall objective of performance review is not only to offer the top management an honest and ethical assessment of employee, but also to help the employees improve their efficiency and effectiveness for developing the organization.

Institutional Culture:

Every institution has a distant culture. Institutional culture reflects the core values of the institution and forms the basis of how people work together. Institutional or corporate culture is blend of ideas, conventions, customs and practices of the company and shared ethical values that define accepted behavior for every employee in an organization. Organization culture reflects the informal procedures that emerge in the organizations culture which is determined by the institutions vision and core values. The CEO and senior managers and management heavily influence the culture. Efficient and effective HR system is important to mould the work culture.

6.7 ETHICS IN FINANCIAL MANAGEMENT

Finance is lifeblood of any organization and it plays a dominant role for successful running of any business. The whole world runs after finance. Financial management includes resource management, finance operations and accounting operations.

Resource management is the efficient and effective deployment of organizational resources at the right time in right proportions when they are required. Such resources may include financial resources like cash, raw material, inventory, human skills, plant snd machinery or information technology etc.

Financial operations involve providing financial advice and guidance, support of the procurement process, providing pay support and providing disbursing support. Financial management is a broad area which covers the following functions:

1. Financial analysis and planning.
2. Investment decisions.
3. Financing and capital structure decisions.
4. Dividend decisions and
5. Short term asset management.

6.7.1 ROLE OF FINANCE MANAGER

The finance manager heads the finance department. The finance manager in every organization plays a key role like a hub of a wheel. Normally, a financial manager's role involves in the following activities.

1. Providing and interpreting financial information.
2. Business modeling and forecasting.

3. Monitoring performance and efficiency.
4. Risk analysis
5. Strategic financial planning.
6. Formulating long-term business plans.
7. Pricing related decisions.
8. Developing complex financial models.
9. Budgetary control
10. Monitoring cash flow.

According to The Companies Act, 1956 the management of any organization is the custodian of the owner's funds. These funds are managed by the financial managers to maximize the wealth of the shareholders. Compensation and other incentives of managers are tied with the profitability of the business and hence, there is a scope for managers to involve in fraudulent activities to maximize their payments.

Ethics in Finance:

Ethics in general is concerned with human behavior that is acceptable or "right" and that is not acceptable or "wrong" based on conventional morality. General ethical norms encompass truthfulness, honesty, integrity, respect for others,. fairness, and justice. They relate to all aspects of life, including business and finance. Financial ethics is, therefore, a subset of general ethics.

Ethical norms are essential for maintaining stability and harmony in social life, where people interact with one another. Recognition of others' needs and aspirations, fairness, and cooperative efforts to deal with common issues are, for example, aspects of social behavior that contribute to social stability. In the process of social evolution, we have developed not only an instinct to care for ourselves but also a conscience to care for others. There may arise situations in which the need to care for ourselves runs into conflict with the need to care for others. In such situations, ethical norms are needed to guide our behavior. As Demsey (1999) puts it, "Ethics represents the attempt to resolve the conflict between selfishness and selflessness; between our material needs and our conscience."

Ethical dilemmas and ethical violations in finance can be attributed to an inconsistency in the conceptual framework of modern financial-economic theory and the widespread use of a principal-agent model of relationship in financial transactions. The financial economic theory that underlies the modern capitalist system is based on the rational-maximizer paradigm, which holds that individuals are self-seeking (egoistic) and that they behave rationally when they seek to maximize their own interests. The principal-agent model of relationships refers to an arrangement whereby one party, acting as an agent for another, carries out certain functions on behalf of the other. Such arrangements are an integral part of the modern economic and financial system, and it is difficult to imagine it functioning without them.

The behavioral assumption of the modern financial-economic theory runs counter to the ideas of trustworthiness, loyalty, fidelity, stewardship, and concern for others that underlie the traditional principal-agent relationship. The traditional concept of agency is based on moral values. But if human beings are rational maximizers, then agency on behalf of others in the traditional sense is impossible. As Duska (1992) explains it, "To do something for another in a system geared to maximize self-interest is foolish. Such an answer, though, points out an inconsistency at the heart of the system, for a system that has rules requiring agents to look out for others while encouraging individuals to look out only for themselves, destroys the practice of looking out for others"

The ethical dilemma presented by the problem of conflicting interests has been addressed in some areas of finance, such as corporate governance, by converting the agency relationship into a purely contractual relationship that uses a carrot-and-stick approach to ensure ethical behavior by agents. In corporate governance, the problem of conflict between management (agent) and stockholders (principal) is described as an agency problem. Economists have developed an agency theory to deal with this problem. The agency theory assumes that both the agent and the principal are self-interested and aim to maximize their gain in their relationship.

A simple example would be the case of a store manager acting as an agent for the owner of the store. The store manager wants as much pay as possible for as little work as possible, and the store owner wants as much work from the manager for as little pay as possible. This theory is value-free because it does not pass judgment on whether the maximization behavior is good or bad and is not concerned with what a just pay for the manager might be. It drops the ideas of honesty and loyalty from the agency relationship because of their incompatibility with the fundamental assumption of rational maximization. "The job of agency theory is to help devise techniques for describing the conflict inherent in the principal-agent relationship and controlling the situations so that the agent, acting from self-interest, does as little harm as possible to the principal's interest" (DeGeorge, 1992). The agency theory turns the traditional concept of agency relationship into a structured (contractual) relationship in which the principal can influence the actions of agents through incentives, motivations, and punishment schemes. The principal essentially uses monetary rewards, punishments, and the agency laws to command loyalty from the agent.

Most of our needs for financial services such as management of retirement savings, stock and bond investing, and protection against unforeseen events, to name a few are such that they are better entrusted to others because we have neither the ability nor the time to carry them out effectively. The corporate device of contractualization of the agency relationship is, however, too difficult to apply to the multitude of financial dealings between individuals and institutions that take place in the financial market every day. Individuals are not as well organized as stockholders, and they are often unaware of the agency problem. Lack of information also limits their ability to monitor an agent's behavior. Therefore, what we have in our complex modern economic system is a paradoxical situation: the ever-increasing need for getting things done by others on the one hand, and the description of human nature that emphasizes selfish behavior on the other. This paradoxical situation, or the inconsistency in the foundation of the modern capitalist system, can explain most of the ethical problems and declining morality in the modern business and finance arena.

According to Professor John Boatwright of Business Ethics and Management School at Loyola University, Chicago, The Theory of Ethics in Finance revolves around three broad areas.

1. Financial markets.
2. Financial services.
3. Financial people in the organization.

6.7.2 FRAUDS IN BANKS

Legal authorities define fraud as a crime that involves the use of dishonest or deceitful conduct in order to obtain some unjust advantage using dishonest means with an intention to cheat other persons or institutions, to make them part with something of their own. It is assumed that the fraudster knows that his or her act is false or is without belief in its truth and knowing it he/she includes others to act upon the matter. This will deprive them of their possessions.

a. Financial services sector that is fraud in credit cards, cheques and other types of identity related services.
b. Insurance sector that is internal fraud committee by employees against the insurer, fraud by policy holder and claim fraud.
c. There are other types of frauds such as those related to telecommunication, securities and the computer.

A study of bank frauds brings into light several types of frauds with or without the connivance of bank employees. Authorities on the subject identify four elements responsible for the commission of bank frauds.

1. Active involvement of the staff - both supervisory and clerical either independent of external elements.
2. Failure on the part of the bank staff to follow scrupulously the instructions and guidelines laid down by regulators like the RBI.
3. External elements perpetrating frauds on banks by forgeries or manipulation of cheques, drafts and other negotiable instruments.
4. Collision among businessmen, top bank executives, civil servants and politicians in power to flout rules and regulations and to throw banking norms to the winds.

6.7.3 TYPES OF BANK FRAUDS

Unauthorized extension of credit facilities such as cash credit, pledging, hypothecation of goods against bills or book debits, pledging of spurious goods hypothecating goods to more than one bank, inflating the value of goods, removing goods with the convenience of the bank employees, pledging of goods belonging to a third party and accepting obsolete and inadequate stocks are all done with a view to cheat banks for illegal gratification.

Apart from frauds committed by outsiders on banks or their clients, banks themselves resort to unethical practices, against the guidelines provided by the RBI.

The National Consumer Disputes Redressel Commission at New Delhi has recently issued a notice to the RBI and 88 commercial banks including the foreign banks operating in the country for delaying the crediting of cheques. Based on a complaint it is found that the banks in the country are allegedly earning nearly Rs 6,210 million in interest everyday due to delays in crediting cheques sent for clearance. According to the complaint, a gross violation of the rights of millions of consumers was taking place in the banking industry. It was pointed out that there was a huge time gap between when the cheques of a bank customer was paid by the drawee bank and the bank actually credited its consumers account and there is a still further time gap if we consider when funds were made available for withdrawal.

The complaint said that during the financial year 2005-2006 nearly, 1,300 frauds were made. Million cheques were cleared by the 88 banks operating in India through their branches across the country amounting to about Rs.113.4 million. Even if it assumed that the banks enjoyed the benefit of fund float only on 50% of the cheques deposited, the daily rate of interest would come to Rs. 6210 million a day at 4% of interest. It was submitted that as per RBI guidelines a local cheque was to be credited on the 3rd working day from the date of acceptance of cheques at the counters and that an outstation cheque drawn on a bank in any of the four metropolitan cities was to be credited within seven days.

Frauds are also committed in the areas of granting overdraft facility in the current account of the customers. A large number of frauds have been and are being committed through bank drafts, mail transfers and telegraph transfers. In recent times several banks frauds have come to light in the use of credit cards and also in the extension of home loans. The same property is pledged to more than one bank by using original look-alike another documents made possible by color photocopies.

Some inherent weakness in the web browsers and the internet make users susceptible to phasing attacks. Fraudsters use emails to persuade users to part with sensitive information like passwords for websites, financial information etc. In a typical attack a user receives an e-mail message from the attackers with the address and logo or image of a bank or financial institutions making him or her believe that the messages has come from these institutions.

Measures:

For a long time especially after the adoption of licensing policy, restrictive imports and import substitution rationing by Foreign Exchange Regulation Act (FERA), 1973 there was a large degree of smuggling and money laundering in the country. Half hearted attempts by the government at different times did not yield any tangible result in curbing this menace and this caused huge losses to the exchequer. Prevention of Money Laundering Act, 2002 is a comprehensive legislation to curb the evil of money laundering.

Section 12 of the Prevention of Money Laundering Act (PMLA) casts certain obligation on the banking companies with regard to preservation and reposition of the PMLA. Each bank has to furnish information of transactions to the Director of the (FIU-INO) within the prescribed time, where the principal officer has reasons that a transaction or a series of transactions are integrally connected so as to defeat the provision of this section. The branches shall have to maintain a register containing information of the following types of transactions.

a. All cash transactions of the value of more than Rs. 1 million or its equivalent in foreign currency.

b. All series of cash transactions integrally connected to each other which have been valued below Rs. 1 million or its equivalent in foreign country.

c. All cash transactions, where forged and counterfeit currency notes or bank notes have been used as genuine and where any forgery of a valuable security has taken place.

d. All suspicious transactions whether or not made in cash.

6.8 UNETHICAL ISSUES PREVALENT IN INDIA

As we discuss business ethics from the Indian perspective, it is important to look at ethical violations in their various forms that are rampant in the country. Harshad Mehta Stock Market Scam, Insider Trading of L&T vs. Reliance, 2G Scam, are some of the unethical practices taken place even in reputed organizations. Research studies show that organizations are involving in several unethical issues such as bribery, deception, theft, unfair discrimination etc.

Bribery:

Bribing is commonly practiced in India even today and is considered to be part of conducting everyday business. According to a Times of India opinion poll, 76% rated business as a corrupting force, right after 'politicians and ministers', which 98% considered being the most corrupt. Bribes or personal payments, gifts or special favours are mainly given to influence the outcome of decisions. Bribes have to be paid for almost anything a company wants to do, whether it is expanding, obtaining a contract or exporting or importing goods. Most government officials receive low remuneration and expect bribes, to improve their personal state.

Bribery is a manipulative method where one buys the power or the influence of other person in order to satisfy his or her selfish need. Bribes create a conflict of interest between the person receiving bribe and his or her organization. This conflict would result in unethical practices when somebody is bribed for something.

Bribery:

- It raises the cost of goods sold.
- Leads to perceptions of unfair treatment of some companies and groups at the expenses of others.
- Decreases the level of trust across groups.
- Different forms of bribery also lead to differential perception that can further decrease trust.

Corruption:

With so much corruption prevalent in the country any Indian citizen is forced to wonder what has happened to the country's leaders. There seems to be no doubt that the principal reasons responsible are first, the type of governance, we the people gave ourselves and second, the type of economy that was imposed on us. First, we choose an electoral process in which the spending of millions to win a seat was forbidden, yet necessary. This single factor made corruption and black money a substantial part of the electoral process, and therefore, of government and industry.

Transparency International which prepares the Corruption Perception Index (CPI) every year placed India, 71st among 102 countries it surveyed in 2002 and estimated that by way of corruption, officials at various levels siphon of an astounding sum of Rs. 267680 million every year.

Bribery is what contributes to corruption and takes the forms of

- Demand and acceptance of money by officials for doing what they are expected to do.
- Stealing public funds.
- Demanding and accepting 'commissions'.
- Offering bribes, especially for undo and out-of-turn favours and use of public office for personal pecuniary gains.

Black money:

Black money refers to the illegal earning made by people, whether they are businessmen or others, in violation of legal channels of earning income. Black money generation is a consequence of the system of controls, permits, quotas and licenses. Considerable amount of black money was also generated in the administration of controls and licenses.

The genesis of the so-called black economy in India can be traced to the Second World War when the country had to export several essential commodities to the war prone areas in Europe, which resulted in severe shortages within the country leading to controls and regulations.

The generation of black money comes through various sources:

- Under reporting of output or sales or over reporting of the costs or misclassification of personal expenses by manufacturing and trading enterprises.
- Black income generated in relation to capital receipts on sale of assets, that is the registered value of property represents only 60% of its true value.
- Through leakages, that is the registered value of property often represents only 60% estimates cost of construction, plant and machinery off as black income.
- Black income generated by corporations in the private sector to the extent of 10-15% in relation to their kick backs.

Coercion:

'Coercion is forcing a person to act in a manner that is against his or her personal beliefs.' It is an external force or a man -made constraint created that compels the other to act against his free will. The authority of the person who demands such activity plays an important role. It may be in the form of blackmail to an individual in an organization. It may be in the form of a threat of blocking a promotion or loss of a job. This sort of unethical practice in the organization will beget more unethical behaviour from the individual.

Insider trading:

This is one form of misuse of official position of an individual in the organization. Here, the employee leaks out certain confidential data to outsiders or to insiders, which in turn, ruin the reputation of the company. Insider trading may lead to the bad performance of the company in the long run. If the employees trade confidential matters, the competitor may intervene and make use of the opportunity.

Tax evasion:

There are major unethical practices of tax evasion. Many large corporations hire the services of professional tax consultants to take advantage of loopholes in the law and evade taxes to the extent public. The reason the attribute for such behavior is the prevalent rate of corporate taxation, which is very high. In fact, this has generated a parallel economy in spite of government's continuous endeavors to channelize this money towards legitimate development purposes.

Conflicts of interest:

Even the most loyal employees can find that their interests conflict with that of the organization. Sometimes this clash of goals and desires can take a serious form. In an organization, conflict of interest arises when employees at any level behave with private interests that are substantial enough to interfere with their job or duties. This would result in the individual's interest acting against the interest of the employees. Conflicts of interest are morally perturbing, especially when it causes an employee to act to the detriment of the organization.

Pollution:

The unethical practice of pollution affects society and population to a major extent. The high level of pollution due to the indiscriminate and improper disposal of effluents by industries has rendered the world a highly unsafe place for living.

Why should Indian Business be Ethical?

- ***Ethics responds to the best in us:***

  Most of people want and even need to be ethical in their private lives and also in their business affairs. People want to work in an organization they can respect and be publicly proud of.

- ***Values create credibility for the company with the public :***

  People will purchase their goods and subscribe to their issues if companies are seen to be ethical.

- ***Values give management credibility with its employees :***

  Only perceived moral uprightness and social concern bring employee respect. The management of such companies is held in high esteem by their employees. In such companies, attrition rate will be low.

- ***Values help better decision making :***

  Hard decisions which have been studied from both ethical and economic angles are more difficult to make, but they will stand up against all odds, because the good of the employees, the public interest, and the company's own long term interest would have all been taken into account.

6.9 REASONS FOR UNETHICAL PRACTICES AMONG INDIAN CORPORATIONS

- The Indian public has considered business people as corrupt, untrustworthy and profiteering.
- The government's policies and new projects, giving a chance to some politicians, beaurocrats and industry people to amass huge wealth at the cost of the exchequer.
- The industrial licensing policy was also responsible in the past for increase in unethical practices.
- Unethical and corrupt practices are ruling the roost as there is no proper check or severe punishment for the wrong doers.
- With the boom in the financial sector and organizations facing various kinds of challenges, the risk faced by corporations is increasing several folds.
- Another area where Indian corporations are subject to fraud risk is from cyber mafia.

6.10 BUSINESS ETHICS IN INDIA

- With the onset of globalization and the huge foreign institutional investment in India, Indian corporations can no longer turn a blind eye to the needs of the hour.
- An ethical corporate can contribute to serve the community around it directly and indirectly, in many ways.
- A corporate expects others in the line of business to be ethical in their dealings; else the entire trust upon which business is conducted will be lost.
- Ethical business must be adhered to by the entire business community. It is the foundation for conducting business.
- A trust worthy company that has over the years earned good reputation and the goodwill of people through its ethical conduct stands a much greater chance of attracting more business than the others. Ex: Tata Group

Corporations in India cannot afford to be Ethical:

- Even companies that started off with intentions to do business in an ethical manner had to compromise their principles due to the highly politicized and bureaucratic business environment in the country.
- The growing corruption, increasing disparity between people and rapidly reducing profit margins add to the woes of organizations that want to be ethical

Indian Companies face two types of Corrupt Practices:

- Political corruption in which money is paid in return for favors done by politicians- 'quid pro quo'.
- Companies are greasing the palms of bureaucrats to make them do things. They were not supposed to do, but now corruption, has graduated to such an extent where both the parties are not at all feeling guilty.

Business Executives listed three major obstacles to Ethical Behavior:

1. Company policies.
2. Unethical industry climate.
3. Corruption in government.

The other factors affecting Ethical Dilemmas of Indian Corporations:

- Socio-cultural factors such as the sense of hospitality and reciprocity.
- The psychological fear of losing jobs.
- Government tax structures and regulations.
- Sanctions and discriminations in a society that can be offset with accumulations of wealth by fair or foul means.
- Uncertainties and fears about the future.
- Strong family traditions and laws of inheritance in which parents want to leave substantial assets to their children.
- Overall scarcity of resources and the difficulty of amassing wealth through normal and legitimate means.
- An inequitable and scorching tax system which discourage hard working and honest tax payers and lead them to bribe tax-collector.
- A tendency to adopt an easy option when confronted with difficult ethical choices.

Survey conducted by Indian Institute of Public Opinion (IIPO):

An open survey was conducted by a team of IIPO in the four metropolitan cities by interviewing 1500 literates on the corruption issue.

- A large percentage (88.8%) are of the opinion that corruption is the serious problem in the country
- Regarding Government owned business 89.3% accepted corruption as a serious problem, while 73.2% felt that corruption is a serious problem in private owned business.

Similarly the opinion of the business man and the retail traders are:

- Corruption in Government owned business (59.8%)
- Corruption in privately owned business (40.2%)
- Corruption is higher in government owned business organizations due to:
  - ✓ Role of business executives.
  - ✓ Influence of politicians.

SHORT QUESTIONS

1. Concept of ethics in general.
2. Definition of ethics and its nature.
3. Objectives of ethics.
4. Concept of business ethics
5. Characteristics of business ethics
6. Benefits of ethics in work place
7. Ethics and target marketing
8. Ethics and sales
9. Ethical issues in HRM.
10. Ethical issues in Finance.
11. Moral responsibilities in advertising.
12. Unethical issues of advertising.
13. Black money and corruption.

ESSAY QUESTIONS

1. Explain the concept of ethics in general. Discuss its nature and goals.
2. Define ethics and explain the objectives of ethics.
3. What is business ethics? Explain the need and characteristics of business ethics.
4. Discuss the role of values and virtues in business ethics.
5. Explain the importance and relevance of business ethics.
6. Define business ethics and explain various ethical models guiding decision making.
7. Explain various ethical theories in relation to business and management
8. What is the relationship of ethics and marketing? Discuss the ethical issues in marketing.
9. Explain ethical issues in target marketing, product placement and sales.
10. What is meant by business ethics? Clearly explain the ethical issues related to advertising.
11. Explain the ethical issues involved in human resource management.
12. Discuss the ethical issues relating to financial management.
13. Explain the ethical issues relating to financial markets, financial services and financial people in the organization?
14. Write briefly the bank frauds occurred in India and abroad in the recent past.
15. Discuss various factors responsible for unethical practices by Indian corporations.
16. Why should Indian business be ethical? Explain.

❖ ❖ ❖

UNIT - VII

BUSINESS COMMUNICATION

7.1 ***Fundamentals of Communication***

- 7.1.1 Concept and Definition of Communication
- 7.1.2 Nature of Communication
- 7.1.3 The Process of Communication
- 7.1.4 Characteristic Features of Communication:
- 7.1.5 Classification of Communication
- 7.1.6 Business Communication
- 7.1.7 Types of Business Communication

7.2 ***Report Writing***

- 7.2.1 Meaning and Definition
- 7.2.2 Formats for Presenting Reports
- 7.2.3 Types of Reports
- 7.2.4 Classification of Reports
- 7.2.5 Parts of Report
- 7.2.6 Techniques of Writing Report
- 7.2.7 Essentials of Good Report Writing

7.3 ***Cross Cultural Communication***

- 7.3.1 Concept of Culture and Cross-Culture
- 7.3.2 Cross-Cultural Misperception
- 7.3.3 Cross-Cultural Misinterpretation
- 7.3.4 The Realities of Communication Across Cultures
- 7.3.5 Effects of Cross-Cultural Communication
- 7.3.6 Problems in Cross Cultural Communication

7.4 ***Presentation Skills***

- 7.4.1 Concept
- 7.4.2 Structuring the Presentation
- 7.4.3 Oral Presentation Skills

7.1 FUNDAMENTALS OF COMMUNICATION

The Creator by creating nature and various creatures started the era of communication. The sounds, smells and sights are in fact signals of communication. Right from small creatures like ants to the ultimate human being, communication is common. We have been communicating from birth to death. In all our institutions- family, society, schools, hospitals, temples, churches, military or business organizations communication is essential. In fact we cannot imagine any activity without communication. But in reality, success stories of communication are very less when compared to failures. That makes the subject complex and hence an in depth study is needed.

7.1.1 CONCEPT OF COMMUNICATION

The word "communication" is derived from the Latin word ***'communis'*** which means commonness. It creates a common ground of understanding. In other words, it is the transmission and interacting of facts, ideas, opinions, feelings or attitudes. Communication involves the creation of meaning in the listener, the transfer of information and thousands of potential stimuli.

There is no mutual understanding without communication; mutual understanding is the core of human relations. In nature man alone has the power to communicate. There are different communication modes like expressions in words, sight, sound, touch, smell and taste etc., Gestures and movements are called body language. Even silence is a mode of communication in some contexts. Communication is the story of man and his efforts to communicate effectively. Civilization and culture progress to the extent communication develops.

Definition:

"Communication is an exchange of facts, ideas, opinions, or emotions by two or more persons. Communication is also defined as interaction by words, letters, symbols, or messages and as a way that one organization member shares meaning and understanding with another."

– *Newman and summer*

"Communication is the sum of all the things one person does when he wants to create understanding in the mind of another. It involves a systematic and continuous process of telling, listening and understanding."

– *Allen Louis A.*

"Communication is the process of passing information and understanding from one person to another. It is the process of imparting ideas and making oneself understood by other."

–*Theo Haiemann*

"In exhaustive theory of organization, communication would occupy a central place because the structure, extensiveness, and scope of organizations are almost entirely determined by communication techniques."

– *Chester Barnard*

Scope of Communication

The broad policies and objectives flow downward from top management to a lower level. Both written and oral or verbal media can be used to transmit messages. Written media consists of instructions, orders, letters, memo's, journals, posters, bulletins, boards, information racks, handbooks, manuals, annual reports, union publications, etc. Verbal media may consists of face-to-face conversation, lectures, conferences, meetings, interviews, counseling, public address system, telephone etc. Sophisticated communication technologies like SMS, E-mail, Internet etc., have emerged.

7.1.2 NATURE OF COMMUNICATION

The purpose of communication is to make others to understand and act accordingly. Communication is effective when the message is shared and understood with one another. There can be no communication, if the information is not understood by the receiver in the same sense as it was intended to be by the communicator.

Communication is an Art and a Science:

It is obvious that communication contains both the elements those of a science and those of an art. Then, communication is both art and science. The science of communication provides a body of principles which can guide the managers to find a solution to specific problems and objectives evaluation of results. Communication is a creative art and few people are masters at it. It develops new situations, new designs and new systems needed for further improvement.

Communication is a Social Process:

Communication process involves the sender of the message and the receiver of the message. In between, encoding and decoding of symbols takes place; reception, listening and knowledge represent the reception stage. Communication is also a special process because there is interpersonal communication process in which two or more people are involved. In case of a written communication, the sender is a writer and receiver is a reader. In case of oral communication the speaker transmits the message and the receiver is the listener. In the case of visual communication, the function of the receiver is observation.

Communication as a social process affects the entire society. It is a tool that enables everyone in the society to satisfy his basic needs and desires and to get along with other people.

Communication is a Human Process:

The art of getting things done through and with the people in a formally organized group cannot be achieved without a proper communication network. The job of management is to disseminate as much detailed information by various networks and media so as to enable the management groups to understand objectives, policies, procedures and rules to accomplish organizational objectives. On the other hand, it is the function of the management together detailed information from appropriate channels which helps managers in making sound decisions and in turn to communicate.

Communication is a Universal Process:

The principles and techniques of communication are universal in application but not necessarily and exclusively applicable to only business. They are applicable to social, religious, charitable, chairman, managing director, heads of various functional areas and subordinates have successfully, to use the same communication skills and principles in their inter-personal group and organizational situations.

7.1.3 THE PROCESS OF COMMUNICATION

Communication is a process of exchange of ideas, facts, opinions, and manner by which the receiver of the message shares meaning and understanding with another. It is the whole sequence of transmission and interchange of facts, ideas, feelings etc.

Communication is a process that uses a set of media to transmit ideas, facts and feelings from one person to another. Media challenge the communicator to select them with an awareness of their purpose to the listener or reader. So, a good communicator must understand the receiving and understanding capabilities of the recipient not only of the transmitting message but also their effect.

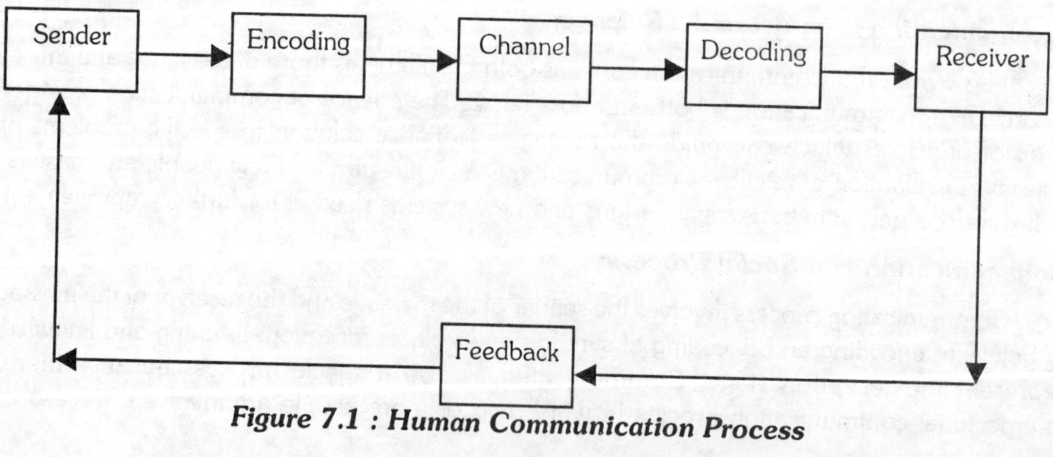

Figure 7.1 : Human Communication Process

Elements of Communication Process:

According to David K. Berlo, the whole sequence of communication (called communicating process) involves the following steps.

- Ideation
- Encoding
- Transmission
- Receiving
- Sender
- Decoding
- Acting

Message:

It is a piece of information, spoken or written, to be passed from one person to another. It is the subject matter of communication. It may involve any fact, idea, opinion, figure, attitude, or course of action, including information. It exists in the mind of the communicator.

Transmitter:

He is the sender of message or communicator or spreader, a person who transmits the message. In the case of mechanical devices used for communication, para transmitter is an operator that transmits message. The person who conveys the message is known as the communicator or sender.

Encoding:

Encoding process translates ideas, facts, feelings, opinions into symbols, signs, words, actions, pictures and audio visuals etc.

Communication channel:

Communication channel means the medium or media through which the message passes. The words, symbols or signs selected should be transmitted to the receiver or listener through certain channel or medium. There are various forms of written media like letters, reports, manuals, circulars, notes, questionnaires etc. The forms of oral media include face to face conversation, Dictaphone, telephone, meeting, conferences, internet chatting, video-conferencing etc.

Receiver:

Receiver is the person to whom the message is meant for by the sender. A person who receives the message is called receiver. It is the receiver who receives and tries to interpret, perceive, understand and act upon the message.

Decoding:

Decoding is the process of translation of an encoded message into ordinary understandable language. Receiver converts the symbols, words or signs received from the sender to get the meaning of the massage.

Feedback:

Communication is an exchange process. For exchange to be complete the information must go back to communicator, so that he can know the reaction of the receiver. Feedback enables the communicator to carry out corrections or amendments or change the message to achieve the objective of communication. Communication is a mechanical system consisting of following elements. They are:

1. Information – source (sender)
2. Transmitter – to convert a message into transmittable sign.
3. A channel – vehicle to communicate like a cell phone
4. A receiver – who reconstructs the message to whom it is intended.
5. The message – data-words or signs etc.,
6. Noise – disturbance either at the sender or receiver or channels technical competency

New skills for resolving interpersonal conflicts.

a) Increased productivity even under adverse conditions.
b) Improved interviewing and consulting techniques.
c) The ability to create an organizational climate of support and trust.
d) The flexibility to understand co-workers.
e) Active, accurate listening habits.
f) The enthusiasm to create team spirit, company pride and goal congruence.
g) Enhanced powers of interpersonal motivation.

Essentials of Good Communication

i. Clarity
ii. Information.
iii. Completeness.
iv. Emphasis on attention.
v. Consistency.
vi. Integration.
vii. Use of informal organization.
viii. Two way communication.
ix. To know the receiver.
x. Time.

xi. Simplicity

xii. Communication network

xiii. Use of media

xiv. Feedback

Ten Commandments of Good Communication:

1. Clarity of ideas before communication.
2. Examine the true purposes of communication.
3. Take the entire environment, physical and human into consideration
4. When valuable, obtain advice from others in planning communiqués
5. Beware of the overtones as well as the basic content of the message.
6. When possible, convey useful information
7. Follow up on communication
8. Communicate with the future as well as the present in mind
9. Support words with deeds
10. Be a good listener

7.1.4 CHARACTERISTIC FEATURES OF COMMUNICATION

1. Credibility.
2. Context.
3. Content.
4. Clarity.
5. Continuity
6. Channels.
7. Concise
8. Capability
9. Crispness
10. Consistency.

Objectives of Communication

1. Human relations.
2. Empathy.
3. Persuasion.
4. Dialogue.

5. Information.
6. Motivation.
7. Understanding
8. Problem solving
9. Grievance redressal.
10. Fostering attitude.

Purpose of communication (Functions)

1. Integration function.
2. Informing function.
3. Evaluation.
4. Directive function.
5. Influencing function..
6. Incidental function.
7. Teaching function.
8. Image projection function.
9. Orientation function.
10. Interview function.

Reasons for growing importance of Communication:

- Large – size organizations
- Technological advancements
- Growth of trade union activities
- Emphasis on human relations
- Importance of public relations.

Advantages of Communication to Management:

1. Co-ordination.
2. Smooth working.
3. Effective decision making.
4. Managerial efficiency.
5. Co-operation.
6. Effective leadership.
7. Job satisfaction.

8. Increases productivity.
9. Morale building.
10. Achieving goals of the organization.

7.1.5 CLASSIFICATION OF COMMUNICATION

Communication is broadly classified into following groups.

a) Interpersonal communication.
b) Intrapersonal communication.
c) Group communication.
d) Small group communication.
e) Large group communication.
f) Organizational communication.
g) Informal communication.
h) Mass communication.

Interpersonal Communication

Exchange of information between two persons is called "interpersonal communication." Dialogue is a powerful medium of communication. Interaction with people gives rise to interpersonal communication. This is one of the earliest media of exchange of information between two persons which normally takes the form of oral and face-to-face communication. It is quite different from other media, like written, mass or group communication.

Communication is a transaction process where people relate meanings, select arbitrary symbols and exchange of symbols. Transactions have an important role in the interpersonal communication. This helps to improve interpersonal skills in communication with other people in one or another communication. Two people contact simultaneously and share the sentiments, ideas and beliefs etc., and develop expectations of each other's behavior. It helps in building relationship which may be positive or negative.

Intrapersonal Communication

Intrapersonal communication implies communication within the self or inside one's self. An individual's communication depends upon his knowledge, experiences, beliefs, confidence level, fears, dilemmas etc. The honesty in communication depends upon the mutual trust and confidence developed with the other person. The quality of interpersonal communication is affected by these intrapersonal factors.

Communication Noise

Shannon identified that noise affects the quality of communication. Noise may be the result of technical aspects like channel competency or capacity or psychological aspects present in the sender or receiver like superiority or inferiority complex or mistrust against the other etc.,

In his communication model, he opined that noise may start right from the sender because of the failure of encoding process. As a result it sends wrong signals in the transmission of the message to the receiver. Already some noise may exist with the receiver in the form of fears, mistrust, confusion and poor knowledge about the encoded message. The final fatal result is that the receiver of the communication fails to decode.

Filtering and Distortion of Message

Filtering with reference to communication refers to a part of interpretation process of communication. When a message is transmitted from one person to the other this problem occurs. The sender while encoding the message may commit mistakes by choosing inappropriate words or poor symbols which may not convey the real meaning intended but at the same time may give totally a distorted version. At the receiver's end because of poor knowledge or psychological predisposition, the message gets filtered to suit to his ego needs. The ultimate result is failure to understand the communication in the true spirit. Soon after receiving the message, the receiver has to interpret the impulse or idea of the sender. The accurate interpretation will depend upon the past knowledge, experience, beliefs, attitudes, etc.

It is the interpretation process; a person may filter some bits of information. When the idea pass through the mind, some pieces of information are ignored or filtered out and others are added. In the words of Leland Brown, certain beliefs, likes and dislikes, have programmed certain behavior pattern that serves as the basis for individual's *Cognitive structure, which* refers to a set of values, attitudes, knowledge and expectations. That in turn causes rejection or acceptance of the information.

Honesty in Communication

Honest communication involves a sense of obligation to one's self, to other people, and to the Society.

One of the noblest words among the social virtues is "honesty". It is an essential quality in binding people together in the family, in community, and in society. All civilizations gave high value and esteem for honest and sincere communicators.

Persuasion:

Persuasive communication plays a vital role in getting the things done through others. Instead of forcing a person to do the work without preparing him mentally, creates negativeness and leads to dissatisfaction. A superior by proper counseling and persuasion of his subordinates can achieve wonderful results.

Dialogue:

It is sharing: It is the participation of people in the search for common values and ideas as they deal with problems of joint concern. Dialogue is conversation between two or more persons with a view to reaching an amicable agreement. It is for sharing the information to have a clear understanding. This helps in forming common ideas, values and beliefs for creation of common work culture.

7.1.6 BUSINESS COMMUNICATION:

Communication is used to promote a product, service, or organization; relay information within the business; or deal with legal and similar issues. It is also a means of relaying between a supply chain, for example the consumer and manufacturer.

Business Communication is known simply as "communications". It encompasses a variety of topics, including marketing, branding, customer relations, consumer behavior, advertising, public relations, corporate communication, community engagement, research & measurement, reputation management, interpersonal communication, employee engagement, online communication, and event management. It is closely related to the fields of professional communication and technical communication.

In business, the term communications encompasses various channels of communication, including the Internet, Print (Publications), Radio, Television, Outdoor, and Word of mouth.

Business Communication can also refer to internal communication. A communications director will typically manage internal communication and craft messages sent to employees. It is vital that internal communications are managed properly because a poorly crafted or managed message may create problems of misunderstanding. There are several methods of business communications including:

- Web-based communication - for better and improved communication, anytime anywhere
- Video conferencing which allow people in different locations to hold interactive meetings;
- E-mails, which provide an instantaneous medium of written communication worldwide;
- Reports - important in documenting the activities of any department;
- Presentations - very popular method of communication in all types of organizations, usually involving audiovisual material, like copies of reports, or material prepared in Microsoft PowerPoint or Adobe Flash;
- Telephoned meetings, which allow for long distance speech;
- Forum boards, which allow people to instantly post information at a centralized location; and
- Face-to-face meetings, which are personal and should be succeeded by a written follow-up.

Business communication is somewhat different and unique from other types of communication since the purpose of business is to make money. Thus, to develop profitability, the communicator should develop good communication skills. Knowing the importance of communication, many organizations train their employees in communication techniques.

7.1.7 TYPES OF BUSINESS COMMUNICATION

Knowing the different types of business communication is important for using the right type at the right moment. The following are the different types of business communication.

- ***Verbal communication:*** Verbal communication is a type of communication that involves use of words for communicating.
- ***Non-verbal communication:*** Non-verbal communication is a mode of communication which uses body language and various other physical gestures as a means for communicating.
- ***Written communication:*** Written communication is a type that only includes written forms for communicating.
- ***Employment communication:*** Employment communication is a mode of communication that is particularly used for accepting the applicants for a job.
- ***Electronic communication:*** Electronic communication is the modern way of communication that includes electronics and latest technology for communicating such as teleconferencing e-mail etc.,

Steps for implementing self-confidence in common problems of communication:

1) Prepare the message carefully.
2) Practice aloud, rehearse more times and imagine audience.
3) Hear your own voice by tape recorder.
4) Use appropriate dress for the occasion.
5) Think about your audience and their level of understanding.
6) Begin slowly, stage fright disappears after starting.
7) Speak louder than ordinarily.
8) Speak as often as you can. The more the practice, earlier it is to speak with confidence.

A few tips:

i. Avoid using slang words
ii. Use "I" statements, not "You" statements
iii. Listen as much, if not more, than you speak
iv. Respect silence in a conversation
v. Do not judge someone based on accent
vi. Do not interrupt or try to finish someone's ideas

7.2 REPORT WRITING

For the higher level management positions in govt., and non-govt., organizations report-writing is an essential and very important task. Before taking a final decision on any big project or to introduce a change in the existing situation, then the top management requires detailed information to study the repercussions of such a decision. In one way report-writing is a test to identify the intelligence and potentiality of a manager. Report-writing requires a lot of background work of studying, writing, collecting facts and figures and doing research to analyze the problem or problems associated with the report. Writing the report in a readable way is an art and also a science which only professional managers can handle.

7.2.1 MEANING AND DEFINITION

"Report is a textual work usually of writing, speech, television, or film made with the specific intention of relaying information or recounting certain events in a widely presentable form".

Report means a statement or description of what has been said, seen, done etc. It is a treatise containing facts, figures, information, analysis, opinions, suggestions, recommendations, maps, graphs, charts, pictures, statistical tables, specially complied for a particular purpose.

C. A. Brown defines a report as a communication from someone, who has to inform someone who wants to use that information. It describes the events or individuals to someone who requires it.

Written reports are documents which present focused, salient content to a specific audience. Reports are often used to display the result of an experiment, investigation, or inquiry. The audience may be public or private, an individual or the public in general. Reports are used in government, business, education, science, and other fields.

Reports are written to be read, this may be by one person or an entire audience. Keep this in mind as with most all forms of writing you have an intended target audience. A report contains research specific to your questions as well as a hypothesis to build. Remember that organization of the report with clear and precise structure is mandatory. Coming off topic or not properly combining the parts of the report will not only throw the reader off the topic but also the purpose of writing it will be defeated. Stay rhetorical, remain on key and, keep to your outline and research in writing your report.

7.2.2 FORMAT FOR PRESENTING REPORTS

Reports should contain graphics, images, voice, or specialized vocabulary in order to persuade that specific audience to undertake an action. One of the most common formats for presenting reports is ***IMRAD***:

i. ***I***ntroduction,

ii. ***M***ethods,

iii. ***R***esults and

iv. ***D***iscussion.

Though this structure is generally followed as a standard format, reports may vary on the basis of contents. Reports may have alternative patterns like the problem-solution format etc.,

Additional elements used for report writing:

i. Headings,

ii. Charts,

iii. Tables,

iv. Figures,

v. Pictures,

vi. Abstracts,

vii. Summaries,

viii. Appendices,

ix. Footnotes,

x. Hyperlinks, and

xi. References.

7.2.3 TYPES OF REPORTS

The following are the various reports commonly observed:

i. Scientific Reports,

ii. Recommendation Reports,

iii. White Papers,

iv. Annual Reports,

v. Auditor's Reports,

vi. Workplace Reports,

vii. Census Reports,

viii. Trip Reports,

ix. Progress Reports,

x. Investigative Reports,

xi. Budget Reports,

xii. Policy Reports,

xiii. Demographic Reports,

xiv. Credit Reports,

xv. Appraisal Reports,

xvi. Inspection Reports,

xvii. Military reports etc.,

7.2.4 CLASSIFICATION OF REPORTS:

I. On the basis of usage by parties:

1) External reports:

These reports are prepared for the use of external parties.

2) Internal reports:

Reports prepared for the use of internal parties at various levels of management.

II. On the basis of importance:

1) Routine reports:

It involves continuous comparison of actual with standards, to know the deviations and to take remedial measures.

2) Specials reports:

Special reports are prepared and supplied for special purposes. Certain long-term decisions like expansion, modernization, change in method of production, or make decision to replace labor by machine etc.

III. Reports to different levels of management:

1) Reports to top management:

These should provide detailed data and other information for planning and formulation of basic policies.

2) Reports to middle / functional management:

The middle level management is concerned with the task of implementation of basic goals and objectives formulated by the top management and hence the reports contain the specific information required at that functional level viz., production, marketing, finance, HR etc.,

The following are various reports prepared at respective functional levels for usage.

A. Production reports:

i. Installed capacity.

ii. Idle capacity.

iii. Capacity utilization.

iv. Actual production.

v. Standard production.

vi. Manpower availability.

vii. Manpower utilization.

viii. Number of hours worked.

ix. Output.

x. Cost of production.

xi. Scrap.

xii. Quality aspects.

B. Sales reports:

a. Actual sales.

b. Budgeted sales.

c. Area-wise and product-wise sales figures and analysis.

d. Expected sales.

e. Analysis of difference between actual and expected.

f. Comparison of sales with the corresponding earlier periods.

g. Number, value and quality or orders booked.

C. Purchase reports:

Reporting on purchases involves periodical reporting on transactions that form part of quality, cost of production and blocking of capital.

D. Financial reports:

Interest, taxation sources of finance, cost of capital and number of other items which do not find a place under any other reports.

3) On the basis of functions:

(a) Operation reports

(b) Financial reports

4) Corporate reports:

1) Statuary reports: Reports which are required to prepare under law are called statuary reports.

2) Board of Directors Report: Annual reports of the directors attached to every balance sheet is called Directors report.

3) Auditors Reports: The auditor's report should be attached to the balance sheet, including the auditor's separate, special and supplementary.

4) Non statuary reports: Reports which are not required to prepare under law are known as Non statuary report.

IV. Other reports:

1) Review reports: The management reports must have utility and use for decision making and policy formulation of plans.

2) Cost audit report: It contains the matter about security of cost records.

3) Interim reports: A committee or a commission may submit an interim at any time before submission of final report.

4) Oral report: Presentation of written matter before a group.

7.2.5 PATTERNS OF REPORT

1) Letter form:

This type of report is written in letter form. It is written in the first person, i.e., I believe….., I am personally of the opinion……, I suggest……. etc.

2) Letter-text combination form:

Both letter structure and text forms are combined in this type.

3) Memorandum form:

It avoids all formalities to be followed for the purpose of preparation and presentation of report as required in case of letter form.

Parts of Report:

Generally, a typical formal report usually incorporates the following parts:

A) Preliminary part:

1) Cover.
2) Title.
3) Authorization.
4) Covering Letter
5) Acceptance of message.
6) Preface
7) Acknowledgements.
8) Content page.
9) Lists of tables and figures.
10) List of abbreviations.

B) Body of the report:

1) Abstract.
2) Introduction.
3) Body of the report.
4) Discussion.
5) Headings and subheadings.
6) Findings.
7) Recommendations.
8) Conclusion.

C) Supplementary part:

1) Bibliography.
2) Appendix.
3) Glossary.

Parts of a Research Report:

1) Statement of problem:
2) Objectives for writing the report
3) Review of literature
4) Research methodology
5) Universe of study.
6) Sampling frame.
7) Sampling procedure.
8) Units of observation and sampling size.
9) Data collection
   I. Primary data
   II. Secondary data
10) Data processing
11) Data Analysis
12) Findings
13) Suggestions
14) Conclusion

7.2.6 TECHNIQUES OF WRITING REPORT

1) Comprehend what you are required to report.
2) Ascertain all possible sources of information.
3) Decide upon what sources to draw.
4) Gather information and explanations.
5) Sift the evidence.
6) Synthesis the acceptable evidence.
7) Abstract what is to the point and discard the rest.
8) Throw what is left into report form.

9) Summarize the findings

10) Finalize the report.

7.2.7 ESSENTIALS OF GOOD REPORT WRITING

1) Right selection of title.
2) Clarity of ideas
3) Completeness of the data.
4) Conciseness in presentation
5) Simplicity of language
6) Understandable language.
7) Courtesy in reporting objectively
8) Accuracy of figures and facts
9) Brevity in the analysis part
10) Coherence of the events
11) Honesty in writing
12) Sequence.
13) Emphasis on most important points
14) Cost minimization in completing the report
15) Timely presentation.
16) Adaptability.
17) Attractiveness.
18) Comparability

7.3 CROSS CULTURAL COMMUNICATION

7.3.1 CONCEPT OF CULTURE:

Common values and perspectives shared by people who are conditioned by similar education and life experience.

Characteristics of culture:

1. Culture is not inherent, but learned
2. Cultures are rooted in deep seated beliefs
3. Culture is the basis for self-identity and community
4. Cultures are dynamic

Cross-Culture:

Each person is an individual with their own ways of doing things, their own style of speech and their own way of communicating. However, there are some common ways in which different cultures communicate. Depending on where you were raised, who taught you to communicate, and whether the language you are trying to use is your native language, your communication style develops in a unique way. From situation to situation, this style may work well, or it might not. Sometimes in communication, you may get frustrated with your co-communicator for differences in style. But before you get frustrated, remember that difference is not necessarily a bad thing. It might take a little extra effort, but you can still be successful in communication and by making that extra effort, you might just learn and gain a lot.

Some Common Differences to Consider in Cross-Cultural Communication:

1. Frequency of eye contact
2. Assertiveness
3. Use of hands while talking
4. Physical distance between communicators
5. Speed of speech
6. Use of first names vs. titles
7. Volume of speech
8. Use of facial expressions

Always Remember:

Culture is not the same as race, ethnicity, or country of origin. Although all of these things contribute to culture, many other things do as well. You may have differences in communication style with someone who looks just like you and may have the same style as someone who looks much different. The bottom line is: don't assume and remember that everyone is an individual. When communicating with someone whose first language is different than your own, you may want to remember the following ideas. Speaking louder or elongating words is not usually helpful. Instead, speak a little slowly, and ask questions to clarify the meaning of what they are saying. If they are having difficulty in understanding you, try to rephrase your point. Most importantly, be patient and don't be afraid to ask for their patience too. By working together, you will be able to communicate with each other well.

All international business activity involves communication. Within the international and global business environment, activities such as exchanging information and ideas, decision making, negotiating, motivating, and leading are all based on the ability of managers from one culture to communicate successfully with managers and employees from other cultures. Achieving effective communication is a challenge to managers worldwide today.

Cross-Cultural Communication

Cross-cultural communication occurs when a person from one culture sends a message to a person from another culture. Cross-cultural miscommunication occurs when the person from the second culture does not receive the sender's intended message. The greater the differences between the sender's and the receiver's culture, the greater is the chance for cross-cultural miscommunication.

Communication does not necessarily result in understanding. Cross-cultural communication continually involves misunderstanding caused by misperception, misinterpretation, and misevaluation. When the sender of a message comes from one culture and the receiver from another, the chances of accurately transmitting a message are low. Foreigners see, interpret, and evaluate things differently, and consequently act upon them differently. In approaching cross-cultural situations, one should therefore becareful till similarity in between the two parties takes place. It is also important to recognize that all behavior makes sense through the eyes of the person behaving and that logic and rationale are culturally relative. In cross-cultural situations, labeling behavior as bizarre is quite possible. Communicating across 'cultural barriers' usually reflects culturally based misperception, misinterpretation, and misevaluation.

7.3.2 CROSS-CULTURAL MISPERCEPTION

Do the Americans and the Chinese see the world in the same way? No two national groups see the world in exactly the same way. Perception is the process by which each individual selects, organizes, and evaluates stimuli from the external environment to provide meaningful experiences for one's self.

Perceptual patterns are neither innate nor absolute. They are selective, learned, culturally determined, consistent, and inaccurate.

- Perception is selective. At any one time there are too many stimuli in the environment for us to observe. Therefore, we screen out most of what we see, hear, taste, and feel. We screen out the overload and allow only selected information through our perceptual screen to our conscious mind.
- Perceptual patterns are learned. We are not born seeing the world in one particular way. Our experience teaches us to perceive the world in certain ways.
- Perception is culturally determined. We learn to see the world in a certain way based on our cultural background.
- Perception tends to remain constant. Once we see something in a particular way, we continue to see it that way.
- We therefore see things that do not exist, and do not see things that do exist. Our interests, values, and culture act as filters and lead us to distort, block, and even create what we choose to see and hear. We perceive what we expect to perceive. We perceive things according to what we have been trained to see, according to our cultural map.

7.3.3 CROSS-CULTURAL MISINTERPRETATION

Interpretation occurs when an individual gives meaning to observations and their relationships. It is the process of making sense out of perceptions. Interpretation organizes our experience to guide our behavior. Based on our experience, we make assumptions about our perceptions so we will not have to rediscover meanings each time we encounter similar situations.

For example, we make assumptions about how doors work, based on our experience of entering and leaving rooms; thus we do not have to relearn each time we have to open a door.

Similarly, when we smell smoke, we generally assume there is a fire. Our consistent patterns of interpretation help us to act appropriately and quickly.

Categories

Since we are constantly bombarded with more stimuli than we can absorb and more perceptions than we can keep distinct, we only perceive those images that may be meaningful. We group perceived images into familiar categories that help to simplify our environment, become the basis for our interpretations, and allow us to function in the complex world.

Stereotypes

Stereotyping involves a form of categorization that organizes our experience and guides our behavior toward ethnic and national groups. Stereotypes never describe the individual behavior but the common behavior of a group. Stereotypes help in understanding the groups and act appropriately in new situations.

Sources of Misinterpretation

Misinterpretation can be caused by inaccurate perceptions of a person or situation that arise when what actually exists is not seen. It can be caused by an inaccurate interpretation of what is seen; that is, by using one's meanings to make sense out of reality. Sources of cross-cultural misinterpretation include subconscious cultural "blinders," a lack of cultural self-awareness, projected similarity, and parochialism.

Subconscious Cultural Blunders

Most of the interpretations go on at a subconscious level. Hence, we lack awareness of the assumptions we make and their cultural basis. Our home culture never forces us to examine our assumptions or the extent to which they are culturally relevant.

Lack of Cultural Self-Awareness

Although we think that the major obstacle in international business is in understanding the foreigner, the greater difficulty involves in understanding one's own culture and in conditioning the behavior to it.

Edward Hall, a famous anthropologist remarked that we are generally least aware of our own cultural characteristics and are quite surprised when we hear foreigners' descriptions of us. For example, many Americans are surprised to discover that they are seen by foreigners as hurried, overly law-abiding, very hard working, extremely explicit, and overly inquisitive.

7.3.4 THE REALITIES OF COMMUNICATION ACROSS CULTURES

Different words may mean different things to different people. In addition to different vocabularies, cross-cultural communication is made difficult by the fact that in different languages even the same word can mean different things.

Communication problem will arise because of alien language and unfamiliar body gestures. In international perspective, two issues namely, language and coordination are relevant.

Some words are understood differently in different countries. General Motors produced a car called the Nova, which did not sell well in Italy where "No va" means "does not go". In China, Coco-Cola means "bite the head of a dead tadpole". Even different colours signify different sentiments in different cultures.

Communication varies across cultures. Body language, for example, can convey quite a different message in one culture than in another. Thus, managers should be forewarned that they cannot take everything for granted while dealing with people from another culture. They must acquire familiarity with verbal and nonverbal languages of that culture.

Communication across countries has another dimension namely, the need for time coordination. For example, when an Indian executive talks to his or her counterpart in USA, he must coordinate with a time difference of several hours depending upon the region and location of that place.

Studies suggest that even when both persons in an international transaction know each other's language, communication may still suffer. In addition to the most basic verbal communication skills, non-verbal communication may create serious misunderstandings. Even though we share many values, beliefs and attitudes, we misinterpret and misunderstand each other. This is so even when we are dealing with our own people. The problem simply becomes accentuated when we deal with persons of foreign origin.

7.3.5 EFFECTS OF CROSS-CULTURAL COMMUNICATION

Cross-cultural communication endeavors to bring together such relatively unrelated areas as cultural anthropology and established areas of communication. Its core is to establish and understand how people from different cultures communicate with each other and provide with some guidelines for better communication in between two cultures.

Cross-cultural communication is a combination of many other fields. These fields include anthropology, cultural studies, psychology and communication. The field has also moved both toward the treatment of interethnic relations, and toward the study of communication strategies used by co-cultural populations.

The study of languages other than one's own can not only help us to understand what we as human beings have in common, but also assist us in understanding the diversity which underlies not only our languages, but also our ways of constructing and organizing knowledge, and the many different realities in which we all live and interact. Such understanding has profound implications with respect to developing a critical awareness of social relationships. Then only globalizing business becomes a reality.

It is imperative that the speaker understands the grammar of a language, as well as how elements of language are socially situated in order to reach communicative competence. Human experience is culturally relevant, so elements of language are also culturally relevant.

7.3.6 PROBLEMS IN CROSS CULTURAL COMMUNICATION

The key to effective cross-cultural communication is knowledge. First, it is essential that people understand the potential problems of cross-cultural communication, and make a conscious effort to overcome these problems.

Secondly, it is important to assume that one's efforts will not always be successful, and adjust one's behavior appropriately.

One should be patient and forgiving, rather than hostile and aggressive, if problems develop. One should respond slowly and carefully in cross-cultural exchanges, not jumping to the conclusions.

Active listening is essential to avoid misunderstanding. If words are used differently between languages or cultural groups, learning the nuances of that language is essential.

Often, intermediaries who are familiar with both cultures can be helpful in cross-cultural communication situations. They can translate both the languages and create awareness for better understanding. A mediator or intermediary can explain the problems and make appropriate procedural adjustments.

Cross-cultural communication limits our perceptions, our interpretations, and our evaluations. Cross-cultural perspectives tend to render everything relative and slightly uncertain. Entering a foreign culture without any idea on it creates many problems. Hence, a study and training to the employees who work with other cultures help the organization bailout itself from cross cultural barriers.

7.4 PRESENTATION SKILLS

7.4.1 CONCEPT

Presentation is the practice of showing and explaining the content of a topic to an audience or learner. Presentations come in nearly as many forms as there are life situations. In the business world, there are sales presentations, informational and motivational presentations, first encounters, interviews, briefings, status reports, image-building, and of course, the inevitable training sessions.

Presentation skills are the essential techniques useful for presenting an idea or set of ideas to another. Wikipedia defines it as: "the process of showing and explaining the content of a topic to an audience." It goes on to say that normally these presentations are accompanied by a visual aid such as a power point, charts, hand-outs, etc.

Presentation skills are imparted through basic training for any manager or any trainee executive. They are critically important and cannot be passed over.

There are many techniques on how to present something effectively. Many books have been written and lectures have been given on the same. Presentation skills can be gotten by just a little effort and conditioning yourself to step out of your 'safe, normal bounds' and achieve the public speaker role.

It may be difficult in the case of shy people. But People like Abraham Lincoln and George Bernard Shaw struggled in the beginning to speak but later on became excellent orators. This became possible because of the regular positive instruction given to their mind.

Although individuals most often think of presentations in a business meeting context, there are countless occasions when that is not the case. For example, a non profit organization presents the need for a capital fund-raising campaign to benefit the victims of a recent tragedy; a school district superintendent presents a program to parents about the introduction of foreign-language instruction in the elementary schools; an artist demonstrates decorative painting techniques to a group of interior designers; a horticulturist shows garden club members or homeowners how they might use native plants in the suburban landscape; a police officer addresses a neighborhood association about initiating a safety program.

Presentations can also be categorized as vocational and non- vocational. In addition, they are expository or persuasive. And they can be impromptu, extemporaneous, written, or memorized. When looking at presentations in the broadest terms, it's more important to focus on their purpose. There are three basic purposes for giving oral presentations:

1. To inform
2. To persuade
3. To build goodwill

7.4.2 STRUCTURING THE PRESENTATION

Structure is important because a well organized presentation creates a positive impression among the audience. The presentation gains the audience's trust and they will be more likely to listen to you. A structure provides a logical flow so that you can provide the information that the audience needs to follow your presentation. The structure will help you become more comfortable following this flow. There is a natural structure to presenting and the following structure formalizes this process.

- ***Purpose:*** To determine your purpose ask "What are the main points I want my audience to take away from my presentation"? This provides focus for you and the audience is clear on what they will gain listening to your presentation.
- ***Audience pre-assessment***: It is important to identify the characteristics, knowledge and needs of your audience so that you are delivering the 'right' presentation to the 'right' audience. Know who your audience is, what they want to know and what their background is. This step is done before the presentation or during the course of presentation.
- ***Opening your Presentation/Bridge:*** This is also known as the hook. It is designed to grab the audience's attention and provide them with a reason to be interested in the presentation.
- ***Body of Presentation:*** This is the major portion of the presentation. It is necessary that it connects directly to your purpose or bridge. Cover enough points to achieve your purpose and be sure to support your points clearly and concisely.
- ***Closing your Presentation:*** This is the final impression that you will leave with your audience. Make sure it is a strong one. Connect back to your purpose and let them know where you have been. Leave your audience with a clear understanding of your points.

7.4.3 ORAL PRESENTATION SKILLS

1. PREPARATION AND PLANNING

1.1 Essential Preparation And Planning

CHECKLIST

This is a checklist of the essential elements to consider in preparing and planning an oral presentation.

QUESTIONS TO ASK YOURSELF

1. What is the aim?
   - to buy my product
   - to adopt my recommendations
   - to join the club
   - to give me a job
2. What is my title?
   - The new Nokia 2001
   - How to reduce production costs
   - The INT Chess Club
3. Who am I speaking to?
   - What are the benefits to the audience of my product/report/speech?
   - Are these people the decision makers?
   - What do they know of the subject?
   - How does this change my approach?
   - What sort of questions will they ask me? What are the answers?
   - What aspects will they be interested in?
4. What are the main points I want to make? 1, 2, 3; first, second, third; point a, point b, point c.
5. What do I want the audience to do after listening to my presentation? We must invite them:
   - to buy my product
   - to accept my findings
   - to join the club
   - to give me a job

1.2 Other questions concerning physical aspects.

- Who is the audience?
- How many people will there be in the audience?
- Check beforehand, if you can, the place where you are going to make your presentation.
- Where will it take place? How big is the room?
- What equipment is there in the room? What equipment do I need?
- Does the equipment work?
- Are you going to need a black or whiteboard?
- Have you got chalk and / or a felt tip pen?
- Do you need an overhead projector or a screen?
- Are they in place? Is there a podium? Where are you going to put your notes / papers /transparencies?
- Do you need an adapter or extension lead?
- Can the information be seen?
- Can you present the information and not get in the way?
- Do you need a pointer?
- Will you need to dim the lights or draw the curtains?
- Are you going to need handouts or any other documents? How many? Do they present a good image of you and your company?

When?

What time of day is it? What day is it? Will the audience be more or less receptive when listening?

How long?

In relation to what the audience knows or time constraints, what can I eliminate if necessary?

Other

Appropriately? Shoes polished? Are my hands and fingernails clean?

2. STRUCTURE OF AN ORAL PRESENTATION

A good oral presentation is well structured; this makes it easier for the listener to follow.

Basically there are three parts to a typical presentation: the beginning, the middle and the end (or introduction, body and conclusion). We are going to look at each part in turn and present the language needed to express both the structure and the content.

2.1 THE BEGINNING OR THE INTRODUCTION

The beginning of a presentation is the most important part. It is when you establish a rapport with the audience and when you have its attention.

2.1. A. Get the audience's attention and signal the beginning.

- Right.
- Well.
- OK.
- Let's begin.
- Good.
- Fine.
- Great.
- Can we start?
- Shall we start?
- Let's get the ball rolling.
- Let's get down to business.

In English-speaking countries it is not uncommon for the speaker to begin with a joke, an anecdote, a statement made to surprise or provoke in order to gain the audience's attention, to make people listen, to feel relaxed and even to introduce the subject. This may or may not be appropriate in your country; you are probably the best judge. Certainly humour is difficult to convey and would not be appropriate in all contexts.

A good technique is to try to get your audience involved in your talk either by asking direct or rhetorical questions. Ask for a show of hands for example, in response to a question or, present information in such a way that the audience can identify with it. You can give an anecdote, unusual or surprising facts, or an illustration from real life could be employed here.

2.1. B. Greet audience.

It is important to greet the audience by saying something like:

- Hello ladies and gentlemen.
- Good morning members of the jury.
- Good afternoon esteemed guests
- Good evening members of the board
- Fellow colleagues Mr. Chairman/Chairwoman
- Thank you for your kind introduction

2.1. C. Introduce yourself - name, position, and company

Do this not only to give important information so people can identify you but also to establish your authority on the subject and to allow the audience to see your point of view on the subject. For example you may be a student, researcher, manager or director of a company

It is a good idea to put your name, company's name, company logo, title and date of the presentation on all the transparencies or handouts.

- Good morning everyone, I'd like to start by introducing myself.
- My name is———
- I am a student at———
- I am a doctoral candidate in———
- I am the manager of———
- I am a researcher from———I've been working on the subject now for X years...
- I've had wide experience in the field of———
- Good morning, my name is ———. I am a student at ——— and I would like to talk to you today about some of my findings in a study I did on——— ——- Sometimes, especially when invited to speak, the host introduces the guest, gives the same information as above and then gives the floor to the guest speaker. In such a situation you need not once again repeat the same. Instead you can directly thank the host for his introduction and start your presentation directly.

2.1. D. Give title and introduce subject

What exactly are you going to speak about? Situate the subject in time and place, in relation to the audience and/or its importance. Give a rough idea or a working definition of the subject. You can choose any of the following expressions to start your presentation.

- I plan to speak about...
- Today I'm going to talk about...
- The subject of my presentation is...
- The theme of my talk is...
- I've been asked to give you an overview of...

Cultural aspects may be important here; scientists want to demonstrate their work and findings while managers and humanities people want to share ideas and reflections with their audience. It may be the result of a desire to persuade and convince. It may be comparison of two or more products, plans or proposals.

Why are you going to speak about it?

- I have chosen to speak about this because...
- I was asked to speak about X because...

Have you set any limits on the scope of your talk? What won't you speak about?

It may be very useful to eliminate certain areas before you start so as to avoid confusion or deviation from your main task. It also protects you from criticism later for not covering certain aspects or issues.

Have you estimated the time it will take? It is useful to give the listeners some idea of how long you will speak so as to maintain their attention better.

- I will not speak about...
- I have limited my speech to
- My talk will last about 15 minutes

Concerning time, professional people are very often pressed for time. The average person's attention span is also very, very short. Conclusion: the shorter the better!

- I will speak for 15 minutes.

You may want to give acknowledgements here too. If you have been sponsored, supported or encouraged by a particular firm, organization, professor, etc. you may want to recognize their contribution. Your research and paper may have been the work of a collaborative effort and you should acknowledge this too giving the names of all the participants.

At some point you should ask a question or somehow try to determine the attitude and knowledge of the audience. How do they feel about the subject? You will then have to modify the contents, as you never know exactly what they expect. Then you can use any one of the expressions given hereunder:

- Have you ever heard of...?
- You may already know...
- I feel sure that some of you...
- Every day you encounter...

To get the audience's attention and perhaps to find out where they are you could introduce the subject by saying:

- Have you ever heard of/seen X?
- You've probably seen countless times...
- You may have wondered...

2.1.E. Give your objectives (purpose, aim, goals)

The main purpose of an informative speech is to have the audience understand and remember a certain amount of information. You should therefore have two purposes: a general purpose and a specific one. The former is to inform: to give an overview, to present, to summarize, to outline; to discuss the current situation or to explain how to do something or how something is done. The latter is what you want the audience to take away with them after listening to you, what you want them to do, what they should remember.

- What I would like to do today is to explain
- To illustrate...
- To give you the essential background information on...
- To outline...
- To have a look at...
- What I want my listeners to get out of my speech is...
- If there is one thing I'd like to get across to you today it is that...

Once you have established your specific objectives you may go on to giving your content.

2.1.F. Announce your outline

You want to keep the outline simple so two or three main points are usually enough. Concerning grammar the headings of the outline should be of the same grammatical form.

- I have divided my presentation into —— parts.
- In the first part I give a few basic definitions.
- In the next part I will explain the pros and cons of the concept
- In part three, I am going to show the solutions to the problems
- In the last part I would like to give a practical example

2.1. G. Questions and comments from the audience.

You should also let the audience know at some point in the introduction when they may ask questions.

- I'd ask you to save your questions for the end.
- There will be plenty of time at the end of my speech for a discussion.
- You may interrupt me at any moment to ask questions or make comments.

Make a transition between the introduction and the body.

You should refer to your transparency or outline.

Now let us turn to point one. Let us now move on to the second part, which is, as I said earlier....

2.2 THE MIDDLE OR THE BODY

2.2. A. Content.

What information should you give in your speech? All your information should support your purpose. In most cases you will have to limit the content, as time is usually precious!

2.2. B. Quantity

How much information should you give? Enough to clearly develop your ideas. Don't forget to illustrate through examples.

2.2. C. Sequencing your ideas.

Here are a few possibilities for organizing your ideas: logical; chronological order; from general to specific; from known to unknown; from accepted to controversial; cause/effect; problem/ solution.

Whatever sequencing you choose, the headings should be clear.

2.2. D. Keeping the audience's attention

The beginning and the end or the first and last parts of a talk are what listeners will remember best. Think of ways you can keep the audience's attention throughout the rest of the speech.

2.2. E. Signposting or signaling where you are

Just as when you are driving along a road that you don't know very well, you depend on signs to guide you, you need to guide the listener by using expressions to tell him/her where you are going. That is to say, first announce what you are going to say. Give an example to lighten the subject. And then say what you want to say. Indicate when you have finished one point and then go on to the next one. It is very useful in oral presentations. Experienced presenters will also clearly pause; change their stance and the pitch of their voice as they move from one part of a presentation to another.

Listing information

Lists are often a necessary evil. Vary your language whenever possible and avoid reading directly.

Linking ideas, sections/making transitions

Indicate the end of one section and the beginning of the next.

- That's all I would like to say about...
- That we've seen... let us turn to...

Does not use, in a first time, at first, at last, firstable.

Outlining options.

If there are alternative ways of looking at a topic or proposal, outline them to show you are familiar with the different ways of dealing with a situation.

- There seem to be two possible ways of dealing with this...
- We've looked at this from the point of view of the manufacturer but what about if we were to...
- A number of options present themselves at this point....

If what you are dealing with demands a comparison of strengths and weaknesses indicate clearly the different aspects and underline the points you feel are important or secondary. According to the demands of the context, you can choose an expression from the following:

What exactly are the benefits?

- On the plus side we can add...
- This is not the only weakness of the plan...
- We cannot ignore the problems that such an action would create...
- We do not need to concern ourselves with…
- Of lesser interest are…

To be clear and concrete. Use examples, rephrasing, summaries etc.:

To give an example:

- Now let's take an example.
- An example of this can be found...
- To illustrate this…
- Let's see this through an example.
- For example,
- For instance,

To rephrase:

- Let me rephrase that,
- In other words
- Another way of saying the same thing is
- That is to say

To summarize:

- To summarize
- To sum up,
- Let me summarize by saying
- So that concludes my overview
- In conclusion
- Briefly said
- In short,
- What I've tried to show in this part...
- To recap what we've seen so far...

To emphasize

- What is very significant is...
- What is important to remember...

- I'd like to emphasize the fact that...
- I'd like to stress the importance of...
- to highlight...
- to underline...
- What I tried to bring out...
- What we need to focus on...

To refer to what you have said previously:

- As I have already said earlier...
- As we saw in part one...
- To repeat what I've said already...

To refer to what you will say:

- We will see this a little later on.
- This will be the subject of part 3.
- We will go into more detail on that later.
- For now, suffice to say...

To refer to what an expert says:

- I quote the words of ...
- In the words of...
- According to...
- Here I'd like to quote...
- As Mr. X says in his book...
- There is a famous quotation that goes...

To refer to common knowledge:

- As you all may well know...
- It is generally accepted that...
- As you are probably aware (of)...

STEPS IN CONCLUDING THE PRESENTATION

The end of a talk should never come as a surprise to an audience; it needs special consideration.

Content

The end or the conclusion of your talk should include four parts:

A brief reminder of what you tried to show in your speech and how you tried to do so, a short conclusion, thanks to the audience for listening and an invitation to ask questions, make comments or open a discussion. At the end you should briefly summarize your speech in a few lines to make sure the audience has retained the main points. Then you should give some kind of conclusion. That is to say you should give a message that logically comes out of the ideas developed in your speech. This could be a commentary, the lessons learned, some recommendations, or the next steps. You could also make a call to action; the audience should have to do something. Thirdly, thank the audience for being there.

Finally, ask for questions and comments or invite a discussion. If you choose the former, you put yourself in a superior position compared to the audience and should be considered as an expert. You will need to be very prepared intellectually and psychologically to transfer control to the audience and be able to answer any questions.

However, in the case of the latter, you put yourself more or less on equal terms with the audience and do not have to be the expert with all the answers! The audience may have some clear ideas or some practical knowledge about the subject themselves! Naturally you need to signpost the end of your talk. This may take the form of a recapitulation of the main points.

- I'd like to summarize/sum up
- At this stage I would like to run through/over the main points...
- So, as we have seen today....
- As I have tried to explain this morning BT finds itself in....

Or there may be recommendations or proposals that you wish to make;

- As a result we suggest that...
- In the light of what we have seen today I suggest that...
- My first proposal is...

Above all when you conclude do not do it abruptly or as if surprised to get to the end of your talk.

- In conclusion I would like to say that...
- My final comments concern...
- I would like to finish by reminding everyone that...
- Do not introduce new information.

You may at this point wish to distribute a vocabulary list or more detailed information that you wish to make available.

- I've prepared a slim folder of the proposals...
- In the sheets that are now being distributed you will find a breakdown of the...

And finally you may well have to deal with questions.

- I'd be happy to answer any questions....
- If there are any questions please feel free to ask.
- Thank you very much for your attention and if there are any suggestions or comments

Dealing with difficult questions

1. Make sure you understand the question.
   - Ask a question to see if you understand
   - Repeat the question in your own words to check that you have understood.
   - If not, ask the questioner to repeat
2. In answering:

   Delay the answer (ask for time and/or repeat the question)
   - Just a minute please. What is a...?
   - How can I put it?
   - I'm glad you asked that question.
   - That's a good question/point/remark.
   - Can I answer that question later?

   Admit that you are not responsible.
   - I saw that in the work of...

   Agree but give an alternative point of view
   - I agree with you but there is another way of looking at it.

3. ***VISUALS***

   What are visuals?
   - Graphs charts
   - Maps photos
   - Drawings images
   - Models video/film
   - Objects

   What media are used?
   - Transparencies/slides
   - Power point slides
   - Video projection/projector
   - Handouts

It is often a good idea to give out a paper copy, called a handout, an outline, a glossary of key words, sources, any other visuals you plan to use, so people can take them away, not waste time in taking notes on key concepts.

What is the vocabulary of the equipment used?

- Blackboard, whiteboard, paperboard
- Chalk, felt tip pen or marker, eraser
- Podium, lectern, overhead,
- Overhead projector system (OHP)
- Screen
- Pointer
- Microphone, mike
- Opaque projector

What should you put on a visual?

- Key words
- Technical words
- Lists
- Examples
- Diagrams
- Charts

Vocabulary of graphs/chart

- Line graph
- Bar chart
- Flip chart
- Diagram
- Pie chart
- Flow chart
- Organization chart

Why use visuals?

- To focus the audience's attention
- To illustrate points easier to understand in visual form but difficult in a verbal form (e.g. statistics)
- To reinforce ideas
- To change focus from oral to visual
- To involve and motivate the audience

- To involve all the senses
- To serve as logical proof
- To save time and avoid putting information on a board
- To avoid turning your back to the audience when writing on a board
- To help the speaker

Text to put on a visual

- Name, conference/company and company logo, date, title of presentation. Try to do this consistently but not to the detriment of a table or image.
- Full sentences are not to be used, unless a quote is given, give round figures
- Keep text to a minimum

Size, layout, font, size and colors.

- Size - A4
- Layout should be pleasant and easy to read: horizontal/landscape layout is preferable.
- Fonts: Ariel, Helvetica, Times New Roman, Futura, Optima, Verdana, New Century,
- Schoolbook and Courier. Some companies impose a particular style.
- Font size – may be 20 or more depending on the size of the room you will be speaking in.
- A good idea is to use different sizes for different types of text: i.e. 20 for main headings, 16 for subheadings, 14 for other text.
- Use CAPITAL LETTERS, **bold face**, italics, underlining, (white on black) or shading
- To highlight if possible, use color transparencies (unless you are just showing text).

How many?

One every two minutes is sufficient. To show too many slides is worse than none at all.

General and miscellaneous tips.

- Have the slides ready and in order.
- Check to see if the OHP is plugged in, in working order and in focus.
- Test the visual to see if people at the back of the room can see it.
- Stand to the side of the screen and face the audience.
- Mask to reveal only what you want the audience to see.
- Use a pointer or a pen to draw attention to a specific point.
- Visuals should be adjusted to the audience.
- Visuals should supplement the spoken message.

- Large enough for everyone to see. (Good idea to give out a paper copy, i.e. a handout, not at the same time though, as the audience may not look at you)
- Don't display too much information, too many colors.
- Does the layout work?
- Check spelling mistakes or grammatical errors.

How should you present a visual in a presentation?

It is not sufficient just to put up a transparency on the screen and expect the audience to turn its attention to it, to understand it and make the link with what you are saying.

It is important to prepare your audience for what they are going to see. This keeps the audience on their toes and gives you the opportunity to position your visual correctly.

- o Let's look at the current distribution of the market, as you can see...
- o I'm going to show you now the most recent figures available...
- o My next slide concerns the method by which...

Remember to draw the attention of the audience to the points that you wish to highlight but avoid redundancy by describing everything that is in the visual!

- As you can see....
- The first line of figures is the most revealing..
- Observe how the increase has had an effect on the...
- What is important here is the way that...

You can also try to rephrase your point to give it emphasis, giving the audience time to absorb the information.

- In other words the number of employees has a direct effect on the...
- Or to look at it in another way every time you...
- That is to say no matter what technique is used, the results remain

4. CREATING INTEREST AND ESTABLISHING A RELATIONSHIP WITH THE AUDIENCE

Do not assume the audience will be interested in what you have to say. Even if they are, minds wander and get distracted. From the very beginning you need to create interest and continue the tempo throughout your speech. You need to put everything on your side to promote knowledge acquisition. In informing an audience you have to adjust to what people think. Use attractive supporting materials. How can you do this?

Arouse listeners' interest from the beginning. In the introduction show how your subject or what you are going to say affects or may affect their lives. In other words, make it personal.

Other techniques are:

- Give an unusual fact or statistics.
- Illustrate with a real life story or anecdote.
- Ask the audience to do something. "Raise your hands if you know."
- Ask the audience direct or rhetorical questions.
- Other tips:
- Be brief and clear in giving the subject and purpose.
- The speaker's attitude is important - knowledge, personality, openness.
- Be lively and enthusiastic.
- Use a variety of media sources.

Rhetorical questions

What is a rhetorical question? It is a question that you ask without expecting it to be answered. Why use such a question? In using such a question the speaker appears to be having a dialogue with the listeners. It also should catch their attention.

- Have you ever seen/heard/experienced...?
- How can we explain this?
- What does that mean?
- What can be done about that?
- What does this imply for you, as a consumer?

Emphasizing/highlighting

Say something is important.

- The important thing to remember is...
- The essential element is...

Stress verbs with your voice.

Add auxiliary verbs for emphasis.

Change the word order

- What I'd like to show today is the difference between the two products.
- Good it may be, easy it isn't.

Repetition

- As I've said before...
- Let me repeat

Tripling, chunking and other techniques of word play and emphasis should be used as you become more fluent and confident.

5. BODY LANGUAGE

The golden rule is "Be natural and relax!"

What is body language?

Eye contact, facial expressions, posture, movements, gestures.

Why is it useful?

It is a natural part of communication:

- To clarify meaning; it is very visual
- To vent nervousness
- To maintain interest
- To emphasize and regulate

Below are just a few examples of both positive and negative body language:

Positive body language

- Eye contact to keep audiences' attention (Asian audience might feel aggressed.)
- Facial expressions should be natural and friendly. Don't forget to smile.
- Raise eyebrows to show surprise
- Open eyes wide
- Squint your eyes
- Knit your eyebrows to show consternation or puzzlement
- Posture – stand straight but relaxed (do not slouch or lean)
- Movement - to indicate a change of focus, keep the audience's attention
- Move forward to emphasize
- Move to one side to indicate a transition
- Gesture
- Up and down head motion or other movements to indicate importance
- Pen or pointer to indicate a part, a place (on a transparency).
- Shrug of the shoulders to indicate "I don't know!"
- Hands - back and forth = two possibilities, more or less
- Arm - movement back, forth

Negative body language

- o Loss of eye contact: looking at notes, looking at screen, at the board, at the floor
- o Don't stare, or look blankly into people's eyes
- o Swaying back and forth like a pendulum
- o Back turned to the audience
- o Nervous ticks
- o Hands in pockets

6. VOICE AND PRONUNCIATION

Correct pronunciation is important if one is to be understood correctly. Incorrect pronunciation is perhaps the first cause of communication breakdown. If the listener is not accustomed to the speaker's native language, he/she will not understand a mispronounced word. Mispronunciation also tires the listener's ear and he/she will perhaps even stop trying to understand the speaker if it becomes too difficult.

6.1 What is pronunciation?

There are two important aspects of pronunciation of individual words, word stress and the individual sounds themselves called "phonemes".

Suggestion: make sure you know how to correctly pronounce at least the key technical words or words that you repeat over in your speech. Just as in the case of individual words in English a particular syllable receives stress, so do particular words in a sentence. Sentence stress concerns stressing particular words in a sentence usually at regular intervals. English speakers stress words that are important for meaning such as: nouns, verbs, adjectives, adverbs, negatives, demonstratives and interrogatives. Unstressed ones include articles, auxiliary verbs, prepositions, and conjunctions.

Linking - (as in French) between a consonant and the following vowel and grouping words into ***thought groups*** - needs to be practiced.

6.2 Voice

The voice, or more precisely the qualities of the voice, should be used to its fullest. Qualities include loudness, speed (fast or slow), variety, pitch (high or low), silent moments or pauses.

The voice is important:

- To indicate importance, meaning
- To create atmosphere and to avoid sounding monotonous and putting the audience to sleep!

7.5 INTERVIEWS:

An interview is a conversation in which the interviewer questions the interviewee in order to gain information. Interviews can be formal or informal, structured or unstructured. They can be conducted one-to-one or in groups, face to face or by telephone. Interviews are a very common research tool in the social sciences, and as such, attract a great deal of commentary and discussion. Interview technique is the oldest selection tool still practiced by almost all the organizations as it serves the purpose of testing the knowledge and observing the behavior of the candidate.

Interviews are a useful method for the following purposes :

- To investigate issues in an in depth way
- To discover how individuals think and feel about a topic
- To investigate the use, effectiveness and usefulness of information or services quality
- To inform decision making, strategic planning and resource allocation
- To interact on sensitive topics which people may feel uncomfortable discussing in a open forum or group
- To add a human dimension to impersonal data

7.5.1 TYPES OF INTERVIEWS:

- ***Informal, conversational interview*** - no predetermined questions are asked, in order to remain as open and adaptable as possible to the interviewee's nature and priorities; during the interview the interviewer "goes with the flow".
- ***General interview guide approach*** - intended to ensure that the same general areas of information are collected from each interviewee; this provides more focus than the conversational approach, but still allows a degree of freedom and adaptability in getting the information from the interviewee
- ***Standardized, open-ended interview*** - the same open-ended questions are asked to all interviewees; this approach facilitates faster interviews that can be more easily analyzed and compared.
- ***Closed, fixed-response interview*** - all interviewees are asked the same questions and asked to choose answers from among the same set of alternatives. This format is useful for those not practiced in interviewing.

7.5.2 ADVANTAGES OF INTERVIEWS:

The main advantages of interviews are:

- They are useful to obtain detailed information about personal feelings, perceptions and opinions
- They allow more detailed questions to be asked
- They usually achieve a high response rate
- Respondents' own words are recorded
- Ambiguities can be clarified and incomplete answers followed up

- Precise wording can be tailored to respondent and precise meaning of questions clarified
- Interviewees are not influenced by others in the group
- Some interviewees may be less self-conscious in a one-to-one situation.

Disadvantages of Interviews

The main disadvantages of interviews are:

- They can be very time-consuming: setting up, interviewing, transcribing, analyzing, feedback, reporting
- They can be costly
- Different interviewers may understand and transcribe interviews in different ways.

7.5.3 INTERVIEW PROCESS

Stage 1: Determine what information is required. What do you want to find out?

Stage 2: Decide on the method of data collection and the audience for the interviews e.g., students, academicians and administrators.

Stage 3: Draft the interview schedule, considering content, wording, format, structure and layout

Stage 4: Pilot/test the interview schedule with colleagues or a sample of potential interviewees and revise as necessary

Stage 5: Conduct the interviews

Stage 6: Transcribe interviews

Stage 7: Analyze the transcripts

Stage 8: Write up, present and use the findings

7.5.4 INTERVIEWING

Interview methods of data collection for organizational diagnosis purposes is used mostly when an organization engages outside consultants for diagnostic and development purposes. Sometimes interview methodology is also used by internal teams and/or change agents. Interviews have the major advantage of providing an opportunity for face-to-face interaction with the participants of the organization. In fact in medical diagnosis interview is the first step and forms the basis for subsequent testing. In organizational diagnosis studies, interviews may form the first step as well as the last stage of diagnosis. They could be exploratory interviews, hypotheses testing interviews, change inducing/idea testing interviews. There could be individual interviews or group interviews.

The spoken word is usually the greatest source of investigative evidence and often the best evidence. The primary goal of an interview is to elicit and record information from the complainant, subject, and every important witness. Your investigation is not complete until you have accomplished this goal.

Effective interviewing is a skill that must be learned by specialized training and/or experience. Most people learn to interview by watching others or constant practicing. Learning the basic concepts is the proper way to conduct an interview and practicing these methods is critical to success as an interviewer.

7.5.5 INTERVIEWING GOALS

Some rules to follow in interviewing are:

1. ***Establish rapport :*** Establish rapport with the interviewee to make her/him feel comfortable and at ease.
2. ***Seek only the truth :*** Emphasize that you seek only the truth.
3. ***Listen attentively :*** Listen attentively, evaluate the interviewee's responses to your questions carefully and take good notes.
4. ***Be objective and unemotional during the interview :*** Remain objective and unemotional **throughout** the interview, although it can be difficult if the witness is uncooperative or reluctant.

7.5.6 INTERVIEW PLAN

Preparing an Interview Sequence Plan :

Preparation is the ***key*** to a successful interview. Before you conduct any interview, create an Interview Sequence Plan

- o Who you will interview
- o The order of the interviews
- o The category of interviewees
- o The questions you intend to ask

The Interview Sequence Plan is an Interview Plan that includes the order you intend to conduct the interview.

The Interview Plan for each candidate:

1. Type of Interview
2. Physical and Psychological Factors
3. Questioning Techniques
4. Topic Outline
5. Number of Interviewers
6. Recording
7. Rights and Responsibilities

1. *Type of Interview :*

Your approach will differ depending on the category of interviewee and the subject of interview. Some interviewees require a slightly different approach, so you may need to employ specialized interview techniques, depending on the type of interviewee. Plan your approach and make a note in your Interview Plan.

2. *Physical Factors and Psychological Factors :*

a. *Physical Factors*

The physical environment can have a tremendous impact on your ability to conduct a successful interview. Keep the following in mind when conducting an interview:

- Choose an appropriate location to minimize noise, movement, interruptions etc.,
- When possible, choose a room located away from the subject's work area.
- Choose an appropriate office to conduct the interviews.
- You can enhance the interviewee's focus with a well-lighted, moderately sized, private room in comfortable settings.
- Minimize noise and interruptions. Do not accept phone calls or visitors during the interview.
- Choose the room furnishings and the position of the furniture based on the needs of the interview.

Eliminate communication barriers such as desks, tables, and personal items.

b. *Psychological Factors*

You have an influence on psychological factors (e.g., fear, excitement, intimidation) that impact the success of the interview. Be aware of this influence and try to eliminate negative factors and foster positive interview conditions.

3. *Questioning Techniques :*

Evaluate the interviewee to determine which interviewing techniques to employ. The more familiar you are with the details of the case and the personalities involved, the better you will be able to tailor your interview techniques. Document the types of questions you plan to ask in the Interview Plan.

4. *Topic Outline :*

An outline of topics provides clear-cut goals and objectives for the interview. You do not include the actual questions you intend to ask, only a description of each topic you want to discuss with each interviewee. An outline helps you to:

- Avoid reading the questions during the interview;
- Focus your attention on the answers to ensure they are responsive; and,
- Ask appropriate follow-up questions.

5. *Number of Interviewers :*

Make a note in your Interview Plan whether a second investigator will be present during the interview and the role that investigator will play. If a second investigator is not available, another trustworthy person may be used as a stand-in.

When two investigators are available, the lead investigator:

- Introduces the interviewers
- States the purpose of the interview
- Asks the first series of questions
- Sets the tone and the parameter of the interview

The other investigator:

- Takes notes
- Observes the interviewees' body language
- Ensures the investigator covers all of the topics in the outline
- May ask follow-up questions

As a rule, the interviewers do not interrupt each other, but may switch roles as topics change.

6. *Recording the Interview :*

Document the method you used to record information using one of these methods:

- Note taking
- Sworn Statements
- Results of Interview
- Tape recording
- Videotapes

7. *Interviewee's Rights and Responsibilities :*

Be prepared for the interview. Determine in advance the rights and responsibilities of each interviewee. Include this information in the Interview Sequence Plan.

7.5.7 PHASES OF AN INTERVIEW

The interview may be divided into five phases or segments, each with its own purpose. The phases are:

PHASE 1 : Introduction

PHASE 2 : Building Rapport

PHASE 3 : Questioning

PHASE 4 : Summarization

PHASE 5 : Closing

PHASE 1 : Introduction

The Introduction phase sets the tone of the interview. Follow these procedures :

- Introduce yourself and the office you represent.
- Ask the interviewee to introduce him or herself.
- Explain the purpose of the interview to allay the interviewee's fears and apprehension.
- Provide an overview of what to expect during the interview.

PHASE 2 : Building Rapport

Before you ask the first question, build rapport with the interviewee. Establish a sincere and trusting relationship from the beginning and a method of non-verbal communication to enlist their full support and cooperation.

Some important tips for successful interviewing

- Greet the interviewee with a firm, friendly handshake.
- Set the tone with your voice , gestures, and facial expressions.
- Treat everyone with dignity and respect.
- Use neutral terms and non-threatening mannerisms and body language.
- Express empathy or sympathy, when appropriate.
- Avoid making sarcastic comments which hurts the interviewee.

PHASE 3 : Questioning

Communication, both verbal (language, speech, words) and non-verbal (conduct, expression, attitude), is the key to a successful interview. The ability to question effectively is central to eliciting verbal responses from interviewees. Good questioning is a four step process that involves:

Step 1 : Ask a question.

Step 2 : Receive the answer.

Step 3 : Evaluate the answer.

Step 4 : Record the response.

STEP 1: Ask a Question

Keep the following in mind when asking a question:

- Ask one question at a time.
- Use who, what, when, where, why, and how questions.
- Ask questions that develop or explain facts.
- Ask questions in a conversational manner.

- Use terms that are familiar to the interviewee, and avoid using acronyms.
- Sequence the questions from general to more specific.

General questions require a narrative response; specific questions require a yes or no answer.

Example of question sequencing from general to more specific:

- Tell me about ....
- Describe the events...
- When did you...
- Who was there...
- Where was the...
- What time did...
- Why were you...

STEP 2 : *Receive the Answer*

When receiving answers to your questions:

- Listen carefully.
- Keep an open mind.
- Paraphrase responses to show the interviewee you are listening before moving on to another question.
- Concentrate on what the interviewee is saying.
- Maintain control of the interview at all times.
- Control, but do not dominate, the discussion.
- Summarize the key points.
- Let each person tell his/her story with minimal interruptions.
- Use silence to force a response.
- Keep your talking to a minimum and encourage responses by using gestures and eye contact.
- React to disclosures appropriately.

STEP 3 : *Evaluate the Answer*

- Compare the accuracy of responses.
- Keep the interviewee focused on the issue.
- Use direct questions to fill in missing details and to test the interviewee's sincerity and commitment.

STEP 4 : Record the Response

Accurate note taking is critical to the success of an interview. You should take notes even when taping an interview in the event an interviewee challenges the accuracy of the interview. Keep the following in mind when taking notes:

- Always indicate the method of interview (in person, by phone, tape recording), purpose, place, date and time, and attendees and their phone numbers.
- Your notes should be factual, objective, concise, clear, and complete.
- A tape-recorded interview must include both your questions and the interviewee's answers.
- Review your notes several times during the course of the interview.
- Retain your notes and tapes.

PHASE 4 : Summarization

During this phase, the investigator summarizes the salient parts of the interview to ensure continuity and accuracy. This phase is even more important in the one-interviewer interview. Review your notes.

- Clarify or add to the information provided in the interview.
- Use this opportunity to prompt further recall, ask additional questions and verify critical information.
- Provide an opportunity for the other investigator to comment or ask questions.
- Ensure you have recorded all important information accurately

PHASE 5 : Closing the Interview

At the conclusion of the interview:

- Provide the interviewee an opportunity to discuss information not covered during the interview.
- Reassure the interviewee about any concerns raised during the interview; At the conclusion of the interview:
- Thank the interviewee for the cooperation.

7.5.8 INTERVIEW GUIDELINES

- o Greet the interviewee in an appropriate manner.
- o Establish rapport.
- o Define or state the purpose of the interview.
- o Maintain control; don't let the interviewee interview you.
- o Ask one question at a time.

- Evaluate each piece of information or allegation on its own merit.
- Maintain strict impartiality and keep an open mind.
- Keep your talking to a minimum.
- Keep the interviewee at ease.
- React to disclosures appropriately.
- Be non-judgmental.
- Limit barriers between you and the interviewee.
- Don't let the interviewee interview you.
- Avoid arguing with the interviewee.
- Listen before taking action.
- Take your time. Don't hurry.
- Be a good listener.
- Accept the interviewee's feelings.
- Use appropriate questioning techniques, as described in this chapter.
- Use silence, when appropriate to force a response.
- Make no promises.
- Ask questions that develop or explain facts, such as questions that begin with Who, What, When, Where, Why, and How. Ask questions in a conversational manner.
- Use transitions to connect thoughts, starting with known information and working toward areas of undisclosed information. Use leading questions as a technique for making transitions from one topic to another.
- Use terms that are familiar to the interviewee and avoid using acronyms.
- Ask a general opening question.
- Match the interviewee's verbal pace.
- Ask questions in a logical progression based on the sequence of events.
- Follow open-ended questions with specific questions.
- Ask what the interviewee expects or wants to happen as a result of the information he/she provides.
- Take breaks often.
- Don't argue.
- Ask if there is any other information the interviewee would like to add.
- Extend your appreciation.
- Close the interview appropriately.

7.5.9 INTERVIEW CAUTIONS

Effects of Cross-Cultural Communication

When conducting interviews, avoid:

- Revealing personal prejudices - destroys your objectivity and credibility.
- Hurrying - encourages mistakes and omissions.
- Making Assumptions/jumping to conclusions – you may fail to obtain important information and allow false or unverifiable information to be introduced into the investigation.
- Making promises you can't keep – destroys your credibility and reputation.
- Degrading the interviewee or talking down to him/her - encourages unnecessary emotional barriers and antagonizes the interviewee.
- Placing too much attention on minor or irrelevant issues - impedes the progress of the interview; and,
- Allowing the interviewee to control the interview or become angry - distracts from the information gathering process.

7.6 VIDEO CONFERENCING:

7.6.1 Concept:

Videoconferencing is the conduct of a videoconference (also known as a video conference or video teleconference) by a set of telecommunication technologies which allow two or more locations to communicate by simultaneous two-way video and audio transmissions. It has also been called 'visual collaboration' and is a type of groupware.

Videoconferencing differs from videophone calls in that it's designed to serve a conference or multiple locations rather than individuals' It is an intermediate form of video telephony, first deployed commercially in the United States by AT&T during the early 1970s as part of their development of Picture phone technology.

With the introduction of relatively low cost, high capacity broadband telecommunication services in the late 1990s, coupled with powerful computing processors and video compression techniques, videoconferencing usage has made significant inroads in business, education, medicine and media. Like all long distance communications technologies (such as phone and Internet), by reducing the need to travel to bring people together.

7.6.2 NEED FOR VIDEO CONFERENCING

a. Reduced Travel Costs:

In today's globalized economy, travel is often a prerequisite for leveraging new market opportunities. Journeying to distant locales to engage in face-to-face interactions with customers, partners, and colleagues is a time-honored business ritual, and nothing will ever replace the impact of live interactions. But a large percentage of routine or regular business trips with all their attendants' expenditure can be eliminated by communicating over video. With vast improvements in quality, availability, and ease of use, and with the ability to interact and share content in high definition video conferencing technology has reduced the costs and risks of travelling to long distances. The majority of organizations will see a single outlay of annual travel expenses far outweighing the entire video conferencing investment, easily justifying the implementation.

b. *Increased Productivity across Dispersed Workforces and Teams is possible through videoconferencing:*

Teams normally interact with their members using phone, e-mail, instant messaging (IM), or workflow applications. However, with 80 percent of communication consisting of non-verbal visual cues, the ability of teams to understand, process, and collaborate over distance using these methods is severely impeded. Wherever video is added to a meeting, participants are more likely to stay focused, because they can be seen as well as heard. Expressions of satisfaction, concern, confusion, understanding and so on, can easily be seen and addressed, speeding and informing the group more effectively than myriad e-mails, voicemails, and IMs. The result is that the decisions are made faster, projects completed sooner, and productivity increased across the organization.

c. *Improved Hiring and Retention of Top Talent possible:*

Hiring processes can be very lengthy and costly, especially when candidates are located in other cities or when multiple people are involved in the interview process. Organizations with video conferencing systems in their offices can reduce expenses and time by bringing candidates into the nearest facility and allowing interviews to be conducted both in person and over video. Video interviews can also be recorded, enabling persons unable to be part of the live interview process to see and evaluate the candidate over video. Video communication helps in employee retention by following an evaluation procedure which is just and positive. Examples include improved cooperation by allowing remote employees to become closer faster with other team members; helping employees retain work/life balance by mitigating travel so they can spend more time with their families; allowing employees to work partially or full time from home, to alleviate the impact of commuting; or simply engaging in real-time face-to-face interactions that are richer and more fulfilling than any alternative short of a live in-person meeting.

d. *Sustained Competitive Advantage:*

Video communication offers multiple paths for creating and maintaining competitive advantage. Teams communicating over video share knowledge more widely, resulting in faster and more informed decisions that reduce the time to market new products and services. Support teams leverage video to create more personal, one-to-one relationships with their customers, encouraging a loyalty far beyond the capabilities of a traditional call center agent. Manufacturing organizations use video conferencing and content sharing to verify product quality, make revisions, and ensure accuracy throughout the supply chain, while their competitors continue to rely on next-day delivery of services. Video enables sales executives to clearly and immediately appreciate the status of the pipeline, beyond the rows on a spreadsheet. Public relations and human resources departments can promote the organization's use of video as proof of corporate efforts to protect the environment.

e. *Environmental Initiatives:*

Video conferencing is an obvious "green" technology, allowing organizations to mitigate energy use by dramatically reducing the need to travel. By communicating over video, organizations can also substantially reduce their carbon footprint and help ensure a basis for regulatory compliance. With tools that provide a powerful way to enable conferences and other video content to be streamed live or on demand around the world, employees, customers, partners, and students can use video to communicate, engage and interact with others across distance at any time, from wherever they are.

7.6.3 ADVANTAGES OF VIDEO CONFERENCING

- Faster decision making
- Retention of highly-skilled workers
- Standardizing work processes and keeping staff up-to-date on frequently-changing policies
- Keeping the product development teams in coordination with client needs
- Reducing hiring cycle and recruitment costs
- Leveraging technical expertise across different locations
- Improving employee satisfaction, productivity and boosting meeting efficiency
- Finding and screening new offshore partners and clients
- Monitoring the quality process and manufacturing

Disadvantages:

- Limited to a certain number of users at the same time
- Audio quality with large groups.
- Stability of your connections
- High price.

With the explosion of bandwidth after the Dot Com era, the resources are now available to provide more interaction in the virtual classroom via video conferencing. Using the various technologies available for video conferencing, educators can provide a more interactive distance learning experience by delivering real time video, voice, and data communications to their distance students. Administrators of both government and private organizations can interact with their subordinates for review of various activities to take a quick decision and to order for implementation simultaneously.

SHORT QUESTIONS

1. Explain the concept and definition of communication.
2. Explain the scope of communication.
3. Explain briefly the process of communication.
4. What are the essentials of good communication?
5. What are the ten commandments of good communication?
6. What are the objectives of communication?
7. Explain the purpose of communication.
8. Briefly explain the types of communication.
9. Explain the concepts of communication and business communication.
10. What are the types of business communication?
11. What is report writing?
12. Explain the most common format of presenting reports.
13. What is cross cultural communication?
14. How do you structure a good presentation?
15. What are the various types of interviews?
16. Explain briefly the process of interview.
17. What is video conferencing?

ESSAY QUESTIONS

1. Explain the concept and definition and scope of communication.
2. Define communication? Explain briefly the process of communication.
3. Explain the concept of communication? What are the essentials of good communication?
4. What are the objectives of communication? Explain the purpose of communication.
5. Define communication? Explain the types of communication.
6. Explain the concepts of communication and business communication. What are the types of business communication?
7. What is report writing? Explain the most common format of presenting reports.
8. What is cross cultural communication? How do you structure a good presentation?
9. What are the various types of interviews? Explain the process of interview.
10. What is video conferencing? What are its advantages and disadvantages?

❖ ❖ ❖

UNIT - VIII

CONTEMPORARY MANAGEMENT PRACTICES

8.1	Management Information System (MIS)
8.2	Materials Requirement Planning (MRP)
8.3	Just-In-Time (JIT) System
8.4	Total Quality Management (TQM)
8.5	Six sigma Approach
8.6	Capability Maturity Model (CMM) Levels
8.7	Supply Chain Management (SCM)
8.8	Enterprise Resource Planning (ERP)
8.9	Performance Management
8.10	Business Process Outsourcing (BPO)
8.11	Business Process Re-engineering (BPR)
8.12	Benchmarking
8.13	Balanced Score Card

8.1 MANAGEMENT INFORMATION SYSTEMS

Introduction

An information system contains information about an organization and its surrounding environment. Three activities – input, processing and output produce the information organizations need. Feedback is returned to appropriate people or activities in the organization to evaluate and refine the input. Environmental factors such as customers, suppliers, competitors, stockholders and regulatory agencies interact with the organization and its information systems. The function of an information system is shown in figure 8.1. Information systems can be either computer based or manual. Manual systems use paper and pencil technology. Computer based information systems rely on computer hardware and software technology to process and disseminate information.

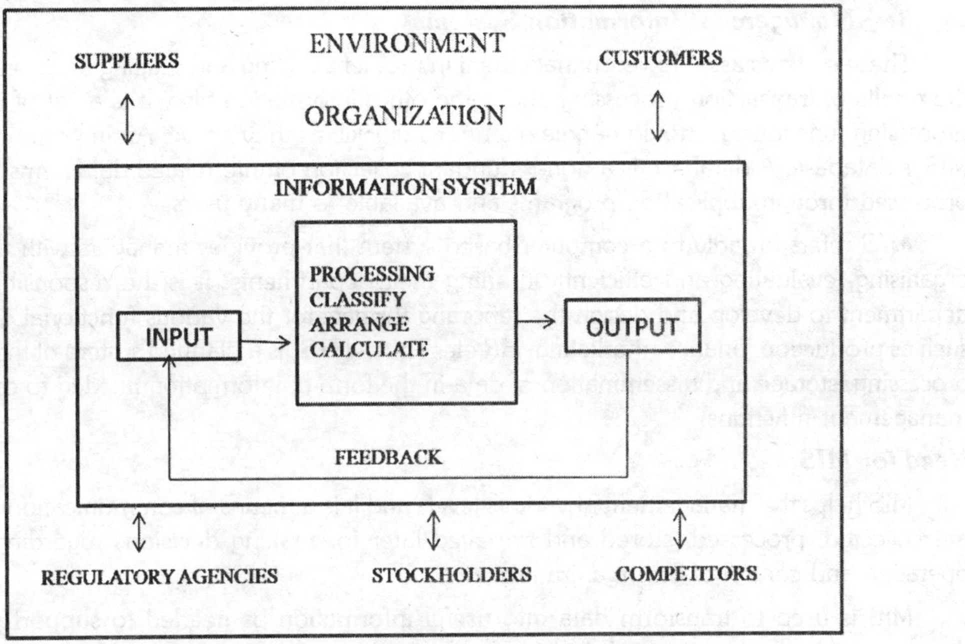

Figure 8.1 : Functions of Information System

Types of Information Systems:

The three major information systems are

1. Transaction Processing Systems
2. Decision Support Systems
3. Management Information Systems

1. Transaction Processing Systems:

TPS process business transactions of the organization. Transaction can be any activity of the organization. Transactions differ from organization to organization. For example, take a railway reservation system, booking, canceling, etc are all transactions. Any query made to it is a transaction. This provides high speed and accurate processing of record keeping of basic operational processes. These include calculation, storage and retrieval.

Transaction processing systems provide speed and accuracy and can be programmed to follow routine functions of the organization.

2. Decision Support Systems

These systems assist higher management to make long term decisions. These type of systems handle unstructured or semi structured decisions. A decision is considered unstructured if there are no clear procedures for making the decision and if all the factors to be considered in the decision cannot be readily identified in advance.

These are not of recurring nature. Some recur infrequently or occur only once. A decision support system must be very flexible. The user should be able to produce customized reports by giving particular data and format specific to particular situations.

3. *Management Information Systems*

These systems assist lower management in problem solving and making decisions. They use the results of transaction processing and some other information also. It is a set of information processing functions. It should handle queries as quickly as they arrive. An important element of MIS is database. A database is a non-redundant collection of interrelated data items that can be processed through application programs and available to many users.

MIS refers broadly to a computer-based system that provides managers with the tools for organising, evaluating and efficiently running their departments. It is the responsibility of MIS department to develop and design the reporting formats for the various functional departments such as production, finance, marketing, HR etc. Thus, '***MIS***' is a planned system of the collection, processing, storage and dissemination of data in the form of information needed to carry out the management functions.

Need for MIS:

MIS helps the management at various levels and it is a means of communication where data are collected, processed, stored and retrieved later for making decisions regarding planning, operation and control of an organization

MIS is used to transform data into useful information as needed to support managerial decision making with structured decisions.

MIS is network of communication channels and information processing centres used for

- Storing, updating, collection and processing information and
- Applying the processed information to various users managing the information.

Role of MIS in Business:

- It provides information about the various aspects of business.
- It helps the executives to avail the information regarding the functional areas quickly.
- The database helps in conducting research.
- It provides sound information regarding the financial health of business organization.
- It helps the HR manager in finding out the requirement of manpower, their wages and salaries, performance appraisal, training, promotion and employees turnover etc...
- It helps the production manager in deciding capacity utilization, number of rejections per batch, frequency of break down and status of shipment etc...
- Regarding marketing, it provides information relating to the product, price, promotion, segmentation, sales etc. and ensures smooth functioning of the department.

Characteristics of MIS:

- It is management oriented
- Management directed
- Integrated system (5M's- man, money, methods, material and machine)
- Common data flow
- Avoids redundancy and duplication in data storage

- Heavy planning element
- Subsystem concept
- Common database
- Flexibility and ease of use
- Computerisation

Classification of MIS:

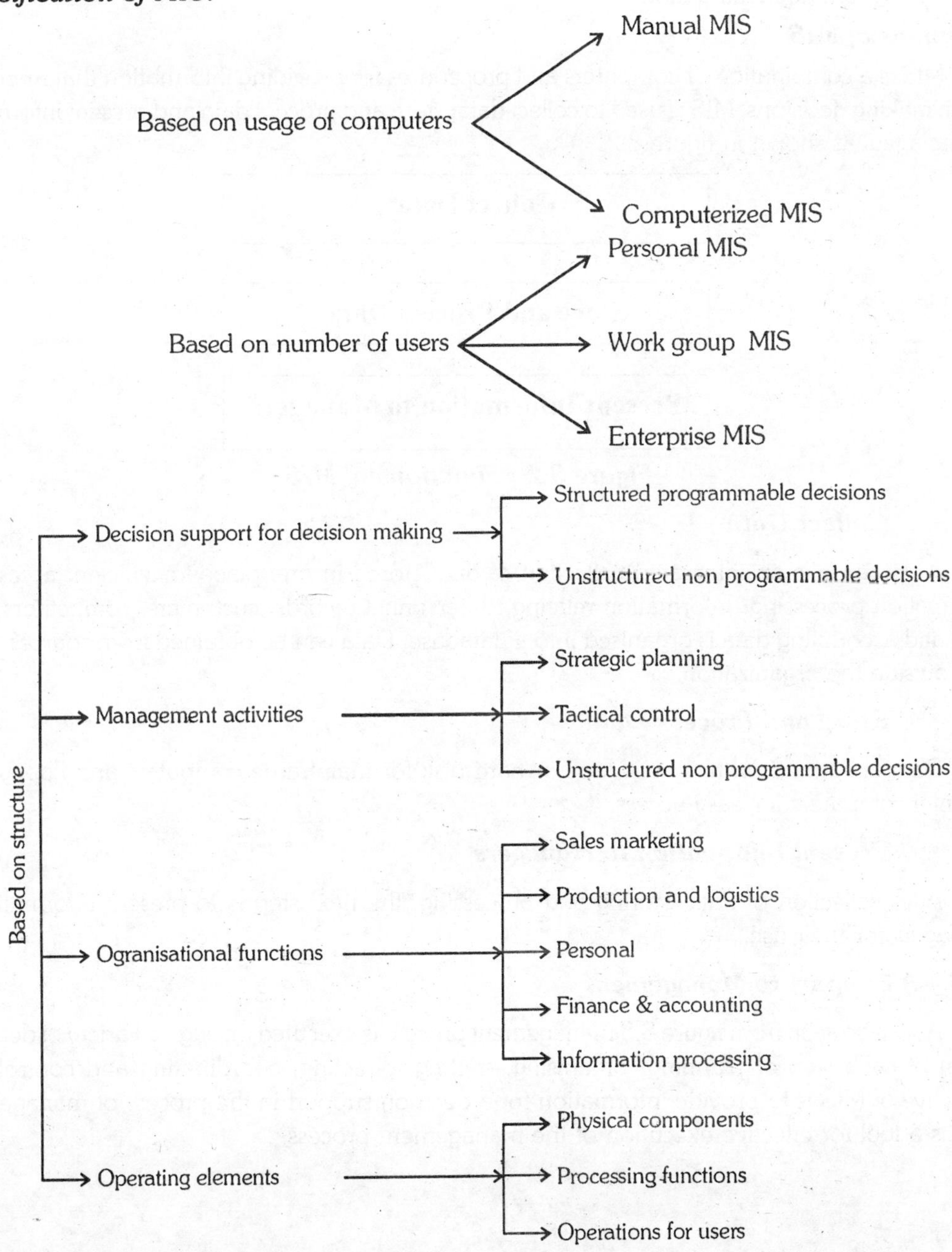

Major Components of MIS

The typical MIS is based on the four components

- Data gathering
- Data entry
- Data transformation
- Information utilization

Functions of MIS

MIS is a combination of computers and procedures for providing information that manager's use in making decisions. MIS is used to collect data, store and process data and present information to managers as shown in figure 8.2.

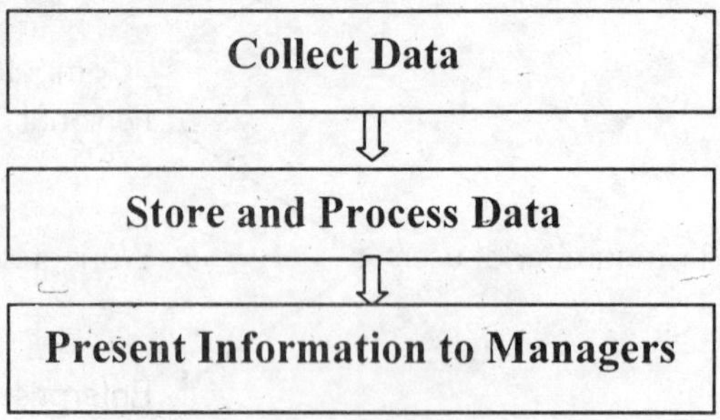

Figure 8.2 : Functions of MIS

- ***Collect Data***

A database is an integrated collection of data stored in one place for efficient access and information processing. Information relating to personnel records, customers, competitors, sales data and accounting data is organised into a database. Data can be obtained from sources within and outside the organization.

- ***Store and Process Data***

Data are stored on magnetic tape or hard disk for mainframe computers and floppy disks for mini computers for easy access.

- ***Present Information to Managers***

After collection of data, storing and processing, the next step is to present information to managers for their use.

MIS – A Support to Management

As can be seen from figure 8.3 management process is executed through a variety of decisions taken at each step of planning, organising, staffing, directing, coordinating and control. The objective of MIS is to provide information for a decision support in the process of management. MIS is a tool for effective execution of the management process.

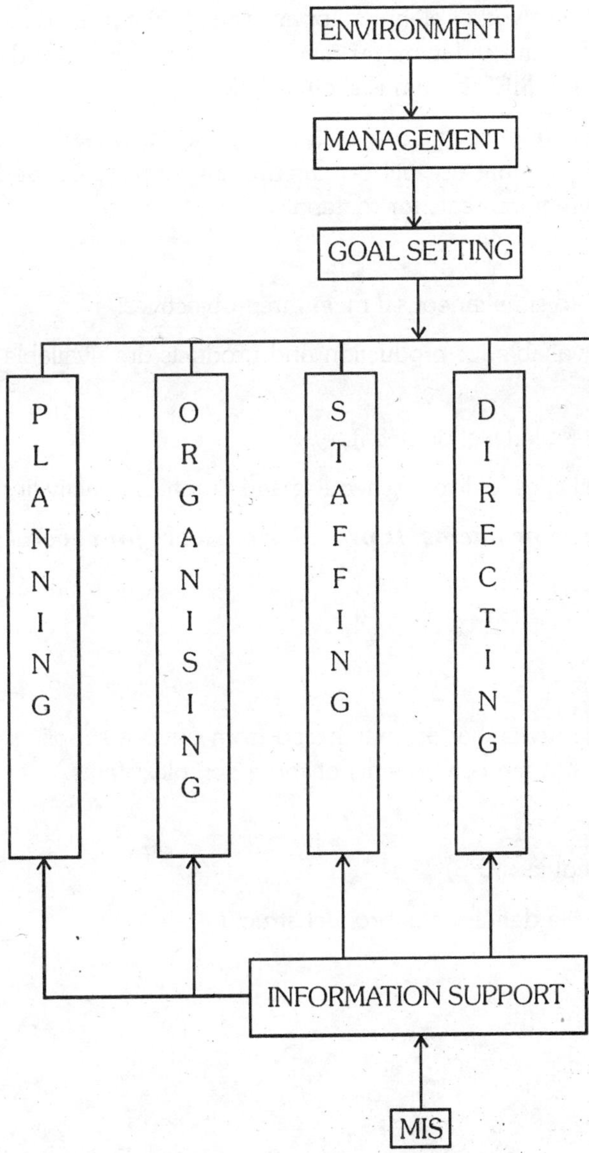

Figue 8.3 : MIS support to Management

8.2 MATERIAL REQUIREMENT PLANNING (MRP)

It is an internal production process designed to ensure that the materials, components, parts, subassemblies are available as and when required. MRP is time phased priority planning system. These systems calculate the requirements of materials and schedule supply demand pattern. Material Requirement Planning is a production planning and inventory control system used to manage manufacturing processes. Most MRP systems are software based, while it is possible to conduct MRP by hand as well.

MRP is defined as a scientific method of planning for arriving at time phased requirement of materials, components, parts, self contracted items for meeting demand for finished goods at the stipulated time. The structure of the MRP system is shown in figure 8.4.

American Production and Inventory Control Society (APICS) defines MRP as that which constitutes a set of techniques that use bill of material, inventory data, and the master production schedule to calculate requirements for materials.

Objectives of MRP

An MRP system is intended to simultaneously meet three objectives:

1. Ensure materials are available for production and products are available for delivery to customers.
2. Maintain the lowest possible level of inventory.
3. Plan manufacturing activities, delivery schedules and purchasing activities.

MRP is a tool to deal with these problems. It provides answers for several questions:

1. What items are required?
2. How many are required?
3. When are they required?

MRP can be applied both to items that are purchased from outside suppliers and to sub-assemblies, produced internally, that are components of more complex items.

Pre-requisite Inputs for MRP:

- Master production schedule (MPS)
- Bill of material (BOM) file defining the product structure.
- Inventory status file

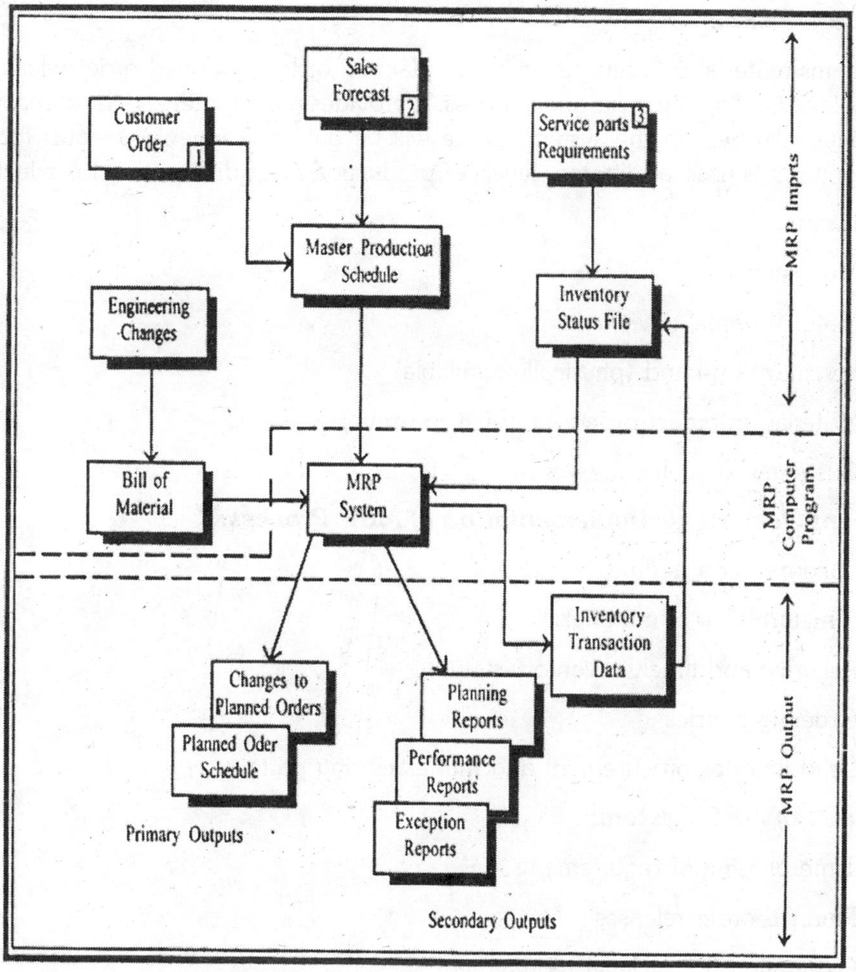

Figure 8.4 : Structure of MRP System

Master Production Schedule

It expresses the overall production plans. It is a schedule, which shows the number and timing of all items to be produced over a planning horizon. It is stated in terms of end items which may be products or assemblies.

Bill of Material:

It is a document which process for a given time, the list of materials required, and unit consumption and location code. BOM refers to splitting requirements for the product to be manufactured into its basic components with the codes and specifications. Bill of material file is a file containing the bills of material for all end items. It contains listing of all raw materials, parts, sub-assemblies, and assemblies that go into an end item. The amount of each component that is required to produce one end item is included.

Inventory Status File

It contains material on hand or on order, planned orders, planned order release, lot sizes, safety stock levels, lead time costs and supplies. It provides a computerized list of records of each material, physically held in the system. There will be only one inventory status for individual material, even if it is used at different levels of production or in different end products.

It indicates:

(i) Material code

(ii) Material name

(iii) Inventory on-hand (physically available)

(iv) Material on-order (ordered but yet to arrive)

(v) Customer order for the item

Requirements for Proper Implementation of MRP Process:

- Valid master schedule
- Structured bill of materials
- Accurate and timely inventory status
- Ordering policies
- Lead time for procurement and manufacturing parts

Key Features of MRP System:

- Time phasing of requirements
- Planned order releases
- Generation flower level requirement
- Rescheduling capacity is provided

Benefits of MRP system are:

- Customer service is improved
- Reduction in lead time
- Reduction in work-in-process
- Reduction in past-due orders
- Elimination of annual inventory
- Reduction in finished goods inventory, raw material, components and parts and safety stock
- Increase in productivity
- Capacity constraints are better understood

- Inventory turn-over increases
- All the above benefits are due to correct tracking of inventory and accurate estimation of planned order for each time horizon

Drawbacks of MRP

The greatest advantages of MRP are its straight forwardness and established procedure. However, the simplicity in MRP calculations often leads to many problems in real life.

(i) Incorrectness in Supplier's Lead Time

MRP depends heavily on correctness of the lead-time stored for each item. Correct estimate of lead-time depends upon supplier's familiarity with the product, vendor reliability, etc. In case this goes wrong, the component or raw material will not reach in time, causing incorrectness in other calculations also.

(ii) Incorrectness in Inventory Data

This causes incorrectness in the calculations of net requirements. This may happen very frequently due to:

(a) Miscounting

(b) Scrap, not being accounted for

(c) Items lost in transit

(iii) Inaccuracy in Manufacturing Lead Time

The in-house production is often rescheduled or adjusted due to:

(a) Change in customer's demand

(b) Change in workload of factory, causing changes in lead time of manufacturing.

Busy factory causes more work-in-process and queue before operations, resulting in higher lead times.

(iv) Inaccuracy in BOM Structure

This causes the inaccuracy in the estimates of gross requirements to the calculated. This can happen when:

(a) There is a design change.

(b) Component substitution is implemented without proper recording.

Some other problems of MRP are due to highly computational-intensive approach of MRP. This causes over-dependence on MRP outputs. Any inaccuracy causes failure of MRP to a great extent.

8.3 JUST - IN - TIME

Just-in-time production is "philosophy that focuses attention on eliminating waste by purchasing or manufacturing just enough of the right items just in time". JIT is a Japanese production management philosophy of manufacturing based on planned elimination of all waste and continuous improvement of productivity. Proper use of JIT manufacturing has resulted in increased quality, productivity and efficiency, improved communication and decrease in cost and wastes. Thus, JIT stands for purchasing / producing necessary quantities at the necessary time.

Just-in-time (JIT) is an inventory strategy that strives to improve a business's return on investment by reducing in-process inventory and associated carrying costs. Just in time production method is also called the Toyota Production System. To meet JIT objectives, the process relies on signals or kanban between different points in the process, which tell when to make the next part. If implemented correctly, JIT can improve a manufacturing organization's return on investment, quality, and efficiency.

Definition:

A "demand-pull" approach that produces only what is necessary to satisfy the demand of the ensuing manufacturing process." – ***Accounting Dictionary***

Just in time inventory is the minimum inventory that is necessary to keep a system perfectly running. With just in time (JIT) inventory, the exact amount of item arrives at the moment they are needed, not a minute before or not a minute after.

Goals of JIT:

- Increasing the organisation's ability to compete with rival firms and remain competitive over the long run.
- Increasing the degree of efficiency within the production process.
- Reduce the level of waste materials, time and effort involved in the production process.

Other Goals:

- Identifying and responding to customers' needs.
- Aiming for the optimal quality / cost relationship.
- Eliminating unnecessary wastes.
- Trusting relationships between the suppliers.
- Designing the plant for maximum efficiency.

Components / Elements of JIT:

These elements can be grouped together into 3, people, plant and systems.

1. *People Involvement:*

Employees at different levels in the organisation as well as the following groups are involved.

- Stakeholders and owners of the company.
- All employees and labour unions.
- Management.
- Government.

2. Plant:

Numerous changes occur about the plant which includes plant layout, multi function workers, demand, pull production, kanbans and continuous improvement.

3. Systems:

Systems within an organisation refer to the technology and process. Two such systems are MRP (Material Requirement Planning) and MRP II (Manufacturing Resource Planning). The system designed should allow production smoothing and standardization of job leads to more uniform output rate.

Push / Pull Production:

Basically production is classified into two categories.

- Produce on demand (Pull system)
- Produce to forecasts of demand or make for stock (Push system)

Kanban Pull System:

Kanban system is a kind of production system which operates based on the information contained in cards, called "kanbans". Kanban is a Japanese word meaning signal or message or communication used to control the flow of items through the production process. Waving hands or shouting, sending a card are a few examples for kanban. A kanban system is a system of inventory and production control (Pull inventory system) which uses kanbans as the principle information transmission device.

Basically, there are two types of kanbans:

- Withdrawal kanban (WK)
- Production order kanban (POK)

The withdrawal kanban is used to indicate the type and amount of product which the next process should withdraw from the predicting process.

The production kanban specifies the type and quality of product which the next process must produce.

Basic Principles:

A set of possible reasons for maintaining high stock is listed below:

- Unreliable or unpredictable delivery
- Poor quality from suppliers
- Increased variety of materials
- Machine breakdown
- Labour absenteeism

Benefits of JIT:

- Reduced setup time
- Reduction of wastes (defects, scrap, rework).
- There is a massive reduction in work-in-process which results in lower space requirements.
- Stronger and more reliable working relations with suppliers.
- Reduction in lead time
- Employees with multiple skills are used more efficiently.
- Improved working relations between employees.
- Fewer inventories of raw materials.
- Increased flexibility, lower costs and higher productivity.
- Production scheduling and work hour consistency synchronized with demand
- Improved quality and customer satisfaction
- Higher profits

Thus, the main advantages of JIT are:

- Lower stock holding means a reduction in storage space which saves rent and insurance costs
- As stock is only obtained when it is needed, less working capital is tied up in stock
- There is less likelihood of stock perishing, becoming obsolete or out of date
- Avoids the build-up of unsold finished product that can occur with sudden changes in demand
- Less time is spent on checking and re-working the product of others as the emphasis is on getting the work right first time

Limitations of JIT:

- Cultural differences.
- Loss of individual autonomy.
- Success of JIT depends upon co-operation between employees.
- There is no flexibility.
- There is no safety stock to offset inaccurate demand forecast.
- JIT production is effective only when the daily demands are fairly stable.

The main disadvantages of JIT are

- Production is very reliant on suppliers and if stock is not delivered on time, the whole production schedule can be delayed.

- There is little room for mistakes as minimal stock is kept for re-working faulty product.
- There is no spare finished product available to meet unexpected orders, because all products are made to meet actual orders. However, JIT is a very responsive method of production.

8.4 TOTAL QUALITY MANAGEMENT (TQM)

The term TQC was coined by A.V. Freignbaum in 1983 in Japan, TQC has later become TQM. It is a corporate business management philosophy which recognizes that customer needs and business goals are inseparable.

Definition of TQM: It is the process of integration of all activities, functions and processes within an organization in order to achieve continuous improvement in cost, quality, function and delivery of goods and services for customer satisfaction.

TQM is the quality of features and characteristics of a product or service that bears on its ability to satisfy customers. ***– American Society for Quality Control (ASQC)***

TQM can be defined as managing the entire organization so that it exceeds in all dimensions of products and services that are important to the customer.

TQM is the control of the transformation process of an organization to best satisfy customer needs in the most economical manner.

TQM can also be defined as creating an organizational culture committed to the continuous improvement of skills, teamwork, processes, product, service quality and customer satisfaction.

Following are some other definitions of TQM:

- TQM is a way of managing to improve the effectiveness, flexibility and competitiveness of a business. TQM is managing the entire organization so that it excels in all dimensions of products and services that are important to the customer.
- TQM is both a philosophy and a set of guiding principles that represent the foundation of a continuously improving organization.
- TQM is an integrated organizational approach in delighting both external and internal customers by meeting their expectations on a continuous basis through everyone involved with the organizational working on continuous improvement in all products, services and procedures along with proper problem solving methodology.

Thus, Total Quality Management is about

- Total customer satisfaction
- Total functions in the organization
- Total range of products and services offered
- Addressing all aspects of and dimensions of quality
- Addressing total organizational issues such as retaining customers, improving profits and generating new business for the future

- Involving all in the organization to achieve total customer satisfaction
- Demanding total commitment from all in the organization to achieve total customer satisfaction

The goal of TQM is customer satisfaction, by means of continuous improvement Thus, TQM is not just about quality but it is about organizational excellence. It is about turning all products, all services, all processes and all people into gold (perfection).

Elements of TQM:

a) Total employees involvement

b) Total company wide quality control

c) Total waste elimination

Principles of TQM:

Following are the principles of TQM:

1. Performance measurement is a must at organization, department and individual level.
2. Customer's orientation is a must.
   - Customer complaints, surveys, questionnaires, feedback, retention.
3. Continuous improvement is must.
   - Reduction is scrap, rework, inventory costs, waste of human, potential, product, queuing, over production, unnecessary processes, excess workers movement.
4. Total employees involvement is must.
   - Appraisal system, customer impact, competence reward system, motivation,
   - Empowerment - empower people to act and evaluate their action.
5. Purchasing and supplier management is must.
6. Management involvement is must.
7. Communication with staff at all levels regularly both formally and informally is must. Promote two way communication at all levels.
8. Classifying people's skills is must. Keep pace with organizational needs.
9. Identifying training needs and relating them with individual capabilities and requirements is must.
10. TQM cannot afford weak links/processes. Weak links or processes have to be improved.

The main principles that underlie TQM are summarized as below:

- ***Prevention*** - Prevention is better than cure. In the long run, it is cheaper to stop defects in products than trying to find them.
- ***Zero defects*** - The ultimate aim is no (zero) defects or exceptionally low defect levels if a product or service is complicated.

- ***Getting things right first time*** - Better not to produce at all than produce something defective.
- ***Quality involves everyone*** - Quality is not just the concern of the production or operations department. It involves everyone, including marketing, finance and human resources.
- ***Continuous improvement*** - Businesses should always be looking for ways to improve processes to help quality.
- ***Employee involvement*** - Those involved in production and operations have a vital role to play in spotting improvement opportunities for quality and in identifying quality problems.

TQM Mission:

a) Exceed customer's expectations

b) Use best in class practices

c) Eliminate defects

d) Eliminate wastes

e) Motivate all employees.

Benefits of TQM

1. Customer satisfaction oriented benefits
2. Economic improvement oriented benefits.

Customer satisfaction oriented benefits

- Improvement in product quality
- Improvement in product design
- Improvement in production flow
- Improvement in employee morale
- Improvement in quality consciousness
- Improvement in market place acceptance
- Improvement in product service
- Improved quality and productivity

Economic improvement oriented benefits

- Reduction in operating costs
- Reduction in operating losses
- Reduction in field service costs

- Reduction in liability exposure
- Reduction of rejection, scrap and wastage, reworking.

Four Cs of TQM:

These are:

1. Commitment
2. Competence
3. Communication
4. Continuous improvement.

Tools for Continuous Improvement:

- Statistical Tools
- Zero-defects Programme
- Quality Circles
- Just-in-Time(JIT) Manufacturing
- Benchmarking
- Business Process Re-engineering
- Value Analysis/ Value Engineering
- Six-sigma Approach
- The Deming Cycle of Plan-Do-Check and Act (PDCA)
- Kaizen Practice for Continuous Improvement
- Poka-Yoke (Mistake-Proofing)
- Taguchi's Quality Loss Function

8.5 SIX SIGMA APPROACH

This technique is the latest and highest form of quality management and surpasses ISO 9000. This is a business management strategy originally developed by Motorola, USA in 1980s. Six Sigma concept has been coined by a Motorola engineer Bill Smith in the early and mid 1980's. Since then hundreds of companies around the world such as Motorola, General Electric (GE), Godrej, Wipro, Tata Steel etc., have adopted six sigma approach.

The term six sigma originated from terminology associated with manufacturing, specifically terms associated with statistical modeling of manufacturing processes. The maturity of a manufacturing process can be described by a sigma rating indicating its yield, or the percentage of defect-free products it creates. A six-sigma process is one in which 99.99966% of the products manufactured are statistically expected to be free of defects (3.4 defects per million). Motorola set a goal of "six sigma" for all of its manufacturing operations and this goal became a byword for the management and engineering practices used to achieve it.

Six sigma is a quality improvement programme with an objective to reduce the number of defects to as low as 3.4 parts per million. Six sigma quality is a bench mark of excellence for product and process quality. The Greek letter sigma is the statistical representation for standard deviation. Six sigma level indicates that product or service delivered is 99.99966% defect free. This means that only 0.0000034% times the product or service delivered is defect prone.

Six sigma seeks to improve the quality of process outputs by identifying and removing the causes of defects (errors) and minimizing variability in manufacturing and business processes. It uses a set of quality management methods, including statistical methods, and creates a special infrastructure of people within the organization ("Black Belts", "Green Belts", etc.) who are experts in these methods Each six sigma project carried out within an organization follows a defined sequence of steps and has quantified financial targets (cost reduction or profit increase).

Approaches for Six Sigma

There are two approaches for achieving six sigma

1. DMAIC - used for projects aimed at improving an existing business process.
2. DMADV - used for projects aimed at creating new product or process designs.

1. ***DMAIC*** means Define, Measure, Analyse, Improve and Control. The Six Sigma DMAIC process is an improvement system for existing processes falling below specification and looking for improvement

The DMAIC project methodology has five phases:

- ***D***efine the problem, the voice of the customer, and the project goals, specifically.
- ***M***easure key aspects of the current process and collect relevant data.
- ***A***nalyze the data to investigate and verify cause-and-effect relationships. Determine what the relationships are, and attempt to ensure that all factors have been considered. Seek out root cause of the defect under investigation.
- ***I***mprove or optimize the current process based upon data analysis using techniques such as design of experiments, or mistake proofing, and standard work to create a new, future state process. Set up pilot runs to establish process capability.
- ***C***ontrol the future state process to ensure that any deviations from target are corrected before they result in defects. Implement control systems such as statistical process control, production boards, and visual workplaces, and continuously monitor the process.

2. ***DMADV*** means Define, Measure, Analyze, Design and Verify. The six sigma DMADV process is an improvement system used to develop new processes or products at Six Sigma quality levels.

The DMADV project methodology, also known as DFSS ("***D***esign ***for S***ix ***S***igma"), features five phases:

- ***D***efine design goals that are consistent with customer demands and the enterprise strategy.

- ***M***easure and identify product capabilities, production process capability, and risks.
- ***A***nalyze to develop and design alternatives, create a high-level design and evaluate design capability to select the best design.
- ***D***esign details, optimize the design, and plan for design verification. This phase may require simulations.
- ***V***erify the design, set up pilot runs, implement the production process and hand it over to the process owner.

Both DMAIC and DMADV are executed by six sigma green belts, six sigma black belts and six sigma master black belts.

Sigma Level	***Defects per Million Opportunities***	***Yield (%)***	***Competitive Level***
One	***6,90,000***	***30.9***	***Non – Competitive***
Two	***3,08,537***	***69.2***	***Non – Competitive***
Three	***66,807***	***93.3***	***Industry Average***
Four	***6,210***	***99.4***	***Industry Average***
Five	***233***	***99.98***	***World Class***
Six	***3.4***	***99.99966***	***World Class***

Six sigma level indicates that the product produced or service delivered is 99.99966% defect free. This means that only 0.00034% times the product or service delivered is defect prone. When 0.0000034 is multiplied by one million it comes to 3.4 defects per million opportunities (DPMO). Thus, a process is said to be at six sigma level provided the process is not producing more than 3.4 defects per million opportunities.

Some organizations—such as Toyota, Solectron and General Electric—have adopted the quality program and goal of ***six sigma,*** which means eliminating defects to the level of 1 per 3.4 per million opportunities—or a process that is 99.99966 percent defect free. Five sigma is 233 defects per million, and four sigma is 6,210 per million. Most firms operate at the four sigma level. A key theme in six sigma programs is the reduction of waste. Toyota trains all employees to seek opportunities to reduce waste in seven areas—called Toyota's Seven Wastes. They include:

- Waste of overproduction (also irregular production),
- Waste of time on hand (waiting),
- Waste in transportation,
- Waste of processing itself,
- Waste of stock on hand (inventory),
- Waste of movement, and
- Waste of making defective products.

Example: General Electric (GE) recently developed a quality program based on the six sigma goal. One element involves training "black belts" for four months in statistical and other quality enhancing measures. The black belts then spend full time at GE plants and set up quality improvement projects. Jack Welch, GE's CEO, is giving this program his strong personal support. The following example illustrates the difference this program has made. Customers of GE's Milwaukee-based medical division were frustrated by the short life of the tubes in GE's CT scanners. The tubes lasted for about 50,000 to 100,000 x-rays and took about four hours to replace. GE assigned a team of six-sigma black belts to the problem. Their job was to measure and analyze each phase of the tube manufacturing process to determine how waste could be reduced and product improvements made. They reduced by nine months the time needed to perfect new models of the x-ray tubes and increased the life of the tubes by five times. The new tube provided sharper and more complete pictures allowing physicians to examine images of the entire brain of a stroke victim, rather than just slices at a time. GE estimated companywide savings from the six sigma program at about $600 million.

Types of Six Sigma Teams

Six sigma teams are formed for implementing in true spirit keeping in mind both managerial as well as technical aspects.

1. Top management
2. Program champions
3. Master black belts
4. Black belts
5. Green belts
6. Yellow belts

- ***Top Management:*** They are responsible for setting up a vision for the six sigma implementation in the organisation. They also empower the employees with the freedom and resources to explore new ideas for breakthrough improvements.
- ***Program Champions:*** Business leaders who lead six sigma by sponsoring projects are called Champions. They are responsible for its implementation across the organisation in an integrated manner. Champions also act as mentors to black belts.
- ***Master Black Belts***: Identified by the program champions, they are the persons with highest level of technical and organizational proficiency. They act as in-house expert coaches for the organisation and train black belts and green belts.
- ***Black Belts***: They operate under master black belts to apply six sigma methodologies to specific projects. They are leaders of teams, responsible for measuring, analyzing, improving and controlling the processes that influence customer satisfaction and productivity growth.
- ***Green Belts***: Six sigma green belts are the employees capable of forming and facilitating six sigma teams and managing six sigma projects from concept to completion. They operate under the guidance of black belts and support them in achieving the overall results.

- ***Yellow Belts***: They are the employees who have been trained in six sigma techniques as part of the corporate-wide initiative though they are not expected to actively engage in the quality improvement activities.

Application of Six Sigma Programs

Six sigma programs are always directed towards quality improvement, cost cutting and time saving. Six sigma programs are employed in design, production, service, operations management, inventory management and delivery.

- ***Six Sigma Management concepts*** find greater appreciation and application in recent times. The Six sigma management characteristics include:
  1. Providing strong leadership.
  2. Defining performance merits.
  3. Selecting projects likely to succeed.
  4. Selecting and training appropriate people.
- ***Six Sigma Technical aspects*** form a part and parcel of managerial strategy and aids in cost cutting and defect minimization. The technical aspects of six sigma include
  1. Improving process performance
  2. Reducing variation
  3. Utilizing statistical models
  4. Designing a structured improvement strategy

Benefits of Six Sigma:

1. It introduces rapid and almost radical improvements.
2. It transforms the entire organization.
3. It ensures enhanced product quality.
4. It helps to achieve higher productivity.
5. It helps to have rapid response to changing needs of the customers and market.
6. It is a continuous improvement process

Obstacles to implementing Six Sigma includes the lack of:

1. Company-wide definition of quality.
2. Strategic plan for change.
3. Customer focus.
4. Real employee empowerment.
5. Strong motivation.

6. Time to devote to quality initiatives.
7. Leadership.
8. Poor inter-organizational communication.
9. View of quality as a "quick fix".
10. Emphasis on short-term financial results.
11. Internal political and "turf" wars.

8.6 THE CAPABILITY MATURITY MODEL (CMM)

The Capability Maturity Model (CMM) was originally developed as a tool for objectively assessing the ability of government contractors' processes to perform a contracted software project. CMM is a collection of instructions an organization can follow with the purpose to gain better control over its software development process. Though the CMM comes from the field of software development, it is used as a general model to aid in improving organizational business processes in diverse areas; for example in software engineering, system engineering, project management, software maintenance, risk management, system acquisition, information technology (IT), services, business processes generally, and human capital management. The CMM has been used extensively worldwide in government offices, commerce, and industry and software development organizations. The Capability Maturity Model Integration (CMMI) is a new version of CMM.

Structure of CMM

The structure of Capability Maturity Model involves the following aspects:

- ***Maturity Levels***: A 5-level process maturity continuum - where the uppermost (5th) level is a notional ideal state where processes would be systematically managed by a combination of process optimization and continuous process improvement.
- ***Key Process Areas***: A key process area (KPA) identifies a cluster of related activities that, when performed together, achieve a set of goals considered important.
- ***Goals***: The goals of a key process area summarize the states that must exist for that key process area to have been implemented in an effective and lasting way. The extent to which the goals have been accomplished is an indicator of how much capability the organization has established at that maturity level. The goals signify the scope, boundaries, and intent of each key process area.
- ***Common Features***: They include practices that implement and institutionalize a key process area. There are five types of common features: commitment to perform, ability to perform, activities performed, measurement and analysis, and verifying implementation.
- ***Key Practices:*** The key practices describe the elements of infrastructure and practice that contribute most effectively to the implementation and institutionalization of the KPAs.

Levels of the CMM

There are five levels defined along the continuum of the CMM and, according to the Software Engineering Institute (SEI) : "Predictability, effectiveness, and control of an organization's software processes are believed to improve as the organization moves up these five levels. While not rigorous, the empirical evidence to date supports this belief."

Level 1 – ***Initial*** - At this maturity level 1, processes are usually adhoc and the organisation usually does not provide a stable environment.

Level 2 – ***Repeatable*** - At this maturity level, software development successes are repeatable. The organisation may use some basic project management to track cost and schedule.

Level 3 – ***Defined*** - At this maturity level, processes are well characterised and understood, and are described in standards, procedures, tools, and methods.

Level 4 – ***Managed*** - Using precise measurements, the management can effectively manage and control the software development effort. In particular, it can identify ways to adjust and adapt the process to particular projects without measurable losses of quality or deviations from specifications.

Level 5 – ***Optimising*** - This maturity level focuses on continually improving process performance through both incremental and innovative technological improvements.

Within each of these maturity levels are key process areas (KPAs) which characterize that level, and for each KPA the five definitions identified are goals, commitment, ability, measurement and verification.

People Capability Maturity Model (PCMM)

In order to improve their performance, organizations must focus on three things – people, process and technology. With the help of the capability maturity model for software (CMM) many organizations have made improvements in their software processes and practices. Yet many of these organizations have discovered that significant changes are required in the way they manage their people. To provide guidance to organizations that want to improve the way they address people issues, the SEI developed the people capability maturity model (PCMM) in 1988. PCMM is a framework patterned after the structure of CMM, to help organizations successfully address their critical people issues. The primary objective of the people CMM is to improve the capability of the entire workforce. The people CMM consist of five maturity levels. Each maturity level is as evolutionary plateau at which one or more domains of the organization's processes are transformed to achieve a new level of organization capability.

People CMM is intended for executives and managers, systems and software professionals, those responsible for improving work force management practices, human resource professionals, software engineering process group members who want to accelerate the achievement of higher CMM maturity levels, and those who aspire to be managers of technical professionals. Since its initial release in 1995, the people CMM has been used throughout the United States, Canada,

Europe, Australia, and India to guide and conduct organizational improvement activities. Small and large commercial organizations, as well as government organizations are using people CMM. Moreover, once executives identify an organization's strategic objectives, the people CMM provide guidance that improves the organization's ability to satisfy those objectives through a competent, capable workforce.

8.7 SUPPLY CHAIN MANAGEMENT

Supply chain encompasses all activities associated with the flow and transformation of goods from the raw material stage to the end user as well as associated information flow, material flows both up and down. It is the integration of these activities through improved SC relationship to achieve a sustainable competitive advantage. It is thus, the sequence of organization's facilities, functions, and activities that are involved in producing and delivering a product or service.

Supply Chain Management (SCM)

SCM is defined as the "design, planning, execution, control, and monitoring of supply chain activities with the objective of creating net value, building a competitive infrastructure, leveraging worldwide logistics, synchronizing supply with demand and measuring performance globally."

Supply chain management is the systemic, strategic coordination of the traditional business functions and the tactics across these business functions within a particular company and across businesses within the supply chain, for the purposes of improving the long-term performance of the individual companies and the supply chain as a whole.

Thus, supply chain consists of the network of organization that connects supplier and end-users. It provides the route through which raw material is converted into finished good/services into the hand of consumers. Supply chain management, in turn, covers the "flow of goods from suppliers through manufacturing and distribution chains to the end users"

Objectives of Supply Chain:

- To maximize the overall value generated.
- To achieve maximum supply chain profitability.
- To reduce supply chain costs to the minimum possible level.

Activities of Supply Chain

Supply chain activities can be grouped into strategic, tactical, and operational levels.

Strategic Level

- Strategic network optimization, including the number, location, and size of warehousing, distribution centers, and facilities.
- Strategic partnerships with suppliers, distributors, and customers, creating communication channels for critical information and operational improvements such as cross docking, direct shipping, and third-party logistics.

- Product life cycle management, so that new and existing products can be optimally integrated into the supply chain and capacity management activities.
- Information technology chain operations.
- Where-to-make and make-buy decisions.
- Aligning overall organizational strategy with supply strategy.
- It is for long term and needs resource commitment.

Tactical Level

- Sourcing contracts and other purchasing decisions.
- Production decisions, including contracting, scheduling, and planning process definition.
- Inventory decisions, including quantity, location, and quality of inventory.
- Transportation strategy, including frequency, routes, and contracting.
- Benchmarking of all operations against competitors and implementation of best practices throughout the enterprise.
- Milestone payments.
- Focus on customer demand.

Operational Level

- Daily production and distribution planning, including all nodes in the supply chain.
- Production scheduling for each manufacturing facility in the supply chain (minute by minute).
- Demand planning and forecasting, coordinating the demand forecast of all customers and sharing the forecast with all suppliers.
- Sourcing planning, including current inventory and forecast demand, in collaboration with all suppliers.
- Inbound operations, including transportation from suppliers and receiving inventory.
- Production operations, including the consumption of materials and flow of finished goods.
- Outbound operations, including all fulfillment activities, warehousing and transportation to customers.
- Order promising, accounting for all constraints in the supply chain, including all suppliers, manufacturing facilities, distribution centers, and other customers.
- From production level to supply level accounting all transit damage cases and arrange to settlement at customer level by maintaining company loss through insurance company.

Importance of Supply Chain Management:

Supply chain management integrates the supplier, distributor and customer logistics requirements into one cohesive process to include demand planning, forecasting, materials requisition, order processing, inventory allocation, order fulfilment, invoicing and bills payment.

Of late, supply chain management is gaining more importance because of the following reasons.

- The total time for materials to travel through the entire supply chain can be quite long (say 6 months to one year or more). Since the materials spend so much time waiting in inventory at various stages in the supply chain, there is a great opportunity to reduce the total supply chain cycle time leading to a corresponding reduction in inventory, increased flexibility, reduced costs and better deliveries.
- Many companies have drastically improved their internal operations and now find it necessary to consider relations with external customers and suppliers in the supply chain to gain further improvements in their operations.
- Supply chain thinking is an application of system thinking and provides a basis for understanding processes that cut across a company's internal department and processes that extend outside the company as well.
- The goals of supply chain management are to reduce uncertainty and risks in the supply chain, thereby positively affecting inventory levels, cycle time, processes and ultimately end-customer service levels.

The term supply chain may also imply that only one player is involved at each stage. A manufacturer may receive material from several suppliers and then supply to several distributors. Thus, most of the supply chain activity is actually network. A typical supply chain involves a variety of stages which may include customer, retailer, distributors, manufacturers and raw material suppliers. Each stage in a supply chain is connected through flow of product, information and funds. These flows often occur in both direction and may be managed by one of the stages or intermediary.

Need for Supply Chain Management

1. Improve operations
2. Increasing levels of outsourcing
3. Increasing transportation costs
4. Competitive pressures
5. Increasing globalization
6. Increasing importance of e-commerce
7. Complexity of supply chains
8. Manage inventories

Problems addressed by Supply Chain Management

Supply chain management must address the following problems:

1. ***Distribution Network Configuration:*** Number, location and network missions of suppliers, production facilities, distribution centers, warehouses, cross-docks and customers.
2. ***Distribution Strategy:*** Questions of operating control (centralized, decentralized or shared); delivery scheme, e.g., direct shipment, pool point shipping, cross docking.
3. ***Trade-Offs in Logistical Activities***: The above activities must be well coordinated in order to achieve the lowest total logistics cost. Trade-offs may increase the total cost if only one of the activities is optimized. For example, full truckload (FTL) rates are more economical on a cost per pallet basis than less than truckload (LTL) shipments. If, however, a full truckload of a product is ordered to reduce transportation costs, there will be an increase in inventory holding costs which may increase total logistics costs.
4. ***Information:*** Integration of processes through the supply chain to share valuable information, including demand signals, forecasts, inventory, transportation, potential collaboration, etc.
5. ***Inventory Management:*** Quantity and location of inventory, including raw materials, work-in-progress (WIP) and finished goods.
6. **Cash-Flow**: Arranging the payment terms and methodologies for exchanging funds across entities within the supply chain.

Elements of Supply Chain Management

Element	*Typical Issues*
Customers	Determining what customers want
Forecasting	Predicting quantity and timing of demand
Design	Incorporating customer wants, manufacturing and time
Processing	Controlling quality, scheduling work
Inventory	Meeting demand while managing inventory costs
Purchasing	Evaluating suppliers and supporting operations
Suppliers	Monitoring supplier quality, delivery and relations
Location	Determining location of facilities
Logistics	Deciding how to best move and store materials

Benefits of Supply Chain Management

1. Lower inventories
2. Higher productivity
3. Greater agility
4. Shorter lead times

5. Higher profits
6. Greater customer loyalty

8.8 ENTERPRISE RESOURCE PLANNING (ERP)

ERP is an integrated enterprise – wide information system. It integrates the information system of an organization and automates most of the business functions. Enterprise is the group of people with a common goal, which has certain resources at its disposal to achieve this goal. In an enterprise way, the entire organization is considered as a system and all the departments are its subsystems. Information about all aspects of the organisation is stored centrally and is available to all the departments. Each sub system knows what others are doing, why they are doing it and what should be done to move the company towards a common goal.

ERP refers to the techniques and concepts for integrated management of business as a whole from the view point of the effective use of management resources to improve the efficiency of enterprise management. As shown in figure 8.5 ERP is an integrated computer-based application used to manage internal and external resources, including tangible assets, financial resources, materials, and human resources. ERP is a high – end sophisticated software solution that reduces the pressure and workload of the managers and provides accurate, timely information for taking appropriate business decisions. ERP systems help to make this task easier by integrating the information systems, enabling smooth and seamless flow of information across departmental barriers, automating business process and functions and thus, helping the organization to work and move forward as single entity.

The purpose of ERP systems is to facilitate the flow of information between all business functions inside the boundaries of the organization and manage the connections to outside stakeholders. Built on a centralized database and normally utilizing a common computing platform, ERP systems consolidate all business operations into a uniform and enterprise-wide system environment. Originally ERP packages were targeted at the manufacturing industry and consisted functions for planning and managing the core business such as sales management, production management, accounting etc. However, in recent years ERP packages are adapted to diverse types of industry and the expansion of implementation is progressing on a global level. ERP if properly implemented can improve the efficiency and competitive advantage of an organization to a large extent. The activities supported by ERP systems include all core functions of an enterprise including financial management, production and operations, HRM and marketing.

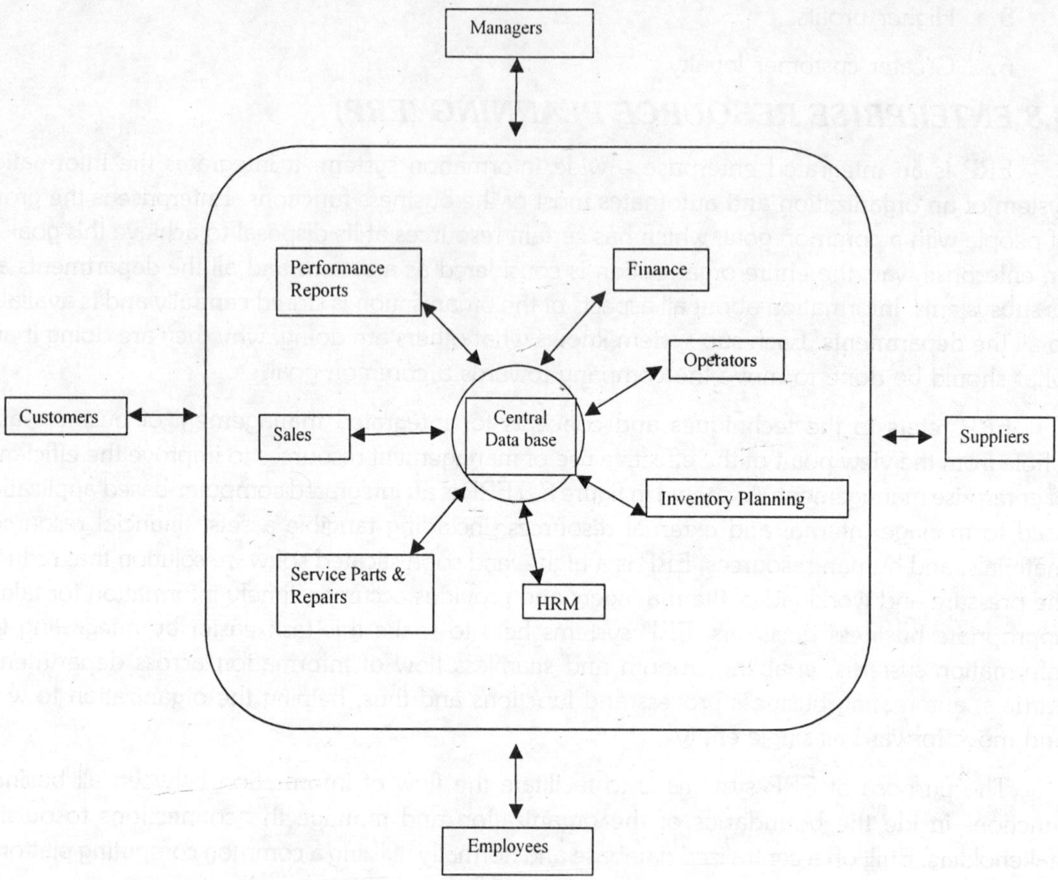

Figure 8.5 : Enterprise Resource Planning

Evolution of ERP

It can be observed from figure 8.6 that the ERP model took years to emerge and is still emerging. The concept began in the 1960's with MRP or materials requirement planning that assisted manufacturing companies in planning and scheduling.

MRP - In the manufacturing industry MRP became the fundamental concept of production management and control. MRP was an outgrowth of the bill of material (BOM) processing. MRP began in 1960's and became very prominent in the 1970's. The production people were searching for better and more efficient methods of ordering material and components. MRP was a perfect answer for their needs.

Closed – loop MRP – Along with materials requirement planning it involves a series of functions for automating the production process. It contains tools and techniques to address both priority and capacity and supports both planning and execution.

Manufacturing Resource Planning II (MRP II) – The third stage in the evolution of ERP is MRP II. It is the next logical step of closed – loop MRP and contains additional capabilities such as sales and operational planning, financial interface and simulation capabilities for better decision making. MRP II is made up of a variety of functions such as business planning, sales and operational planning, demand management, production planning, master scheduling, materials requirement planning, capacity requirement planning etc., each linked together.

ERP - The final step in the evolution is the emergence of ERP. Fundamentals of ERP are the same as that of MRP II. However, the enterprise software makes ERP broader in scope, capable of dealing with more business functions and better integration with the finance and accounting functions. ERP system is capable of integrating with other tools like customer relationship management, supply chain management etc. ERP is a direct outgrowth and extension of MRP and as such includes all of MRP II's capabilities.

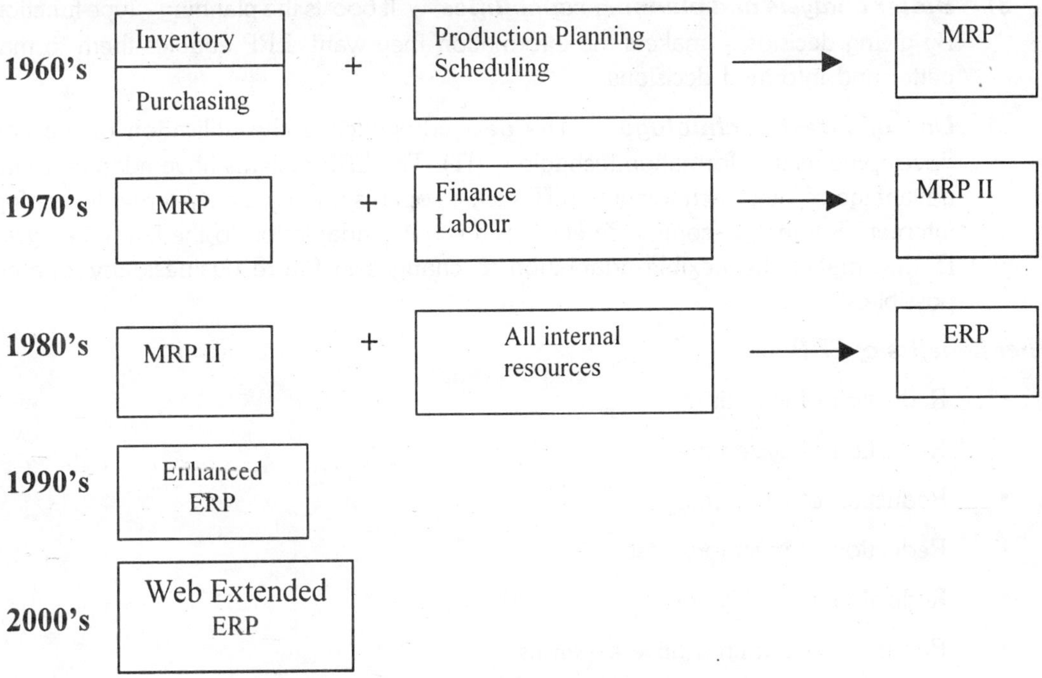

Figure 8.6 : Evolution of ERP

Advantages of ERP

Installing an ERP system has many advantages both direct and indirect.

The direct advantages include

- ➢ Improved efficiency
- ➢ Information integration for better decision making
- ➢ Faster response time to customer queries etc.

Indirect benefits include

- ➢ Better corporate image
- ➢ Improved customer goodwill
- ➢ Customer satisfaction etc.

Direct benefits of an ERP system are

1) ***Business integration*** → The first and most important advantage lies in the promotion of integration and automatic data updating between related business components since data is automatically updated at the transaction time, various management decisions can be made in a timely manner.

2) ***Flexibility*** → Diverse multinational environments such as language, currency, accounting standards etc., are covered in one system and functions that can manage multiple locations are packaged and can be implemented automatically.

3) ***Better analysis and planning capabilities*** → It boosts the planning – type functions. By giving decision – makers the information they want, ERP enables them to make better and informed decisions.

4) ***Use of latest technology*** → The next advantage is the utilisation of the latest developments in information technology (IT). The ERP systems have adapted to take advantage of latest technologies in IT such as open systems, client / server technology, internet / intranet, e–commerce etc. It is this quick adaptation to the latest changes in IT that makes the flexible adaptation to changes in future business environments possible.

Other benefits of ERP are

- Reduction of lead time
- Reduction of cycle time
- Reduction of labor cost
- Reduction of inventory cost
- Reduction in quality costs
- Reduction of administrative expenses
- On – time shipment
- Productivity improvement
- Quality improvement
- Customer services improvement
- Improved resource utility
- Improved supplier performance
- Better customer satisfaction

ERP systems create value through

➢ Integrating organizations activities

➢ Forcing the use of best practices

- Enables organizational standardization
- Eliminates information asymmetries
- Provides online and real time information
- Allow simultaneous access of data
- Facilitates intra – organization communication
- Facilitates inter – organization collaboration

ERP - The Business Modules

ERP systems help the management by making the planning process more productive and efficient. All ERP packages contain many modules. The number and features of the modules varies with the ERP package. Rather than catering to the needs of their own departments, functioning in isolation, the different modules in an ERP system are integrated. They send and receive data across departmental barriers. Another feature is the automation of the various procedures and tasks. With the procedure automation and modules integration, the same task will be completed within minutes by a single person.

ERP software is made up of many software modules. Each ERP software module deals with a major functional area of an organization. Common ERP modules include modules for finance, manufacturing, production planning, human resources, plant maintenance, materials management, quality management, marketing, sales and distribution, purchasing, inventory control, product distribution, order tracking, financial accounting, etc. Organizations often selectively implement the ERP modules that are both economically and technically feasible.

Commercial Applications

Manufacturing: Engineering, bills of material, work orders, scheduling, capacity, workflow management, quality control, cost management, material and capacity planning, shop floor control, manufacturing process, manufacturing projects, manufacturing flow

Supply chain management: Order in cash inventory, order entry, purchasing, product configuration, supply chain planning, supplier scheduling, and inspection of goods, claim processing, and commission calculation

Financials: General ledger, cash management, investment management, investment budgeting, accounts payable, accounts receivable, fixed assets

Project management: Costing, billing, time and expense, performance units, activity management

Human resources: Payroll, training, time and attendance, benefits and salary administration

Customer relationship management: Sales and marketing, commissions, service, customer contact, call-center support

Data services: Various "self-service" interfaces for customers, suppliers and/or employees

Access control: Management of user privileges for various processes.

The ERP vendors are shifting their focus from big – fortune 1000 companies to different market segments (medium size companies, small companies etc) which will lead to a fierce battle for market share and mergers and acquisitions for strategic and competitive advantage. The ultimate winner in this race will be the customer, who will get better products and services at affordable prices.

8.9 PERFORMANCE MANAGEMENT

Introduction

The word "performance" can be split up as "performance" plus "management". Performance means what is expected to be delivered by an individual or a set of individuals with in a time frame in terms of results or efforts, tasks and quality, with specifications of conditions under which it is to be delivered.

Performance management is the process of creating a work environment or setting in which people are enabled to perform to the best of their abilities and talents. Performance management is basically a managerial process which consists of planning performance, managing performance and rewarding performance. It is holistic and disciplined approach which includes planning, monitoring, developing, rating, and rewarding employee performance. This function is carried out by each manager with help and support of the HR specialist. HR creates the framework for an organization's internal environment.

Performance management is about enabling managers to perform better in order to succeed. This means creating a motivating work environment through appropriate incentives, feedback and rewards. Performance management has become a popular vehicle for attempts to integrate the management of human resources with the organization's wider strategy.

Performance management includes activities to ensure that goals are consistently being met in an effective and efficient manner. Performance management can focus on the performance of an organization, a department, employee, or even the processes to build a product or service, as well as many other areas.

Purposes of Performance Management:

1. ***Informational Purpose***
   - To let an employee know his performance compared with job standards.
   - To assist in identifying special talents and abilities
   - To identify employees needing performance improvement
   - To allow employees to evaluate management.
2. ***Motivational Purpose***
   - To establish closer employer-employee relationships and communicate the job requirements and standards of performance in a periodic basis.
   - To provide financial rewards or recognition for well done job
   - To work out plans to solve performance problems
   - To encourage initiative, creativity and develop a sense of ownership amongst the employees.

3. ***Developmental Purpose***

   - To identify individual employee training needs
   - To identify individuals for potential development
   - To help the employee strengthen current performance and prepare for higher responsibilities
   - To show organizational interest in attracting and retaining capable employees

4. ***Managerial Purpose***

   - To translate organizational goals into individual job/performance objectives
   - To communicate management's expectations regarding employee performance
   - To provide feedback to the employee about job performance in the light of managements' expectations
   - To diagnose the employee's strength and weakness.

The specific purpose of performance management is:

- To achieve sustainable improvements in organizational performance.
- To increase the motivation and commitment of employees
- To enable individuals to develop their abilities, increase their job satisfaction and achieve their full potential to their own benefit and that of the organization as a whole.
- To develop constructive and open relationships between individuals and their managers.
- To provide framework in terms of targets and standards of performance.
- To focus attention on the attributes and competencies required to perform effectively.
- To provide an opportunity for individuals to express their aspirations and concerns.
- To serve as a two-way channel for communication about roles, objectives, relationships, work problems and aspirations.

In brief, performance management aims to:

- Identify expected performance levels
- Encourage high levels of performance
- Measure and evaluate individual performance
- Provide feedback on individual performance
- Extend necessary assistance for performance improvement
- Confer reward or punishment depending upon actual performance.

An organization's overall performance management begins with the development of organizational strategy. Before any assessment of individual performance can be made, the organization's direction must be articulated and communicated.

Advantages of Automated Performance Management Systems:

There are many ways and methods to measure employee performance but one of the most effective ways is using automated tools. The following are the advantages for using automated performance management systems:

1. ***Automation of processes:*** Organizations can improve their HR reporting and analytics with the automation of their performance measurement process. It also saves time and money.
2. ***Goal clarity and alignment:*** Everyone in the organization is clearly aware about the common organizational goals and objectives. Once the goals are clearly defined, everyone works for the growth of the organization.
3. ***Remote Workers (out of office operations):*** Technological advancements have led to the growth of alternate working arrangements. With an EPM, employees working out of offices can coordinate their efforts with their managers.
4. ***Flexibility and customization:*** The employee performance management solutions can be customized according to the needs of the organization.
5. ***Competency management:*** Every organization has some competencies around which their business operations revolve. An efficient and effective employee performance measurement solution ensures that the competencies are managed well.
6. ***Talent management (retention and growth):*** Employee performance management is an important factor for talent management. It helps to identify known competencies, develop succession plans, notice talent gaps and establish compensation scales based on employee assessment.

8.10 BUSINESS PROCESS OUTSOURCING (BPO)

Business Process Outsourcing means handing over the work of the company to an outside company or agency for completion on contract basis. It is the delegation of one or more IT intensive non core business processes to an external service provider that owns, administers and manages the selected process based on defined and measurable performance metrics. It is the process of hiring another company to handle business activities for the company. BPO is a source of outsourcing that involves the contracting of the operations and responsibilities of specific business functions or processes to a third-party service provider.

Originally, this was associated with manufacturing firms, such as Coca Cola that outsourced large segments of its supply chain. In the contemporary context, it is primarily used to refer to the outsourcing of services.

BPO is typically categorized into back office outsourcing - which includes internal business functions such as human resources or finance and accounting, and front office outsourcing - which includes customer-related services such as contact center services. BPO that is contracted outside a company's country is called offshore outsourcing. BPO that is contracted to a company's neighboring (or nearby) country is called near shore outsourcing.

An advantage of BPO is the way in which it helps to increase a company's flexibility. However, several sources have different ways in which they perceive organizational flexibility. Therefore, business process outsourcing enhances the flexibility of an organization in different ways.

BPO is distinct from information technology (IT) outsourcing, which focuses on hiring a third-party company or service provider to do IT-related activities, such as application management and application development, data center operations, or testing and quality assurance. In the early days, BPO usually consisted of outsourcing processes such as payroll. Then, it grew to include employee benefits management. Now it encompasses a number of functions that are considered "non-core" to the primary business strategy. Now it is common for organizations to outsource financial and administration (F&A) processes, human resources (HR) functions, call center and customer service activities and accounting and payroll.

These outsourcing deals frequently involve multi-year contracts that can run into hundreds of millions of dollars. Often, the people performing the work internally for the client firm are transferred and become employees for the service provider. Dominant outsourcing service providers in the BPO fields (some of which also dominate the IT outsourcing business) include US companies IBM, Accenture, and Hewitt Associates, as well as European and Asian companies Capgemini, Genpact, TCS, Wipro and Infosys. Many of these BPO efforts involve off shoring - hiring a company based in another country to do the work. India is a popular location for BPO activities.

Frequently, BPO is also referred to as ITES — information technology-enabled services. Since most business processes include some form of automation, IT "enables" these services to be performed.

Features of BPO

Nature of Employment

BPO is the processing of the low end non core business functions which the people with minimum skills can do. Generally fresh or reasonably experienced B.Com, B.A., B. Sc. graduates with good communication skills are preferred by BPO companies. Training is generally given by these BPO companies or by some outside training agency to the newly recruited graduates to make them suitable for the onshore as well as offshore.

Professional Approach

BPO works on the process expertise. The process of routine work is managed by BPO more efficiently and effectively than the client companies if they do it in-house.

Career Difference

Employment in BPO companies is still considered by people as job and not as a career. Generally graduates work in BPO in their initial working years to earn good money and then they either try to go for higher education or to go for other jobs. Thus, jobs in BPO are still not recognized by society as a career.

•

Working Hours

BPO industry mainly works on the basis of 24 × 7 × 365. Especially in offshore services provided to USA the vendor has to work round the clock. Thus, in BPO there are abnormal working hours and working in shifts.

Employees Turnover

In case of BPO industry, employee turnover rate is very high. Generally people work for one or two years in call centers and BPOs and then for various reasons like taking to higher education or better jobs in other industries or due to abnormal working hours they leave the job.

Knowledge Process Outsourcing (KPO)

An offshoot of BPO is KPO — knowledge process outsourcing. Considered by some to be a subset of BPO, KPO includes those activities that require greater skill, knowledge, education and expertise to handle. For example, whereas an insurance company might outsource data entry of its claims forms as part of a BPO initiative, it may also choose to use a KPO service provider to evaluate new insurance applications based on a set of criteria or business rules; this work would require the efforts of a more knowledgeable set of workers than the data entry would.

Knowledge Process Outsourcing is the field where the service providers, by using their specialized domain expertise, process the information in the most professional way and convert it into the most useful form for the client user and then deliver this processed information to client company for making most crucial decision in the core business functions. In other words it is outsourcing of the core activities such as research and development, analysis and crucial decision based function. The current definition of KPO encompasses R&D, product development and legal e-discovery, as well as a number of other business functions. Also coming into use is the term BTO — business transformation outsourcing. This refers to the idea of having service providers contribute to the effort of transforming a business into a leaner, more dynamic, agile and flexible operation.

BPO and KPO

The functions covered under BPO and KPO are moderately different as shown in the table 8.1. These functions are basically different in its natural form as the BPO covers non core functions and KPO covers core functions. The functions covered under BPO are shown in figure 8.7.

Table 8.1 : BPO Turns into KPO

Feature	*BPO*	*KPO*
Functions	Non core and routine	Core
Nature of Employment	For fresh graduates with good communications skills	For professionals like CA, MBA, Engineers, PhDs etc.
Professional Approach	Works on process expertise	Works on domain expertise
Career Difference	Considered by people as job not as a career	Considered by professionals as career
Working Hours	24×7×365 type of working	Normal 8 hours working
Employees Turnover rate	Very high (almost 40%)	Comparatively very less
Growth Rate	Expected to be 26%	Expected to be 46%

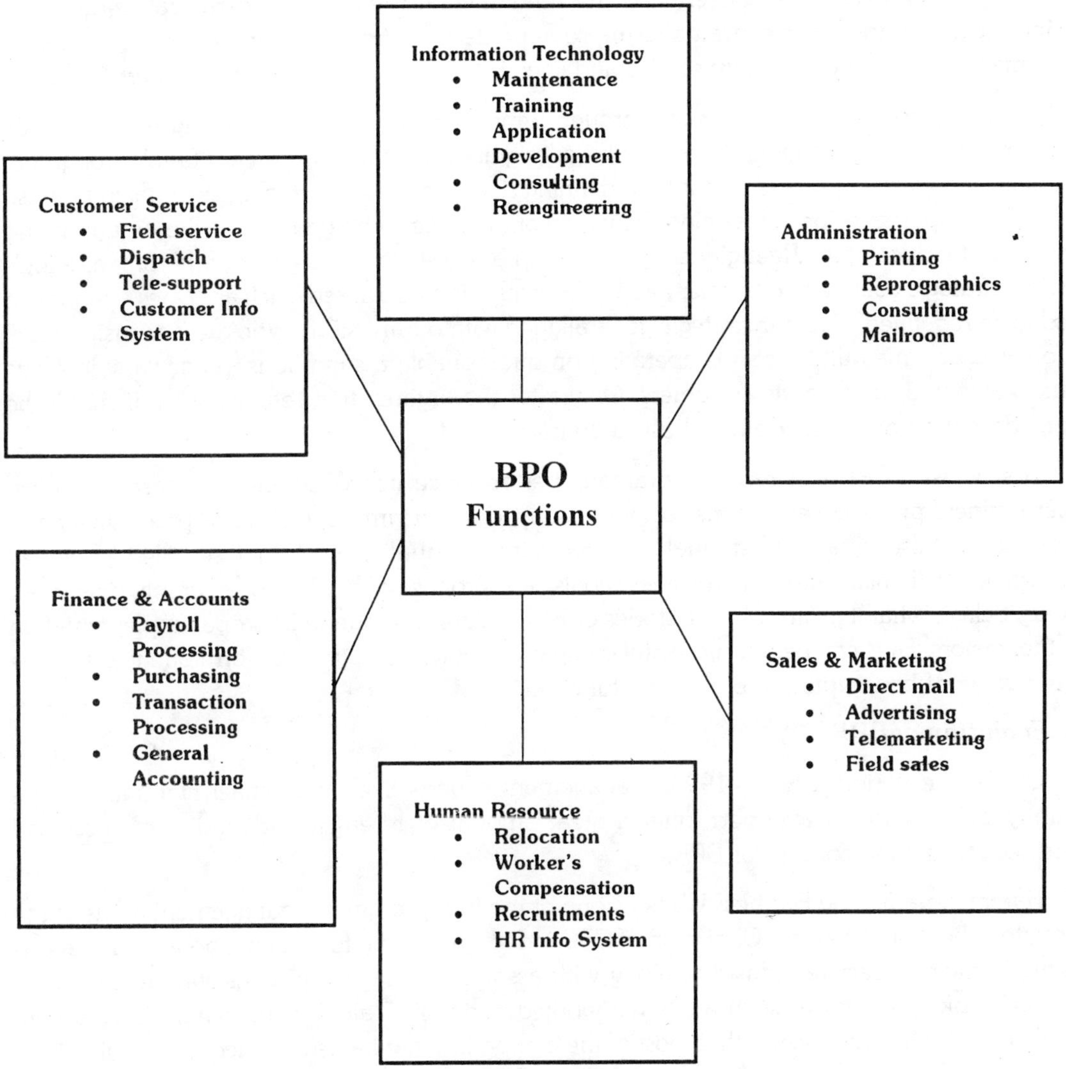

Figure 8.7 : Functions Covered under BPO

8.11 BUSINESS PROCESS REENGINEERING (BPR)

Introduction:

The term is also known as "Process Re-engineering ". Business Process Reengineering (BRP) means not just change – but dramatic change and dramatic improvements. This is achieved by the overhaul of organizational structures, management systems, job descriptions, performance measurements, skill development, training and most importantly, the use of information technology. BPR impacts every aspect of how the organization runs its business. Change on this scale can cause results ranging from enviable success to complete breakdown and failure.

"Business Process Reengineering is the fundamental rethinking and radical re-design of business process to achieve dramatic improvements in critical, contemporary measures of performance such as cost, quality service and speed". **– *Dr. Michael Hammer***

BPR is a powerful tool for break through improvements. It means starting all over again from scratch. It is not reorganizing or simply redesigning. Reengineering seeks breakthrough not by enhancing existing processes, but by redefining the processes and strategies by taking a fresh tool. It is an approach for redesigning the way work is done to better support the organization's mission and reduce costs. Reengineering starts with a high-level assessment of the organization's mission, strategic goals, and customer needs. Basic questions are asked, such as "Does our mission need to be redefined? Are our strategic goals aligned with our mission? Who are our customers?" An organization may find that it is operating on questionable assumptions, particularly in terms of the wants and needs of its customers. Only after the organization rethinks what it should be doing, does it go on to decide how best to do it.

A successful BPR can result in dramatic performance improvements, increase in profits, better business practices, enormous cost reductions, dramatic improvements in productivity and so on. It can also create substantial improvements in quality, customer service, employee satisfaction, profitability and other business goals. The promise of BPR is not an empty one; it can actually deliver what it promises. The stories of BPR failures are due to improper implementation or other factors. BPR can help a successful company to stay on top or transform one that may be on the verge of bankruptcy, into a successful one.

The Evolution of BPR:

During the period 1990 – 1993, management experts like Dr. Michael Hammer, James Champy, and Thomas Davenport, after a great amount of research and studies of successful industries created the concept of BPR.

Hammer, named by Business Week as one of the four prominent management gurus of the 1990s, together with Champy, Chairman of CSC index, gathered information about organizations thriving in their respective industries, along with assorted management consulting experiences. They were asking questions such as, "what worked and why?" along with "what didn't it work and why not?" They discovered that most of the companies that had succeeded in changing their processes had used a similar set of tools and tactics. They called this set of procedures as business process reengineering.

Today, many organizations have acquired extensive experience in performing BPR. Many of these experts are still not in agreement on every activity necessary for this; yet, the core activities have remained stable during the continuous debate. The disagreements may be, in part, due to the uniqueness of each organization. However, since organizations differ, the activities necessary to successfully perform BPR may also differ.

Principles of Re-Engineering:

- Organize the process around outcomes, not tasks
- Eliminate non-value adding steps

- Link parallel activities instead of integrating their results at the end
- Involve key people early
- Put the decision point where the work is performed
- Have those who own the output of the process, perform the process
- Capture information at the source and avoid redundant data compliance at different points

Steps for Re-Engineering:

- Identify and map all the processes required for the business
- Decide the critical ones
- Form cross-functional teams with empowerment
- Understand the current process
- Brainstorm and redesign the process
- Verify the re-engineering process

Hammer and Champy (1993) suggested the following steps.

1. ***Develop business vision and process objectives:*** This step involves prioritizing objectives and setting targets for the future. A BPR vision statement describes the ideal state of a process.
2. ***Identify processes to be redesigned:*** This involves identifying critical or bottleneck processes and envisioning the steps to avert shortcomings in them.
3. ***Understand and measure the existing processes:*** This involves identifying current problems and setting a base line.
4. ***Identify information technology levels***: This involves bringing those involved in the process to a brain-storming session to identify new approaches.
5. ***Design and build a prototype of the process:*** This includes implementing organizational and technical aspects.

The focus is mostly on customer and value addition to the customer, viewing the material transformation process in terms of those activities tied to transforming material into something of value to the customer.

BPR - The Different Phases:

According to Peter F. Drucker, "reengineering is new, and it has to be done". The task that experts agree upon to successfully perform BPR can be grouped into seven steps, or phases. All successful BPR projects begin with the most critical requirement-communication throughout the organization.

1. Begin organizational change
2. Building the reengineering organization

3. Identifying BPR opportunities
4. Understanding the existing process
5. Reengineering the process
6. Blueprint the new business system
7. Perform the transformation

The three R's

Janson states that every reengineering effort involves 3 basic phases.

1. ***Rethink:*** This phase require examining the organizations current objectives and underlying assumptions to determine how well they incorporate the renewed commitment to customer satisfaction.

2. ***Redesign:*** This phase requires an analysis of the way the organization produces the products and services it sells – how jobs are structured, who accomplishes what tasks and the results of each procedure.

   Then, a determination must be made as to which elements should be redesigned to make jobs more satisfying and acceptable to customers.

3. ***Retool:*** This phase requires a thorough evaluation of the current use of advanced technologies, especially data processing systems, to identify opportunities for change that can improve services and customer satisfaction.

Challenges faced by Reengineering Efforts

Unfortunately, all BPR projects are not as successful as those described. Most of the BPR projects will fall short of expectations. Even BPR supporters admit the likelihood of a project failing is greater than it succeeding. Companies that begin BPR projects face many of the following challenges.

➢ ***Resistance*** – change, especially radical change, always meets a great deal of resistance. In many cases this is the most serious problem companies' face in BPR.

➢ ***Tradition*** – Traditional ways of doing things do not die easily; they are often a part of the organization's culture. This means the culture and beliefs held by individuals will also have to change.

➢ ***Time requirements*** – BPR is a lengthy process, almost always taking two or more years to complete.

➢ ***Cost*** – It is costly to examine thoroughly the way business is handled and to question the way everything is done in order to find a faster and more efficient way to accomplish it.

➢ ***Scepticism*** – Some people are sceptical about BPR. Some view it as traditional systems development, but in a new wrapper with a fancy name. Others do not believe it can be done. A big obstacle is outlasting those who say it cannot be done.

- ***Job losses*** – BPR often results in employees being laid off. Some estimates range as high as 25 million jobs being eliminated before BPR runs its course.

Maximising Chances for BPR Success

There are guidelines that can be followed to maximize the chances for success in a BPR effort.

- Realize that not every company needs to re-organise itself. Do not embark on a BPR project simply because it is the thing to do. Do not try to fix something you should not be doing in the first place.
- Expect strenuous resistance and manage it properly. Sell the change by constantly stressing the positive aspects of the change and the benefits to be derived by employees and the company.
- Surround the project with a sense of urgency, since projects tend to die unless the need to change is urgent and is constantly re-emphasized.
- Get top management to fully support the project and have them make it clear that everyone is expected to support the project.
- Keep the lines of communication to employees open to prevent damaging and inaccurate rumours and misunderstandings.
- Create an atmosphere of trust and co-operation. Allay fears and provide assurances that the company is genuinely concerned about employees.
- Make sure the people who are affected by or are going to use the new system are involved in the change process.
- Change the way employees are evaluated and rewarded to motivate them to support the system.
- Staff the project with the best people and provide them with resources they need to be successful.
- Design the system from the customer's point of view, not from that of the company. Eliminate processes or steps that add no value to the customer.
- Make sure employees are adequately trained on how to use the new system.
- Be prepared to change the company's culture and its organizational structure and to re-organize the information systems function.
- Go for small success at first. Go for more dramatic projects once you have gained some experience in BPR.

Observing these guidelines is time-consuming and expensive. As a result, some people skip the more difficult steps to speed up the BPR process. Unfortunately, ignoring these guidelines usually results in a project failing to meet its intended objectives or in the project being unduly delayed. The old adage, "take time to save time," certainly applies when considering a BPR project.

8.12 BENCHMARKING

Introduction:

World-class performance starts with competitive analysis, but goes far beyond it. While competitive analysis focuses on product comparisons, bench marking looks beyond products to the operating and management skills that produce the products. It is the process of comparing one's business processes and performance metrics to industry bests and/or best practices from other industries. Dimensions typically measured are quality, time and cost. Improvements from learning mean doing things better, faster, and cheaper.

Benchmarking is continuous quality improvement technique for products, processes and services. Benchmarking is finding and implementing best practices that lead to superior performances of an organization. Robert C. Camp first coined the term "benchmarking" in 1980 while he was engaged in studying the improvement programme at Xerox Corporation, USA. Benchmarking has captured the attention of many industries, researchers and consultants.

Benchmarking means measuring one's own performance against that of competitors' performance. It is the continuous process of measuring products and services against the toughest competitors or those companies recognized as industry leaders. In other words, Benchmarking is the search for industry best practices that lead to superior performance.

Benchmarking is a process of comparing and measuring one's own business processes with those of business leaders (best) anywhere in the world to gain information and understand their methods and processes and then adopting it in their own organisation for improving performance at a higher level.

- Benchmarking is a continuous quality improvement technique for products, processes and services.
- Benchmarking is the continuous systematic process of measuring products, services and work processes or practices against the toughest competitors or those companies recognized as industry's best.

➢ Benchmarking is the search for the industry's best practices and the adoption of such practices to ensure superior performance – ***Robert Camp***

The objective of benchmarking is to understand and evaluate the current position of a business or organisation in relation to "best practice" and to identify areas and means of performance improvement.

Benchmarking is a general approach to business improvement based on best practice in the industry, or in another similar industry. It can provide a useful quality improvement target for a business. This can be a helpful approach for services as well as for products – for example a fast food business selling fish and chips could decide that it wanted to aim to equal McDonalds' speed of meeting customer orders for takeaway food. A financial services firm might want its call centre staff to answer 95% of telephone calls within six rings, if this is the practice of the best in the industry.

Types of Benchmarking: Benchmarking is classified on the basis of the type of partner selected for the benchmarking. The partnership team (or, organization/groups/system/process) may be from the same company or from different organization. Based on the approaches, benchmarking is classified as:

1) Internal Benchmarking
2) Competitive Benchmarking
3) Functional Benchmarking
4) Best Practice (Generic) Benchmarking

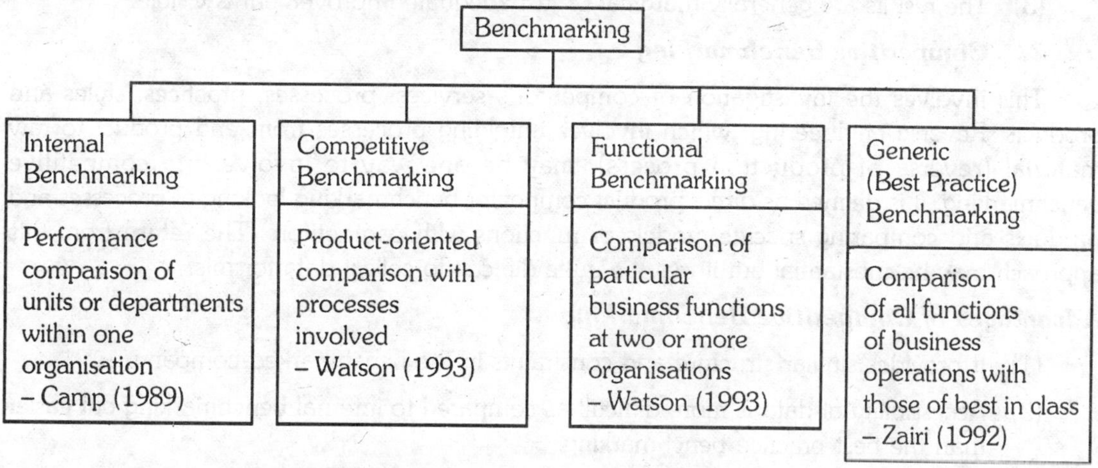

Figure 8.8 : Types of Benchmarking

1. *Internal Benchmarking*

It is performed within one organization by comparing the practices and performance of similar business units or business process located at same or different places. This approach is the most accessible one as the comparison is conducted between similar operations in other parts of the same company. Internal benchmarking is defined as "performance comparison of units or departments within one organization". In the internal benchmarking, there is no problem of confidentiality and, therefore, it should be attempted first before embarking on any other type of benchmarking.

Advantages of Internal Benchmarking

(1) It uses similar language, mechanism, system, culture, mind-set and top-management support.

(2) There is considerable ease in the access to data.

(3) There are no problems in establishing communication between units.

(4) The process does not involve confidentiality problem in accessing data.

(5) The returns of benchmarking efforts are relatively quick.

(6) The approach is relatively silent, low profile, and a low threat affair.

(7) It provides a test bed for quicker improvement.

(8) Along with transfer of data, expert services from the benchmarked unit are easily available.

Disadvantages of Internal Benchmarking

(1) It lacks external focus and may foster complacency and lack of seriousness.

(2) Internal weaknesses, such as cultural problem, leadership problem, etc., tend to remain unaltered.

(3) The results are generally marginal or just adequate improvement is visible.

2. *Competitive Benchmarking*

This involves the investigation of competitor's services, processes, practices, styles and products. Reverse engineering, which involves unfolding processes from end product to raw material (reverse of production process), may be one way to involve into competitive benchmarking. It is defined as direct product competitor benchmarking looking at processes and products and comparing specific models or functions with competitors. The return from this approach may be substantial but it may be quite difficult to collect data for this.

Advantages of Competitive Benchmarking

(1) It provides similar structure and constraints in the benchmarked company.

(2) Accessibility of data is more difficult as compared to internal benchmarking but easier than the best practice benchmarking.

(3) Threats are relatively less.

(4) Confidence in the decision makers mind due to similarity with competitors.

(5) The disadvantage in internal benchmarking is the chance of complacency and arrogance. However, this is overcome in this approach.

Disadvantages of Competitive Benchmarking

(1) It is difficult to convince the competitors for sharing data.

(2) Many constraints, such as legal, ethical and trade secrets prevent the success.

(3) It restricts the creativity in the process of improvement.

3. *Functional Benchmarking*

It is the application of process benchmarking that compares a particular business function in two or more organizations. It may be defined as specific function comparison with best practice or a comparison of specific function with best in industry and best in class. It can also be a comparison of particular business functions at two or more organizations.

Advantages of Functional Benchmarking

1. Higher chances of breakthrough as the functions are similar and comparison is with best in class.

2. Moderately sensitive to ethical/political reservation due to similar functions.
3. Widens the perspective of the corporate.
4. There are very high chances of stimulating changes.
5. Similar functions provide opportunity to map the world class on a much easier

Disadvantages of Functional Benchmarking

1. Due to similar functions sometimes data accessibility is less.
2. Activity becomes high profile due to involvement of best in class.
3. There is greater ramification for change.
4. Expectations are far more.

4. *Best Practice (Generic) Benchmarking*

In this, the practices of identified leaders are considered, irrespective of the business sector, where benchmarking is performed against very specific activities. This approach initiates great opportunities for companies to collaborate and exchange information as it can only be advantageous to both parties.

Key Features of Benchmark Company (Best Practice)

- Any organization, regardless of sector, location or activity
- Must be the best practice company in own.

Advantages of Best Practice Benchmarking

1. The possibility of breakthrough achievements is tremendous.
2. It is less sensitive to either ethical or political reservations.
3. It may widen the perspective of the company.
4. It is more useful for stimulating change.
5. Due to lack of competition among the two companies, it is easy to exchange information as compared to external benchmarking in similar sector.

Disadvantages of Best Practice Benchmarking

1. There is greater ramification for change.
2. As compared to internal benchmarking, the access of information is difficult.
3. It is a high profile activity due to involvement of world class (best practice) corporate.
4. High expectation for change.

Phases of Benchmarking Process:

Following are the four phases of Benchmarking process.

1. Planning Phase
2. Analysis Phase

3. Integration Phase
4. Action Phase

1. Planning phase:

- Identify what is to be benchmarked –which process? why?
- Identify comparable companies
- Determine data collection methods
- Collect data

2. Analysis phase:

- Determine the current performance "gap". Analyse data to compare actual with standards
- Project future performance levels. Identify the desired levels of performance of your company in future.

3. Integration phase:

- Communication benchmarking findings and gain acceptance from top management and people concerned

4. Action phase:

- Develop action plans - prepare schedules, budgets and procedures for implementation.
- Implement specific actions - assign tasks supervise and get feedback from time to time.

Benchmarking Process:

1. Plan 2. Search 3. Observe 4. Analyse 5. Adopt

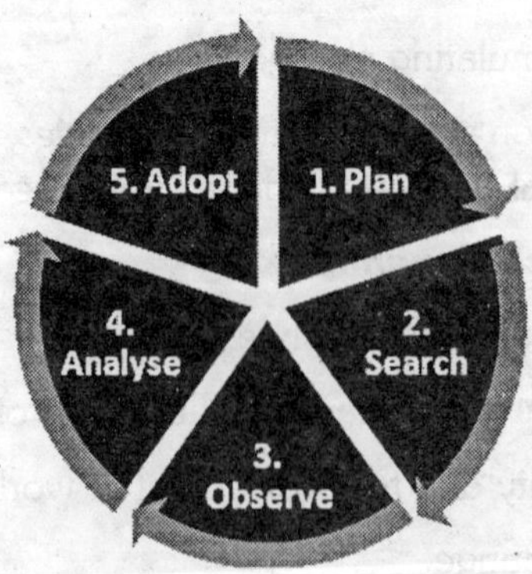

Figure 8.9 : Benchmarking Process

The major steps involve:

1) Measuring the performance of best – in – class relative to critical performance variables.
2) Determining how the levels of performance are achieved and
3) Using the information to develop and implement a plan for improvement

Advantages of Benchmarking:

1. Best practices may be incorporated in the company operations, thus, productivity, sales and profitability will increase.
2. It provides targets that have been achieved by others.
3. Technical breakthrough can be identified early and quality of product increases.
4. It helps a company to learn its strengths and weakness and those of other organizations.

Benchmarking Pitfalls:

1) Proper infrastructure of total quality such as information system, process control and human resources programme should be provided first before starting benchmarking.
2) Involve the employees fully in the process. Participation will lead to enthusiasm.
3) Define your own process before gathering others data.
4) Perceive benchmarking as an ongoing process.
5) Expand the scope of the companies studied. Confirming benchmarking firms to your own area, industry or to competitors is probably too narrow approach in identifying excellent performers.
6) Perceive benchmarking as a means to process improvement, rather than an end in itself.
7) Set goals for closing the gap between what is (existing performance) and what can be (benchmark).
8) Empower employees to achieve improvement.
9) Maintain momentum. Credibility is achieved by quick and enthusiastic action.

8.13 BALANCED SCORECARD

The balanced scorecard is a strategic planning and management system that is used extensively in business and industry, government, and nonprofit organizations worldwide to align business activities to the vision and strategy of the organization, improve internal and external communications, and monitor organization performance against strategic goals. It was originated by Drs. Robert Kaplan (Harvard Business School) and David Norton as a performance measurement framework that added strategic non-financial performance measures to traditional financial metrics to give managers and executives a more 'balanced' view of organizational performance.

"The balanced scorecard retains traditional financial measures. But financial measures tell the story of past events, an adequate story for industrial age companies for which investments in long-term capabilities and customer relationships were not critical for success. These financial measures are inadequate, however, for guiding and evaluating the journey that information age companies must make to create future value through investment in customers, suppliers, employees, processes, technology, and innovation".

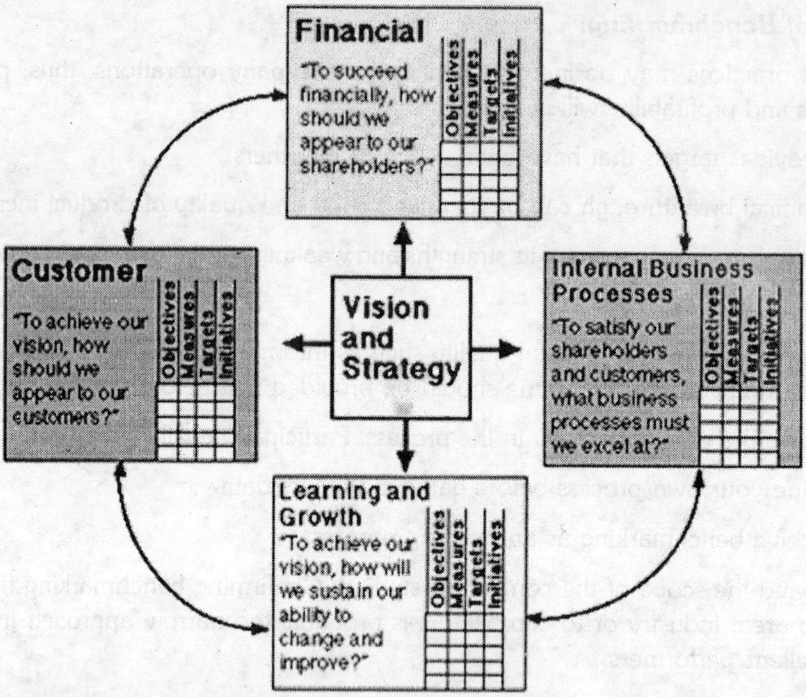

Figure 8.10 : Balanced Scorecard - The Four Perspectives

Balanced Scorecard - The Four Perspectives

The 1st Generation design method proposed by Kaplan and Norton was based on the use of three non-financial topic areas as prompts to aid the identification of non-financial measures in addition to one looking at financial. The four "perspectives" proposed are shown in figure 8.10. They are :

1. ***Financial:*** encourages the identification of a few relevant high-level financial measures. In particular, designers were encouraged to choose measures that helped inform the answer to the question "How do the firm look to shareholders?"
2. ***Customer:*** encourages the identification of measures that answer the question "How do customers see the firm?"
3. ***Internal Business Processes:*** encourages the identification of measures that answer the question "How well does the firm manage its operational processes?"
4. ***Learning and Growth:*** encourages the identification of measures that answer the question "Can the firm continue to improve and create value?" This perspective also examines how an organisation learns and grows.

For each of the four perspectives, it is necessary to identify indicators to measure the performance of the organisations.

- ***Internal perspective*** – how well does it manage its operational processes?
- ***Innovation and learning perspective*** – can the firm continue to improve and create value? This perspective also examines how an organisation learns and grows.

Financial Perspective – This is concerned with the shareholders view of performance. Shareholders are concerned with many aspects of financial performance. Amongst the measures of success are:

- Market share
- Revenue growth
- Profit ratio
- Return on investment
- Economic value added
- Return on capital employed
- Operating cost management
- Operating ratios and loss ratios
- Corporate goals
- Survival
- Profitability
- Growth
- Process cost savings
- Increased return on assets
- Profit growth
- Cash flow
- Net profitability ratio
- Sales revenue
- Growth in sales revenue
- Cost reduction
- Share price
- Return on shareholder funds

Customer Perspective - This focuses on the analysis of different types of customers, their degree of satisfaction and the processes used to deliver products and services to customers. Particular areas of focus would include:

- Customer service
- New products
- New markets
- Customer retention
- Customer satisfaction
- What does the organisation need to do to remain as customer's valued supplier?

Potential goals for the customer perspective could include:

- Customer satisfaction
- New customer acquisition
- Customer retention
- Customer loyalty
- Fast response
- Responsiveness
- Efficiency
- Reliability
- Image

The following metrics could be used to measure success in relation to the customer perspective:

- Customer satisfaction index
- Repeat purchases
- Market share
- On time deliveries
- Number of complaints
- Average time to process orders
- Returned orders
- Response time
- Reliability
- New customer acquisitions
- Perceived value for money

Internal Perspective - This perspective is concerned with assessing the quality of people and processes. This seeks to identify:

- How well the business is performing.
- Whether the products and services offered meet customer expectations.
- The critical processes for satisfying both customers and shareholders.
- Activities in which the firm excels
- And in what must it excel in the future?
- The internal processes that the company must be improved if it is to achieve its objectives.

Potential goals for the internal perspective include:

- Improve core competencies
- Improvements in technology
- Streamline processes
- Manufacturing excellence
- Quality performance
- Inventory management
- Quality
- Motivated workforce

The following metrics could be used to measure success in relation to the internal perspective:

- Efficiency improvements
- Reduction in unit costs
- Reduced waste
- Improvements in morale
- Increase in capacity utilisation
- Increased productivity
- Percentage of defective output
- Amount of recycled waste
- Amount of reworking

Innovation and Learning Perspective

This perspective is concerned with issues such as:

- Can we continue to improve and create value?
- In which areas must the organisation improve?
- How can the company continue to improve and create value in the future?
- What should it be doing to make this happen?

Potential goals for the innovation and learning perspective include:

- New product development
- Continuous improvement
- Technological leadership
- HR development
- Product diversification

The following metrics could be used to measure success in relation to the innovation and learning perspective:

- Number of new products
- Percentage of sales from new products
- Amount of training
- Number of strategic skills learned.
- Value of new product in sales
- R&D as % of sales
- Number of employee suggestions.
- Extent of employee empowerment

Main benefits of using the balanced scorecard

- Helps companies focus on what has to be done in order to create a breakthrough performance
- Acts as an integrating device for a variety of corporate programmes
- Makes strategy operational by translating it into performance measures and targets
- Helps break down corporate level measures so that local managers and employees can see what they need to do well if they want to improve organisational effectiveness
- Provides a comprehensive view that overturns the traditional idea of the organisation as a collection of isolated, independent functions and department.

ESSAY QUESTIONS

1. Explain the major functions and classification of MIS.
2. Explain some of the causes that can result in the failure of an MIS.
3. What is material requirement planning (MRP) Illustrate? What are its pre requisite inputs?
4. What is material requirement planning? What are the benefits and drawbacks of MRP?
5. What are the main principles of total quality management? Discuss the tools used for continuous improvement.
6. What is TQM? Discuss the elements and benefits of TQM
7. What do you understand by total quality management? How does this concept differ from quality control techniques?
8. Explain the philosophy behind total quality management, customer satisfaction and continuous improvement. What are the objectives of TQM?
9. What is six sigma? Discuss the approaches for six sigma and state its benefits
10. State the need and importance of supply chain management (SCM) and explain the problems addressed by supply chain management.

11. Explain the steps in the evolution of enterprise resource planning. Discuss the commercial applications of ERP.
12. What is performance management? Explain the purposes of performance management.
13. What is business process reengineering? Explain the steps of Michel Hammer relating to re-engineering.
14. What are the challenges faced by reengineering efforts? Discuss the guidelines to be followed to maximize the chances for success in BPR.
15. Explain what is meant by benchmarking and compare the different types of benchmarking.
16. What are the steps in benchmarking process? State the advantages and pitfalls of bench marking.
17. Discuss briefly the four perspectives of balance scorecard.
18. Write short notes on following :
    a) Management Information System
    b) Business Process Outsourcing
    c) Supply Chain Management

FILL IN THE BLANKS

1. ERP systems help to make this task easier by ....the information systems. (Integrating)
2. ERP is an abbreviation for .... (Enterprise Resource Planning)
3. Management information system serve the .... level of the organization. (Management)
4. Total Quality Management is about .... (Customer satisfaction)
5. Six sigma quality is a bench mark of .... for product and process quality. (Excellence)
6. Six sigma level indicates that product or service delivered is.................. defect free. (99.99966%)
7. .... is an inventory strategy that strives to improve a business return on investment by reducing in-process inventory and associated carrying costs. (Just-in-time)
8. Capability Maturity Model consists .... Maturity Levels. (Five)
9. An advantage of BPO is the way in which it helps to increase a company's .... (Flexibility)

❖ ❖ ❖